PARLIAMENT, PARTY AND THE ART OF POLITICS IN BRITAIN, 1855–59

Books published by Macmillan in association with the London School of Economics

Michael R. Bonavia
THE NATIONALISATION OF BRITISH TRANSPORT
H. M. Drucker
THE POLITICAL USES OF IDEOLOGY
George Feaver and Frederick Rosen (*editors*)
LIVES, LIBERTIES AND THE PUBLIC GOOD
Graeme J. Gill
PEASANTS AND GOVERNMENT IN THE RUSSIAN REVOLUTION
Angus Hawkins
PARLIAMENT, PARTY AND THE ART OF POLITICS IN BRITAIN, 1855–59
Tony Hayter
THE ARMY AND THE CROWD IN MID-GEORGIAN ENGLAND
Marian Kent
OIL AND EMPIRE: BRITISH POLICY AND MESOPOTAMIAN OIL, 1900–1920
L. H. Leigh (*editor*)
ECONOMIC CRIME IN EUROPE
Andrew Linklater
MEN AND CITIZENS IN THE THEORY OF INTERNATIONAL RELATIONS
Michael Malet
NESTOR MAKHNO IN THE RUSSIAN CIVIL WAR
C. A. W. Manning
THE NATURE OF INTERNATIONAL SOCIETY
Terence H. Qualter
GRAHAM WALLAS AND THE GREAT SOCIETY
OPINION CONTROL IN THE DEMOCRACIES
Leonard Schapiro
THE ORIGIN OF THE COMMUNIST AUTOCRACY
David Seckler
THORSTEIN VEBLEN AND THE INSTITUTIONALISTS
Nicholas A. Sims
THE DIPLOMACY OF BIOLOGICAL DISARMAMENT
W. von Leyden
ARISTOTLE ON EQUALITY AND JUSTICE
HOBBES AND LOCKE

Series Standing Order

If you would like to receive future titles in this series as they are published, you can make use of our standing order facility. To place a standing order please contact your bookseller or, in case of difficulty, write to us at the address below with your name and address and the name of the series. Please state with which title you wish to begin your standing order. (If you live outside the UK we may not have the rights for your area, in which case we will forward your order to the publisher concerned.)

Standing Order Service, Macmillan Distribution Ltd, Houndmills, Basingstoke, Hampshire, RG21 2XS, England.

Parliament, Party and the Art of Politics in Britain, 1855–59

Angus Hawkins

Associate Professor in Modern British History
Loyola Marymount University, California

M

MACMILLAN
PRESS

in association with
THE LONDON SCHOOL OF ECONOMICS
AND POLITICAL SCIENCE

First published 1987

Published by
THE MACMILLAN PRESS LTD
Houndmills, Basingstoke, Hampshire RG21 2XS
and London
Companies and representatives
throughout the world

Typeset by Acorn Bookwork, Salisbury, Wilts.

Printed in Hong Kong

British Library Cataloguing in Publication Data
Hawkins, Angus
  Parliament, party and the art of politics in
  Britain, 1855–59.
  1. Great Britain—Politics and government
  —1837–1901
  I. Title
  320.941   JN216
  ISBN 0–333–42257–0

For my parents and Esther

Contents

Acknowledgements

A large number of debts of different kinds are incurred during the writing of a study of this kind. First, I would like to thank those who made available copyright material, especially the Marquess of Salisbury, the Earl of Clarendon, the Earl of Dalhousie, the Earl of Derby, the Earl of Harewood, Viscount FitzHarris, Baron Monk Bretton, Sir Andrew Duff Gordon, Sir Charles Graham, Cmdr F. H. M. FitzRoy Newdegate, the Hon. David Lytton Cobbold, Mrs J. E. Goedhuis, Mr D. C. L. Holland CB, Mr T. D. G. Sotheron-Estcourt, as well as the Trustees of the Broadlands Archives Trust and the Trustees of the National Library of Scotland. I am also grateful to the staff of the National Register of Archives, both in London and Edinburgh; the Clerk of the Records, the Record Office, House of Lords; Ms Amanda Arrowsmith, the Suffolk Record Office; Mr E. G. W. Bill, Lambeth Palace Library; Mr M. A. F. Borrie, the British Library; Mr Alan Cameron, the University of Nottingham Library; Mr W. J. Connor, Leeds District Archives; Miss R. C. Dunhill, the Hampshire Record Office; Mr J. M. Fenton, the Department of Palaeography and Diplomatic, University of Durham; Mr Dudley Fowkes, the Staffordshire Record Office; Mr G. M. Furlong, University College, London; Mr James Galbraith, the Scottish Record Office; Mr Iain Maciver, the National Library of Scotland; Mrs Patricia Moore, the Glamorgan Archive Service; Dr J. B. Post, the Public Record Office; Mr Derek Shorrocks, the Somerset Record Office; Mr D. J. H. Smith, the Gloucestershire County Record Office; Mr Peter Walne, the Hertfordshire County Record Office; Mr C. C. Webb, the Borthwick Institute of Historical Research, York; Mr W. N. Yates, the Kent Archives Office; and the archivists and staff of those libraries and record offices I have consulted. I am grateful to the editors of *Victorian Studies* and the *Journal of British Studies* for permission to use material which first appeared in their journals in a rather different form. I apologise for any inadvertent infringement of copyright.

Debts of a more personal kind exist. Dr Andrew Jones revealed to me the fascination and complexity of Victorian politics. I owe him my love for the subject. Mr Alan Beattie, who supervised the doctoral thesis from which this study came, challenged, encouraged and cared. Any worth in what follows owes much to him. I value highly the time,

Acknowledgements

advice and true friendship both have given me. Dr Robert Self offered companionship, scholarly criticism and emotional support when it mattered most. Mr Patrick Davis and Mr Tim Farmiloe took the manuscript under their wing. My professional colleagues have saved me from many errors; particularly Mr Stephen Lawrence, Dr Joseph Tiedemann and Dr Lawrence Tritle whose good nature I have tested with my demands. The comments of Professor John Vincent and Professor J. B. Conacher at various stages in the development of this study were invaluable. Indeed, three books informed my work in a way that cannot be adequately recognised in notes: John Vincent's *The Formation of the Liberal Party, 1857–1868*; J. B. Conacher's *The Aberdeen Coalition, 1853–1855: A Study in Mid-Nineteenth-Century Party Politics*; and D. E. D. Beales' *England and Italy, 1859–60*. Needless to say, my debt to them in no way commits them to any of my views. For any errors I am solely responsible.

Finally, and most importantly, I would like to thank those to whom this book is dedicated for their love, support and patience. Accept this as a token of my appreciation for many blessings.

Angus Hawkins

Note on References

All manuscript references are to those catalogue systems in use at the time of my consulting the manuscript. Five figure references to collections housed in the British Library are to Additional Manuscripts. I have followed the injunction in operation when I consulted the Holland House Mss. not to use any catalogue reference, as cataloguing and foliation were still in progress. Those strokes taken to represent ampersands have been transcribed as 'and'. Capitalisation has been standardised. Question-marks preceding words, names or dates indicate illegibility.

ABBREVIATIONS

BIHR	*Bulletin of the Institute of Historical Research*
EHR	*English Historical Review*
HJ	*Historical Journal*
JBS	*Journal of British Studies*
QVL	*The Letters of Queen Victoria*, A. C. Benson and Viscount Esher (eds) (London, 1907)
TRHS	*Transactions of the Royal Historical Society*

Amid the multitude of grave, grand, historical and business like aspects of the House of Commons, it must not be forgotten that it is the first Club in the World – an unrivalled sphere of original shining gossip, news, guesses, predictions, surprises, surmises, probabilities, improbabilities, affirmatives, denials, delightful calumnies, immediate vindications, undulations, strophes and anti-strophes of all kinds. It has not, as the showman says, 'its equal in the civilised world'. . . . There is a perpetual succession, not exactly of fresh actors, for the dramatis personae *remain a good deal the same, but of fresh acting; they appear in new positions and attitudes, and take their parts in fresh scenes; the occasion and the dialogue are fresh from day to day. . . . [W]e have a true and living scene acted before us in the solid spectacle of Parliament, where real men fight the real battle of political life, give and parry real blows, aim at real prizes, struggle for real victory. . . . You may be quite sure you see nature here; the artist does not delude you; . . . you need not suspend your admiration till by some scientific rules and tests laid down by critics you have decided whether this or that character is 'natural' or not; whether all is high or generous, or even decent or not, all is certainly natural. Political life has its disguises and masks of course, but so has nature also; it is real life – not a sham or mere representation.*

J. Mozley, an anonymous leader in *The Times*, 4 February 1859, p. 9.

Introduction

The world of contingency and political combination is much larger than we are apt to imagine. (Note in Russell's hand, n.d. (?1858) Russell Mss. PRO 30/22/13/E, fol. 143)

[T]he difficulty of solving a problem of political causation consists not so much in the obscurity and uncertainty of the facts themselves, as in the necessity of disentangling the ravelled skeins into which they are formed, and of discerning a clue in the labyrinth of human action. (George Cornewall Lewis, *A Treatise on the Methods of Observation and Reasoning in Politics* (London, 1852) p. 332)

The 'principle of parliament', Walter Bagehot celebrated in 1867, 'is obedience to leaders' and 'party is of its essence'.[1] With these words Bagehot affirmed the central role of party in modern British politics. Parliamentary parties and their leaders provided the prestigious centrepiece of Victorian politics. Yet the function of party within the political system was never static. Since the 17th century, parties have assumed a shifting reference to the monarchy, the notion of ministerial responsibility, loyal opposition, a changing electorate and extra-parliamentary organisation. The mid-19th century was a crucial period in this long process of change. During these years parliamentary politicians redefined their relations with the national political community, while within Westminster itself party alignment was being redefined so as to shape the political configurations of the future.

The 1850s are important because of the apparent confusion that accompanied this crucial redefinition of party connection. The historical problem is the more urgent when one of the modern sages of the Victorian era confesses that 'after 1852 it is not very easy to read any intelligible meaning into the party system at all'.[2] The pursuit of meaning highlights those events preceding the emergence of a relative clarity and, in retrospect, lasting cohesion in party connection in 1859. The historical importance of that year lies in the public reaffirmation of a bi-partisan alignment of parliamentary opinion. More specifically, the events of June 1859 saw the fusion of a Liberal party under Palmerstonian leadership, with Radical and former Peel-

1

ite support, confronting a Conservative party shorn of many prominent Peelites. The preceding years of confusion and uncertainty
demand explanation.

Events between the Corn Law crisis of 1846 and the death of Sir
Robert Peel in 1850 disrupted established parliamentary party connection. Thereafter two critical factors perpetuated instability. First,
Conservative leaders favoured a passive strategy in opposition which,
after the relinquishing of Protectionism, sought advantage in not
adopting a forthright stand on any single question of policy. Thus,
inactivity came to conceal the relative cohesion of Conservative party
sentiment. At the same time non-commitment denied others the
opportunity to define a clear non-Conservative position with reference to specific issues. Secondly, amongst Whigs, Peelites, Liberals
and Radicals there were a large number of prominent individuals with
claims upon the leadership of non-Conservative sentiment. Outside
the Conservative party there existed little distinction in being distinguished. During the session of 1855, sixty-three actual or past cabinet
ministers took part in debate.[3] If the principle of parliament was
obedience to leaders, then a surfeit of leadership found natural
expression in party confusion. The parliamentary instability of the
1850s was *not* the result of disillusion with the principle of party.
Rather the pursuit of that principle by too many, in too many
differing forms, determined that existing party connection could not
be anything other than unstable.

The essential difficulty of parliamentary politics in the 1850s was
the delineation of Conservative intent in the presence of a Whig–Liberal–Radical crisis of leadership. Thus, as Kitson Clark observed, it is
not 'very easy to say what specific opinions were uniquely organised
in the middle of the century by the Conservative party'.[4] While on the
other side of the House there occurred 'the intricate personal man-
oeuvres of a select group of statesmen and a curious *pas de deux*
danced by Lord John Russell and Lord Palmerston'. The relative
clarity of party alignment that emerged in 1859 had profound importance for the future. Not only was the character of the Conservative
party, in the aftermath of the Protectionist crisis of the 1840s, more
clearly defined. Not only was it decided which prominent Whig,
Liberal and Radical claims to pre-eminence were to be substantiated.
But these developments required a Liberal redefinition of purpose
accommodating the results of realignment which, after Palmerston's
death, became associated with William Gladstone's sense of personal
mission. In important ways 1859 set the scene for the parliamentary
party politics of the later 19th century.

I

By the late 1820s parliamentary politics had become embodied in party politics. No longer was the possession of office the result of being chosen by the King to constitute a non-party coalition which subsequently acquired Commons support. Parties did not have essential constitutional status. But executive government could no longer be sustained by either the monarch alone or by the crown's ability to return a favourable House of Commons. Increasingly, ministerial stability became dependent upon predictable parliamentary support.[5] The substance of the crown's prerogative was being held by ministers in office at the pleasure of parliament. Bagehot's emphasis on the nature of party in the Commons by the 1860s reflected the prevailing belief that ministers could no longer rely on either the monarch or the Lords for their sustenance. 'The moment, indeed, that we distinctly conceive that the House of Commons is mainly and above all things an elective assembly, we at once perceive that party is of its essence.'[6]

The clarification of political positions in the wake of the Catholic and reform crises of 1828–32 brought new distinction to parliamentary parties. Having assumed office and having passed the 1832 reform act, Whigs sought executive substance for that brilliant social and rhetorical millieu that had constituted Whiggery excluded from power.[7] Victorian political zeal nearly always sought inspiration in the past. The Whigs' problem existed in the fact that the present need for a governmental purpose focused upon the past model of their opposition rhetoric. Prior to 1827, Whigs were in the anomalous position of being a solitary party in a non-party system.[8] They were sustained by a belief in the primacy of parliament, the virtue of party connection, the repressive evils of executive power as embodied in the royal prerogative, and a notion of liberty and honour subordinated to a hierarchical social structure. After 1830 this jealously guarded Foxite tradition was adapted to the responsibilities of office. This accommodation was the more difficult in the presence of earnest evangelicalism and doctrinaire utilitarianism. Yet the weight of that Foxite tradition restored faith in parliament as the authoritative arena of national politics, and belief that the authority to govern came from the support of organised opinion in parliament. Thus parties were an essential element of parliamentary government. William IV's actions in November 1834 were portrayed as the final protest of a tyrannical executive conclusively quashed by the election of 1835 and Lord Melbourne's resumption of the premiership.[9]

Immediately after 1832 the issue of the Established Church in

England and Ireland created further difficulties for Whigs in office, but also revitalised a dispirited Conservative party in opposition.[10] Sir Robert Peel's minority ministry of 1834–35 and his Tamworth Manifesto regenerated Conservative purpose in terms of 'good' and 'responsible' government assimilated with Burkean notions of reforming in order to preserve. There existed, however, a central irony to Peel's leadership. While he became the focus for a reinvigorated Conservative party he also remained firmly committed to an increasingly anachronistic executive notion of government. Reissuing William Pitt's lines learnt from Lord Liverpool and Canning, Peel portrayed constitutional authority as emanating from a government acting as loyal ministers of the crown, and motivated by considerations of national interest. While focusing politics at the cabinet level, this view suggested that ministers should not be obligated by servile tenure to those who supported them while in office. Executive authority did not come from organised parliamentary opinion, but from being selected as the servant of the crown.[11] Appropriately, Peel's leadership of the Conservative party was not confirmed by Conservative backbench opinion, but by the preferences of William IV in 1834.

Thus Peelite Conservatism came to be defined in terms of duty and responsibility, rather than in terms of property in which there existed little distinction. Romantic Tory rebels such as 'Young England' might present the onus of duty as descending through a social obligation to 'the people', but Peel forcefully portrayed that onus as ascending towards the monarchy and the government's executive function as the ministers of the crown. This Peelite definition, in turn, placed an obligation on followers to follow, and obviated any divisive discussion about the social and moral function of land. Peel gave the revitalised Conservative party a ministerial ethic, not a party doctrine.[12]

The Lichfield House Compact of February 1835 brought together Whig, Radical and Irish MPs, and confirmed that trend towards a two-party system observed by Namier.[13] The writings of Norman Gash, D. E. D. Beales and David Close affirm that by the late 1830s 'politics were dominated by two major parties to an extent previously unknown in British history'.[14] In 1841 Peel became head of a Conservative government that enjoyed a majority of eighty in the Commons. Yet the essential paradox of 1841 was that it was a great party triumph for an anti-party view of government. The events of 1841 to 1846 played out the implications of this paradox.[15]

Conflict is implicit in the agonistic vocabulary of politics. It is also an implicit part of such language to suggest clarity where vague or divergent opinion may exist. The perceptual clarity that the rhetoric of two-party alignment brought to parliamentary sentiment in the 1830s overlay such differences. Peel's rhetoric of ministerial responsibility and strong government had, by 1841, been assimilated with notions of progressive improvement, the enlargement of the Conservative's social base and constituency organisation.[16] Once in office such rhetoric allowed prominence to questions of executive moment, as exemplified in annual budgets, at the expense of legislative issues or foreign affairs. Moreover, such Peelite emphasis overlay the consolidation of the agricultural interest, a more muscular Anglicanism, and an intense anti-Catholicism that accompanied Peel's years as premier after 1841.[17]

The disruption of the Conservative party in 1846 dramatically revealed the limitations of Peelite priorities as a palliative for Conservative differences. Conservative backbenchers discovered that Peelism meant scant regard for their religious, economic or social sensibilities. Peel found the demands of party obligation incompatible with his elevated executive notion of constitutional authority. The divisions within the Conservative party in 1846 were never simply differences over economic policy between the landed interest and free trade converts. It was a split between official Conservatism, as associated with the priorities of Peel's frontbench, and a backbench sentiment attached to the rhetorically flexible opposition pose of pre-1841. It was a split between two opposed interpretations of ministerial authority. Peel's embarrassing disdain for Peelite party organisation after 1846 was entirely consistent. Perhaps 1846 also witnessed a split between an instinctive Conservatism associated with the prestige of property, and a Peelite Conservatism that, at the highest level, found sustenance in a morally elevated concept of public responsibility. In any event, the Corn Law crisis of 1846, Peel's constitutionalism and free trade policy shattered that well defined two-party alignment that had emerged during the previous decade.[18]

Conservative dislocation prompted a crisis of purpose within Whig, Liberal and Radical ranks. After 1846, under the premiership of Lord John Russell, Whigs and Liberals found themselves in office. They were sustained by a vague rectitude over notions of 'progress', 'improvement' and 'liberty' that appeared the more vague in comparison to the hard-headed administrative character of Peelism. The prominent Whig Lord Clarendon considered his political creed 'to be nearly effete, and as the means of governing, a matter of history rather than fact'.[19] Increasingly between 1846 and 1852 Whig policy became a series of shifts and compromises that betrayed liberal impulses devoid of coherent purpose. An absence of young Whig talent, expropriations in Ireland, Lord Palmerston's foreign policy, retrenchment, fiscal plans, religious issues and parliamentary reform, as well as the presence of Peelites, Irish Liberals, Manchester Radicals and organised Nonconformity revealed the increasing bankruptcy of Whig doctrine. Russell, as the personification of Whig rectitude, found the extension of free trade, through repeal of the Navigation Acts, insufficient to consolidate Whig–Liberal–Radical sentiment. His revival of the reform question in 1848, bearing similar hopes, only further undermined his leadership. Russell's failure to unite non-Conservative opinion emphasised Peel's authority, although Peel's executive beliefs dissuaded him from translating that authority into party alignment. Furthermore, Russell's failure to consolidate progressive parliamentary sentiment in the late 1840s left that possibility open in the 1850s.[20]

Peel's death in 1850 proved to be of profound yet paradoxical importance. While it allowed party support to be openly acknowledged as the source of executive authority in parliament, it also removed the parliamentarian best able to impose a distinct delineation of party upon increasing political disarray. Thus Peel's death created a fundamental problem: the translation of faith in organised party support, as a constitutional precondition to effective government, into distinct and stable party alignment. In the following years other circumstances emphasised the difficulty. Easing social tensions, abundant harvests and rising prices and rents secured the prosperity of the propertied. There existed no acute fear of imminent social revolution. No single issue came to dominate debate as had occurred in previous decades. Meanwhile, especially amongst moderate political opinion, it was accepted that many issues of importance in the divisive debates of the 1830s and 1840s were no longer of practical concern. It was against this background that Conservative inactivity and a Peelite, Whig, Liberal and Radical crisis of leadership assumed such significance.[21]

The immediate impact in Westminster produced symptoms of political fluidity. Between 1850 and 1852 Russell sought, ineffectively, to restore his leadership and Foxite birthright with a revived concern for parliamentary reform. Palmerston challenged Russell by advertising differences over foreign policy. Lord Grey adopted expertise over colonial affairs. Other Whigs, impatient with their leaders' caprice, searched for alternatives to Russellite concerns. The Peelites allowed a belief in their own indispensability to conceal growing differences of intent. Radicals suffered ostracism and internal division. The Irish Brigade emerged, pledged to be Celtic thorns in the side of any Anglo-Saxon ministry, while seeking responses to Irish land grievances.[22] Meanwhile Lord Derby adopted masterly inactivity, preparing to wean the Conservative party from commitment to protection in 1852, but offering no alternative diet to sustain distinctive endeavour. The realignment of party connection seemed a constant threat to those wishing to preserve the *status quo*, but an encouraging solace to those excluded by existing arrangements.

In 1851 Russell was planning to bring the Peelite Sir James Graham into his cabinet.[23] During 1852 a Derby–Palmerston alliance was widely anticipated. The Radical John Roebuck tested Graham's reaction to the Liberal leadership.[24] Palmerston 'opened a negotiation for placing Lansdowne at the head of a government, which would include many of the Whigs, all the Peelites willing to join, and possibly some of the Derbyites'.[25] Russell appeared to go 'knocking on everyone's door . . . in total forgetfulness of his own dignity'.[26] Disraeli and Derby's son, Lord Stanley, believed an alliance with the Irish Brigade to be 'always a desirable object'.[27] In the event, a minority Conservative government was followed, in December 1852, by a Whig–Liberal–Peelite coalition under the premiership of Lord Aberdeen.[28]

There can be little surprise in the fact that party nomenclature assumed unprecedently complicated forms during the 1850s. Yet it would be a great mistake to see this as revealing disillusionment with the principle of coherent party connection. A moral sense of party was retained which, rather than dismissing party as a sapping of energy better devoted to national ends, perceived party as being in the national interest and the safeguard of strong government. The 'golden age of the backbencher' is an erroneous, though seductive, vision compounded of nostalgia and polemic.[29] A common conviction prevailed that 'parliamentary government is a government of political parties', and that independent voting substituted 'the rule of the few and the wise, by that of the many and the foolish'.[30] Belief survived that 'if parliamentary government be prolonged in this country . . . it must rest on the basis of party'.[31] This, in turn, enforced the practical truth that 'nothing unless under a head, can . . . be of use'.[32] Gladstone observed in 1856:

[T]he disorganisation of political parties has for the last ten years, greatly impaired the strengths of the Executive. This capital evil discredits Government, encourages faction, retards legislation, diminishes the respect necessary for the efficiency of Parliament, and is thus unfavourable to the stability of our institutions.[33]

In a crowded House of Commons Disraeli affirmed that 'party, well defined and well appreciated, is the best guarantee for public and private honour'.[34] In 1852 Queen Victoria predicted:

One thing is pretty *certain* – that *out* of the present *state* of confusion and discordance, a sound state of *Parties* will be obtained, *and two Parties*, as of old, will again exist, without which it is *impossible* to have a *strong* Government. *How* these *Parties* will be formed it is impossible to say at present.[35]

Confusion and discordance attended both the Aberdeen coalition and Palmerston's subsequent administration, formed in February 1855. Derby's minority Conservative ministry, formed in February 1858, tried to exploit the flux of party connection. It was not until the summer of 1859 that a stable two-party alignment re-emerged. By June 1859 it 'was possible to rally 637 MPs into a party division in which there was little cross-voting'.[36] On 6 June 1859 a meeting at Willis's Rooms was attended by leading Whigs, Liberals, Radicals and a number of former Peelites. 'That meeting may fairly be called "a turning point" in English political history. . . . The meeting marks the real beginning of that union of Whigs, Peelites and Liberals which became the Liberal party of the later nineteenth century.'[37] Indeed, it 'may be legitimately regarded as the formal foundation of the Liberal party'.[38]

II

The important transformations that took place in the function of party during the 1860s and 1870s, as parliamentary parties became national parties, emphasised the importance of the alignments that emerged during the late 1850s. The association of parliamentary personnel that attended the meeting in Willis's Rooms provided a Liberal focus for an emergent cheap daily press, militant Nonconformity and organised labour.[39] The power of Gladstone's oratory fused that popular Liberalism with a previously existing, though morally recharged, tradition of administrative progressivism. In response, the Conservative party extended constituency organisation and devised a rhetoric stressing social need and imperial prestige.[40] Thus Disraeli sought to mediate social grievances, affirm Conservative governing capability, and distinguish his own political presence amongst the working and middle classes. The importance of these developments suggest that earlier historical judgements, which dismiss the political events of the late 1850s, create an historiographical difficulty. An intellectual problem is the product of an antagonism between empirical evidence and accepted knowledge; an historical problem exists when *idées reçues* fail to explain evidence *extant*.

Surveying the 1850s nearly thirty years later, Gladstone 'touch[ed] very lightly and briefly on events which happen[ed] between the Crimean War and the year 1860'.[41] One politician's avoidance of an embarrassing perplexity became historical orthodoxy. McCarthy sensed 'a sort of langour' in parliament and the public mind during the period.[42] G. M. Trevelyan and J. R. M. Butler perceived, 'in that easy-going period', an 'inertia' that revealed politics to be 'placid'.[43] G. M. Young's verdict was unequivocal: 'Domestic politics [were] languid.'[44] More recently, J. B. Conacher has sustained the outline of received narrative by describing the late 1850s as years of 'political doldrums'.[45]

Simple historical empathy demands dissent from such orthodoxy. The circumstances of behaviour were just as forceful and intentions equally as powerful between 1855 and 1859 as in 1832 or 1846. The perception of inertia and inaction only renders the immaculate conception of the Liberal party in 1859 the more miraculous; 1859 can only be explained by taking events after 1855 seriously. The diarist Charles Greville commented in May 1858:

In my long experience I do not recollect to have seen so much political bitterness and violence (except perhaps during the contests of the Catholic and Reform questions), and certainly there never was a great Parliamentary battle distinguished by so much uncertainty and so many vicissitudes and in which the end corresponded so little with the beginning and the general expectation.[46]

The verdict remained valid for succeeding months. Gladstone, at the end of the same session, was certain that 'all commentators must in fairness admit, that at least it has not been an insipid year'.[47] Disraeli confessed that 'I don't know I ever passed thro' a period of so much excitement, labour and anxiety, encouraging the desponding and animating the timid'.[48] This intensity of political activity underlines the importance of the late 1850s in the development of Victorian parliamentary parties.

The greater historical problem exists in discerning the meaning of party nomenclature in the confused circumstances of parliamentary politics after 1850. Sir Edward Bulwer Lytton observed that 'in politics, as in religion the bigot generally hates those most from whom he really differs least'.[49] This aphorism warns against readily subordinating human nature to purely rational precepts and imposing doctrine upon sentiment. Attempting to define the terms Conservative, Whig, Liberal or Radical in purely doctrinal terms can create as many problems as it solves. First, avowed allegiance must be surrendered to an implied superior ideological reality. Secondly, there is the danger of locating an association of complex attitudes along a continuum representing a single ideological dimension that the involved nature of human thought defies. The comprehension of motive and intention is only possible within the untidy pattern that the evidence presents, while enforcing the truism of the individuality of individual behaviour. As W. O. Aydelotte warned at the beginning of his statistical analysis of the Commons in the 1840s, 'anyone who has worked closely with his materials must be conscious that as soon as he begins to sort men into categories he is departing from reality. General labels are never accurate or satisfactory: they obscure important differences and describe only partially circumstances that are complex and varied.'[50] For the purposes of this study, politicians' self-avowed designations have been taken as authoritative. Where these might seem anomalous or deceptive, the intent behind such discrepancy is further stimulus to historical curiosity.

The practical nature of argument and thought within Westminster placed a premium on persuasion rather than logical precision. This is a further warning against the search for clearly defined doctrinal distinctions. A characteristic of thought in parliament was a lack of concern with first principles. Abstract reasoning, a cause for suspicion rather than respect, was seen as a subversive activity that obscured the politic limits of the possible. A typical reaction to an untypical mind was Lord Overstone's apprehension about Robert Lowe: 'a dangerous man' because 'an abstract reasoner – with no practical experience nor any respect for it'.[51] Another Whig perceived Lowe 'to be a man full of the wildest theories of a nature most inapplicable . . . rendering him, if he possesses any influence, a very dangerous person'.[52] The sober Sir George Cornewall Lewis 'filled the House with amazement' by explaining his 'abstract theories on the Rights of Property'.[53] Bright quickly learned that the Commons 'hates to be lectured – and it also hates subtlety, long trains of reasoning and nice distinctions and qualifications'.[54] The subtle nuance of intellectual precision was an anathema in circumstances where language served the purposes of persuasion and practicality could highlight the virtues of ambiguity. The 'intellectual haze' of 'abstract argument diluted and dissolved in real life' forcefully obscured the ready acknowledgement of doctrinal nicety.[55]

It is of little surprise that party nomenclature after 1850 offered ample opportunity for those who felt inclined to cry out that the Emperor had no clothes. Politicians desiring new alignments found it 'mere child's play and an idle abuse of words to talk about Liberalism, Conservatism and Radicalism at all' when political opinion had reached 'such an . . . absolutely chaotic and disorganised state'.[56] New arrivals at Westminster found 'it was perfectly impossible to see one's way' as 'there is no party who have any fixed principle for their watchword or any definite political object in view'.[57] Thomas Milner Gibson, seeking a rationalisation of Liberal attitudes and the survival of an independent Radical party, declared that he had 'but a hazy perception of what constituted the exact difference' between Conservatives and Liberals. 'It did not appear to him to be at all useful or necessary to enter into any investigation of that kind.'[58]

For the historian, the investigation is both necessary and useful. Terms of party distinction were universally used and intended to evoke an impression or convey meaning. Despite party connection being in apparent flux, party nomenclature was still used as a means of identifying purpose. The search for meaning is the central problem for the political historian of the mid-19th century. Aydelotte has undertaken a similar enquiry, using quantitative methods, for the comparatively cohesive parliament of 1841–47. By collating biographical details with MPs voting behaviour in crucial divisions, Aydelotte established that political attitudes were not determined by social or economic factors, but were the product of political and ideological considerations.[59] It was also confirmed that parties were divided internally, but on many occasions acted in unanimity. Thus the existence of intra-party tensions belied by a rhetoric of two-party alignment was affirmed.

Historical enquiry, however, is a response to the historian's questioning of his own material; he is both observer and an aspect of that observed. The onus this response places upon the historian is inherent in his method, and statistical enquiry readily reveals the effect of this methodological reflex. By ordering his data in ideological terms of party orientation, over a wide number of issues, Aydelotte found 'that there existed, between the two main party groups . . . substantial ideological differences'.[60] The data presented, however, yields equally conclusively to a chronological analysis that blurs distinct ideological terms of reference. In more recent writing Aydelotte has tested data against just such temporal criteria. This suggested an alternative interpretation of events 'couched less in ideological terms and more in strictly political terms'.[61] It also confirmed that the meaning of party nomenclature resided in the particular intent of specific situations. Thomas Sotheron-Estcourt, an 'independent Conservative', touched on the essential dilemma: 'Whig and Tory, I am persuaded are the only distinctions that Englishmen will accept, because like a Domino at a Masquerade, they mean nothing and cover everything.'[62] Party nomenclature was more a means of inner rationale than a tool of ideological analysis.

Computer analysis of commons voting behaviour between 1852 and 1859 undertaken by J. R. Bylsma and R. G. Watt, reveals the surprising resilience of two-party voting amongst backbenchers in major political divisions after 1850.[63] This confirms a prevalent faith in the virtue of party, the illusion of backbench independence and the force of habit. It also emphasises the importance of frontbench purposes and the prevailing idiom of political debate. Aydelotte showed that a rhetoric of distinct two-party alignment in the 1840s overlay intra- as well as inter-party tensions. Bylsma and Watt reveal that similar tensions in the 1850s were overlaid with a rhetoric of party flux. The perception of party flux in the 1850s was given credence by the very generalised character of party opinion, as well as the absence of one dominating issue, Conservative inactivity, and a crisis of leadership amongst non-Conservatives.

Bylsma and Watt's suggestion of the broad contours of backbench opinion show that fluidity was not shapelessness.[64] But some other points need to be made. First, without disrupting resilient two-party alignment, bi-polarity could be defined in different ways. Therein lay the strategic complexity of events after 1850 focusing upon individuals such as Derby, Palmerston, Lord Stanley and Lord Grey. Secondly, the contours of backbench opinion shifted over time with changes of government and circumstance. Thirdly, quantification, without reference to private sources but only public statement, misses whole levels of political intention. With reference solely to his division votes in 1857, Russell emerges as a stalwart 'Palmerstonian'. Yet Russell behaved in that way precisely because, as revealed in his private correspondence, he was looking to Palmerston's imminent demise. The public appearance of Russell's behaviour was a conscious concealment of his private intent. The intricate and subtle nuances of political activity often elude precise measurement.[65]

What emerges from the variety of public and private sources is that the meaning of party nomenclature lay in broad generalised doctrinal positions framed within shared attitudes towards other sections of political opinion. The imprecise doctrinal definition of party labels prompted Graham to note that 'Paley's maxim in matters of religion is true also in politics: "men often change their creed, but rarely the name of their sect." '[66] Party labels were useful for what they excluded as much as being guides to what was positively included. More than being reducible to coherent principle, party nomenclature was associated with tone, style, personal reputation and past positions. This was all the more true when a party 'comprises, within itself, far greater discernities of political principles and tendencies, than can be noted as dividing the more moderate portion of one from the moderate portion of the other'.[67] Indeed, for Gladstone, the 'great characteristic of this singular state of things is that political differences no longer lie between parties, but within parties'.[68] It was common experience producing common attitudes to other politicians that clarified the doctrinal vagueness of party labels. Collective identity sprang from shared perceptions of opponents.

By the 1850s two predispositions or attitudes of mind distinguished the Whig rhetorical formulas of rational liberty, honour and due deference. The first was a contemptuous disregard for the Conservative party shorn of Peelites. When Whigs looked at the benches opposite them they saw 'brute votes', the machinations of 'the stupid party' and prejudice posing as principle. After 1846 it became a Whig truism that the Conservatives, without Peelite talent, lacked the ability to form an administration. It did not appear possible that 'the Derby crew [could] ever again be taken to man the ship. . . . Lord D. and Dizzy [had] both shown themselves totally unfit to take the helm'.[69] The thought came easily that 'conservatism [was] not little more than a name. There [was] no cause and no leaders that the party care[d] to follow.'[70] Whigs felt contempt mixed with fear, however, of a complete Conservative demise.[71] The absence of an alternative party suitable for Whig denigration as the vehicle of reactionary sentiment might expose Liberal poses concealing conservative concerns.[72]

A fear of Radicalism was the second shared attitude that coalesced Whig opinion. Radicalism threatened the Whig wish to appear as a 'safe' and 'respectable' party of government. Radicals found 'the Tories more civil in the intercourse of the lobbies and the refreshment rooms than the Whigs' who 'always thought it necessary to snub the Radicals to satisfy the Tories they were not dangerous politicians'.[73] Whig reluctance to use their large financial resources for the benefit of extra-parliamentary organisation sprang from the same fear of populism and an instinctive belief in the respectability of parliamentary preoccupations.[74] Radicals lacked honour, generosity of spirit and lofty ideals inherited through rank and breeding, historical awareness and, in portraying responsible concession as capitulation, gratitude.

Liberals subscribed to similar attitudes. That a backbencher described himself as a Liberal, rather than a Whig, was indicative less of distinctive opinion than the social circles from which he was excluded and the political ethos with which he wished to associate. Thus Gladstone could observe in 1855 that Liberalism had come to consist of old associations and a dislike of partisan Tory attitudes.[75] Moreover, Russell could be confident that even those Liberals whose opinions matched those of avowed Radicals would 'give their practical support to men less extreme and more judicious'.[76] The flavour that avowed Liberalism lent personal opinion was of an inclination for 'reasonable' and 'constitutional' 'progress' and 'liberty': no more and no less than this. Avowed Liberals differed over the franchise, the ballot, disestablishing the Church of England, fiscal plans, retrenchment and those religious issues, such as the Maynooth grant, which touched upon Protestant–Catholic relations.[77] What change was 'reasonable' or 'constitutional' was determined by personal bias and specific circumstances. Yet Whigs and Liberals also perceived themselves to be the 'natural' party of government. They 'derive[d] wonderful security from the absence of men fit to take their places'.[78] As much as one shared doctrinal principle cohering Whig–Liberal opinion, it was shared perceptions of others that delineated a common purpose.

A similar diversity of opinion and concerns existed within Radical circles. The remnants of Philosophic Radicalism, the Manchester School, Dissent, an emergent temperance movement, and pressure groups such as the Administrative Reform Association, attested to Radical differences.[79] Utilitarian patriots such as John Roebuck shared little with free trade internationalists like Richard Cobden. What all did share, however, was contempt for Whigs and their Foxite axioms. Whigs and Liberals, Radical opinion chorused, voiced the rhetoric of reform and progress in order to protect the worst vested interests of an oligarchic system. '[W]hen reformers get on the cushion of office they usually blow fresh air into it and sit much after the same fashion as their predecessors.'[80] Roebuck attacked the Whigs as 'an exclusive and aristocratic faction. . . . When out of office they are demagogues; in power they became exclusive oligarchs.'[81] Cobden affirmed that the Whigs only kept office by 'the prostitution of the Radicals'.[82] Consequently Cobden feared vehemently opposing a Conservative government only to be committed to 'a Whig restoration'.[83] Similarly Bright, in his strongest demagogic fervour, attacked privilege so as to focus his venom upon a Whig clique and its pretensions. The ballot, more than any other single issue, cohered Radical opinion because it was a reform aimed directly at the deferential corruption of oligarchy.

The Peelites after 1850 sustained a sense of camaraderie through the pious cult of a dead leader and a self-adulatory sense of superiority. There was, Gladstone intoned, 'scarcely one among them who was not, for one reason or another, much above *par* as a Member of Parliament'.[84] Political hauteur was made manifest in 'their intense self-satisfaction'.[85] Those not Peelites placed a less charitable view upon the Peelites' sense of worth; 'they are a Sect–entre nous *Prigs*. There is a snobbism that runs from their deceased head all down thro' his tail.'[86] As the inheritors of a ministerial ethic, not a party doctrine, the circumstances of sharing power and the domestic repercussions of the Crimean War did fatal damage to Peelite cohesion. High morality proved an ineffective bond as Peelite intentions diverged under adversity.

The Conservative party had as much diversity of opinion within its ranks as the benches opposite. At one extreme were men such as Lord Stanley, who made more extra-parliamentary speeches during the 1850s than either Cobden or Bright on the needs of the working man and the towns. Stanley was 'in favour of the admission of the Jews into Parliament, of the Maynooth grant, and of the exception of

Dissenters from the Church Rates'.[87] At the other extreme were 'ultra-Tories' such as Charles Newdegate and William Beresford; the latter being a self-confessed 'bigoted Protestant'.[88] Within 'ultra-Tory' circles, fellowship was nurtured by a close-textured religiosity, constant suspicion, Anglican fervency and an oppressive sense of being men *contra mundum*.[89] Between these extremes lay a body of opinion that shared a tender sensitivity in varying degrees to change. The pragmatic nature of Conservative doctrine more easily tolerated such divergence after 1852 and the relinquishing of Protectionism. There remained precious little else to cohere Conservative sentiment except habit and loyalty to Lord Derby.

The absence of a distinctive Conservative purpose was the conscious product of Derby's opposition strategy. It was a strategy that looked to exacerbating Peelite, Whig, Liberal and Radical differences in the void created by Conservative passivity.[90] In doing nothing Conservatives could emphasise the divisions amongst non-Conservative opinion and the obstruction to Peelites, Whigs, Liberals and Radicals acting together. The importance of Derby's actions as Conservative leader after 1846 consisted in what he chose not to do. He did not commit the party irrevocably to Protectionism, despite economic inducements. He did not identify the party as the zealous defender of the Established Church in an Anglican Constitution under threat, despite the sectarian excitement of Russell's Durham Letter in 1850. He did not commit the party to rigid obstruction to an artificially induced, and Whig-inspired, revival of parliamentary reform after 1848. He did not fire the party with outraged patriotism during the Crimean War, despite the much publicised mismanagement of the war effort. This was not a confession of doctrinal impotence, but a deliberate avoidance of any commitment which might consolidate non-Conservative opinion. The critical question was whether habit and personal loyalty could sustain Conservative unity long enough to bring about Whig, Liberal and Radical dismemberment.

Conservative non-commitment and the fact that shared attitudes defined party feeling gave credibility to the belief in party flux. The relation between foreign policy, the condition of England question, religious issues and party policy provided further plausibility. The only major and innovative doctrinal challenge to existing parliamentary opinion in the 1850s merely confirmed Radical differences and consensus elsewhere. Richard Cobden and John Bright decried traditional foreign policy in terms of a moral internationalism founded upon free trade, in sharp contrast to the concepts of power politics and national interest that defined established perception. Free trade and finance, the latter always central in Cobden's thought, demanded peace abroad so as to allow reform at home. Moral internationalism formed the natural corollary to Cobden's economic tenets.[91] Notions of 'balance of power' and 'spheres of interest', Cobden and Bright claimed, constituted an inadequate and dangerous understanding of international affairs promoting disharmony and war. The challenge was ineffective. It failed because it was at once so radical and yet repudiated by other Radicals. Roebuck, voicing an older 18th-century patriotic Radical tradition, poured scorn on Cobdenite ideas and Bright's rhetoric.[92] Thus, while the Crimean War ensured that foreign policy dominated debate during 1854 and 1855, it also had two important implications for the discussion of policy. First, popular resentment at inefficiency did not prompt reappraisal of the terms within which foreign policy was couched. It merely confirmed that the ultimate test of foreign policy was success.[93] Ineffectiveness was the Aberdeen coalition's besetting sin. Secondly, it revealed that differences over foreign policy did not complement party differences, but fractured parliamentary opinion in disruptive ways. This defined Palmerston's political opportunity in 1855, and ensured that the axiomatic utterances of Pitt and Canning survived the intellectual challenge of Cobdenite thought.

Two other areas of executive and legislative concern were conspicuous by their absence in the context of party policy. First, social legislation remained a non-party issue.[94] Factory legislation, with its cry of social justice, did not sit easily with the Whig–Liberal cry for rational liberty. Nor did it always overcome the vested interests of middle-class Radicalism. The condition of England question, and even the condition of Ireland question (despite the efforts of the Irish Brigade), did not create a bond of compassionate high-mindedness between Whigs, Liberals and Radicals. The incompatible elements of paternalism, evangelicalism, humanitarianism and liberty ensured that the condition of England did little to determine the condition of parliamentary parties.

Secondly, religious questions were impossible to fit into defined party positions. Though Church Rates or the admission of Jews into parliament, which could be seen to have legal and political significance, allowed the Liberals some unanimity through the cry of civil and religious liberty; other issues such as the Maynooth grant sharply divided Liberals from each other.[95] For all other sections of parliamentary opinion, religious questions were a source of constant disruption. Aberdeen in 1853, newly appointed as prime minister, railed against 'these confounded Church matters'.[96] The coalition minister, Sir Charles Wood, reviewing the 1854 session, found 'mostly every question on which we were beaten involved religious feelings more or less. You cannot reason about them and control men's feelings on such subjects.'[97] The Peelite, Sir James Graham, looking to the 1857 session, noted that 'unhappily religious questions are likely to be prominent and there are sources of difference which it is always most difficult to reconcile'.[98] Lord Stanley anticipated nothing with greater certainty than 'a great ecclesiastical crash'.[99] Ultra-Tories, after 1846, interwove Protectionism and strict Anglican belief 'into a dogmatism which rasied . . . an artificial zeal in the name of religion'.[100] Church Rates, the Maynooth grant, marriage law amendment, Sunday trading and the selling of church property all divided Conservative opinion.[101] Peelites disagreed over Church Rates, Maynooth and Russell's education resolutions in 1856.[102] It was clear that 'Protestantism [was] too dangerous a bond for practical men who look to form a government'.[103] In an age of religious revival religion was too important to be important in defining party differences.

The difficulty of religious questions, the absence of social issues, a conceptual consensus over foreign policy, and the definition given to doctrinal positions by shared perceptions of others, refined the meaning of party nomenclature. Equally important, such meaning gave credibility to a prevailing sense of party instability prompted by Conservative passivity and a non-Conservative struggle for leadership. It meant there was little doctrinal absurdity in the variety of speculated realignments entertained during the 1850s. Criteria of plausibility existed in the intentions and perceptions of those participating, excluded, or requiring to be reconciled to such realignment.

III

Four modes of Victorian thought on politics informed parliamentary activity to varying degrees and were fused through the medium of rhetoric; first, those associations of abstract ideas or first principles comprising doctrine; secondly, the implementation of executive or legislative action as policy; thirdly, that understanding of constitutional realities describing the source of political authority; and finally, those strategic concerns looking to translate intent into effective action. In reality the relation between these modes of thought was neither distinct nor in any prescriptive or hierarchical order. But their interrelation in the 1850s brought Conservative strategy and Peelite, Whig, Liberal and Radical antagonisms to the fore. Within a parliamentary system bestowing constitutional authority upon stable party support the effect of indistinct doctrinal differences on policy intensified the strategic complexities of a surfeit of party leadership and Conservative evasiveness.

Within Westminster, in the 1850s, there were 'many men of power and eminence, but great difficulties arising from various causes, present and past relations, incompatibilities, peculiar defects of character or failures, in bringing them together'.[104] As Prince Albert observed: 'the difficulty of obtaining any strong government consists, not in the paucity of men, but in the oversupply of Rt. Honourable gentlemen'.[105] The practical implications of too much talent and ambition were clear. '[O]ffice has the quality of charity: it blesseth him that has and him that hopes: it maintains without difficulty two sets of incumbents, an actual and a prospective: but it cannot well maintain four or five.'[106]

Political correspondence will always reveal dissension and disquiet. Squeamishness should not obscure the fact that such tensions can as easily be symptoms of political vitality as party fragility. What is important is that such feeling during the 1850s cast an eye towards a wide variety of future contingency. The events of 1852 produced a wealth of speculation. Russell had committed himself to the issue of parliamentary reform as the means of reasserting his diminishing control over Liberal opinion. Graham offered support. The greater body of Whigs moved away from Russell, impatient with his fickleness. Palmerston appeared to be moving towards a union with the Conservatives while disparaging Russell as 'factious and querulous'.[107] The Conservatives, in office from February to December 1852, publicly forsook Protectionism which appeared to open up possibilities of future additions from Whig and Peelite ranks. Disraeli speculated on a Conservative–Radical alliance on an anti-Whig platform. Radicals, meanwhile, found themselves increasingly excluded from important political counsel.

The formation of the Aberdeen coalition in December 1852 exacerbated as many antagonisms as it attempted to appease. That the Peelites, while numerically small, took the 'lion's share' of high offices infuriated Whigs and Liberals.[108] Russell entered the coalition with 'scarcely a personal or even a party friend in it'.[109] A token Radical in the cabinet, Sir William Molesworth, did little to conceal the expendability of extreme Liberal opinion. Palmerston's presence in the cabinet denied any immediate Derbyite fusion. Yet there was the danger to the Peelites that a coalition government would 'not so much make the Liberals rich as make us poor indeed'.[110] When Disraeli represented the Whigs as the subservient pawns of the Peelites, and the Radicals as the tools of both, it was 'a most skilful and ingenious rubbing up of old sores'.[111]

Gladstone safeguarded the early months of the Aberdeen coalition in an axiomatic Peelite manner. His budget of 1853 appeared to substantiate the government's claim to executive talent and administrative efficiency. The onset of the Crimean War in 1854, however, shattered Peelite pretensions to managerial professionalism. Diplomatic difficulties and military mismanagement fell heavily upon a cabinet presumed to be packed with administrative talent.[112] Moreover, the cabinet found itself struggling with the internal problems created by the bitter antagonism between Russell and Palmerston. Russell's attempt to bring forward a reform bill in 1854 was Palmerston's opportunity to exploit 'the explosion of feeling' against Russellite priorities.[113] Russell's stock fell as he provided confirmation for those who wished to see him as 'wayward, uncertain and querulous'.[114] Meanwhile Palmerston continued to associate himself popularly with a 'bustling foreign policy' so as to 'stave off constitutional questions' and a recognition of Russell's authority.[115] Derby chose not to take up the Conservative's golden opportunity of assailing the coalition on an outspoken patriotic platform. This left political options open in 1855.

In January 1855 the Aberdeen coalition came to a fractious and ignominious end. The fall of the coalition affirmed two fundamental practical truths. The coalition was defeated on Roebuck's motion by Conservative unity and utter Whig, Liberal and Radical disarray.[116] This set the scene for the intricate negotiation that followed. Derby's failure to form a ministry with Palmerston closed off the immediate opportunity of transforming Conservative unanimity into a majority by absorbing centrist opinion. Russell's failure to form a ministry confirmed the deep divisions and disgust within non-Conservative ranks. This threw Palmerston forward as the temporary arbitrator of immediate differences. Picking up on Derby's deferred opportunity of the previous year, Palmerston came through as the popular representative of patriotic fervour.[117] But Palmerston's pre-eminence, his age and his lack of a stable following in parliament, did little to remedy the basic ills of party connection.[118] The fundamental difficulties remained: the future political role of a unified minority Conservative party, and the reconciliation of a surfeit of leadership fragmenting Peelite, Whig, Liberal and Radical support.

Events between 1855 and June 1859 produced two general elections, the fall of two governments, the formation of two others, and a succession of complex situations manipulated by subtle political minds. They also produced that bi-partisan alignment of parliamentary opinion celebrated at Willis's Rooms and embodied in Palmerston's second ministry. This study examines the manner in which that alignment of political opinion took shape. Its premise is that the actions of individual politicians and parties cannot be isolated from the perceived intentions of others and the contingent shift of events. This is not narrative in default of explanation. It is party, policy and personality developing within an intimate parliamentary context of rapidly changing circumstances.

1 Palmerstonian Politics

I believe [Lord Palmerston] is where he is because the public thought him the right man for the post . . . and I do not believe there is a more able and patriotic statesman than Lord Palmerston. (Kinnaird at Perth, *The Times*, 26 December 1856, p. 10)

Palmerston . . . is the only public man in England who has a name. Many criticise, many disapprove, but all, more or less, like him and look on him as the only man. He has on his side that which is the strongest element in the mental organisation of all human society, namely the public's national prejudices. Someone said, 'Give me the national songs and I will rule the nation'; and Canning said, 'Don't talk to me of the "sense of the nation"; give me the *nonsense*, and I will beat it hollow'. (Herbert to Gladstone, 4 January 1857, Gladstone Mss. 44210, fol. 292, cited in A. H. Gordon, Baron Stanmore, *Sidney Herbert, Lord Herbert of Lea: A Memoir*, 2 vols (London, 1886) II, p. 68)

Palmerston's political career was a triumph of diligence, style, longevity and luck. His leap to the premiership in February 1855 was an opportunity presented by the miscalculation of others seized with alacrity. Derby, at the head of a unified Conservative party, looked to gaining power on his own terms, and gambled on Russell and Palmerston failing. Russell, facing Whig–Liberal disarray, failed, but tried to keep his options open for the future. The rapid succession of confused events that occured during the cold months of January and February 1855 acquired, in retrospect, a gloss of certainty. Palmerston had become prime minister because he was the only leading politician capable and popular enough to do so. In part this interpretation of events was convincing because it provided Derby with an alibi for what others might perceive as the result of his own inadequacy. Thus Derby provided corroboration with the statement that Palmerston was 'the man called upon by the voice of the country to take the management of affairs'.[1] It was also convincing because Palmerston recognised in this belief a means of mobilising support. He fashioned it into a basis for his continued control of political affairs.

During 1855 and 1856 a body of 'Palmerstonian' rhetoric was

constructed that proved a persuasive portrayal of Palmerston's triumph and an effective constraint on others. The essential tenets were simple, yet more telling for their simplicity. Palmerston was indispensable because other politicians, primarily Russell and Derby, were either unworthy or incapable. This projected the personality of the premier as the central element in his appeal for power. Palmerston was associated with diplomatic expertise and effectiveness in foreign affairs – an imperative need in the midst of a mismanaged Crimean War. Legislative domestic issues, therefore, were subordinate to executive foreign policy. Such rhetoric provided the vehicle for Palmerston's skilful use of the press and tapped genuinely popular support in the country. Ministers, seeking re-election in March 1855, proclaimed Palmerston's indispensability.[2] After August 1855, once Robert Lowe became Paymaster General, *The Times* forsook its initial hostility and brought the new orthodoxy to the breakfast tables of the political public.[3] 'The country had needed a man, and in Lord Palmerston it found the man it needed.'[4] A compelling need was defined out of popular desire.

This rhetoric, however, is *not* an explanation of Palmerston's political ascendancy following the fall of Aberdeen's coalition. It tells us how Palmerston wished matters to be seen. To that extent it describes a reality outside parliament and Clubland. But it tells us very little about the reality of Palmerston's situation within Westminster. In truth 'Palmerstonian' rhetoric was the product and need of the premier's situation in parliament. Both the distinction and relation between Palmerstonian language and parliamentary circumstance are crucial to an understanding of the true nature of Palmerston's pre-eminence during 1855 and 1856.

'Palmerstonianism' consisted of the axioms of Chatham and Pitt injected with a distinctive and energetic jauntiness. That 'Palmerstonianism' reiterated the established concepts of foreign policy strengthened the premier's political position, as the phrases he used were familiar and prescriptive. The Crimean War had not modified established domestic understanding of foreign policy. Within the Aberdeen cabinet, Herbert noted, they were 'all agreed as to the objects in view'.[5] Disagreement existed over divergent means to a common end, and temperament, age and experience exacerbated such differences.[6] Yet, when forming his ministry, Palmerston had a long interview with Aberdeen on foreign affairs. Aberdeen declared himself 'satisfied' with Palmerston's intentions, and encouraged Graham, Gladstone and Herbert to join Palmerston's cabinet.[7] Such concurrence ensured that the established notional depiction of foreign policy remained intact.[8]

Orthodox axioms were more an apparent than real constraint on political activity. It was a practical maxim that 'with regard to occurrences likely to have international consequences, no general rule could be uniformly applied. In each case the government had to exercise its own discretion.'[9] Despite a rigidly held public purpose, 'it [is] unwise to settle too long beforehand what course [is] to be pursued in regard to future and hypothetical events which [may] never happen and with respect to which, intervening events and concomitant circumstances [will], if they should come to pass, very materially determine the course to be pursued'.[10] What should be recognised as a threat to 'British interests', an 'insult' to 'honour', a disturbance to 'the balance of power', or necessary for the 'preservation of peace' remained vague and ill-defined. In parliament it was the testing of rhetorical credibility against specific decision that mattered. Palmerston's greatest executive resource existed in the freedom that presentation allowed in practice.

'Palmerstonianism' left 'foreign affairs . . . elevated as the chief, if not the sole department of national politics and interest'.[11] During the 1840s foreign policy had not been a preoccupation; this had been Peel's need and achievement.[12] After 1850, and his 'Don Pacifico' speech, Palmerston made known his dissent from Russell's leadership through foreign affairs. In December 1853 Palmerston managed the announcement of his short-lived resignation from Aberdeen's coalition so as to suggest foreign policy as the reason for his going, rather than reform which was the actual source of his dissatisfaction.[13] During 1854 Palmerston allowed it to be understood that deep divisions existed within the government over the conduct of the war. Argyll remembered that Palmerston 'had been quite as unforeseeing as any of us as regards the unexpected contingencies', but 'popular superstition' saw him as the man to lead the war effort, and the man 'who could have prevented it'.[14] This public belief, which had little private substance, allowed Palmerston to escape the acrimony that fell upon Aberdeen's discredited coalition in January 1855. As premier, after February 1855, the tolerance rhetoric allowed to actual decision permitted Palmerston to alternately emphasise 'peace with honour' and 'war with victory'. This denied a Peelite–Conservative union, effective Conservative opposition as either a party of peace or war, and frustrated any attempt by Russell to coalesce Liberal–Radical opinion.[15] During the session of 1855 and early months of 1856, debate was naturally preoccupied with the Eastern Question and the Crimean Commission Report. The Conference of Paris dominated parliamentary discussion during April and May 1856. But the conclusion of the Crimean War did not signal a return to the consideration of domestic issues. Relations with the United States became of concern, but by the end of the session there 'appeared nothing to keep one awake, but the drowsy hum of the Italian question'.[16] America, Persia, Neuchâtel, Anglo–French relations, and China formed the diet of political controversy at the beginning of the 1856 recess.

'Pamerstonian' rhetoric was not without domestic reference. But such domestic reference as it did contain only emphasised the primacy of foreign relations. 'Progressive improvement' was that which every man sought in his private affairs. With an inductive logic Palmerston's language offered 'progressive improvement' abroad as the proper object of national interest. Fundamental to 'Palmerstonianism' was a determining relation between international affairs and national strength and prosperity. The emphasis on foreign policy was sustained in an argument that pointed to social stability in progressive wealth, and progressive wealth in the defence of British interests abroad.[17] The audience 'Palmerstonianism' described was a national community of shared interest subsuming offensive class politics and divisive social grievances. A national appeal suggested the easy assumption of policies of social appeasement. Diplomacy became the touchstone of domestic, as well as foreign, policy. At the same time domestic freedom, stability and prosperity gave Britain 'moral force' abroad and provided 'a bright example' to others.[18] Equally importantly, this language portrayed the main purpose of government as executive, rather than legislative, and the main area of executive decision to be foreign affairs.

Palmerstonian rhetoric defined the public portrayal of government policy delivered to eager audiences at Manchester, Salford and Liverpool during 1856.[19] It preached Palmerston's indispensability, the primacy of foreign affairs, an executive notion of government, and imputed inadequacy to other prominent parliamentarians. It described a stable and free national community of interest, less concerned with the distribution of wealth than the securing of greater prosperity. It allowed a flexibility of executive decision within the tolerant rhetorical constraints of traditional policy. Yet 'Palmerstonianism' was only a powerful force outside parliament as part of what Cobden called the snobbish flunkeyism of the provinces. The fickle loyalty of a pliable public and that proclaimed by *The Times*, merely suggested that Palmerston might too easily mistake popular opinion for real political support.[20] The true purpose of Palmerstonian policy lay in parliamentary circumstance.

As prime minister, Palmerston's immediate concern was parliament. He was no longer 'Cupid', the 'alpha and omega of the War Office', a 'juvenile Whig', or 'Lord Pumicestone', but a shrewd, dispassionate and resilient manager of men. If, as a young man, he often fell short of expectation, in old age he constantly surpassed it. Aged seventy-one in 1855, Palmerston, Russell suggested, only reached maturity after his biblical span of three score years and ten. 'Had he died at seventy he would have left a second class reputation. It was his great and peculiar fortune to live to right himself.'[21] Having 'achieved the object of his ambition' in becoming premier, Palmerston 'put off the old man and became a babe of grace with his altered position'.[22] Seeming to 'eschew all pleasure' he stuck 'to the House as a diligent tradesman sticks to his shop'.[23] His expertise in foreign affairs became the resourceful response to a parliamentary need. A disarming *présence d'esprit*, an affable manner and an enviable vigour enhanced administrative talent. Palmerston's triumph of social manner was admirably complemented by Lady Palmerston's parties at Cambridge House.[24] Lady Palmerston was an accomplished political 'grand dame' with 'the remains of great beauty'.[25] This mattered because it compensated for other difficulties.

Palmerstonian policy stressed foreign policy not merely because diplomacy was Palmerston's forte, but because the government had no stable parliamentary support on domestic issues. Nor was it the character of Palmerstonian policy because Palmerston was a one-dimensional political presence. His moving away from France, anti-Russian statements, actions over the Hungarian question and support for Polish nationalists in the late 1840s and 1851 had won Radical support.[26] His exertions as Home Secretary between 1852 and 1855 suggested another facet to his public persona.[27] The circumstances of 1855, however, precluded developing these alternative styles of appeal. The sessions of 1855–56 threw up a number of disruptive domestic questions. During 1855, bills of exchange, a loan bill and newspaper duties in March and April, administrative reform in July, and in 1856, monetary reform, law amendment and the appellate jurisdiction bill, as well as the crisis over the Wensleydale peerage, divided Whig–Liberal support.[28] Religious issues, marriage law amendment and Sunday trading in 1855, Maynooth, Sunday music in parks, the Bishops of London and Durham retirement bill and education (doubly dangerous because associated with Russell) cut across government votes. Herein lay the purpose of a Palmerstonian preoccupation with foreign affairs. Many domestic measures introduced by the government were either inherited or unavoidable. The newspapers duties bill came out of a resolution moved by the Radical Milner Gibson in May 1854, who also introduced the oath of abjuration bill in 1856.[29] The government's Scottish education bill and Cambridge University bill were based upon measures drawn up by Aberdeen's cabinet. The appellate jurisdiction bill was the proposal of a select committee created in response to a motion by Derby in the Lords. In April 1856 Palmerston shelved the local dues bill in a select committee. Though he was 'in the abstract against the system', the question of the purchase of military commissions was laid aside.[30] By the end of the 1856 session the ministry had discarded a limited liability bill, a public health bill and an agricultural statistics bill, and postponed law reform. No wonder Derby found the government's legislative programme 'rendolent of water gruel'.[31] Bright characterised Palmerston's purpose as 'to do nothing at home and to pretend to be doing something abroad'.[32] Cobden declared 'a state of *universal sham*'.[33] Disraeli believed that 'after six months of idle phantoms and of empty noise, it is no longer "measures not men", but it is men without measures'.[34]

Without a stable parliamentary following on domestic issues Palmerston was forced to stake his governing capability on foreign affairs. It was a political necessity to suggest the absence of critical domestic questions, while heralding foreign events as suitable occasions for decisive parliamentary debate. News of the capture of Kertch in June and the fall of Sebastopol in September 1855 prevented Russell leading a peace offensive after his resignation from the government. Palmerston portrayed the fall of the fortress at Kars as a question of confidence in April and May 1856, and secured a straight party vote.[35] This floated the government through the remainder of the session and made the practical moral clear. While domestic issues defined no reliable Palmerstonian support in parliament, foreign policy could galvanize scattered Whigs, Liberals and most Radicals into the necessary unanimity. Moreover, foreign affairs offered strategic advantages to Palmerston within Westminster, who was well practised in using them. Forced to debate decisions *post facto*, opposition was conscious of its isolation from events. The government 'must be in possession of much information of which we are ignorant'.[36] Furthermore, injured patriotism offered the ultimate retort to criticism, while preserving the necessary reserve attending diplomatic activity. During February 1856, in 'the interests of diplomacy', Palmerston was coyly reticent as to whether or not a state of war existed with Persia.[37] Parliamentary discussion of the Paris Conference was curtailed by Palmerston's statement that he did not wish to 'impede or embarrass negotiation by premature discussion'.[38] In such strategy lay that which Disraeli dubbed 'the patrician bullying of the Treasury bench'.[39]

It was Palmerston's achievement to align avowed Whigs and Liberals, who had formerly defined their Liberalism in terms of domestic and legislative reform, with an executive notion of government that disregarded legislation in a preoccupation with foreign policy. This was possible because such an accommodation did not require a denial of collective Whig–Liberal attitudes of mind. 'Palmerstonianism' did not challenge Liberal contempt for Conservatives, fear of Radicals, or their sense of being the natural party of government. Indeed, it skilfully re-enforced such beliefs. This accommodation, however, also confirmed the vulnerability of Palmerstonian policy if domestic issues should push aside foreign affairs.

At the beginning of 1856 it seemed that Palmerstonian rhetoric had an authoritative hold over the perception of political affairs. There appeared to be 'no parties, and Palmerston and the war are the only banners'.[40] Even after the Treaty of Paris in March 1856 there seemed to be 'no great principle for which anybody is ready to give battle'.[41] But Palmerston, for one, was aware of the deceptive nature of appearances, and parliamentary prudence contained an instinctive bellicosity. When a dispute broke out with the United States over British Honduras and the behaviour of the British Ambassador in Washington, Palmerston, although privately outraged, adopted a conciliatory pose in the Commons.[42] In June 1856 Palmerston made concessions to Washington that pre-empted Disraeli and Gladstone forming a hostile alliance.[43] Similarly, Palmerston sought to appease sections of parliamentary opinion with low-church ecclesiastical appointments. Yet if these appointments, suggested by his son-in-law Lord Shaftesbury, attracted some Tory support and did little to offend Liberal sensibilities, they only further inflamed Peelite anti-Palmerstonianism.[44] The essential truth remained. Viewed from afar 'Palmerstonianism' was an impressive achievement. Close to, Palmerston's political standing exhibited feet of clay.

I

That 'Palmerstonianism' was in essence Palmerston not only characterised ministerial rhetoric, but also shaped the pattern of cabinet
relationships. Cabinet meetings were less an occasion for the poten-
tially disruptive discussion of policy, than an opportunity to consolidate a sense of official cohesion. 'Aberdeen had introduced the habit
of settling everything *out* of the cabinet which suited Palmerston
exactly.'[45] The ostensible authoritativeness such congeniality suggested, however, concealed the fact that Palmerston's authority had
as much to do with the compliance of colleagues as with personal
prestige. Just as the apparent ascendancy of 'Palmerstonianism'
belied a precarious parliamentary reality, so Palmerston's ascendancy
within the cabinet belied the necessary acquiescence of his ministers.
During 1855 and 1856 the cabinet formed a tolerant and accommodating phalanx of 'Palmerstonian' support. Ministers remained
content that Palmerston was the best arbitrator of 'Palmerstonian'
policy as long as such policy had credence. Once such credibility was
lost, however, with the withdrawal of ministerial compliance, Palmerston's indispensability would vanish.

The presence of prominent Whigs in Palmerston's cabinet – Lords
Clarendon, Granville, Landsdowne and Sir Charles Wood – signified
disgust with Russell. Whig 'Palmerstonianism' was, in truth, anti-
Russellism. Clarendon, as Foreign Secretary, was a genial and non-
doctrinaire purveyor of Palmerstonian thought. Eager to 'smooth
rough edges', and sometimes suspected of 'insincerity and cowardice',
colleagues at times found Clarendon 'uneasy and inclined to throw
the blame on everyone'.[46] Such pessimistic alarm was diagnosed as a
lack of political nerve.[47] Granville, aged thirty-nine in 1855, personified Whig principle as an accommodation of discretion. Able and
agreeable – his nickname was 'Pussy' – Granville led the government
in the Lords, and was a link between Palmerston and the court.[48] Not
only disillusioned with Russell, but suspicious of the Peelites, Granville's presence provided a guarantee of tact. Lansdowne, aged
seventy-five in 1855, was the patriarch of Whiggism. Before 1830,
alongside Lord Holland, he had presided over the brilliant social
milieu that had constituted Whiggism isolated from power. Embody-
ing 'good sense, experience, temper, and moderation', Lansdowne,
though 'very ill . . . very lame and crippled by gout', directed Whig
loyalty away from Pembroke Lodge to Cambridge House.[49] Wood

served a similar purpose in 1855, though he found his responsibilities at the Admiralty exacting and onerous. By the autumn of 1855, Wood 'was looking ill and not well, appearing harrassed', but remained loyal to Palmerston because he believed Russell had 'abandoned' the Whigs in 1852.[50]

Lord Panmure, a 'great man in Scotland', represented a Whig section, formerly supporters of Russell, alienated by exclusion from the Aberdeen coalition.[51] Granville, however, thought Panmure 'one of the dullest men he ever knew . . . by far the least able man in the cabinet . . . prejudiced, slow, and *routinier*'.[52] Sir George Grey, aged fifty-six in 1855, as Home Secretary was considered by Bright to be 'the head of the moderate party in the cabinet'.[53] In 1850, along with his cousin Lord Grey, he had opposed Russell's reform proposals and, a year later, had opposed junction with the Peelites believing Gladstone's presence would outrage backbench opinion.[54] In 1852 Wood hoped Grey would become Liberal leader in the Commons with Russell in the Lords and Palmerston heading the Conservatives in the lower House. In fact Grey sought the Speakership of the Commons, which offered 'an income and no great cause of anxiety or uneasiness'.[55] Joining the Aberdeen coalition in 1854, Grey gratefully accepted office under Palmerston the following year. Forcible rather than eloquent, and eristic rather than rhetorically effective, Grey 'did not speak to you as a great man'.[56]

Two ministers were marked out by their personality and intelligence from their 'Palmerstonian' Whig colleagues: Sir George Cornewall Lewis and the Duke of Argyll. Regarded by some as the most learned Englishman of his generation, Cornewall Lewis was the author of a treatise on 'The Method of Observation and Reasoning in Politics', and was privately engrossed in Classical study.[57] His intellect intimidated and, in its esoteric inclinations, occasionally amused his colleagues. Not entering parliament until the age of forty-one in 1847, Cornewall Lewis quickly rose to frontbench prominence with a reputation for financial sagacity. Editor of the *Edinburgh Review* between 1852 and 1855, he returned to the Commons in that latter year and immediately succeeded Gladstone as Chancellor of the Exchequer. Cornewall Lewis' 'singularly cold' manner was the antithesis to Gladstone's voluble moral style.[58] Cornewall Lewis was also the foremost representative of the safe and judicious orthodoxies of Liberal finance opposed to the complex ingenuity of Gladstone's 1853 scheme. Appearing 'calm, philosophical, and destitute of passion' Cornewall Lewis' mind resembled 'a registering machine with a patent index'.[59]

The Duke of Argyll, aged a mere thirty-two in 1855, possessed a youthful intellectual vigour that led Granville to consider him 'a clever little fellow'.[60] With a well-earned reputation for a disposition to controversy, as a former Peelite, Argyll had advocated 'activity' as 'the best Conservative policy'; 'it being the only way of guiding that progress which [was] inevitable in a safe direction'.[61] In 1855, however, Argyll was content to acquiesce to 'Palmerstonian' premises. During 1856 Argyll, 'neither in the House or the cabinet, ... work[ed] as [he] had worked'.[62] During the 1856 recess he confessed himself to be *'in great ignorance'* and unable to write 'one word on politics'.[63] Such uncharacteristic passivity pointed to that ministerial compliance upon which 'Palmerstonian' authority depended.

Three other cabinet appointments – Robert Vernon Smith, Henry Labouchere and Matthew Talbot Baines – revealed Palmerston's wish to associate Whig anti-Russellism with the interests of the commercial classes. Upon such names rested the credibility of the Palmerstonian alignment of national prestige with middle-class prosperity. Yet if the appointments served a political purpose their executive effects were far less beneficial. Granville expressed his opinion that Vernon Smith, as President of the Board of Control, was 'a fool, a damned fool'; the 'worst of the Cockloft'.[64] Despite Palmerston's insistence upon the appointment, Vernon Smith proved 'very unpopular and totally useless'.[65] Labouchere, as Colonial Secretary, neither astonished his friends nor alarmed his enemies. Derby thought the 'appointment add[ed] nothing to the strength of the cabinet', and was 'in fact a very negative sort of move'.[66] Baines, as Chancellor of the Duchy of Lancaster, was associated with the Nonconformist communities of West Yorkshire, though himself an Anglican. But because of ill health his limited energies had little effect upon government policy.[67]

Remaining members of the cabinet, such as Lord Stanley of Alderley, offered little enough aspiration or ability to disturb the *status quo*. Lord Cranworth, as Lord Chancellor, 'was a good executive – but no lawyer, and withal obstinate consulting no one' but his Solicitor-General.[68] Lord Harrowby, as Lord Privy Seal, proved to be 'a tiresome troublesome colleague'.[70] Yet such personal irritations were willingly subsumed during 1855–56 by a genial accommodation of 'Palmerstonian' priorities. 'Palmerston left the departments pretty much to themselves' and 'did not attend to much beside foreign affairs'.[71] Foreign policy, in turn served 'Palmerstonian' purposes within Westminster. Colleagues agreed that 'no leader ever so devoted himself to the business of the House'.[72]

The easy compliance of colleagues was also reflected in the fact that in the Commons Palmerston took the greater responsibility of ministerial speaking upon himself. Critics saw this as proof of ministerial inability. The government appeared 'most ill-off in spokesmen', while 'the divers opposition speakers arrayed against them appeared almost unprecedented'.[73] Disraeli observed that 'with the exception of Palmerston, who for a man of seventy-one still displayed astonishing energy, the cabinet [had] neither an orator nor a debater'.[74] Parkes, 'tabling out the speaking public men for and against', could 'never remember such a deficit in any government'.[75] This was, in part, true. The 'Palmerstonian' frontbench was certainly not a distillation of talent. Names like Vernon Smith or Baines did little to substantiate official authority. Yet the acquiescence of men like Cornewall Lewis and Argyll showed that Palmerston offered, for the moment, a convenient cause in the absence of any clear alternative purpose. Such was the cutting edge to Disraeli's jibe at 'majorities collected God knows how, voting God knows why'.[76]

II

While 'Palmerstonian' rhetoric defined political positions it was the prime minister who, 'between the various members of his administration . . . personally form[ed] the sole connecting link'.[77] The crucial question was how long 'Palmerstonian' rhetoric would continue to be seen as a credible response to the public need. 'Insecure' at its inception, the prospects of the ministry caused constant concern to the government frontbench throughout 1855 and 1856.[78] Observations that the ministry was 'very shaky' complemented cabinet anxiety about 'the rickety state of the government'.[79] During August 1856 'in the London Clubs the talk [was] that matters [were] not going straight with [the] government'.[80] The ministry, Clarendon confessed to Brougham, 'has no majority upon which it can depend except the Tories owing to their internal dissensions'.[81]

The major threat to 'Palmerstonianism' from the government side of the House was Lord John Russell. Russell, Whig premier from 1846–52, was the foremost political victim of 'Palmerstonian' axioms. By 1852 'a great many Whigs even objected to Lord John'.[82] Palmerston, Lord Grey, and other prominent Whigs had openly dissented from Russell's leadership.[83] Upon the fall of his government, Russell had apparently confirmed 'a character of rashness and obstinacy' which betrayed 'a great want of the milder of those qualities'.[84] Russell's personality encouraged disillusionment. He appeared clannish, distant, and aloof. 'Johnnie would have made an excellent Indian chief'[85] as 'the weakness of Lord John is not that only does truth not reach him, but that he's ever surrounded only by those who dare not tell it him'.[86] Even sympathetic Whigs were forced to regret 'Johnny's want of communication'.[87] After 1850 Russell did 'nothing to stain his moral reputation tho' enough to render his countrymen skeptical of his common sense and his political disinterestedness'.[88] The impression prevailed that 'if he were not conceited, ignorant of human nature, [and] a wee selfish, he had all the characteristics and experiences of a very superior man of his age'.[89] Many of Russell's flaws were attributed to the ambitious intrigues of his wife and her relations – the large Eliot and Romilly families. Gladstone likened Russell to 'the soldiers of the Crimea, *overrun with vermin*'.[90] Clarendon wished 'some *safe* man could be placed in bed between Lord and Lady John'.[91]

The difficulties of the Aberdeen coalition were attributed by colleagues to 'the incessant attempts of Lord John to keep up party differences'.[92] His presence in the cabinet gave 'the strongest party colour to the neutral combination'.[93] His motives 'were not exactly malicious, nor wholly base, but dangerous in the extreme and subversive of all faith and union among public men'.[94] Russell's attempt to form a government in February 1855 was 'still born' as the leading Whigs 'virtually ostracised him'.[95] Russell's failure was Palmerston's opportunity. At Clarendon's insistence Palmerston appointed Russell as the British delegate to the Vienna Conference. Derby believed Palmerston had 'laid a trap for J. R.'[96] Alternatively Russell may have hoped to emerge as the prestigious architect of European peace and stability; a powerful 'liberal' response to Palmerston's imputed bellicosity. In the event, in July 1855, Russell was forced to resign 'in a storm', Palmerston insisted, 'too strong . . . to be resisted'.[97] Russell became the victim of differing diplomatic interpretations of '*limitation* and *counterpoise*'.[98] Clearly 'very much depressed' Russell felt the Whigs had 'behaved ill, so few have at once firmness of purpose and honesty of intention that the whole concern seems doomed to rottenness'.[99] Russell concluded the 1855 session by 'throwing every present and future obstacle in the way of the government'.[100] The question of the Papal States he raised 'as an apple of discord never having mentioned the word while in government'.[101] Full of 'uneasiness' at the beginning of 1856 Russell reportedly refused 'to be galley slave to any administration!'[102] After Palmerston 'gagged' his education resolutions in April 1856 Russell was 'a concentrated essence of Lemon.'[103]

Russell's threat to Palmerston was that he personified exactly that elevated Liberal consciousness that 'Palmerstonianism' conspicuously lacked. Russell's rectitude exposed the soft underbelly of Palmerstonian rhetoric. The Foxite and legislative progressivism that Russell offered was in sharp contrast to the official diet of Canningite axioms and material prosperity. Moreover, Russell might coalesce those parliamentary elements, particularly Peelites and Radicals, antagonised most by Palmerstonian rhetoric with a rejuvenated Liberal intent made manifest in domestic reform. Disraeli observed that despite Russell's 'loss of character' he was 'one of the few men who [could] do without that necessity'.[104] An impression grew that 'Russell's Downing St. friends have made a Jonah of Johnny'.[105] Backbench Whigs 'openly expressed the opinion that [Russell] had been far worse treated by his *friends* in cabinet . . . than they had been treated by him'.[106] Among 'the underlings at Brooks's . . . abuse was shifting to regret', and turning to 'approbation'.[107] In August 1856 Russell travelled to the continent, it being his intention, it was suggested, to return 'à la Peel . . . from Egypt'.[108] Certainly Russell was adamant that his 'place [was] in the H. of C. but not as a servile adherent'.[109] Those close to Russell noted that 'there is no political damnation irrevocable in England'.[110]

An alternative focus for discontent was the third Earl Grey, son of the Whig premier. Grey, however, marred impeccable credentials with a suspect temperament and judgement. Caring little for honours he confessed to 'a great liking for power'.[111] A cantankerous manner repeatedly denied him the power he sought. In Melbourne's government Grey had 'made the cabinet a bear garden'.[112] As Colonial Secretary in Russell's ministry he displayed an obstinate temper that intensified his personal feud with Russell. In April 1853, Disraeli suggested an alliance between the Conservatives and the 'discontented Whigs' led by Grey. With typical disdain Grey 'decidedly rejected the offer'.[113] During the Crimean War, Grey advocated administrative reform so as to strengthen aristocratic control of political institutions; he 'did not see that abler men [were] rising in the democracy'.[114] These actions affirmed Grey's idiosyncratic position. But after February 1855 Grey's anti-Palmerstonianism promised a possible common cause with others. In agreement with Aberdeen, Grey was 'disgusted with the incessant interference with other countries, and the intention of keeping a large peace establishment'.[115] He believed 'every public man ought to be careful not to say anything which [could] excite the pugnacious temper of John Bull, whose blood was far too hot'.[116] By 1856, while his non-interventionist views were specifically 'anti-Palmerstonian', Grey provided an alternative Whig threat to 'Palmerstonian' ascendancy.

One threat to 'Palmerstonian' ascendancy, from the Radical benches, was conspicuous by its absence. Only a strong animosity to the Whigs provided any common Radical cause.[117] Bright, acting his usual role as the publicist of Cobdenite thought, declared that if 'the phrase of "the balance of power" [was] to be always an argument for war, the pretence for war [would] never be wanting, and peace [would] never be secure'.[118] This challenge failed because its postulates were 'supposed to be so extravagant as to carry with them their own refutation', and because it was a view itself vehemently opposed by other Radicals.[119] Roebuck and Layard adopted rhetoric that enforced the established notions of foreign policy.[120] What was divisive was not so much friction between degrees of radical intent as conflict between differing forms of radical belief. This divergence of outlook was compounded by ill health, bereavement and insolvency.

The contempt which his denunciation of diplomatic axioms received brought Cobden 'to the most complete state of political scepticism. I have no faith left. Nothing will surprise me, or disappoint me, or displease me or greatly please me any more'.[121] Bright found Cobden acting as if he wished to 'abdicate' as a political leader and 'shrinking from the fight in which he had for so long been engaged'.[122] The support of Radicals such as Roebuck for the Crimean War only added bitterness to futility. A 'heart-sickness' was prompted by the spectacle of the Radical party having 'thrown away its principles and committed suicide'.[123] Living in seclusion as a gentleman farmer in Sussex, Cobden became lost in private musing: 'sick of [the] everlasting attempt out-of-doors to give the semblance of an agitation that [did not] exist'.[124] Any public endeavour was 'merely beating the air'.[125] The sudden death of his fifteen-year-old son, in April 1856, left Cobden the more preoccupied with mortal purpose than public policy. At the beginning of 1856 Bright suffered a nervous breakdown: 'anything which excit[ed] and irritat[ed]' him caused 'pain and weakness in the brain'.[126] Finding that 'walking or standing at the Club, or doing much of anything, [brought] on the sensation of unsteadiness', Bright remained, throughout 1856, 'a favourite voice pitched at a low key'.[127]

During negotiations to form a government, in December 1852, the 'Manchester School' had been totally ignored; 'Bright, Gibson, Keogh, Cockburn, Osborne, etc.' were left 'all furious at not having been consulted'.[128] Bright attacked the Aberdeen coalition because, as he admitted to Lord Stanley, 'a change of hands would probably put the Tories again in power – then parties would be reconstructed – the Whigs and the Radicals would once more come together – and theirs must be the next turn'. Bright added 'that he should like an avowedly Tory government better than this one'.[129] Bright favoured the formation of a Derby ministry in February 1855. Once again, however, Radical wishes carried little weight. Cobden's disillusion and Bright's ill health left patriotic Radicals, in particular Roebuck, to direct extreme Liberal opinion. Yet Roebuck's utterances only enforced 'Palmerstonian' axioms and emphasised the irrelevancy of Cobden and Bright.

That Roebuck's language affirmed the apparent ascendancy of 'Palmerstonian' rhetoric, however, did little to strengthen the party fragility that existed beyond appearances. Even the premier's age and health encouraged the supposition that 'Palmerstonian' concerns were merely a temporary party arrangement presaging future realignment. In December 1852 Wood had noted that 'Palmerston [was] too old to wait very long for office, and his health seem[ed] to be breaking'.[130] By 1853 Graham thought 'Palmerston much changed and much more feeble, his energy much less, and his best days gone by'.[131] Greville thought it 'too late for [Palmerston] to look out for fresh political combinations and other connections'.[132] During 1854 Disraeli was willing to surrender the Conservative leadership in the Commons to Palmerston confident that Palmerston was so old that 'the real power should always remain with himself'.[133] During the 1856 session Palmerston was hobbling into the House on one, sometimes two, sticks with his foot bandaged from gout.[134] By September 1856 Lord Shaftesbury, his son-in-law, starkly observed that 'Palmerston is old: he may die'.[135] Even though Clarendon, by 1856, through hard work and tobacco, seemed 'not long for this life,'[136] colleagues expected him to live longer than the premier. Yet Palmerston's delicate health was a contingent factor that could also tell in his favour 'since statesmen [were] willing to accept terms from him, which they would otherwise decline, thinking the arrangement must of necessity be only temporary'.[137] The important fact was that 'Palmerston's age (now past 70) enter[ed] as an element into all calculations on the duration of his government'.[138]

2 Milton's Fallen Angels

Do not let us be told the question is whether we are to have
Palmerston or no Palmerston. (Gladstone to Aberdeen (? March
1857) Gladstone Mss. 44747, fol. 57)

[A] new and parti-coloured opposition took the field: Mr. Gladstone, Sir James Graham, Mr. Herbert, Lord John Russell, and Mr.
Disraeli. The war cloud under which they had cowered had drifted
by, and they raised their heads, like Milton's fallen angels, from the
oblivious pool, to plot anew for the recovery of all that the last two
years had cost them. (R. Lowe, 'The Past Session and the New
Parliament', *Edinburgh Review*, 204 (April 1857) p. 562)

Palmerston's achievement was the actual dominance of foreign
affairs, the apparent paucity of domestic issues, and the prominence
of the personality of the premier in parliamentary rhetoric and debate
during 1855 and 1856. Palmerston successfully donned 'Chatham's
mantle'. This created the imperative need, among hostile sections of
political opinion, for a policy of opposition distinct from mere anti-
Palmerstonianism; an opposition policy to shift the political focus
away from the person of the premier. This in turn, pointed to that
which opposition groups perceived to be their distinctive concern.
The Peelites typified both the critical need among government
critics for a distinctive policy, and the eager cultivation of such
policies during the autumn of 1856. Since 1852 'the rot' had been in
the Peelite party, 'the real diminution of the Peelites, considered as a
middle party, . . . [being] even greater than the apparent one'.[1] The
Aberdeen coalition realised Gladstone's fear that sharing power
'would not so much make the Liberals rich as make us poor indeed'.[2]
After 1852 Whigs came to despise the Peelites 'as much as they
love[d] their pocket boroughs'.[3] Graham, Gladstone, and Herbert's
resignations from Palmerston's cabinet in February 1855, only two
weeks after accepting office, were seen as confirmation of Peelite
duplicity. At the same time many Conservatives disliked the Peelites'
'Puseyism' and resented their claim to be the embodiment of intelligence and talent.[4] By 1856 most Whigs, Liberals, and Conservatives
were content to leave the Peelites 'in an elevated and ridiculous
position'.[5] The Peelites themselves were left to lamely lament that
'isolation has become more isolated'.[6] With heavy irony Robert Lowe

observed that 'our dear friends the Peelites . . . are falling into . . . contempt and disrepute'.[7]

A collective sense of superiority could not conceal, as Cardwell confessed in November 1856, the Peelites' 'want of a definite position'. They suffered from 'the absence of an object, distinctly understood, openly avowed, and capable of being defended on grounds of public interest'.[8] Aberdeen appreciated that any attempt to overthrow Palmerston required 'some specific and arguable cause'; a 'strong apprehension of a mischievous policy, and general disapprobation and distrust' was, in itself, insufficient.[9] The embarrassments and misfortunes of the Aberdeen coalition, the conclusion of the Crimean War and the reconciliation of diplomatic differences with the United States, left the Peelites with Gladstone's budget of 1853 as their credible claim to distinction.[10] That Cornewall Lewis had fundamentally differed from the tenets of Gladstonian finance in his own budgets of 1855 and 1856 gave the issue substance.[11] Thus the budget of 1853 became, three years later, the *magnum vectigal* of Peelite purpose, and Peelite cohesion became Gladstone's fiscal practice writ large.[12] While 'friends [were] few and daily becoming fewer', and the 'Little Band' was threatening to 'be soon dissolved into [its] first elements',[13] Graham, Gladstone and Aberdeen, during the recess of 1856, alighted on the immediate reduction of the income tax to a peacetime rate as 'the grand object' of Peelite policy.[14] Graham urged on Gladstone that 'the opinion of the House should be taken over' with regard to the reduction of the income tax, thus providing 'a bridle in [Palmerston's] mouth'.[15] If Palmerston remained prime minister there was 'no safety but in the stoppage of supplies, so as to make a war expenditure impossible; and the reduction of the income tax, from the 5 April next, present[ed] this opportunity'.[16] Aberdeen expected 'little from the House of Commons or from the public in support of a wise, just and moderate foreign policy', but a defence of the 1853 financial scheme, which Gladstone might assume with perfect consistency and justice, would divert attention away from Palmerstonian diplomacy.[17] In the January 1857 *Quarterly Review*, Gladstone, with stark and uncharacteristic austerity, brought the issue of income tax to the fore, portraying it as the overriding question of the coming session.[18]

Gladstone was an appropriate spokesman for Peelite policy. Not only was he the self-appointed guardian of Peel's financial tenets, but, personally, he crystallised much of the collective unpopularity of the Peelites. Jowett once remarked that Gladstone was not dishonest, but it was natural that those who did not understand him should think him so.[19] In 1856 very few persons understood Gladstone. His position in the Commons, Aberdeen conceded, was 'very peculiar'. With an 'admitted superiority of character and of intellectual power Gladstone did not possess the sympathy of the House at large'; he had incurred 'the strong dislike of a considerable portion of Lord Derby's followers' and was 'very unpopular'.[20] Detractors found in Gladstone a weakness for sophistry and verbosity; 'a fatal gift that serve[d] to expose infirmities'.[21] Despite 'his unquestionable powers of intellect', Parkes concluded that Gladstone was 'politically ill-educated and his principles loose and changeable'.[22] Colleagues found in Gladstone an earnestness that denied politic sense. There was 'no "perspective" in [Gladstone's] views. All objects, great and small, [were] on the same plane; and consequently the tiniest sometimes assume[d] the largest dimensions.'[23] Peelite backbenchers, with an uneasy blend of respect and uncertainty, found that 'Gladstone, with all the qualities which [made] one admire and love him, baffle[ed] all calculation by the great individuality of his mind, at once conscientious and ambitious, subtle and vehement, impulsive and discriminating . . .'[24] In 1856 Gladstone was aged forty-seven. At a critical stage in his political career he enjoyed status rather than effectiveness, while a dubious prestige in default of influence corresponded ill with his wish for executive responsibility.[25] Gladstone was, Graham noted, 'without sufficient occupation of that high order, for which he pant[ed] and for which his abilities pre-eminently qualified him'.[26] A presence in politics nurtured on Thomas à Kempis, Aristotle, Homer, Dante, Pascal and Bishop Butler, Gladstone's complex and earnest inner life only intensified the anguish of isolation. In February 1856 Gladstone drew up twenty-one reforms comprising a comprehensive financial programme. It demonstrated the central importance of finance in Gladstone's political plans, was a clear affirmation of executive ambition, and implied a financial offensive against Palmerston once a Crimean peace was concluded. Gladstone admitted that he 'greatly felt being turned out of office, I saw great things to do, I longed to do them. I am losing the best years of my life out of my natural service.'[27]

The question of the income tax offered the Peelites, and in particular Gladstone, the opportunity to re-restablish their authority within Westminster. It also offered Gladstone the opportunity to pronounce a policy over which he might expect Conservative support. Since the death of Peel, Gladstone had urged Aberdeen to 'be liberal in the sense of Peel, making out a liberal policy through the medium of the Conservative party'; junction with the Liberals was the Peelite's 'least natural position'.[28] By 1856 Gladstone believed Palmerston's government to be 'an organised hypocrisy', with the Liberal party 'content to travel towards the Dust of Death'.[29] Therefore it was 'the first duty of every independent member of parliament', upon the Commons meeting in February 1857, 'to do his best towards displacing Palmerston'.[30] Through the pages of the *Quarterly Review*, Gladstone exhorted Conservatives to express their opposition to Palmerston's policies by avowing retrenchment. By December 1856 both Aberdeen and Graham expected the coming session to open 'with Gladstone on the frontbench of the opposition',[31] both considering 'Gladstone's concert with Lord Derby as pretty well established, or on the point of being so'.[32] Yet Gladstone was subject to one determining circumstance. The Conservative party was more important to Gladstone than Gladstone was to the Conservative party.

Conservative aversion to Gladstone rendered union a questionable benefit for the Conservative leadership. Malmesbury preferred Palmerston to Gladstone, believing the former 'to be a gentleman – Gladstone cannot be *that*. He is a Jesuit tout caché'.[33] During his unsuccessful attempt to form a Conservative ministry in February 1855, Derby invited Gladstone to join his cabinet. Gladstone, after consultation with his colleagues, declined Derby's offer. Much historical attention has been given to Derby's invitation; less attention has been given to Derby's reaction to Gladstone's refusal. Derby believed 'that Gladstone's refusal saved [him from] some imminent risk of great disaster' for, had Gladstone joined a Conservative cabinet, Derby 'should not only have had to encounter great dissatisfaction, but possibly the loss of fifty or sixty votes and some of them men [Derby] had destined for office'.[34] The Conservative whips could only view the alliance, after 'putting the Peelite combination in every shape', with 'terror and dismay. Gladstone alone would be an almost impossible pill for our best men to swallow'.[35] Derby's considered verdict was succinct and decisive: 'It is very well, therefore, as it is'.[36] What was true in February 1855 became no less pertinent during succeeding months as it became apparent that 'half the Tories' preferred a Palmerston government to the prospect of being led by Gladstone.[37]

A brief triangular correspondence during November and December 1856, revealed the readiness with which Gladstone was prepared to respond to any hope of 'understanding' with Derby, while demonstrating the reticence Derby entertained about concert with Gladstone. In November Derby wrote a polite reply to an enquiry from the editor of the *Quarterly Review*, the Rev. Elwin. Looking to play the part of a broker in politics at the highest level, Elwin took Derby's letter as authorisation to negotiate the possibility of a Conservative reconstruction in the Commons.[38] Elwin looked to Gladstone as 'the competent leader' around whom 'the hollow alliance' of the Conservative party in the Commons might 'be broken up that it may be remodelled and united'.[39] In response Gladstone stated that he would be 'ready to speak to [Derby] in confidence and without reserve on the subject of public affairs'.[40] Derby, however, failed to react with the promptness Elwin desired or Gladstone had been led to expect. After a lapse of a month Derby relayed to Gladstone a non-commital 'pleasure' at the possibility of an inter-view.[41] Derby made his purpose plain to Jolliffe:

> Gladstone is, I know, expecting to hear from me, and *very hungry*, though very cautious. I shall write to him shortly, but only to express my readiness to talk with him confidently upon the state of public affairs. I am sure it is good policy not to seem too eager to effect an understanding at which, after all, we may never arrive.[42]

'So far so well!' was the chief whip's succinct response.[43]

Peelite concern with the income tax not only suggested differences between Gladstone and Derby, but concealed the divergence of intent between Peelites. Both Graham and Aberdeen were agreed that the question of finance, 'especially if the abatement of the income tax [were] included in it, would soon cover in the eye of the public general cooperation, and ultimately lead to new party combinations'.[44] The new combinations they envisaged, however, were very different from those sought by Gladstone. Aberdeen and Graham looked to Russell, rather than Derby, as Peel's spiritual heir. Graham, aged sixty-four in 1856, tempered a firm belief in the benefits of political economy with the conviction that the harsh principles of self-help be alleviated by education. Support for a peaceful foreign policy, religious and civil liberty and parliamentary reform, Graham often expressed in an extreme language that belied the moderation of his belief.[45] Bold in word, but reticent in action, Graham could be 'at once rash and timid . . . a warm friend and a dangerous adviser'.[46] Peel's 'right-hand man'[47] from 1841 to 1846 and a first-rate administrator, as a politician Graham proved 'decided in manner, but irresolute in mind'.[48] Thus his talents were 'neutralised by his reputation for inconsistency'.[49] Graham himself admitted 'that the great fault of his political life had been his *versatility*'.[50] Granville thought him wanting in 'pluck'.[51]

In 1852 Graham had believed 'the question of free trade would be lost in that of reform and the constitution',[52] and to Gladstone, in something nearing 'matured resolution', indicated a readiness 'to join with John Russell and the Liberal party as such'.[53] By July 1852, in regular correspondence with Russell, Graham looked towards 'a definite policy' of alliance, based on finance, franchise and education; religion and the ballot remained 'the stumbling blocks'.[54] In December 1852, Graham opposed any reconciliation with Palmerston, 'aggravating every difficulty, magnifying every obstacle . . . and acting the part of a firebrand to perfection'.[55] Within the Aberdeen cabinet Graham gave loyal support to Russell's proposals.

By 1856 Aberdeen came to share Graham's belief in Russell as the most effective political reply to 'Palmerstonian' policies. In December 1856 the Duke of Bedford, Russell's elder brother, wrote in friendly terms to Aberdeen.[56] The Peelite leader replied that all asperity of feeling between Russell and himself was at an end.[57] Subsequently Russell wrote to Graham disclaiming any confidence in Palmerston's government and declaring the state of the revenue unsatisfactory, unless the government adopted retrenchment. This, Russell supposed, they would not do.[58] The problem lay in forming another government to succeed Palmerston's apart from Derby who 'would make infinite confusion.' The solution of this problem, Graham and Aberdeen were agreed, was dependent upon 'the attitude which Lord John [might] assume towards the government'.[59] Russell, Graham emphasised, was the one person who might give the *coup de grâce* to Palmerston.[60] Russell would play the premier 'a slippery trick' if he had the opportunity, and would prove 'a more formidable adversary than either Derby or Disraeli'.[61]

Sidney Herbert, who lacked Gladstone's ability but was 'a much better manager of men', dismissed Derby and was disillusioned with Russell.[62] '[O]ne never knew when Lord John was steady, he changed his mind, gave up a thing and came back to it, in the most capricious and unaccountable way.'[63] Herbert chose to see Palmerston's ascendancy as 'more popular and stronger than ever'.[64] The Duke of Newcastle, who after Peel's death 'coveted' the Peelite leadership, by 1856 little influenced Peelite counsel.[65] During the Aberdeen ministry Newcastle as War Secretary had been the foremost victim of allegations of administrative inadequacy, possessing a putative 'affinity for fools'.[66] By February 1855, Newcastle was 'discredited in public estimation',[67] and friends advised a prudent and temporary withdrawal from political prominence; he 'could afford to wait'.[68] Yet Newastle found himself in little 'active accord' with the remnant of Peel's friends.[69] Edward Cardwell, excluded from Aberdeen's cabinet and expecting an offer of office from Palmerston, favoured 'a junction between [the Peelites] and the great body of the Liberal party'.[70] The divergent opinion of Herbert, Newcastle and Cardwell emphasised Peelite differences.

Graham and Aberdeen encouraged Gladstone's pronouncements over the income tax as purveying unity of purpose, while discouraging communication with Derby.[71] If, Aberdeen warned, Gladstone assumed 'a decided opposition at the beginning of the session, without any intelligible or assignable cause', his exertions would be deprived of their full effect.[72] Graham predicted that any admission of previous concert with Derby would 'mar the whole game' and Gladstone would 'stand alone'.[73] While Derby delayed responding to Gladstone's offer of consultation, Graham, with barely concealed relief observed that 'Rupert [had] lost his opportunity by delaying his charge'.[74] As the 1857 session approached, Aberdeen found Gladstone's 'indignation against the government [to be] extreme'.[75] The article in the January *Quarterly Review* was 'not only a declaration of war, but the plan of campaign'.[76] Graham urged on faltering colleagues that finance and expenditure remained Gladstone's 'strong ground', and was 'more likely to win public favour and to stand the test of a general election than any other great question [then] open'.[77]

I

Conservative inactivity had, by 1856, brought personalities and their attributed flaws to the fore. Impelled by a nagging sense of inconsequence, Conservative doubt and self-searching revealed inevitable differences. Backbench observation that 'none of [the opposition] were nearby',[78] complemented comments that the Conservative party appeared 'full of jealousies, personal and political, and [had] no principles upon which to found a consistent opposition'.[79] In January 1856 Jolliffe, the chief whip, contemplated resigning, finding his position intolerable without any intelligible cause or distinct principle to advance.[80] The 'great dissatisfaction expressed by the Conservatives ... against their leaders' and the charge that 'the Conservatives do not put forward a distinct policy',[81] was both the natural consequence and an unconscious acknowledgement of Derby's opposition strategy.

Historical judgement has given much weight to those not privy to Derby's thought; those offended by a bluff social manner, excluded by a restricted circle of confidants, or chronicling a Beaconsfield Conservative tradition.[82] The portrait has been preserved of 'a man lacking the qualities of ambition and dedication normally necessary for successful party leadership'.[83] Those who enjoyed Derby's confidence, however, recognised those qualities that earlier in his career had marked him out as Lord Grey's successor as Whig leader. Macaulay found in him 'a knowledge of the science of parliamentary defence and attack' resembling 'rather an instinct than an acquisition'.[84] Bulwer Lytton thought him the '*cleverest* public man I ever met. Others have had more genius, more knowledge, more pure intellect, but no one ever seemed to me to rival his cleverness.'[85] The rapidity with which he conducted business impressed his colleagues. Disraeli found Derby's 'mind always clear, his patience extraordinary. He rises in difficulty and his resources never fail.'[86]

From his Whig and Foxite apprenticeship, Derby brought the basic tenets of a public doctrine that continued to inform his leadership of the Conservative party. A belief that parliament was the authoritative arena of national politics prescribed the parameters of political activity. This encouraged disdain for extra-parliamentary organisation and the press, sustained a belief in aristocracy as the natural political leadership of the country, and identified stable party support in parliament as the source of the constitutional authority to govern.[87] This public doctrine defined the objectives of Derby's leadership. To keep the Conservative party unified, when the opportunity arose to assert their role as a credible party of government, and to assimilate moderate support when it promised to be permanent and represented by prominent names. Backbench fractures or temporary alignments, although convenient, did not fulfil that lasting redefinition of bipolarity Derby desired. The final element in Derby's public doctrine was a truly Conservative scepticism. But even when he felt the 'game was lost', he remained determined that 'it ought to be played, and I will play it out to the last'.[88] It was this commitment that was unappreciated by many contemporaries, and has been obscured for historians by Derby's chosen strategy.

Derby's personality further obscured his political purpose. His weakness as Conservative leader was a disinclination to translate political sensitivity into social familiarity. Only those sharing his pleasures and offering an aristocratic camaraderie, such as Lord Malmesbury, became intimates. His famous sense of humour kept others at a distance from the private self. Moreover, a remarkable single-mindedness and total absorption in the activity of the moment was often misinterpreted by political subordinates in social situations as indifference or incapacity. He was fond of using the expression, 'One thing at a time'.[89] All this concealed the subtle complexity and earnest commitment of Derby's political thought. Isolated from the total party context, viewed as merely part of Conservative circumstances, what was astute does appear vacuous. Divorced from his policy in office, Derby's opposition strategy could appear to be a confession of doctrinal impotence. But such impressions seriously misread Derby's actions.

Derby believed that doing nothing could succeed like success. In searching for unity Derby anticipated that Peelites, Whigs, Liberals and Radicals would only discover their incompatible differences. Conservative offensives in opposition would only provide an artificial bond of agreement between non-Conservatives. In doing nothing, Conservatives could allow any Peelite, Whig, Liberal and Radical association to fall apart of its own volition.[90] The Conservative ministry of 1852 had not fallen in the defence of any principle that might serve as the rallying point for any single party. In opposition to the Aberdeen coalition Derby decided 'to kill [the government] with kindness'.[91] By the end of 1854 those outside the ministry were receiving 'a lamentable account of the internal condition of the government'.[92] Since 1851 Derby's patience policy had been primarily intended to adhere Palmerston as Conservative leader in the Commons.[93] Although the Peelites might rejoin the Conservative party, Palmerston was 'worth the whole lot'.[94] In January 1855 Derby did not believe that Palmerston was a prospective premier.[95] Palmerston's unexpected success, excluding both Russell and Derby, made Derby's actions, in retrospect, appear a self-confession of Conservative inability.[96] It left the Conservative party, moreover, in the artificial position of confronting its best ally. In opposition to Palmerston's government, Derby immediately resumed his patience policy, deeming it unpatriotic to criticise the ministry's diplomatic attempts to conclude a peace in the Crimea.[97] Between 1852 and 1855 Derby had believed that parliamentary reform, rather than foreign affairs, would dismantle the coalition.[98] After 1855, reform and other domestic issues remained unresolved promising a future realignment.

Derby's inaction, his demeanour, and slack attendance during the 1856 session were seen by some as a wish to retire: a suspicion that might persuade 'the more ambitious [to] desert to other leaders'.[99] It was observed that if Derby continued 'to hold aloof, [did] nothing . . . communicating with nobody, it [was] only natural that many of our best men should complain . . . [and] ride off on their own hobbies'.[100] Dissatisfaction, however, never hardened into disloyalty. Jolliffe could assure Derby 'that what [was] wanted to unite all sections [was] a certainty that it [was Derby] who direct[ed]; and that nothing [was] done without consultation, and unless it [had] received [his] approval'.[101] Nor should Conservative carping and anxiety detract from the fact that they were the single most unified and cohesive body of votes in parliament throughout the 1850s.

It has become an historical platitude, nonetheless true for being so, that Disraeli during the 1850s was unpopular with many Conservatives and insecure in his position as Conservative leader in the Commons.[102] The most important implication of this was that many Conservative backbenchers found it easier to dislike Disraeli than to be disloyal to Derby. Disraeli provided an obvious target for the discontent created by Derby's strategy. Because of this, and Disraeli's need for Derby, ultimate authority within the party never came under question. The fertility of Disraeli's strategic thought disturbed many. Malmesbury believed that 'to get office [Disraeli] would do anything, and act with anyone.'[103] In 1852 Disraeli expressed a wish to approach the 'Manchester School', believing that they were '*hot* for *organic* changes but only required office'.[104] During 1853 he became 'full of a project of alliance with Lord Grey and the discontented Whigs'.[105] Disraeli also believed in a possible alliance with the Irish Brigade and, in 1855, revived 'the old topic' of concert with the 'Manchester School'.[106] Such plans confirmed belief that Disraeli, although 'ambitious, most able and without prejudices', was 'unable to comprehend the morality of [a] political course'.[107] Derby's relationship with Disraeli was born of contingency, rather than trust. Not invited to Knowsley until 1853, Disraeli was offended, in 1856, by Derby's failure to extend a similar invitation to his wife.[108] Admiring Disraeli's 'temper, tact and ability', Derby, 'jealous lest [Disraeli] should aim at the first place . . . sneered at his tendency to extremes of alternative excitement and depression'.[109] Such private doubt became prudent caution when Whigs gave credence to the suggestion that Disraeli, in truth, 'despise[d] and dislike[d] Derby, think[ing] him a good "Saxon" speaker and nothing more'.[110]

Disraeli, needing Derby's support to retain his authority in the Commons, was prepared to voice the appropriate sentiment at the appropriate time. Before going to Paris, in August 1856, while rumours of 'a great intrigue to shelve Dizzy' were rife,[111] Disraeli, 'in a fixed and satisfactory state of mind', declared himself to Jolliffe to be Derby's 'devoted follower'.[112] As Disraeli hoped, this was reported to Knowsley. In Paris, however, 'Dizzy [was] very low and his more open-mouthed wife anything but complimentary about Lord Derby'.[113] Disraeli retained a suspicion that 'Lord D. only employed without trusting him'.[114]

Those around Disraeli in the Commons were both a benefit and threat to his position. Lord Stanley, Derby's son aged thirty in 1856, was 'very able, besides working hard', and '*in fallor* someday [would] be someone'.[115] Colleagues found Stanley had 'a most powerful brain', with 'high intentions, great industry and ambition'.[116] It was becoming a prevalent assumption that Stanley was 'the only man to look to'.[117] In 1853 Malmesbury stated his belief, while Stanley was still aged only twenty-seven, that the Conservative leadership in the Commons was a position 'reserved' for Stanley and was a position he might assume when he pleased.[118] Stanley discerned that 'Tory Democracy' which Palmerston left as a legacy to Disraeli. Experiences in Lancashire, where he 'found remaining an almost feudal respect for the [Stanley] family, which [had] not been duly cultivated',[119] convinced him of the necessity of attending to emerging 'interests'. Among the 'self-made industrialists', whose 'force' and 'shrewdness' of character greatly impressed him, Stanley observed, except in Church matters, 'many Conservative tendencies'. It was, he concluded, only the 'mingled timidity and pride of the country gentlemen' which kept them aloof from the Conservative party. Making extra-parliamentary speeches more frequently than Cobden or Bright during this period, on the advantages of study for working-men, the needs of the large towns, Mechanics Institutes and work for women, within Westerminster Stanley supported competitive examinations for the Civil Service, the abolition of purchased commissions in the Army, the securing of the property earnings of married women, the admission of practising Jews into parliament and the abolition of Church Rates.[120] Bright, with uncharacteristic jollity, declared Stanley to be more radical than himself.[121]

Constantly 'angry' with Disraeli, the Conservative party became 'displeased' with Stanley, 'suspecting him to be coquetting with the Manchester party'.[122] It was Whig opinion that Stanley was 'more allied with Bright than with any other public man'.[123] Conservatives courting respectability deemed Stanley 'bad company', many calling him 'the greatest Liberal in the House'.[124] Prepared to stand by his father while he remained Conservative leader, Stanley wished to retain, in the event of Derby's retirement, the independence 'to hold [himself] free to form any connection that might then seem suitable'.[125] 'From any wish to lead the Conservative party the fate of Peel [was] enough to set [him] free'. Increasingly after 1854 Stanley, while distancing himself from Disraeli, sought to represent scrupulous public integrity. In November 1855, from filial loyalty and political prudence, he declined a position in Palmerston's cabinet. From November 1855 on Stanley was seeking an independent position of informed and intelligent moderation. Certainly he could not be relied upon 'with too much confidence, as an out and out party man'.[126]

Sir John Pakington, previously 'known only as an intelligent and active country gentleman',[127] in 1852 sought Palmerston's succession to Disraeli in the Commons.[128] Disraeli, in response, treated Pakington 'with much contempt'.[129] Pakington drew attention to a want of 'constructive and effective action' in Disraeli's neglect of 'preconcert and prearrangement'.[130] He also became closely associated with the education question – an involvement that placed Disraeli's leadership in 'an inconvenient and embarrassing position'.[131] During 1856, while finding common cause with Russell and Cobden over education, Pakington was an annoyance to Disraeli and a fellow-spirit to Stanley illustrating the spectrum of opinion contained within avowedly Conservative allegiance.[132] Such diversity of opinion emphasised for many the need for a sense of purpose absent in inaction.

Initiative amongst those of lesser prominence became a threat to party unity. Heathcote, anxious lest another session should 'just fall away without some attempt at producing by systematic conference some unity of action', urged identification between those 'who by their position, as country gentlemen, and their habits of thought as Conservative politicians, could be eventually led to take up the same general (?) stance on affairs'.[133] Such pleas were less subversive in intent than dangerous for being undirected. In such circumstances Derby's coolness towards Gladstone was good sense. In January 1857 certain 'young madmen' declared their refusal 'to submit to a junction with Gladstone', assurances accompanied by the veiled threat that they were not only speaking for themselves.[134] Malmesbury remembered 1855 when, after Gladstone had been offered a place in a Conservative cabinet, 'no less than eighty members of the House of

Commons threatened to leave [Derby]'.[135] The task before the Conservative leadership was to preserve party unity while proving that 'Toryism [was] not necessarily antagonistic to progress'; the strategy being 'to sever Palmerston qua Tory, which he [was], from his Whig followers, and [to] make him yell when he [fell], not on arms'.[136]

'[C]onsultation and conference in high quarters' during December 1856, prompted optimism in Jolliffe and the belief that Derby had 'set the wheels agoing'.[137] Malmesbury had been lamenting the party's *'destitute'* condition; a 'miserable £500 a year' had been collected from twenty peers. Derby donated a sum of money to the party's political fund which was seen as a sign of new determination. Though disclaiming ambition for office Derby declared himself 'ready to accept the responsibility of it if [he saw] a chance not only of taking but keeping it'.[138] On 19 January 1857 a conference was held at Knowsley; its composition betrayed the nature of Derby's intention. Walpole, Pakington, Bulwer Lytton and Stanley participated. Disraeli was invited, but as he was abroad it was known he would be unable to attend. Pakington, 'hampered by his engagements with the Manchester folks on the subject of education',[139] refused to accept Derby's proposal to adopt the issue as an 'open question'.[140] Derby appeased Pakington by promising further discussion and the possibility of conciliation in the arrangement of details.[141] Stanley, though his invitation to Knowsley was intended to remind him of his filial obligations, showed his independence by refusing Disraeli's invitation to a parliamentary dinner immediately prior to the session. Unable to consider himself a representative of 'agricultural Conservatism' Stanley speculated on the future necessity for 'a coalition all moderate politicians might join'.[142] His 'real reason was simply a wish to be free as regard[ed] political action, especially on the subject of income tax'.[143] By mid-January 1857 Disraeli returned from Paris with knowledge of a 'secret treaty' between England and Austria safeguarding Austria's Italian dominions. Before the start of the session Disraeli 'appeared in highest exultation', 'alluded mysteriously to certain disclosures' and stated that 'by this day fortnight [the Conservatives would] be in office'.[144] Disraeli also prepared two financial resolutions to be placed before the Commons, complementing Gladstone's cry over the income tax and the settlement of 1853. Derby, who appeared to be 'in high force', was ready to consider these as part of an 'intended financial attack upon the enemy'.[145]

While Derby saw Conservative opportunity in having no distinct policy and the Peelites sought distinction in fiscal concerns, the Irish

Brigade translated one specific issue into a general political attitude. The hard core of twelve Irish MPs that, by 1856, constituted the remnant of the Irish Brigade were pledged to effect some reform in landlord–tenant legislation and redress Irish agrarian grievances. This programme assumed the character of anti-Palmerstonianism. But the alliance between the Tenant League and the Catholic Defence Association upon which the party was based was an uneasy one.[146] Once within Westminster, members of the Irish Brigade sought to define their political purpose in broader terms, yet the small number of votes they controlled restricted their influence. They lacked a leader with the qualities that Parnell was later to provide for Irish grievances. Rural prosperity dulled the edge of their invective. Moreover, religious questions, with which the Irish Brigade were also much concerned, had become a matter most prominent politicians preferred to ignore. All this eroded the ground of 'independent opposition' upon which the Irish Brigade attempted to stand.

II

In politics the choice between alternative courses and the selection of that to be preferred is influenced by the conduct of others acting in an adverse sense. It is difficult, however, to anticipate the precise response an opposing party will adopt in any particular situation. Cornewall Lewis observed an analogy with chess. 'The nearest approach to a sure prediction which can be made is, to reduce [an opponent's] choice to a limited number of foreseen alternatives.'[147] Those moves considered or anticipated but never played can be as important as those actually made. During the recess of 1856 prominent politicians reaffirmed their opposition to 'Palmerstonian' orthodoxy with what they perceived to be their own distinctive concern in anticipation of certain contingencies. They sought standpoints sufficiently defined so as to provide distinction, while at the same time imposing constraints on others.

To pronounce the established axioms of diplomacy was to be 'Palmerstonian'. The dominance of 'Palmerstonian' rhetoric was the repudiation of Cobdenite doctrine. To parade a liberal rectitude was to be Russellite. The apparent paucity of domestic concerns and lack of concern with the Papal States was the guarantee of Russell's isolation. To preach the necessity of retrenchment was to be Peelite, and the 1853 budget became the *magnum vectigal* of Peelite purpose.

Derby's refusal to identify the Conservatives with a distinct rhetorical position he saw as future opportunity rather than an immediate disadvantage. Non-commitment offered the maximum of contingent possibility. The relative importance of such concerns within Westminster was the measure of real effectiveness; the manipulation of the concerns of the majority, the yardstick of political success.

Within Palmerston's cabinet it was Russell's exact intentions that excited the most acute disquiet. Lady Palmerston, in December 1856, when congratulated on the aspect of affairs observed that 'things [were] not at all as smooth as [they] could wish. Lord John is coming home.'[148] Lady Palmerston was not to be consoled; Russell was 'coming home and he [had] promised to stay abroad'. Rumour in the Clubs was 'that Lord John [had] been getting up materials for an anti-ministerial display on Italy' and was in 'open rebellion'.[149] Brougham was told that Russell was 'coming home to run out Palmerston'.[150] Some members of the cabinet suggested appointing Russell as leader in the Lords; a pre-emptive elevation that would avert hostility in the Commons. Aberdeen thought such a move 'would be a great stroke for Palmerston',[151] but Palmerston thought 'Johnny safer out of his government than in it'.[152] More to the point, Russell had no intention of accepting such a debilitating promotion.[153]

The ministry repeatedly tried to discern Russell's exact intentions. Clarendon asked Lord Normanby in Florence to ascertain 'in what sense [would Russell] return'.[154] On learning that Russell was coming home full of hostility and 'Mintoism', Clarendon charged the Ambassador at Paris to discover 'what [Russell] intend[ed] to do'.[155] With relief the cabinet learnt that Russell was 'not meditating a reform bill'.[156] Yet the threat appeared all the more ominous for remaining indistinct. As the 1857 session approached the Conservatives happily noted the unease at Cambridge House. Such apprehension made it 'the more desirable that [Derby] should be at the head of his army . . . if Lord John comes home with mischievous intent and Gladstone has the same intent as regards the government'.[157]

3 Finance, Reform and China

The House of Commons is as unstable as water. But the people have great qualities and they may in time cease to bow before the idols, and resume their ancient love of truth. (Russell to Minto, 22 July 1855, Minto Mss. 11775, fol. 102)

The active part of the session lasted barely a month, and never, we apprehend, was so much faction crowded into so small a space of time. (R. Lowe, 'The Past Session and the New Parliament', *Edinburgh Review*, 204 (April 1857), p. 562)

By January 1857 the 'agitation against the income tax was growing and becoming loud'.[1] Cornewall Lewis warned cabinet colleagues that there was 'nothing the country would dislike so much as keeping up high taxation', and that it was 'hatred of high income tax which [would] animate the people'.[2] During January Cornewall Lewis required 'extravagant'[3] ministers to reduce their departmental estimates enabling him to propose a lower rate of income tax such as would 'satisfy the House and the public'.[4] Gladstone 'was reported to be overflowing with economical venom, and Aberdeen admitted to Argyll that Graham meant to do all the mischief he could'.[5] Russell's 'hostility to the government seem[ed] to be pretty well known', and '[h]is arrival [was] regarded with apprehension'.[6] In private Lord Grey declared his intention to make the Persian question 'his great "cheval de bataille"'.[7] Clarendon anxiously noted that 'Persia, Naples and China [stood] in awful array next to each other' promising to 'give rise to never ending debates'.[8]

The Queen's Speech which opened parliament on 3 February 1857, in 'containing as little as it was possible to put together',[9] betrayed government anxiety and intent.[10] Framed within what was portrayed as the 'normal' function of executive government, domestic reference was minimal while diplomatic comment sought to be reassuring. Malmesbury's response, that the speech 'told us nothing',[11] was the calculated effect of an address that 'was all foreign, apart from a paragraph very general on amendment of [the] law'.[12] In the 'meagre bill of fare for the coming session' Derby found but a 'vague and shadowy portraiture of the measures' the government intended to introduce,[13] while Disraeli found in the speech nothing but 'wars and rumours of wars'.[14] Derby challenged the government to make 'a positive pledge that beyond the year 1860 the income tax should not be maintained'. Followed by a general indictment of Palmerston's diplomacy the denunciation of the financial standing of the government was a specific attack that prepared the ground. Although he 'moved no amendment and deprecated any being moved' Derby 'condemned severely the conduct of the government'.[15] Lord Grey's amendment on the government's policy in Persia was negatived by 45 to 12; opposed by Derby yet, of greater significance, supported by Aberdeen.[16] '[S]uch an invidious thing for an ex-prime minister to do, that his intention must have been to show his disapprobation of the government.'[17]

In the Commons, Disraeli disclosed revelations of a 'secret treaty' with Austria, with which he hoped to prove diplomatic duplicity, and gave notice of two resolutions recommending a reduction in the income tax and an adherence to the financial settlement of 1853.[18] The accusations of a signed agreement to protect Austria's dominions in Italy 'fell rather flat'.[19] But Gladstone declared support for Disraeli's financial resolutions and urged, in earnest phrases, a return to the settlement of 1853.[20] From the Radical benches Milner Gibson echoed Gladstone and, while denouncing the hostilities in Persia, asked 'who was to pay for this war?'[21] Russell's statement to the House, his having arrived from the continent only the previous evening, proved to be a delicate balance of independent support and covert hostility. While disparaging Disraeli's resolutions, and approving of the government's policy in Persia, Russell delivered an extended criticism of the cabinet's policy over Naples.[22] Returning to the 'apple of discord' he had thrown down in 1855, Russell revealed his allegiance as something to be sought rather than presumed. The price at which loyalty might have to be bought was that which most acutely exercised ministerial anxiety. Clarendon 'complained bitterly'[23] of Russell's speech, which was 'by no means friendly in tone to the government'.[24] While Palmerston, suffering from 'a slight return of gout',[25] privately impressed upon Panmure the need to reduce estimates,[26] Cornewall Lewis scheduled his budget statement for 13 February so that it came before the debate on Disraeli's resolutions on the 17 February.[27] The general impression of the debate on the address was 'certainly unfavourable to the position of the government',[28] and it was 'obvious from the whole tone of the proceedings in both Houses that the government [was] threatened with very serious difficulties'.[29]

On 4 February 1857, in 'a strictly confidential' meeting with Derby, Gladstone declared that he was 'content to act [against Palmerston] without enquiring who was to follow', decried his isolated position, denounced the Peelites as 'a great evil', and described himself 'as a public nuisance'. To his 'separate position [he] felt most anxious to put a period'.[30] In reply Derby drew attention to 'much bitterness or anger' felt towards the Peelites 'among a portion of his adherents'. In private, with less tact, leading Conservatives noted that if Gladstone 'joined [the] party, he would only benefit [them] by his talents, for on the other hand, [they] should lose many of [their] supporters'.[31] Disraeli also warned of the threat of abstentions from the financial debate in the Commons; the sort of 'undercurrent which [led] to shipwreck'.[32]

To strengthen Conservative unity, Derby arranged a council of 'both Peers and Commons, but only four of each – *not* including Henley'.[33] Henley's absence was calculated to ensure Pakington's ease. Confident that Palmerston's government was 'becoming very unpopular', Derby believed that the question of the income tax offered the best opportunity of dislodging the cabinet.[34] The call for 'reduction of taxes [was] loud and general', the issue would enlist Gladstone's oratory while care was taken to deny any prearranged concert and, on such a question, the cabinet would be reluctant to dissolve parliament.[35] Derby also made efforts to ensure that the attack on the government's fiscal policy retained the public appearance of Conservative enterprise by rejecting alternative resolutions proposed by Gladstone.[36] Insistent that prior consultation should not be allowed 'to interfere with our entire freedom as to our future course', Derby encouraged Gladstone's 'spontaneous' support of a Conservative motion while steadfastly avoiding prior commitment to any Peelite resolutions.[37] Derby's studied evasion only exacerbated the divergence of intent which existed, despite Gladstone's assurances, amongst his Peelite colleagues.[38]

While 'the economical fit [was] on very strong',[39] and Palmerston was showing 'some symptoms of physical weakness' which might become 'very serious at the beginning of a long and arduous session',[40] the nature of the government's budget became critical. Moreover, Cornewall Lewis 'cold-blooded as a fish, totally devoid of sensibility [and] of an imperturbable temper', was seen as 'just the man to encounter and baffle' Gladstone.[41] The budget the Chancellor announced to the Commons on 13 February 1857 was, indeed, designed 'not to suit the book' of either Gladstone or Disraeli 'out of whose sails the wind [was] taken'.[42] Proposing a reduction of the income tax from 16d to 7d in the pound – the fixed rate originally introduced by Peel – Cornewall Lewis also recommended a gradual diminution of the tea and sugar duties.[43] The reference to Peel was the artful touch of malicious irony emphasising the proposal withdrawing the main plank from Gladstone's platform. '[V]ery well received'[44] by the Commons, 'notwithstanding Gladstone's notorious determination to attack it on every vulnerable point',[45] the budget dramatically pre-empted opposition attack. It denied Gladstone any opportunity to advocate the fiscal question as a means of reuniting the Peelites and the Conservative party. Graham repeated his wish to see Gladstone 'lead the Commons, under John Russell as prime minister in the Lords' and his conviction that Derby would find it impossible to discard Disraeli 'like a sucked orange'.[46] In any combined initiative over finance, Graham warned, Gladstone could only appear subordinate on that in which he wished to seem pre-eminent. The budget also weakened Derby's commitment to the fiscal question as a means of overthrowing Palmerston. Jolliffe received reports that some backbenchers, finding Gladstone 'the most objectionable man in the House', would 'almost sooner keep away from the [financial] division than help to be the means of restoring [Gladstone] to office'.[47] Derby began to perceive the China question as the more effective issue with which to dismantle Palmerston's precarious following.[48]

I

A parliamentary session presents an untidy spectacle to those wishing to preserve distinction between differing issues. 'Narrative', Carlyle declared in an early essay, 'is *linear*, action is *solid*'.[49] A third dimension is suggested by the shifting political intent that connects differing aspects of policy. While Derby, once finance appeared an increasing political liability, cast his attention to the China question, the issue of parliamentary reform revealed new aspects to the difficulties of Palmerston's cabinet. Since the beginning of the session Russell had been 'the person whose movements [had] attract[ed] the greatest attention'.[50] The 'higher ministerialists [were] very civil in what they said of him' while 'the lower alternat[ed] praise and abuse according to the opinion he express[ed] approving or disapproving the course taken by the government'.[51] Shrewdly those close to Russell saw encouragement in such attitudes. 'All the abuse, praise and concession is ... a great proof of the strength of [Russell's] position and if he continues as he has begun this strength will increase daily until he may not improbably become practically the leader of the House out of office.'[52] During the first weeks of the session Russell appeared 'in good spirits'.[53]

On 19 February, the Radical Locke King introduced into the Commons his motion, proposed annually and previously promptly negatived, to establish an identical £10 parliamentary suffrage in both counties and boroughs.[54] During the subsequent debate Russell declared an unqualified support for the motion, thinking it 'a safe improvement' calculated to 'consolidate the institutions of the country'.[55] The cabinet, accepting George Grey's opinion that the motion was impossible to amend so as to proceed with what they thought unobjectionable (a county franchise of persons occupying tenements rated at £20),[56] opposed the motion.[57] Russell took 149 Whigs and Liberals, 8 Radicals and 8 Peelites into the division lobby in support of the motion leaving a frontbench rump of 37 Whigs and Liberals to oppose the proposal. Although, because of Conservative opposition the motion was negatived, the message for the ministry was simple and clear. On a question such as reform where Liberal backbenchers' perception of themselves as the party of 'progress' and 'improvement' might be appealed to, Russell was a figure whose authority surpassed that of the cabinet. By his support for Locke King's motion Russell also revived reform as a live political issue engaging political calculation. Russell's actions over Locke King's motion proved the single most important event of the 1857 session. It threw Russell's earlier ambivalent independence into perspective, and confirmed the subversive potential of liberal rectitude upon Palmerstonian support.

Immediately after the Locke King debate the fragile nature of party connection was further illustrated by discussion of the Maynooth grant – one of those matters, Palmerston urged, 'which ought to remain between man and his own conscience'.[58] Again the government vote was split with many backbenchers voting against the Treasury bench. The party heterodoxy of religious sentiment, despite the cabinet's opposition to Spooner's motion for an enquiry, further emphasised the delicate state of Palmerstonian support.

The conclusion of the finance debate on 20 February, served to confirm the divisive pressure concert with Gladstone placed upon Conservative unity, and the ineffectiveness of Gladstone's appeal to his settlement of 1853. Gladstone 'made a very long and furiously excited speech, in which he fiercely attacked [Cornewall] Lewis',[59] 'his idolatry of his own budget of '53 the secret of it'.[60] Lord Overstone, a wealthy Whig peer interested in monetary reform, considered Gladstone's 'able and brilliant' speech to have been 'very illogical' and a 'not very fair attack on the financial department of the government'.[61] Cornewall Lewis himself 'spoke of it as so personally bitter that he was quite amazed'.[62] From the Conservative back-benches George Bentinck, supported by the 'ultra-Tory' Newdegate, declared he was not prepared to support either Disraeli's motion or the budget proposals until the estimates had been discussed in the Committee of Supply.[63] Refusing to compromise his 'distinct right to exercise [his] own unfettered judgement on any question', Bentinck warned Derby of 'the dangerous consequences to the welfare of the party if certain *unnamed coalitions* should be carried out'.[64] Malmesbury could only lament that Bentinck seemed to amuse himself by opposing everything.[65]

The budget debate dispelled Gladstone's carefully cultivated illusion of Peelite unanimity. The Peelite section had split over Locke King's motion: when Graham supported the motion, and Herbert opposed it,[66] Gladstone deemed it 'a bad night for Peelism'.[67] Eleven colleagues, including Graham and Herbert, followed Gladstone's support of Disraeli's financial resolutions, but another eleven, headed by Cardwell, supported the government. As the *magnum vectigal* of Peelite purpose, the financial settlement of 1853, and by implication Gladstone's desire for a Conservative reunion, was in the event no less subversive a cry than Conservative fear of Gladstonian intent. When Disraeli's resolutions were negatived by a majority of eighty,[68] the cabinet viewed the victory as 'the benefit of a junction between the haters of Gladstone and the haters of Disraeli'.[69] The defeat of Disraeli's resolutions not only facilitated the passage of the budget, but discredited the issue of finance as the expression of unified opposition hostility.

The debate on the budget strengthened Derby's conviction that the Conservatives '*must* bring forward the case of China, in some shape or other'.[70] Bowring, the British representative in China, had resorted to armed force in demanding reparations for a technical insult to the British flag and the fulfilment of treaty rights allowing access into Canton. Despite the warning of the Attorney-General that 'a very serious case against [the government] on the points of international law could be, and probably would be, made out in the House of

Commons',[71] the cabinet fully supported Bowring's action.[72] Yet, while China offered the opportunity for the reiteration of 'Palmersto-nian' orthodoxies it also offered differing sections of anti-Palmerstonian opinion the opportunity for a 'grand onslaught'.[73] On 16 February, after corresponding with Lord Grey, Derby gave notice in the Lords that as soon as the papers relating to Canton were laid on the table of the House he would move a specific motion in reference to it.[74] Lord Lyndhurst, the elderly doyen of Conservative peers, was known to be in 'high force, with the Blue Books before him, getting up the China case'.[75]

At the opening of the China debate in the Lords on the 24 February, Derby, in a 'very powerful and admirable' speech,[76] drew attention to the 'proceedings of a most violent kind [which] had occurred at Canton', describing the behaviour of British officials as 'menacing, disrespectful and arrogant'.[77] Carnavon, 'in a very good speech indeed for a beginner',[78] on every principle of humanity and justice disavowed the acts committed at Canton,[79] while Malmesbury, both on grounds of policy and morality, considered the proceedings at Canton unjustifiable.[80] The government in response pronounced the axioms of 'Palmerstonian' rhetoric. Derby's criticism, Clarendon claimed, would endanger the lives and property of all British subjects in China, would cast dishonour on the British flag and would bring ruin upon the Oriental trade.[81] Derby's motion was negatived by thirty-six.[82] But of much greater significance was the public promi-nence Derby's motion gave to the China question. Both Aberdeen and Grey accompanied Derby into the division lobby and demon-strated the common cause which sections of the opposition might find in refuting Palmerston's Chinese policy.

The subsequent China debate in the Commons, on a motion moved by Cobden denouncing the government's policy, confirmed the wide range of opinion that might come together over the issue. The 'arrogance and presumption' of the cabinet's policy, Cobden declared on 27 February, over the 'chimera' of access to Canton, violated international law and politic sense.[83] The 'great event of the first night', however, was Russell's 'powerful attack on the government' which, in 'one of his very best efforts', was 'exceedingly bitter and displayed his hostile animus'.[84] The success of the speech found itself measured in Palmerston's unease; 'the cheering ... and the temper of the House was disagreeable and John Russell's speech was unqualified hostility'.[85] As the China question became 'uppermost in men's minds and on men's tongues', to those with a distaste for the harsh realities of political action all appeared 'falsehood, in its various phases and degrees'.[86] But those with greater sensitivity for the practical aspect of public pronouncement foresaw future contingency. Russell was 'straining every nerve to mislead and seduce the supporters of Lord Palmerston'.[87] Such understanding also revealed the logic of recent debate: 'in truth, the vote of Lord John and his supporters on Locke King's motion put an end to the majority of Lord Palmerston', and the attack on the government's China policy 'followed up [Russell's] first success'. Therefore, 'Lord John will now try to get a party on the principle of parliamentary reform, and with the prospect of a dissolution near he may very possibly succeed'.[88] The 'tone and tenor' of Russell's speech 'was calculated to impress everyone who heard it with the feeling that his object was to turn the government out'.[89] Goderich's speech, alluding to the need for reform of the colonial administration, signalled the support Russell might gather to himself.[90]

Statements from Bulwer Lytton[91] and Lord Robert Cecil[92] provided an extended exposition of international law to which all sections of the Conservative backbenches might subscribe, as was confirmed by Warren[93] and Whiteside.[94] Disraeli, however, having failed to press home either his secret treaty accusation or his finance motion, appeared 'very sulking' and discouraged debate on the China question.[95] Disraeli was forced to realise, however, that while Derby's disinterest in his own schemes ensured ineffectiveness, his own apathy for a line being pressed by Derby was irrelevant. Disraeli's need for Derby was far greater than Derby's need for Disraeli. On 28 February, Derby held a meeting of the Commons Conservative party at which he reiterated the obligations of subordination. Derby:

> began by alluding to the defection of a few members of the opposition on the budget, which he understood had been occasioned by a report of his having coalesced with Mr. Gladstone. He denied such being the case, but declared in the most emphatic manner that should any member of the Conservative connection attempt to dictate to him the course he should pursue with regard to political personages, he would regard it as an insult, and no longer recognise that member as attached to his party.[96]

The declaration was received 'with long continued cheering and the greatest enthusiasm' while 'the most complete confidence in Lord Derby [was] expressed'.[97]

As the China debate in the Commons continued Clarendon considered the outcome 'very doubtful', dependent 'as much upon those who stay[ed] away as on those who vote[d]', and it remaining 'difficult to ascertain beforehand what people [would] do'.[98] Gladstone 'inflamed by spite and ill humour', appeared 'ready to say and do anything and act with anybody if he [could] only contribute to upset the government', while Russell had given way 'to all the bitter feeling that [was] within him, and [had] cast all moderation to the winds'.[99] Predictably, Graham gave unqualified support to Russell.[100] Herbert, in turn, censured the government for 'commending the judgement, fairness and moderation of those who had inflicted so much suffering on the Cantonese'.[101] At a meeting of the Commons Liberal party on 2 March, Palmerston 'harangued them cheerily', but Goderich 'spoke for those who, giving a general support to the government, intend[ed] to vote against them' on Cobden's motion.[102] With the ostensible stoicism that '[h]uman fortunes [were] a mixture of good and bad', Palmerston received Hayter's calculation of a government defeat by 8 to 12: '[t]wenty Conservatives will vote with us, and fifty from our own side, including in that number 14 Peelites, will vote with Cobden'.[103] As the debate continued, however, private summons were sent by telegraph to every government vote that could be brought to the House, even those abroad, that might save them from a minority.[104] While the result was 'uncertain' and rumours were rife, much significance was seen to depend upon Palmerston's speech.[105]

'[I]ll both with gout and cold',[106] Palmerston's statement on the evening of 3 March[107] proved 'very dull in the first part and very bow-wow in the second; not very judicious, on the whole bad, and it certainly failed to decide any doubtful votes in his favour'.[108] Grey found the speech 'in the lowest tone of mere party speaking and bad jokes, full of misrepresentation, and an appeal to all the worst feelings and prejudices of his hearers' with 'some clever claptrap in it'.[109] In a malicious response Milner Gibson noted that Palmerston's party meeting was remarkable for the absence of certain prominent men such as Russell, while the government's conduct had forsaken the Liberal watchword of 'Peace, Retrenchment, Reform' for the motto 'Bombardment of Canton and no Reform'.[110] Roebuck and Disraeli, in concluding the debate, portrayed Cobden's motion as a vote of censure implying lack of confidence in the government.[111] Disraeli challenged Palmerston to appeal to the country with the programme 'No Reform! New Taxes! Canton blazing! Persia invaded!' In the division the government were defeated by a majority of sixteen, 'more than any of them expected'.[112] Gladstone felt the vote did 'more honour to the H. of C. than any [he] ever remember[ed]'.[113] Conservative analysis of the division discovered a consolidated body of 204 Conservative votes, augmented by 36 Whigs and Radicals, 18 Peelites supporting Cobden, with only 24 'self-called Conservatives', headed by George Bentinck, voting for the government.[114] Derby felt the manner in which the party had been 'brought to the post' reflected 'the very highest credit on [Jolliffe's] good management', numbering the 'Bentinck malcontents' at five, with the rest either 'very low Church' or 'loose fish who [might] be had by any government'.[115] The *Edinburgh Review* noted the 'curious fact' of the division that every MP who had held office in a former cabinet, with the exception of Edward Ellice, voted against the government.[116] As with Roebuck's motion in January 1855, the government were defeated in March 1857 by Conservative solidarity and Whig, Liberal, Radical, as well as Peelite disarray.

At a cabinet meeting on 4 March, the government promptly chose to portray Cobden's motion as a vote of no confidence, to dissolve parliament, and to call an election. Resignation 'was out of the question'.[117] The appeal to popular 'Palmerstonianism' realised a threat Palmerston had been wielding within Westminster since the summer of 1855. Clarendon disclosed that Palmerston 'would have been quite ready to dissolve last year, but there was no good excuse for it'.[118] Cobden's motion provided both the excuse and a favourable issue with which to exploit 'Palmerstonian' feeling beyond Westminster and Clubland. Moreover, the cabinet's determination to dissolve parliament as soon as possible would prevent others raising alternative issues with which to complicate a simple electoral sanction of 'Palmerstonian' axioms.[119] Any complex issues raised in continuing debate would be 'very disagreeable with men so reckless and uncompromising as Gladstone, Disraeli, Lord John and others'.[120] Cobden acknowledged that 'the premier [had] lived for the last year upon terror of a dissolution'.[121] Argyll smugly observed that never was 'a penal dissolution more thoroughly deserved, and [he] was quite excited by the confident expectation that Palmerston would be supported by the country'.[122]

Palmerston's announcement of the cabinet's decision to dissolve parliament in the Commons on 5 March alluded to the 'peculiar circumstances' of the government defeat.[123] Previous divisions, particularly over the budget, had upheld government policy while Palmerston conjectured that it would be very difficult for any alternative ministry to be formed from the 'combination of parties' which had supported Cobden's motion. Disraeli welcomed the opportunity to achieve 'well defined and well appreciated' party opinions as pronounced on the hustings,[124] but the accusation of combination stung those, such as Russell and Gladstone, anxious to protect their integrity.[125] The ministry seized the moment to portray the majority over Cobden's motion as 'a combination among all the scraps and debris of parties which had resulted from many fractures and which had nothing in common except an unreasoning antipathy to Palmerston'.[126]

During the final weeks of debate until parliament was prorogued on 21 March, confident that Palmerston's popularity was 'red hot',[127] the cabinet sought to prevent any manipulation of issues that might overshadow a simple appeal to Palmerston's personal standing. Liberal backbenchers declared that Palmerston was 'very popular – people troubling themselves very little about the justice or injustice of the [China] war and angry at the supposed coalition'.[128] To enforce that perspective Clanricarde was urged not to initiate a debate on revenues for the war in Persia,[129] and Clarendon placed before the Lords the chief stipulations of the treaty recently signed between the British and Persian governments.[130]

Cobden, with an agitator's faith in agitation, believed the attempt to pass Palmerston off 'as a policy in himself' was 'a hollow business' that would 'collapse under the effort of a few genuine public meetings'.[131] Cobden prepared to fight Palmerston on the ground of the China question. Others with greater scepticism about the 'popular will', however, sought alternative concerns with which to divert attention from the personality of the premier. Gladstone's attempt to revive the financial issue only provided further proof of his isolation. 'Times', Gladstone succinctly noted, 'are changed, and men!'[132] Herbert, weakening further Gladstone's bargaining position, admitted to Malmesbury that the Peelites were 'much divided, there being hardly a subject on which they agreed'.[133] Conservative backbenchers felt the need for a distinctive 'cry' that 'should not only be popular in the country but *adopted by the party generally*'.[134] A need created by the expectation that 'the elections [would] be so put that no principle [was] at stake'.[135] Such an election would produce a 'liberal gain to support Palmerston for a time', but would give way to 'a movement ministry' of which they would 'not be surprised to see Lord John the head'.[136] Recognition that 'R's success would be the defeat of Palmerston',[137] however, recommended to Derby the resumption of a patience policy reliant on inaction rather than initiative. In his final parliamentary statement of the session Derby did little to develop the standing of the issues that had arisen during the previous weeks.[138] While suspicion of a coalition with Gladstone remained to do 'irreparable mischief', the possibility of a Whig and Liberal schism offered advantage in repose.[139] Indeed, visitors to Cambridge House were told that the 'unprincipled coalition' that had united over Cobden's motion had made a 'mixed party' on the government side, in which 'blue and orange [might] fuse with some other colour or sink into white'.[140]

II

Disraeli declared to one lady admirer that '[p]ublic appeals in favour of a *name* and not a *policy* are convenient, but at the same time deceptive'.[141] Certainly the general election of 1857 has been conventionally perceived as a triumphant 'plebiscite' in support of Palmerston's premiership.[142] This study is not primarily concerned with the psephological truth of such an assertion, but rather with the perception of the election that politicians themselves entertained. Even so a few comments are necessary. Particularly as historical orthodoxy, which in truth has been repetition of the reading imposed by *The Times* upon the election, is misleading. First, local issues were prominent in all mid-Victorian elections. In 1857 they were more influential than in most. Secondly, the appeal to the opinion of the country was very limited. The number of candidates standing for election was the lowest in any general election since 1832. The number of uncontested constituencies was higher than in any election since 1832 with the exception of 1847.[143] When one looks at the local picture what is striking is how peripheral (with perhaps the exception of Norfolk) the issue of Palmerstonianism was to the election results. Moreover, where Palmerstonianism was an issue it was such a vague appeal that it was easily adapted to particular local situations.[144] In England no one issue dominated the elections, although parliamentary reform was mentioned by nearly all candidates. In Leicester and Aylesbury religious issues overshadowed the China vote. In Leominster religion and reform were the dominant concerns.[145] In Wales religion emerged as the single most important issue.[146] In Scotland, more strikingly than in England, no single question prevailed and generalities are impossible.[147] In Ireland, religion, the Maynooth grant and patronage in the form of tenant rights dominated hustings activity.[148] In sum, the 1857 election was *not* a plebiscite in support of Palmerston's premiership. This makes sense of the variety of contemporary readings of the election. It also allows the historian to make sense of political events in parliament after May 1857.

Cabinet confidence at the beginning of the election suggested that Palmerston was 'dictator for the moment' and set 'on a bed of roses'.[149] But the considered opinion of Lord Normanby, as the election drew to a close, contrasted strongly with the 'Palmerstonian' confidence of three weeks earlier. The election, Normanby concluded, had been 'a series of surprises and [had] tended rather to show in succession the weakness of each party than the strength of any.... [Palmerston] had mounted on the British Lion whom he had got into capital condition for the occasion, but it [was] lucky for him the race [was] only in *one heat*.'[150] The heterogenous character of those Liberals successfully returned to parliament confirmed Normanby's comment.[151] 'The cry for Palmerston alone ended in a cry for Palmerston and reform.'[152] Increasingly disturbed by the pledges Liberal candidates were making to reform and the ballot, Palmerston came to suspect that the Ryder St Committee, who were sponsoring government candidates on behalf of the party, was 'trying to pack the parliament with ballot men willing and unwilling'.[153] This 'bit of treachery' he saw as a suggestion that some Liberals were anticipating 'a radical parliament with John Russell as its head'.[154]

Received historical opinion has emphasised the rout of Radicalism in the face of an overwhelming 'Palmerstonian' reaction. Cobden, Bright, Milner Gibson, Layard and Miall lost their seats. But to what extent do their electoral contests in Lancashire, Manchester and the West Riding, reflect a 'national' sentiment? Greenwich, Bolton, Bristol, Carlisle, Stockport, Stoke and Sheffield returned anti-Palmerstonian candidates, while at Lambeth a motion was carried against the sitting 'Palmerstonian' member.[155] That Radicalism lost its most prominent personalities has continued to attract attention, but they were as much the victim of local circumstances as national opinion.[156] The drawing of general psephological conclusions from the variety of local activity is difficult. But what was of crucial importance to contemporary politicians was that the implications of the election for the future were of sufficient ambiguity as to allow credibility to differing expectations.

III

Cabinet reaction to the election results was an ambivalent acknowledgement of immediate success and future difficulty. *The Times* announced the government majority to be 105.[157] Conservative calculations discerned 284 committed 'government men', 74 Radicals and 36 Liberal–Conservatives or 'half-government men'.[158] Conservative appreciation of the distinctions within the government majority pointed to the source of ministerial disquiet. Immediate cabinet gratification was drawn from the belief that the Peelites had been 'broken' and 'smashed as a party, which was good'.[159] The elections, it was noted with satisfaction, would take the conceit out of the Peelites.[160] Moreover the 'expulsion of Bright, Cobden, Milner Gibson and Layard from parliament was, in itself, worth a dissolution'.[161]

The recognition of future difficulty, however, focused upon the question of reform. At Nottingham on 13 March, and five days later in East Norfolk, Liberal candidates pledged themselves to an extension of the franchise.[162] On 19 March, in London, Russell delivered an extended argument for necessary reform and appealed for promotion of the cause of 'progress'.[163] Thereafter a number of successfully elected Liberal backbenchers avowed support for Palmerston while also pledging themselves to further reform. Granville recognised that the 'danger consist[ed] in the probable formation of a numerous and respectable Liberal party opposed to the present government. The game [was] not an easy one for anybody [with] regard [to] reform.'[164]

Argyll, believing 'they [could not] too early, or too carefully consider the course to be pursued', urged Palmerston to think on reform 'with a view to the preparation of a measure of their own in the *next* – not *this* – session'.[165] This would 'resist any attempt on the part of Lord John Russell, or others, to force on a discussion prematurely'. Similarly Clarendon, advising Palmerston of the demand for some limited reform, was confident that it need not be 'an unconservative measure if it is done with prudence and organic changes . . . avoided'.[166] His own scheme of enfranchising degrees and commissioners, while requiring every man in giving his vote to sign his name, would, he believed, disfranchise as many as would be enfranchised, and 'guard against the spurious agitation that will be got up upon the question by a few individuals for personal objects'. The proposal stands as testament to the conservative sentiment that gave impetus to Whig notions of progress. Granville, in a different line of argument, hoped Palmerston, while appearing reasonable and 'moderate', might allow Russell to bring forward his own reform scheme first. It being 'almost impossible to concoct a [bill] which will please everybody', Russell would then stand 'unmasked'.[167] Colleagues reminded Palmerston that there was 'nothing [the prime minister had] ever said or done to entitle anyone to assume that [he was] not in favour of reform'.[168]

Reluctant to use 'ambiguous words which would be capable of opposite interpretations',[169] the 'programme of ministerial intention'[170] which Palmerston delivered to his constituents at Tiverton rested on established points of appeal.[171] Palmerston declared it to be 'unbecoming' in him 'to enter into detailed pledges or hold out distinct promises' upon any point of domestic 'improvement'.[172] Cabinet anxiety, however, argued that neglect preferred little but the acrimony born of neglect. Silence would be tested against the scepticism of those who remembered Palmerston's opposition to Russell's reform bill in 1854 and Locke King's bill a few weeks earlier. Newcastle held that Palmerston 'was anything but a reformer'.[173] Lord Dunfermline could 'not believe there [was] a single person in the cabinet, unless it was Mr. Baines, who would not willingly have declined the task of proposing a reform bill', and had no doubt 'that if Palmerston had felt he had the power to beat Lord John and reform he would cheerfully have done so'.[174] Certainly Lady Palmerston proved anxious to impress upon political acquaintances that 'P. had not pledged himself to any great measure of reform, but only to remedy acknowledged defects'.[175]

Newcastle believed 'that Palmerston [would] be disappointed with his new parliament'.[176] 'Many acute politicians' predicted that 'ministerial exaltation' would be short-lived as 'the elements of discord among Liberals [were] countless and impracticable'.[177] It became apparent that the new House of Commons had 'an unwieldly and unmanageable weight of Liberalism in it'.[178] Newcastle deemed it 'all nonsense to suppose that the China vote [had] really influenced the decision of the country, but there [was] one question which alone Palmerston care[d] about (and that in an *adverse* sense) which [had] gained ground everywhere and [was] now established as the question of the day – reform of parliament'.[179] Those close to Russell felt his 'position [was] greatly changed for the better, and with discretion on his part he [would] be again the master of the situation'.[180] The implications of the election results were clear: 'the immediate victory is Palmerston's, the second is the Liberal Party's and the third will be Lord John's'.[181]

That Russell, immediately after the election, presented differing opinion to different persons should cause less consternation for the historian searching for motive than an appreciation of the antagonistic pressures acting upon Lord John. To members of the cabinet Russell declared himself 'very much' pleased with the composition of the new parliament in which he saw 'a revival of Whig county representation'.[182] A few weeks later, during a *tête à tête* of more than an hour with Lady Clarendon, Russell impressed her 'with the notion of his friendly intentions towards the government'.[183] In contrast, while writing to the recently defeated Radical Layard, Russell was less sanguine about public affairs, fearing 'that Lord Palmerston and his supporters [would] seek to evade their obligations, and the opposition [would] be delighted to disparage the Liberal party as their only chance of regaining public favour'.[184] Yet also anxious to avoid the impediment of popular clamour Russell warned that 'indignation "out of doors" [might] exceed all just limits, and produce a heady flood of innovation rather than sound reform'. To former colleagues Russell recalled that, when leading Whigs had repudiated him and took Palmerston as their leader, he had done nothing but acquiesce and act with the party. But, while admitting that 'Palmerston had done very well for them for a time', he felt the premier's speech at Tiverton 'must put his old friends to the block'.[185] To his closest confidants Russell disclosed that he was 'not inclined to play [the government's] game for them' with regard to reform 'as he had with the budget'. Content that there was little possibility 'of going thro' the short session . . . without some discussion on extension of the suffrage', Russell was prepared to let the government 'get through as they can'.[186] He preferred to 'wait to see what Palmerston proposed and mean[t] to carry . . . but it was quite clear that P. [could not] be a reformer without losing Bentinck and his band, or a conservative without losing the Liberals'.[187] Government had to be by party and, Russell insisted, there could 'only be two parties, a reform party and a conservative party'.[188]

The differing facets of Russell's behaviour were a response to the need, in a pose of principle independence, to avoid offence to too many. Some believed that the City of London election had 're-endorsed [Russell] in such a manner which [might] make him an early successor to Lord Palmerston'.[189] Ellice, though opposed to extensive or rapid reform, 'did not conceal his opinion that [Russell] would again have the opportunity of being at the head of a government'.[190] Some new Liberal MPs made it clear that they looked to Russell 'as the head of their party, and from [him], rather than from Lord Palmerston, [they] expect[ed] Liberal measures'.[191] Against such expectation was counterbalanced the alarm of some Whigs, discomforted 'at the quantity of Radicals in the new parliament', who were apprehensive of the 'inevitable reform bill John Russell [would] propose for the government to swallow'.[192] Trimming his declared intentions allowed Russell time to procure the 'hangers back' so that 'the party [might] be preserved in its entirety and for *Lord John's use*'.[193] The conviction grew that Palmerston could not 'last very long, and the great thing [was] to let him go to pieces legitimately not factiously'.[194] Experience enforced prudence when Lord Holland declared his belief that Russell's 'succession to the premiership [was] obvious' if Russell did not act too soon and 'split up the Liberal party again'.[195] Ultimate success would depend upon Russell 'allow[ing] events to develop a little'.[196] A cabinet that had begun by 'being very Palmerstonian as to reform' would end 'by being very Russell'.[197]

One of the few aspects of the election that found general acceptance within Whig and Liberal circles was that the Conservative party had been 'smashed'.[198] Conservative opinion differed. Jolliffe estimated a secure section of 260 Conservative votes in the new parliament as compared with 256 prior to the dissolution.[199] Such solace rested on a distinction between certain and doubtful allegiance. Finding comfort in the same distinction, Disraeli celebrated that all 'the sections, all the conceited individuals, who were what they styled themselves, "independent", [were] swept away, erased, obliterated, expunged'; a state of affairs he felt 'much more wholesome and agreeable'.[200] The Conservatives emerged from the election 'much more compact and united', able, when the occasion arose, to 'bring a larger force into the field than in the last parliament'.[201] '[H]aving regard to the materials of which the Palmerstonians exist[ed]', the Conservative backbencher Hamilton believed 'an advent to power [was] almost a certainty' if the Conservatives did not 'run at it too soon'. It appeared 'impossible that the 2 sections of which the Palmerstonians [were] made up [could] hang together after the commencement of the session of 1858'.[202] Jolliffe lent ready credence to the conjecture that a reform bill was inevitable 'and that [the] government [would] not last six months!!!'[203] Derby foresaw the opportunity for 'a very formidable opposition' if the Conservatives remained 'united, and moderate and not crotchety', while if the rumours of a reform bill were to be believed another early dissolution seemed possible.[204]

The results of the election recommended a resumption of that patience policy Derby had advocated while opposing the Aberdeen coalition. Disraeli's wish for a more immediate and dynamic strategy illustrated differences of temperament and outlook. To Disraeli's suggestion that 'a bold and decided' course over reform would place the Conservative party on its 'legs',[205] Derby made an authoritative statement of his views that served to confirm that Conservative policy was decided at Knowsley. Palmerston's majority was 'of a heterogeneous character' and though Palmerston had 'at present the game in his hand' Derby's object was 'to make him play it in our sense':

> The Peelite and Manchester men are obliterated: but it would be a mistake to say that the House is divided into two parties only; among the Liberals there are two divisions differences between whom must shortly become more marked than they are at present. The old Whigs are far less numerous than the Radicals, and are proportionately afraid of them. Pam has ousted Johnny from the command of the Whigs, and the necessities of the latter's position will make him bid for the support of the Radicals with whom, however, he will never obtain a cordial acceptance. Palmerston on the other hand will not be sorry to see him take this course; and if he finds him committed to it, will take the line of great moderation, and lean upon Conservative support. To encourage this tendency on his part, if it exists, and to ferment divisions and jealousies in the Government majority must be our first objective; while we should carefully avoid multiplying occasions for their voting in concert, in opposition to motions brought forward by us.[206]

For Derby, confined by an attack of gout to his bed at Knowsley, the immediate merits of inactivity remained. On the issue of reform, Derby expected the premier not to introduce a bill in the coming session, but rather 'that Palmerston [would] try to turn John Russell's flank by compelling him to show his cards, and then promising to bring forward the subject of parliamentary reform, after mature consideration by the government, in the session of 1858'.[207] Thus, with 'two rival [Liberal] chiefs in the field', immediate Conservative policy appeared 'obvious': 'to wait till both of them had opened their budget, or at all events committed themselves to some course'. Moreover, restraint, rather than any overt desire to promote the question, would be more palatable to backbench Conservative sensibility.

Where the calculation of others and self-perception met was in the position of the Peelites after the election: the Peelite party, Herbert starkly declared to Aberdeen, is 'extinct'.[208] Yet, the manner of their extinction, its implications for the future and the constraints it placed on the present were, as always, matters of disagreement amongst the Peelites themselves. In a 'radical' speech at Carlisle, Graham portrayed Palmerston as the obstacle to reform who had opposed Russell in 1853 and Locke King in 1857.[209] In reply to Palmerston's imputation of faction, Graham observed that '[n]o accusation [was] so easily made or so readily believed by knaves as knavery'. This emphasis, born of Graham's sympathy for Russell's claim as the authoritative voice on reform, warned cabinet Whigs of hostile intent,[210] and lent impetus to the severance of Peelite connection. Gladstone, as the prominent Peelite least inclined towards Russell, felt that 'by adopting reform as a watchword of present political action, [Graham] had certainly inserted a certain amount of gap' between himself and some of his colleagues.[211] Herbert, 'weary of the evils which the existence of a third party, which [Gladstone] called a public nuisance, created', declared his intention to take his place 'on the liberal side of the House'.[212] Graham believed the 'Peelites as a party [were] gone'.[213] Aberdeen echoed 'the conviction that there [was] no such thing as a distinctive Peelite party'.[214] Gladstone, whose mind had 'been wrought into a state of sensitiveness which [was] excessive and morbid', gave way to expressions of desperation: 'You will never be able to get away from me so long as I can cling to you . . .'[215]

Future hope came to shape understanding of the past so as to indicate an immediate course of action. Graham and Aberdeen agreed that the Peelites as a party had ceased to exist in 1852 when a coalition had been formed with Russell on 'the avowed bases [of] fusion and reform'.[216] In this 'age of progress', Aberdeen declared to Gladstone, 'the liberal party must ultimately govern the country'.[217] The use of the adjectival form was crucial; while 'liberalism' pointed to Russell, 'Liberalism' as represented by the Liberal party, pointed to Palmerston. In correspondence with Cobden, Graham acknowledged the importance of 'honest reformers' coming to an understanding and prophesied official prevarication. 'Time [was] of value to every minister in possession of power and it [did] not sink in value when weighed by a premier at the age of seventy-three'.[218] A concert among 'honest reformers' Graham envisaged as excluding Gladstone, but possibly including Herbert. For his own part, however, Herbert perceived 'conservative progress' as best practised by Palmerston rather than Russell. Though 'Palmerston hated reform as he hated the Devil', Herbert argued, 'the country had returned a parliament to support Palmerston and reform – or the former [would] go to the wall'.[219]

Disagreeing with Graham and Aberdeen, Gladstone also dissented from their interpretation of recent events. Denying that 'a real and final amalgamation with the Liberal party' had occurred in 1852, Gladstone observed that over foreign policy, expenditure and taxation, while 'sharply opposed to Lord Palmerston', the Peelites were in 'general agreement with Lord Derby and the bulk of his party'.[220] On the other hand, Gladstone had no doubt that Russell was persuaded that 'the country must be governed by the Liberal party . . . that he must be at the head of it [and] that reform or education . . . or some other question must be employed as an instrument for these higher purposes'.[221] This 'total inversion of means and ends', Gladstone concluded, denied any possibility of union with Russell. Forced to acknowledge, under Aberdeen, Graham and Herbert's insistence, the end of the Peelites as a party, Gladstone confessed a fear lest the Peelites should not only be 'extinguished', but put out 'with a stench'. This disaster, the personal implications it held, and the comment it contained on the public effectiveness of his fiscal policy, to one of such a highly strung and complex nature as Gladstone's, occasioned a profound personal crisis. The more so as, during the previous weeks, he had 'seemed in the highest excitement'.[222] In the months after April 1857, theology and Homer sustained Gladstone during a period when failure rendered politics profoundly distasteful. With an anguished emotional intensity he reflected on the demands of 'Balaam'.[223] Finding himself 'isolated',[224] Gladstone declared a wish 'in pain and distress . . . to keep quiet'.[225] He would 'leave the management of public affairs to others'. He informed Aberdeen: 'I do not look to spending in political life the last of my strength. I only await the day when the evidence of the facts shall convince me that I have no reasonable expectation of doing good there, and certainly both the fact and the manner of the severance that is now hanging over [the Peelites] are the most significant indications that have yet been afforded me towards a proof, which I dare say the next few years will carry to demonstration.'[226]

While Gladstone engaged in an anguished purgative withdrawal from active politics, both Cobden and Bright saw public confirmation of their own personal sense of barren isolation. Prior to the election Cobden had been certain 'there [was] no safer battle-ground than the

Chinese business', and though he expected their 'opponents [to] try to escape the issue', they 'must rub their noses in it'.[227] On the hustings Cobden portrayed the Chinese war as 'a blunder and a crime', while denying that his motion had been the factious vehicle for a coalition of parties, and refusing 'to do the humble dirty work of the minister of the hour'.[228] As the election progressed, however, Cobden found it necessary to acknowledge the question of reform. Cobden's subsequent emphasis on redistribution, rather than the franchise, which anticipated Bright's later campaigns to educate the people, formed the guiding wisdom of 'Manchester School' orthodoxy on reform.[229] When Milner Gibson and Bright were not re-elected at Manchester and Cobden was defeated at Huddersfield, post-mortems diagnosed popular 'ignorance, passion and credulity' as the instruments of their defeat.[230]

Comfort was found in a sense of isolated moral righteousness. They were, Bright consoled Cobden, 'ahead of the public opinion of [their] time'.[231] They were 'ostracised because [their] political creed [was] in advance of, and [their] political morality higher than that of the people for whom [they had] given up the incessant labours of nearly twenty years'.[232] Cobden believed that the 'flunkeyism' of the manufacturers, having given way 'to a paroxysm of snobbishness', inclined them to go down 'on their bellies, and throw dust on their heads and fling dirt at the prominent men of their own order'.[233] Bright, 'bringing philosophy to comfort [him] in [his] misfortunes',[234] did not despair of a complete change, ten years hence, on the questions on which the public mind [had] been recently so active and so much mistaken'.[235] Cobden, however, unable to repeat the labours of twenty years earlier and once again begin a life of agitation, acknowledged himself to be past his prime.[236] It was left to Bright to actively contemplate the future of Radical policy and, in particular, reform.

While providing the commitment to future Radical activity, Bright enunciated Cobden's thoughts as the wisdom of 'Manchester School' policy. The key to any reform bill lay in the principle of redistribution that accompanied any extension of the franchise: 'redistribution was the difficulty and the danger'.[237] Thus, Bright speculated, 'Lord John would be disposed to correct the democratic tendency of suffrage extension by retaining an unjust redistribution of seats – and by offering a wide suffrage along with a mischievous arrangement of seats' would obtain 'some liberal support, as in 1854 ... ready to support the very worst bill that was ever contrived'.[238] A £10 suffrage in the counties and a household rating suffrage in the boroughs

would, Bright believed, with the ballot, provide a parliament favourable to an 'honest' redistribution of seats, but the present parliament
would not vote for such reforms. Cobden, meanwhile, worried about
his health and, deeply disillusioned with the judgement of the country, retreated into a rural obscurity and advised Bright to abstain from
controversy and debate.

Roebuck, like Cobden and Milner Gibson, during his election at
Sheffield had presented the China question as the dominant issue.
Dwelling upon the legal ambiguities of the question and resorting to
the patriotic axioms that distinguished his Radical position, Roebuck
portrayed the Chinese war as the pretext for England's 'renown
[being] cast into the dust, degraded, [and] made dishonourable'.[239]
Once successfully re-elected, however, and with Cobden, Bright and
Milner Gibson removed from parliament, Roebuck perceived in the
growing concern with reform an opportunity for a concerted Radical
initiative under his own auspices. Towards this end Roebuck's
lieutenant, Samuel Morley, sounded out Cobden's response to a
'preliminary chat' as to the 'best course to be pursued by advanced
Liberals under present circumstances'.[240] Such a meeting might be
followed by 'a large and influential meeting' at the Reform Club 'at
which some of [the] smaller men [would] gladly cooperate'.[241] The
need to organise was all the greater because some believed that
'Palmerston [would be] drowned ere long in the stream of Liberals
now rushing into the House all pledged to move ahead while [Palmer-
ston] seem[ed] resolved to stand still'.[242] Milner Gibson and Miall
accepted Roebuck's overtures; Cobden, disparaging Roebuck's
'inordinate vanity' to always secure the first place, declined. There
seemed, Cobden declared to Morley, 'little life anywhere', the 'working classes [were] dead to politics' and 'literally seem[ed] to have no
leaders'.[243] The abstention of Cobden, who had provided the most
coherent substantive Radical statement on the question of reform,
was a great blow to Roebuck's attempt to lead a Radical initiative. No
less than the Whig–Liberal party, Radical unanimity suffered from
the inherent antagonism of distinct ambition and prominent personalities.

The election results, the meaning that politicians saw in them and
the action they saw as appropriate, produced a consensual strategy
springing from widely divergent intention. Waiting upon events pro-
ferred a positive policy in the light of an assumption that others would
be forced or inclined to act. Though electoral oratory had initially
focused upon the premier and 'Palmerstonianism', the advocacy of

Liberal backbenchers and, most importantly, Russell, had brought reform to a new public prominence. Thereafter reform provided for protagonists the key to future action. While the cabinet was secure for the present, reform promised to be the issue to undermine the government's authority; Argyll, Clarendon and Granville's anxiety was acknowledgement of the problems reform might create. Government embarrassment over reform offered Russell hope for the future. Moreover, the emergence of the reform issue had shown Radicals responding to, rather than initiating, demands for change. Reform had prompted a Radical response which had been only belatedly forthcoming. Similarly reform had defined Aberdeen's and Graham's leanings towards Russell, Herbert's sympathy for Palmerston, and Gladstone's isolation. Conservative inactivity, and the shrewd strategic assumptions on which it rested, became aligned with the immediate intentions of other pre-eminent politicians. For Gladstone, Disraeli, Cobden and Bright, inactivity was a savage comment upon their own ineffectiveness; for Palmerston, Derby and Russell it was a chosen policy that promised future reward. A pose of watching and waiting was adopted by most, was convenient for many, and sustained a variety of differing hopes.

4 Reform Deferred

> Thus far the votes in Parliament indicate, to a casual observer, a large and firm Palmerstonian majority. Knowing ones, however, say significantly 'wait a little' – and they mean by 'a little' a whole year at least. By that time the strong infusion of Reform into the new House will have fermented, found its way to the top, and be prepared and able to shake the smooth surface of the Ministerial cauldron. It is astonishing how patiently they bide their time. The power 'to wait' is a great one. (Dallas to Cass, 26 May 1857, cited in G. M. Dallas, *Letters from London, 1856–1860*, I, p. 169)

Political events during the remainder of 1857 serve as an explanation as to why the question of reform was deferred. The historical need for an organising principle exists in this negative concern. Why did reform, the imminent focus of political concern during the months of March and April, become, after the election of 1857, an issue of ostensible neglect? In short, a consensual strategy of inaction ensured inactivity.

The Queen's Speech[1] opening the new parliament on 1 May 1857 was a statement 'expressio minus' that betrayed government unease in reticent design.[2] The speech, focused 'chiefly on foreign affairs and containing no mention of reform',[3] promised legislation on law reform, divorce and a measure checking fraudulent breaches of trust which might safeguard 'the continued well-being and contentment of [the] people and progressive development of productive industry'.[4] Upon an enquiry from the Liberal backbencher Buchanan,[5] which Palmerston found 'injudicious',[6] the premier pledged the government to a reform bill in the next session.[7] Palmerston then asked for 'forbearance' during the present session, avoided 'any declaration upon particular points in reference to representative reform', and declared it 'highly inexpedient to engage in discussions upon the large and sweeping question of a change in the representation of the people in parliament'.[8]

Buchanan's enquiry confirmed the observation of those who saw 'an unwieldly and unmanageable weight of Liberalism' in the new Commons which, if 'solidified as a party distinct and "prononcée"', would 'rush into reform'.[9] It substantiated the opinion of those who believed that Palmerston's 'personal appeal' had 'produced a House which [had] no particular personal inclination to Palmerston and in which he [had] no personal party'.[10] Palmerston's statement, Greville noted, 'put the House in good humour by promising a reform bill next year'.[11] Before the meeting of parliament Russell had 'doubt[ed] the possibility of going thro' the short session . . . without some discussion on extension of the suffrage'.[12] This had been both his expectation and hope. Palmerston's statement held the question in abeyance and denied Russell the immediate opportunity he had anticipated.

The consensual strategy of inaction, and the particular manner in which Palmerston adopted it, had a soporific effect on party calculation. Greville, diagnosing opposition inactivity as impotence, predicted that 'the session [was] going to pass away in the most quiet and uneventful manner'. The 'only men who might be formidable or troublesome seem[ed] to have adopted the prudent course of not kicking against the pricks'.[13] Malmesbury concluded that 'Lord John and the Radicals [were] evidently convinced that the shortness of the session and Palmerston's strength remove[d] all hope at present of a demonstration on their part'.[14] He did 'not believe there [would] be any question of consequence in the H. of Lords for a long time',[15] while Derby concurred that the 'session seem[ed] likely to be a quiet one'.[16] To at least one foreign observer there appeared to be 'quite uncommon serenity . . . in the political heavens. Parliament [was] coolly discussing domestic topics, the camp at Aldershot, the law of divorce, penalties on fraudulent trustees, improvement of parks, reformatories, etc.', while the 'ministry appear[ed] wonderfully at ease'.[17]

Appropriately for a period of 'high political' inactivity, religious questions came to the fore. By negativing Spooner's annual motion[18] the Commons 'escaped the dreary miseries of a Maynooth debate'.[19] A bill to withdraw the Edinburgh annuity tax was withdrawn, while the Burial Amendments Act enabled more unconsecrated burial ground to be made available for the use of dissenters. On 15 May 1857 Palmerston introduced a bill allowing practising Jews to take their seats in the Commons. It must remain a moot point whether the bill was introduced in the expectation that it would be defeated in the Lords. In the light of past experience such a fate was more probable than any other and, indeed, the measure was rejected by the Upper House. Certainly, as constitutional practice decreed, the government were not obliged to pursue the measure once it received the Lords veto. The effect of the government initiative, and its predictable failure, was to hold in abeyance another issue closely associated with

Russell. It was cogent comment on government strategy that Russell, persevering with the question, 'resembled an inexpert swimmer trying to buoy himself with awkwardly entangled bladders'.[20]

The political significance of long debate in the Commons over the government's divorce bill was the confirmation it provided of Gladstone's isolation. During the session Stanley noted that Gladstone, 'either from ill-health, pique or prudence', stayed away from the House.[21] To Cobden, Gladstone admitted himself 'very unwilling during the present session either spontaneously to take up, or to assume any leading part in any discussion'.[22] Around the clubs went the report that Gladstone's head was in a bad state and that he was not likely to be much in the House.[23] The debate over the divorce bill provided Gladstone with a religious focus for his energies as he contended that parliament could not 'take upon itself by its sole authority to determine religious and spiritual matters'.[24] In speeches that seemed to the Speaker 'to outrun the Transatlantic cable',[25] Gladstone showed 'great ability . . . but as usual [did] himself more harm than good'.[26] The obvious comment was provided by Lord Dunfermline: 'Gladstone seem[ed] to stand quite alone and . . . [had] no weight in parliament. This [was] very strange considering the great powers he possess[ed].'[27] On his forty-ninth birthday Gladstone plaintively noted: 'On this day I close my 48th year. How long a time for me to cumber the ground: and still not know *where* to work out the purpose of my life.'[28]

The strategic unimportance of religious discussion allowed Stanley to suggest that 'within the House party-spirit [was] dead'.[29] Yet, how 'the considerable Commons Liberal majority [would] range or act on any change of premiership, or how it [would] settle the ugly question of further parliamentary reform remain[ed] to be seen'.[30]

I

There exists no simple relation between events occurring outside Westminster and the response within. Parliamentary perception passes through the medium of language, established policy and party circumstance, creating less a refractive distortion of events than a new dimension to their understanding. The first news of a mutiny in India reached London on 26 June, reporting the rising of native troops at Meerut. Details of the seizure of Delhi, Cawnpore, the seige of

Lucknow, and horrifying tales of atrocity and torture followed. A sense of deep moral outrage swept the country. Yet the anguish and alarm the Indian Mutiny excited in Britain had surprisingly little immediate effect on the political scene in Westminster.[31] The acknowledgement of an inability to immediately influence events, the fact that the latest intelligence took six weeks to reach London from India, and a confident optimism about the final result typified cabinet attitudes.[32] Only Clarendon, and later Argyll, came to doubt the adequacy of the government's response to the crisis.[33] Clarendon's alarm, however, had little impact on those ministers directly, if distantly, involved in the suppression of the revolt: Palmerston, Vernon Smith, Panmure and Wood. The small number of debates in parliament on the situation in India were occasioned by opposition enquiry and quickly curtailed by ministerial assurances.[34] The cabinet consistently sought to exclude the question of the mutiny in India from the field of political controversy. Amongst the opposition only Lord Ellenborough in the Upper House and Disraeli in the Commons, both men without a substantial following pronouncing a line for others to follow, sought distinction by attacking the government's response or lack of response to the revolt.[35] 'Palmerstonian' argument suggested that the present crisis demanded a patriotic, i.e. non-partisan, confidence in the administration.[36] Though his rhetoric did not acknowledge it, Palmerston's appeal to patriotic duty was not a prescriptive political right. That in July 1857 it might be understood as such was tacit, yet powerful, comment on political circumstance in Westminster. With the Indian Mutiny the government faced what it presented as a 'national crisis' because too few of influence wished to make it the occasion for a 'political crisis'.

Initially Palmerston had hoped to keep parliament sitting until some decisive news arrived from India; a 'general desire' prevailing that 'the grouse [could] wait for a fortnight'.[37] On 5 August, however, in the absence of any news of military successes in the subcontinent, the premier informed the Speaker he wished 'to wind everything up, allowing ample time for the divorce bill in Committee, and [to] prorogue on the 20 or 22 . . .'[38] At the end of the session Granville felt confident that the government had 'done pretty well in the House of Lords where there [was] no great object for any peer to be troublesome, when they [were] convinced the government [was] safe for a time . . .'[39] During the recess, cabinet confidence was evident in ministerial absence. In September, Dallas found '[n]ot a single member of the ministry in town: unless he [had] strayed in for a few hours to or from scenes of social enjoyment'.[40] Four weeks later Parkes was still able to report that '[n]ot a minister was in London'.[41]

While holding the question of the government's response to the Mutiny in abeyance, during October 1857 Palmerston tested the reaction of the cabinet to the immediate abolition of the East India Company and the establishment of a new administrative system in India. Granville discerned that '[o]ne of Palmerston's motives [was] to do something great, which [might] distinguish his premiership, [and] another to have something that [would] act as a damper to reform'.[42] Argyll agreed with Granville 'that Pam's great object in mooting the East India Co. question [was] to damp the reform of home institutions'.[43] Despite the objections of Clarendon to 'a change in the midst of a great crisis', Palmerston became increasingly committed to the question of Indian government as a matter of alternative political concern.[44] To his junior ministers Palmerston appeared 'very sanguine', although nothing 'oozed out' from the cabinet of their intentions.[45] On the Indian administration question Granville hoped there would exist one opinion, 'Conservatives as well as radicals'.[46] Russell, Cornewall Lewis believed, would 'be much influenced by the course which Mr. Fox took on this subject'.[47] Palmerston, in response, firmly rejected Fox's India Act of 1803 as a basis for the new India bill.[48] Although Cornewall Lewis found it difficult to predict the course of the Derbyites they would 'doubtless take advantage of any weakness in the position of the government'. But he doubted their 'having any strong sympathy with the Company'.[49] Parkes had 'no doubt [that] the Tory opposition [would] anxiously expect such a chance in opposition to *any* India bill; and in which they might be joined by a ministerial division'. In this event Russell would 'chuckle at his possible change out of the new rupee'.[50]

Awaiting the legitimate fracture of Liberal party connection, Russell's position during the summer of 1857 remained intentionally vague. To anxious Whig enquirers Russell let himself be understood to be 'very reasonable'.[51] During August speculation arose as to Russell being made a peer. But Russell was 'too sagacious to accept being more or less shelved. There [was] a great opening for him as soon as Pam [broke] down.'[52] In May 1857 Lady Palmerston was 'very anxious' about the premier's health. 'He [was] so weak as to be unable to take any exercise even on horseback and he [had] an open sore on his foot very dangerous at his age.'[53] During June Clarendon admitted that he was uneasy about the sore on Palmerston's leg which had been found very difficult to heal.[54] In October, while at Broadlands, the premier had 'an attack of shingles which lasted more or less until Christmas, and at first was very painful and depressing'.[55] Throughout the year Palmerston's health remained a contingent factor in Russell's calculation. Appearing 'calm' about the Mutiny in India and the cabinet's efforts for its suppression, Russell remained content to comment 'that the most real difficulty would begin when the Mutiny was subdued'.[56] If reform was to be held in abeyance, the future government of India was an issue that, despite ministerial hopes, offered opportunity for confrontation. Others anticipated that 'scarcely two men [would] agree as to what ought to be the best form of government for India . . .'[57] Aberdeen believed 'the future government of India present[ed] a problem of which the solution [was] impossible'.[58] Although the question of the government of India might 'swamp' reform,[59] as Palmerston intended, Russell was prepared to await an opportunity that might still be offered by Liberal dissension.

A future opportunity for Russell was evidenced in Granville's fear that '[n]othing would be more fatal than to attempt to buck all reform'.[60] Wood believed that after Palmerston's pledge the government could not 'avoid something in the reform line'.[61] Palmerston's hope that the issue of the government of India might delay any consideration of the reform question during the 1858 session cabinet colleagues found an impracticable, even desperate, expectation.[62] It was clear that if the government took 'the line of doing nothing they [would] have to reckon upon the active hostility of Lord John'.[63] Even if 'a moderate measure' were proposed the ministry would 'have much trouble about it'.[64]

During the 1857 recess, much Whig anxiety came to focus upon the momentarily deferred, yet invidious, question of reform. Lords Grey and Brougham seemed to stand 'in much fear' of 'the obvious disposition of Lord John and Graham to try and outbid the government'.[65] Grey prepared an essay to be published in the autumn on the whole subject of reform 'to point out the danger of either increasing the strength of the democratic element in [the] constitution or of allowing parliamentary reform to become again a subject of party strife'.[66] Dunfermline counselled Brougham on the necessity to consider reform 'with calmness, with a consciousness of the benefits . . . under the present reform bill and of the dangers of rash changes, especially in the direction of increasing unintelligent numbers'.[67]

During August 1857, though publicly calm over India, in private Russell was 'very hostile' to the government and 'long[ing] to supplant Palmerston'.[68] Russell suspected that the cabinet might bring in 'a *large* reform bill' in the expectation of its rejection by the Lords, that 'the Commons would [then] vote confidence in the ministers; parliament would not be dissolved, and so the question would be shelved for another year!'[69] Graham's surmise that India might be used to displace domestic questions, so that 'Johnny's hobby [would] be brought to a standstill, before he mount[ed] him',[70] was more closely aligned with cabinet thinking. During September 1857 Russell framed a reform scheme that was agreeable to Graham.[71] Having established that 'little or no difference of opinion'[72] existed between them, however, Graham was apprehensive that the issue of reform would offer Russell 'no chance if he is over eager and makes the first move. His game is to wait on Palmerston, compel him, if he can, to produce the government bill and then tear it to rags as worthless and inefficient'.[73] In response Russell declared it unnecessary to discuss specific points about reform until the question arose in 'a more practical shape', and avowed his intention that the government should be censured by 'the light of events'.[74] Graham observed that '[t]he disposition to fight [was] quite apparent: the fear of consequences [was Russell's] only restraint'.[75]

Looking to parliamentary debate in 1858, Russell believed that 'reform [would] certainly be brought in, but the Indian bill, and Indian enquiries [might] last 3 months of the session'.[76] He decided that there was no obstacle to the cabinet introducing a reform bill by March, but if they failed to do so he would attempt a measure of his own and probably move a vote of want of confidence. If, on the other hand, the measure the government brought forward was 'a sham, public indignation would dispose of it'. Russell watched for indications of cabinet opinion. At the end of October he believed the cabinet 'had not discussed either reform or India . . .'[77] A week later he was 'inclined to think that the question of reform [would] be shortly brought before the cabinet', and that Palmerston would yield to the wish of one or two members of the government in favour of reform.[78] Russell remained confident that some members of the cabinet believed that they could not violate Palmerston's reform pledge without loss of honour or credibility. 'This', Russell insisted, 'should be driven home.'[79]

That Whigs identified Russell and Graham as the source of alarm was tacit comment on Radical impotency. As a gentleman farmer in Sussex Cobden found the 'proceedings of the House [had] ceased to interest [him]'.[80] Old colleagues found him 'deeply immersed in farming' and clearly indisposed to re-enter parliament. While spend-ing the summer fishing in the Highlands, Bright received an un-expected invitation to represent Birmingham in parliament. Despite being too ill to address a public meeting, early in August Bright was elected, in his absence, as MP for the city. Cobden saw the result as proof of Birmingham's 'exemption from aristocratic snobbery', and '[i]f Bright should recover his health and be able to head a party for parliamentary reform . . . Birmingham would be a better home for him than Manchester'.[81] More immediately, however, Cobden was still concerned about Bright's 'swimming in the brain'. Bright himself admitted in November 1857 that his 'nerves [were] not yet strong', and if he could manage to attend parliament occasionally he 'could not yet venture to speak'.[82]

The only Radical initiative came from Roebuck, who saw an opportunity for asserting his personal authority in directing Radical efforts over reform. Morley, relaying Roebuck's wishes, informed Cobden that 'there [was] only needed a calm, distinct, full utterance to ensure such a response as would convince Lord Palmerston that trifling with the question [would] not do'.[83] At a meeting in June 1857, attended by Ayrton, Clay, Trelawny, Platt, Philips, Gilpin, Miall and chaired by Roebuck, a formulation of Radical aims was undertaken.[84] A meeting held in November 1857, again chaired by Roebuck, examining the Radical manifesto prepared during the intervening months, served only to affirm the differences existing over even the familiar tenets of Radical belief.[85] Ayrton, for one, took exception to the proposition extending the county franchise to £10 occupiers because he felt it would swamp the legitimate influence of property and tend to array town against country. Bright, Cobden and Milner Gibson's absence only emphasised Radical dissension.

Little concerned with Radical plans, but greatly concerned with Russell's intention, the cabinet discussed reform during October 1857. In the following weeks Palmerston consulted the opinion of his colleagues, in particular Argyll. Granville, observing that the cabinet were 'to reform the government of India but [were] horribly puzzled about reforming [them]selves', believed Palmerston to be in favour of a reform bill, 'but a small one'.[86] The scheme the premier presented to the Queen on 18 October was intended as 'a moderate measure' confining the franchise to men of 'intelligence and independence'.[87] While the borough franchise would remain at £10, the county suf-frage would be lowered to £20. The vote would also be given to officers of the Army and Navy, lawyers, physicians, clergymen and to 'all clerks of merchants, bankers and manufacturers and to any other classes who might be found to come within the same principle'. In deference to cabinet opinion Palmerston also agreed to limited disfranchisement of a number of small boroughs. The scheme was one calculated to appease the greater part of Conservative opinion, reassure Whigs and allow Liberal exhortation for 'safe progress' to appear substantiated. No avowed commitment or parliamentary schedule accompanied the scheme, however, and where the government of India might defer consideration of reform Palmerston could be expected to be diffident.

The scheme of reform Palmerston framed in October 1857 betrayed his expectation of Conservative support. This belief complemented the object of Derby's own policy: to show Palmerston that his friends sat on the benches opposite rather than alongside him. Derby's commitment to this strategy hardened as sources of Conservative dissension became apparent. Disappointed by his failure to be elected Speaker of the Commons, Spencer Walpole provided a querulous and vehemently anti-Disraelian presence in Conservative counsel.[88] Disraeli's active interest in the government's response to the mutiny threatened to become a disruptive issue, more because of its source than the line of argument adopted. The question of reforming the government of India also threatened to reveal deep divisions within Conservative ranks. While Stanley feared 'hasty legislation about India even more than apathy',[89] Disraeli argued for a Conservative initiative establishing 'one of the mainsprings on which any ministry must be formed' and exploiting defections from the commercial ranks of the government.[90] Disraeli reminded Lennox that the Conservatives had criticised the existing system of Indian administration in 1853.[91] Directly at odds with Disraeli's wish for an initiative was the desire of those such as Henley to see the Conservative party defend the East India Company.[92]

In response to Disraeli's desire for a positive move, early in May 1857 Derby had been insistent that the opposition be kept 'quite at liberty', and 'must "combine" with the government to protect them against their Radical supporters'.[93] Growing Conservative dissension enforced Derby's commitment to this policy. Moreover, 'neuralgic gout', which kept Derby at Knowsley in May, despite a show of pugnacity, restricted his political exertions during the session.[94] By the autumn Derby was again confined by gout and appeared to be 'in very low spirits – quite without his usual *entrain*'.[95] These physical problems contributed to the quiescent attitude Derby adopted over

India. Ill-health, party dissent and established intent ensured the Conservative party's inactivity; an inactivity of which Disraeli was the foremost victim.

II

In September 1855 the news of the fall of Sebastopol had given Palmerston's government sufficient credibility to survive a critical political situation within Westminster. Two years later, in September 1857, military events abroad, over which the government had no direct control, once again eased the cabinet's difficulties at home. The recapture of Delhi and the first relief of Lucknow appeared to substantiate Palmerston's jaunty optimism and confound the prophets of doom. The news also ensured that the question of India would assume the form of administrative reform, over which the government could retain the initiative, rather than a difficult post-mortem into the cabinet's handling of the crisis.

As the tide of events seemed to turn in India, however, a financial crisis in Europe caused acute alarm. During the autumn of 1857 a monetary scare prompted an extensive stoppage of banks in the United States which, in turn, excited consternation in London. 'A feverish anxiety pervad[ed] the mercantile classes.'[96] During the first week of November 1857, Cornewall Lewis considered the 'alarm and uneasiness' to be so great that he restricted the number of deputations he received on 'this delicate subject'.[97] On 12 November Palmerston and Cornewall Lewis authorised the Governor of the Bank of England to issue extra notes, which required a bill of indemnity from parliament.[98] Thus, despite the shrewd surmise that 'Palmerston [would] not call parliament together sooner than he [could] help', the premier found it necessary to reassemble parliament at the beginning of December.[99] Consistent with his original intention, however, Palmerston was determined to confine debate 'strictly to the indemnity bill and congratulatory speeches on the Indian victories'.[100]

As a ready recipient of gossip 'Groucher' Greville, looking to the tranquil appearance of past debate, declared that 'Pam [was] more of a dictator than ever'.[101] Those better informed and of greater political weight dismissed such complacency. Wood talked 'despondingly of a disagreeable session which he did not see his way through'.[102] New-castle believed that the 'tide [was] turning against [the] government' and forecast that 'the coming short session [would] sow the seeds of much mischief to [Palmerston's] popularity and power'.[103] Derby, who by November 1857 was once again in 'high force',[104] deemed it 'impossible . . . to confine [parliament's] attention to the currency question'.[105] Derby urged Disraeli, in an unusual reversal of roles, 'not to allow this early session to be made a mere matter of form to suit the convenience of the government'. Russell prophesied that the government would 'be exposed to a great pressure from *within* to postpone the performance [of reform] indefinitely', but insisted that it was 'very necessary to keep up a counter-pressure and remind ministers of obligations . . .'[106] Herbert confirmed that if the government hoped to postpone reform the session would be 'disagreeable with a vengeance'.[107] Graham believed that the 'financial difficulties [had] overtaken the Dodger, and [had] assumed a shape and dimensions, from which neither bluster nor buffoonery [would] afford a ready escape'.[108] Parkes noted that though unforeseen contingencies had 'staved [reform] off for a while . . . Lord John [was] a pointer dog – a setter at the game'.[109]

It is a testament to the prerogative of the Treasury bench in directing debate that, despite hostile intent, Aberdeen concluded that after seven days of the emergency session in December 1857 'the government [had] had an easy session and were satisfied with their success. In the House of Commons India was scarcely touched upon; the commercial crisis engaged all attention.'[110] What those seven days of debate up to 12 December 1857, when parliament was adjourned until February 1858, did reveal was that the consensual strategy of inaction no longer commanded acceptance. Palmerston's apparent dominance had been as much the product of opposition compliance as of ministerial authority. By December 1857 the opposition was no longer content to wait upon events and engage in masterly inactivity. Bessborough, the government whip in the Lords, anticipated 'a good deal of exertion when parliament [met] in February. The tone of the opposition seem[ed] more than ordinarily bitter. Derby especially, and when our blessed reform bill is launched we shall have very few friends.'[111] Similarly Granville began to 'dread' the coming session 'as a great breaker up of parties and making the future very difficult'.[112] Ministerial apprehension was a sincere acknowledgement of Russell's position: 'waiting for an inheritance at 66 years of age is a sorry game'.[113]

5 'A Breaker-up of Parties'

The varieties of the aspects of public affairs have been like the figures in a kaleidoscope, and one ought to catch each fleeting symmetrical arrangement, before it is changed into some other, equally fleeting, in order to comprehend the rapidity and importance of the changes which are going on. (Greville Diary, 20 February 1858, Greville Mss. 41122, cited in C. C. F. Greville, *The Greville Memoirs* H. Reeve (ed.) (London, 1888) VIII, p. 165)

C'est le commencement de la fin. (Derby to Disraeli, n.d. (?16 February 1858) Hughenden Mss. B/XX/S/204)

Palmerston observed that the autumn weather of 1857 was 'like the squares on a chess board alternately black and white – one day beautifully fine the next . . . cloudy and rainy'.[1] Yet as an unusually mild Christmas season approached, Palmerston's political outlook grew increasingly threatening. He had survived the months since the 1857 election with an apparent ease that obscured the real precariousness of his position. Anxiety about the Indian Mutiny had been subsumed within a moral outcry against the perpetrators of atrocity. Reform legislation had been deferred. Potential sources of political threat had been content that this should be so.

But as the parliamentary session of 1858 drew closer the passive compliance that had tolerated Palmerston's pre-eminence dissipated. The wind of change was sensed by Bessborough when he became uneasy about the coming session and the extraordinarily bitter tone of the opposition. Granville's dread of a difficult future was a similar recognition of the hardening of hostile intent. The imminent lapse of tolerance sensed by many had an immediate effect within the intimate context of the cabinet. The Duke of Bedford, while acknowledging that 'Pam's luck [was] wonderful and [had] carrie[d] him through many a difficulty', reported to his brother, Russell, that '[o]ne of [Palmerston's] colleagues, an important member of his cabinet and a good man, [had] not a very elevated opinion of [the premier]'.[2] Such doubt was given greater urgency by the government's commitment to legislate upon Indian administration and parliamentary reform. During December 1857, as appreciation of future difficulties increased within the cabinet, the established pattern of cabinet decision-making began to break down. The cabinet became conscious, Granville disclosed, 'of the diminution of Palmerston's energy and power'.[3] When Lord Grey pointed out to Wood some of 'the great difficulties' of those questions upon which the cabinet were committed to legislate, he noticed that Wood did not doubt the justness of his views.[4]

What was revealed as apprehension to those outside the ministry assumed the form of anxious rancour within the cabinet. Early in January 1858 Cornewall Lewis decried the outline of the proposed India bill as 'wholly insufficient' meeting 'only a fraction of the case'.[5] In a conversation with Greville, Cornewall Lewis betrayed 'an exceedingly mean opinion of [Palmerston's] intrinsic value'.[6] The Chancellor declared his belief that the government's 'great misfortune' had been their throwing out of Locke King's motion, this being 'regarded as a fatal error, to which they owed the dilemma in which they found themselves placed'. In reply to Greville's comment that Disraeli considered Palmerston's popularity to be of a negative character and rather more from the unpopularity of every other public man than from any peculiar attachment to him, Cornewall Lewis simply observed that '[Disraeli] *estimated Palmerston at his real worth*'.[7]

In January 1858 Argyll expressed his general unease and anxiety about the measures being prepared for the approaching session. The India bill, he thought, 'had not been fully enough considered; and that there [was] little enough time to master it before parliament [met]'.[8] Success over the India bill, Argyll deliberated, would depend on how the government were prepared on other questions, especially reform. By adopting India as the first business of the session the cabinet would be open to the charge of choosing that question as a means of postponing reform. Already Lord Grey was among those saying the cabinet had no real intention of reform at all. Argyll 'thought it essential to [the government's] position that we should be able to state that the *promised* measure of reform is ready, altho' it will not be introduced until we think there is a fair prospect of being able to proceed with it'. The discretion inherent in such an assurance was crucial: '[t]his [might] not be the case this session *at all*'. But 'it is equally necessary that [the government] should be able to rebut with truth the charges which are sure to be brought in support of resistance to the India bill'.[9] Argyll was 'annoyed to think that Palmerston [did] not seem fully alive to the necessity of advancing on this matter beyond the point at which [they had] already arrived'. The discrepancy, in Argyll's mind, between politic necessity and Palmerston's capability was growing.[10]

Cornewall Lewis concurred in Argyll's misgivings about the priority given to India, before the insurrection had been subdued, and Palmerston's 'shy' and 'procrastinat[ing]' attitude towards reform.[11] Similarly, Sir Richard Bethell, the Attorney-General for whom 'the India bill [had] absorbed almost [his] whole time and attention', came to 'deeply regret the resolve to introduce the bill . . . It [was] indeed a suicidal measure.'[12] Bethell also came to regret 'the tone and language of the premier', particularly on religious questions.[13] Lord Lansdowne, Palmerston's latterday mentor, was 'evidently much alarmed at the prospect of the India bill and its Imperial Government'. Lansdowne, Herbert reported, 'said very little, but by shrug and gesture he implied a very modified satisfaction'.[14]

Beyond the cabinet such anxiety became the subject of intense speculation. Lord Grey heard from all quarters 'that Palmerston [had] fallen into more unpopularity since parliament adjourned than [he had] supposed possible'.[15] There was 'a growing impression of the instability of the government and of its having become so discredited that even the fear of a Derby–Dizzy government [would] not be sufficient to support it'.[16] Even Greville, looking towards the meeting of parliament in February, predicted that if Palmerston meant 'to rest upon his popularity, and to endeavour to conjure it by his habitual offhand manner and assurances that they had done all they could, expecting that such assurances [would] be accepted as a matter of course . . . he [would] be greatly mistaken'.[17] Delane, sensing the shift of attitudes, 'thought the government would not remain long in office . . . and he ridiculed the idea of its not being practicable to form another'.[18] Delane's opinion was significant, less because of its influence than as a barometer responding to the changing mood. Outside the pale of the government it was 'admitted that Palmerston was not the man he was, and the diminution of his popularity was visible universally'.[19] Parkes, noting that the '*Future* [was] dark and gloomy', marvelled 'that under such circumstances the cabinet should design, inopportunely and absurdly . . a spick and span new form of India government'.[20] Lord and Lady Palmerston, he concluded, were 'intoxicated' with popularity, and 'too old to recollect its treachery'.[21]

The event that dramatically affirmed the precariousness of Palmerston's cabinet was the appointment of Lord Clanricarde as Lord Privy Seal in succession to Lord Harrowby. On 9 December 1857 the ill and rapidly ageing Harrowby, on the advice of his doctors, tendered his resignation to Palmerston. Palmerston accepted on the condition that the resignation be kept secret until a successor was appointed.[22] Lord Overstone refused Palmerston's offer of the vacant office and Lord Clanricarde accepted on condition that the cabinet meant to abolish 'the E[ast] I[ndia] Co. and the Directors in their present functions'.[23] The government, Palmerston assured Clanricarde, were 'determined to propose to parliament to sweep away that phantom the East India Company and to place the administration of India under the direct authority of the Crown through the responsible Minister of the Crown'.[24] Clanricarde, brother-in-law of the Indian Governor-General, Lord Canning, had pursued an energetic private campaign, via correspondence with Granville, in defence of the Governor-General and his policies during the mutiny.[25] Abolition of the East India Company Clanricarde perceived as a just vindication of his brother-in-law's actions.

It was Clanricarde's public reputation that outraged Palmerston's colleagues. Clanricarde had been involved in a scandalous court case during 1854 and 1855 containing all the ingredients of avid popular interest: sexual immorality, child cruelty and alleged murder.[26] Although not directly charged, the evidence given in court revealed Clanricarde to be closely implicated in much disreputable activity. Lord Grey thought it 'the worst case, by many degrees, against a man of rank that had come out in [his] time'.[27] On receiving news of Clanricarde's appointment in December 1857 Landsdowne, it was reported, 'wrote to Palmerston to ask him if he was out of his senses'.[28] Granville's response was no more favourable, noting that the appointment was 'much criticised' and was 'ill-managed' in that it should have taken place 'when there was nothing else to talk of'.[29] As news of the appointment became public Granville's alarm increased. He came to believe the appointment was 'the most unpopular act of Palmerston's official life'[30] and, immediately before parliament met, found the subject 'in a dreadful mess'.[31]

The response to the news of Clanricarde's appointment to the cabinet was immediate and universally hostile. Parkes observed that the 'selection of Clanricarde *vice* the Saint Harrowby [was] really a strange act in the premier', and it 'was talked of as an outrage of public opinion . . . to place Clanricarde in a cabinet about to deal with India and reform'. Moreover, in a more purely political sense, 'with so many Liberals out of office, [it] was a very mischievous act' by Palmerston which was 'a heavy draft on his political capital and public status'.[32] Lord Grey believed that Clanricarde's appointment had done more to undermine Palmerston's popularity than any other event during the recess.[33] Greville thought there was 'a feeling of universal indignation against it'.[34]

The manner of Clanricarde's appointment typified much in Palmerston's leadership. The appointment was made with little reference to the misgivings of ministerial colleagues and, indeed, it was viewed as '*anti*-Whig and Palmerston's personal gain'.[35] Disraeli reported the rumour that Lady Palmerston had been primarily responsible for the successful selection of her 'protégé'.[36] Bethell believed that three months hence Palmerston's government would become 'an historical fact' to be referred to only in the past tense.[37] The hope that such talk would be dissipated by Lady Palmerston's parties and the opening of parliament appeared a lame response to acute anxiety within the cabinet and open hostility outside it. Parkes noted the cardinal circumstance. 'Clanricarde's nomination makes people think better of Lord John; and it is feared it will move the latter to more spleen against the ministry.'[38]

I

While Downing Street became the scene of growing apprehension during the winter of 1857–58, Pembroke Lodge became the focus of intense speculation. Russell's position as Liberal heir-apparent was acknowledged by Whigs in increasingly frequent moments of unease. Graham, in Cowes mourning the recent death of his wife, sought the consummation of that Russell–Peelite alignment he had coveted since 1850. Aberdeen provided a guarded impetus to Graham's intention. Both acknowledged the crucial significance of Russell's plans for the future.

The Duke of Bedford showed Lord Broughton 'a letter from someone connected with the government about Lord John – advising him to be quiet and assuring him that all Palmerston's colleagues would act *under* him if P. should retire'.[39] Ellice began to share the belief that 'John Russell, if he surviv[ed] Palmerston [was] sure of being prime minister'.[40] Security of inheritance, however, was dependent upon Russell's immediate actions. Was Russell prepared to wait until Palmerston retired before wresting control from the premier's hands? Was Russell prepared to cultivate his relations with the ministerial frontbench so as to establish his claim? Was the established pattern of party connection adequate to safeguard Russell's future position?

The desire of many prominent Whigs that all these questions be answered in the affirmative was little guide to Russell's own intention. Indeed, in December 1857 after his elder brother, the Duke of Bedford, had paid £15 000 of Russell's debts and settled on him an annual allowance of £2000, the strength of Russell's independent position was enhanced.[41] Russell's lack of income had always necessarily coloured his attitude towards office: the possession of a ministerial salary enabling him to fulfil the social obligations of his political position. Bedford's renowned meanness had often handicapped Russell's political influence.[42] The Duke's handsome endowment, in the winter of 1857, however, extended Russell's freedom of action.

Immediately after parliament was adjourned in December 1857, Russell, exploring a variety of openings, sent a searching letter to Graham.[43] Though Graham was still at Cowes mourning the death of his wife, Russell assured him that India and reform were questions 'well worthy of [Graham's] efforts' upon which he might 'qualify generally for a leading part'. Over reform, a refusal by the government to legislate on the question, or a 'sham' measure, would dissatisfy the Commons. Postponement, however, would not produce the same effect and this, Russell suggested as an interpretation of the Manchester School's silence, was Bright's game, 'with a view to a more complete triumph of the democracy'.[44] The letter, which intentionally left Russell's intentions undisclosed, ended with mention of the thought that remained with Russell throughout the recess. Palmerston was 'failing in mind though not in body'. Previous conjecture about the premier's health had assumed that his mental faculties would fall victim to physical infirmity. Russell believed he discerned in Palmerston's recent actions signs of mental decline that might anticipate physical incapacity.

In his reply, Graham assured Russell of his animosity towards Palmerston. A 'sweeping ill-digested India bill and a sham reform bill' were the 'visitations most to be expected and dreaded'.[45] But Graham stressed that the state of parties was 'the real evil'. Amongst the Liberals, who were 'much divided at heart', Graham saw distinct and antagonistic sections of opinion most clearly pronounced over the issue of reform. '[T]he advanced portion would carry democracy further than our institutions could bear: the time serving portion would do, or not do, anything rather than quit their hold in Downing

St.'[46] The support for a redefinition of Liberal policy Graham saw in the 'band of honest men', standing 'between these two extremes', who were sincerely attached to the existing forms of government, but well aware of the necessity of timely reforms as the surest means of averting revolution. This band, Graham lamented, was 'confounded with the mass, [had] no organised existence or accredited leaders, and [was] impotent in consequence'.[47] This conscious prompting antici- pated a self-evident response. Russell might distinguish such an 'honest band' from the mass, provide an organised existence, and be that accredited leadership.

Just as Cobden, by emphasising the importance of redistribution, provided the touchstone for Radical views on reform, disfranchise- ment became the touchstone for that concessionary spirit of Liberal progress that Russell and Graham looked to represent. Both Russell and Graham agreed 'that any measure which fail[ed] to include disfranchisement must be regarded and treated as a sham'.[48] Moreover Graham was satisfied that Russell would 'never again accept office under Palmerston; and [Russell's] brother's generosity . . . establish[ed] his independence and greatly strengthen[ed] his position'.[49] Aberdeen remained cautious. He distrusted Russell's own judgement and, 'clever and adroit as [Russell] certainly [was]', he had 'invariably been struck by [Russell's] extreme ignorance'.[50] Aber- deen's caution revealed a nagging doubt. Russell might, by acting hastily, compromise his own position.

In fact Russell betrayed an astute awareness of the ambiguity of his own situation. The sympathy of those Whigs anxious not to violate gratuitously the claims of party loyalty recommended to Russell a prudent, rather than overt, dissent from Palmerston's policy. What Graham or Aberdeen might see as damaging compromise Russell saw as the conciliation of divergent support. At the request of Vernon Smith Russell gave the cabinet his views on future Indian govern- ment. As to reform, Russell, on hearing that the government would 'do a great deal in a *lateral* direction', have no disfranchisement, and propose a £20 franchise in the counties and £5 in towns, declared his intention to avoid opposition on the second and third reading while taking his own line during the Committee stage.[51] Graham, in response to Russell's politic accommodation, could only observe that Russell's relations with the government were different from his own.[52]

The deliberate ambiguity of the position Russell assumed aggra- vated Graham and Aberdeen's fears. A second letter from Russell,

after he found the first 'coming', Graham reported to Aberdeen as 'a
step in the opposite direction'.[53] Russell's avowal of the fear of
'entangling alliances' Graham considered 'very cool and hardly civil'.
Russell agreed with the argument that 'much communication with the
ministry would be more embarrassing than any entangling alliance',
but insisted such communication was 'very rare, and never on the
subject of general policy'.[54] Further, Russell explained that although
he had given his views on India to Vernon Smith, the cabinet had not
outlined their intended measure to him and therefore he was not
committed beforehand, except by his own expressed opinions.[55]
While anxious to avoid 'entangling alliances' Russell continued to
protest to Graham 'that he [was] *not* the humble servant of the
government'.[56]

In truth Russell was adamant about his future prospects. In Whig
circles it became apparent that Russell was acting 'under the influence
of a fresh feeling of antipathy to Palmerston', thinking 'it not worth
his while to wait for the chance of Palmerston being withdrawn from
the field . . .'[57] He had 'fully made up [his] mind not to serve under
anyone again. [He could] do very well without office, but [would] not
accept any subordinate situation.'[58] Understanding of Russell's
motive exists in the light of this resolve. Rather than indecision it is
the pragmatic conciliation of contrary expectations that Russell's
correspondence reveals. Never having known a 'more formidable
prospect for a parliament' with 'three most important questions –
India, finance, reform' – to be discussed, Russell saw Palmerston as 'a
prime minister with little knowledge to inform him, and no principle
to guide him'.[59] He repeated Graham's opinion that it would 'require
many low church appointments to restore to the government the
odour of sanctity after Clanricarde's appointment'.

Graham also sought to prepare both Ellice and Cardwell for
Palmerston's demise. Both might be influential members of an
'honest band' of Liberals reasserting a traditional Liberal policy of concessionary progress. Omitting to mention his own strong 'anti-
Palmerstonian' feelings Graham suggested to Ellice that it would be
'a charity to arrest [Palmerston] in his jumping and tumbling career'.
For such action Palmerston 'would have reason to be grateful in the
end'.[60] In response Ellice was sympathetic to the suggestion that
reform should be the first priority of the next session. In a similar tone
Graham also suggested to Cardwell that loyal dissent would be a less
factious design than the obligation of honest apprehension.[61]
Graham's attempts to repair relations between Russell and potential

support, however, were nullified by an insensitive letter Russell sent
Ellice in late January 1858. In the letter Russell suggested that Ellice
had been disloyal to Foxite principles when he had not agreed to a
Committee of Enquiry into the conduct of the Crimean War. On
being told that he was a 'Palmerstonian' and Russell was a 'Foxite',
and no two things were more different, 'Bear Ellice was roused . . .
and growled fiercely'.[62] Russell's blunder sabotaged the earnest
endeavours of Graham, his self-appointed intermediary.

At the beginning of January 1858, Russell requested a meeting
with Aberdeen.[63] On 13 January Aberdeen reported to Graham
Russell's apparent determination to avoid any embarrassing com-
mitments. Although the government claimed 'to have secured Ld.
John's support, and profess[ed] to have prepared all their measures in
concert with him', Aberdeen was optimistic that Russell might 'slip
his neck out of the collar'.[64] Russell also shared with Aberdeen his
suspicion that 'there was a material failure in Palmerston's mind –
although his bodily health might be good'. The meeting removed all
doubts Aberdeen entertained about Russell's precise intentions and
he noted, with approval, that Russell 'seemed anxious to have Gladstone's opinion'. Graham provided a characteristically vivid metaphor.
Russell had 'reason to believe that there [was] some screw loose in
the cabinet, and he intend[ed] to furnish the lifeboat and to take the
crew under his own special protection'.[65] Graham extended the
metaphor to Russell. 'A false step in present circumstances would be
irretrievable. The storm will run high: to jump into the boat requires
that it shall be brought alongside without it being swamped or stoved
in the attempt: and there are Pirates in the offing, ready to board the
ship, as well as friends, who are desirous to save the sinking crew.'[66]
There also existed, one might add, of no less political moment, the
tradition of the captain going down with his ship.

The days remaining before parliament met followed the pattern of
previous weeks. Russell, 'willing to wound, but yet afraid to strike', in
'great spirits and in very good health', sought the uncompromised
pose that might conciliate support.[67] The situation, Russell warned
Graham, required 'the most mature reflection'. While not 'insensible
to the dangers which Palmerston's levity and presumption' caused,
'on the other hand it [was] desirable not to give any colour to the
charge which [Palmerston] professed so groundlessly, but so successfully . . . of factious combination against him'.[68] In turn Graham
warned Russell that although Russell might appear to have 'Palmerston on the hip', much would depend on 'the spirit of the country' and

the 'line to be taken by Lord Derby'. Russell would 'be rash and ill-advised if he [fought] too roughly at the commencement'.[69]

One other significant attempt to sound out opinion took place. On 17 January 1858 Palmerston had an interview with Aberdeen[70] during which the 'conversation was commonplace enough, but tolerably easy and unconstrained'.[71] Over India, the main topic of discussion, Palmerston appeared to have 'no definite views on the subject' except that he wished to substitute the Crown for the Board of Directors. Although, as Aberdeen acknowledged to Graham, there must, 'in [Palmerston's] opinion be some measures of detail . . . he did not seem to think them very important; nor did he seem to know very well what they were . . .'[72] 'Nothing', Graham thought, 'could be more characteristic. All smooth and all easy on the surface; the rocks ahead either unseen, or utterly disregarded.'[73] Graham confessed that he 'should like to see Palmerston's cards on the table before [he] put into the pool'. He felt as 'if surrounded by sharpers'.

II

On 15 January 1858 the cabinet received reports of an attempted assassination upon the French Emperor Louis Napoleon in Paris. The Italian leader of the attempt, Orsini, it was discovered, had planned the assassination while resident in England, the bombs with which the attempt had been made were manufactured in England, and Orsini himself had reached France with an English passport in an English name. Popular feeling in France immediately became aggressively anti-British. Strong expressions of this Anglophobia appeared in the French press and still more unfriendly comments on the character and policy of the English people were contained in congratulatory addresses presented to the Emperor by certain Colonels in the French army. Additional force was given to the language of the addresses by their insertion in the official columns of the *Moniteur*. On 21 January 1858 Clarendon received a despatch from Count Walewski, the French Foreign Minister, calling on the British government to assist France in suppressing 'those demagogues who violate[d] the right of asylum, by affording [France] a guarantee of security which no State [could] refuse to a neighbouring State, and which [they] were authorised to expect from an ally'.[74] Clarendon sent no formal answer to the despatch.

The cabinet felt itself caught between the critical and contrary demands of diplomatic necessity abroad and political caution at home. Clarendon in particular feared that French outrage would forge an anti-British alliance in Europe led by France and Russia. This fear, complemented by the private confession that French anger was not unjustified, emphasised the necessity for some gesture of reconciliation.[75] On the other hand, any conciliatory gesture would enrage feeling in Britain in the hostile portrayal of a British cabinet amending British laws in response to Gallic dictates. This would expose the government to criticism from a vigilant domestic opposition possibly couched, ironically, in 'Palmerstonian' terms. To do nothing was diplomatically impossible. To do too much, however, would be politically disastrous. Bethell, as Attorney-General, recommended strengthening the Treason Laws.[76] A new extradition treaty was also proposed, but both suggestions were rejected. Palmerston drew up a full blown alien bill.[77] But when he presented it to the cabinet on 22 January the majority of ministers judiciously advised against it.[78] In the end a conspiracy to murder bill was framed that introduced no new laws, but increased existing penalties for proven conspirators.[79] This, the cabinet hoped, would be the diplomatic maximum and the political minimum that need be done. Bethell, 'in his niminy-piminy manner',[80] was left to weakly complain of the speed with which he had had to prepare the measure.[81]

The parliamentary strategy Palmerston envisaged for the conspiracy bill was dependent on Conservative support. The cabinet, Palmerston informed Clarendon, 'ought to communicate privately with Derby and Disraeli and get their previous consent', which he thought they would not refuse.[82] Though Palmerston expected to have the Radicals in the House of Commons 'and perhaps some of [the government's] friends' against him, with Conservative assistance he hoped to carry the measure. This strategy was the exact realisation of Derby's long-held aim to dissolve Palmerston's majority with kindness.

Derby's openness to Palmerston's plan was facilitated by the nebulous character of Conservative intent. Party meetings had been arranged during the recess, but Jolliffe was resigned to the fact that '[t]he attendance [would] not be very large'.[83] Rumours that the government intended 'a very "stiff" reform bill', with long schedules of partial and complete disfranchisement, Derby had dismissed as improbable as well as impracticable.[84] Disraeli contented himself with sounding out reaction to a possible coalition between 'the most moderate of the Whigs, especially the younger ones such as Granville and Argyll' with the Conservatives if Palmerston were displaced, while remaining 'hazy' about the means by which Palmerston was to be defeated.[85] An opposition policy, dependent on government initiative and the differences within government support, offered an amenable vehicle for Palmerston's strategy.

On the evening of 30 January 1858, Clarendon 'had a long and upon the whole satisfactory conversation' with Derby on the subject of the conspiracy bill and the necessity of maintaining the Anglo–French alliance by placating public opinion in France.[86] Derby appeared to Clarendon as anxious about the refugee question as if he himself had been in office, and agreed to the kind of measure that would be desirable.[87] Yet Derby warned that he believed parliament would not invest the government with the powers they might outline in a bill. Despite this scepticism Derby declared a wish to treat the question as a national, rather than party, concern and offered 'to consider with [the cabinet] beforehand any measure which the government determined upon introducing'.[88] Both Clarendon and George Grey urged acceptance of this offer.[89] Palmerston's tactics and Derby's long-term strategy had merged.

The government's arrangement with Derby to safeguard the passage of the conspiracy bill assumes its proper significance when placed in the context of apprehension about India and a wish to postpone the question of reform. As a guarantee of legislative success amid increasing doubts, both within and without the cabinet, about the government's governing capabilities, Derby's 'handsome offer' did much to bolster cabinet confidence. George Grey remained aware, however, that caution would be necessary with the conspiracy bill.[90] Greville predicted that 'if Pam were kicked out [they] should have Graham, Cardwell, John Russell, Sidney Herbert, Clarendon and Granville'.[91]

On 2 February 1858 George Grey sent Russell details of the conspiracy bill, amended in a cabinet meeting earlier that day, in the hope that its passage might be safeguarded further by Russell's prior agreement.[92] Russell, however, returned the prompt answer that he would oppose it 'to the utmost of [his] power'.[93] Reporting the same sentiment to Graham, Russell was informed that the Peelites also felt revulsion 'at the idea of altering the law of England, in obedience to the dictation of France'.[94] Palmerston dismissed Russell's letter as 'childish', confident that Russell would not 'find much support in an opposition founded upon such grounds as he state[d]'.[95] The bill, Palmerston cajoled colleagues, would 'do well'.[96] The patriotic umbrage that Derby had seen as a powerful obstacle to the bill, however, offered increasingly fertile ground for those who resented 'the dull despotism with which [Palmerston] weighed down his contemporaries'.[97] Accompanied by apprehension about India and awareness of the complexity of reform, patriotic righteousness also encouraged hopes for Russell's future success. 'Will Lord John seize the opening that has now been made so unexpectedly for him, to regain his place as a Liberal Constitutional Statesmen and so to recover his hold upon public opinion in the country? If he likes he has an immensely popular game, wholly devoid of faction, to play; and such an opportunity as present, does not fall to the lot of man twice in a single life.'[98]

III

During January 1858 popular interest was engaged in the elaborate preparations for the first Royal wedding in eighteen years. The wedding between the Princess Royal and Prince Frederick William of Prussia, on 25 January, in the Chapel Royal, St James, provided an excuse for uninhibited national celebration. The second relief of Lucknow brought good news from India, but details of the bloody massacre at Cawnpore revived anguished outcries against the barbarous sepoy. The pages of the *Moniteur* further inflamed patriotic sensibilities. Against this backdrop of popular excitement, Palmerston's political position became increasingly perilous. When the parliamentary session opened on February 1858, Greville could 'never remember parliament meeting with greater curiosity and excitement. The situation of the government is generally regarded as so precarious and the revolution in Palmerston's popularity and therefore his power is so extraordinary, that everybody is expecting some great event will occur, and the hopes of all who wish for a change and who expect to profit by it are reviving'.[99] Palmerston's announcement in the Commons, on the evening of 4 February, of the government's intention to amend the law of conspiracy was received with desultory cheers and an ominous absence of enthusiasm.

On 5 February Roebuck introduced a motion for a debate on the attacks upon the English people contained in the pages of the *Moniteur*, attacks which stigmatised England as 'a den of conspirators'.[100] Roebuck, 'exceedingly violent against L[ouis] N[apoleon]', was 'reproved' by Palmerston while 'Horsman reproached Palmerston'.[101] This was an inauspicious illustration of Whig–Liberal dissension. Yet Graham, for one, was relieved that Russell had declined to act in open concert with Roebuck. Sensing that 'the inclination on "the Liberal side" of the House [was] quite in favour of allowing the conspiracy bill to be brought in', Russell refused to 'risk a very bad division in opposing what [was] almost a right of the ministers', and warned Roebuck that 'he [would] not commit himself to divide'.[102]

On 8 February Palmerston introduced the conspiracy bill into the Commons and debate continued for two successive nights. Much discussion echoed the misgivings ministers had expressed in cabinet.[103] In the House, however, Palmerston forcefully advocated the measure as a necessary modification of the existing law while refusing to abstain from altering the law because other nations had given way to impulses of passion or perhaps fear.[104] Palmerston maintained a fundamental distinction between the bill as a piece of law reform and the political circumstances in which it had been brought forward. Inoffensive as a measure of law reform, Palmerston stressed that it had not been introduced because of French diplomatic pressure.

Immediately after Palmerston's speech, A. W. Kinglake, celebrated author of an eight-volume history of the Crimean War in which he showed great animosity to Louis Napoleon, moved an amendment postponing legislation until the production of the correspondence between the two governments subsequent to Walewski's despatch.[105] Kinglake saw the bill as a concession to the pressure put upon Palmerston by Walewski's despatch. Horsman seconded the amendment.[106] The government backbenchers Hadfield, Fox and Gilpin denounced the bill, arguing that it was unnecessary and would prove a dead letter unless it provided for means of detection. The variety of Whig and Liberal speeches that followed illustrated the dilemma that H. A. Bruce described to his wife: 'Reason says in favour of it – feeling argues against it.' Bruce had 'been talking over the matter with Goderich who [was] just as full of doubt . . .'[107] Lord Elcho, as often before, found he could vote for neither motion.[108]

Roebuck, that same evening, portrayed the French Emperor as the failed assassin of the Duke of Wellington.[109] After his speech Roebuck made it his boast that its consequence would be a war with France in six weeks, 'and the foundation of a government of which Lord John Russell should be the head, and he himself a member'.[110] Russell, on the second night of the debate, denounced the measure as contrary to the whole course of 'modern enlightened legislation'.[111] It would have been better, he continued, to have stated the 'plain truth' that the asylum, which the French called 'a den of assassins', would remain as part of English liberty not to be given up to gratify the French government. Before the debate Russell had assured Graham that he did not intend to divide against the conspiracy bill.[112] Once the general feeling of the House became apparent, however, Russell announced to Graham 'a change of purpose and the determination to divide'.[113] Graham, still at Cowes, was left to lament that it was 'not easy to act on the spot with one who changes so often and so suddenly. It is quite impossible at a distance.'

It is not clear whether Derby informed Disraeli of his conversations with Clarendon, but Disraeli's speech in the Commons on 9 February did little to compromise Derby's arrangement with the government. Conversely, it left sufficient opportunity for criticism and opposition to satisfy Conservative backbench animus. From the Conservative backbenches Gathorne Hardy concluded that Disraeli's speech had been 'admirable', those of the government 'most wretched' and Russell's 'mischievous and not in good style'.[114] As Disraeli made clear, a vote to introduce the bill was not to be seen as a pledge to future support. It was a vote to discuss, rather than approve, the bill.

In a division on 9 February the first reading of the bill was carried by 299 against 99. The partition of votes, on a stage of legislation that was usually passed over as a formality and that many saw as an established ministerial right, revealed the erosion of Palmerstonian support. Russell and Roebuck divided against the bill.[115] Dissentient Whigs such as Lord Elcho, Horsman, Viscount Melgund and George Byng (the eldest son of Lord Stafford), followed Russell into the lobby accompanied by Radicals and advanced Liberals such as Ayrton, Milner Gibson, Kinglake, Bulkeley and Scholefield. Sir Robert Peel (son of the premier and widely regarded as a buffoon) and Kinnaird represented that body of formerly avowed Palmerstonian Liberal sentiment that increasingly sympathised with the manifest liberalism of Russell. On 10 February Russell made a peremptory statement on the parliamentary oaths bill and, the following day, made a similarly authoritative liberal contribution to the education debate. Such declarations reaffirmed that Russell represented those traditional attitudes and cherished Liberal principles that Palmerston had neglected.

The latent hostility of Conservative sentiment artfully concealed by Disraeli's speech on 9 February had found expression in Lyndhurst's question to the government in the Lords on 8 February.[116] Parliament, Lyndhurst insisted, was entitled to look towards the French government for a retraction of the insults published in the *Moniteur*. Moreover, 'if the object of any bill brought in by the government [was] merely to increase the punishment for conspiring to commit murder without facilitating the means of detection . . . it [would] be considered as having been introduced for the mere purpose of soothing that unjust and uncalled for irritation in France which [had] led to the insults' to which he referred. Lyndhurst's attack on the anticipated form of the government measure indicated the growing hostility within Conservative ranks that, as Dallas noted, 'exhibited great feeling and vindicated the popular clamour'.[117]

Debate over India was offering further opportunity for demonstrations of opposition to the government. On 5 February Vernon Smith introduced the East India loan bill enabling the East India Company to raise money to meet the expenses occasioned by the mutiny.[118] Strong objections were raised at every stage of the measure. Cornewall Lewis stressed that the bill involved no new principle or any prospective charge on the Exchequer.[119] Only prolonged clause-by-clause debate, however, ensured the bill's passage.

On 8 February Panmure in the Lords and Palmerston in the Commons moved a resolution for a vote of thanks to the Governor-General, the civil officers of India and military commanders for the energy and ability shown in the suppression of the mutiny.[120] The Conservatives, in both Houses, immediately objected to the inclusion of Lord Canning's name in the motion and an acerbic discussion followed. What subsequent debate illustrated was the absence of any consensus over the question of India that might offer the government a safe alternative to controversy over the conspiracy bill. To emphasise the point Lord Grey, in 'a very fine speech',[121] presented a long and elaborate petition deprecating the government's apparent intention to abolish the East India Company,[122] a petition that was introduced into the Commons by the backbench Conservative Thomas Baring.[123]

The divergent and contrary opinions prompted by the issue of India found their first extensive expression when Palmerston introduced the government's India bill to the Commons on 12 February 1858. Not intended as an act of hostility to the East India Company, the premier urged the abolition of the system of 'double government' on the grounds of convenience and the dangers of conflicting responsibility.[124] Anticipating objections, Palmerston denied that a minister responsible to parliament would render Indian affairs subject to party passions and factious purpose. Thomas Baring immediately moved an amendment against legislation on India, defended the record of the East India Company and warned against converting a Dominion of the Queen into 'the shuttlecock of party'[125] – a line reiterated by the politically unattached Monckton Milnes and the Conservative Vansittart who demanded enquiry before legislation.[126] Sir James Elphinstone and the 'Palmerstonian' backbencher Charles Mangles, attacked the measure.[127] Once again it was left to Cornewall Lewis to provide the forceful ministerial statement that kept the bill alive.[128]

At the opening of the second night of debate, on 15 February, Roebuck declared his support for the government measure.[129] The statement lent hope to ministerial expectation. Yet what remained to cause dissent was the strength of the East India Company interest and the line adopted by Russell. While the former made constant demonstrations of their disapproval, Russell gave no indication of his intent but remained content to watch the response the government's measure might elicit. In private he told Graham of his intention to vote with the government on the second reading, while Graham, who had decided to vote against the bill, noted that if Baring's motion was carried against the government 'Palmerston must fall and Derby take his place'.[130]

Conservative aversion to the government's India bill emphasised the cabinet's vulnerability to criticism from its own rank and file.[131] Exploiting that weakness, Russell's speech, as the debate drew to a close, was a careful statement of qualified approval.[132] What was said belied that which was left unsaid. Russell emphasised the urgent necessity to legislate upon the question; he could not consent to leave the matter in doubt for another year. The long-term strategic considerations implicit in this sentiment were consistent with Russell's private purpose. India, as a 'damper' to reform, needed to be removed from the arena of political debate. But although Russell voted for the bill his speech did not contain a specific commitment to the terms of the measure. The opportunity for modification was promised in Committee while the possibility of extinction in the Lords, under the combined animus of Lord Derby and Lord Grey, was strong. The speech also let it be understood that if Russell should become prime minister he would not use reform to postpone dealing with India. The forebodings of Lord Minto threw light on Russell's expectation. 'The government seem[ed] unbroken in a cause which [was] likely and certainly ought to deprive it of the most respectable portion of its support – yet any other [would] be for the worse, and the Whig party [would] be divided.'[133]

The India bill passed its second reading by 318 votes to 173 with a majority of 145.[134] Reaping the benefit of Russell's and Roebuck's ostensible support the government lost a rump of only 37 votes to the East India Company interest, while gaining the temporary allegiance of 27 dissentient Conservative votes. After the division, however, Bethell, well aware of the deceptive character of the vote, suggested to Palmerston that, like a Roman consul at a Triumph, he ought to be accompanied by a slave to remind him that he was 'a minister mortal'.[135]

On 19 February Palmerston moved the second reading of the conspiracy bill and again stressed that the measure was proposed as a law amendment.[136] The premier also defended the cabinet's failure to answer Walewski's despatch by assuring the House that an answer had been given by word of mouth. A written communication of their intention to amend the law would only have led to irritating and controversial discussion and the appearance that the government was submitting to a foreign power. Immediately after Palmerston's statement Milner Gibson, in a speech that Palmerston admitted to be of 'considerable ability',[137] moved 'a clever and cunning amendment', not attacking the bill directly, but deprecating the government's failure to answer Walewski's despatch.[138] The government, Milner Gibson asserted, had in an admission by silence agreed that England sheltered assassins. Milner Gibson then embarked on a prolonged and damaging critique of Palmerston's inconsistency in his dealings with foreign powers, quoting passages from the speeches of Sidney Herbert and Disraeli to show that the despatch might have been answered. Milner Gibson's amendment, Lord Grey recorded, 'was received with cheers from all sides, and Baines who got up to answer him was very little listened to'.[139] From the Conservative benches both Disraeli and Walpole spoke out in favour of Milner Gibson's motion. Gladstone, in 'a good piece of declamation',[140] made a 'vehement and eloquent speech' against the conspiracy bill.[141]

Members of the cabinet subsequently accused Derby of reneging on his undertaking to safeguard the conspiracy bill. In truth, Derby adhered to the letter rather than that which the cabinet saw as the spirit of the understanding. As Derby later assured Clarendon, 'no measures were taken on [his] side of the House to obtain an attendance hostile to the government – no meeting was held – no "whip" was out'.[142] But neither had Derby made any apparent effort to communicate his agreement with the cabinet to Conservative back-benchers. No meetings were held at all. In the absence of direction, Disraeli's non-committal declarations during the first reading of the bill allowed differing opinions to be entertained without the suggestion of intra-party division. Derby referred to the division on the first reading as testimony of his good faith; 'of the 299 who formed the majority, 112 at least were from the Conservative ranks'.[143] Derby did not refer, however, to the conditional character of much of that support. Moreover, Milner Gibson's motion did not attack the principle of the bill but the government's conduct over Walewski's despatch. Thus Disraeli's support for the motion could be portrayed as compatible with, because it was distinct from, support for the government's measure. Derby pointed out to Clarendon that Milner Gibson's motion was 'most skilfully framed. It did not interfere with the passing of the bill. It did hit the weak part of [the government's] case.'

For members of the cabinet such niceties smacked of sophistry. 'It [was] supposed that no orders were given in the morning by Derby to his party, but being under the gallery and seeing the effect of Milner Gibson's speech he gave the word "charge".'[144] Palmerston's bitterness was evident in his report of the debate to the Queen. 'Lord Derby', he asserted, 'had caught at an opportunity of putting the government in a minority. [Lord Derby] saw that there were ninety-nine members who were chiefly of the Liberal party, who had voted against the bill when it was first proposed and who were determined to oppose it in all its stages. He calculated that if his own followers were to join those ninety-nine the government might be run hard, or perhaps be beaten, and he desired all his friends to support Mr. Milner Gibson.'[145]

Palmerston, in closing the debate, 'lost his temper, attacked Milner Gibson more violently than wisely, and rather damaged his cause'.[146] The attack elicited murmurs of dissent and Palmerston 'quite lost himself'.[147] Palmerston's anger was the more vehement because the cabinet had expected little opposition before the discussion began. 'So confident were the government whips that they made no exertions, and Hayter actually allowed some of his people to go away unpaired, telling them that they were quite safe, and their presence was not necessary.'[148] The prevalent opinion was 'that the game had been ill-played by the government and that Palmerston spoke as ill as possible'.[149]

Russell chose not to speak in the debate. Finding 'the state of politics [was] strange' he believed that 'never [had] the honour of England been so tarnished . . . and [they were] to be satisfied and kiss rod!'[150] Before the debate Russell expected 'the followers of the ministers' to carry the bill only 'to retain a sense that they [had] been kicked and [had] not resented it'. The course of the debate, however, revealed the widespread support for Milner Gibson's motion.[151] In the division lobby Russell accompanied Milner Gibson and Roebuck, leading 89 Whig, Liberal and Radical votes.[152] The motion was carried by 234 to 215; a majority against the government of 19.[153] The relatively low number of Conservative votes in the division reflected the lack of leadership given by Derby. Conservative opposition to the bill arose from what Derby chose to describe as 'spontaneous conviction'.[154] The government's defeat was as much due to the defection of Whig, Liberal and Radical support as Conservative animus. Wood 'admitted that the battle had been miserably ill-fought by the government' and sought solace in the belief that 'a more vigorous defence and adjournment would probably have led to a different result'.[155]

The announcement of the result of Milner Gibson's motion was met with a 'burst of cheering'.[156] 'Disraeli's face', Malmesbury observed, 'was worth anything – a mixture of triumph and sarcasm that he could not repress.'[157] 'Graham was in raptures, and as [Bright] took [his] seat after the division, he seized [Bright's] hand with enthusiasm, as if he had met with a great deliverance.'[158] Bright himself celebrated that '[t]he imposter [was] once more overthrown, and the victory [was] apparently complete'.[159] Lord Grey, with characteristic indiscretion, reminded Russell of 1852, 'when Palmerston had tripped up Lord John's heels . . . saying [Russell] had now paid off Palmerston – a joke [Russell] by no means like[d]'.[160]

IV

At a cabinet meeting on the afternoon of 20 February it was decided unanimously that the government should resign.[161] But this decision should not be accepted as dutiful compliance with the verdict of what Palmerston always insisted was a chance defeat. Of all the difficult issues facing the government, the Orsini affair, India, and reform, the first perhaps offered the most favourable question on which to go out. It identified Russell with a Radical faction and associated Palmerston with the moderate section of Whig–Liberals. Moreover, it did not incite unified Conservative opposition. India and reform fractured Palmerstonian support in much more damaging ways. In particular the alternative issues might offer Russell the opportunity to appear moderate.

The act of resignation, in such circumstances, assumed the character of a deliberate attempt to embarrass the 'accidental combination of parties' that had opposed the ministry over Milner Gibson's motion. As Lady Palmerston observed to her husband:

> The House has behaved so abominably that I am glad they should find the difficulties of what they have done, and you go out on a subject to which no blame attaches, merely a sham reason and an excuse used by the crafty to catch the fools. In my belief I think Derby will not be able to form a government that will stand, and if they try a dissolution the cry will be Palmerston and no base coalitions.[162]

Derby subsequently confessed to the Queen his fear that 'the resignation of the Palmerston cabinet might only be for the purpose of going through a crisis in order to come back again with new strength, for there existed different kinds of resignations . . .'[163] If such considerations lay behind the Palmerstonian cabinet's prompt decision to resign they were to be disappointed.

Immediately after the cabinet meeting Palmerston went to Buckingham Palace to tender the resignations of his government. On the subject of his successor Palmerston 'declined giving advice, but explained the state of parties in parliament'.[164] The premier's portrayal of options betrayed his own inclination. 'Derby [was] at the head of [a] large party in both Houses – John Russell with scarcely any. Derby might join Peelites or without them make a government and [the] Liberals might take him up.'[165]

The Queen immediately sent for Lord Derby. Insistent that he went to the palace only 'to *consult*' Derby laid 'fully before the Queen the existing situation, and . . . begged Her Majesty to take some time to consider her course'.[166] Stating surprise at the result of the division on 19 February, Derby ascribed it to 'the work of Lord John Russell and Sir James Graham in the interest of the Radicals'.[167] Looking towards the immediate obstacles to forming a Conservative ministry, Derby observed that 'nothing but the forbearance and support of some of his opponents would make it possible for him to carry on any government'. Moreover, the 'position of Lord Palmerston was a curious one, the House of Commons had been returned chiefly for the purpose of supporting him *personally* and he had obtained a working majority of 100 (unheard of since the reform bill), yet his supporters had no principles in common and they generally suspected him: the question of the reform bill had made him and Lord John run a race for popularity which might lead to disastrous consequences.'[168] As an adjunct Derby added that 'if on full reflection [Her Majesty] made up her mind to command [his] services, [he would] feel it [his] imperative duty to obey'.[169] Derby's tone was deliberate. By ascribing Palmerston's defeat to the activity of Russell and Graham, Derby refuted accusations against himself and protected his claim to public loyalty. By drawing attention to the obstacles to his forming a ministry, Derby safeguarded himself against failure. Also the 'person who was asked first by the Sovereign had always a great disadvantage'.[170] If the Queen subsequently offered Derby office he could accept 'with advantage in our favour. If not we have not declined office.'[171] Derby was determined to accept power on terms other than sufferance.

Derby's reserve with the Queen was an acknowledgement of the possible combinations of party connection that might be sought. Bright observed to his wife that the prospect of 'revenge' was offered to the 'Manchester School'. 'Palmerston has been our great enemy, and we have slung the stone which has brought him down.'[172] Ellice, after loyally supporting Palmerston over the conspiracy bill, in conversation with Bright admitted that he gave up Palmerston and would go with anyone else who could lead the party.[173] Russell demanded consideration. 'Johnny', Bright noted, '[was] all alive, and [thought] himself the coming man.'[174] The radically minded Whig, Lord Goderich, believed 'the only possible combination, except the present government', to be 'an administration composed of Lord John and the principal members of the present cabinet, with some of the Peelites and some "new blood"'.[175] Such a government, Goderich maintained, was 'dependent upon Palmerston's colleagues being ready to desert him'. Doubting this to be possible Goderich expected 'to see the present government restored to office, *faute de mieux*, and weakened by their defeat'. Newcastle, 'in ignorance of everything beyond Lord P.'s resignation', presumed Lord Derby would be sent for and 'form *a* government. The Whigs [would] soon rally round Johnny', but Newcastle could not see where were Russell's 'materials'.[176]

On 21 February the Queen informed Derby that further reflection had only confirmed her earlier resolve.[177] Derby accepted the task of forming a government, '*as regard[ed] the Court*, to more advantage than if [he] had at once, and without giving [the Queen] time to weigh the difficulties . . .'[178] The indulgence of the Court Derby believed to be the more necessary because he wished to look to 'extraneous assistance' in the formation of a government: assistance which might be largely dependent on his having the freedom to offer particular offices.[179] He was 'anxious to frame the new cabinet upon a comprehensive basis, availing [himself] of the services of eminent men of Liberal–Conservative opinions, who [were] not . . . fettered by engagements, which would render their cooperation hopeless'.[180]

On receiving the Queen's commission, Derby wrote to Lord Grey, the Duke of Newcastle and Gladstone. In his letter to Gladstone, Derby explained that he would willingly include Sidney Herbert in his cabinet, but feared that Herbert was 'too intimately connected with John Russell to make it possible for him to accept'.[181] Derby's offer conveyed little enthusiasm. Aware that Gladstone would not enter a Conservative cabinet alone, Derby could also be confident that none of Gladstone's colleagues would come with him. Gladstone, who had been expecting such an offer from Derby, guardedly refused a seat in the cabinet.[182] '[T]he reconstitution of a party', he answered, '[could] only be affected, if at all, by the return of the old influences to their places, and not by the junction of one isolated person.'[183] Gladstone himself noted the circumstances of which Derby was well aware. 'There is a small but active and not unimportant section, who avowedly regard me as the representative of the most dangerous ideas. I should thus, unfortunately, be to you a source of weakness in the heart of your own adherents, while I should bring to you no party or group of friends to make up for their defection or discontent.'[184] This comment was corroborated by Delane's remark to Disraeli that a Derby ministry would 'do much better without Gladstone'. The Conservative Lord Galway enforced the point on Jolliffe. 'What rascals these Peelites are, a thorn in the side of *both* parties. Shall we lose much by Gladstone not joining? He carries so few *votes* with him . . .'[185]

Gladstone sent his answer to Derby after discussion with Aberdeen, Graham and Herbert during which slight modifications to Gladstone's draft were made. The gist of these alterations resulted in a more forthright refusal than Gladstone had originally intended. A passage declaring Gladstone's willingness to have a private interview with Derby was deleted.[186] A promise of qualified support was retained. Gladstone declared that any government formed by Derby would have 'strong claims' upon him, and could expect 'favourable presumptions' in 'the absence of conscientious differences on important questions'.[187]

Gladstone received a letter from Bright which, although it had no effect on a decision Gladstone had already taken, revealed the anxiety certain Radicals felt at the prospect of a coalition Derby government. If Gladstone joined a Derby government, Bright warned, he would 'link [his] fortunes with a constant minority, and with a party in the country which [was] every day lessening in numbers and power'.[188] More pertinently, a Peelite–Conservative cabinet would fail to serve as a reactionary focus for the polarisation of opinion that might revive Radical fortunes. In 1854 Bright had objected to the centrist aspirations of the Aberdeen coalition: '[t]o neutralise parties [was] to neutralise agitation'.[189] Once the Conservatives came into power, Bright maintained, 'parties would be reconstructed – the Whigs and Radicals would once more come together – and theirs [would] be the next turn'. Opposition to a government of a 'moderate' complexion boded ill for Radical hopes. Beyond concern with Gladstone's interests, Bright's advice revealed concern with Radical prospects. Bright's anxiety was momentarily allayed by Gladstone's assurance that he saw no immediate prospect of reunion with the bulk of the Conservative party.[190]

Observers perceived another contingent factor in Gladstone's decision not to enter a Derby cabinet: the question of the leadership in the Commons. Lord Grey later suggested that Gladstone would have joined the government had he been offered the leadership of the Commons.[191] Practically, such an offer was impossible. In February 1857 Graham had noted that it would not be possible for Derby to throw away Disraeli, 'like a sucked orange'. A year later those constraints still existed, enforced by the antipathy towards Gladstone that existed among the Conservative backbenches. The governing circumstance that the Conservative party was more important to Gladstone than Gladstone was to the Conservative party, prevailed. What was left to the Peelites was the odium of obstructive impassivity. '[T]his small clique', Lord Grey concluded 'remain[ed] consistent to the end in making any strong government impossible by refusing to go into or succeed another they [had] destroyed.'[192] 'We shall be charged, as usual', Graham complained, 'with "putting ourselves up and buying ourselves in".'[193]

Problems of personality, rather than substantive policy, determined Lord Grey's and the Duke of Newcastle's refusal of Derby's offer of cabinet posts. Avowedly surprised by Derby's proposal, Newcastle declined on the ostensible grounds that by joining the government he would neither give strength to the ministry nor render any real service to the country.[194] In private he admitted that he 'could not tell Derby the real reason for [his] refusing to join him – [he] could not say one of your colleagues is a rogue and the other a fool – Dizzy and Malmesbury to wit'.[195] Lord Grey 'had no hesitation as to [his] decision in consequence of the wretched leaders Derby [had] for his party in the H. of C. – had there been a different set of these and especially if Disraeli had been out of the way, [his] view of the question would have been altered'.[196] Personal considerations were all the more crucial because Lord Grey felt the time had come when he agreed 'more with Derby and his friends in political questions than with those who call[ed] themselves the Liberal party'. The Liberals, Grey continued, wanted 'to abolish Church rates – to shorten the duration of parliament – ballot etc. etc. all of which [he] was against whereas all the questions on which [he] differed with Derby and Co. [had] been settled in [his] favour and [could] not now be disturbed'.[197] In replying to Derby, Grey referred to 'the present state of affairs and the materials at [Derby's] disposal (especially in the House of Commons) for forming an administration', and declared that it would be neither useful to Derby nor honourable to himself for him singly to join Derby's government.[198] What, in truth, Grey was looking to was 'a new division of parties, with the old-fashioned Whigs . . . or at all events the moderate Liberals on one side, and the radicals on the other'[199] – a thought he found echoed by Charles Wood and Newcastle.

The refusals by Newcastle, Grey and Gladstone, although Derby did not think the latter's 'very conclusive', prompted severe doubts about the possibility of his forming a ministry.[200] Doubts were all the more acute as Derby sensed the importance for the party's credibility of being seen to be able to form a ministry. Failure to accept the Queen's commission, Derby explained to the Duke of Northumberland 'would have been the signal for the utter and final dissolution of the party' and failure to form a ministry would be 'almost, if not quite, as disastrous'.[201]

Lord Stanley hesitated to accept office in his father's government, hoping that it would be formed upon a broad basis. A pure Conservative government, Stanley felt, that might be portrayed as reactionary, would only 'unite every section of the Liberal party in opposition'; without names to refute the charge of intractable Toryism, the Conservatives' bid to govern would prove untenable.[202] Ironically the inclusion of Stanley's name in the cabinet was the one most likely to rebut allegations of Conservative obduracy. Stanley noted one advantage in joining a Conservative cabinet: any liberal measure adopted 'will by the public be ascribed mainly to me, while to measures of an opposite tendency I shall be regarded as having been opposed'. Stanley's hesitation drew from Disraeli, in his correspondence with Derby, a flood of indulgent prose. 'There is really only one sorrow in all this: it draws tears from my eyes, and from your heart, I am sure, drops of blood. What mortifies me most is that I feel [Stanley] is making a great mistake.'[203]

Amongst loyal party members Derby's offers of office had a success that encouraged him to continue. Malmesbury, always amenable, accepted the Foreign Office. Henley, representing 'ultra-Tory' sentiment, accepted the Board of Trade. The Earl of Hardwicke consented to become Lord Privy Seal. Ellenborough, after the Court raised objections to his taking the War Office, accepted the President of the Board of Control, while Disraeli, it was agreed, should resume the Chancellorship of the Exchequer. Pakington, who had no previous experience of naval matters, accepted the Admiralty and the joke circulated the Clubs that Derby chose him *'because he [was] sure to be at sea when he [got] there'*.[204] General Jonathan Peel, after some initial hesitation, took charge of the War Office and, as the brother of the former Conservative leader, availed the government of the political asset his name provided. After Pemberton Leigh had refused a peerage and the Lord Chancellorship on account of his age, Derby appointed Sir Frederick Thesiger with the title of Lord Chelmsford.[205]

A problem arose when Walpole, still embittered by his failure to become Speaker, raised objections to Derby's offer of the Home Office. The failure to adhere Peelite sentiment, Walpole argued, denied the Conservatives 'increased weight and additional authority' sufficient to ensure ministerial stability. Moreover, he felt disinclined to join a government which he maintained was not united on the three main questions of the year: '1. the renewal of the Bank Charter Act. 2. the government of India. 3. reform of parliament'.[206] In the event Derby persuaded Walpole to accept the post of Home Secretary and to waive his immediate misgivings about the government's possible divergence over details of future policy.

Bulwer Lytton, who had accepted the Colonial Office, proved a further difficulty. On 24 February Lytton informed Jolliffe that he would be unable to guarantee his re-election for Hertfordshire.

Derby understood this as a move, on the part of his 'refractory friend', to obtain a peerage.[207] Insistent that no elevation could be conferred, Derby began to consider other names for the post. Disraeli, thinking Lytton 'too impudent' suggested Lord John Manners who would 'do *very well*, better than Labouchere'.[208] '[I]nstead of sending for Lytton or communicating with him personally, [Derby] sent a message to him, saying he could not expose the government to the danger of a contest. Lytton of course withdrew, but he was very much annoyed ... [A] fortnight afterwards he prophesied a speedy dissolution of the administration and denounced Disraeli's financial intentions.'[209] Disraeli noted that he 'never contemplated that Lytton should have been in the cabinet' until Derby had taken 'too gracious notice' of Lytton in February 1855.[210]

Lord John Manners consented to take the Colonial Office, but made it clear to Derby that he would 'infinitely prefer resuming his seat at the Board of Works'.[211] When, on 25 February Malmesbury persuaded Stanley to join the government, Derby offered his son the Colonial Office and Lord John Manners became First Commissioner of Works.[212] Disraeli considered Stanley the single most important accession to the ministry. A similar importance was attached to Stanley's appointment by those outside the party, greatly enhancing the ministry's standing.

The arrangement of offices outside the cabinet revealed the same concerns and similar difficulties that Derby had experienced in constructing his frontbench. In an attempt to appease 'ultra-Tory' sentiment and anxieties Derby offered Newdegate the Presidency of the Board of Health. After consultation with Henley, Newdegate declined the offer on the grounds that in the past he had opposed the Board of Health as unnecessary and, if he accepted, his re-election for North Warwickshire would be difficult.[213] Newdegate also alluded to his personal objections to Disraeli. Disagreeing with Disraeli over many important questions, Newdegate informed Derby that he felt he might best serve him remaining 'an independent supporter of his government'. Newdegate's subsequent doubt about his decision betrayed the latent 'ultra-Tory' sympathies upon which Derby might be able to presume, if the appearance of his actions corresponded with what was portrayed as inevitable.

Disraeli's insistence that 'Hamilton must be greatly provided for' and that it was '*quite impossible* that Henry Lennox [could] be thrown over',[214] secured a Financial Secretaryship to the Treasury for the former while the latter became a Junior Lord of the Treasury. Both posts were associated with Disraeli as Chancellor of the Exchequer. Lennox held the post dealing mainly with Scottish business despite warnings of ill-feeling amongst Scottish Conservatives that an Englishman sitting for an English borough was in charge of Scottish affairs.[215] Sotheron-Estcourt accepted the Presidency of the Poor Law Board while reminding Derby that he 'had not been a partisan of his since he last went out of Office' and stipulating that when Derby 'went out [he] must again be independent'.[216] Derby was content to accept such conditions while gaining avowedly independent support. As a promising young backbencher Gathorne Hardy accepted the office of Under-Secretary for the Home Department under Walpole.[217] Lord Naas as Chief Secretary for Ireland was an appointment calculated to please Irish and more particularly Irish Brigade opinion.

The wish to embrace as comprehensive a basis of support for the government as possible was not only expressed in Derby's appointments, but was also energetically pursued by Disraeli in correspondence with Delane. *The Times* had condemned the conduct of the Orsini affair and, on 23 February 1858, there appeared a panegyric of Palmerston which, on the occasion of his resignation from office at the age of seventy-three, resembled an obituary.[218] On 22 February Disraeli sent 'almost as impudent a letter as was ever written' to Delane reminding the editor of the 'old spirit of camaraderie' and 'generous support' the paper had given in 1852.[219] Delane remained initially sceptical about the merits of the new government, however, and skilfully incorporating information Disraeli had communicated in his letter in a leader on 24 February, described the list of ministers as 'a penitential sheet' and the formation of a Conservative government as 'a suicidal act'.[220] Undeterred, Disraeli sent to Delane on 25 February the final list of the ministry which included Stanley in the cabinet.[221] Disraeli did not think 'at any time the secondary appointments were so strong. Hardy, S. Fitzgerald, Sotheron-Estcourt, Edward Egerton, Carnarvon, Hardinge – all very good. Legal-good. Irish good.' Delane was also promised an exclusive early copy of Disraeli's address to his Buckinghamshire constituents. In *The Times* leader on 26 February the final list of ministers was reviewed cordially and Disraeli himself was singled out for special praise.[222] By 16 March Malmesbury noted that *The Times* was 'most complimentary' towards the government.[223] Palmerston was not the only leading politician who could play the press.

V

Whig and Liberal response to the formation of a Conservative government was shaped by one determining circumstance and one formative attitude of mind: the mutual antagonism between Russell and Palmerston, and the fundamental belief that the Conservatives were not a credible party of government. Newcastle, characteristically estimating Conservative support in the Commons at a low figure, acknowledged that Derby was 'resolved to form *some* government this time in spite of every consideration short of impossibility', but he had little expectation of it lasting.[224] Given this expectation Newcastle saw '[t]hree things . . . on the cards – 1. Palmerston returns with 2 or 3 changes in his cabinet – 2. Lord John Russell with a mixed cabinet from the Liberal party – 3. Some other less prominent member of the same party who might possibly combine some who would not join either of the other two.' The first possibility Newcastle thought the least likely with much depending on how long Derby's government lasted and the interval in opposition that might be afforded for personal bitterness to subside.

Granville observed that Stanley's initial reluctance to join the cabinet was 'good heir apparent tactics'.[225] The cabinet was 'respectable enough', but with, as Granville calculated, under 200 Derby supporters in the Commons, much would depend upon the Liberals who were 'very much divided'.[226] Lord Grey noted the changed regard for the new cabinet once it was known it would include Lord Stanley.[227] Such enhanced standing put greater pressure upon internal Whig and Liberal relations. Cardwell anticipated that 'J. Russell and Palmerston in their rivalry with each other [would] run a race in violence to get the lead'.[228] Similarly Clarendon supposed that Derby's 'only plank of salvation [would] be the divisions of the Liberal party'; a party which was 'split into factions more bent on cutting each other's throats than disposed to unite against the Tories'.[229] The consequences appeared plain. 'If this state of things is turned to account dexterously and Palmerston and J. Russell fire into each other every night as it is expected they will do Derby may have a longer innings than people generally suppose.'

Russell's chagrin at Derby succeeding in forming a government suggested to some that Russell had been 'act[ing] under the impression that he must inevitably be asked to try to make one of his own – and that he was disappointed by Lord Derby undertaking the task in spite of his lack of supporters'.[230] What is more likely is that Russell acted in the hope of future rather than immediate advantage. Russell considered the 'Derby-Dilly [would] be very ill-kissed' and that he would be 'more disposed to act with Gladstone than before' as he saw 'no present prospect of a union of the Liberal party'.[231] In six months' time, however, Russell prophesied there might be 'a union of the Liberal party which [might] be a foundation for the future'. The Palmerston ministry, he felt, had been 'a sham Liberal ministry having no heart even when their head was for reform'.[232] A future union of the Liberal party would be dependent upon a reaffirmation of Liberal principles which only Russell could provide. In the meantime Russell was content to 'keep below the gangway that [he might] not appear to compete for the lead with Palmerston', while watching the new ministry which would have 'but a fretful existence'.

Lord Minto, Russell's father-in-law, preferred similar advice founded upon the same assumptions. The Derby ministry could not last long enough to do much harm, but would be useful if it afforded time for 'a revision of parties to furnish better materials for another administration'.[233]

> The object of everybody now should be to make the most of the probably short reign of the Tory Administration; to reconcile the divided sections of the Liberals. This will I think depend wholly on Lord John. If he stands on his own ground neither courting nor avoiding his colleagues, but bringing forward his own genuine views on great questions, irrespective of party interests or personal feelings, he will very soon be master of the position – and they who are now running him down will beseech him to place himself at their head. Anything like a separate alliance with such as Gladstone, Graham or the Peelites, would be discreditable as founded on personal rather than public considerations. Lord John should be seen *as himself* – neither Grahamite, Peelite or Radical – but the old Whig leader round whom others may cluster if they please.[234]

Increasingly such thoughts became orthodox Whig hopes.

Russell himself, as well as Graham, envisaged any 'cluster' that looked to him for leadership as including Peelites. Such an association might not only lend strength to a Russellite cabinet, but prevent wavering individuals such as Gladstone lending strength to a Derby government. During the negotiations that accompanied the formation of the Conservative government, Russell was alarmed by rumours that the Peelites had given an assurance to Derby that they would not cooperate with Russell and that it was on this understanding that Derby had persevered in his attempt to form a ministry.[235] These rumours, which were consistent with what Derby understood to be the inconclusive tone of Gladstone's reply to the offer of cabinet office, Graham emphatically denied.[236] Russell's anxiety revealed the immediacy of his concern with Peelite intentions.

Graham, who had exerted the greatest influence on Gladstone not to join Derby's cabinet, regarded 'the return of Palmerston to the head of affairs [as] the greatest evil which [he could] contemplate, and [was] the danger most to be guarded against at the present moment'.[237] Gladstone shared Graham's fear. 'A great public good [had] been achieved in the overthrow of Lord Palmerston. It remain[ed] an intolerable question whether he [would] get back again. On this only one thing seem[ed] clearer than the rest – everyone agree[d] it must be this year or never.'[238] Yet Gladstone was adamant that neither he nor anybody else he knew would help Palmerston return to power.

When the Commons met on 5 March 1858, the position on the benches taken by the principal protagonists poignantly symbolised the state of political feeling. The Conservatives, after six years of opposition, were once again 'on the sunny side of the House': a move which 'seemed to have imparted new life to them'.[239] Graham 'planted himself resolutely, and without hesitation, in his old place' below the gangway on the government side of the House, where he was joined by Gladstone and Sidney Herbert.[240] This position demonstrated, Granville noted, 'that they will not join Palmerston and that they are prepared to defend Derby from factious opposition; ready when the proper moment comes to join J. Russell in forming a government'.[241] Palmerston positioned himself directly opposite Disraeli in a course that was 'straight and unwavering'.[242] Around him sat members of his former cabinet with Cardwell sitting on the benches behind amongst the supporters of the late government. The rump of the Irish Brigade positioned themselves alongside Graham, Gladstone and Herbert, below the gangway on the government side of the House.[243] Dramatically Russell arrived in the chamber late and, for a time, seemed undecided where to sit.[244] After some hesitation Russell finally took a seat on the front bench of the opposition, just below the gangway, among the Radicals and 'independent' Liberals.[245]

6 Derby and Conservative Defiance

[Lord Derby] I am free to say has constructed an Administration which, as far as the personal characters and abilities of the Members of the Government are concerned, is equal to any Administration I have seen in this House. But the question is, what have been their principles, and what is to be their policy? (R. Bernal Osborne, 15 March 1858, *Hansard*, 3rd series, CXLIV, 182)

[I]t is essential to the well working of our system of Parliamentary Government that the people should not suppose there is only one man who can guide the state, or only one party who can be entrusted with the public interests. (Sir J. Pakington at Worcester, February 1858, Palfrey Mss. 3762/8)

The formation of a Conservative government in 1858 was a direct assault on Whig and Liberal belief; a fundamental repudiation of that which Whigs and Liberals held to be true. The Liberals had come to regard themselves 'in some degree as the heirs in fee simple of power'.[1] They were loath to credit the Conservatives, shorn of Peelites, with the resources or ability to form an administration. Sir Francis Baring, the Whig backbencher, even urged on Russell that 'the *existence* of the [Conservative] ministry [was] contrary to parliamentary government'.[2]

Derby's statement of ministerial policy in the Lords on 1 March 1858 was an intentional negation of Liberal attitudes. '[T]here can be no greater mistake', Derby informed the Lords, 'than to suppose that a Conservative ministry necessarily means a stationary ministry.'[3] Derby promised a policy of:

constant progress, improving upon the old system, adapting our institutions to the altered purposes which they are intended to serve, and by judicious changes meeting the increased demands of society.

Derby's statement echoed the spirit of Peel's 'Tamworth Manifesto'. It sustained the same purpose; to identify the Conservative party as a centrist party of 'good government'. Dallas noted that Derby had 'relaxed the rigid character of his Conservative party by defining it as ready to introduce safe improvements of every sort'.[4] Lord Grey found Derby's statement 'very reasonable and the course [Derby] [was] going to take [was] nearly if not quite what [he] should have recommended'.[5] Derby observed that the broad distinctions of political parties no longer existed. Such being the case he hoped to obtain for measures of progressive improvement the support of those not usually associated with him.[6] With regard to the Orsini affair Derby promised that without exception the right of asylum would be maintained inviolable, although it remained an intolerable grievance that persons having that protection should by their acts involve or embroil England with her allies. With regard to India he declared the government's intention, in accordance with the expressed opinion of a majority of the Commons, to transfer the supreme authority from the East India Company to the Crown. In conclusion, Derby explained his government's attitude towards reform. It was, he declared, 'highly inconvenient' that 'it should perpetually be kept dangling before the Legislature'. Avoiding any specific pledge the premier hoped, if the pressure of parliamentary business allowed, to introduce a reform bill in the next session: a measure which might 'be accepted as fair and reasonable . . . by all moderate, impartial and well-educated men'.

Goderich viewed the statement with a mixture of disbelief and dismay. 'It was a curious one as the declaration of the policy of a Conservative administration; but its evident meaning was let us go on till next session, and then see if we won't give you nice little reforms.'[7] Palmerston noted, with a sense of grievance rather than triumph, that Derby had 'adopted all [his] measures with more or less modifications'.[8]

The spirit of Derby's speech was echoed in the hustings speeches of ministers seeking re-election. At Belfast, Cairns denied that Conservative policy was 'something opposed to improvement . . . [and] for retrograding', but held 'that governments had a right . . . to progress and go on improving'.[9] At Droitwich Pakington offered 'a better and more legitimate definition of the word reform than that suggested in the merely party sense.'

The signification in which it is taken to mean careful revision and cautious improvement of all our institutions, whether representative or otherwise. In that larger and better sense I think I am justified in saying the present Administration are ardent reformers. (Cheers.)[10]

Sotheron-Estcourt, in North Wiltshire, emphasised his independence of party and the liberal character of some of his views only to express his agreement with Derby's policy.[11] Lord Stanley, without the need to alter his recognised opinions, reiterated the theme.[12] The peroration of Disraeli's speech at Aylesbury was an elaborate and forceful working of the established text.[13]

The House of Commons reassembled to meet the new government on 15 March 1858 and immediately Bernal Osborne challenged the Treasury bench to state their policy and principles.[14] In the event Bernal Osborne 'made a fool of himself'.[15] Disraeli, in response to the challenge, seized the opportunity to extol the 'moderate' aims of the government.

> We wish to support and maintain the institutions of the country, but we also wish to improve them. We believe that the best way to maintain the institutions of the country is to improve them; and therefore we can't permit the Hon. Gentleman to be such a monopolist of all plans for the amelioration of society as he and his friends on all occasions, in a manner so greedy and covetous, aspire to be considered.[16]

The taunt was pointed and well aimed.

'Palmerstonian' credibility was assailed by the speech with which Horsman followed Disraeli. Horsman, 'who had the touchiness of an old maid',[17] had resigned from Palmerston's ministry in April 1857. The bulk of his speech Horsman devoted to the character of Whig–Liberal dissension and, in particular, the responsibility of Palmerston for the schism. The downfall of the late government and the consequent disorganisation of the party were, Horsman urged, the inevitable result of Palmerston 'relying too much on adroitness and dexterity for that permanent strength which could only be acquired by solid fidelity to principles'.[18] Religious freedom, for the first time in a Liberal cabinet, had become an 'open question'. The question of Church rates had been neglected. The principle of administrative reform and the 'pure' dispensation of patronage had given way to 'shabby nepotism'.

Horsman believed that 'the interests of truth and progress would be more surely promoted by real liberality in opposition than by professed liberality in office'.[19] The fortunes of Liberal principle reflected the respective prospects of Palmerston and Russell. Palmerston was anxious for an immediate return to power while Russell's influence over the rank and file was uncertain. 'The old government [were] evidently impatient to resume their places. . . .'[20] Conversely, Russell, looking to reunion in six months' time, favoured a period of opposition during which he might re-establish his authority at the expense of a discredited Palmerstonian leadership.[21] Horsman declared that 'the prospect of fixity of tenure on the part of the government for five or six months did not appear very disheartening; and by the majority on the opposition side of the House, who preferred principles to place, and the character of a party to the location of its chiefs, it would not be viewed with very great dismay.'[22] Palmerston, with characteristic optimism, though galled by Horsman showing 'his piratical colours', remained confident that he would not 'rally any large fleet of Junks around him'.[23]

Russell, speaking after Horsman, further defined the threat to Palmerston.[24] Russell anticipated a Conservative–Liberal confrontation over reform, and referred to Disraeli's description of the 1832 settlement as an attempted 'consolidation of Whig power'. Conservative invective provided a ready handle for Liberal and, in particular, Russell's righteousness. Disraeli's charge, Russell declared, was proof of the spirit in which a Conservative government would frame a reform bill. Russell's speech gave a clear indication of his preferences; a caretaker Conservative government of sufficient longevity to ensure Palmerston's demise, and of a sufficiently reactionary character so as to provide a stimulus for reaffirmed Liberal rectitude over the issue of reform. The feasibility of this strategy was confirmed by Palmerston's brief speech concluding the debate exonerating his ministerial policy.[25] 'His speech was tamely received and furnished a fresh proof of the loss of his popularity and influence.'[26]

The force of Russellite argument that a period of opposition was both necessary and desirable, lay in its claim to be the sensible response for a party threatened by faction. Granville, still professing loyalty to Palmerston and distrustful of Russell, accepted the need for Whigs and Liberals to agree amongst themselves before they attempted to return to office. Ellice made known his disinclination to 'join in any attempt to oust [the government] till he saw his way to the formation of a better government, and [thought] time ought to be afforded for a reunion of the Liberal party'.[27] Bruce resigned himself to opposition with the thought that 'the Liberal party [would] have time to forget its present jealousies, and to be consolidated, so that the next ministry [might] be drawn from its ablest members'.[28] The situation became more complex, however, with the possible promotion of conciliatory figures such as Clarendon or Granville if intra-party wrangles were prolonged beyond immediate expectation. With two ostensible leaders unable to lead, either independently or in conjunction, third or fourth names might recommend themselves.[29]

The Conservative government was in a numerical minority in the Commons. But it looked across at an opposition rife with dissension which, in fact, rendered the Conservatives the single largest political group in the Commons. Whig and Liberal disaffection offered a Conservative ministry professing moderation accessions of strength. Radicals, also, could possibly swell the ranks of those who, despite ostensible doctrinal incompatibility, might display sympathy for the new ministry. Two contradictory, but equally practicable, considerations encouraged this response. First, if the government failed to fulfil its rhetorical promise, it might provide a reactionary focus for a polarisation of attitudes. Bright deemed the Derby government a 'transition ministry, to be followed, I trust, by one more entitled to the confidence of the great Liberal party in the country'.[30] Secondly, and more immediately, while the Conservative tenure of office gratified Radical 'anti-Whig' sentiment, being a minority in the Commons might make the Conservatives more willing to concede reforms in return for support than an avowedly Liberal majority government. This was the realisation of Cobden's wish in December 1856 to see the Conservatives on the Treasury bench so that some 'thorough practical reforms' might be passed.[31]

Malmesbury and Derby, in discussion with the French ambassador de Persigny, arrived at a settlement of the disagreement between Britain and France early in March 1858 which preserved dignity on both sides. Malmesbury sent a conciliatory answer to the Walewski despatch which the French government answered in a similarly conciliatory spirit. The latter arrived immediately before Disraeli went to speak in the Commons on 12 March.[32] By 15 March, Disraeli was noting that the ministerial benches were in high spirit.[33] Broughton recorded the 'general impression' that Derby would '*pull through* the session'.[34] Greville also noticed that 'there [was] a growing opinion that [Derby] ought to have fair play and no vexatious opposition, and Granville [remarked] that he thought [Derby] would get on very well'.[35] Dallas provided a non-partisan comment on events. 'Parliament has got along with the new ministry pretty well. Prodigious efforts to propitiate members by their attentions and blandishments of private intercourse are obviously unremitting. They will have their effect – and probably that will be first seen in the care with which a test question will be avoided by the extreme Liberals.'[36]

I

The moderate stance of progressive Conservatism which the government had defined in their rhetoric and personnel, required translation into legislative detail. The question of Indian government, left in legislative limbo by the resignation of Palmerston, remained a question of immediate concern. The concern was all the more immediate because of the suspicion that 'some of Lord Palmerston's people' were preparing 'to move *his* bill if an *opening* should occur'.[37]

The bill to which Derby's cabinet agreed revealed the lengths to which the Conservative government was prepared to go in demonstrating the absence of reactionary inclination. The character of the bill also bore the marks of its author, Lord Ellenborough. Ellenborough had an air of enlightened opinion and administrative efficiency, marred by a putative weakness of judgement.[38] The bill did, indeed, project a fabian tone. Ellenborough introduced the elective principle into the nomination of the executive and recommended a representation of the commercial interest. The system of 'double government' was to be abolished and a Minister of the Crown, occupying the rank and fulfilling the duties of a Secretary of State, would be President of a Council of India. The composition of this council characterised the ministerial design. Half the council of eighteen would be nominated by the Crown, the other half elected. Originally Ellenborough proposed to give three elected members to large cities in India, but, upon Stanley's advice, the constituencies were changed to urban areas in Britain and their number increased to five.[39] Members would be elected by the cities of London, Manchester, Liverpool, Glasgow and Belfast, the constituencies to return these members being the same as the existing parliamentary constituencies. The remaining four elected members would be chosen by a constituency formed from those resident in India for ten years who had been either in the Civil Service or had been a resident proprietor of £2000 stock – a constituency estimated at about 5000 persons.

When, on 26 March 1858, Disraeli introduced the government's India bill – India bill No. 2 as it came to be known[40] – an incredulous surprise typified reaction. An enlarged council of eighteen with nine of its members elected, and five of those by popular urban constituencies, accorded ill with the expectation of a Conservative scheme.[41] Nor did the bill elicit the cross-bench support the government had hoped. Roebuck attacked the bill as 'a sham' from beginning to end with the electoral principle introduced to conceal the despotic character of the bill.[42] Bright declared the provisions relating to popular election as 'claptrap.'[43] If the message was unwelcome to the government, the tone of Bright's speech was friendly, it being understood as a request to be allowed to vote in favour of a Conservative India bill rather than revive Palmerston's scheme. The measure, Bright privately noted, resembled Ellenborough, 'all action and no go'.[44]

Despite Ellenborough's belief that the bill would be 'a great success', Greville noted that the measure was 'received with general aversion and contempt ... The only people who [were] pleased [were] the Palmerstonians. They think that when this bill has been rejected or withdrawn theirs will pass, and this will, *ex necessitate*, compel Derby to retire and open the way to Palmerston's return to office.'[45] Broughton dismissed the measure as 'a crazy scheme'.[46] 'Nobody hereaway', Forster reported to Goderich, 'Tory, Whig or Radical [stood] up for the bill or the constituency dodge.'[47] The government backbenches did little to disguise their dismay. As a junior minister, unaware of the details of the measure until Disraeli introduced it into the House, Gathorne Hardy was 'startled' by its 'absurdities ... Such a set for executives-pledged! What bribery, what corruption! What a mess altogether! ... Such a measure from the collective wisdom of our cabinet amazes me.'[48]

On the same evening that Disraeli introduced the government's India bill the Commons adjourned for the Easter recess. The interval provided the opportunity for protagonists to prepare. Prevalent opinion anticipated that the government would find it impossible to pass India bill No. 2 and the uncertainty that would result promised potential advantage to a variety of groups. The recess occasioned various attempts to sound out opinion and align support.

The most intense activity was within Whig–Liberal circles with the rival pretensions of Russell and Palmerston determining discussion. During March 1858 the Duke of Bedford had vainly attempted to reconcile the two men, but found 'the estrangement between Palmerston and Lord John great as ever'.[49] It had been made clear to Bedford, by Aberdeen, that most Peelites were 'verging towards a union with Lord John, some more, some less; Graham [was] devoted to him, Sidney Herbert and Cardwell perfectly well disposed. The Duke of Newcastle gradually becoming so, and Gladstone at present the least friendly ...'[50] Aberdeen informed Bedford that he was doing all he could to bring about such a union. After the introduction of the India bill Russell sought out the Peelite response and, in particular, confessed himself 'anxious to know what Gladstone [was] disposed to *do* about the new India bill'.[51] For his own part Russell believed the bill ought 'to be got rid of on the second reading'. Russell 'did not see how Derby could go on'.[52] Aberdeen and Gladstone, however, were hesitant to overthrow the Conservative ministry while the possibility of Palmerston succeeding Derby seemed a likely eventuality. Gladstone, Aberdeen informed Russell, although differing little from Russell's objections to the bill 'at the same time would be unwilling to destroy bill No. 2, in order to revive bill No. 1, and still less to reinstate its author'.[53]

Graham shared Aberdeen's and Gladstone's caution and suspected that Russell misjudged his standing with the Whigs.[54] Newcastle concurred in the Peelite's general wish to wait upon events. He had hoped the government 'would pull through [the] session for [he] could see no change which would be so much for the better as to compensate for the disadvantages of another ministerial fall'.[55] But he feared that the ministry had 'committed suicide' with its India bill. Newcastle was aware that 'Pam [was] both willing and anxious to turn [the government] out immediately. This [was] of course *his* best, if not only chance of a return to office – but he [would] find himself in a very different position. His popularity out-of-doors [was] gone and he [would] not be *tolerated* as he lately was in parliament, when the Liberals [felt] that he [had] forced himself upon them.'[56] In the face of Peelite reticence Russell assured Aberdeen that he was 'by no means so desirous, as [Aberdeen] suppose[d], that the government should go out', although he retained the option, if he found 'a pretty general support', to move the rejection of bill No. 2.[57]

Whig visitors to Pembroke Lodge found 'the small man . . . talkative and friendly' and came away with the impression that he was 'much against the India bill'.[58] While sounding out Peelite opinion Russell sent George Byng, a respectable Whig intermediary, 'to invite [Granville] to say what he thought would be the most eligible course to adopt in the present state of affairs, and with reference to the government bill'.[59] Granville, according to Byng's account of the interview, seemed 'a good deal surprised', but 'rather pleased' at the overture. Granville declined to give any immediate answer, but agreed to send Cornewall Lewis to Pembroke Lodge to talk with Russell. Granville's response, however, also showed that, as Graham had feared, Russell's claim on Whig loyalties was less secure than Russell himself imagined.

On the morning of 29 March, a meeting was held at Cambridge House attended by Palmerston, Lansdowne, Cranworth, Clarendon,

Cornewall Lewis, Labouchere, Vernon Smith and Granville 'to consider what should be done about the govt. India bill'.[60] All were
'unanimous that the scheme [was] detestable, [was] unpopular and
ought not to pass, but there [were] some differences of opinion as to
the most judicious course on the 2nd reading'.[61] Palmerston, Cornewall Lewis, Cranworth and Vernon Smith declared themselves
ready to oppose the second reading; Granville, Lansdowne and
Labouchere appeared rather more 'timid'.[62] In view of their differences it was resolved 'to decide nothing till [they had] ascertained
what was the opinion of some of the leading men of [the] party',[63] i.e.
Russell's exact intentions.

Greville noted that it was 'easy to understand that Palmerston
[could] desire nothing so much as that Lord John should take the lead
in opposing the India bill, and he should support him, because in that
case, [with] the defeat of the bill by a large majority ... and the
government going out, [Palmerston] would infallibly be sent for
again, and in reforming his government, he would no doubt invite
Lord John to join it'.[64] By encouraging Russell to act decisively and,
more importantly, promptly, while at the same time remaining closely
associated with any initiative, Palmerston might allow Russell to do
his work for him. What members of the former government feared
most, however, was that Russell's liaison with the Peelites might, as it
had in 1852, deprive them of ministerial precedence.

After the meeting at Cambridge House George Byng visited Granville and informed him that 'Lord John had at first thought that it
would not do to oppose the India bill, but upon reflection [Russell]
was convinced that it was imperative to do so'.[65] The day's earlier
meeting had, however, revived the former cabinet's collective sense,
and Russell's intention of approaching Whigs individually, without
reference to their loyalty to Palmerston, foundered on a reaffirmed
camaraderie. Granville replied that if Russell moved the rejection
of the second reading of the bill he would be 'warmly supported'
by Lord Palmerston and his late colleagues, as a group.[66] Only
Clarendon, who still felt a strong personal animosity towards
Russell, thought there were 'objections to [Russell] taking the lead
in it'.[67]

Lord Stanley of Alderley, as a member of Palmerston's former
cabinet, believed Russell's proposal to move the rejection of the bill
relieved them of many difficulties and had several advantages.[68] 'It
[took] away the charge of impatient attack upon the government from
the late ministry.' It also might be seen to suggest 'an agreement to

common action between Lord John and Palmerston'; an agreement that might be understood as a reconciliation 'without the inconveniences of Gladstone's cooperation'. But the difficulties, in the event of a 'joint government' being formed, remained. In particular, the question of who was to lead the House of Commons. Stanley of Alderley hoped this might be solved 'by the fact of either of them being sent for by the Queen to form a government and the one who was entrusted with the formation of the government might naturally lead the Commons without reflection on the other'. Such innocent hopes, however, bore little relation to Russell's determination and Whig desire to exclude any Peelites from the spoils of office. Russell believed it to be 'impossible' that he should take office again under Palmerston and declared his conviction that the only ministry entitled to stand was one containing Whigs, Radicals and Peelites.[69]

Faced with the decision of Palmerston's late cabinet to act together, and Peelite fear of reinstating Palmerston through premature opposition, Russell began to reconsider his decision to reject the second reading of the Conservative India bill. Cornewall Lewis, when visiting Pembroke Lodge on 31 March, found Russell 'undecided as to his course'.[70] At a party, that same evening, held 'for the purpose of bringing John Russell and [Palmerston] together', Palmerston found Russell 'civil and generally friendly but wavering'.[71] Russell made it very clear that he was '[f]earful of turning the government out if he succeeded in throwing out their India bill. He was not', Palmerston ruefully observed, 'so squeamish when we were in.'

Russell's change of intention, once it became clear that prominent Whigs would not immediately disavow Palmerston, eased the government's difficulties. Ralph Earle, formerly Disraeli's secret factotum at the Paris embassy and now employed as Disraeli's private secretary, calculated that Palmerston, with possibly 364 supporters, would easily be able to negative the second reading of the bill. 'Lord Palmerston [would] not dare to put ministers in a minority unless he [had] a good pretext for doing so – the support of the section of the Liberal party friendly to the government [would] furnish him with such a pretext.'[72] Amongst that support Earle included 'Roebuck, the Peace party, Ayrton, Horsman, Kinglake'; all former sympathisers of the Derby government alienated by the details of the India bill.

The moral to be drawn from such calculations was obvious. 'It [might] be damaging to the government to withdraw or change their bill, but it would be fatal to the government and *to the party* to run the risk of its rejection by the House.'[73] Ellenborough was obliged to agree with Derby that the five popularly elected members of the council formed the weakest part of the bill, and suggested their being reduced to two, thus enabling the government to retain some 'commercial men in the Council'.[74] Derby approached Bulwer Lytton, a Conservative with established personal connections with the Radical section, to ascertain what Bright and Milner Gibson objected to in the bill and what they would find acceptable.[75] The Radicals, Bulwer Lytton discovered, had 'met on the very day the bill was introduced and went down to the House with the unanimous resolution to support the government bill if possible'.[76] They were unanimous, however, in opposition to the details of the measure the government proposed, but retained their hostility to Palmerston and their reluctance to dislodge Derby's ministry. Bright, approached 'indirectly, yet directly', insisted on 'the uselessness . . . of retaining the election principle' and also decried 'the wretched system of jobbery . . . in existence'. If the government reduced the council to twelve, to be nominated by the Crown, the names to lie on the table of the House thirty days before the appointments became final, Bright believed he would vote for the second reading.[77] Bright's compromise complemented his colleagues' fear that Palmerston might 'slip in again',[78] and the desire to see 'something . . . done to prevent Palmerston's return'.[79] If Palmerston were to form a government it was predicted that he would 'ride roughshod' over the Radical section. Thus the Radicals would be very glad, Bulwer Lytton reported, to see the government's bill put into such a shape as would enable them to assist in carrying it. Revision of the question of patronage and a reduction of the council so as to number thirteen, Bulwer Lytton suggested, might not only find favour with Radicals, but also win the support of Russell. The withdrawal of the town representatives afforded the government the opportunity to make a concession as to patronage which would make 'the safest and most popular distinction between the principle of [the new] bill and that of the last government'.[80]

The government's readiness to amend their bill opened the way to cross-bench negotiation. Milner Gibson communicated Bulwer Lytton's proposals to an increasingly sympathetic Russell stating that the Radicals 'would like to be invited to a course which would avoid any sanction to Lord Derby's bill, preserve them from a Palmerston restoration, and offer a fair chance of a good bill for India'.[81] Milner Gibson himself, although convinced that the government's original plan was 'quite out of the question', objected to the notion that those who could not vote for India bill No. 2 should 'be made use of to give

Palmerston a political triumph over Derby – perhaps even to restore the former to office'.[82] Such concessions as Bulwer Lytton suggested, Milner Gibson assured Bright, would 'extricate [the Radicals] from the Palmerston danger'.[83]

On 2 April 1858 Disraeli informed Derby of a clandestine suggestion he had received from 'the Independent Liberal Party' that, in order to prevent the defeat of the government, 'some person of commanding position' should move a series of resolutions as to the opinion of the House of the principles on which a bill for the government of India should be framed.[84] Disraeli had no doubt that Russell was both the prominent person referred to and the author of the suggestion. Disraeli numbered Liberals willing to follow Russell in such a move, those 'most anxious to prevent the triumph of P.', as 'about ninety to a hundred'. On 5 April Derby made a speech at the Mansion House courting the cooperation of parliament and the country, and deprecating the fact that the government of India 'should be made the sport of political parties or the battlefield of rival disputants'.[85] Derby also adopted Ellenborough's suggestion of announcing, during the speech, the government's readiness to relinquish popularly elected membership of the Council.[86] Clarendon understood Derby's speech as a declaration that the India bill was 'no life and death question for the government and that it [might] safely be cut up or kicked out'.[87]

The same day that Derby made his speech at the Mansion House, Russell wrote to Cornewall Lewis. Russell informed Cornewall Lewis that Bulwer Lytton had communicated with the Radicals, and that the offer of 'large concessions' had been made.[88] Observing that the Radicals were 'very loath' to give any vote which might endanger the government and that the government were prepared to 'take a beating on the Second Reading without resigning or dissolving' Russell confessed himself inclined to 'pause' before acting. He believed the government wished 'to stay in for the session and recess, and [would] live upon dirt if they [could not] get better fare'.[89]

On 6 April 1858 Russell received an 'intimation' from Milner Gibson that if he were 'to propose a committee of the whole House ... the government would not only agree, but would postpone the consideration of their bill'.[90] Russell declared such a course 'admirable'. Aberdeen, whose 'chief interest in the whole matter [was] that whether Russell succeed[ed], or whether [he] failed[ed], the result should not prove injurious to [Russell's] present position', advised that no decision should be made without previous concert with

Graham. The conciliatory nature of the plan, however, found favour not only with Graham, but was also supported by Gladstone, particularly as Milner Gibson's involvement suggested that Bright and his friends would safeguard the passage of resolutions in Committee.[91] Yet Graham could not help commenting on 'the rashness and audacity of the little man, "drawing his resolutions", and having them cut and dry without consulting anyone and then expecting that they [were] to be adopted and supported by common concert as a matter of course'. Graham repeated his belief that the 'smaller the advance and the more gradual the steps the wiser [would] be the proceeding'. But that 'Little Body like[d] to move with mighty strides'. Graham's fear was that Russell was '*over*-active; his strength [was] to sit still; to point out errors on whichever side they [were] committed, and to correct them'. Once it became apparent that both the Conservative and 'Palmerstonian' India bills were unacceptable, the subject was open to compromise by Russell. After this either 'Palmerston or Johnny [would have to] withdraw their stake and go to another table'.[92] The opportunity to rise above party in public reaffirmed Russell's sense of party grievance in private.

> [T]he Whig leaders, after 20 years service ... discarded me because I was for a constitutional enquiry. I can never serve or act with them until I am returned to my proper position. There is *my* point of honour ... If bill No. 2 is thrown out, and no other proposal made, bill No. 1 and its author seem inevitable. Gladstone, Gibson and 100 more in the H. of Commons are not prepared for this result.[93]

The strength of Russell's resolve bore a direct relation to his confidence in success.

When parliament reassembled on 12 April, the first night of Commons debate was devoted to India and what had emerged as the plan of conciliation, with Stanley negotiating directly with Russell, was acted out.[94] Disraeli opened the debate with a statement that the second reading of the India bill would be proposed as soon as possible.[95] Immediately after Disraeli had finished speaking Russell proposed that both India bills be withdrawn and that resolutions as a basis for a government of India bill be discussed in a committee of the whole House.[96] Disraeli found Russell's speech 'in a spirit most calm and conciliatory to the House and to [the] ... government'.[97] Then, 'wishing to defeat the prospects of Lord Palmerston' and hoping 'himself to occupy a great mediatory position', Russell announced his intention 'to propose the *mezzo-termine* of Resolutions!'[98] In reply Disraeli accepted Russell's proposal and intimated that, considering Russell's experience and ability, the undertaking could not be in better hands.[99]

Subsequent debate, however, disrupted the plan to allow Russell to take the Indian issue under his own wing.[100] Wood intervened and expressed himself astonished that a subject of such importance should be left in the hands of a private member and saw the introduction of the resolutions by Russell as an abdication of its duties by the government.[101] Disraeli, in response to Wood's censure and with a copy of the resolutions already privately received from Russell, agreed to move the resolutions from the Treasury bench.[102] Disraeli understood Wood's statement as an attempt 'to deprive Lord John of the mediatory position'. Although Russell was 'greatly mortified' at not introducing the resolutions himself Disraeli immediately accepted the task without giving grounds for any charge of 'arrogance and intrusion' into Russell's personal initiative.[103] Palmerston's urging that debate should be confined to the two bills already proposed was overtaken by events.[104] It was only left to Palmerston to jeer that Disraeli, 'like Anthony came to bury his bill and not to praise it', while it appeared that the Chancellor had been 'assisting at a sort of Irish wake'.[105]

Russell's rescue of the government from their Indian difficulty inflamed opposition antagonism. Privately Palmerston confessed his belief that 'Horsman [was] persuading John Russell that if the present government [could] be kept in for a sufficient time Johnny and Horsman [would] be able to form a party amongst the Radicals that upon any reverse happening to the Tories John Russell would be in a position either to claim to form a government of his own, or if he joined [a Palmerston] government to bring into the cabinet with him a sufficient body of his new adherents.'[106] Russell, in turn, recognised that 'the gentlemen who expected to come back into office [were] of course very angry'.[107] Greville noted that *The Times* 'attacked [Russell] with the utmost bitterness, and there [was] a general clamour against him on the part of the late government and their friends'.[108]

It appeared as though there was nothing 'but confusion, perplexity and irritation in the political world'.[109] Particularly bitter were those who had served as junior ministers in Palmerston's ministry, men such as Robert Lowe, Benjamin Hall and Edmond Pleydell Bouverie, who had no prospects in a Russell government. In turn Russell was determined not to help 'the Lowing herd . . . back to their stalls and provender'.[110] It was clear that 'the breach between [Russell] and the Palmerstonian Whigs [was] much widened, and [had] become more difficult to heal'.[111] Russell conjectured that 'fifty lies, 300 invectives and 900 lashes from The Times' would be 'ordered as a fit punishment' for his apostasy.[112]

II

The ready withdrawal of their India bill demonstrated a Conservative wish to avoid crisis by compliant concession. A similar response was prompted by other issues that challenged the public posture and private unanimity of Derby's cabinet. There were, Disraeli warned Pakington, 'plenty of rocks ahead', and the cabinet should avoid 'sinking ships to increase the difficulties'.[113] The question of Church rates bitterly divided the cabinet. Agreement would be impossible, Disraeli complained, even if 'the Angel Gabriel himself were to draw up a Church Rates Bill'.[114] As a result, the cabinet postponed any legislation on the issue for the present session. A deputation from the Protestant societies, campaigning for the repeal of the Maynooth grant, was received by Derby, on 27 April 1858, with studied aloofness.[115] The composition of an Education Commission alarmed Henley, who threatened resignation. With consummate tact Derby placated both Henley and Pakington, while appointing the Duke of Newcastle as head of a commission that included the economist Nassau Senior, the Radical dissenter Edward Miall, and William Charles Lake, later Dean of Durham and a friend of Gladstone.[116] But it was the government's budget that, concurrent with debate over India, most successfully substantiated official rhetoric.

Disraeli's budget of 1858 confirmed the dispensability of Gladstonian expertise. It was a Gladstonian budget without Gladstone. Sir Stafford Northcote saw the session of 1858 as 'the critical moment for deciding whether the scheme of 1853 should or should not be carried into effect'.[117] Disraeli was faced with a deficit of £3½ million, incurred by war expenditure and interest on loans raised by Cornewall Lewis. Disraeli's choice lay between the liquidation of the debt or complete abandonment of the 1853 scheme. Disraeli decided to write off the debt, thus enabling the government to propose a return to the rate of income tax Gladstone had scheduled in 1853. 'The increased liabilities arising from the war', Disraeli declared, did 'not furnish reasons strong enough to make [parliament] regard the scheme of

1853 as visionary and fantastic.'[118] Gladstonian in substance, but more importantly Conservative in authorship, the budget, announced in the Commons by Disraeli on 19 April 1858, affirmed the government's administrative credibility.[119] The budget was 'received with favour and excited no opposition in any quarter'.[120] Gladstone was left to express a general approval adding a warning against excessive expenditure.[121] Indeed, Gladstone was lamely left with neither the political opportunity to exercise his executive talent, nor the political opportunity to advertise executive ambition in fervent opposition.

The timing of the budget did not pass unnoticed by Cornewall Lewis. That Disraeli was to announce his budget before debate on the India resolutions suggested that he thought he had got something 'captivating'.[122] If the budget was 'a tolerably safe and quiet one, the House [would] agree to it' and the stage would be set to reconcile differences over India. Thereafter, the government would be able with confidence to prorogue. '[A] simple restoration of the late government', Cornewall Lewis lamented, '[was] quite out of the question.' Disraeli himself felt the budget had been 'a complete success' and had 'met with universal approbation'.[123] Derby congratulated the Chancellor on 'the signal success of the budget'.[124] The triumph of the budget, moreover, confirmed a growing impression that 'the ministry [were] gradually getting firmer in their seats . . . They [had] dodged an open breach with France. They [had] steered their India bill, piloted by Lord John Russell, into smooth "no party" waters.' And, finally, Disraeli had 'introduced his budget, which [was] praised and accepted by the practical financiers of the City'.[125]

The strengthening of the position of the ministry emphasised Whig and Liberal difficulties. Ellice believed Russell had 'gained nothing by his mutiny but more anger from his friends. . . . Pam [was] in better humour, but not disposed to abdicate his Throne – Johnny determined to usurp it.'[126] Therein lay ministerial hope. 'While the game lasts', Ellice noted, 'Derby is quite safe.' Between 12 and 28 April 1858 the Indian resolutions, '[t]heir substance, and their very phraseology, were carefully considered, and decided on, by the cabinet'.[127] Using Russell's proposed plan as a framework, a form of words was composed which Derby 'laboured' to 'impress upon the minds of the party' was that 'without which [they could not] go on', and stood as proof of the 'perseverance of [their] intentions once announced'. This was a necessary rebuff to the Palmerstonian charge that the government could not govern.

In introducing the resolutions on 16 April, Disraeli reviewed the history of the debate on the Indian issue and compared the main features of the two India bills presented to parliament.[128] The advocates of the bill of the late government, Disraeli noted, had boasted of its simplicity, it consisting of the appointment of a minister with individual responsibility sitting in the Commons with the assistance of a limited number of nominees. But the more he reflected upon the simple plan, Disraeli declared, the more he was convinced of its danger and impracticability. India bill No. 2 recognised a necessary virtue in complexity and the advantage of introducing the elective principle into the appointment of the council. The point was stressed: if there was to be a real council for India, recourse must be had to the elective principle, which was an all-important portion of any scheme. Other questions, such as finance and patronage, were, comparatively, matters of detail.

The perspective that Disraeli's speech gave to the problem of Indian government emphasised the 'liberal' character of the Conservative bill and the readiness of the government to compromise. Palmerston characterised the speech as 'a funeral panegyric' upon a bill Disraeli had murdered himself, and contended that the argument in favour of the elective principle was founded upon a fallacious analogy between Indian government and the British constitution.[129] Gladstone saw in neither plan any elements of a good scheme and urged a greater awareness of the problems of attempting to govern by one people another people, separated not only by distance, but by blood and institutions.[130] The only private sympathiser for Gladstone's views was Bright who was 'keen and decided . . . that no India bill should pass which [did] not limit the dangerous and much misused discretion of the Ministers of the Crown in the use of the Army of India'.[131] Disagreeing with Russell and Disraeli over the resolutions, Gladstone also made clear his dislike for Palmerston's plan and, as so often, gave negative clarity to his idiosyncrasy. In response Russell urged that the Commons earnestly continue with the resolutions and arrive at a necessary settlement of the Indian question.[132]

The vague and non-committal nature of Russell's speech, concentrating on procedure rather than the principles of any particular bill, was deliberate. It was Russell's intention to play the role of 'umpire' rather than become 'a party in the suit'; it being prudent not 'unnecessarily to show [his] hand and to lay [his] cards on the table'.[133] Graham reminded Russell of the realities of statesmanship: '[T]hough party objects are universally disclaimed, yet in reality it is a struggle for power.'[134]

7 India: 'A Startler'

> The Liberal Party in the Commons resembles a pack of hounds in full cry when the huntsman and the whipper-in have been thrown at a fence or immersed in jumping a wide brook . . . In fact there is at present no Liberal leader, and not a single man to denounce the headless condition of the party, or demand the selection of a third man if the two will not come to an agreement. (Parkes to Brougham, 3 May 1858, Brougham Mss. 20080)

> We are now endeavouring to reconstruct the party on a wider basis, and trying to lay the foundation of a permanent system. (Disraeli to Derby, 13 August 1858, Derby Mss. 145/5, cited in W. F. Monypenny and G. E. Buckle, *The Life of Benjamin Disraeli, Earl of Beaconsfield* (London, 1910–20) IV, p. 183)

During March and April 1858, government concession created the deliberate impression that 'a positive conflict upon a cabinet question' would be 'hard to bring about'.[1] There existed limits to concession, however, defined by executive, rather than legislative, decision. On 12 April 1858 Lord Ellenborough received from Lord Canning, the Governor-General of India, the draft of a proclamation to the people of Oudh that, with certain exceptions, 'the proprietary right in the soil of the province [was] confiscated to the British government which [would] dispose of that right in such manner as it [might] deem fitting'.[2] Canning, as yet unaware of the change of ministry, sent the despatch accompanying the draft to Vernon Smith in the belief that he was still the responsible minister. Vernon Smith failed to forward this private letter to Ellenborough. This neglect on the part of Vernon Smith was consistent with his general reticence to exchange details of policy with his successor.[3] Thus Ellenborough received the apparently punitive draft with an incomplete understanding of its purpose and character. Ellenborough's reaction to the proclamation, placing a literal interpretation upon its wording, was as severe as his understanding of its intent. Declaring that threatening the disinheritance of a people would create almost insurmountable obstacles to the re-establishing of peace in India, Ellenborough forcefully rebuked Canning. The reprimand was sharp, severe and, in retrospect, appears heavy-handed.

Ellenborough had shown Derby his reply to Canning's proclamation on 17 April, the day after the cabinet had discussed the matter.[4] Derby, as Ellenborough remembered, approved it 'saying it was very proper and not too strong for the occasion'. Disraeli, Pakington and Manners also read the reply, either that evening or the following morning. Pressure of business, however, prevented Ellenborough submitting his despatch to the whole cabinet on 24 April; nor was the despatch submitted for the approval of the Queen. Misjudgement compounded procedural oversight when Ellenborough sent, in anticipation of approval, copies of his despatch to Granville in the Lords and Bright in the Commons. Publication at once became inevitable and the subject was exposed to hostile political scrutiny.

Ellenborough's intemperate, if partially uninformed, despatch provided the opposition with an opportunity for 'positive conflict'. Canning was cast as the abused martyr to Conservative folly, while Ellenborough became the personification of ministerial incapacity.[5] Moral rectitude was further inflamed when, in early May, different versions of Ellenborough's despatch were laid before the two Houses. In the Commons it was presented *in extenso* and, through what Ellenborough subsequently described as an administrative accident, in the Lords the despatch was presented with omissions. The City went into 'a state of frenzy', as did the Directors of the East India Company. 'All the government people', Granville noted with satisfaction, '[said] it [was] a very bad case.'[6]

During the first week of May 1858, there appeared to be nothing 'but negotiations and communication' between Whigs and Liberals 'to effect a coalition between the rival leaders and their friends for the purpose of their at least uniting in one great hostile vote'.[7] It was noted that Palmerston, early in May, expressed a wish to have a conversation with Russell, but then regretfully observed that he apparently changed his mind and shrank from it when the opportunity presented itself. It was noted that one day when it was raining Palmerston took Russell to Pembroke Lodge in his coach, but regretted that Palmerston did not get out and enter the Lodge 'when he might have had the conversation he had expressed a wish for, and so it ended'.[8] The Duke of Bedford arranged a meeting between Russell and Clarendon to resolve the personal animosity that existed between them. When called on by Clarendon, however, Russell 'did not allude to Vienna, which [was] the real gist of his grievance and the source of his hostile feeling, so that with that reticence it [was] not strange that they should have parted much as they met'.[9] Charles Wood communicated with Russell on behalf of the 'Palmerston cabinet', but little was achieved.

At a meeting in Cambridge House on 9 May, Palmerston and Granville decided to move 'a motion of regret and alarm at the despatch being published, tending to weaken [Canning's] authority, and increasing the difficulty of governing India'.[10] At Granville's suggestion the motions were given to two independent members, Cardwell in the Commons and Shaftesbury in the Lords. Granville estimated that the motion would be beaten by seven or eight in the Lords, but was confident of 'a majority of 100 in the Commons'. On 10 May, Cardwell and Shaftesbury both gave notice of their motions. The limited terms of the motion revealed the desired focus of discussion. No reference was made to Canning's despatch; no comment passed on the Governor-General's policy of confiscation; no allusion made to Ellenborough's ignorance of Canning's correspondence with Vernon Smith. What might be neatly avoided in the composed form of a motion, however, was little protection against the unpredictable course of a parliamentary debate.

Of paramount importance was the timing of this opportunity for 'positive conflict'. The ten weeks that the Conservatives had been in power was sufficiently short a time for Palmerston to believe he was acting before his popularity was dissipated by opposition division, but also sufficiently long a time for Russell to believe that it was the moment to assert his authority over a leaderless opposition. These contrary and incompatible intentions underlay an ostensibly concerted manoeuvre. While not present at the Cambridge House meeting, Russell made it known he would be willing to vote for Cardwell's motion. But Lennox's report of Russell's decision to Disraeli showed political insight imparted by innuendo: 'no arrangement has been entered into by Palmerston and John Russell except their *simple vote* for Cardwell'.[11] Russell was subsequently 'irritated' by Bright's suggestion in the Commons of a 'renewed political alliance' between Palmerston and himself. He was only dissuaded from publicly denying such an association by it being pointed out to him 'that it would be very far from being in his interest to do so'.[12]

Shaftesbury's notice of his motion in the Lords, on 10 May, forced Ellenborough to defend his actions.[13] Copies of his despatch to Canning had been sent to Granville and Bright out of courtesy as some friends of Granville were already aware of Canning's intentions. Lord Grey, however, enquired whether the government had been in possession of any other information beyond that received directly from Canning.[14] Ellenborough was then subsequently forced to admit that the government did not know with certainty that the proclamation had been published in India at all.[15] They had received no direct communications from the Governor-General for nearly a month. Such admissions prepared the way for an impassioned debate on Vernon Smith's conduct.

Both Derby and Malmesbury pressed the point that Vernon Smith failed in his 'bounden duty' to furnish Ellenborough with the information contained in Canning's letter.[16] Granville's reply that Vernon Smith received the letter too late to change Ellenborough's condemnation of Canning's proclamation was swiftly refuted by Ellenborough detailing the dates of subsequent correspondence.[17] Ellenborough then accepted total responsibility for the tone of his despatch and the fact that it was published. He then made the dramatic announcement that his resignation from the government had been accepted by the Queen. This act of self-sacrifice on the part of Ellenborough, Derby hoped, would prevent Cardwell's motion being debated in the Commons.[18] Even if Cardwell continued with his proposed censure, however, Derby anticipated that, in the light of Ellenborough's resignation, a division would 'almost certainly result in a majority for the government'.[19] That Shaftesbury's motion in the Lords was not withdrawn was mainly due to Grey's private insistence on continuing with the debate.[20] The motion was subsequently defeated, on 14 May, by a majority of nine. But the greater challenge to the government existed in the Commons.

The opposition expected a majority of 100 on Cardwell's motion.[21] Dallas saw Cardwell's motion as 'a battery suddenly and indiscreetly provoked to open its deadly fire on an administration already tottering'.[22] Though some ministers affected 'to regard the self-immolation of Ellenborough as an adequate atonement', the government's 'great hope ... seemed to be the extreme difficulty, if not impossibility, of combining a sufficient number of Radical votes with the Whigs'.[23] Such difficulties would be exacerbated by the prospect of an election. The possibility of a dissolution had existed ever since Derby formed his ministry with a decided minority in the Commons. '[A] march to the last Tory pitched battle', only twelve months after the previous election, was calculated to excite pecuniary and local anxieties.[24] Many Whig and Liberal backbenchers were uncertain of re-election and anxious to avoid the expense and uncertainty of the hustings.

On 11 May 1858 Derby visited the Queen and requested a promise that a dissolution would be granted if the government were censured.

The Queen, however, refused to commit herself, informed Derby that she would confer with others, and commented on the inconvenience of frequent dissolutions. Derby, 'very much disappointed and mortified', waited upon the inclination of the Queen's advisers.[25] The Queen turned to Aberdeen. Aberdeen's advice revealed much about Peelite intention. Aberdeen informed the Queen that if Derby resigned then Palmerston would have to be recalled, but could think of no precedent that would justify refusing a dissolution if it would automatically dismiss the prime minister.[26] Granville detected the influence of Gladstone's 'more powerful and youthful mind' in the elderly Peelite's portrayal of options.[27] Certainly Aberdeen's depiction of events omitted that which he held dearest: a Russell–Peelite collaboration appeasing Radical sentiment. The first requirement, however, to deprive Palmerston of his rapidly diminishing influence, ensured that Aberdeen protected Derby's immediate interests.

With shared intention Graham and Aberdeen came to advocate differing courses of action, while Aberdeen and Gladstone, with differing intent, advocated the same course. Graham, in agreement with Russell himself, believed that Russell was in a sufficiently strong position to displace Palmerston if the government were defeated over Cardwell's motion. Thus initially Graham supported Cardwell's initiative. Aberdeen, in contrast, believed that Russell would have to wait and not act prematurely if he was to dislodge Palmerston, and did 'his best to dissuade Cardwell and Shaftesbury from going on with their motions'.[28] Gladstone opposed the motion because it might herald Palmerston's return to office, while remaining the Peelite least sympathetic to Russell. After the announcement of Ellenborough's resignation, Herbert, who had at first supported Cardwell, became 'very much against going on'.[29] Favouring Palmerston's return to power, Herbert's reticence was the result of a belief that, the primary target of Cardwell's motion having gone, the motion would be defeated and such a defeat might be fatal to Palmerston's position.

Ellenborough's resignation, as Derby had hoped, led many backbench Liberals to question the wisdom of continuing with Cardwell's motion. 'But the die was cast, the Palmerstonians were quite confident and eager for the fray, and would not hear of stopping in their career.'[30] At a meeting at Cambridge House on the morning of 13 May, Palmerston, 'determined to go on with Cardwell's motion notwithstanding Ellenborough's resignation', found that Russell was in agreement with this decision. Hayter and Brand anticipated a majority of from 40 to 50 against the government.[31] A 'numerous and noisy' meeting of the Liberal party at Cambridge House the following day was 'well attended'. Palmerston assured himself that it 'went off well'.[32] Though Headlam, Roebuck, Divett and Rich 'made some complaints' Palmerston believed that 'the general temper of the meeting [had been] good'. What the meeting did prove to Palmerston was that a simple restoration of the former 'Palmerstonian' cabinet was no longer possible. If he were returned to power his ministry would have to be on 'a broader basis, and more liberal measures should be adopted'.[33]

Cardwell introduced his motion to the Commons on 14 May with the spirited contention that, despite Ellenborough's 'chivalrous' declaration, the criticism of Canning's proclamation was 'the collective act of the Ministry'.[34] In reply the Solicitor General, Sir Hugh Cairns, made 'the most remarkable speech' which struck listeners as 'very clever and effective'.[35] The form of the resolution, Cairns contended, contained a complex proposition.[36] First, it proposed to express no opinion upon the policy of Lord Canning; secondly it was a censure upon the government for having expressed an opinion upon Canning's proclamation; and, thirdly, it censured the government for having sanctioned the despatch conveying that censure. But, Cairns continued, if the House was to avoid expressing an opinion upon the policy of Canning, it was impossible to approach the other portions of the resolution. This speech, Disraeli celebrated in great excitement, 'completely destroyed the whole case. Cardwell a failure.'[37] Palmerston conceded that Cairns had 'ably answered' Cardwell's statement.[38] Concluding the first night of debate, Russell, speaking 'very well and vigorously [and] quite in his old style',[39] observed that the House was reduced to two alternatives; either to censure the government, or to declare Canning to be deserving of the most severe reprobation.[40] It was the duty of the government, however, not to hamper Canning in performing his difficult duties. Yet he had been the subject of a condemnation resembling a lampoon rather than a grave rebuke, full of sarcasms and reproaches. The speech helped repair the opposition case although the impression remained that 'the speaking [had been] all along better on the government side'.[41]

Following the first night of discussion Disraeli made up his mind to continue the debate till 21 May.[42] '[E]very day [the ministry's] prospects as to the division appeared to be mending and public opinion more and more inclining against the opposition and the Proclamation, though still blaming Ellenborough's letter.'[43] Disraeli did not see how the opposition could 'press for the close of the debate, or shrink from maintaining the indictment which they [had] preferred against [the government]'.[44] He was confident, moreover, that the ministry would 'not be under the necessity of spinning out, having sufficient of first-rate men on the subject from the government, Gladstonians, and Gibsonites'. The only thing that made the result of a division doubtful, Disraeli believed, was 'the general incredulity as to a dissolution'.

On 16 May, Derby once again had an interview with the Queen and declared that the government 'could be saved if it were known that the Queen had not refused a dissolution, which was stoutly maintained by Lord Palmerston's friends'.[45] Reaping the benefit of Aberdeen's advice, Derby learnt that a dissolution would not be refused to him. The Queen 'trusted that her honour would be safe in his hands as to the use he made of that knowledge'. Derby 'seemed greatly relieved'. In the event of a dissolution Derby felt confident of 'a large gain', the country being 'tired of the "Whig family clique"; the Radicals like Mr. Milner-Gibson, Bright, etc., would willingly support a Conservative government'.[46]

One section of opinion the government hoped to influence, armed with the Royal sanction for a dissolution, were the Peelites who, 'with the exception of Gladstone, [were] all wrong'.[47] If, Disraeli suggested, Derby were to open 'pomparlers' with Aberdeen, 'materials now hesitating and hostile might be fused and appropriated'; what was wanted was 'the word of command from their Director-General'. In the attempt to appropriate Peelite support Disraeli opened a correspondence with Graham who, Disraeli believed, meant to abstain from the vote on Cardwell's motion. On 17 May, Disraeli was able to assure Graham that 'Lord Derby [had] not the slightest doubt of his power of dissolving'.[48] This assurance had the anticipated effect of fusing Peelite opinion. Graham came to share not only Aberdeen's intention, but concurred in the means Aberdeen believed might secure that shared aim; support for the Derby government as a safeguard against the restoration of Palmerston. Only Herbert continued in his support of Cardwell's motion, prepared to accept the return of a modified 'Palmerstonian' ministry.[49]

In retrospect much importance was given to the threat Derby was able to make of a dissolution, which not only consolidated Peelite opinion, but further fragmented Whig and Liberal sentiment. The threat of a dissolution, however, was only one factor that undermined the fragile unanimity of opposition strategy. The passage of time, as

Disraeli had hoped, also served to exacerbate differences.[50] These differences became obvious during the second and third nights of debate on 17 and 20 May. Roebuck delivered 'a violent speech against Cardwell and the Whig party'.[51] Bright dismissed the motion as a disingenuous attempt to lead the House into an unfortunate dilemma.[52] In a peroration that proved 'a startler', Bright portrayed the attack upon the ministry as a party manoeuvre and with bitterness and sarcasm laid bare the 'arcana' of the 'Palmerstonian opposition.[53] Sir Arthur Elton, from the Liberal backbenches, declared that Ellenborough's despatch, though deficient in courtesy, was 'substantially right'.[54] There was 'some solvent at work that [was] rapidly disintegrating the opposition'.[55] Amid increasing opposition disunity, Graham's speech was recognised to have been of 'very great effect'.[56] Graham's '[h]atred of Palmerston', Fortescue shrewdly noted, 'probably decided his course'.[57] Graham found the proclamation 'impolitic' and the despatch condemning it, though employing harsh and unjustifiable terms, indiscreet, but nothing more.

Graham's argument was substantiated by the arrival on 20 May of further mail from India showing that Sir James Outram, the military commander in India, disapproved of Canning's proclamation. Derby immediately allowed these new despatches to be laid on the table of the Commons insistent that 'nothing should be done in the way of production or of omission which [could] justly be complained of by opponents'.[58] Their submission, Derby believed, 'exercised a powerful influence' on the opinion of the House.[59]

On the morning of 21 May, Disraeli received a letter from Cardwell requesting agreement to withdraw his motion, and subsequently Palmerston desired to confer with Disraeli putting forward the same question.[60] To these enquiries Disraeli replied, 'in a very lofty tone, that he would hear of nothing which could possibly be construed into any admission on [the government's] part of their meriting any part of the censure which the opposition had been labouring to cast upon them'. Disraeli was determined that the abandonment of the motion by the opposition should be public and self-avowed. At a meeting held on the morning of 21 May, attended by Palmerston, Wood, George Grey, Cornewall Lewis and Russell, it was decided to continue with the motion unless the 'temper of the House [was] against doing so'.[61] What Pamerstonians came to fear, however, was the 'particularly mortifying' spectacle of Palmerston 'involved in inevitable defeat, and without the power of rallying a second time'.[62]

Events on the evening of 21 May realised exactly Palmerstonian fears and Disraeli's wish to make a spectacle of opposition embar-rassment. At the beginning of the debate the Radical James Clay appealed to Cardwell not to press his motion to a division.[63] To those 'old birds' within Westminster it appeared that Clay was 'only open-ing a farce, the programme of which was prearranged'.[64] The 'Irish Independent' George Bowyer seconded Clay's appeal.[65] Cardwell, however, declined to accede to Clay's demand.[66] Acting the part of 'a coy lady' who must at first refuse, Cardwell, it was predicted, would withdraw once Palmerston asked him personally to do so. Thereafter there followed a long succession of appeals from the opposition backbenches for Cardwell to withdraw his motion. Duncombe warned Cardwell that if he insisted in continuing he would 'leave [Cardwell] to the tender mercies of the honourable gentlemen oppo-site'.[67] Danby Seymour and other members expressed doubts whether the proclamation had ever been issued at all.[68] Locke King, Wyld, Joseph Locke, Lord Harry Vane, P. O'Brien and Sir William Jackson, amongst others, then proceeded to insist that the division proposed would be on a false issue and that the wisest course was to withdraw the motion. Disraeli could only liken the scene on the opposition benches 'to one of those earthquakes in Columbia or Peru of which we sometimes read. There was a rumbling murmur, a groan, a shriek, distant thunder; and nobody knew whether it came from the top or the bottom of the House. And then the whole of the opposition benches became one great dissolving view of anarchy!'[69] Derby believed that 'no exaggeration could be applied to that extraordinary scene.'

Waiting for his cue, Palmerston, after hearing the appeals from the backbenches, rose to ask Cardwell to withdraw his motion.[70] To this request Cardwell agreed, expressing his wish to act in conformity with the general feeling of the House.[71] Disraeli then seized the opportun-ity to celebrate the ministerial victory. The government, Disraeli declared, had looked without apprehension to the result of a divi-sion.[72] The government moreover, had abstained from the debate as much as possible; the motion had been opposed by members uncon-nected with the Treasury bench and their eloquence had led to the strange result at which they had arrived.

The debate over Cardwell's motion and its withdrawal was a watershed for the Derby ministry; the 'affair [had] been the battle of Marengo of political warfare'.[73] Gathorne Hardy rejoiced that the opposition 'bubble [had been] burst'.[74] Disraeli excitedly observed that when 'the very best of the fight was to rage, the enemy suddenly

fled in a manner the most ignominious! Never was such a rout!' Derby
found the debate analogous to 'the explosion of a well constructed
mine, under the feet, not of the assailed, but of the assailants'.[75] Nor
was such importance granted to the debate solely in Conservative
circles. Broughton, attending a party at Cambridge House on 22 May,
found it 'pretty well attended but very different from the gay happy
circle of a week before'.[76] Knatchbull-Hugessen, a Liberal supporter
of Russell, acknowledged the withdrawal of Cardwell's motion to be
'a great triumph to [the] Ministers [which] strengthened their position
for the time'.[77] Palmerston himself recognised the debate to be 'a
great triumph for [the] government'.[78] Grey found 'a general feeling
that the party had received a most mortifying defeat, and that the
business had been deplorably managed'.[79] Graham believed 'the
faction fight', which had 'ended in a farce', would 'carry Derby over
the session if [the premier made] no great mistakes. At all events the
danger of [Derby] being trodden down by his own "wild Elephant" is
at an end; and Johnny will think twice, if he ever thinks twice, before
he embarks on a second Cambridge House foray.'[80]

II

'The Whigs', Greville observed, 'are in the condition of a defeated
army, who require to be completely reorganised and reformed before
they can take the field again. The general resentment and
mortification is extreme. They have naturally lost all confidence in
their leaders, and they are now all ready to complain of the tactics of
which they entirely approved till they found that defeat had been the
consequence of their adoption.'[81] Dallas discerned three effects of the
'abortive impeachment'.[82] First, it had 'permanently split, and so
kill[ed], the Peelite party'. Secondly, it postponed for 'a considerable
time any further assault'; and, finally, it went 'very far to produce
throughout the country the impression that the men at present at the
helm understand steering a little better than their opponents and can
safely be permitted to command the ship until some other enquiry
occurs'.

Carnarvon observed that after the failure of Cardwell's censure
'the government floated on top of the wave. [They] suddenly found
[them]selves in the confidence apparently of the country, the newspapers, and the House of Commons, where [they] hardly ever [after]
then met with a defeat.'[83] The remaining weeks of the debate,

suffered in record heat and an evil stench from the Thames that forced members to abandon the Committee rooms, afforded the government a comfortable respite. Lyndhurst's observation in July 1858 that the 'Tories [were] getting on admirably' with '[n]othing to oppose them, and majorities in every division' was an accurate verdict on debate throughout June and July.[84]

The resumed debate on the government for India bill, based upon Russell's resolutions, during June 1858, provided ready illustration of Whig and Liberal dissension. 'When Lord John proposed that the number of the Council for Indian Affairs should be 12 instead of 15 . . . many Liberals . . . voted with the government, and he was beaten by 50 or 60 votes. When in Committee Lord Palmerston proposed that the clauses relating to the Council should only be in force for 5 years . . . Lord John opposed him and the result was that 25 Liberals followed [Russell] and the government had a majority of 34 against Lord Palmerston. And when, on the same evening, Russell proposed to negative the clause which provided that secret orders might be sent out without the knowledge of the Council, Lord Palmerston opposed him – was followed by about 30 Liberals, and the government had a majority of 173 to 149 upon a point which, one would have thought, should have united all Liberals against them'.[85] Not only was the obvious discord worthy of note, but also the paltry number of votes either Palmerston or Russell could lead into the division lobby was a striking indication of disillusion. Grey found the most telling aspect of the debate to be the 'extreme unpopularity of the ex-Ministers'.[86] Despondent Liberals felt compelled to point out the obvious truth that the government were 'gaining majorities entirely through the want of unity among their opponents'.[87]

The debate over the Indian resolutions also confirmed Stanley's reputation as a politician of integrity and talent. Stanley succeeded Ellenborough at the Board of Control and steered the India bill through the Commons. Carnarvon believed that 'a considerable part of [the government's] success [was] due to Stanley and the manner in which the India bill [had] been carried through'.[88] Disraeli came to recognise his thirty-two year old colleague as 'a source of great strength and popularity'; 'a man of first-rate abilities and acquirements'.[89] Within Westminster, Stanley established his reputation as 'a calm, philosophical statesman', not inclined to give 'to party what [was] meant for mankind'.[90] Greville received reports of Stanley's 'indefatigable industry, his businesslike qualities', courtesy, affability, candour and patience. He noted that Stanley was 'completely *the man* of the present day, and in all human probability [was] destined to play [an] important and conspicuous part in political life'.[91] The altruistic aspect of this public impression corresponded closely with Stanley's private thought; there existed little discrepancy between political rhetoric and private intention. But though the unimportance of political calculation is essential to an understanding of Stanley's own motive, the public perception of Derby's son formed part of the currency of Conservative high political strategy. Stanley was a vital part of that ministerial desire to affirm Conservatism as the creed of 'moderate progress' and 'safe' government.

That desire was also evident in a second invitation sent to Gladstone to join the government immediately after the withdrawal of Cardwell's motion. Walpole, on 22 May, with Derby's authorisation, asked for Gladstone's cooperation, placing either the Board of Control or the Colonial Office at his disposal and indicating that the offer 'should be taken to signify the wish of the government progressively to extend its basis'. Gladstone, repeating his argument of February, provisionally declined, but agreed to discuss the offer with Graham and Aberdeen before giving a final answer. Graham's advice was markedly more enthusiastic than in February; the offer was 'a tempting one' and the moment chosen 'opportune'.[92] The difficulties Graham saw in acceptance were, first, separation from 'friends' and, secondly, 'the question of the lead in the House of Commons'. Graham believed the first difficulty hardly existed. An 'intimate alliance' with Derby, moreover, was an alliance which Gladstone 'might form with perfect honour'. Gladstone complained of being 'at the bottom of a well, waiting for a ladder to be put down . . . Derby tender[ed] this ladder'.[93] The question of the leadership in the Commons, however, remained. Gladstone, Graham asserted, could not 'without humiliation and dishonour accept a seat on the Treasury bench with Disraeli for [his] leader'. Yet neither could he make it 'a condition *precedent*' that Disraeli should abdicate. 'Side by side', however, Graham was confident that Gladstone would 'soon virtually supercede [Disraeli]'. Graham felt certain that 'in the Commons pre-eminence would be [Gladstone's], let the official arrangements be what they may'. Graham ended his advice with a warning, 'Time is running fast away – You have attained the utmost vigour of your understanding and of your powers. Present opportunities are not to be neglected in the vain hope that better *may* arise, but which may also never come.'[94] 'The truth [was]', Graham confided to Aberdeen, 'that Gladstone wish[ed] to join, and to carry with him Herbert and his most intimate friends.' Gladstone forgot he was 'master of his own decision; and he [mistook] his influence over them when he [believed] that he [could] overcome their fixed determination'.[95]

Further attempts to persuade Gladstone to accept Derby's offer were evidenced by a letter Disraeli sent to Gladstone on 25 May. After declaring that it had been his wish since 1850 to reunite the Peelites and the Conservative party, Disraeli stated that he was 'actively prepared to make every sacrifice of self for the public good, which [he] thought identical with [Gladstone] accepting office in a Conservative Government'.[96] Now was the moment, Disraeli believed, to be 'magnanimous'. In a frigidly aloof reply to Disraeli's letter, however, Gladstone alluded to that consideration Graham believed to be the decisive factor in Gladstone's intentions: 'what change would be requisite in the constitution of the present government in order to make any change worth a trial[?]'[97]

Stanley understood Gladstone's reply to be a *response argumentative* rather than a *refus categorique*, and saw the letter as an attempt to prompt Derby to invite Aberdeen into the Conservative cabinet.[98] Gladstone's sense of his own worth, however, exceeded Derby's estimation of Gladstone's value to the government. Derby did not believe he could approach Aberdeen 'with any proposition which [would] not be either an insult to him or a degradation of [the government]'. Both Disraeli and Stanley hoped that Gladstone might 'take India under the shield and cover of Lord Ab[erdeen] joining the cabinet ... without office'.[99] Such hopes were rendered illusory, however, by Derby's disinclination to have Aberdeen in his cabinet and Aberdeen's unwillingness to accompany Gladstone in reunion. As in February 1857, Gladstone was the victim of the discrepant intention of others. Graham, lamenting the inconclusive end of the negotiations, predicted that Gladstone would be 'unhappy and dissatisfied', renewing 'impossible efforts with his friends', with the result that he would be 'more isolated than ever, estranged from his present friends, and cut off from a new alliance'.[100]

The Commons debate over the Roumanian question on 4 May had lent further definition to Gladstone's isolation. In an impassioned speech (anticipating the central tenets of the Midlothian campaign) Gladstone decried the policy of shoring up the decaying Ottoman Empire as a constraint on Russian expansionism, because it preserved an obstacle to national autonomy in south-eastern Europe. Refusing to share in the hope of a regenerated Turkey, Gladstone not only gave new expression to his anti-Palmerstonianism, but clashed swords with Disraeli. In his article in the *Quarterly Review* of October 1858, Gladstone's passionate attack against Turkish barbarity was the climax of his journalistic outcry against Palmerston's Crimean policy.[101] Yet this line of attack proved to be a cul-de-sac in 1858, only emphasising Gladstone's isolation. The loud plea for the emancipation of subject peoples was to be quietly dropped when a Conservative overture of a rather different kind was made in October 1858.

Reorganising his cabinet in May 1858 without Gladstone, Derby appointed Stanley to the Board of Control and Bulwer Lytton as Stanley's successor at the Colonial Office. Earlier in his life Bulwer Lytton had been a Radical, but, it was suggested, became a Conservative once he inherited his mother's estates in Hertfordshire. Bulwer Lytton had 'no great capacity for business or method in the small details and arrangement of the daily work', while his ideas, once he had keenly taken up any subject, came 'too rapidly [with] his plans under[going] too many changes'.[102] But despite this lack of administrative talent, Carnarvon found Bulwer Lytton capable of taking a broad view of any question before him while remaining far more human in his sympathies than Stanley. Bulwer Lytton represented the flamboyant face of progressive Conservatism, manifesting concern rather than efficiency and a certain Gothic colourfulness in lieu of capability.

The public character of the government, enhanced by the growing reputation of Stanley and the appointment of Bulwer Lytton, was further established by a series of 'liberal' measures. During April 1858 the Radical, Locke King, introduced a private bill to abolish the property qualification for MPs.[103] Walpole, as Home Secretary, gave the measure his active support on the grounds, first, that the existing law required no such qualification from Scottish members and, secondly, that it was unbecoming to parliament to maintain a system universally understood to be an unreality and a sham.[104] Despite the public opposition of one cabinet member, Henley, and backbenchers such as Newdegate, Knightley and Bentinck, the measure quickly passed through the Commons and was supported by Derby in the Lords.

In December 1857 Russell, reaffirming his adherence to the principle of religious tolerance, had introduced an oaths bill into the Commons with the object of allowing practising Jews admission to parliament. Two amendments, one to enable Catholic MPs to subscribe to the same oath as others, and another, moved by Newdegate and seconded by Spooner, attempting to strike out the fifth clause allowing Jews to take the entrance oath omitting the words 'upon the true faith of a Christian', were both defeated by large majorities. The bill duly passed the Commons and was debated in the Lords during April 1858. In the ensuing discussion Derby compromised his formerly unqualified opposition by promising only to object to the crucial fifth clause if opposition to it was shown in Committee.[105] Lord Grey warned, however, that if the Lords rejected the bill a conflict with the Lower House would result with the Commons enforcing their opinion on the Lords. The second reading was allowed to pass on 22 April, but five days later the Lord Chancellor Chelmsford carried an amendment by 118 votes to 80 omitting the fifth clause. Predictably the subsequent debate in the Commons re-inserted the fifth clause, rejected Chelmsford's amendment, and constituted a committee to investigate the reason for disagreement with the Lords. Provocatively, Baron Lionel de Rothschild was made a member of the committee in spite of his official exclusion from the Commons.

Concomitant with the debate over Cardwell's motion in the Commons, Derby saw the confrontation between the two Houses over the oaths bill as a serious threat to the government's position. Early in May 1858 Derby informed Disraeli of a possible compromise solution which Disraeli without authorisation, but perhaps as intended, communicated to Russell. Russell made it clear that any amendment moved as a compromise would be better made in the Lords and that, if a compromise was not found, he would be forced to continue the debate by means of resolution.[106] On 18 May Derby received from the Conservative peer Lord Ellesmere a proposed solution similar to Derby's own: that the Commons should be allowed to admit Jews while the Lords continued to exclude them from their counsel.[107]

While in private Derby was actively seeking a compromise, in public he carefully maintained a passive pose to satisfy the Anglican sensibilities of his backbenchers. On 31 May 1858, the Conservative Lord Lucan proposed an amendment in the Lords that would enable each House to alter the oath with regard to its own members.[108] Derby, in turn, consented to the consideration of Lucan's amendment.[109] It was also agreed that Lord Lyndhurst, another Conservative who had long advocated Jewish relief, should prepare an alternative bill thus providing parliament with two alternative plans. Derby's public pose of reluctant concession to others' initiatives preserved confidence in him amongst a variety of backbench opinion, principally amongst 'ultra-Tories' such as Newdegate and Spooner. But recalcitrance was notably absent from private cabinet counsel. In a letter sent to prominent 'ultra-Tories' and noted zealous Anglicans, Derby further prepared the way for compromise. Derby pointed to the dangers of a constitutional crisis.[110] The 'question [had] resolved itself in[to] one whether it [was] desirable to continue without attempt at compromise . . .; or whether a solution [might] be formed, which [might] save the dignity, and to a certain extent maintain the principles, of both Houses.'

Consistent with his conscious attempt to avoid offence to 'ultra-Tory' feeling, Derby came to favour Lucan's amendment to the measure Lyndhurst was preparing, which suggested that each House be empowered to admit not only Jews but all non-Christians. Thus, during the debate on both proposals in the Lords on 1 July 1858, Lyndhurst agreed that Lucan's bill should be given priority.[111] The second reading of Lucan's bill was subsequently carried by a majority of forty-six votes with Derby and other ministers supporting the measure. Russell adopted the measure in the Lower House where, once again, Newdegate and Spooner opposed the bill and castigated the Lords for a concession 'worse than 1846'. The ministerial line was reasserted, however, by the Conservative backbencher Henry Drummond who saw the bill as the least mischievous means of resolving an inescapable problem.[112] The bill subsequently passed its second reading and received its third reading on 21 July 1858; a measure that one historian has described as 'the most symbolic religious liberty measure of the 1850s'.[113]

Religious concessions were also made to Roman Catholics. The Irish Brigade gave consistent support to the government during the 1858 session in return for a number of reforms. Catholic chaplains in the army were given permanent rank and salary; a contract was negotiated for a direct mail service between Ireland and America which was expected to create a commercial boom in Galway; the Home Secretary allowed easier access to prisons and workhouses for Catholic priests; and it was made known that the cabinet was considering the question of the Irish landlord and tenant law.[114] Such concessions, in particular the last, allowed the Irish Brigade to justify a Conservative government and modify their position of independent opposition; a position that, in practice, retained the character of anti-Palmerstonianism. To protect Catholic sensibilities the Home Secretary also quickly cut short debate over Spooner's annual motion regarding the Maynooth grant.[115]

Two divisions in June 1858, meanwhile, were significant for anticipating the question of reform in 1859. Locke King again proposed the equalisation of the county and borough franchise and a ballot proposition was brought forward. Although defeated, both issues provided clear indications of Whig, Liberal and Radical feeling on the major question of the forthcoming session. In contrast to February 1857, by June 1858 non-Conservative opinion (including Palmerston) was solidly in favour of equalising the franchise. The question of the ballot, however, deeply divided Liberals and Whigs while Liberal Conservatives and Conservatives unanimously opposed the reform.[116] These divisions suggested a game plan for reform that Derby was to remember during the recess: a stratagem designed to exploit the evident collapse of opposition unity.

Disraeli, by the end of July 1858, was confident that the government had been successful, 'not withstanding all the disturbance and hostility of the early part of the session . . . [S]eldom', he rejoiced, '[had there] been [a session] in which a greater number of excellent measures [had] been passed than the present.'[117] Dallas, 'as a stranger, a mere looker-on', observed the close of the session and the state of political feeling:

> Lord Derby has shown wisdom, tact and statesmanship, far beyond what was expected of him, and the natural result is a corresponding triumph over public opinion. The spirit of exterior conciliation is quite distinct. He soothes and satisfies everywhere: France, United States, Naples. At home he has ceased to fight with the age, concedes more liberally than he ever promised. . . . Surely there is nothing equivocal in these traits of a six month policy – shown too in the midst of difficulties.[118]

Dallas predicted that in the event of a dissolution 'it would not surprise [him] to find the new House of Commons more disposed than the present one to sustain the existing government'.

8 Opposition without Form and Void

[T]he aspect, with regard to parties, is hazy and I can form no opinion as to what is likely to happen. Lyndhurst, I hear, says that it will all depend on a chapter of accidents, and that those accidents are as likely to be in favour, as against, the government. (Bedford to Brougham, 30 September 1858, Brougham Mss. 30406)

I would far rather help Derby against the Radicals than work with the latter, by whose help I fear some of our Liberal friends would seek to recover power at any sacrifice of their principles. (Argyll to Aberdeen, 19 August 1858, cited in Duke of Argyll, *Autobiography and Memoirs* (London, 1906) II, p. 123)

The people were never better disposed, or the nation less inclined to rash and dangerous measures, yet there is every prospect that a course of legislation will be commenced which will lead us by short and easy stages to a wild democracy. (Grey Diary, 31 December 1858, Grey Mss. C3/21)

By August 1858 the testimony of opposition despondency and division was overwhelming. In July 1858 Charles Wood was eloquent about 'the miserable condition of the [party] and condemned Palmerston's recent conduct'.[1] Criticism and carping continued throughout the recess. Argyll observed that the Whigs and Liberals were 'still in chaos and [with] no prospect of an end to this condition of things'.[2] Cornewall Lewis came to accept that the government was, for the moment, unassailable.[3] Graham intoned that the 'broken fragments of the old Whig party [were] so shattered that they [could not] be pieced together again. The old stagers [had] known each other too long and too well; and they dislike[d] each other too much'.[4] In January 1859 Herbert could still see no prospect 'of the formation of an efficient party, let alone government, out of the chaos on the opposition benches'.[5] Charles Villiers echoed the verdict from the Radical benches. 'The Liberal party is too much divided and scattered at present to offer the least expectation of returning to power next year, and the people who are now in must be great blunderers if they cannot at least secure themselves for another year or two'.[6]

In May 1858 Clanricarde believed it 'indisputable that Palmerston [was] greatly disliked by a number of Liberal MPs and that Clarendon [was] so unpopular that he could not be reappointed to the F.O.'[7] It became a suggestion that 'P. himself and J.R. ... might as well retire',[8] while, in a more assertive tone, it was acknowledged that 'Palmerston [had] lost his chance'.[9] Gladstone and Lord Grey made dinner-table conversation out of the change of opinion in the Commons with regard to Palmerston; Gladstone observing that 'nothing like it had ever been seen before'. The force of Gladstone's comment was confirmed by Wood 'distinctly' remarking 'that *P*. would *never* again be prime minister'.[10] Despite the appearance of a reconciliation over Cardwell's motion in May, by the end of the session it became apparent that 'the feud between [Russell] and Palmerston was likely to last'.[11] Russell repeatedly asserted his determination not to serve again under Palmerston during the recess.[12] In January 1859 Wood wearily lamented that there was 'no appearance of drawing together in any of our chiefs. P[almerston] [was] not at all prepared to abdicate the position which he [held]. Lord. J. Russell, Graham, Gladstone, as well as Bright and others [were] as determined he [would] not be head of a Liberal government – and this render[ed] the event almost, if not quite, impossible.'[13]

The continued rivalry between Russell and Palmerston, however, had wider consequences than merely dividing loyalties. Prominent Whigs, who had formerly been content to support Palmerston, began to assert their own claims; some individuals came to perceive a vested interest in instability. In May 1858, Delane found Granville 'diffuse on the difficulty of exclusion' and his fear that there would be 'too many of the ancients in the next [Liberal] cabinet'.[14] Increasing disillusion stimulated alternative ambitions. Newcastle, in an association of opinion that revealed more than his stated intent, 'agreed it was time to find new leaders – but would not aspire to the post himself'.[15] In private conversation Newcastle continued to deny any aspiration sufficiently strongly so as to recommend himself for advancement. When a conciliatory figure was desired, self-effacement paraded its own merit. By the close of the session speculation recognised the claims of Cornewall Lewis as a future premier and it was noted that Lady Theresa Lewis, with more than conjugal pride, hinted as much.[16]

Between the months of August 1858 and January 1859 prominent

Whigs and Liberals were reacting to events not as a group with a coherent unified response, nor even as sections of similarly inclined opinion, but as individuals. The landmarks of collective action had disappeared. In March 1858 Bedford concurred in Lord Grey's belief that 'one of the great difficulties in forming a strong and united Liberal party was the absence of any important public questions. Those on which the Whig party was formerly united hav[ing] been settled'.[17] Men such as Bedford and himself, Grey suggested, were 'far nearer in [their] political opinions to Derby and his friends than to a great many of those who pass[ed] under the common name of Liberals – such persons as Milner Gibson'.

Increasingly during 1858, a number of Whigs and Liberals came to see advantage in opposition to a Conservative government prepared to appear progressive. Knatchbull-Hugessen, who had acted as a teller for Russell in a number of Commons divisions, concluded that, in retrospect, it was 'advantageous to Liberal principles that [the Conservatives] should have been in office ... There were certain questions which could hardly have been solved by a Whig cabinet, but which [had] found their solution.'[18] Greville and Broughton, in a similar vein, both agreed that the government 'ought not to be disturbed'.[19] Herbert warned Granville that, 'on the whole, it [was] best for the country that [the Conservatives] should go on. It [was] a great mistake to take office before your opponents [had] made blunders enough to efface the memory of one's own and new governments [made] fewer than old ones.'[20] By August 1858 Palmerston himself admitted that if he 'was to make a bet about the government's chances [he] would rather back them in, than out, for next session – [the opposition] gangway men [were] not disposed to supporting any but a yielding Tory government'.[21]

The moment found its measure even if the chosen men remained obscure. During the recess of 1858 and January 1859, fragmented opposition opinion, in the question of parliamentary reform, focused on an issue fully capable of reflecting political complexity in legislative difference and programmatic utterance. Reform offered to subtle minds in complex circumstance infinite opportunity to advertise and distinguish differing positions. '[T]he reform puzzle', Graham plaintively confirmed, was 'a perplexity on every side'.[22] Derby's government was publicly committed to consider reform during the session of 1859, and it became increasingly apparent that the government neither wished to, nor was to be allowed to, revoke that commitment. Parliamentary reform would define future party connection.

I

Befitting his personal commitment to the question, Russell made the first preparatory move regarding reform. Late in July 1858, in a short private talk with Palmerston, Russell ascertained that a £12 county and £6 borough franchise would be unacceptable at Cambridge House.[23] In a subsequent meeting with Graham, Russell 'struck off . . ., apparently without much premeditation, and without any consultation', a scheme of reform he knew Palmerston would find objectionable.[24] Russell recommended extending the franchise to £12 occupiers in the counties and £5 occupiers in the boroughs; further rights of voting contained in his bill of 1854; no total disfranchisement; disfranchisement of one member from all boroughs not having 500 £10 voters – about thirty – and granting those members to counties, large towns and 'learned bodies' such as universities in England and Scotland.[25] Russell expected reform to create a bi-partisan realignment with the Conservatives, Palmerston and conservative Whigs coming together. 'A perilous conjunction for the Whigs, but they [might] be mad enough to try it.'[26] As important to Russell, however, was a corresponding redefinition of Conservative allegiance. In particular, the potential that reform offered of severing Stanley's filial loyalty. In devising a government scheme Derby must, Russell predicted, 'in the one case . . . sacrifice his son, and in the other his party'.[27]

Recognising that Russell was 'fidgety and always on the out-look for "break-ups" ', Graham was aware that Russell 'wish[ed] to make Lord Stanley a stepping-stone to power; but Lord Stanley [had] quite as good a chance of using Lord John, as Lord John [had] of leading the young one'.[28] By creating an opportunity for Stanley to associate himself with his Liberal rhetoric Russell also lay himself open to the possibility of Stanley using such an association to give greater weight to his own pronouncements. Aberdeen observed that 'Lord Stanley [was] the only popular man in the country; there being entire indifference about all other public men, although Lord John's position [was] improved'.[29] Graham acknowledged that Stanley's 'views and opinions [were] sincerely Liberal, and he [could not] long remain a member of his father's cabinet'. But, Graham added, it was hard to foresee Stanley's 'future destiny' and it was once before thought 'that "Lord Stanley" was the "decus et tutamen" of the Whigs'.[30]

In an oft-repeated sermon, Graham decried Russell's desire to be active. '[I]t would be more creditable to him to rest on his laurels than

to embark on a new enterprise, in which disgrace [might] be incurred
... But to "sit still" which was "the strength of Egypt", [was]
regarded by Lord John as a proof of impotence.'[31] The attempt 'to
satisfy Conservatives and Liberals [was] a task beyond the powers of
Lord John'. Herbert echoed 'the imprudence of producing a reform
bill'.[32] Bedford admitted to Clarendon 'that John's state of mind
worried him to death and made him wish to have nothing to do with
politics. [Russell] was in the habit of writing his impressions to the
Duke, who [said] he immediately put the letters into the fire in order
that there [might] be no record of such foolishness and injustice.'[33]
Bedford recalled that their father had said 'that John's failure thro'
life would be want of judgement'. Bedford considered the prophesy
to have been fulfilled.

During August 1858 Russell repeatedly invited Stanley to Pembroke Lodge[34] and, at the beginning of September, while 'his large
and little family' was staying at Woburn, Russell, with the Duke of
Bedford's permission, invited Stanley to the ancestral home.[35] 'The
old and the young statesman', Bedford observed, 'appeared to be on
the best terms', although 'their conversation related to the past rather
than the present or the future'. But this social intimacy was, Bedford
believed, a preparation for 'a fresh organisation and combination' of
parties which seemed 'almost inevitable'.[36] Early in October 1858
Russell kept 'himself before the public',[37] delivering speeches at
Liverpool and, at Stanley's invitation, stayed two days at Knowsley in
the company of the prime minister and his son. Russell found Derby
'in boyish spirits ... but not one word of politics'.[38] Russell left
Knowsley with the impression that Derby would not consent to 'any
democratic movement' such as Stanley and Disraeli might suggest.
There was, therefore, the probability of a split in the government with
Stanley joining Russell in a measure of 'real' reform. That measure of
reform, Russell hoped in the face of Derby's obdurance, need not 'go
very far', but he would 'be governed by circumstances'.[39]

Responses to the growing intimacy between Russell and Stanley
were varied. Wood believed that 'a government comprised of Johnny,
Pakington and Stanley etc.' was not 'quite off the cards'.[40] Cornewall
Lewis could not believe that Russell wished to join the government,
but suspected an intention 'to supersede them by a successful reform
bill, and to enter Lord Stanley and perhaps Pakington into his
Cabinet'.[41] In a similar vein Stanley of Alderley believed that over the
question of reform one might see 'Stanley, Dizzy, the Manchester
Party including a ? of Peelitism, and possibly Johnny against Derby

and Palmerston . . .'[42] Lord Holland, in contrast, shared Graham and Aberdeen's apprehension. The government were constructing 'a trap' by 'trying to win over Johnny' and bringing out a reform bill he would support; a trap Russell might fall into 'out of spite to Palmerston'.[43]

The political wisdom was cited that 'a great man' kept himself 'in his own dignity, and wait[ed] until he [was] wanted; a little man, wanting to make himself of importance, [was] always restless'.[44] Stanley was 'a dangerous minister' and, if he had capacity, 'the cards [are] in his hands'; if Russell were 'but quiet and patient, his day will come'. After his visit to Knowsley, Russell, indeed, came to regard any initiative on his part with diminishing enthusiasm. After 'the Liverpool Congress' Parkes found that Russell's *present* intention [was] very decidedly to wait'.[45] After the correspondence of August and September, Graham found Russell 'silent' towards him.[46] Graham translated Russell's new caution into a characteristically graphic metaphor:

> Your race is a waiting race. The play will be made by others; great mistakes will be committed; an opening will be afforded for you . . . The channel will be buoyed for you by the wrecks, right and left, of the ships leading in . . . You are no bad pilot when the waves run high; but in this case it is wiser to await than to seek the storm. Derby will soon find himself in the midst of it without chart or compass; and friend Bright is no helmsman in extremity.[47]

Confirmation of the wisdom of Russell's new-found patience was provided by Bright's own decision, in October 1858, to pronounce a programme of radical parliamentary reform.

During the session of 1858, while Cobden in his rural Sussex retreat disavowed any interest in politics, Bright recovered his health and nurtured an optimistic hope in a Radical resurgence.[48] Bright refused his annual autumn invitation to Haddo from Lord Aberdeen, where he saw 'no good to be done', and decried both Aberdeen and Graham's 'lack of courage in their general course'.[49] Bright and Milner Gibson had been content during the 1858 session to help Derby and prevent 'a Whig restoration'. But now Bright saw in the reform question 'a means to prove himself a Giant refreshed'.[50] A 'Derby bill', Bright anticipated, 'would be something rather worse than nothing'.[51] Bright also feared that 'the Whig families [might] find out that it [would] be best for them to help the Tories to carry something called a reform bill'. Cobden agreed that any government measure, even if it professed to be a 'real reform bill', would 'drop out of existence' when its details were examined.[52] During 1857 Cobden had provided Bright with the radical *principum* that in any scheme of reform redistribution was of greater importance than suffrage. During 1858 Cobden added the ballot to the prerequisites of radical reform, and these perspectives were faithfully reflected in Bright's rhetoric.

During the autumn of 1858 Bright made a number of public speeches on reform and foreign policy. His intention was to put the question of reform 'on the right track . . . so as to warn the people of the pit-falls which Disraeli [was] . . . digging for them'.[53] Bright received an 'amusing note' from the Reform Club which advised moderation, pointed out that Russell agreed with Bright on foreign policy, and noted that Russell was 'free on the suffrage'.[54] The letter suggested it was 'not worthwhile to make things difficult by dwelling on the distribution of seats and the ballot', and by this emphasis denying a possible concert between Bright and Russell. Bright's rhetorical response brooked no compromise. 'What is reform without a redistribution of seats and the ballot?'[55]

Bright delivered his first speech on reform at Birmingham on 27 October 1858. *The Times* sent 'a special engine' so that a report of the speech might reach the press for the morning edition.[56] Bright, with renewed vigour, stressed the seriousness of the reform question and emphasised the necessity to provide 'a satisfactory' bill; 'a delusion and a sham' would render feeling on the question both bitter and malignant.[57] Bright then continued to define what radical opinion might find satisfactory. A borough franchise equivalent to the parish and poor law union suffrage which, although short of 'manhood suffrage', was immediately practicable; nor could he see any obstacle to an equally extensive county franchise, but it was of great importance that the 40s franchise should be extended to all the United Kingdom, not only England and Wales.[58] Then, indulging in the numbers game that afforded endless permutations, he argued that the metropolitan boroughs and all large boroughs ought to have double, treble, or quadruple their present number of members. After attacking the constitutional check embodied in the House of Lords, Bright then warned his audience of the danger of a Conservative redistribution bill giving greater influence to the landed interest. This warning Bright accompanied with a declaration that any reform bill which pretended to be generally satisfactory must concede 'the shelter and the protection' of the ballot.

Bright's profession of faith was significant not only as a definition of

Radical opinion, but also as the first public commitment to any specific scheme of reform by any prominent politician since 1854.[59] Yet the tone of Bright's appeal detracted from its content. In particular, in his attack on the House of Lords, Bright had predicted that every peer, whether of good character or bad, would vote against every measure of reform, including that 'creature of . . . monstrous, nay, even of adulterous birth – a spiritual peer'.[60] Such language was seen as an incitement to 'class' hatred and 'democratic' rule. Graham concluded that 'Bright [had] aided Derby, by pitching the key-note too high: harmony [would] be produced by a lower strain. But who [was] to be Leader of the Band?'[61]

Bedford found Ellice 'anti-American and therefore anti-Bright', while Aberdeen wondered whether 'a rapid course of "Americanisation" ' would be their 'euthanasia'.[62] Clarendon found the Court, 'on the whole, pleased with Bright's speech as likely to promote Conservatism and so prevent him walking arm-in-arm with cabinet ministers'.[63] At Edinburgh, Cowan deprecated Bright's attack on the House of Lords, the tendency of which was, he feared, 'to incite the humbler against the upper classes of society'.[64] The thought was echoed by Shaftesbury and given more eloquent form by Argyll at Dundee on 11 November 1858.[65] '[T]he surest symptom', Argyll expounded, 'of national progress . . . was the various classes of society uniting together . . . for the purpose of rectifying the evils of our political condition'.[66] Less magisterially, but with as happy a rhetorical effect, Bouverie, at Kilmarnock, took up Bright's challenge to indulge in numbers. If, as Bright recommended, Bouverie mused, redistribution was determined by population they must at once give 50 additional members to Ireland. 'He respected the Irish members, but he did not think nor did he think they were prepared to say that the Irish element should be increased by so much (Hear, hear!).'[67] Backbench Radicals also regretted 'to see [Bright] enact the demagogue rather than the statesman'.[68] Lord Goderich, with his radical designs for social emollition, 'deeply regretted the attempt to stir up once more the extreme class hatreds of 20 or 30 years ago'.[69] Goderich wished to maintain the difference between the political intelligence of the town and country populations, while accepting 'the present *municipal* suffrage . . . for boroughs and a £10 household suffrage for counties'. Goderich regarded the ballot, however, as 'a mere piece of election machinery, which there [was] no chance of carrying' and objected to the shortening of parliament as 'all nonsense'.

On 29 October 1858 Bright made a speech at Birmingham, concerned with both reform and foreign affairs.[70] His statement on foreign policy formed a natural adjunct to his pronouncements on reform. Bright decried the established portrayal of foreign policy, couched in terms of the balance of power and Protestant interests, as merely the means by which, since the Glorious Revolution, the material interests of the great territorial families of England had been protected. Thus, in his famous dictum, he saw foreign policy as 'a gigantic system of outdoor relief for the aristocracy of Great Britain'.

On 5 November, Bright attended a 'Reform Conference' held at the Guildhall Coffeehouse, London. The meeting was chaired by James Clay, MP for Hull, with Roebuck, Roupell, Cox, Mosley and Muntz also in attendance.[71] What the Radical party could unanimously accept as satisfactory, however, remained conveniently ill-defined. A motion to adopt the principle of manhood suffrage was rejected. Roebuck then suggested with ostensible deference, after observing that all former reform bills had been 'the child of aristocratic condescension', that Bright be given the responsibility of drawing up a reform scheme. What paraded as deference, however, concealed the dangers inherent in individual authorship. What was known to be Bright's bill, ultimately, was a commitment for none but Bright.

The evolution of Bright's scheme and the attendant vagueness of many details, reflected the difficulties of assimilating disparate Radical opinion. At the time of the London Conference, Bright was decided on the details of a new franchise: a rating suffrage for the boroughs, a £10 occupier's suffrage in the counties and a 40*s* franchise for Scotland and Ireland as already existed in England and Wales.[72] But what Bright considered to be of greater importance and crucial to any scheme of reform, namely redistribution, remained embarrassingly, or perhaps prudently, ill-defined. Bright even revealed to Cobden a degree of ambivalence about the ballot. Ironically under pressure from the Ballot Society 'not to touch their question', and aware that 'if omitted we should have less difficulty with Lord John Russell', Bright also had cause to believe that 'the Whigs [were] yielding on the point, and [were] comforting themselves with Lord Althorp's saying "that it would not make much difference"'. In the last resort, however, he arrived at the conviction that if they omitted the ballot they would 'run the risk of being thought insincere and [would] weaken [their] friends'. Bright, moreover, reaffirmed his commitment with the suspicion that Graham was advising Russell to regard the ballot as 'merely part of the machinery' rather than a 'principle'.[73]

The loss to Bright by Cobden's withdrawal from politics was pathetically revealed in the former's lack of facility with legislative form. While arranging the schedule of his bill Bright 'went through the old reform bills of 1852 and 1854, and found that many of the clauses [met the present] case, filling up the *blanks* differently . . .'[74] In contrast with such artlessness, Cobden expected Disraeli to 'produce something so ingeniously complex and paradoxical that he [would] make captive many a willing boroughmonger on [the opposition] side of the House'.[75] Bright's handling of the statistical and historical aspects of the reform question also revealed Cobden's much missed contribution to Radical effectiveness. Villiers warned Bright that many, not 'the pedants of the "Saturday Review", but men who were good reformers besides', accused him of mistakes with regard to parochial rating and the qualification required for electing guardians.[76] Criticism of Bright's analysis and statistics became widespread. Cornewall Lewis, with cool intellectual disdain, found Bright to be 'a wonderfully ignorant man. His knowledge of facts [was] limited and superficial'; an obstacle he overcame by exuding 'confidence'.[77] Such deficiencies confirmed Disraeli's verdict that Bright lacked 'the subtleness of Cobden, but he [had] far more energy, and his talents [were] more practically applied'.[78]

Speaking at a large public meeting in Manchester, on 10 December 1858, Bright again stressed his belief that a House of hereditary legislators could not be a permanent institution in a free country and portrayed the Commons as 'a sort of deputy to the House of Lords, and an organ of the great territorial interest of the country'.[79] Such language again excited Whig alarm and fear of 'class' antagonism. In a speech at Glasgow on 21 December 1858, Bright announced a reform scheme he understood to be 'a rational and substantial project' that contained 'nothing made up of conundrums and tricks'.[80] The franchise was the same as that recommended at Birmingham: a borough franchise conferred on all who were rated to the relief of the poor, and on all lodgers who paid a rent of £10; a county franchise reduced to £10 rental and the vote protected by the ballot. For the first time, however, Bright publicly described his proposals for redistribution. The disfranchisement of fifty-six English, twenty-one Scottish and nine Irish boroughs; the removal of one member from thirty-four other boroughs; the seats obtained by this disfranchisement to be distributed according to population among the larger

towns, counties and divisions of counties in the United Kingdom.
Finally Bright added a plea for revision of legislation in regard to
primogeniture on entails and settlements which, he argued, kept vast
estates in one hand through successive generations.

Bright's language, in particular about the House of Lords, power-
fully shaped response to his reform scheme. Some perceived a
discrepancy between the violence of his rhetoric and the more
moderate nature of his reform proposals. In private Bright complained 'bitterly that he [was] misrepresented', declared that he was
'against any unnecessary change; and most of all change for change's
sake'. His wish was to be seen as 'very moderate and practical'.[81]
Some surmised that Bright 'express[ed] himself more strongly than
his real views would justify, and then complain[ed] of misrepresentation when the ordinary meaning [was] put upon his words'. Cornewall
Lewis, taking the reverse view, however, suspected that 'in the
excitement of speaking [Bright] let out his real opinions'.[82] Then,
finding that these gave 'offence, create[d] alarm, alienate[d] supporters and deterr[ed] other Liberals in his boat', and being 'desirous of
making himself a Leader', in his 'cool moments' Bright retracted
'what he said in public, and complain[ed] that he [had] been mis-
understood and misrepresented'. That, in private, Bright also talked
of Granville as premier and Russell as leader of the Commons in a
future Liberal government, however, suggested Bright's earnest
desire to be understood as 'moderate' once the threat of a 'radical'
constitutional change was seen to be real.

II

Bright's activity during October, November and December 1858,
placed reform at the forefront of political concern, and established
Bright's claim as the foremost representative of Radical opinion.
Bright was aware of Russell's wish to 'wait patiently the introduction
of the government bill . . . before he should say what he thought or
would do'.[83] Graham believed that ' "free born John" [had] made a
move in advance for the express purpose of forestalling [Russell]'.[84]
Such an initiative would have been consistent with a wish to appear
'moderate', once alarm and apprehension had been excited, while
pre-empting Russell's conciliation of 'safe progressive' opinion.
Graham also approved of 'Bright, without intending it, [having]
rendered great assistance to Lord Derby, and [having] made Lord

John prudent by compulsion to an extent his wisdom would not have dictated'.[85] Parliament would 'be disposed to talk about what the government offered in preference to what Bright threaten[ed]'.

Bright's initiative pressed Clarendon to define a distinctive Whig position.[86] Clarendon acknowledged 'the necessity of some understanding being come to by the *discerptu membra* of the Liberal party about reform'.[87] Bright had challenged a previously studied and vague non-commitment. During October 1858 Argyll also began to urge 'moderate Liberals' to come to 'some general understanding among themselves as to what they wish[ed], and *what they* [*would*] oppose, in the principles of new reform bills'.[88] In correspondence with Russell, Argyll urged 'some general understanding, and some plan of action, agreed upon by those who wish[ed] to avoid either a Tory or a Radical reform bill'; the present state of parties '*throw[ing] out of gear* all the usual constitutional checks of parliamentary opposition'.[89]

Lord Grey responded to Whig anxiety and confusion by emphasising the need to raise the reform question above party conflict.[90] Decrying political differences as being dependent 'more than formerly on personal feelings and interests' Grey adopted a conciliatory pose of supra-party centrism substantiated by the publication of his pamphlet on parliamentary reform.[91] Grey's line could come to appeal to those such as Ellice, who looked to a Whig restoration; Clarendon, who feared 'radical' reform and Conservative chicanery; Granville, who saw a need for new leadership; and Lowe, looking for democratic checks and cabinet office. Grey's language skilfully played upon that anxiety voiced by one Whig hostess who wished 'some man of reputation, courage *and* property, to get up and say he [would] *not* consent to place the government of this old country in the hands of the "greatest number"'.[92]

The reform scheme that Grey outlined to Ellice early in January 1859 was intended to establish 'a clearly ascertained principle' that would prevent 'a Dutch Auction [with] each [party] outbidding the other in concessions to popular clamour for possession of office'.[93] The proposal of a £5 town franchise, by Aberdeen's government, had made 'it very difficult, if not impossible, to prevent a reduction of the franchise to [that] extent at least'.[94] Thus Grey suggested the adoption of 'the old municipal qualification – namely payment of rates for three years'. Those seats reallocated in redistribution would go not only to 'large towns or the great manufacturing districts', but also to constituencies of such professional bodies as barristers, solicitors and medical men. The significant recommendation, so as to remove reform from 'the party battlefield', however, was to insist upon an enquiry by a parliamentary committee before any legislation was passed. Such a committee, moreover, would settle the question before the displacement of the Conservative ministry; 'a change of government before reform [was] settled would greatly aggravate the difficulties and dangers of that question'.

The attempt to prevent reform becoming 'a conflict of parties for power' would, in the short term, 'be favourable to the maintenance of Lord Derby's government'. But Grey was content that the Liberals should remain in opposition until a satisfactory 'reconciliation' of their leadership revived their political effectiveness. He believed Russell would be 'little fit' to lead such a realignment, while politely disclaiming Ellice's natural, if not obvious, suggestion that Grey himself might direct and be seen to personify 'moderate' Whig and Liberal sentiment. The desire to see a permanent solution to the reform question coming from a consolidated body of 'moderate' opinion was a prevalent concern amongst Whigs during the recess. This pressing issue, however, failed to elicit a common response. Although Grey's intention might be acceptable to others, his personality and past militated against concerted action. Moreover, Grey lamented that the previous year had done more than any other to bring upon him the infirmities of age' and he felt 'his life [was] slipping away'.[95]

Cornewall Lewis and Clarendon came to see themselves as victims of Whig rivalry, Conservative hypocrisy and Radical recalesence. During the recess each sought the other's opinion and approval and, in private correspondence, established a common resolve.[96] After his decision, in October 1858, to await a government bill before announcing the details of any measure, Russell disclosed to Clarendon that it would be 'useful to come to an understanding as to points which should be maintained, amended or rejected'.[97] This confidence Clarendon took as his cue to act as intermediary between Cambridge House and Pembroke Lodge. Bedford granted extra momentum to Clarendon's purpose by informing him that Russell was in correspondence with Argyll and Wood, that Russell 'abused Dizzy' and was predicting that 'none of *us old Whigs*' would be able to act with Bright.[98] Clarendon 'could see no objection to asking his old friends' to consider a reform bill he believed Russell 'had ... more or less ready'. On 29 November 1858 Clarendon wrote to Palmerston observing that Russell 'would be utterly discredited by acting either with the government or with Bright and he would be comparatively powerless if he [could not] get the support of the moderate Liberals who on their part [had] an interest in acting with him and *keeping him strait*'.[99] In an uncompromising, if candid, reply Palmerston observed 'that Lord John [was] more likely to be looked to about reform than himself and that he [had] no intention to play 2nd fiddle to said John'.[100] This response Clarendon understood to be confirmation of Palmerston's belief 'in an ultimate junction between moderate Whigs and non-Radical Tories, but even if such a feeble alliance as that were possible the prospect of it [was] too distant for a man of P.'s age to speculate upon prudently'.

Clarendon's fear remained that if Whigs could not 'serve the purpose of keeping [Russell] strait', either Bright would 'eat the amount of dirt necessary' to make 'Lord John fraternise with him', or the government would recruit Russell's aid in the formulation of their scheme.[101] He anxiously noted that 'there [was] always some member of the government at Pembroke Lodge – if it [was] not Stanley it [was] Peel', a 'sly fellow' who did 'not waste his time there for nothing'. They might 'manage to extract what Lord John [thought] necessary and the government [would] try to meet his wishes'.

The attempt at reconciling Palmerston and Russell having failed, Clarendon and Cornewall Lewis began to brood upon the need for some 'central point round which a large portion of the scattered Liberals might cluster'.[102] Lord Howden, in writing to Clarendon, stressed the need to 'chalk out something for themselves as a visible sign of existence', but 'it [was] not easy to say what'. Howden lamented that 'such [had] been the immorality and unnatural commerce going on lately that [they would] still appear Radicals to the Conservative gentlemen and regular old Spoonies to such a fast association as Stanley, Bright and Co.'[103] Reeve's anxious wish to have an article in the forthcoming number of the *Edinburgh Review*, that might 'do much to guide opinion' without 'actually proposing a measure' on reform, was an opportunity to define 'a central point' around which 'scattered Liberals' might gather.[104] Cornewall Lewis would be able, Clarendon urged, to 'rig [the Whigs] out in new uniforms and make them look decent for parliament by an article which should well pepper the Tories, and show how accurately in 1832 the Whigs estimated the requirements of the country'. Cornewall Lewis received the suggestion favourably and agreed that 'an article in the E.R. at [that] moment ought to be more than an essay – it ought to be a party manifesto'.[105]

The difficulties of defining 'a central point' around which Whigs might 'cluster' remained insurmountable, however, because of the desire of Russell and Palmerston for non-commitment. Russell showed a 'petulant opposition' to any such article,[106] subsequently agreeing to 'an historical sketch' which could not be mistaken for 'a party manifesto'.[107] 'Palmerston too', Clarendon predicted, '[would] probably deprecate an article as embarrassing to himself'.[108] The failure of even this limited initiative occasioned acute despondency. 'It [was] difficult', Clarendon lamented, 'to know how to steer among a parcel of men who [were] guided only by personal motives. Their rivalries set the reform question in motion, and upon them the government [would] be safely floated over the question and the session.' Clarendon confided in Reeve his belief 'that a telling review of Tory illiberality and hindrance-spirit for the last 30 years, of Radical rashness and the Americanism and inconsistencies of Bright would have brought the public by induction to look to the Whig party for protection from the extremes and that this might have spliced together the mangled remains of the party and galvanised them into life again.'[109] But if Russell and Palmerston were 'to repudiate the article and . . . the former [was] to be angry and perverse when parliament [met] it [would] be better to have none at all'. In the event, Cornewall Lewis wrote an article for the January issue of the *Edinburgh Review*, but 'confined [himself] to general considerations without entering into any details of a plan'.[110]

During the recess both Clarendon and Cornewall Lewis retained their belief that, despite the government being 'essentially dishonest and [with] no other principle than that of remaining in office',[111] during the coming session 'the fate of the government bill [would] depend on the Whigs and moderate Liberals who, by throwing their weight into either scale, [would] determine the inclination of the balance'.[112] Cornewall Lewis anticipated 'a varigated measure – [the government would] put in a few touches to please their own party, and add one or two strong things, which it would be difficult for Liberal members to vote against'. It was, therefore, imperative that Whigs judge the bill '*as a whole*: its general character and tendency ought to be estimated, and the decision made accordingly'. Further caution was demanded by the suspicion 'that Dizzy and not Derby [was] the real master of [the] cabinet, and that he [would] continue . . . to have his way'.[113] 'Dizzy' had 'knocked every atom of principle out of his party and the Tories [were] in fact ready for anything that they believe[d] [would] keep them in power'.[114] Distrust of the government, and in particular Disraeli, warned Cornewall Lewis against 'driv[ing] any one principle to excess in framing a representative system', however seductive to Liberal sensibilities such a principle might be, and the necessity to look to 'the general character' of any 'motley production' the ministry might bring forward.[115] What was to be avoided, however, was the abolition of 'all moderate sized boroughs', with more influence granted to 'the trading classes' by transferring members from abolished constituencies such as Arundel and Calne to 'manufacturing towns', leaving 'nothing but counties and large towns'. Furthermore, a 'great reduction of the borough franchise' would, Cornewall Lewis feared, 'create an extremely venal constituency – men whose votes, if not obtained by direct bribery, would be purchased by a blanket at Christmas'.

The wish for limited reform and an acute distrust of the cabinet's intentions heightened Whig alarm at the possibility of Bright finding common cause with Russell. It was noticed that since his Birmingham speech Bright had modified some of his public pronouncements and, in private, professed moderate aims. Early in December 1858, Clarendon began to suspect that Bright, 'feel[ing] the dangers of his isolated position', sought a *rapprochement* with Russell.[116] This suspicion was confirmed by the news that Russell had 'received some applications . . . from Bright *since* his Birmingham speech, enquiring after [Russell's] opinions on the subject of reform'.[117] Russell's answer '*not* to produce his promised bill' was, Cornewall Lewis noted, 'the advice of a well-wisher of Bright'. Since his decision in November to quietly wait for the government's measure before declaring his own scheme, Russell had appeared to be in 'a conservative vein', and Clarendon found comfort in the circumstance that 'it [was] strange that [Russell] should become more hostile to Bright as Bright approach[ed] nearer to him'.[118] Lack of trust in Russell's judgement, however, rendered such thought shallow solace. Palmerston, with less personal apprehension than either Clarendon or Cornewall Lewis, acknowledged that Russell deemed Bright 'a dangerous ally', but believed that Russell was not 'enough alive to the dangerous tendency of the measure with which Bright [said] he would be content as a first step towards his further objects'.[119]

The Whig inference that Bright was becoming alarmed by his own isolation was astute. Prominent Radicals such as Roebuck were adopting vague postures that intimated much, but affirmed little. None of Roebuck's political correspondence for the period survives; there remains only the fragmented extracts from Roebuck's letters contained in Leader's biography. Only two aspects of Roebuck's behaviour during the early part of the recess are known. First, that during October 1858 he visited Ireland and renewed a social intimacy with prominent Conservatives. Having had a meeting with the Conservative Attorney-General for Ireland, Whiteside, Roebuck dined with Lord Naas, the Chief Secretary for Ireland and, on a different occasion, with Lord Eglinton the Lord Lieutenant – a round of social activity that included a meeting with the cabinet minister Spencer Walpole.[120] Secondly, in London at the beginning of November 1858, Roebuck committed Bright to producing a specific scheme of reform; a public act that possibly concealed a malicious private intent behind pious self-effacement. If all this is seen as part of a common strategy, then Roebuck was attempting to isolate Bright in a manner that left himself as a conciliator of Radical aspiration and Conservative discomfort. Certainly, by January 1859, Roebuck was 'talk[ing] in disapproval of [Bright's] movement'.[121]

At the end of December 1858, Bright requested a meeting with Russell, which Russell arranged for 4 January 1859.[122] After a 'very long' interview Russell admitted that he was 'pleased with [Bright's] confidence', but supposed that Bright was not 'equally pleased with [his] refusal of all partnership in [Bright's] proceedings'. Although the reform scheme Bright had produced at the meeting had been 'a very large one, but not a very extreme one [Russell] could not help telling [Bright] that if he had brought out his plan without its supposed levelling effects he would not have created a quarter of the alarm he [had] done by his speeches'.[123] Russell was certain that association with Bright 'would destroy all [his] influence with what Ellice call[ed] the sane part of the community'. He retained a wish not to act until the government had announced their measure which, he was confident, would not 'be one the Whigs ought to support'.[124]

Russell's view that Bright had 'made his bed and [would] be obliged to lie in it' pleased Clarendon and Cornewall Lewis, who noted that Russell was equally insistent that 'Derby [could not] be trusted with a reform bill'.[125] Russell's rejection of Bright's overtures not only saved him from a dangerous association, but also, Cornewall Lewis celebrated, would be 'a great mortification to [Bright's] inordinate vanity, and a great tumbledown to a man who consider[ed] himself censor of all politicians'.[126] However 'confident [Bright might] be in his language, there [was] no doubt that he [was] disappointed as to the result of his campaign, and [was] conscious of his failure. He expected to be able to dictate terms to others – but he [was] now reduced to beg assistance from Lord John, and so negotiate with the vile Whigs.' Yet Russell's exact intentions still caused Cornewall Lewis and Clarendon disquiet. 'Lord John seem[ed] to be in a state of feverish excitement scarcely knowing "à quel saint se vouer".'[127] He abused Derby, Malmesbury and Disraeli; ' "ergo", the government must go out – "ergo" he must come in'. 'But', warned Clarendon, 'between John's lip and cup . . . many a thing may happen.'

Through private correspondence Russell sought to rally those who might support a 'Russellite' solution to reform. During Christmas 1858 Russell wrote 'a feeler' to Grey denouncing Bright's oratory. Grey, 'little disposed' to 'become again one of [Russell's] political followers', condoned Bright's speeches as doing 'more good than harm by alarming people about a democratic reform act'.[128] In the attempt to assuage Clarendon's fears Russell discounted the threat from Bright and pointed to the existence of 'a good set of Whigs and some good Tory country gentlemen in the House of Commons'.[129] At the same time Russell informed Graham of his desire to act in concert with Herbert, Cornewall Lewis and himself.[130] Arguing for the revival of his own 1854 bill, Russell warned Graham that if Derby's bill stood for a second reading, 'and there [was] no alternative but Bright's, shabby people [would] vote for Derby, as their only refuge from the Radicals'.[131] Graham accepted the 1854 bill as the basis for a settlement, but urged Russell not to act 'prematurely'. When they came to 'the critical moment', Graham assured Russell, 'no one [had] knowledge and experience on [the] subject equal to [Russell's], and [he was] the natural leader'.[132]

Russell also cultivated Argyll's desire for a settlement and elicited a commitment to the bill of 1854 as 'a substantial, just and liberal measure'.[133] Such a scheme provided an alternative to a government bill which, Argyll feared, would be what 'the Yankees call[ed] a "Dunkum measure" ' with 'plenty of cork in it'. On 25 January 1859 the former Attorney-General, Sir Richard Bethell, held a dinner attended by Liberals and Whigs, at which 'he spoke like a true Christian and prescribed good will and union among Reformers'.[134] The mood of the meeting Bethell then reported to Russell.[135] Russell, Bedford observed, was 'fully healthy and must take an important part in the coming session. On the reform question he [would] be looked to and turned to as the greatest authority on that subject'.[136]

By the end of 1858 Palmerston appeared a spent political force. Since the withdrawal of Cardwell's motion in May 1858 it 'appear[ed] more and more evident that Palmerston's political career [was] drawing to a close, and he alone seem[ed] blind to the signs that denoted it'.[137] By October 1858 Russell felt sufficiently confident of his position to adopt a patronising tone towards Palmerston:

> I do not want to meddle with Palmerston or his position. He has done good service to the country, and should be respected while he is quiet and leaves his friends alone.[138]

Reflecting widespread opinion, Delane, in November, advised Osborne that he might 'safely recant' his allegiance to the two 'luminaries' Palmerston and Clarendon. 'No star [shone] very bright above the horizon, but these two seem[ed] to have hopelessly set'.[139] Palmerston's demise was publicly announced by Lowe in December 1858; the observation being the more telling coming from one whose career had been closely associated with Cambridge House. Palmerston, Lowe declared, was 'no longer in power and [would] probably never return to it'.[140]

In October 1858 Palmerston was obliged to accept an unsolicited invitation to visit Louis Napoleon.[141] Anti-French feeling in England had been growing since the beginning of the year. Clarendon accompanied Palmerston to Compiègne in November, and a flood of criticism followed.[142] The visit weakened an already weak political position. After his return to London, Palmerston assumed a prudent obscurity. He advised Clarendon that, with regard to reform, they 'ought to lie still'. Any 'attempt to come to an understanding with John Russell or anybody else, would answer no good purpose'.[143] The inevitability of disagreement over specific details of reform suggested that '[b]y far the best way [was] to wait and see what the government bill [might] be, and then deal with it according to its merits'; a passive role further recommended by a basic distrust of Russell's intentions. 'John Russell on the one hand and the Radicals on the other, [were] too dogmatical and pertinacious in their separate views to concede anything to those who [were] not disposed to go to their lengths', and Palmerston was decided he would not 'tie [him]self as a kettle to the tail of either of those sections'.[144] He suspected that Russell wanted 'to add a million to the existing voters' which 'would do very much to swamp property and intelligence'.[145] The 'introduction of such a mass of ignorance and poverty [would] tend to alter that constitution in which [Russell] want[ed] to give them an interest, and alter it, not for the better, but for the worse'.[146] Believing that no 'stable government' was possible 'until either the Radicals [had] beat down all other parties, or until all other parties [had] waited to beat down the

Radicals', Palmerston anticipated 'a union between the better part of the Whigs and the conservative section of the Tories'.[147]

III

Anglo–French relations and Italy saved politicians from an exclusive preoccupation with reform during the recess. But in contrast to the complexity and subtle speculation involved in framing a new system of representation, the question of Italy elicited widespread agreement. The dissent of Lord John Russell, Gladstone and, in some company, Palmerston, sprang from differences of emphasis and political prospects rather than ideology. Three powerful factors influenced the thinking of both Conservatives and Liberals, and shaped common thinking on the Italian question in the winter of 1858–59.[148] First, a deep suspicion of Louis Napoleon. This was expressed at governmental levels in diplomatic misgivings and fear of a hostile Franco–Russian alliance, and at a popular level in increasing fear of an invasion threat. Secondly, a concern for the balance of power in Europe should Austria suffer humiliating defeats. Thirdly, a deep rooted anti-Catholicism that saw in papal temporal sovereignty a glaring example of illiberal political corruption embodied in Pope Pius IX. The response to Austrian control of Lombardy and Venetia, and the Piedmontese desire to annex these provinces, was shaped by these concerns into consensus. Sympathy for liberal Italian nationalism existed. But if it entailed Napoleonic aggrandisement, Austrian humiliation, and had wider consequences far beyond desirable local reforms, without striking at the real root of repression in the Papal States and the Kingdom of the Two Sicilies, then it was the wrong time and the wrong situation in which to excite nationalist feelings. A strong wish for non-intervention prevailed.

After Louis Napoleon's meeting with Count Cavour, prime minister of Piedmont, at Plombières, on 21 July 1858, it became obvious that Napoleon was intending to aggravate a war against Austria on behalf of the Kingdom of Piedmont–Sardinia and Italian 'liberty'; a belief confirmed by French military preparations and Piedmontese diplomatic activity. France came to be seen as 'the wanton disturber of the peace of Europe'.[149] 'Many little circumstances mark[ed] the probability of serious disturbance in Italy . . . Piedmont', it seemed 'only await[ed] the signal from France to commence the fray.'[150] Cornewall Lewis, voicing common opinion, disliked the prospect of

England 'joining the march in a war against Austria for ceeding Lombardy to Sardinia'.[151] Austria, he recalled, '[had] behaved very well to [England] in the winter of 1854', while France continued to be 'a perpetual source of disquietude . . . with her enormous army and her unprincipled gambling government'.

Aberdeen, with personal memories of an earlier Napoleonic conflict, observed that he had 'always anticipated as much evil as good from the French alliance'.[152] An attack on Austrian provinces in Northern Italy by France and Piedmont would 'be so manifestly in the wrong' and 'the whole war [would] be so perfectly gratuitous on their part', that Britain would be forced to adopt a 'neutral or hostile' role.[153] The 'best' that could be hoped for, Aberdeen opined, was 'an avowed neutrality' on the part of England 'at the commencement; with the certainty that ambition, injustice, and the perfidy of the parties engaged [would] soon become apparent'.[154] Graham admitted that he was 'never sure of anything where France [was] concerned' and was 'by no means certain Louis Napoleon [would] not encourage Piedmont "to eat the Artichoke"'.[155] Newcastle concurred in the hope that the government's policy would be 'to keep out of the Italian mess' for as long as possible.[156]

Cornewall Lewis, Aberdeen, Graham and Newcastle were not unsympathetic to the cry for Italian independence. All saw in Piedmont a liberal and anti-clerical foundation for Italian unity that, in time, might rescue the peninsula from foreign domination. But scepticism about Napoleon's true motives, and a belief that a strong Austria was vital to European equilibrium, contained Italian sympathies. Lord Minto 'trembl[ed]' for the young liberties of Piedmont in any partnership with Napoleon and [did] not see much Italy [could] gain by the substitution of French for Austrian dominance'.[157] Although he regretted 'to see our "soi-disant" French alliance replaced by hostile feeling', like Aberdeen, Minto had 'long thought this inevitable while L.N. ape[d] the ambition of his uncle'. As former Liberal Foreign Secretary, Clarendon also saw 'a real danger to Piedmont' in ostensible French sympathy and assistance.[158] '[I]f a French army once gets there to assist [Piedmont] in Italy L. Napoleon will soon put in a claim to interfere with her form of government and request the suspension of such liberties as do not harmonise with those enjoyed by the French people.' Clarendon entirely agreed with Minto's opinion that 'Italy would not gain by the substitution of French for Austrian dominion', and despite the Emperor's adoption of a pacific pose 'there [was] no change in his intention and he [meant] to have a war'. Cornewall Lewis declared that his 'sympathies are all with the Italians against their foreign masters, but Naples or Rome are worse governed than Lombardy – and if Italy has to be governed by either the Austrians or by Louis Napoleon, I prefer the Austrians as having a better spirit, and being less tyrannical'.[159] Graham impressed his distrust of Napoleon upon Russell. Graham could understand 'the ambition of Piedmont', and the desire 'to eat the artichoke leaf by leaf; but a battle for *Liberty*, under the banner of Louis Napoleon, pass[ed] [his] comprehension'. 'For who loves *that* must first be wise and good, and tho' [Louis Napoleon] is *wise* as a serpent, he is not harmless as a Dove.'[160]

In the Clubs, Villiers found that 'the feeling against war, or great disturbance abroad . . . appear[ed] to be universal',[161] while 'the people in the City [were] decidedly against meddling in all this rascally French–Italian concern, and indeed to keep entirely and rigidly aloof'.[162] *The Times* leaders, still occasionally written by Lowe, declared the accepted axioms of educated opinion.

> The Liberal party in Europe has no good will to Austria . . . But the notion of letting loose the bands of another French Empire and the Old Monarchies of Europe . . . all in the name of Liberty was too much for the consciences of Europe.[163]

Urging England to 'stand aloof from this desperate iniquity', *The Times* described Napoleon's complaints against Austria as 'pretexts . . . not motives'.[164] The 'French Ruler [had] achieved the wonderful task of turning nine-tenths of the English Liberals into sympathisers with the Power which was their favourite object of denunciation'.[165]

In contrast to commonplace cynicism about Louis Napoleon, Russell 'doubt[ed] the Emperor's steadiness about Italy' and observed that any 'movement [would] diminish the power of the priests'.[166] In 1855 Russell had pricked Liberal consciences and embarrassed Palmerston's cabinet by bringing forward the question of the Papal States. In Piedmont, Russell identified a force for liberal constitutionalism and reform, an antidote to Papal servility and a bastion against foreign despotism, in particular Austria. In January 1859 Russell retained his belief that 'Italy [would] never rest again till it [had] independence'.[167] Furthermore, his association with the cause of Italian unity led Russell to feel the need to distinguish his own position from that of his colleagues. Although Russell agreed with Aberdeen's wish that 'if there [was] a war with Austria and France

[they] ought not to interfere, but reserve [their] interposition to a later period in the struggle', Russell believed Aberdeen's 'sympathies [were] with the Austrians' while his own were 'with the Italians'.[168] Russell felt that 'the Emperor [had] indeed made a mess of it. Instead of exhibiting himself as the breaker of peace, he ought to have waited until the state of Italy called for, and justified his interference.'[169] As it was, Russell found Louis Napoleon to be 'like a tailless rocket; you [could not] tell which way he [would] throw his destructive force'. In the face of an almost universal distrust of Napoleon and wish for non-intervention, Russell regretted that the Italian question had 'present[ed] itself in the worst way possible'.[170] An 'aggression on Austria, in her own dominions, prompted by the ambition of the House of Savoy, aided by the ambition of the House of Bonaparte would be very ill looked upon by Europe'. There was 'no excuse for attempting by force of arms to alter the provisions of a treaty, nor [could] anyone believe that a fierce love of liberty animate[d] the Emperor'.[171]

Regretting that they differed as much as they did, Russell sought to reassure Clarendon of his aims: that England, France and Russia 'should come to an understanding' whereby Austria gave up Milan, Venice, Bologna, while keeping Verona, and possibly Mantua.[172] This would prevent Austria losing her frontier fortresses. If these were taken 'the Tyrol and Vienna would be open'; Austria's 'only resource would be to go to war to maintain her[self] as a great power in Europe' and, as a result, 'France and Russia would divide the east'. But if 'Austria [would] not go back unless forced she [would] be left to fight it out as best she [could] – her villainy about Venice would make it just that she should lose all she received as stolen goods'.[173] Russell wished England 'to propose a good plan – formally and officially – aggrandising Sardinia, Tuscany and Naples – and leaving Rome with a garrison (Swiss if you like) to the Pope'. If such a plan was rejected then England should 'decline to use force and leave fools to their folly'. The 'best chance for peace', Russell believed, was 'the strong distaste for war in France, and the readiness to meet it in Austria'.[174] Russell's wish for a diplomatic safeguarding of Italian independence, however, was countered by Clarendon's suspicion of Louis Napoleon. Noting Russell's own admission that 'Napoleon and Cavour [were] playing with foils for Lombardy's Crown' and 'both wait[ing] for a revolt in Italy', Clarendon observed that 'the Emperor seem[ed] disposed to pick a quarrel with Austria'.[175] Thus the laudable aim of Italian liberty became merely an expedient vehicle for Napoleon's ambition.

Graham disliked Russell's tone on the Italian question, while Aberdeen deemed it 'hardly creditable that [Russell] should look with complacency towards a French invasion of Italy, in order to promote the unprincipled ambition of Sardinia'.[176] It was with relief that Aberdeen noted that Clarendon would 'certainly not be inclined to join Lord John in a Cavour crusade'. Indeed, Clarendon found Russell's 'ends [were] desirable enough, but his means of arriving at them [were] wild and impractical'.[177] Such antipathy forced Russell to defer what, in differing circumstances, might have been an opportunity to embark upon a crusade for Italian unification. Instead, Russell accepted the necessity 'to be quiet' and avoid involvement in 'a European war'.[178] He acknowledged that Britain had 'only to look on, and wish the Italians saved both from their enemies and their friends'.[179] To an anxious Whig, Lord Melgund (his brother-in-law), Russell admitted that he would 'be very glad if the Italians obtain[ed] their independence, but [he was] not disposed to lay out an English shilling to obtain that object'. They had, Russell reassured Melgund, 'fish enough of [their] own not yet fried'.[180] It was with 'great relief' that Cornewall Lewis was given to understand that Russell did not want England 'to fight for Louis Napoleon and *liberty*'.[181] Decided that he would not 'wring his hands and cry Peace, Peace', Russell was left to lament that the question had not been 'taken up by the handle – namely foreign occupation in the Roman states'.[182]

Palmerston shared the wish 'to see the Austrians out of Italy', but he did not wish 'to see Austria crippled as a German power'.[183] Avowing himself to be 'very Austrian north of the Alps, but anti-Austrian south of the Alps', Palmerston noted that 'in politics as in other matters, it [was] not enough to show a desirable end, one must also be able to point out means of arriving at it, the objectionable nature of which [could] not counter balance the advantages of the result to be accomplished'.[184] A war initiated by France and Piedmont to drive Austria out of Italy would 'infallibly succeed in its immediate object', but it 'might and probably would lead to other consequences much to be deplored'. It was 'for the interests of Europe that Austria should continue to be a great power in the centre of the Continent'. Palmerston agreed with Granville that if war were to break out 'the only course for England [was] neutrality'. Although he 'should heartily rejoice to see Italy relieved from the iron rule of Austrian dominion and influence' Palmerston admitted that he 'would not take upon himself the responsibility of advising or contributing in any way to bring about war which when once begun might extend beyond its intended range'.[185]

The political significance of the Italian question lay in its potential, dependent upon the development of events, to suggest new configurations within Westminster. As Russell recognised, the manner in which the issue had arisen dictated only one immediate policy: an armed neutrality holding England aloof from any European embroilment. Given the personal association with the question of certain prominent personalities, however, changing circumstances might suggest differing policies and an opportunity for distinction. Villiers observed that either Russell or Palmerston might bring forward the Italian question as a means 'of turning out the present government and giving the public something rational to think about instead of muddling themselves about internal reform'.[186] It became Bright's immediate concern that Italy might 'cast [reform] in the shade'.[187] Ellice saw the opportunity to 'threat[en] . . . the revival of the Palmerston ministry in the event of a European war'.[188] But Graham, echoing prevalent opinion, agreed 'in "Fudge" as the right answer to Palmerston's divine mission as the minister of England in the event of war'.[189]

9 Cabinet Craft and Reform

The opposition now found all their hopes on the dissensions which they expect to arise in the Tory government and camp, which is a very uncertain prospect. . . . [Disraeli] gave me to understand that he was well aware the opposition relied on this contingency, but that it was not likely to happen. (Greville Diary, 5 September 1858, Greville Mss. 41123, cited in C. C. F. Greville, *The Greville Memoirs*, H. Reeve (ed.) (London 1888) VIII, p. 210)

It is possible to consider Whig and Liberal attitudes towards reform, during the 1858–59 recess, in isolation from government plans. Not that ministerial intention had little relevance for opposition thinking; quite the contrary. But rather the cabinet's scheme remained quite unknown to those outside it. Indeed, as testament to Derby's skill, it remained obscure even to some within the cabinet. As Cornewall Lewis mused, in formulating their own thoughts the opposition were forced to discuss 'what ought to be done about an unknown bill, producing an unknown effect upon public opinion and parties in the House'.[1] Whig and Liberal ignorance was the intended effect of ministerial silence. Even when the Conservative Lyndhurst met Derby in November 1858, he found the premier 'spoke a good while but said as little'.[2] In October Derby had reminded Disraeli of the merits of ministerial evasiveness. 'Nothing has so disconcerted our opponents, especially of the peers, as the silence we have kept as to all our intended measures.'[3]

What members of the cabinet did disclose was that the government measure would be an adequate and satisfactory response to the issue of parliamentary reform. While staying at Hatfield, Clarendon learnt from Derby, who 'was in great spirits and endlessly making jokes', that the government bill would 'not be a sham otherwise [they should] create an angry feeling and an extensive demand'.[4] At the same gathering Hardwicke informed Clarendon that 'in his opinion no government would be justified in bringing in a bill which would not settle the question for many years to come'. Such sentiment, Clarendon observed, 'showed progress in a man who a year ago was the Toriest of all living Tories'.[5] Such comment, given to one who it was known would relay hearsay to Cambridge House, served its own

177

political purpose. The details, extent and basis of any measure, however, remained obscure. The 'only *fact*' that Parkes noticed during the recess was a speech by Henley which merely 'committ[ed] his colleagues to a measure', intended 'to influence the stiffer Tories out of doors'.[6]

Palmerston inferred from Clarendon's report of 'Derby's language about reform that their bill will be a moderate one, though as Dizzy will have a hand in it, it is pretty sure to have some absurd provisions'.[7] Even the 'ultra-Tories', Clarendon noted, 'seem[ed] determined to give the government a generous confidence which means eating the same dirt as them'.[8] Therefore, Clarendon predicted, if the cabinet produced 'a measure that is at all decent I have little doubt that they will carry the 2nd reading'.[9] What Clarendon feared was a Tory bill which would contain 'some radical measure' accepted by 'Whigs and moderate Liberals' from trepidation of 'the measure which Bright [would] try to cram down their throats'.[10] This fear was exacerbated by a belief that 'Henley and others have told Derby that his principles and position inspire them into such confidence that they will agree to any bill that he sanctions, but Dizzy is the real master of the cabinet and he means to be popular'.[11]

Cornewall Lewis expected the government to reduce the county franchise to £20, with an aggregation of towns to old boroughs, ostensibly to balance constituencies, but in reality to appease the fears of their county members. He also admitted that he would not be surprised 'if they reduced the borough even more, in proportion, than the county franchise', while resorting to 'the method of contributory boroughs, for the purpose of saving their smaller seats'. However, the government would 'be tender about disfranchisement'.[12] This expectation was apparently confirmed by Lord Henry Lennox's uninformed conjecture that 'the reform bill would be a Liberal one and brought in at an early stage'.[13] Russell saw in Palmerston's expectation of a moderate measure, Palmerston's readiness to support the government. Russell saw fit to warn that 'a measure too small in extending the franchise would only whet the appetite and prepare the way for a larger enfranchisement'.[14]

I

Discussion of parliamentary reform within the Conservative cabinet revealed Derby's unobtrusive mastery, Disraeli's reliance on Derby's authority, and the differing opinion that found in Derby an acceptable arbiter of differences. At the beginning of August 1858, Derby decided to appoint a cabinet committee to consider the question of reform.[15] Disraeli, who had already left London for Hughenden, had been unaware that the premier's thoughts were 'so advanced' on the question and found consideration of the issue initiated without his preparing others for his views.[16] Meanwhile Phillip Rose, as unofficial party agent, came away from his first interview with Derby on reform in August 'quite convinced that no one ought to venture to talk to Lord Derby who does not thoroughly understand his subject'.[17] Derby's thinking on the issue, meanwhile, revealed that the lessons of June had been learnt well. The equalisation of the county and borough franchise would match avowed and unified Whig, Liberal and Radical opinion. The ballot, in splitting that opinion, revealed the limits of the demand for liberal reform. These thoughts stayed with Derby throughout the recess. Derby's perception of the measure became apparent in his appointments to the cabinet committee: Salisbury, Pakington, Stanley, Disraeli, Manners, Jolliffe and himself.[18] Those members of the cabinet not appointed – Walpole, Henley, Hardwicke, Chelmsford and Peel – represented that recalcitrant body of opinion most strongly opposed to extensive reform. Malmesbury was excluded because of pressure of work. Thus the character of the committee Derby selected pointed to the character of the measure to be framed. It revealed that Derby was no less anxious than Disraeli to propose a moderate rejoinder to accusations of sham, and demonstrated that Derby could more efficiently give effect to his wishes.

At the beginning of August 1858, Stanley also began to prepare the ground using suggestions mooted by Philip Rose. Rose, Disraeli's solicitor, had since 1853 acted as 'a confidential medium' between the constituency organisations and the Westminster leadership, in particular Jolliffe.[19] Rose largely supervised Spofforth as 'the ostensible agent of the party'.[20] In June 1858 Rose prepared a memorandum on the subject of the ballot, urging that 'no reform bill, however comprehensive, [would] satisfy a large section of the Liberal party unless some attempt [was] also made to deal with the ballot question'.[21] Although there was no 'real demand for the ballot' many Liberal members had adopted it as 'a cardinal point in their creed' and were, 'for consistency sake . . . compelled to aye it, and it serv[ed] as a standing grievance to which they [could] resort'. In response Rose believed that the adoption of 'a mixed system, partly of open voting, partly of ballot' – although difficult – was not insuperable. Moreover, if the ballot was tested in constituencies where a desire was expressed to adopt it, the effect 'would probably be that the experiment would be tried in a few places, and would signally fail, disappointing none so much as its most earnest advocates'. Thus it would 'continue as an experiment . . . and would not become part of a permanent system'.

Stanley expressed to Disraeli entire agreement with the substance of Rose's memorandum, believed Pakington would 'easily come round', wished 'to sound Lytton, who [was] prepared to concur', and suggested Disraeli 'influence John Manners'.[22] If the government gave up a reform bill altogether, but introduced 'an optional ballot', Stanley continued, 'the party of reform would be better satisfied than with a large measure of reform that left the manner of voting on its present footing'. No less importantly, Stanley believed the 'difference between what Rose suggest[ed] and that which Lord D. express[ed] himself ready to assent to, [was] so small that [he could] not conceive serious difficulty arising in that quarter'.

During August 1858, while defining a personal position on the reform question and cultivating relations with Russell, Stanley also came to share Russell's scepticism about the ability of the cabinet to agree on a reform scheme. As the 'most delicate' of all the questions facing the government, the longer that Stanley considered reform 'the greater . . . appear[ed] the difficulty of meeting parliament with a practical scheme on which the whole cabinet [would] agree'.[23] Thus ostensibly innocent conversation at Knowsley and Woburn became imbued with serious political purpose. As a symptom of the resilience of established connection, however, Stanley also noted that the premier spoke 'in terms of warm praise of Rose which [was] a good sign'.[24]

Derby retained 'good hopes' of a Conservative reform bill and communicated an optimistic tone to Disraeli.[25] Derby also communicated a considerable flexibility on the question of a new franchise, being prepared to adopt an £8 rating suffrage in the boroughs. This did not go as far as Rose's wish for a £6 rating franchise, but was a considerable concession to 'progressive' opinion within the cabinet. What Derby considered to be a necessary 'keystone of the whole', however, was a proposal 'making freeholders in boroughs voters for the boroughs and not for the counties as at present'.[26] Derby reiterated Tory fears of the swamping of the agricultural constituencies by a mass of miscellaneous urban freeholders. To prevent further dilution of the agricultural interest in the counties, especially in industrial areas, was for Derby a more crucial aim than restriction of the franchise. Around this vital issue Derby was prepared to accommodate the franchise; the territorial character of the enfranchised electorate remaining of the paramount importance. This was the Conservative version of Cobden's gospel that the distribution of voters, rather than their number, mattered most.

Disraeli, in response to Derby's initiative and as a result of his own unpreparedness, also adopted a pragmatic line over the franchise; the definition of a new borough franchise being dependent on 'the general character of [their] measure'.[27] If the £10 franchise were retained in the boroughs and the franchise extended in the counties, Disraeli argued that there would be 'a strong case in favour ... of confining borough freeholders to borough voting. Indeed, this [would] be the only mode by which even a tolerable balance could be maintained between the county and borough constituencies.' Although a £6 rating suffrage might be a 'safe' proposal, he believed 'the wisest measure ... would be to retain the £10, because in that case [they] would have the £10 interest on [their] side, while an £8 rating would not enlist many supporters, or any fervent support, while the 10 pounders would join the 5 and 6 pounders in opposition to [the] project'. Disraeli believed that if the proposal to make county freeholders residing in boroughs part of the borough constituency was to be the 'keystone' of their scheme, a uniform £10 franchise was the 'wisest' course.

At the beginning of September 1858, Walpole became alarmed that the government was preparing 'for *Radical* reform'.[28] Walpole's alarm, however, demonstrated the convenience to Derby of distrust of Disraeli. Walpole felt compelled to warn Derby that Disraeli was in favour of assimilating the county and borough franchise to £10, which, he felt, would be 'a fatal step'.[29] The objective irony of Walpole's alarm was, in political terms, an important aspect of Derby's authority. Men such as Walpole found it easier to believe in Disraeli's lack of principle than in Derby's apostasy.

Walpole's response to Disraeli's putative radicalism, moreover, revealed the conservative intent that might lie behind apparently extensive proposals. The assimilation of the borough and county franchise, Walpole claimed, would not provide 'an intelligible principle' for reform, and would not offer 'a fair settlement of this important question'.[30] He discerned 'two main principles which [had] hitherto marked [the] representative system in counties and boroughs, that [was] to say property in the one and occupancy in the other'. Acting on these principles Walpole suggested a county franchise 'to everyone who had the House Tax' and the borough franchise 'to tenants rated at £6 upwards', with proof of eighteen months' or two years' residence. In addition he proposed enfranchising 'all who had realised such a sum in any Public Securities as would yield an interest of £6 a year'. Such a plan, Walpole argued would offer 'an intelligible principle' to safeguard permanency. Its conservative purpose lay in its permanence becoming an obstacle to household suffrage. If Disraeli's scheme was followed, Walpole warned, 'Lord John would immediately bid for a £6 rating. Palmerston would be satisfied with £8: the Radicals would still demand household suffrage'.

Stanley's activity and Walpole's apprehension revealed the complex difficulties that members of the cabinet either found, or created, in the reform issue. Pakington adopted a position of politic ambiguity. To Derby, Pakington reported 'a talk with Walpole in London . . . about reform' where he was 'glad to find that [their] views were very similar – in principle quite so'.[31] To Disraeli, Pakington admitted a suspicion that 'Ellenborough, Stanley, [Disraeli] and [himself had] little in common with the party behind [them] . . . [and] little in common with Derby, Walpole, John Manners and Henley. Lytton [he] presume[d] should be added.'[32] The discerning of motive behind such ambiguity is difficult. Until choice became necessary Pakington may have been attempting to please all. While Pakington's correspondence did little to illuminate, but much to serve his intention, all that remains certain is that his response reflected the circumstantial difficulties of a cabinet grappling with the complexities of reform.

During September and early October 1858, Derby was forced to stay at Knowsley and convalesce following an attack of gout. Disraeli endeavoured to keep 'the Knowsley gout . . . secret',[33] noting that '[n]othing disharten[ed] a party so much as an invalid chief, and [the party was] always afraid he [was] going to die and break up the ministry'.[34] By 23 October, however, Malmesbury found Derby to be once again 'in great force'.[35] Sotheron-Estcourt came away, after visiting the prime minister, fired with the determination 'to show people that [they were] in earnest; so resolved to proceed for a [reform] bill forthwith'.[36] By the end of October, Derby was preparing to return to London, assured Disraeli that he was aware of his anxiety to have 'an early cabinet on finance',[37] and declared his intention to 'set the finance and reform committee actively to work'.[38]

While Derby recovered from his gout and was reassuring his

colleagues of his determination, Stanley received from Jolliffe an invitation to stand as MP for Manchester. Sir John Potter, Liberal MP for Manchester since April 1857, was known to be dying and Jolliffe believed 'a requisition of Liberals to oppose the League which was beaten at the last election' would make Stanley's election as Conservative member 'a certainty'.[39] Jolliffe's wish to exploit Stanley's reputation and acquire a seat formerly associated with Radicalism had obvious merit. Stanley, however, looked upon 'the enterprise [as] hopeless'.[40] Derby, confirming the bias of Stanley's own mind, advised his son '*not* to stand for Manchester'.[41] On 27 October, despite knowing 'the place and the people thoroughly' and being 'alive to the importance of the issue',[42] Stanley declined Jolliffe's offer.[43] This decision, concurrent with Bright's speech at Birmingham, encouraged Conservatives such as Talbot in the belief that reform might 'divide the world into 2 parties again'.[44]

While maintaining a public silence over reform during September and October 1858, the cabinet drew Gladstone into the activities of the Colonial Office. Resting at Hawarden during the recess, involved in Homeric study and family business, Gladstone appeared 'full of animation and apparently very well'.[45] Graham observed 'a restless anxiety for a change of position. I cannot wonder at his hankering for power at his age and with his abilities.'[46] Journalistic attacks on Britain's policy of supporting the Ottoman Empire, however, threatened to elevate passionate anti-Palmerstonianism into complete ostracism. On the question of reform, Gladstone hoped for a Conservative settlement and disclosed a preference for 'a very short affair of only a few clauses and limited enfranchisement'.[47] In correspondence with Brougham, Gladstone accepted the 'principal propositions that we must have a considerable admission of artisans to the franchise, that we must maintain the distinct character of county and borough representation, and that we should try to have a new franchise in favour of knowledge and station'.[48] The fulfilment of these limited propositions Gladstone had reason to expect from a Conservative government.

In September 1858, with Disraeli's approval, Lytton offered Gladstone the charge of a mission to negotiate a new constitutional settlement for the Ionian Islands.[49] Graham advised Gladstone to decline the offer.[50] Aberdeen declared that 'the only part of the affair [he] should regard with real pleasure would be the means it might afford [Gladstone] of drawing closer to the government, and of naturally establishing [him]self in a more suitable position'.[51] After consideration of the offer, during October, Gladstone perceived his 'Lilliputian die [was] cast'[52] and accepted Lytton's commission. Graham believed that the truth was that:

> [Gladstone] longs to establish more intimate relations with the government. ... But the occasion ought to be worthy of the measure. Reform is most likely to afford some such opportunity and I wish for his sake that he had waited for it.[53]

Subsequently Graham came to understand that 'Gladstone's acceptance ... [was] regarded by the ministers as an open act of adhesion'.[54] Cardwell observed 'that all [Gladstone's] leanings are towards the government and that this is regarded by him as an approximation ... [O]bviously Gladstone is tending rapidly towards a more decided connection with the Conservative party'.[55] Certainly Heathcote, from the Conservative backbenches, understood the mission as the promise of Gladstone's future entry into Derby's cabinet.[56] Graham despondently noted that it was 'no longer a question of how to dispose of Disraeli, but how to bring Gladstone back into the front of the battle'.[57] Russell thought Gladstone's mission 'a curious one' and perhaps the pretext 'to be absent from discussion on reform'.[58]

Gladstone was abroad from November 1858 to March 1859 and while staying on Corfu the complex diplomatic problems of any Ionian settlement diverted his energies and further compromised his reputation at home. Moreover, distanced from Westminster, Gladstone failed to translate his heightened anti-Crimean rhetoric into any proposals for the cession of the Ionian Islands to Greece. Once no longer directly anti-Palmerstonian such language could only be an embarrassment to Conservative policy. The government, Hayward noted, 'pride[d] themselves on having made a prize of Gladstone'.[59] Although, Graham predicted, Gladstone 'fancies that he is not hooked ... if he breaks the line Dizzy's harpoon will be in him'.[60] By December 1858, as further diplomatic difficulties were reported to London, Graham concluded that the 'Ionian mission [was] a sad mess'.[61]

In a cabinet meeting on 3 November 1858, the first since September, Derby appeared to be 'in great spirits'.[62] The cabinet committee on reform carried out its deliberations during November. Backbench unease was soothed by the assurance that it was 'a favourable moment for settling that question for this generation, and Bright's violence and his promised bill [would] probably assist [them] to carry a less sweeping measure'.[63] Walpole, however, found such assurance inadequate. Retaining a loyal belief that Derby might become the unsuspecting victim of Disraelian treachery, Walpole reminded the premier of 'the great good-sense' in the statement that 'Conservatives should have a conservative measure'.[64] Afraid that Derby might 'be beaten in [his] own committee' and forced to propose a more extensive measure than he wished, Walpole suggested that Derby leave 'the committee to collect facts and work out details, but . . . reserve principles for the whole cabinet: and that only'. In truth, the discussion of principles in cabinet was precisely what Derby was trying to avoid.

On 21 November, Derby drew up a draft report of the cabinet committee on reform with propositions which, despite 'individual differences', had 'the sanction of a large majority'.[65] In the first instance it was decided that the bill should be concerned solely with England and Wales. It was accepted that it might 'become necessary to consider Scotland', but it was 'not thought desirable' to disturb the scheme relating to Ireland. It was also decided that, although the subject divided itself into the two distinct branches of franchise and distribution, both would be dealt with in one bill; disfranchisement to precede enfranchisement. The committee decided to retain the existing borough franchise, but 'a majority [were] in favour of a £10 rated franchise' for the counties. Pakington had dissented from the majority decision on the borough franchise and Stanley had made his assent conditional.[66] As a concession a 'Lodger Franchise' based on £20 and a year's residence was recommended which 'in the towns especially', would 'introduce a very large and in many respects, a very respectable class'.[67] On his central concern, ensuring that freeholders residing within the limits of a borough voted in the borough, Derby gained a majority, although once again Pakington dissented.[68] With regard to redistribution, although repudiating any attempt at absolute equality, the committee adopted population, as indicated by the 1851 census, as their basis for removing the worst anomalies. They agreed to totally defranchise those 'very limited number of boroughs' having a population less than 5000, thus gaining sixteen seats and to partially disfranchise those boroughs with a population less than 15 000 but above 5000; 'making, in all, 73 seats disposable for redistribution'.[69] No new constituencies were to be created, with the exception of the West Riding and South Lancashire, but every county constituency with a population above 100 000 was to have three members, and where it exceeded 50 000, two, thus creating forty-eight additional county seats. The same principle applied to boroughs disposed of a

further eighteen seats, while those left might be granted to the
University of London or the Inns of Court. Finally, it was agreed to
disfranchise the dockyards, to recommend the use of polling papers
for postal votes and to resist the ballot 'in any shape'.

The scheme that the committee described was very much the
measure Derby anticipated. It established the restrictions of borough
freehold votes within the borough and, despite 'every variety of
opinion' within the committee regarding the franchise, 'a very general, if not unanimous', assent was given to 'the principle laid down in
the Reform Act establishing a broad and total separation between the
constituencies of the boroughs and the counties'.[70] The report also
adopted the suffrage annually proposed by Locke King and, on
several occasions, supported by a Liberal majority. By incorporating
Locke King's motion into their own scheme the government showed
themselves to be more liberal than Palmerston and worthy of independent Liberal support. At the same time those proposals that
Stanley held dear fared badly: the borough franchise was not reduced
and the ballot was rejected outright. Furthermore, the redistribution
scheme, accompanied by the clause relating to the freehold vote, was
one designed to allay Conservative backbench fears.

If the result of the proceedings of the reform committee realised
Derby's expectation, his wish to minimise cabinet dissension by
discussing principles outside the cabinet immediately proved illusory.
The committee report even failed to secure the commitment of
members of the committee. On 23 November, Pakington informed
Derby of his wish to prepare an identity of franchise between counties
and boroughs 'at £8 *rated* value, rather than the *nominal* identity at
£10'.[71] The reasons for doing so, he believed, were fourfold. First, he
anticipated that the Commons would not accept 'a compromise which
[left] the borough franchise untouched'; secondly, if identity was to
be proposed it should be 'real and complete', and not only identity in
sound; also as regarded the counties, he feared £8 no less than £10,
feeling 'both [were] too low'. Finally, such a proposal would be the
government's own 'and not mere adoption of the long-disputed
motion of Locke King'. Pakington also informed Disraeli of his views
and disclosed that both Stanley and Salisbury agreed with him.[72]
After corresponding with Derby and Disraeli, Pakington then 'had a
conference' with Walpole, at which it was decided that a cabinet
should be held, any measure on reform should 'be resisted as inop-
portune', and legislative energies concentrated on the indemnity bill
and India.[73] Pakington was attempting to prevent Derby presenting

the committee report as an authoritative statement, at once pre-empting full cabinet discussion and obliging compromise.

Jolliffe expressed to Disraeli some dissension from the report.[74] Confessing that he had been unprepared to discuss in committee the propriety of omitting Ireland or Scotland from the scheme, Jolliffe admitted a wish that a 'measure for the three Kingdoms should be proposed, or all would be included in one bill'. He believed that 'a reform bill for England render[ed] a simultaneous one for Scotland the most expedient and safe course'. Also his preference for 'a low rating qualification identical in boroughs and counties, though not wholly adopted by the committee, remain[ed] entirely unchanged'; the government might 'go with safety as low as to an £8 rated franchise'. Finally, Jolliffe regretted that the committee had not gone further in the disfranchisement of 'inconsiderable places' having only one member. Jolliffe's dissatisfaction was expressed in less disruptive a manner than Pakington's. Nonetheless it highlighted the vulnerability of the report as a pre-arranged basis for cabinet unanimity, even though it was framed 'with the greatest care and deliberation upon full information'.[75]

The committee report was presented to the full cabinet on 2 December 1858 and Derby found it 'difficult to exaggerate either the difficulty or importance' of the question as 'many differences of opinion' became obvious.[76] Some immediate concessions were made. Derby found 'it necessary to postpone any absolute determination as to recommending the total disfranchisement of any existing boroughs' and wrote to known malcontents, such as Lord Redesdale, requesting information of 'the actual results which in [their] neighbourhood would be produced by the substitution of a £30, £20, or £10 [county] franchise'.[77] Division in cabinet opinion appeared. Walpole warned Derby 'that the more [he] reflect[ed] on the subject the less [he] like[d] the plan of the committee'.[78] Gathorne Hardy's incisive observation that the cabinet needed 'skill and courage' in dealing with the reform question or else the government would 'break up'[79] complemented Malmesbury's pessimistic observation, early in December, that he had 'little expectation of the government producing a measure that [would] satisfy either themselves or the public'.[80]

Derby's difficulties, during December 1858, were unexpectedly aggravated by Lytton's sudden announcement of his wish to immediately resign for reasons of health.[81] '[I]ndependently from the difficulty of finding a successor', Derby was fully aware that 'the effect of any change in the government in present circumstances would be most disastrous'.[82] Entreating Lytton not to resign, Derby observed that 'while credit [would] hardly be given to the real causes which [had] led to [his] preferred retirement . . . rumours of dissension in the cabinet on the eve of the meeting of parliament [would] both weaken the government in public opinion, and increase the difficulty of filling up the vacant office'.[83] Lytton's response was to stress the dangerous state of his health, accompanied by notes from his doctor, and urge the necessity for his resignation. Disraeli was sceptical that health was 'the cause of this unexpected movement', in which case it would be more difficult to persuade Lytton to remain, if this were desirable.[84] Indeed, Disraeli did not share Derby's apprehension at disturbing the cabinet. '[T]he secession of Bulwer, if in any way connected with the reform question by the world, [would] rather be an indication that the project [was] not liberal enough.' In turn this would 'tend to keep [the] party together, otherwise pleased by seeing the administration much entrusted by men of their own class'. The advantage to be accrued from such an understanding of events also influenced Derby and Disraeli's choice of a successor as Secretary for the Colonies.

Derby believed Sotheron-Estcourt to be 'the best man out of the cabinet', while Jolliffe, who was 'equal to any position', was 'invaluable in his present position'.[85] Derby also noted that Walpole, who had resorted to 'very friendly but ominous language on the subject of the franchise, and the general scheme of the committee', might be gratified by such an appointment. Disraeli suggested Henley as a politic successor whose 'want of preferment', Disraeli believed, was 'at the bottom of [his] crotchety churlishness'.[86] As Secretary of State, Disraeli predicted, Derby would 'find no difficulty with [Henley] in Cabinet', while if another were promoted 'he might probably take the occasion to resign on some principle'. Disraeli approved of Estcourt's promotion to the cabinet as an appointment that 'would greatly control Walpole, and among those country gentlemen who, in default of one of their own set in the cabinet [were] constrained to look at Walpole, who, after all, with them [was] only a lawyer'. Derby doubted Henley's readiness to accept the Colonies and did not wish to make an offer and have it declined.[87] He had no objection, however, 'to sounding Henley confidentially as to what his views would be, in the event of a vacancy occurring at the Colonial Office'. Henley could only take 'the suggestion as a compliment, and it might smooth down his bristles for a time – though one could never be secure against his snapping at one's fingers at any moment'. In anticipation of a negative reply Derby observed that 'Chandos might be the better and simpler arrangement', while, if Henley should ultimately resign, they would have 'Estcourt and Egerton to fall back on'.

Derby's comment about the danger of Henley 'snapping at one's fingers' proved peculiarly prescient. On 24 December 1858, before Derby had been able to 'sound out' the President of the Board of Trade, Henley wrote to the premier offering to resign.[88] The offer was made in anticipation of 'irreconcilable differences' upon 'important and difficult subjects'. Derby found the 'ominous communication', indicating 'rather a dogged feeling as to the details of the reform bill', a promise of 'unpleasant fruits'.[89] In reply Derby sent a plea to 'smooth differences of opinion by mutual discussion and forbearance so as to have practical unanimity of action'. Asking Henley to postpone any decision, Derby informed him of Lytton's imminent departure. This information, the premier hoped, might persuade Henley against resigning and incline him towards accepting the Colonial Office. Disraeli found Henley's 'mode of wishing [Derby] a merry Xmas . . . characteristic' and pictured 'his grim smile'.[90] On 27 December, Henley informed Derby of his decision not to resign, remaining 'content' that he had communicated his opinions to the premier.[91] Henley enclosed, however, 'a memorandum on reform as long as a Chancery brief', written by Walpole and supported by both Henley and Peel.[92] The memorandum, Derby noted, revealed that Walpole would be 'less easy to deal with than [they had] expected'.

During Christmas, Lytton continued to send his 'pathological epistles' to both Derby and Disraeli. Lytton described symptoms he listed under consumption, dropsy and paralysis.[93] Disraeli, with the scant sympathy reserved for the hypochondriac, promised Lytton that if he died before Easter he would receive a public funeral.[94] Modifying his earlier view, Disraeli acknowledged that Lytton's secession 'would enbolden the clique, which [was] drawing up "memoranda as long as Chancery briefs" and would be most mischievous'.[95] On 1 January 1859 Disraeli had 'a long interview' with Lytton convincing him to stay in the cabinet. With heavy irony Disraeli reported to Derby that Lytton agreed to sacrifice 'his life to his party'.

Derby's first concern during December was to prevent any resignation from the cabinet, for the reasons which he had impressed upon Lytton and Henley, and to reach some unanimity over the question of reform. Both these aims he came to see as a necessary condition for the continuance of the ministry. Disraeli came to dissent from both of these precepts. Lytton's secession from the cabinet he had initially judged to be the opportunity for a politic redistribution of cabinet office and only Henley's threatened resignation convinced him of the advantages of stability. Disraeli also claimed surprise that members of the cabinet were 'so fidgety' about 'a measure on which the fate of the government [did] not, in fact, depend'.⁹⁶ He predicted that if the government carried a reform bill they would become 'a powerful ministry; if, on the other hand [they were] unsuccessful, [they would] merely continue in the position [they] now fill[ed]'; a government without a majority but 'one which, on all questions, including even parliamentary reform [was] the most practicable under existing circumstances'. Disraeli also gave ready credence to the rumour that, in Whig circles, it was felt to be 'impossible that parliamentary reform could be made a party question', and that, therefore, 'the difficulties would settle themselves'.⁹⁷ Derby could only confess his belief that Disraeli 'somewhat 'underrate[d] the effect which [would] be produced by [their] failing to carry a reform bill' and pointed to the fact that 'the attempt and not the deed confound[ed them]'.⁹⁸

That which Disraeli wished to be understood as of equal importance as reform was the question of finance and his forthcoming budget; an issue that promised greater personal prominence to the Chancellor than the anonymity of collective responsibility over reform. In September 1858 Disraeli had assured Malmesbury that although 'the difficulties of the reform bill [did] not decrease . . . the revenue flourish[ed] and a popular budget [would] carry [them] thro'.⁹⁹ In October, Disraeli had urged Derby to hold 'an early cabinet on finance'.¹⁰⁰ Disraeli was encouraged 'by the state of the country which, [he] believe[d] [was] as generally prosperous as it ever was at any period of its history. Everything succeed[ed], foreign and domestic, and the Ex[cheque]r [was] overflowing.'¹⁰¹ Disraeli impressed upon Derby the need 'to have a brilliant budget, which [was] scarcely second in importance to the reform bill, and the prestige of which, [would] assist [them] in passing the latter'.¹⁰² Disraeli failed, however, to project finance, as Gladstone had in 1853, into the forefront of political concern. He failed because Derby concentrated attention on reform.

The information that Derby received from Conservatives in the counties as to the £10, £20 and £30 franchise proved 'very contradictory', and he admitted that he had 'much difficulty in making up [his] mind what [would] be the safest to propose'.¹⁰³ Rose's enquiries on the transfer of freehold votes from the counties to the boroughs, in turn, revealed 'more difference of opinion than [Derby] like[d] to see'.[104] Jolliffe retained his 'strong opinion' that the lower franchise was both safe and expedient.[105] On the question of disfranchisement, however, he did not believe it 'possible to carry disfranchisement as low as 35 seats – the discrepancies [would] still be far too great'.[106] Personally Derby favoured an extensive measure of sixty-three seats with ten total disfranchisements, but he was 'not blind to the increased opposition which the bill would have to encounter'. His correspondence also revealed a fear amongst many Conservatives that 'a £10 constituency would be a very radical affair'.[107] Walpole's 'Chancery brief' confirmed the presence of such anxiety within the cabinet.

Walpole's memorandum on reform presented the main objections to the committee report as being 'the assimilation (in amount) of the county and borough franchises, and to *any total*, or more than a very partial disfranchisement'.[108] Walpole did 'not object to the transfer of freehold votes to the boroughs, in itself: but if necessarily attended with a £10 franchise, he object[ed] to both'. Derby learnt that Henley 'would consent apparently to a considerable amount of disfranchise-ment, but object[ed] as strongly as Walpole (and Peel [was] said to do so even more) to assimilation and transfer'. At the end of December, Pakington had informed Derby that his views 'expressed in the cabinet with respect to the transfer to the boroughs of the 40/- voters within them' were unchanged, and had restated his opinion that 'making no concession whatever to the working-classes . . . [would] be considered a great defect in [their] plan'.[109] Derby feared that Henley, Walpole and Peel would be joined in their opposition to the transfer of the freehold vote by Pakington, and also Salisbury and Stanley, if the county vote were not reduced to £10.[110] Walpole, however, favoured a £20 or £16 rating franchise. Derby speculated on the practicality of taking 'an £8 rating as an alternative, but not as a substitute, for the £10 value'. But the feeling evidenced in Walpole's memorandum forced Derby to concede that they might 'not be able to go as low as £10 for the county franchise'.[111]

Divergent opinion within the cabinet had forced Derby, by the beginning of January 1859, to relinquish such political advantage as he had gained by framing a measure in a select cabinet committee. The committee report had adopted two principles as the basis for the bill: an assimilation of the borough and county franchise and the transfer of borough freehold voters to borough constituencies. Recent sessions had proved that the former principle enjoyed wide

support in the Commons that encompassed Liberal opinion. The
latter principle Derby, provided with 'overwhelming' evidence by
Rose, believed to be 'the most conservative provision in the bill'.[112]
By the beginning of January 1859 both principles had come under
attack. The groundwork for cabinet unanimity that Derby had carefully prepared in the committee report was threatened by immediate
and forceful dissent.

II

As Derby witnessed the dismantling of his framework for cabinet
unanimity over reform, the question of Italy became of concern. This
brought further definition to the shifting relations between ministers
engaged in reform and another aspect to the relationship between
government and opposition. Malmesbury's primary aim, despite
moral support for a Sardinian restoration and deep dislike for Papal
despotism, was to preserve peace in Europe.[113] He believed that if
'Cavour [went] to war he ought to be shot because no one [knew]
better than [Cavour] the consequences which [might] follow'.[114] England and France, Malmesbury continued, 'ought to prevent it and not
allow a move to disturb the peace'; an object shared by Derby who
took a continual and supervisory interest in Malmesbury's diplomacy.
In August 1858 Peel informed Derby that France was importing
quantities of saltpetre and sulphur. It became clear that Louis
Napoleon meant 'to place himself in a position to make his power to
be felt, when ever it suit[ed] him that [they] should feel it'.[115] It
became equally apparent, from diplomatic activity between France
and Piedmont, that Napoleon's 'great military preparations [had]
primary reference to Italy'.[116] Derby and Malmesbury's suspicion of
French and Piedmontese intention was confirmed by Palmerston's
communication that Cavour was, indeed, 'a slippery fellow'.[117]

Malmesbury's desire to preserve the European *status quo* was not
born of lack of sympathy for Italian unification, but fear that if
Austria were driven out of the peninsula 'Italy [would] become a
second Mexico'.[118] If there existed a practical opportunity to strike at
what Malmesbury believed (along with most Englishmen) to be the
real source of political grievance in the Italian peninsula – the Pope's
temporal sovereignty – then it was to be seized with enthusiasm. But
England could not support the morality of breaking treaties 'in aiding
to expel Austria from Italy; it would be a breach of faith'. It was

'intolerable' that 'Europe should be deluged with blood for the personal ambition of an Italian attorney and a tambour major, like Cavour and his master'.[119] No policy, Malmesbury maintained, could be more fatal to Sardinia than a change in the distribution of power involving France and Austria.

> The part she would play in a war between France and Austria would be secondary; and it may well be assumed that, like other small states acting in concert with a more powerful ally, her interests would not be consulted either in the prosecution or at the conclusion of the war. The internal prosperity which Sardinia has acquired would disappear before the march of a friendly army; and the Sardinian government must know, even by recent experience, that the liberal institutions on which she justly prides herself would be equally distasteful to friend and foe, on which ever side she might be found in an Italian war.[120]

Such views embraced the common sentiment encompassing almost all sections of opinion within parliament.

As a reflection of prevalent opinion, Malmesbury's policy prevented Italy becoming the immediate subject of adversarial politics. The misgivings and suspicions of Aberdeen, Granville, Cornewall Lewis, Argyll and Clarendon, supported Malmesbury's aim of non-intervention. This broad-based agreement also prevented Russell striking a distinctive pose in opposition to government policy. During December 1858 Derby was confident that, despite Austria appearing to be 'at least as anxious to offend as France seem[ed] careless of giving it', there would be no Italian war and assumed that Russia would 'not be over anxious to engage in new hostilities, especially when she [could] hope for no advantage'.[121] This would enable the government to meet parliament in 1859 with a popular foreign policy, and a declaration of diplomatic intent that would secure majority support in the Commons. Towards this end Derby urged Malmesbury to resolve misunderstandings with America and to prepare details for the announcement of treaties to be concluded with China and Japan.[122]

The absence of sectional conflict over the Italian question did not preclude cabinet confrontation. Denied priority over his budget and forced to accept the urgency of reform, Disraeli, as in January 1857, saw an opportunity for a personal initiative in foreign affairs. As before, armed with secret intelligence gathered by Ralph Earle in Paris – much of it to the detriment of Lord Cowley and the official diplomatic corps – Disraeli challenged Malmesbury's capability.[123] The Foreign Secretary offered an easy target. A contemporary, as well as a devoted lieutenant of Derby, Malmesbury had come late in life to the demands of political office. In 1852 Malmesbury had reluctantly accepted the Foreign Office claiming as his qualification knowledge of the *'verbiage'* of the profession through editing the memoirs, state papers and correspondence of his grandfather.[124] Not until 1851, under the tutorship of Stanley, did Malmesbury become familiar with the mysteries of political economy. Stanley noted that Malmesbury was 'full of zeal, able and willing to work, but [had] never studied this class of subjects'.[125]

In January 1859 Disraeli suggested that Malmesbury was seriously misjudging the situation abroad. On 4 January 1859 Disraeli described foreign affairs to Derby as 'critical' with 'decision and energy [as] absolutely requisite'.[126] Disraeli then noted that Malmesbury had gone to Heron Court in Hampshire for a week when 'he ought to be at the F.O. and nowhere else. Any appearance of negligence and any vagueness of language . . . [would] have the very worst effect.' In fact Malmesbury was holding private interviews with the Austrian ambassador, Count Apponyi, at Heron Court impressing on him British wishes for reform in the Austrian and Papal dominions in Italy. On 7 January, in a long letter discussing foreign policy, Disraeli suggested to Derby that Malmesbury was 'very imperfectly acquainted with the state of affairs'.[127] Disraeli also noted that he found 'difficulty in conversing with Malmesbury on these matters' who adopted 'an incipient reserve and jealousy, as if [Disraeli] were trenching on his manor'. Throughout 'this Italian pother' Disraeli suggested Cowley too had been 'off the rails'. Ever since the Orsini business, Louis Napoleon had been 'fitful and moody, and brooding over Italy'. Cavour was also 'always on the watch', and occasionally talked of placing himself 'at the head of the army of invasion'. But, Disraeli continued, 'perhaps equal with his desire "to do something for Italy" [was] the Emperor's wish . . . to restore the good opinion of the English people in his favour'. The Emperor would 'never risk a war which England disapprove[d]'. There therefore existed, Disraeli insisted, an opportunity for Malmesbury, if he acted promptly and decisively, 'to meet parliament with a feather in his cap'.[128] If Malmesbury were to sanction 'the conciliatory movement of Austria [Louis Napoleon would] agree to the revival of Conferences, and content himself with a diplomatic triumph. All immediate danger of war [would] certainly be averted.' If Malmesbury failed to do this, however, Disraeli feared that an outbreak of hostilities was imminent. Derby conceded that 'Austria and France both seem[ed] so much inclined to fly at each other's throats, that it [would] not be easy to keep matters quiet'.[129] The 'worst [was] that with France longing to pick a quarrel, and Sardinia too much inclined to be made a catspaw of, Austria or rather Buol, [was] only too likely to give them a fair pretext'.[130]

Derby refused to return to London for an immediate cabinet on foreign affairs, as Disraeli wished, because it was 'not the best place for real discussion of any affairs, and especially of foreign relations'.[131] Moreover, 'the consequences, in all probability, [were] at least sufficiently hazardous to induce England to pause' before taking an initiative. Despite Disraeli's 'excessive agitation' and the 'critical' state of matters abroad, Derby assured Malmesbury that they had 'plenty to occupy [their] attention at home'.[132] Subsequent events, however, forced Malmesbury and Derby to acknowledge that Disraeli's forebodings had greater weight than they initially granted them. On 12 January 1859 the Foreign Secretary noted that 'the King of Sardinia [had] made a speech which [could] only mean war', and it began to appear that 'war [could not] be avoided'.[133] By late January open hostilities seemed increasingly certain. In response to growing European tension, and under pressure from the Queen, the cabinet decided on 18 January to increase the strength of the navy. But Derby's steadfast loyalty to his Foreign Secretary saved Malmesbury from falling victim to Disraeli's insinuations. Malmesbury remained confident of Derby's trust and, caring 'for neither Austria nor France', both were 'determined to use every effort to prevent war, which would cost 100,000 lives and desolate the fairest parts of Europe'.[134]

III

After study of the Home Secretary's 'Chancery brief' during the beginning of January 1859, Derby was glad to find that Walpole at least admitted the necessity of introducing a reform bill. This necessity, in turn, demanded that such a measure be introduced as might 'have a chance of being accepted as a fair and reasonable compromise which [might] for many years, at least, put a stop to agitation for further reform'.[135] This demand, Derby urged on Walpole, meant some concession from members of the cabinet so as to arrive at an

agreed measure. The cabinet, Derby continued, had agreed 'unanimously' to two propositions: first, that personal property was to confer
a vote indiscriminately for county or borough; and, secondly, that the
same privilege should be given to lodgers. This commitment, Derby
argued, made it impossible to retain the distinction between the
character of the county and borough franchises as Walpole wished.
Over redistribution Derby believed his differences with Walpole were
questions of degree. Concession was both necessary and possible.

While Derby reminded Walpole of practical requirements, Stanley
'broke ground'.[136] The result of Walpole's preferences, Stanley
assured Derby, would be unacceptable to the House of Commons; 'a
£20 county franchise [had] not a hope of passing'.[137] Furthermore
'parliament would with difficulty believe that a scheme so certain of
rejection was put forth with any intention except that it should be
rejected'. Stanley once again insisted that the Commons had so
identified itself with Locke King's motion that they would accept no
measure of reform which did not adopt that principle. After the
failure of such a measure as Walpole proposed, there also existed the
difficulty of a concerted Conservative response to a bill introduced by
Russell. Some of the cabinet would 'answer readily "Oppose it".' But
others would be placed 'in circumstances of peculiar and painful
embarrassment'. They would 'not be compensated for any abandonment of theory by practical success – for Russell's bill would, a year or
two later, undoubtedly pass. They would not have the satisfaction . .
of sacrificing personal ambition to consistency of principle.'

This divergence of cabinet opinion forced Derby to redefine his
position. 'Any secession from the cabinet . . . on the liberal or
conservative side . . . would enlist in its favour a certain amount of
sympathy and encourage opposition on the part of many who would
be willing to accept, even if they did not wholly approve, a measure
which was sanctioned by a united cabinet.'[138] Beyond cabinet unanimity, setting aside 'the question of abstract merit', there was also the
necessity of the measure's 'acceptance by the great body of the
Conservative party and by moderate Liberals'. Derby came to believe
that, within these constraints, there was room for negotiation.
Accommodation, however, would mean surrendering the principles
he had safeguarded in committee. Derby laid before the cabinet a
scheme 'of an £8 rating with the alternative of a £10 value . . . for the
boroughs, and a rating franchise of £16 for the counties'. To
safeguard this compromise plan, Derby made it clear that his 'continuance at the head of the government must depend upon the

acceptance of this proposal by the cabinet'. As an act of good faith on his own part, however, Derby also conceded that it 'might be difficult, perhaps impossible, to propose the transfer to the boroughs of the freehold votes within them . . . and, for the sake of general concurrance, [he was] ready to sacrifice [his] own wishes and opinions on the subject'.

Two events rendered this alternative scheme redundant and lent new support to the original proposals contained in the committee report. First, both Walpole and Henley persevered in their decision to resign. Walpole, 'a conscientious man and a Tory', declared it 'utterly impossible' for him to countenance the cabinet's preferences for reform, while Henley 'very shrewd and clever, but crotchety and easily offended', found the apprehensions he had expressed 'fully confirmed'.[139] Both men agreed to postpone their resignations until after parliament met, while keeping their 'intentions a profound secret'.[140]

Secondly, Rose submitted a memorandum to the cabinet, containing the results of his enquiries amongst Conservative organisations and landowners, supporting those principles Derby had advocated in committee. Deeming the moment appropriate, in the absence of extreme demands and agitation, 'for proposing to the country a fair, and comprehensive and statesmanlike measure' Rose declared the aim of a reform bill to be finality.[141] The assimilation of the borough and county franchise, Rose argued, would allow 'a broad and comprehensive measure' so as to 'embrace the influence of property, station, and intelligence, without regard *solely* to population'. Moreover, the assimilation of the borough and county franchise would allow 'a broad and comprehensive measure' based upon 'statesmanlike views' with finality for its object. Lowering the county franchise to £10, Rose assured Derby, would not 'swamp' the landed interest. Experience of boroughs with a rural district, such as Shoreham and Cricklade, showed the £20 occupiers to be predominately Conservative. A reduction of the borough franchise, however, '*would only be a certain step* on the road to universal suffrage and *democracy*'.

In the light of Walpole and Henley's insistence upon resignation, Derby seized on Rose's memorandum as authoritative. Rose's endorsement of the committee report proved the basis upon which a modified cabinet might proceed. As Rose recommended, 'the *great object*' should be 'to elevate the borough franchise by placing *it* and the county franchise on the same level'.[142] The promise of perma-

nency, the freehold clause, and any redistribution schedule which
might accompany the scheme, would mitigate the effect of an identity
of suffrage. Moreover, it tailored the measure, in terms of franchise,
to the proposal to which Whigs and Liberals had publicly committed
themselves in June 1858. Thus the desire for permanence, the need
for an intelligible principle and political stratagem merged.

10 'A Rope of Sand'

[Reform] has become a taunt, not a boast. (*The Times*, 8 April 1859, p. 9)

I am anxious that we should carry our measure, and that we should not get the reputation of being theorists, pursuing an ideal perfection, and in that pursuit throwing away the opportunity of achieving a reasonable success. (Disraeli to Stanley, 10 February 1859, cited in W. F. Monypenny and G. E. Buckle, *The Life of Benjamin Disraeli, Earl of Beaconsfield* (London, 1910–20) IV, p. 199)

When parliament met on 3 February 1859 it was clear that Italy was an issue of nominal agreement, and reform a question exciting deep animosity. Whigs, Peelites and Liberals felt 'the importance of the first discussion in the H. of Commons and the mischief which John Russell [might] do [was] almost incalculable if he pronounce[d] in favour of Piedmontese aggression'.[1] In turn, Palmerston would 'not like to be outbid by [Russell]'.[2] Clarendon visited Palmerston and Russell and received assurances that 'both [would] be guarded and moderate in their language' on foreign affairs. But 'no one could answer', Clarendon noted, 'for the effect that a debate [might] have on them, particularly on Lord John'.[3] As some further comfort, it was observed that Minto saw 'no good for Italy in replacing one despotism by another, and that [might] have its calming influence'.

The Queen's Speech expressed the prevalent wish to 'maintain inviolate the faith of public treaties' and to contribute 'to the preservation of the general peace'.[4] There was, Derby assured the Lords, 'no question that could justify recourse to war'.[5] In the 'melancholy' event of war, however, Derby remained confident that the government 'had done all in their power, by friendly remonstrances, to prevent so formidable a calamity', and there existed no secret obligations or treaties that would compromise British neutrality. In response to Granville's raising of the question of the Papal States, whence he had just returned, Derby forcefully declared government dislike of the Pope's temporal power as 'the real plague spot of Italy', and the cabinet's wish for reform in that part of the peninsula. From the opposition benches, Lord Grey and Lord Brougham expressed agreement with Derby's policy.[6]

In the Commons, Disraeli echoed Derby's sentiments, admitted that the condition of affairs abroad was critical, acknowledged the value to England of the French alliance, but emphasised that the government had taken that course which they deemed most conducive to peace.[7] Broughton noted the general response to the Queen's Speech as 'good' and, though 'the chances of war seem[ed] greater', was relieved to know that 'England [was] to be neuter'.[8] This statement of government policy complemented Aberdeen's belief that 'French pretensions [were] scandalous . . . and unjust', and confirmed Argyll's hope that 'we [should] be able to stand aside'.[9] Russell's subsequent speech 'was very spirited and effective and . . . moderate too. He stood up for good faith and treaties as did Palmerston also. They both behaved very well especially Palmerston who made . . . a very honest and manly declaration.'[10] Russell approved of encouraging reform in the Papal States, alluding to popular self-determination, while Palmerston pointed to the difficulty created by the presence of French and Austrian troops in the Papal States as part of his general agreement with Malmesbury's policy. Both speeches were concessions to the 'tone of the House' which 'was strong for peace'.

Following the opening of parliament Russell sought support for a peace initiative, drawing attention to the Papal States as the source of Italian instability. Austria, Russell admitted to Clarendon, was in a difficult position. 'A European Congress [was] the only remedy.'[11] Russell's communication with Clarendon was the prelude to approaching Palmerston. They would, Russell advised Palmerston, 'be wanting in [their] duty if [they] allow[ed] the affairs of Italy to drift to war without urging upon [the] government the necessity of endeavouring to prevent such a calamity while it [was] yet time'.[12] The most effective means of securing peace, Russell argued, was to arrange for 'the withdrawal of Austrian and French troops from the Pope's dominions'.[13] Russell portrayed Palmerston as 'the best person to move in this matter', but provided assurances of his own willingness to do so. The suggestion of 'rapprochement', however, was more apparent than real. While he was willing to act with Palmerston over the Papal States, Russell was also aware that 'the [government's] reform bill aloom[ed] in the distance'.[14] Italy offered the chance for a limited common strategy swiftly dissolved by differences over reform. Palmerston, for his own part, declared his willingness to act in concert with Russell and endorsed the latter's belief that 'conflict in Italy [would] be inevitable unless the Roman States [were] evacuated by the French and Austrians'.[15] On 16 February, Palmerston had 'a very satisfactory talk' with Russell.[16] Rather than stridently advocating the cause of Italian unification, as many Peelites, Whigs and Liberals had feared, Russell prepared to step forward as the skilled advocate of European peace, and the foremost opponent of Papal corruption. Rather than attempting to expose the folly of government policy, this initiative sought to suggest that the government were lax in pursuing their own avowed objects.

Palmerston's agreement to act in concert with Russell over foreign troops in the Papal States was recognition of his extreme dependence on the pronouncements of others on the question of reform. For more than any other protagonist, Palmerston's policy over reform was going to be defined by what the government might propose, and what Russell might provide as a suitable 'liberal' reply. On 2 February 1859 Palmerston gave a dinner for some of his ex-colleagues; a decision that was seen as proof of his determination 'to have another lease' of office.[17] Although Sir George Grey, Cornewall Lewis, Cardwell, Baines and Charles Villiers were amongst those who attended, fourteen of the forty-two invitations Palmerston sent out were refused; Ellice, Bernal Osborne, Moncrieff, Francis Baring and Lord Paget being amongst those who 'did *not* come'.[18] No less significant was the identity of those Members of the Commons, such as Wood, Vernon Smith, Bouverie, Sir Robert Peel, Berkeley, Horsman and Elcho, who were not sent invitations. The restricted Cambridge House guest list confirmed that there was 'little hope for Lord Palmerston in the present state of things. People [had] long ceased to wish for him even as a war minister. His popularity [had] altogether vanished and the Liberal party [was] infinitesimally divided.'[19] Palmerston, it was rumoured, was 'more than ever desirous of making a grand speech on foreign affairs';[20] a wish strengthened by his belief that 'one man only in the ministry, Mr. Disraeli, understands anything about foreign policy and he only a little'.[21] Lennox reported to Disraeli that 'Pam and his friends . . . *hope* to support the government reform bill *if* it comes to a second reading; but Pam and his friends look to the F.O. as the means of an overthrow *before* the reform bill can be brought on'.[22]

Adroit diplomacy, government strategy and domestic consensus denied Palmerston his 'grand speech' on foreign affairs. As Hayward recognised, 'England [was] decidedly for neutrality as long as it [could] be maintained. There [was] no feeling for the Italians out of the highest class. But there [was] a growing feeling against the French and the Emperor.'[23] In the Commons on 25 February, Palmerston challenged the government to defend its Italian policy, describe their efforts to preserve peace, and define their attitude towards foreign military occupation of the Papal States as the obstacle to real political reform.[24] In reply, Disraeli informed Palmerston that the government had received communications giving reason to believe that in the near future the Papal States would be evacuated by foreign troops, and that Lord Cowley had been sent to Vienna on a confidential mission promising peace and conciliation.[25] This announcement 'was uncommonly effective'.[26] Disraeli concluded with an appeal that debate on this 'delicate subject' be postponed for the present, while assuring the House that the government would endeavour to maintain the general peace only on principles consistent with the dignity and welfare of Europe. Prolonged and loud cheering followed. Russell could only offer congratulations, make a few remarks on Italian affairs, and then support the recommendation to refrain from any further discussion of the subject.[27]

Disraeli's dramatic announcement of Cowley's mission to Vienna on 25 February 1859 swiftly pre-empted a Russell–Palmerston peace initiative. By mid-March the likelihood of hostilities seemed to be lessening further as preparations for a five-nation Congress were begun. Granville noted that 'peace [had] made a great stride since February'.[28] 'The fear of war', Hayward inferred from club and dinner-table talk, had 'materially abated as regard[ed] the present, although the proceedings of the Emperor L.N. [were] regarded with suspicion and distrust'.[29] Palmerston and Russell were denied a distinctive stance over Italy, and widespread opposition mistrust of Cavour and the Emperor re-emerged. Aberdeen, it was reported, offended both the Duchess of Argyll and indirectly the Gladstones by referring to the Italian nationalists visiting London as '*vagabonds*'.[30] Clarendon observed that the conduct and policy of the Piedmontese government might 'be summed up in 3 words; it had been audacious, unscrupulous and successful'.[31]

Gladstone, returning to London from Corfu on 8 March, found the feeling in England markedly 'anti-Italian'.[32] More immediately alarming, however, was Gladstone's discovery that although he mistrusted 'every *nostrum* for Italy except that of local freedom', he found himself 'already booked even in high quarters as an *ultra* Italian'. It was noted that Gladstone, returning via Turin, had gone 'to pay his court to that firebrand Cavour'.[33] In an attempt to clarify his own position Gladstone wrote an article for the forthcoming April issue of *Quarterly Review*, despite the fact that 'the great Reviews [were] closed against anything of the sort, under the notion of keeping peace'.[34] In the article Gladstone attempted to mend differences with others by presenting the Italian question dissociated from the suspicion of Napoleonic intrigue. He accepted that France had 'not a rag of title to make war upon Austria in the name of Italy'.[35] But this consideration, Gladstone claimed, had obscured recognition of Austrian villainy and the virtuous thirst for independence and relief from political servitude existing in Italy. The attempt to consider Italian claims apart from French ambition was Gladstone's notion of domestic appeasement. He acknowledged British neutrality to be 'the very highest moral obligation' and Austria's vital place in the equilibrium of Europe. But his impassioned pleas for Italian independence caused a storm of protest from *Quarterly* readers, and confirmed Greville's smug observation that Gladstone had been 'completely duped by Cavour'. Even Aberdeen, it was reported, had treated Gladstone's 'delusions and his credibility with the utmost scorn and contempt'.[36]

Debate on foreign affairs during February and March 1859 also included the dispute between France and Portugal over the latter's commandeering of the French ship, *Charles et Georges*. The political importance of the debate was the criticism of Malmesbury it prompted because of the part the Foreign Office had taken in negotiations.[37] These criticisms confirmed doubts about Malmesbury's competence; doubts Disraeli had privately encouraged in January. Granville noted that 'Malmesbury [was] very generally suspected of being incapable, but this [was] balanced by the belief that both Palmerston and Russell [were] not to be entirely trusted on the Italian question'.[38] Moreover, the Cowley initiative and preparations for the European Congress safeguarded Malmesbury from any immediate allegations of incompetence. Palmerston, who had scant respect for Malmesbury's talents, acknowledged that if France and Austria 'all [met] round a table they [were] less likely to meet on the field of battle'.[39] This belief protected both the government and Malmesbury. After a cabinet meeting on 19 March 1859, Sotheron-Estcourt confidently noted that the prospects of peace were better and a 'Congress likely to be assented to'.[40]

While discussion of Italy and foreign affairs appeared to favour the government, some domestic legislation, unobtrusively introduced into the Commons during February 1859, further consolidated their position. Cairns, as Solicitor-General, introduced two bills to simplify the title to landed estates.[41] This complex subject had long received the attention of parliament and several unsuccessful attempts had been made to remedy the expense and difficulty of the transfer of real property. Cairns' measures and personal capability won approval.[42] On 21 February, Walpole announced a church rates bill which he believed would be 'a just, moderate and reasonable settlement of the question'.[43] The government proposed to make the rate a landlords' rate; to enable the owners of land to charge it with a church rate, extending the power to tenants for life as well as owners in fee; to make incumbents and churchwardens corporations; and to make provisions for aiding this rent-charge by voluntary assistance. Provisions would also be made to exempt Dissenters from the rate, but persons claiming exemption would not be allowed to take part in vestry meetings. The Radical Sir J. Trelawny, who annually proposed a bill to abolish the church rate, acknowledged the conciliatory spirit of the government measure, as did Russell, who, nevertheless, questioned the wisdom of exempting Dissenters.[44] Edward Ball, a Conservative backbencher who opposed the Maynooth grant and was an 'earnest supporter of education based upon the Word of God',[45] considered the proposal a very fair one and admitted that he was disposed to support it.[46] Sir George Grey and Cornewall Lewis, revealing a degree of embarrassment over the government's measure, declined to give any firm opinion until time had allowed for further consideration.[47] Opposition frontbench discomfort attested to the political effectiveness of Walpole's conciliatory proposal. Pakington's introduction of the Navy Estimates drew guarded approval from Wood.[48] And although Stanley's statement upon the condition of finances in India received more prolonged and fundamental criticism, the impression remained that the government represented moderate and responsible concession.[49] 'Things', Jolliffe reported to Disraeli, 'appear[ed] to have gone well in the House of Commons.'[50]

Reform remained, however, the dominant domestic question upon which any redefinition of party sentiment would occur. This was confirmed by the apparent unanimity regarding foreign policy. Parliamentary debate during February 1859 was seen as an engaging prelude before the curtain lifted on the main drama of reform.

I

Reference to reform in the Queen's Speech on 3 February 1859 had been oblique and cursory. Disraeli gave the impression of 'pooh-poohing reform as a secondary affair which must wait until other measures of more importance were settled'.[51] In a similar manner Derby, during February, directed debate in the Lords towards foreign affairs.[52] This reticence irritated the opposition. Argyll confessed himself to be 'astonished at Derby appearing to play so loosely and lightly with the question of reform', feeling that the premier 'ought to have begun with it at once'.[53] Herbert noted that Disraeli's evasion 'produced a very unfavourable effect on the House, the more so as he said the bill was ready'.[54] In the Commons, Russell dismissed Disraeli's declaration as vague and illusive, and could see no excuse for delaying the measure.[55]

Government reticence over reform was the direct result of persistent cabinet difficulties. The cabinet met parliament, despite Disraeli's assurances, without a measure fully framed. Walpole and Henley's agreement to postpone their resignations avoided public acknowledgement of difficulties, while during the first weeks of the session Derby sought some agreement over the principles of a measure. On 7 February Derby circulated a memorandum on reform to all members of the cabinet, including Walpole and Henley, urging that the 'time [had] now arrived, when it [would] be necessary to come to a final understanding with respect to certain provisions of the proposed reform bill, the introduction of which [could not] be much longer delayed'.[56] In view of Walpole and Henley's resignations Derby believed the question of suffrage and the transfer of freehold votes might be considered settled, but the question of redistribution remained a problem 'which increase[d] the more it [was] considered'. Bright's extensive scheme had not gained any approval, while the cabinet had before them various proposals, but, Derby observed, 'none of them resting on any intelligible principle'. The best and safest course, Derby suggested, would be to exclude the subject of redistribution altogether from the government's bill.[57] 'The omission of all disfranchisement will disarm much opposition; the large additions we make to the constituency will secure much public support; the equalisation of the franchise will, partially at least, meet many demands; and the general character of the measure will commend itself to the better class of public opinion.'

On 8 February, Derby 'had separate interviews with [his] colleagues, and ... then held a prolonged cabinet'.[58] Disraeli, who thought public opinion upon redistribution was 'not ripe', Lytton, Walpole, Salisbury, Peel and Hardwicke voiced approval of Derby's proposal; Stanley, Pakington, Manners and 'Henley (by proxy)' dissented.[59] Stanley believed the total omission of redistribution would be 'the first step towards a total escape from [their] pledges of last year'.[60] Manners, in an echo of Bright's central tenet, asserted that no reform bill could 'be regarded as a settlement of the reform question, which exclude[d] altogether a redistribution of seats'.[61] Stanley, Pakington and Manners recommended the introduction of 'two bills, tho' one statement', with the suffrage bill being passed before the second reading of the disfranchisement bill was moved. Thus the fate of the disfranchisement bill would not prejudice the passage of the suffrage proposals and, if only passed by a bare majority, it would 'be open to the government not to proceed with it'.[62] In this way the government might propose the partial disfranchisement of forty-seven seats, the first four acts of distribution going to 'unrepresented places', the West Riding, South Lancashire and Middlesex to be divided and the rest apportioned as had been suggested in January. Derby rejected such an extensive scheme as unacceptable and proposed, with the support of Disraeli, a smaller measure of redistribution affecting only fourteen or fifteen seats. Such a narrow redistribution, the premier believed, might reconcile both those who wished to exclude and those who saw the necessity for some reapportionment of seats.[63]

The attempt at compromise placated Manners and to a certain extent Pakington, but only further alienated Stanley who believed 'petty change' worse than mere delay. In a long candid letter to Disraeli, Stanley admitted his fear that such a restricted scheme of redistribution would 'simply throw [them] back into the old track of obstruction and resistance from which [they had] emerged with so much trouble'.[64] In a barely veiled threat Stanley declared that he had 'had enough of that work, and [he did] not mean to have any more'. Disraeli's reply forcibly pointed out to Stanley 'the *practical* position' and advocated the course of narrow redistribution' as 'the one best adapted to the emergency'.[65] Disraeli was confident that Ellice, Horsman, Lowe and, by report, Cornewall Lewis, had 'all taken the Conservative view of this question'. Also, Disraeli argued, proposals with regard to the franchise rendered their bill 'a large and important measure'. Over the suffrage the cabinet would have to expect 'disaffection and even desertion' amongst the Conservative backbenches, and Palmerston, who desired 'above all things to place himself at the head of the Conservative party', was uncommitted to the population standard. 'What is to prevent him from placing himself at the head of our disaffected and getting a majority against us? And in such a case, what course would be left to us?' While the cabinet's proposals over the suffrage might enlist Whig and moderate Liberal support, a restricted disfranchisement and redistribution, Disraeli urged, might ensure the loyalty of Conservative backbenchers.

At a cabinet meeting on 12 February, with the exception of Walpole and Henley, ministers agreed to a £10 borough franchise, including the occupiers of lodgings to the amount of £20 p.a., those receiving pensions or superannuities of £20 p.a., those with deposits of not less than £60 in Savings Banks, graduates, ministers of religion, barristers, attorneys, registered medical men, certificated schoolmasters, and a £10 county franchise.[66] This suffrage scheme acknowledged the £10 county franchise introduced by Russell in 1852 and 1854, recognised the support shown for Locke King's motion and, with the inclusion of the transfer of freehold votes, realised the principles Derby had secured from the cabinet committee in December 1858. Thus Derby finally managed to safeguard his original propositions, although at the cost of two cabinet resignations. His success was confirmed when it was 'understood by the cabinet that the two measures of equalisation of the borough and county franchise and of the transfer of the freeholds [were] inseparably connected; and should one be carried and the other rejected, they would not consider themselves at liberty to proceed with the bill'.[67] On 12 February 1859 the cabinet agreed 'to confine the question of redistribution of seats within *very* narrow limits; and successfully to resist more extensive changes'.[68] The details of redistribution, however, remained undecided.

On 16 February 1859 Derby circulated a memorandum on disfranchisement based upon the result of Rose's inquiry into the claims of unrepresented towns.[69] Proposing to give one member to each of the unrepresented towns of Barnsley, Stalybridge, Birkenhead, West Bromwich, Croydon, Hartlepool and Gravesend, Derby approved of the division of South Lancashire and Middlesex into two constituencies and the West Riding into three, while rejecting Rose's proposal to give a third member to Liverpool, Birmingham and Manchester. This redistribution, in turn, disposed of the fifteen seats Derby considered it necessary to disfranchise. Cabinet agreement to the proposals was unanimous, with dissent only remaining over the granting of the suffrage to clergymen and schoolmasters.[70] The measure of reform the cabinet finally accepted was testimony to the persuasion and skill Derby had exercised in directing ministerial discussion. The measure fulfilled the broad outlines he had indicated in November 1858.

Although Disraeli and Derby dissuaded Stanley from resigning at different times, the premier came to consider the position of 'Walpole and Henley hopeless'.[71] On 8 February 1859 Walpole renewed his offer of resignation.[72] In the light of Walpole and Henley's determination Derby recognised it was 'time to reconsider our *personnel*'.[73] Reconsideration was rendered the more imperative by Lord Henry Lennox's sudden resignation as a Junior Lord of the Treasury – a resignation Lennox submitted to Derby without stating his reasons for the decision.[74] Disraeli had known of Lennox's discontent over patronage and resignation ended the affection that had formerly existed between the two men.[75]

On 14 February Derby offered the Home Office, to be vacated by Walpole, to Pakington.[76] But Pakington with firm politeness refused the offer.[77] Derby also considered bringing Lord Chandos into the cabinet 'as an excellent man of business', but admitted a reluctance 'to entrust him with the constant speaking and attention to numberless details, which [was] required of the Home Secretary'.[78] In the event Chandos chose to decline, pleading financial difficulties, and retained his Railway Chairmanship.[79] Derby chose Lord Donoughmore, 'a man of the world, a sound partisan' and prominent in the Lords, to replace Henley at the Board of Trade.[80] As a result of Pakington's refusal of the Home Office, Sotheron-Estcourt was promoted from the Poor Law Board: an appointment that ensured the cabinet did not lose 'its *bucolic* character'.[81] Estcourt's appointment to the Home Office was one calculated to 'control Walpole' once outside the ministry.[82] With a similar view to backbench sentiment, Lord March succeeded Sotheron-Estcourt as Chief Commissioner for the Poor Law Board. Disraeli understood there to be 'a cabal brewing by Newdegate' and it was known that March wished for office.[83] Disraeli hoped that March's 'adhesion would tend greatly to neutralise cabal'.[84]

In late January, Sir Stafford Northcote replaced G. W. Hamilton as Financial Secretary to the Treasury. This appointment offset concessions to 'ultra-Tory' opinion. Recognised to be of 'extraordinary industry, good social position [and] excellent character', Northcote, Gladstone's private secretary at the Board of Trade from 1842–45, had absorbed his mentor's financial wisdom, and allied this fiscal faith to firmly held religious views.[85] Formerly a Peelite, but drifting by way of an ill-defined independence towards the Conservative party, Northcote took the path Gladstone was expected to travel. Office encouraged a growing friendship between Northcote and Disraeli.[86]

As a final accommodation of personal feeling, Lord Lovaine, who appeared 'very sulky' and seemed 'bent on going', was promoted to replace Lord Donoughmore as Pay Master General.[87] After the appointments Derby admitted he was 'more sanguine of success than [he had] yet been'.[88]

While the final drafting of the reform bill and negotiations to replace Walpole and Henley occupied the government during February, Disraeli was reminded of the need to 'avoid the suspicion that [they] were afraid of the [reform] question'.[89] The date chosen was 28 February 1859 as being the earliest date upon which the bill might be introduced to the Commons, while it was suggested as prudent 'to have it believed that the measure [was] rather an extreme one, so that the Palmerstonians [might] go on talking conservatism'. To ensure backbench solidarity Derby arranged to hold a meeting of his supporters on 1 March.[90]

A dramatic prelude to the announcement of the bill was the revelation that Delane had acquired a copy of the government's measure. On 27 February, Delane told Earle 'he had heard all about the bill – that he could give it every support – that much depended on [Disraeli's] statement and that in all probability the Palmerstonians would be with [them]'.[91] Earle's response was to warn Disraeli 'to deal tenderly with the borough freeholders' and note that '[n]othing could be more friendly than Delane'. The conversation also confirmed Walpole and Henley's suspicion that, during February, *The Times* was 'writing from distinct information from *within the cabinet*'.[92] On the morning of 28 February, *The Times* published the outline of the government's measure, omitting redistribution, accompanied by a leader written by Lowe.[93] Anonymously, Lowe described the measure 'as proof of the wish of the ministers to deal with the question, if not on very wide, at any rate on honest and intelligible principles'.[94] In conclusion Lowe praised the measure as being 'as strong as any government would be able to carry in the present temper of the House of Commons and the public mind'.

The cabinet leak to Printing House Square infuriated Derby who, in the first instance, suspected Disraeli of giving details of the measure to Northcote who, in turn, informed Delane. This allegation Disraeli vehemently denied.[95] The revelation in *The Times*, Disraeli claimed, 'destroyed' him and he was 'half inclined to resign'. To Lennox, the Chancellor admitted that the 'great "trahison" in *The Times*' so 'completely upset him' that he could 'scarcely rally for the fight'.[96] Delane admitted to Disraeli that he had gained knowledge of the bill from Ellice on the evening of 27 February.[97] Indeed, Ellice had also known of a forthcoming 'crack in the ministerial kettle – to be announced at the same time with their new reform bill'.[98] The reform debate, Ellice predicted, would 'end sooner or later in the fusion of parties – against which we shall have a hot radical opposition'. Although the source of Ellice's information remained unknown, both Ellice and Lowe represented that body of Liberal opinion Derby might expect to adhere in any fusion of parties opposing radical demands. When Lowe fell in with Gathorne Hardy, immediately prior to the reform debate on the evening of 28 February, he described the government's measure as 'a capital bill' and avowed his support.[99]

Disraeli's presentation of the bill to the Commons on 28 February 1859 was one calculated to exploit the opinion, expressed by Delane, that the measure was 'so mild and moderate that all reasonable men ought to concur in supporting it'.[100] In 'a very skilful and adroit speech' Disraeli offered the government's proposals as an opportunity to settle the reform question consistent with the spirit and principles of the constitution established in 1832.[101] The government measure, Disraeli claimed, would ensure the representation not only of the voice of a numerical majority or the influence of a predominant property, but all the various interests of the country.[102] Granville observed that 'the effect on the House during [Disraeli's] speech was to produce immense relief – the whole of the 130 members to be disfranchised by Bright's bill were enchanted with the reprieve'.[103]

After Disraeli made his statement '[a]ll the Whigs above the gangway [remained] silent':[104] the 'Palmerstonians were still and impenetrable'.[105] Russell, however, complained to the Commons that Disraeli's speech had filled him with apprehension; first, because it was proposed to transfer borough freeholders' votes from the county to the borough and, secondly, because little or nothing was said of the working classes.[106] By denouncing the bill and talking of 'honest and hardworking men', nervous Whigs and Liberals noted, Russell used 'language smacking of the Bright school'.[107] Observing that 'Pam and his friends had taken the judicious, sensible line' of allowing the three weeks before the second reading for consideration, Ellice expressed alarm at Russell who 'chimed in with Bright, Roebuck and Fox and complained of the *larger bodies* of the working classes not enfranchised'.[108]

Interpreting silence as assent Dallas saw 'unequivocal symptoms of "rapprochement" between [Palmerston's] followers and those of Lord Derby; and to defeat the ultra-Liberals Bright, Gibson, Roebuck and Russell, they [might] find themselves on a test vote in the same lobby'.[109] Ellice, who disparaged Russell for '[a]s usual . . . playing a personal game', believed Palmerston would vote for the second reading.[110] Disraeli received confident reports that 'the Palmerstonian Whigs consider[ed] the bill in many respects a very good one', apart from the clause relating to the freehold voters. They were, the Conservative leader was assured, 'frightened . . . of a more Radical measure if this fail[ed]'.[111] Hayward had 'a good deal of talk' with Palmerston on 3 March:

> [Palmerston] has not yet made up his mind whether he will join Lord J.R. in opposing the second reading . . . A large body of moderate Liberals, however, have already declared for the second reading, and the country seems perfectly indifferent . . . If Lord P. supports the second reading, and the government breaks up from internal weaknesses, he may have another 'innings'.[112]

Disraeli received the report that Palmerston found 'le bill est *trop liberal*'.[113]

Although Granville noticed that 'the abuse poured on the bill by J. Russell, Bright and Roebuck did not produce much effect', in the days immediately following the debate, more hostile opinion began to marshall itself amongst the opposition.[114] At a dinner on 2 March, attended by Roebuck, Byng, Dunbar, Grenfell, Forster and others, '16 of them [Russell] scarcely knew', Russell decided that a meeting of the Liberal party should be held and opposition to the bill declared.[115] Francis Baring warned Russell of the dangers of a party meeting called under a personal aegis and suggested that 'in the present state of parties it [would] be more expedient that the call should be in no particular name and on neutral ground'.[116] Russell's object in calling such a meeting would be 'to unite as much as possible the scattered elements of the Liberal party'. Russell decided to proceed by resolution. The composition of the resolution, however, was critical. Both Graham and Herbert pressed upon Russell the necessity of excluding 'from the wording of the resolution any phrase which [had] become the catchword of any particular section of reformers'.[117] The term 'industrial classes' was struck from Russell's original draft.[118] The process of refinement shaped a resolution concerned with the transfer, or as the motion implied disfranchisement, of the 40s freehold voters' 'ancient and hereditary right of voting in counties', and concluded with a general adjunct that a measure that failed to lower the borough franchise was unacceptable.

The problems of authorship crystallised the difficulty of Russell's wish to mend scattered Liberal party connection. Russell's speech in the Commons on 28 February, Argyll felt compelled to warn him, had 'rather *frightened* the House . . . – especially by the expression "the *great body* of the working classes" – which [was] exactly what people dread[ed] most – the "great body" swamping everybody else of smaller dimensions'.[119] Nevertheless Argyll was confident that the bill would fail if, as was believed, 'the 40/- clause [was] considered a sine qua non by Derby and his party. By so considering it they [made] it the *principle* of the bill.' The final form of Russell's resolution attacked exactly that principle while avoiding a party meeting which would only prove to be 'a Tower of Babel'.[120]

Russell's decision to move a hostile motion against a particular clause of the bill on its second reading determined the character of the reform debate in 1859. The decision also dramatically highlighted aspects of Russell's situation in early March 1859. First, it revealed the necessity to pre-empt any general discussion of the broad merits of the bill as a whole: a broad scheme tailored, in part, to secure moderate Whig and Liberal support. Secondly, a suitable motion might bring together sections of opposition whose contrary opinions otherwise denied an easy cooperation: the delicate task of composing the motion affirmed the difficulties of conciliation. Thirdly, Russell's authorship of the motion might secure him that authoritative voice in the reform debate which he sought; the authority of Disraeli, Stanley, Bright, Cornewall Lewis, Wood or Palmerston would, at the same time, be denied.[121] Russell's decision also raised important contingent queries. Would the cabinet allow Russell's motion to preclude a general discussion of their measure? And finally, would the success of Russell's motion be portrayed by the cabinet as requiring the withdrawal of their bill?

On the evening of 9 March 1859, Russell and Palmerston both attended a dinner, 'rather in the Grosvenor Square style', with Cornewall Lewis, Granville, Wood, Lansdowne and Macaulay also present.[122] The 'two great men did not shake hands, and only spoke for two minutes to each other', but the following morning Russell showed his resolution, as amended by Graham and Herbert, to Palmerston who declared that he had no objection to it. The absence of any objection was testimony both to the inoffensive form of the resolution and Palmerston's willingness to allow a resolution to test backbench opinion. By design the resolution tolerated a variety of differing interpretations. By diverting attention away from the bill as a whole to the detail of freehold voting, Russell also offered the opposition an opportunity to oppose without commitment to subsequent arrangements. As *The Times* was quick to comment, on the second reading the principle of the bill was in issue, but by forcing parliamentary debate upon specific clauses, which might properly wait until the Committee stage, Russell placed many backbenchers in an ambiguous position.[123]

Palmerston gave it to be understood that he was amenable to 'a dexterous party move', while remaining personally uncommitted. He also provided reassurance for anxious moderate MPs and influential observers such as Delane. To this contrasting audience Palmerston 'had spoken strongly against a resolution'.[124] He gave it to be understood that he 'did not mean to "throw over Johnny", but that he would bear it with great fortitude if others [did] so'.[125] The danger existed of the success of the second reading of the bill creating 'a greater split than ever of the Liberal party'.

While fear of a European war abated during early March, the inconclusive character of initial debate on reform, Whig and Liberal confusion, Russell's resolution and Palmerston's non-committal agreement to Russell's initiative ensured that 'home politics [were] as uncertain as ever'.[126] Hayward observed that '[n]o one [could] foresee the result of Lord J.R.'s motion'. Although likely to be supported by Bright and, apparently, Palmerston, 'there [were] a good many Liberals who [did not] know their own minds yet'. Of crucial importance in shaping backbench opinion was the question of what would follow a majority for Russell's motion. The government might choose to dissolve, resign, or 'withdraw their bill and go on, defying the opposition to try a vote of confidence'.[127] Beyond this speculation lay the uncertain prospects of any new government, and how it might be constituted. '[T]he two Kings of Brentford [would] neither serve under the other. Palmerston without the Peelites, Bright and J. Russell' appeared 'impossible', while Granville and other former members of Palmerston's cabinet held firm objections to Palmerston assuming power with Conservative support.[128] In a conversation with Palmerston on 7 March, Russell ascertained that existing differences between Palmerston, Bright and himself precluded any easy alliance.[129] Palmerston stood out for an £8 value borough and £15 county franchise, while Russell argued the merits of a £6 rating suffrage in the boroughs. To enforce differences, while reporting Bright's willingness to compromise, Russell informed Palmerston of Bright's readiness to accept Russell's scheme in return for the lower franchise and the ballot.

Differences within the opposition were all the more obvious amongst those openly opposed to Russell's motion. Clarendon impressed upon Cornewall Lewis 'that if J. Russell carrie[d] his resolution, it [would] not dó for him to object to the second reading, unless ministers ignor[ed] the obligation which the restoration impose[d] upon them'.[130] Ellice, who expected Derby to 'be succeeded by some coalition like Aberdeen's', found Russell's notice an 'injudicious' attempt 'to catch the demagogue' Bright.[131] At the start of the session Lord Grey declared his hatred for 'Palmerston, J. Russell and Derby', in that order.[132] When news of Russell's intention to oppose the second reading reached Brooks's, Grey made it equally clear that he considered such opposition 'factious'.[133] On 12 March, Grey sent Elcho a letter criticising Russell's resolution as 'highly objectionable'.[134] With Grey's permission the letter was published in *The Times* on 15 March, accompanied by a leader that considered the resolution 'answered no good purpose . . . [and] was an invitation to the Whigs to affirm what [was] superfluous or vague'.[135]

Roebuck's shifting attitudes affirmed Hayward's comment that they were watching 'a game of parliamentary tactics rather than a great constitutional struggle'.[136] Flattering himself that his opposition to the government bill on 28 February had ensured Russell's immediate hostility, Roebuck saw himself as a prime mover in events.[137] He attended Russell's dinner-party at which it was decided to oppose the Conservative measure. But Roebuck was subsequently infuriated by Russell's readiness to consult with Palmerstonians, and by Russell's lack of communication with himself. It was Russell's neglect that prompted Roebuck to change his position over reform. Roebuck, on 18 March, made a speech in the Commons that contrasted sharply with his initial utterances.[138] Appearing 'in the novel character of a peacemaker', Roebuck argued that the prospect of Russell's resolution threatened reform being postponed indefinitely.[139] He proposed to Russell a precedent of his own, and urged Disraeli to propose another bill framed on propositions Russell might introduce as resolutions into the House. Russell dismissed Roebuck's suggestion and Disraeli remained silent.[140]

II

The uncertain Whig and Liberal response to the government's bill proved a partial fulfilment of cabinet intention. Derby's more immediate concern after 28 February, however, was the preservation of Conservative backbench unity. Despite some apprehension that there might be objection voiced to the £10 county franchise, 'led by Walpole',[141] when the bill was announced, Sotheron-Estcourt noted, '[o]ur people took it well'.[142] Walpole and Henley's announcement of their resignations that same evening had been 'full of half-suppressed bitterness towards their colleagues', but appeared to have 'exhibited weakness on the part of the retiring ministers'.[143] At the start of the party meeting on 1 March, Derby 'detailed the pro's and con's' of the measure the government had introduced to the Commons and explained the reference of clauses that might in themselves seem 'liberal' or 'extreme', to each other and the balance of the bill when viewed as a comprehensive whole.[144] Derby 'plumply informed the assembled gentlemen that everyone of them must vote for every part and the entirety of the measure unflinchingly: and that if it finally failed, he would dissolve parliament'.[145] The central message that Derby delivered, 'admirably and with great effect on his supporters',[146] was that the cabinet were 'resolved to go it blind for the bill, the whole bill and nothing but the bill'.[147] Palmer, Trollope and Newdegate voiced their preference for a £20 qualification in the counties, 'but all intimated they should support the bill'.[148] Sotheron-Estcourt found the temper of the meeting '[m]ost satisfactory'. The only note of discord was prompted by discussion of Walpole's and Henley's resignations.[149]

On 5 March, Derby held 'a satisfactory meeting of peers' and, after receiving 'many letters of approval' from the Lords, assured Disraeli that '[t]here [was] no fear *there*!'[150] Disraeli was further comforted by reports of disunity amongst the opposition. Milner Gibson, Disraeli learnt, was informing Liberal backbenchers that Russell intended to oppose the second reading of the bill even should his resolution be carried and accepted by the government and 'he [would] state this to the House if asked the question'.[151] The admission of such an intention, it was suggested, would persuade many Liberals to oppose Russell's resolution if the question was asked by 'an independent man' whose opinion was not known. Russell, it was further reported, was 'annoyed ... by his being supposed to be allied with Lord

Palmerston and Mr. Milner Gibson and others wish[ed] it to be shown that they [did] not concur with Lord P.'s views upon the franchise'.

The apparent unity of the Conservative party at the meeting of 1 March proved deceptive. That clause which Derby believed to be the most conservative proposal in the bill, confining freeholders in the boroughs to borough votes, proved to be the focus for backbench Conservative recalcitrance. On 9 March Derby was informed of a meeting to be held that afternoon at the Carlton Club to discuss the freehold clause and make it known that there existed 'a great wish on the part of some influential county Members' to remove the clause for the second reading.[152] Disraeli duly received a petition urging the withdrawal of the clause.[153] Derby confessed himself to be 'astonished' at the nature and source of the objection.[154] Although acquiescent at the meeting of 1 March, Newdegate wrote to Derby on 9 March and expressed his regret that he should have 'ever appeared in any degree as the advocate of a redistribution which could only be a palliative of the dangers from the proposed reduction and equalisation of the occupation qualification'.[155] The urban freehold vote in the counties, he continued, 'tended to relegate the asperity of class distinction', while the restriction of the freeholders to voting for the boroughs 'would strengthen the claim of the large towns to an addition to the number of their representatives if the claims of property, households and population [were] not entirely to be set aside'. For these reasons Newdegate felt himself 'unable to vote for a bill which [was] based upon the reduction of the county occupation franchise to £10 and upon the equalisation of the franchise'.

The perversity Derby sensed in Newdegate's objections arose from the fact that 'if there were one constituency which, in a Conservative sense, would benefit more than another by the transfer of the borough freeholds it was Newdegate's constituency of North Warwickshire'.[156] Opinion at the Carlton Club, as well as Russell's resolution, gave the freehold clause an increasingly ominous significance.[157] Manners, reflecting cabinet bemusement, could only observe that 'country members who a fortnight ago were so well pleased with the transference of the borough freeholders, now [said] that they [could not] meet their constituents with that principle on their banners'.[158]

At a cabinet meeting on 10 March, a compromise scheme was considered allowing freeholders in the limits of the borough the option of either voting for town or country.[159] It was also arranged for an opposition member 'to put a question to the Chancellor of the Exchequer, which [would] enable him to state the intention of the government without giving any formal notice'.[160] Newdegate, however, remained persistent in his perversity. Concession was received with ridicule. 'Now ain't this wonderful, or ain't it what the Americans call "*smart*". They don't know', Newdegate confided, 'that they can neither mollify nor subdue me by their conduct.'[161] Seeing the bill as Disraeli's means of ejecting 'such stiff old Tories' as himself from the party, Newdegate then took to criticising the cabinet's concession to his first objection as removing 'the only ruled compensation' that might prevent the £10 franchise from 'swamp[ing] North Warwickshire with Liberalism . . . so the bill in its present form [was] Locke King's bill pur et simple'.[162] While Lord March hinted to members of the frontbench that 'some cabal in the party' was under way,[163] on 15 March, Bentinck and Newdegate organised a meeting of Conservative malcontents to request the withdrawal of the bill.[164] A group of 20 backbenchers followed Bentinck and Newdegate's lead and pointed the way to '[s]chism'.[165] On 17 March, Bentinck and Palmer 'went to Derby as delegates from [the] small meeting of disenchanted Conservatives to ask him to withdraw the reform bill'. They were unceremoniously 'snubbed'.[166]

It had become clear that no cabinet concession, short of complete withdrawal of their reform measure, would placate 'ultra Tory' sensibilities. As a result Derby adamantly rejected any further attempts to tailor the bill to backbench opinion. The proposed modified freehold clause was dropped, and a commitment made to 'adhere to the bill'.[167] By 16 March, Derby was parading a firm resolve that brooked no compromise. 'There shall be no mistake! We must command this parliament, or throw the die for the next – and let our friends know that it is the last card.'[168] At a cabinet meeting on 19 March it was decided to confront Russell's motion on the ground of their original bill, and if defeated to 'throw up the bill and dissolve parliament'.[169] This ministerial commitment decided the course of future debate. With the defence of consistency the cabinet would not modify their bill, but faced Russell's motion as a blatant and cynical ploy. This might decide wavering support, but, in the event of a defeat, the government could appeal to the country as the innocent victims of faction. Thus the electorate could endorse a Conservative government as the only party to offer a sincere and comprehensive solution to the *damnosa hereditas* of reform.

III

Russell's notice of his motion in the Commons on 10 March attempted to pre-empt a general consideration of the government's measure and, within the terms of an ambiguous resolution, secure opposition unanimity. The cabinet's decision on 19 March to confront the motion, without concession, as an obviously disingenuous manoeuvre, was calculated to maximise the dilemma of a divided opposition. It was to be 'made clear in the course of the debate that the success of Lord John's motion will be fatal to the bill'.[170] Russell's commitment and cabinet resolve determined the focus of the reform debate that continued from 20 to 31 March. Much attention was given to the borough franchise, the equalisation of the county and borough suffrage, the 'evils' of disfranchisement, and the divergence of opposition opinion. Very little attention was given to redistribution or what Bright dubbed 'fancy franchises'. Moreover, no indication was given of alternative schemes that might replace the government measure.

In introducing his resolution on 21 March, Russell asserted that the establishment of a uniform suffrage in both counties and boroughs, accompanied by the freehold clause, would change the constitution of the country. The speech, by common assent, was 'not effective'.[171] Granville noticed that Russell's statement 'fell as flat as possible on the House. The personal allusions to himself were coldly received.'[172] Stanley's reply made even less impression on the House, though it read well in printed form in *The Times* the following morning.[173] Newdegate announced his opposition to the government measure and promised to support Russell's motion.[174] The 'only speech of importance' on the first night, however, 'was an admirably expressed one by Horsman against the resolution though in favour of amending the bill in many respects'.[175]

Following Horsman's speech, Disraeli wrote to Elcho urging him to 'take a part, an early part, in the impending debate'.[176] He hardly knew, he declared to Elcho, 'an occasion when a man of your position and power of speaking could produce a greater effect on opinion'. Horsman's speech affirmed Derby's intention to establish that the success of the resolution would be a rejection of the bill. This would deny any Conservatives or moderate Liberals who supported the resolution the comfortable option of subsequently voting for the second reading.[177] By allowing Russell's motion to be brought forward as 'the main question' Derby expected to force Whigs and

Liberals to acknowledge that 'there was hardly a single point on which the various sections of the opposition could come to an agreement'.[178] Moreover, prolongation of discussion would 'develop still further the conflicting views of the opposition and show the impossibility of forming a cabinet from their ranks with any hope of permanency'. Continued debate might also allow the settlement of a European Congress over the Italian question to be announced before the vote was taken on Russell's motion. Derby became increasingly confident of a diplomatic coup that might strengthen the government's position in the Commons.[179] Prolonged debate would more clearly demonstrate 'the hollowness of the union opposed to the government and the impossibility . . . of their agreeing on any line of policy'.[180]

The statements of the Conservative frontbench faithfully fulfilled Derby's keen strategic expectation of the debate. Lytton taunted the opposition with the observation that they might, 'by bridging the gangway with a rope of sand', patch up the quarrels of years for the division of a night.[181] Cairns submitted the resolution to a close and extended examination and asked why freehold property in a borough should be dealt with on a principle different from that applied to other property.[182] He challenged Russell to state clearly the specific proposals he would suggest to replace the government bill. Pakington denounced Russell's manner of raising an abstract resolution upon the second reading as irregular and unparliamentary.[183] Thus debate was focused upon Russell's resolution, attention drawn towards opposition differences and discussion was prolonged.

After the first nights of debate, Derby believed the prospects as to a division had 'changed considerably', with the cabinet acquiring hope of a majority against the resolution.

> Already many defections are spoken of from the ranks of the opposition, while the Conservative party are becoming more consolidated, and sinking minor differences as they begin better to understand the provisions and bearing of the measure.[184]

As the cabinet hoped, the commitment to Russell's motion embarrassed and perplexed the wavering. Heathcote was released, by sudden illness, from the difficulty of appealing to the government not to consider an amendment to the franchise as fatal to their bill.[185] This left Gladstone to suggest that there existed a coincidence of opinion on all sides of the House with respect to reform, and that there was no controversy traceable to party differences.[186] Gladstone then gave a negative definition to his idiosyncracy by disclosing that he would give his vote neither to the government nor the party when he voted against Russell's motion. This 'clever speech . . . full of inconsistencies' was received with puzzled amusement.[187]

Palmerston was placed in an acutely embarrassing position by both Russell's and the cabinet's determination for confrontation over the resolution. Palmerston, on 25 March, made a speech which sought to ease the government's position. Palmerston declared his support for Russell's resolution on the understanding that the government would continue to allow consideration of every part of the measure in Committee.[188] This was apparent support that milked Russell's motion of its malignancy. Choosing not to portray the motion as a rejection of the bill, Palmerston reconciled the public need to associate himself with a liberal purpose, in supporting the motion, with the private wish to deny Russell a victory while securing a moderate reform measure.[189] Palmerston's speech came very close to squaring the circle. Believing that the county franchise needed to be lowered, and upon further consideration agreeable to a lowering of the borough franchise, Palmerston commended the government's measure for avoiding a large transference of seats from small constituencies to unrepresented places.[190] The disfranchisement of the freeholders and the identity of the suffrage, however, he saw as provisions totally inconsistent with the principle of the constitution. No longer wishing to oppose the second reading, Palmerston suggested the most expedient course would be to propose the resolution, with the government choosing neither to resign nor to dissolve, but continuing with their bill accommodating Russell's motion. The recommendation confirmed that 'Palmerston and his personal tail', anxious to 'repress the expanding glories of his rival', would not contribute to 'the triumphant premiership of Lord John Russell'.[191]

A study of *Hansard* leaves the historian sympathetic with Lansdowne's comment that 'a week's debating in the House of Commons, tho' it [had] produced some good speeches . . . , [had] thrown little light upon the future'.[192] After a request from Disraeli, Elcho, with Lord Grey's approval,[193] made a speech dismissing the resolution as a party move and, although he did not approve of the details of the government's measure, he believed its rationale, as a representation of interests, was a sound principle.[194] Northcote noted that Russell's resolution was couched in general terms and offered no alternative to the government measure.[195] Ellice thought the Conservative measure 'essentially bad' for its sins of commission and sins of omission.[196]

From behind the Conservative frontbench, Walpole argued in vindication of the small borough constituencies and the varied character which the present mixed elements gave to parliamentary representation.[197] He found it difficult to support the second reading of the bill and, unless the government declared that all clauses were open to consideration in Committee, he would vote for the resolution. Graham suggested that the bill was 'too clever by half'.[198]

If Graham's speech, as so often before, suggested a more extreme intention than Graham privately entertained, Bright's statement proved notable for its moderation and has provided historians with a ready critique of the Conservative bill.[199] Posterity's echoing of Bright's criticisms, however, has not assisted historical understanding of the 1859 reform debate. Bright's objections to the bill reflected his own circumstances and differed from the common concerns of the House. The famous dismissal of 'fancy franchises', which Russell had incorporated in his own bill of 1854, drew attention to a part of the measure most other speakers chose to ignore. Bright's speech was an attempt to placate Liberal opinion, chastened by his radical rhetoric during the recess, and portray himself as an amenable partner in any Liberal administration that might follow Derby. In January 1859 both Russell and Cobden had refused to associate publicly with Bright and his stance on the question of reform. His parliamentary statement, in March 1859, was an attempt to end isolation. Bright did not see any great advantage or disadvantage in uniformity of franchise and thereby avoided the foremost issue of the debate. Moreover, he was not, he declared, 'very democratic'. What Bright pointed to was the popular desire for reform out-of-doors, apparent in public meetings exceeding, he claimed, in number and influence those held by the Anti-Corn Law League. Yet to answer this popular wish, Bright insisted, would be an essentially conservative move. Avowing a conservative purpose in supporting Russell's resolution, and avoiding the language of class antagonism, Bright presented himself as a respectable representative of the *vox populi* acceptable to Liberal sensibilities.[200]

A speech by Roebuck emphasised, once again, Bright's isolation and Roebuck's anti-Whig animus.[201] Acknowledging that the bill did little for the working classes, nevertheless, in opposition to Bright, Roebuck claimed that good might be got from the measure. Expressing no implicit confidence in either Russell or Palmerston as reformers, he asked the government whether, on going into Committee, they would accept an amendment for a £6 borough franchise. If they consented to such a course he declared his willingness to vote for the second reading. Bright considered that Roebuck's attack, 'for the habit of the creature [was] only to attack', did little damage and that Roebuck's 'personal vanity and craving for notoriety and display seem[ed] always to lead him wrong'.[202]

Disraeli's speech, concluding the debate, struck the House as 'calm and dignified, his voice was subdued and at times solemn', and 'in the place of sarcasm, and wit and ingenious phrases' he pronounced 'argument and warning'.[203] The government's bill, he declared, was founded upon three principles: that the constituent body of the country should be increased by the introduction of a large number of persons; that large communities were entitled to representation in the House and, finally, that the present borough system of representation should be preserved.[204] In reply to Roebuck, Disraeli assured the House that the government would give 'a candid consideration' to every proposition, although he could not pledge himself to any specific amendment before debate in Committee. Furthermore, Russell's resolution contained only points of detail which ought to be considered in Committee. Disraeli then drew attention to the subject of the franchise, and taunted Palmerston with his change of attitude towards Locke King's proposal. Russell was for admitting the working classes, but omitted any description of how this should be done, while Graham had pledged himself to the municipal franchise. As the two men collaborated in framing the resolution it was, Disraeli suggested, an unavoidable inference that Russell was pledged to the programme of Graham. Given the tenor of Bright's speech Disraeli could see no obstacle to Bright being adopted as 'a trusted and honoured colleague' by Russell and Graham. But what he could not reconcile was 'the mild Conservatism' of Palmerston and some Peelites with 'the avowed, the determined [and] the advanced policy' of Bright.

Disraeli's statement confirmed the prevalent suspicion that, if they were defeated, the government would go to the country. Bedford had predicted the cabinet would dissolve while 'the question of peace or war seem[ed] pretty well settled'; the association of issues was a shrewd reflection of Derby's thinking.[205] On 23 March the 'cabinet reaffirmed its decision to dissolve if defeated on John Russell's resolution'.[206] Derby assured Eglinton that whatever the result of the division he would 'not be in such a breathless haste to resign [his] office'.

We shall at once drop the reform bill, which will accordingly be lost for the session: but our accounts from the country are so favourable that I shall have no doubt whatever as to having recourse to a dissolution before I give in; and I do not apprehend any difficulty on the Queen's part . . . But there may, and no doubt are, difficulties arising out of the critical state of Foreign affairs, which may render an immediate dissolution inadvisable. In that event it is possible that we may go on for a short time, with the present House of Commons . . . There is no concert among the opposition and no chance of their being able to form a government except one of extreme opinion which the country will not have.[207]

In such an event, Russell could be portrayed as the self-interested saboteur of a moderate reform settlement in 1859.

On 29 March, Broughton noted that there 'seem[ed] little doubt that the amendment [would] be carried'.[208] Two days later he recorded that 'several M.P.s at Whites declared that Derby would have a majority'.[209] Granville considered the result 'certain', and believed 'the government [would] be defeated by 25 and [would] resign the next morning'.[210] Significantly Granville felt apprehensive about such an event. '[A] proper fire [the cabinet] will put us in [by resigning]. I really see no satisfactory way out of it.' Similarly Lord Grey feared 'a decided majority against the government'.[211] Russell, it was reported to Disraeli, 'expect[ed] a majority of 25'.[212] In contrast Earle, while prompting Elcho to adopt 'a confident tone' in his speech, disclosed that 'the government whips [took] a very sanguine view of the division and that their majority [was] more than probable'. They had, Earle claimed, 'more than 300 promises of support'.[213] While Earle's optimism served an obvious tactical purpose, it being feared that 'many members would vote with the government, but for the impression that Lord John's resolution [would] be carried', even in private Disraeli was 'inclined to believe we shall win'.[214] The opposition, Disraeli was informed by 'a spy to be depended on', hoped for '302, but it was described as a vanishing majority'. The 'Palmerstonian' backbencher Beaumont sent word to Disraeli, 'by a very confidential means', that '30 Whigs might be depended upon'. Stanley noted that the Whigs were 'greatly alarmed with the prospect of a dissolution', fearing it would 'increase the radical strength', and hoped this might persuade some to vote against the resolution.[215] Less confidently, Carnarvon considered politics to be in 'a very dark and unsatisfactory state'.[216]

The division on Russell's motion took place at 1.00 a.m. on 1 April. In the event, Russell's motion was carried by 330 to 291; a majority of 39.[217] 'A scene of great uproar and confusion followed from Wyld's persisting in adding the ballot to the resolution. Bright and a great many others walked out.'[218] Subsequent analysis of the division, taken in the fullest House for many years, revealed that, although the Conservative backbenchers had returned a loyal vote, not as many Liberals and Whigs had opposed the motion as the government anticipated. The government, Malmesbury noted, 'polled 265 out of 267 of [their] own men' with twenty-six non-Conservative votes.[219] The cross-bench votes were made up of sixteen Liberals and Whigs and ten of the Irish Brigade.[220] Gathorne Hardy observed name after name that the government whips had believed would support the ministry, voting for the resolution; Lowe, Lord Cavendish, Lord Grosvenor, Fortescue, Howard and other backbench Whigs joined Russell and Palmerston in the division lobby.[221] Roebuck also supported the resolution – probably because of Disraeli's non-committal response to his proposed amendment. Derby admitted that 'the majority was unexpectedly large, even according to the calculation of the opposition', and noted that 'some of the other side who had promised to vote had not kept faith'.[222] The vague wording of Russell's resolution, the vaguer sense Palmerston lent to those words, and a 'general belief entertained on both sides that there would be no dissolution unless the majority should be a very slender one', had its effect.[223]

The success of Russell's amendment left the government with the decision whether to resign, dissolve, or continue with reform deferred for a further session and foreign affairs pressing. Some members of the opposition, such as Granville, feared that a decision to resign would most acutely embarrass and perplex the supporters of Russell's motion. Similarly Clarendon believed that a dissolution would be 'a lesser evil than the government resigning and an extreme measure of reform being brought in by their successors'.[224] Arguing that Derby's government 'alone [would] carry a reform bill this session and the question [would] assume most formidable proportion if it [was] allowed to stand over another year', Clarendon believed 'the patriotic thing therefore wd. be not to resign'.[225] The 'hostile attitude' between Palmerston and Russell had intensified as the former had supported Russell's resolution in a manner so as 'to damage any ambitious hopes its author might entertain very seriously'.[226] Granville's anxiety belied the possibility that he himself might be 'the chief who could

enlist both in an administration and bridge the gulf which divide[d]
them'. Others spoke of 'a Russell reform cabinet' that might be
'stronger' without Palmerston; in such an arrangement Stanley might
find a place.[227] Bright did not see how Russell could form a government 'with much chance of success . . . [H]e can hardly undertake to
form a government without asking me to join him – and others, that
is, the Whigs and aristocratic class, will not go with him, if he has
anything to do with me!' Certainly Bright had no desire to remove
'difficulties in the way of the formation of a government of the old
Whig sort'.[228]

At a cabinet meeting on 1 April, the government 'resolved not to
resign, but to dissolve as soon as parliamentary business permitted.
Only Estcourt and Stanley [were] for immediate resignation.'[229] The
announcement of this decision to parliament on 4 April scotched
further speculation. Despite some Conservative apprehension Derby
was confident of an appeal to the country. The government, during
the past fourteen months, had done much to establish the Conservatives as a party of moderate and capable governing ability, that might
be contrasted with the fragmented and factious character of the
opposition. Queen Victoria, for one, was encouraging Derby by
condemning Russell for his contentious manoeuvre which showed he
was 'ever ready to *make* mischief and do his country harm'.[230]

11 The Constitution and War

In the present unsettled state of parties it is impossible to predict
what may happen any day. (Graham to his electoral agent (? April
1859) cited in C. S. Parker, *Life and Letters of Sir James Graham,
Second Baronet of Netherby* (London, 1907) II, p. 379)

Disraeli saw in the cabinet's decision to dissolve in April 1859 an
opportunity for the Conservatives to make a constitutional appeal
rather than merely recite the government's legislative achievement.
'The real issue – the broad great issue [was] whether parliamentary
government [was] compatible with existing institutions.'[1] The Commons was broken into fragments of party which, although they had no
unity of purpose or policy, could always combine to overthrow the
government however it might be formed. There appeared no reason
why there should not be a dissolution upon a ministerial crisis every
February, and '[o]ne was certain next February if Lord Palmerston
form[ed] a government such as he contemplat[ed] and the Radicals
[were] excluded'. This, Disraeli urged, was 'the state of affairs which
the country ought to be called upon to comprehend and remedy'.
Nothing more completely proved the case, he argued, than 'the total
want of cohesion on the opposition benches', and the fact that
Russell's 'flimsy resolution was the only means by which they could
be brought together for the moment; and that when carried, had we
proceeded with the bill, the two leaders of the coalition were pledged
to an exactly contrary policy: Lord John to defeat the government
measure, Lord Palmerston to support and, with amendments, carry
it'.

In the Lords, Derby, although dissatisfied with his speech, elaborated upon Disraeli's text.[2] The distracted state of parties rendered it
almost impossible to administer the affairs of the nation and, in
attempting to settle the question of parliamentary reform, divergent
sections of opinion had preferred the interests of party to the interests
of the country.[3] With such priorities the 'motley and heterogeneous
materials' that constituted the Liberal party had defeated the government not by fair parliamentary opposition, but by an ingenious
manoeuvre. In the Commons, Disraeli declared the disjointed state of

party connection to be prejudicial to the reputation of parliament, and that it was important that the authority of executive government be supported by the authority of parliament.[4]

In replying to Disraeli on 4 April, Russell took the opportunity to present his own reform proposals as a specific alternative to the government's measure.[5] He proposed a £10 franchise for the counties and a reduction of the borough franchise from £10 to £6 thus admitting a number of the working classes. On the more intractable problem of redistribution, Russell suggested a modest scheme re-allocating thirty seats. The moment chosen to announce this plan was calculated to offer a tangible option shaped to moderate opinion. The character of the proposals reflected Russell's ministerial prospects. In the event of Derby being turned out Russell might go to the Lords as premier with either Sidney Herbert or Sir George Grey as Leader of the Commons.[6]

Anticipating events, *The Examiner* placed 'Russell on the Whig or Liberal throne again'.[7] Certainly a buoyant optimism was evident in Russell's comment that Derby should not have accepted office in 1858.[8] The unavoidable inference from such asides was that Russell saw himself as the rightful successor to Palmerston. The character of that succession, in the circumstance of April 1859, Russell revealed in his moderate reform proposals. He admitted that it was 'a difficult position to stand between extremes and yet that [was] the position which a Whig must always occupy'.[9]

Palmerston assumed an ostensibly non-partisan position. He refused to consider the vote on Russell's motion as a vote of censure requiring the withdrawal of the government's bill or a dissolution.[10] If it had been a vote of censure against the government he would not have supported the motion. The result of an election would create a new parliament more likely than the present to decide that power ought to be transferred to other hands. With both the government and Russell becoming more committed, Palmerston shrouded himself with ambivalence. Those at Cambridge House refused to admit 'the Derby reform bill was a bad bill'.[11] The advice Wood proffered to Palmerston acknowledged the attraction of ostensible disinterest. An attempt by Palmerston to form a government would 'render men indifferent comparatively to reform and anxious for the most competent leader in troubled times'.[12] Any declared commitment to a particular scheme of reform would only raise 'a double standard' and might result in the opposition below the gangway pledging themselves against any lead from Cambridge House.

You were not a party to the bill of 1852 and having the advantage of being committed to no particular details it seems to me that by pledging yourself to *anything* you would, in your peculiar position, be throwing away an advantage over everybody else which you now possess.[13]

The spectrum of opinion that Palmerston might encompass within a conciliatory lead, once conciliation was seen to be necessary, was a wide one. Drawing up a hypothetical cabinet under his own premiership, on 30 March 1859, Palmerston included Herbert, Gladstone, Wood, Cornewall Lewis, Clarendon, Granville, Argyll and Newcastle in his list, with Russell included in the government, but safely isolated as Secretary for India.[14]

Palmerston's wish to conciliate and the attempt by Russell to define differences with the government did not amplify obvious divisions amongst the backbenches. While Wood was willing to believe that Palmerston was 'upper-most', he was also forced to acknowledge 'that neither he nor J.R. had so large a party following as Derby – nor did [Wood] think the Liberals would unite for any party purpose'.[15] Lowe had voted in the belief that the government would not resort to a dissolution, while Fortescue observed that the opposition was 'not united enough for so strong a measure'.[16] Lord Moncreiff came to wish that Russell's resolution 'had never been prepared'.[17] As the decision by the cabinet to dissolve exacerbated confusion amongst the opposition backbenches, so confusion revived the possibility that backbenchers might 'look out for a new chief'.[18]

Lord Grey provided an alternative persona around which party configuration might be realigned. Grey had found Derby's defence of the government's decision to dissolve 'injudicious and in very bad taste'.[19] Wood saw an opportunity to champion Grey's claim to Whig and Liberal loyalty. Reminding Elcho, a potential adherent, of Elcho's loyalty to Peel in 1846, Wood declared his belief that 'Lord Grey more than any other public man . . . represent[ed] the principles of Sir Robert Peel'.[20] Wood also believed that he had 'reason to think this opinion [was] spreading rapidly'. As to the objection that Grey was 'difficult to serve with' Wood observed that it was 'one thing to lead and another to fill a second place in government as *Leader*'. In his 'proper place' as premier Grey would 'work very easily and pleasantly with his colleagues'. The potential appeal of Grey was obvious. His family name proclaimed an association with the Liberal past shared with Russell, but without the latter's putative fondness for

Radicals. His 'moderation' and desire for a settlement of the reform question recommended him as a conciliatory figure more easily capable of adhering Conservatives such as Stanley and Pakington than Palmerston. His being a member of the Upper House had distanced him from the acrimonious reform debate of the previous weeks.

Wood's initiative, in the event, fell victim to Grey's ill health. At the beginning of April 1859, Grey's doctor recommended an operation for the division of some tendons in one foot.[21] Performed on 11 April, the operation put Grey in a wheelchair for all of April and May 1859, denied him sleep and effectively isolated him from political events.[22] Grey's private problems worsened when, at the beginning of May, his wife became critically ill. Such private misfortune precluded Grey from public concerns. The result of Wood's abortive initiative, however, was that Wood himself became a subject of suspicion and mistrust both at Cambridge House and Pembroke Lodge. The subsequent imputation of self-interest may not have been entirely misplaced. If Grey had become premier in the Lords, Wood may have realistically hoped to become a similarly conciliatory Leader of the Commons. Neither Grey nor Wood successfully recovered the strength of their bargaining position so swiftly compromised by the surgeon's knife.

During April 1859 Granville observed that 'Argyll [was] bidding for the post' Wood hoped Grey might fill.[23] Although, as a leader to appease differences, Granville thought Argyll 'would not be a bad one', Granville sensibly 'rather doubt[ed] his getting it'. Wanting in age, reputation and influence, Argyll's claim upon Whig and Liberal loyalties was never more than tenuous. Granville himself was an alternative figure who might more effectively cohere a disjointed opposition. The situation was also favourable for a revival of Clarendon's and Cornewall Lewis's prospects. Wood's attempt to champion the claims of Grey, however, remained the only serious initiative undertaken to realign party sentiment during April as the activity of the hustings and the indeterminate character of the next parliament counselled delay. Delay also ensured the continued confusion of backbench opinion. Wood 'attributed the desertion of 35 Liberals in the late vote [on Russell's motion] to hatred of J.R.', while Broughton 'thought it might be attributed to a dislike of bringing back the Palmerston cabinet'.[24] Moncrieff attempted to prevent Elcho being 'sucked into Dizzy's whirlpool'.[25]

The attitudes struck during the first weeks of April 1859 suggested that in the forthcoming election 'the substantial question [would] be reform or no reform'.[26] Foreign affairs, and in particular Italy, appeared not to be an issue. The government were content that this should be so because of the obstacles they were experiencing in foreign agreement to a Congress. Austria made the previous disarmament of Sardinia, as well as France and Austria as urged by England, a *sine qua non* to negotiation.[27] This insistence on the part of Austria prompted France to once more adopt an intransigent attitude; the 'very bad accounts' from Cowley in Paris led Malmesbury to expect war as 'almost certain'.[28] France agreed to disarm prior to the Congress, but refused to urge Sardinia to agree to disarmament.[29] This refusal the cabinet saw as an attempt by France to sabotage the Congress while preserving a pacific pose, with 'Walewski playing fast and loose about Sardinia'[30] and 'Napoleon clearly playing false'.[31] When Azeglio 'came to complain of [an] Austrian despatch insulting to Sardinia' Malmesbury saw it as '[f]resh proof of the insincerity of France'.[32]

In a debate on Italy in the Lords on 18 April 1859, Malmesbury reiterated Austria's rights by conquest, inheritance and treaty to the province of Lombardy. But he recognised a true cause of complaint arose from Austrian interference in other Italian states.[33] He also acknowledged that a strong feeling existed in the country in favour of Sardinia's assimilation of her own independent institutions. But he found it difficult to understand why France should involve herself in the question. The assembling of a Congress had been delayed by the two questions of the composition of the Congress and prior disarmament. In attempting to solve these difficulties the government, Malmesbury declared, had made every effort to avert a war that would be 'a theatre for the dreams of the wildest theorists and the most unprincipled adventurers'. Derby supported Malmesbury's pronouncement with the statement that neutrality, as the object pursued by the cabinet, had to be an armed neutrality. The chances of peace would be immeasureably strengthened if it were known that England would not remain a passive spectator of any event in which her honour was concerned.[34]

Broad agreement over foreign policy continued, during the first weeks of April 1859, to constrain both Palmerston and Russell. Both 'seem[ed] well aware that any encouragement to war would be most unpopular at home'.[35] In a speech in London on 15 April, Russell devoted nearly all his statement to reform, dismissing the government bill as a 'sham' with no real reforming intent or power, and insisting that to have allowed it into Committee would have been to allow important and unsatisfactory clauses to remain in the measure.[36] As a postscript Russell added that he had 'no reason for distrust with respect to the present Secretary of State for Foreign Affairs. (Cheers.)' Similarly, Palmerston, although he had private doubts about the government's policy, maintained a public acquiescence in the cabinet's aims. He believed Malmesbury was 'putting the cart before the horse by insisting on disarming before the negotiation in Congress', but let it be understood that he shared the government's desire to preserve peace.[37]

The Italian debate in the Commons, on 18 April 1859, affirmed an apparent unanimity. Palmerston's reply to Disraeli's statement of government policy[38] restricted criticism to the insistence on prior disarmament and the suggestion that the Congress might continue to consider the question of the amelioration of Italy in general.[39] The only discordant note introduced into the discussion came from the Radical backbencher Duncombe who declared that the state of Italy was a disgrace to civilised Europe and that Italy must be rid of Austria before the peace and happiness of her people could be secured.[40] Significantly, Gladstone, whom Clarendon had expected to be 'the man most likely to do mischief',[41] deprecated Duncombe's speech as tending to widen inconveniently the field of discussion.[42] The tone of the debate enforced the impression that an agreement over the basic aims of foreign policy existed, allowing antagonistic sentiment to focus upon reform. No less significantly, Russell admitted to 'having no faith in L.N., Buol or Cavour. I think they are all waiting for an occasion to say "you see the war was not my fault".'[43]

The ultimatum Austria sent to Sardinia on 19 April 1859 dramatically changed the political situation. On 19 April Malmesbury learnt of Sardinia's agreement to disarm, thus securing the acceptance of the preconditions by all parties involved in the Congress.[44] On the same day, however, Austria, unaware of Sardinia's sudden compliance, sent an ultimatum to Sardinia demanding disarmament within three days or else open hostilities would ensue. Advised by the French 'to give a haughty reply' Sardinia portrayed the ultimatum as an insult and preparations for war were begun.[45] This diplomatic blunder made 'Austria the aggressor and [gave] L.N. a lift'.[46] It also cast a damaging retrospective light on the pronouncements of Derby's cabinet made in the belief that France would prove to be the instigator of hostilities. Aberdeen observed that the 'tables [were] altogether turned, and the French Emperor, who was preparing for war without the shadow of pretext, will now assume the character of an injured innocent'.[47] Palmerston immediately noted the incongruity of the government's earlier policy.

> Everybody has been open-mouthed about the aggressive attitude of France and Sardinia, about to pounce on the innocent lamb of Austria. Now it turns out that Austria is the aggressor, and it is Austria that is fully prepared.[48]

The Austrian ultimatum, and the false position in which it placed the government, transformed the question of Italy into a political issue.

Diplomatic events between 19 and 21 April, and the subsequent war between Austria and France and Sardinia in Northern Italy had an immediate, if ambivalent, effect upon domestic preparations for the election. Parliament dissolved on 18 April with the government delivering a definitive statement of their foreign policy framed within the assumptions then entertained. Three days later, with the apparently erroneous nature of those assumptions demonstrated, electoral addresses were made as revised comment on drastically altered circumstances. Rewriting his address and reversing his former priorities, Russell made two speeches in London on 23 and 25 April giving scant attention to reform, but dwelling at length on the issue of Italy.[49] Derby's policy of 'armed neutrality', Russell claimed, as was evidenced by his unfounded suspicion of France, concealed a policy favourable to Austria. The great need in any settlement of conflicting claims in Europe, Russell continued, was the desire of the Italian people for freedom and liberty. Therein lay the powerful moral content of Russell's appeal. England in the approaching European war, he concluded, should 'maintain not an "armed neutrality", but a fair, open, honest and peaceful neutrality. (Loud Cheers.)' These speeches proved to be challenging and dangerous restatements of Russell's position. The government, whose policy was being overtaken by events, was left momentarily vulnerable.

Derby responded to Russell's challenge in his Mansion House speech on 25 April. By sending the ultimatum, Derby informed the Queen, Austria had 'deprive[d] herself of all claim to the support or countenance of England'.[50] The cabinet agreed 'to send back a vehement protest and advice to Sardinia to appeal to the Protocol of Paris'.[51] Russell's speeches demanded that this private disapproval be made public. At the Mansion House, Derby restated the government's intention to maintain a strict, though armed, neutrality, and 'abused' Austria for opening hostilities.[52] Derby reported to Malmesbury that he was '*very* well received . . . the country [was] all for peace à tout prix – and Austria's intolerable stupidity [had] completely turned the scale against her'.[53] In the speech 'Derby pointedly disclaimed the view attributed to him by Lord John . . . of placing this country in an attitude of armed neutrality with the intention of ultimately taking the part of Austria'. Lord Grey, for one, found the rebuttal 'satisfactory'.[54]

The significance of Russell and Derby's London speeches at the beginning of the election, was that they drew the question of Italy into the arena of antagonistic debate. Fears of a Franco–Russian alliance, possibly aimed at Britain, as well as a panic collapse at the London Stock Exchange heightened the sense of crisis. Of no less significance, however, was the fact that Derby's denial of Russell's accusations allowed those who wished to exclude the Italian issue from discussion to do so. Italy became a matter of controversy for those, in particular Russell and Palmerston, who saw it as a question with which to define differences. Ellice, seeking to preserve the consensus, believed England's 'position in the affair was equally well stated by Derby in his amended speech . . . and by John Russell in his excellent speech to the electors in the City. There seem[ed] no difference of opinion with respect to a national policy.'[55] Graham, in contrast, predicted that when the government were 'brought to book, it [would] be seen that they [had] been wanting throughout both in sincerity and firmness. This [was] the natural consequence of regarding Malmesbury as the sole prop of the peace of the Empire.'[56] In private Russell pressed upon Palmerston the moral impetus of his newly defined position. The European difficulties were 'all owing to the obstinate pretension of Austria to exclude all freedom from Italy. She is now driven to be the assailant, but she will never succeed in putting down the Italian people.'[57]

The elections, which continued into May 1859, revealed the personal preoccupations and differing emphasis that events offered to individual candidates. Some accepted the Austrian ultimatum and Derby's response, as enunciated at the Mansion House, with an equanimity that kept attention focused on reform. Aberdeen expressed the regret of many:

The final decision seems to have been taken, and no hope of peace now remains. It seems that Austria has been unable to endure the countless delays which have been calculated for her . . . Of course she will meet with no mercy here and the step is greatly to be lamented, however strong the actual inducement. The tables are altogether turned.[58]

Newcastle observed that 'the certainty of war would be in the government's favour where parties [were] equally divided – so many thinking it right to support *any* government at the commencement of a war'.[59] Although in late April 1859 Russell was 'in good spirits' and talked 'a good deal . . . on foreign affairs', Italy remained an issue of contention for the few rather than the many.[60] At Halifax, Wood pronounced the traditional Whig wisdom on reform, 'improvement, but not extensive changes', and found himself embarrassed by the Conservative candidate being as 'liberal' as himself.[61] Graham, although committed to Russell's personal fortunes, when speaking at Carlisle on 28 April, confined his statement to reform.[62] Similarly in Birmingham, on 25 April, Bright concerned himself with reform, making only one oblique reference to the foreign situation: a reference the more oblique for being an assertion of general principle.[63]

Palmerston, in a hastily revised address, assailed the government's Italian policy as part of a general indictment of the cabinet's inadequacy.[64] Aberdeen considered Palmerston's amended hustings statement on Italy the 'most brilliant stroke' of the election. Palmerston's careful dissent from government policy might provide Gladstone with a public justification for reconciliation with Cambridge House, 'notwithstanding the three articles of the *Quarterly*, and the thousand imprecations of late years'.[65] Without adequate reason, Palmerston declared, the government had resorted to a dissolution, but he declined to give details of an alternative reform scheme on the hustings. Meanwhile the government had failed in preserving peace, Austria by invading Sardinia had placed herself in the wrong, and the cabinet, in one short week, had changed their portrayal of Austria as 'dignified conciliators' to one of 'public criminals and offenders'. Such anger, Palmerston asserted, was the pique of men frustrated by their own want of foresight.

Stanley, speaking in Kings Lynn on 30 April, elaborated on the Conservative electoral text provided by Disraeli.[66] Reform was only part of the greater issue of good government and constitutional authority. The prospective European conflict was the product of the ambition of a few men and the independence of Italy was nothing more than a plea. The consensus over England's attitude towards Italy, Stanley insisted, still existed – the isolated pronouncements of Russell, Palmerston and some others notwithstanding. Speaking at

Aylesbury on 2 May, Disraeli reinforced the central message: a Conservative government meant moderation, stability and good government both in foreign and domestic affairs.[67]

The vigour of the Conservatives' electoral appeal reflected a general confidence within the cabinet as to their electoral prospects. Derby noted on 25 April that the elections seemed to be 'going on as well as could possibly be expected, or even better', while Disraeli was 'in high spirits'.[68] Northcote forecast, to Disraeli's delight, 'a clear gain of seven seats in Devon and Cornwall, after allowing for the loss of one at Barnstaple', with a possible total gain of nine or even ten.[69] One week later, in a less optimistic tone, Derby observed that '[m]any of the elections [had] been singularly unfortunate; the government candidates having been defeated in 11 places by less than ten votes'.[70] Despite these setbacks, however, Derby anticipated a gain to the Conservatives of not less than twenty-five seats 'giving a total of rather more than 300, without including a considerable number of independent Liberals' who had promised the government their support.[71] The final tally-sheet of new members that Jolliffe produced at the end of the election revealed that the government had indeed gained thirty-one seats creating a total of 306 Conservative members. But against this avowed Conservative strength Jolliffe listed 349 members of the opposition.[72] Disraeli lamented that the gain of those seats lost by less than ten votes might have set the government on 'a rock of adamant', but without an absolute majority their position remained 'critical'.[73] Derby observed that 'very much will depend on the skill with which we play our game'.[74]

The Conservative party had its greatest successes in English counties and small boroughs.[75] But a further eight seats gained in Ireland vindicated the government's Catholic concessions.[76] Conservative victories in Ireland also offered an obvious opening in any attempt to ensure the government's survival despite being in a continued parliamentary minority. Both Cardinal Wiseman and Archbishop MacHale of Tuam had urged Catholics to support Conservative candidates at the elections. Lord Naas had worked closely with influential Irish Catholics from Dublin Castle, and Derby was 'particularly glad to see, though [he had] no "compact" with Cardinal Wiseman as the newspapers [would] have it, that [they had] received a considerable amount of R.C. support'.[77] Derby persuaded Eglinton that 'the appointment of one or two R.C.'s, even to second rate offices', would be 'of considerable advantage' to the government.

The Irish 'independants' *want* nothing for themselves and would forfeit their position by accepting anything: but they do want an answer to their co-religionists who taunt them with their support of a government who, as it is represented, zealously excludes R.C.'s from offices of profit.[78]

The subsequent politic dispersion of patronage enabled those members of the Irish Brigade favourably inclined to the government to continue their support in the absence of any reference to landlord and tenant legislation.[79] Care would be needed, however, if such concessions were not to alienate 'ultra-Tory' opinion. Having long suspected Disraeli of pursuing 'an Irish Papist alliance', Beresford believed it 'quite preposterous' that the 'ultra-Tories' should be made 'such fools as well as such rogues as to give [their] hearty support to a government that [was] secretly dealing with Cardinal Wiseman and promising the Papists anything they wish and anything they dare demand'.[80] Die-hard sensibility offset Irish Brigade support.

An alternative opening for negotiation rested on that interpretation of events since 1852 that saw Palmerston as the most able Conservative leader in the Commons the party never had. Early in May 1859 Disraeli wrote directly to Palmerston suggesting that if he were to unite with the Conservatives in forming a government, bringing with him 'a following of about 20 or 30', the government 'would have more than an absolute majority of the House'.[81] Palmerston, Disraeli continued, might then be 'entire master of the situation', having an influence over foreign policy, even if he were not Foreign Secretary. On domestic policy, Palmerston might propose his own reform scheme which, Disraeli readily assured him, the Conservatives would support. Disraeli also suggested, with no authority for doing so, that Palmerston might then expect to become leader of the Conservative party in succession to Derby. Disraeli predicted the alternative to be Palmerston finding himself an uncomfortable member of a Russell cabinet with whom he would have neither common opinions nor sympathies. Palmerston's reply, a simple and direct yet polite negative, gave scant recognition to the seductive credibility of Disraeli's proposal.[82] Ellice, finding everything 'in a mess', believed it would result 'in some understanding between the Conservatives, and Whigs under Palmerston'.[83] Graham observed:

Whether Lord John and [Palmerston] will come to terms is more doubtful. But Palmerston, *with Tory support*, will be strong enough to conduct the government without him.[84]

Graham went on to describe the union of Palmerston and Derby as 'the probable solution of existing difficulties'.[85] The 'distribution of power [was] the only real difficulty between them . . . There [was] not . . . much to choose between Derby and Palmerston: the one was a Whig and became a Tory; the other for half a century [had] been a Tory at heart and [was] so still.'

Palmerston's immediate rejection of Disraeli's overture attested to the growing opportunity that he saw of assuming power on his own terms. Such a possibility would only be prematurely compromised by an overt junction with Derby. Clarendon, however, attempted an initiative similar to that desired by Disraeli and seen as likely by Graham and Ellice. On 12 May, Clarendon visited Malmesbury and engaged in a 'long conversation about parties'.[86] Believing that 'Lord John Russell and Palmerston never would join', Clarendon 'agreed cordially' with Malmesbury 'that it would be a great benefit if moderate Whigs and Derbyites would join – there was little difference if any between them'. In Whig counsel Clarendon threw 'cold water' on suggestions of attacking the government;[87] the suggestion that the Liberal party was united he found 'absurd'.[88] In the event of a vote of no confidence being proposed 'a great number of moderate men [would] stay away or vote against a motion until they [knew] what [was] to follow'. All that was certain was that 'Palmerston and Lord J.R. [had] not made up their differences, that they [would] not unite and that neither [could] make a government likely to last a moment without the other'.

Clarendon's discussion with Malmesbury revealed Whig and Liberal opinion which might seek moderation in a Conservative alignment against radical demands. Disraeli sounded out Horsman. In an attempt to assuage Horsman's anxieties, Disraeli, in the expectation of a refusal, offered Horsman a position in the cabinet.[89] As Disraeli hoped Horsman declined the offer, but it 'prevent[ed] him from precipitating himself into any combination against the government'.[90] Lindsay, 'supposed to be the type of some dozen men of doubtful Liberal allegiance', was also sounded and 'replied very favourably'. But the same opposition apprehension that might favour a junction with the Conservatives could also come to recognise in Palmerston an alternative safeguard against radical demands. This encouraged Palmerston to avoid any immediate association with the government. On 3 May 1859 Disraeli had impressed upon Palmerston the assumption that, in the event of the Conservatives resigning, 'it would be impossible for the Queen to send for anyone but Lord J. Russell'.[91] The longer uncertainty persisted, however, the stronger became Palmerston's own claim as a figure of conciliation. On 8 May, Disraeli noted 'the growing impression' that Palmerston might be the new prime minister if Russell was 'starved out'.[92]

Once it was ascertained that Palmerston was unwilling to join the government, Disraeli suggested Lord Elgin and Gladstone.[93] Elgin, however, was known to have little hope for the survival of Derby's minority ministry and, compounded by the difficulty of finding a suitable office, it was expected that Elgin would decline. In the case of Gladstone, Disraeli suggested the India Office as 'the only post which would absorb his superfluous energies'. Derby, however, proved noticeably reluctant to reopen negotiations with Gladstone. He questioned whether Gladstone was 'a desirable acquisition', and noted that Gladstone's 'extreme opinions on Italian affairs' would prove 'very embarrassing'.[94] The premier waited until 19 May 1859 before writing to Gladstone to enquire whether he would object to a private interview on the state of public affairs and parties. In a characteristically ambivalent reply Gladstone, in a self-deprecating tone, questioned the value of such discussion, but nonetheless declared himself ready to 'speak without reserve'.[95] This ambivalence Derby took as his cue to swiftly break off further communication. As Derby declared to Disraeli, 'it would have been useless to waste time by an unmeaning conversation, leading to nothing. I own I hardly regret it.'[96]

The decision of the cabinet, early in May 1859, to propose an alternative reform scheme when the new parliament assembled was an attempt to adhere centrist opinion despite Palmerston's absence from the Treasury bench. It was also an attempt to substantiate the rhetorical claims made on the hustings and illustrate the ministry's ability for good government. Although initially reticent, Derby presided over a cabinet meeting on 14 May at which it was determined 'to bring on another reform bill'.[97] Sotheron-Estcourt spoke 'decidedly in the affirmative 1. on account of our character for consistency 2. because, if we do not, others will carry it'.[98] After further discussion '[a]ll but one', probably Derby, 'agreed: and he only wished to put it off'. Derby found comfort in the expectation that 'the prospect of being able to carry a bill through [was] slight'.[99] Manners observed that 'in reality, it [was] proposed to introduce a reform bill, not for its own sake, nor because we approve of its provisions or hope to pass it, but as a means of checkmating Lord John Russell'.[100] At a cabinet meeting on 17 May it was decided to propose a £12 or £15 county franchise and an £8 or £6 borough franchise with the rest of the scheme the same as the last.[101] The political intent of such a scheme was clear. The modified suffrage was that which Palmerston had declared himself willing to accept, while the restricted redistribution clauses, the most successful part of the government's earlier scheme, were retained.

12 Dénouement

The Liberal party are anxious to have a stand-up fight with Lord Derby as soon as parliament meets. The onward tactics are especially pressed by the ultras. When I mentioned this to Lord Palmerston he did not appear so eager, and I thought I observed a disinclination to turn out the government on reform, which of course would give Lord John Russell the advantage. (Hayward to Gladstone, 7 May 1859, cited in *A Selection from the Correspondence of Abraham Hayward Q.C.* (London, 1886) H. C. Carlisle (ed.) II, p. 33)

No reform bill can pass this parliament which does not suit the taste of Lord Palmerston and Lord Derby. The minimum of the one and the maximum of the other are in such close affinity that the opposite parties on this point will easily come to a settlement. (Graham to Russell, 9 May 1859, Graham Mss. Bundle 135, cited in C. S. Parker, *Life and Letters of Sir James Graham, Second Baronet of Netherby* (London, 1907) II, p. 382)

In January 1859 Russell had seemed poised to assume leadership of a revived Peelite, Liberal and Radical opposition to Conservative reform. The tragic theme in the drama of the next four months was the destruction of Russell's vision of triumphant apotheosis. The Conservative cabinet proposed a more moderate reform scheme, with less internal crisis, than expected. Russell had to forestall general discussion with a motion focusing debate on the freehold franchise. Radicals, in particular Roebuck and Bright, failed to endorse Russell's authority. Palmerston supported Russell's motion in such a manner as to scuttle its authors' ambitions. Forced into an election and taking advantage of European events, Russell took up the lofty cry of Italian liberty only to fail in dislodging a preoccupation with reform. Russell's worsening plight brought the engaging subplot of Palmerston's intentions once again into centre stage. At the opening of the final act in May, Russell faced the critical need to recover his position impelled by one governing circumstance: the longer Russell's difficulties persisted the better Palmerston's prospects became.

Following the election Ellice found the future 'very dark'.[1] In any vote against the government Palmerston was 'just as likely to vote against John Russell, as the Radicals [were] to vote for Derby for fear of bringing in Palmerston'. There was 'no likelihood of agreement over reform' with many in the opposition prepared to 'abet' the government with a modified measure. Lansdowne observed, in exasperation, that 'it was absurd to make efforts for the so-called Liberals without knowing what their objects were and who was to lead them'.[2] Wood energetically, but with little effect, counselled a concerted attack on the government. Betraying prevalent misgivings about both the state of the Liberal party and Wood's reliability, Bedford recalled Melbourne's memorable jibe: 'Wood's always so damned cocksure'.[3] While reform offered little ground for unity, Clarendon's forebodings revealed emerging differences over European affairs. Expecting Austria to be beaten in any military conflict, Louis Napoleon, Clarendon warned, once victorious would 'believe himself omnipotent and capable of realising every dream that [had] ever floated in his own or his uncle's head, and the first of these [would] be to revenge Waterloo'.[4] 'Pam and Johnny', Granville succinctly noted, were 'too Italian'.[5] Russell's private attempts to reconcile his own and Clarendon's views proved unconvincing.[6]

Some Whigs and Liberals, however, saw a crucial need for an immediate hostile vote against the government that would offer the opportunity to appease Whig, Liberal and Radical differences in the distribution of office. Graham, sensing that Russell's moment was passing, urged that 'the reckless wickedness of the dissolution rendered [Derby's] early condemnation inevitable'.[7] Graham suggested to Ellice, 'the nestor of [the] party',[8] that the government might be discredited by a Select Committee enquiring into the use of corrupt means at the elections.[9] As Sir George Grey noted it was becoming increasingly urgent to define opposition allegiance:

The main question is . . . how is union to be secured among those who have been honestly returned to this Parliament as Liberals. . . . Who is to be leader of the Liberals and can they act together as they ought, or are they again to be distracted and weakened by internal differences and jealousies? . . . Is an amendment on the Address expedient and should we carry it? I doubt it. . . . What I am afraid of is that things may be left to take their chance and that all confidence in their leaders will be lost by the party.[10]

Somewhat cryptically, Palmerston observed that although in the event of Derby resigning what was to follow was 'by no means clear', events 'sometimes clear up a state of things which before those events happen appear to be ones of inestimable confusion'.[11]

As before, Graham's inclination, and his wish for an immediate move against the government, reflected Russell's best prospects. Russell found the Liberal party to be 'like the Irishman's blanket; if you want to strengthen the top you must cut off the bottom; if the bottom, you must cut off the top'.[12] But Russell insisted, as the elections came to an end, that a general vote of want of confidence in Derby's government had to be proposed. Armed with 'the elements of calculation' and 'a list of the turncoats and deserters of the 31 March', Russell encouraged confidence in the success of such a motion.[13] Granville recognised the politic sense in Russell's chosen strategy. 'It [would] be difficult to ensure everybody voting on any separate question of immediate reform, or of war, or of the criminality of the dissolution – but for one reason or another all [would] join in on a general vote of want of confidence if moved by an unobjectionable person.'[14] Russell believed there would be the least objection to the motion if it was proposed by 'some leading person' amongst the 'Palmerstonian' set.[15] Meanwhile Russell looked to the character of the cabinet to succeed Derby as the safeguard of his own succession to the premiership. Unless the cabinet included Graham, Gladstone, Herbert and Milner Gibson, with possibly the Duke of Somerset and Sir F. Baring, he would have 'none of it'.[16] Although the Duke of Newcastle, Cornewall Lewis, 'and two or three more of the Palmerston set might complete the cabinet', such a frontbench would require the broad appeal of Russell's leadership. 'Otherwise Palmerston may try to construct a cabinet like the last, and probably fail.'

Russell entered negotiations for a Liberal reunion in mid-May with two strong bargaining points. First, that any real reconciliation would have to be reflected in the broad representation of different sections in the new government. A Palmerstonian restoration was impossible. Radicals and Peelites would have to have cabinet office. Secondly, such a government would have to be agreed upon a reform bill that was a compromise between Whig caution and Radical commitment. Russell prepared the way for negotiation with Palmerston after the 10 May, insistent upon these two points. Concession on other matters accompanied by firm commitment on these two points would hopefully protect Russell's position during the uncertainties of subsequent negotiation.[17]

On the evening of 15 May, Cornewall Lewis delivered to Pembroke Lodge a message from Palmerston that 'he would disapprove any amendment concerning the dissolution, or insisting upon immediate introduction of a reform bill, or concerning the conduct of foreign affairs. But he would approve of an amendment or early notice of a motion declaring want of confidence.'[18] Russell, in response, suggested a resolution 'similar to that carried against Lord Melbourne's government in 1841', but also repeated his commitment to acting in agreement with Graham and Milner Gibson.[19] To Graham, Russell reaffirmed that he could not 'without sacrificing public objects, accept office without power, and allow [him]self to be strangled at any moment by the mutes of the party'.[20] He saw 'two situations of influence, the premiership and the leadership of the Commons, which might be 'divided on fair and equal terms. That is, if Palmerston is prime minister, I should lead in the Commons; if I were to be prime minister he ought to lead in the House of Commons.' Graham perceived the advantage in such ostensible deference whilst commitment was maintained to a liberal reform bill and a Peelite and Radical presence in cabinet. 'Your strength will be greatest if you remain in the House of Commons, making the apparent sacrifice of yielding pre-eminence to an old man of seventy-five, but really removing him from the centre of power, which is in the Lower House.'[21]

It was becoming apparent that Bright held 'the balance of parties' in the Commons with 'some 35 firm adherents in the new parliament'.[22] Yet Russell's position was difficult because, even with the support of 'the old Whigs and the extreme Liberals', he could not 'carry on the government, in the face of 300 Tories, without the assistance of Lord Palmerston and his quasi-Liberal adherents'. Thus the form that any resolution took would have to 'ensure the largest possible support from the entire body of the Liberal party'. On 17 May, Herbert wrote to Russell urging that opposition backbenchers be given 'a good prospect of a fair co-operation among the Liberal party'.[23] Liberals of 'cool heads and cautious tempers' wished for a clearer understanding upon reform before any move was made, although Herbert feared that there would 'be more difficulty coming to an agreement on this subject in this parliament than in the last, and more difficulty in carrying a bill'. Herbert's letter prompted Russell to continue his conciliatory move towards Palmerston, while once again insisting that he could 'see no use in having a ministry like the last [Palmerston government] with no real liberal tendencies'.[24] Moreover, Russell remained sceptical about the possibility of an agreement. 'Palmerston and I should soon agree if there were any serious intention of upsetting the ministry. But my belief is that when we do agree some other pretext will be found for keeping them in.'[25]

On 18 May Russell wrote to Palmerston, enclosing a copy of Herbert's letter, and expressing a readiness to cooperate in a motion of no confidence against the government.[26] Russell also made it clear, however, that such a move would require the support of the Radicals. He reported a conversation with Milner Gibson who might act as an intermediary with Bright. Milner Gibson was doubtful as to numbers and apprehensive of defeat, but believed Bright would overthrow the government if an acceptable motion were proposed.[27] Russell therefore impressed upon Palmerston the need 'to shut the mouths of these men, who do nothing but find fault with all that is done, and not done'.[28] Over reform and foreign affairs he believed some understanding not as to details, but 'as to the spirit in which they should be treated' might be achieved. In a similarly cautious reply Palmerston observed that recent events had made Liberals 'more disposed to unite', but they 'should not be bound one way or the other by general expressions in the resolution', so that 'every person who spoke in support of it might take his own ground for giving his vote'.[29]

On 20 May, Palmerston and Russell met at Pembroke Lodge and seemed to build 'the foundation for a solid agreement'. A 'very fair understanding' was arrived at on foreign affairs and reform, and it was agreed that a resolution 'ought to be direct to the point of want of confidence'. A compromise reform scheme of a £6 rating borough franchise and a £10 rating county franchise was decided upon, and a foreign policy of strict neutrality pronounced.[30] Russell, however, also forcefully reiterated his bargaining points. First, that 'any new government ought to be on a broad basis or bottom as it used to be called', and 'the radicals must be secured' with 'some of their best men in office to support the concern'. Secondly, Russell reserved his freedom 'on all matters connected with acceptance of office'. As Russell explained to Graham, by holding himself 'quite free' as to 'the headship' and observing that it was for the Queen to decide who she would send for, Russell could not 'be blamed if the affair miscarried'.[31]

The meeting of the two rival 'Kings of Brentford' on 20 May seemed to signal the beginning of Liberal reunion promising a revived opposition to the Conservative government. Whig intermediaries were suddenly fired with optimistic hope. But Russell's cautious commitment to reunion gave way to renewed doubts after 20 May. This change was prompted by a number of factors. It was becoming apparent that any proposed resolution against the government was not going to contain a specific commitment to parliamentary reform. It was also becoming clear that Graham was feeling too ill and too old to accept office even if it were offered to him.[32] Any new cabinet would not, therefore, contain the leading Peelite most strongly committed to a Russellite leadership. And most importantly of all, while Russell and Palmerston moved towards a reconciliation, Bright remained aloof and silent. Thus another crucial source of support for a Russellite conciliation of opposition differences was absent. Russell had approached Palmerston confident that commitment to a liberal reform bill and a broad cabinet including Peelites and Radicals would secure his pre-eminence. After 20 May it was no longer certain that these two conditions would apply. Furthermore, the mere occurrence of the meeting on 20 May was an acknowledgement by Russell of Palmerston's influence and a constraint on his own freedom of action. As Wood bluntly informed Russell: 'he could hardly refuse to serve under [Palmerston] after what had passed between them'.[33]

In the days immediately following 20 May, hopeful Whigs eagerly sought to consolidate reconciliation, while Russell became increasingly adverse to any further commitment. Wood suggested to Palmerston '*an overt act* showing to the world the union' in inviting Russell to a dinner at Cambridge House.[34] Both Brand and Bouverie also urged that the agreement be 'demonstrated in the same way to the party'.[35] Such well wishers were then shocked to discover Russell in a 'sour and jaundiced state'.[36] On 25 May, Russell informed Wood that 'it was impossible that he should dine with Palmerston'.[37] The same day, despite Wood urging that it was necessary to stay in London, Russell left for Wilton. Russell was finding himself drawn increasingly reluctantly into a chain of events he neither controlled, nor from which he could dissociate himself. The same day Russell left for the country, Palmerston informed Wood that under no circumstances would he go to the Lords. If he became prime minister in the Lords, Palmerston insisted, 'people would not follow Lord John as [Commons] leader and . . . he could hardly trust Lord J. in a position which gave [Russell] so much power over his chief'.[38] This was one more nail in the coffin of Russellite hopes.

Herbert and Cornewall Lewis chased Russell down to Wilton only to encounter a familiar obstacle to compromise. After having 'talked over all matters very satisfactorily' Russell was apparently 'willing to concur in any reasonable arrangement . . . Lady John interrupted them by sending to say that she must go home. S. Herbert offered to drive her up to the station. Lord John however insisted on driving her himself, and when he came back sent to see S. Herbert and said that all the arrangements they had talked over in the morning *would not do*.'[39] Conjugal pride also defined the limits of private agreement.

Gladstone was another source of potential support looked to by Russell who communicated a damaging vagueness of purpose. When asked, five years later, for the explanation of his behaviour in May to June 1859, Gladstone succinctly replied, 'Italy'.[40] Such retrospection, however, bears a sharp contrast to Gladstone's priorities on 18 May 1859 as disclosed to Herbert. 'Two great questions at this moment predominate: the war abroad and reform at home. But the latter bears most upon immediate duties.'[41] Gladstone made it clear that his 'conduct [would] be principally governed' by the earnest desire to have the reform question 'put in train of settlement'. He had 'hoped to see reform settled by Lord Derby's Government "pur et simple" ', but this had failed. He would 'have been glad if they could have effected it by a combination with moderate Liberals', but he believed this was no longer possible. There only remained 'the alternative of a government founded on the ruins of the present one'. But given his preference, Gladstone felt unable to support a vote of want of confidence, as any 'moderate' measure of reform would require 'the aid of a section of the supporters of the present ministry'. The chances of obtaining such aid would be dependent upon the manner in which the Derby ministry was brought down. 'If the most summary and forcible process then chances will be lessened: Disraeli's force in opposition will be increased: and he will use it, if a judgement is to be gained from the past, with very little scruple.'

After Derby broke off communication in mid-May, Gladstone was forced to await a centrist realignment, preferably including moderate Conservatives, and was anxious to avoid being compromised. Mrs Gladstone advertised the ambivalence of her husband's position. She told Granville that Gladstone 'wished bygones to be bygones, was all for a strong government and was ready to join in forming one'.[42] Two days later she told Wood that her husband did 'not contemplate a junction with Palmerston, but rather that he should join Derby'.[43] What lay behind this vacillation was an earnest desire for a strong government of which he might be a member. A modified Conservative or Whig–Conservative cabinet would best serve his purpose but, as in previous years, Gladstone was not master of his own situation.

By 29 May, Gladstone became aware of the urgent need to repair his relations with the Whig leadership so as to keep his future options open. As Aberdeen had predicted, the 'master stroke' of Palmerston's electoral statements about Italy provided Gladstone, despite his vehement anti-Palmerstonianism of previous years, with one last option. Reversing his priorities of eleven days earlier, Gladstone declared the war in Italy to be 'the paramount question of the day'.[44] As the 'peculiar crisis' developed during the last days of May, Italy provided Gladstone with a bridge to a 'broad-bottomed' government if Palmerston or Russell were the only choices. Certainly Gladstone had no desire to be 'the one remaining Ishmael in the House of Commons'.[45]

Bright was another important source of indecision during late May whose prevarication fatally weakened Russell's position. As Russell observed to Graham, the majority on a vote of confidence would be 'very small' and much would depend upon Bright 'who had not yet pronounced'.[46] Even Milner Gibson, acting as intermediary, confessed that 'Bright was uncertain; that he could not make out "what he was at"'.[47] Bright's enigmatic silence sprang from his anti-Whig sentiment and the realisation that, while uncommitted and holding the balance of parties, the Radicals might acquire a high market value in negotiation. 'It is pleasant to watch this gang of aristocratic conspirators in trouble. We have spoilt their game thoroughly . . . We have the key in our hands and nobody will pass into office by us without paying toll to the people and freedom.'[48] Bright stated to Parkes, in the knowledge it would be passed on, that 'nothing was to be gained by a change except on reform – that the conduct of the Whigs since 1846 had been dishonest and wrong, that Palmerston was incurable [and] Lord John was as changeable as the weather'.[49] Such conversations established that Radical cooperation could only be secured at the cost of concessions over reform; a price Bright believed Whigs and Liberals would soon be willing to pay.

Bright's difficulty was the lack of Radical unity. The most obvious and debilitating division remained that between Bright and Roebuck. On the hustings during April, Roebuck declared that the government's reform measure indicated 'a true reforming spirit on the part of its authors'.[50] At Milford in May, Roebuck denounced Palmerston as 'false and hollow and the great enemy of the Liberal party'.[51] While Bright shared Roebuck's opinion of Palmerston, their opposite responses to the Conservative reform bill remained an irreconcilable difference between them. In May, Roebuck informed Lindsay, who acted as an intermediary with Disraeli, that he was 'quite ready now to receive reform, and a wise foreign policy, from the present possessors of power'.[52]

During May, Bright also found himself increasingly distanced from Milner Gibson. During the previous year Milner Gibson had always indicated a greater loyalty to Cobden than to Bright, which became particularly noticeable when Cobden dissociated himself from Bright's reform agitation at the beginning of 1859. Thereafter Milner Gibson, rather than Bright, was the closest link with Cobden in parliament. During May, while Bright remained secluded, Milner Gibson became actively involved in opposition negotiation and the role of intermediary slowly changed into that of representative. Milner Gibson's involvement created the impression that he was much more ready than Bright to cooperate in Liberal reunion. This perception, in the nature of a self-fulfilling prophecy, confirmed a growing divergence between the two men.

After 20 May, Gladstone's ambivalence, Graham's ill health, Bright's silence and Radical differences critically weakened Russell's negotiating position. Graham, alarmed by Russell's growing difficulties and 'very uneasy with respect to Bright's suspended decision, on which so much [would] eventually turn', urged Russell to negotiate with Palmerston more definite arrangements guaranteeing his position.[53] The agreement 'stops short of the vital point, which is the division of power between you two'. Without agreement on this point 'a misunderstanding' at the critical moment would 'give to a rupture the character of personal jealousies apart from public interests'.[54] But on 26 May, Russell decided against presenting an 'ultimatum'.[55] Having 'more than once been blamed for acting without concert' Russell feared he might 'cool if not alienate the attachment which [he] still possess[ed] by any premature decision'. He had gone through too much to trust himself again 'to the uncertain waves unless in a vessel very strongly built'. Yet, though his freedom of action was becoming increasingly restricted, Russell retained his determination. 'All I say is, I am not ready to engage myself in a future Ministry of which I am not to be the lead.'

While during late May Russell's bargaining position, if not his resolve, was eroded, Palmerston saw the opportunity to be assertive. On 27 May, Palmerston told Hayter 'that he could not serve under Lord John: tho' he would support his government'.[56] Such strategic jostling confirmed the thinly veiled rivalry behind the agreement of 20 May. By the end of May the mood in Whig and Liberal circles was very different from the buoyant optimism of ten days previously.

Hayward observed that whether 'Lord J.R. and Lord P. will sit in the same government is to be doubted', but he hoped they would cooperate 'and take their chance of what is to come'.[57] Ellice disliked moving a want of confidence motion and urged his colleagues 'to be more patient – not to attack a front which, if you fail, will consolidate the government, but to wait until the enemy falls to pieces'.[58] Ellice also had serious misgivings 'as to dividing the spoils after the anticipated victory'. Aberdeen noted, with little surprise, that '[n]otwithstanding the progress made in coming to an understanding, I do not find that matters are finally arranged'.[59] Aberdeen also observed that 'all this may turn out to the advantage of the government, notwithstanding any amount of mischief and incapacity'. On 28 May, Broughton readily believed that 'the rumour of *P*. and *R*. being reunited [was] untrue', and suggested 'they might copy the example of Fox and North and appoint a first Lord as nominal prime minister'.[60] Personal feelings further complicated matters. Lord Grey roundly declared that he would 'oppose any government to which C. Wood belonged', while Clarendon, who appeared 'much excited and rather cross', anticipated that any 'coalition between Johnny and Pam would probably give the F.O. to one of them'.[61]

On 30 May, Wood informed Palmerston that he 'did not think there was much chance of Lord J. being sent for'.[62] Armed with growing confidence, Palmerston wrote to Russell the same day 'offering to serve under him in case the Queen sent for him, if Lord John would do the same by him'. Russell answered 'to the effect that he thought it better that their liberty of action should not be fettered by any such compact'.[63] This exchange, its predictable outcome, and the growing confidence at Cambridge House that it reflected, provided Palmerston, who kept a complete copy of the correspondence, with material to influence wavering opinion. The rejection of such an ostensibly self-effacing offer could be shown as proof of Russell's selfishness. On the evening of 31 May, Russell agreed to attend a dinner at Lord Carlisle's with Palmerston, Granville, Clarendon, Cornewall Lewis, Gladstone and Wood, but 'talked of his friends entrapping him into a cabinet to turn him out afterwards'.[64] It was quite apparent that Russell was in 'an unsatisfactory state of mind'.

In a meeting at Cambridge House on 1 June, Palmerston, Clarendon, Granville, Cornewall Lewis, G. Grey and Hayter, 'decided on having an amendment at all events'.[65] It was also determined to call a meeting of the party at which Palmerston would request Russell's presence. Both decisions were taken in the knowledge that Russell's close supporters, such as Hugessen, were advising 'strongly of the necessity of *continued* union'. Gladstone, it was confidently believed, would 'speak violently against the government, vote for them and join [a Palmerston] government'.[66]

While Cambridge House was increasingly coming to direct events, the Radical section renewed contact with Pembroke Lodge. Milner Gibson made it known to Russell that he was 'unhappy' about Bright's reticence, and that he would join a Liberal government, 'provided he could do so honourably and with a prospect of being in any useful position'.[67] On the morning of 2 June, Bright broke his silence and met with Russell at Milner Gibson's. On the subject of reform Bright made no mention of the ballot, but insisted upon a £6 rental, not rating, franchise for the boroughs.[68] Such a scheme, it might be anticipated, would be attractive to Russell and unacceptable to Palmerston. Russell, for his own part, once again insisted upon the broad character of any Liberal cabinet to succeed Derby. Milner Gibson and Bright subsequently decided that they should demand two cabinet positions in any new government.[69]

The meeting with Bright and Milner Gibson bolstered Russell's flagging hopes. Russell, visited in the afternoon of 2 June by Corne-wall Lewis, 'talked a good deal of how the party had treated him' and 'thought that he ought to have some security against being thrown over again'.[70] Speaking 'with bitterness of the party' Russell declared himself 'now in favour of a meeting which he said that he would attend'. This meeting raised in Cornewall Lewis' mind the possibility of Russell becoming leader in the Commons if Palmerston, as prime minister, could be persuaded to go to the Lords. The 'radicals might not follow Palmerston, but he thought the Whigs would follow Lord John'. Both Wood and Clarendon, however, dismissed such speculation as 'incompatible with P's position'. It was Palmerston himself who authoritatively scotched any further conjecture of this kind by bluntly insisting 'that he could not agree to go to the H. of Lords, that he could not trust Lord J. in the Commons, that he (J.R.) would not receive the support of the party: that . . . as long as he [Palmerston] was well and strong he would not leave the Commons'.[71]

In the evening of 2 June, Palmerston visited Pembroke Lodge, and it was agreed by both leaders that at a party meeting they would declare their readiness to cooperate in forming a government. But, as Wood observed, during the meeting 'Lord John had said nothing to [Palmerston] about arrangement of places'.[72] This meant the agreement was 'in very general terms and I am afraid we are not much nearer the mark'. Herbert felt similar uncertainty. 'People seem very doubtful about the proceeding to be taken, and feel, not without truth, that it is a desperate undertaking requiring much more hearty co-operation and goodwill than we all possess.'[73] On 4 June, invitations were sent out for a Liberal party meeting at Willis's Rooms on 6 June. The invitations were signed by Palmerston, Russell, Herbert, Milner Gibson and others, 'led by Palmerston and Russell like Nelson and Collingwood'.[74] The totting up of numbers followed. Brand, on 31 May, had estimated an opposition majority of fifteen[75] which, by 4 June, he revised to twenty.[76] Government sources, however, calculated a ministerial majority of ten[77] and, as Granville noted, the Conservatives appeared 'sanguine'.[78]

The counselling of doubtfuls ensued. Heathcote gave advice to Gladstone in a situation 'full of difficulty and embarrassment'.[79] If, Heathcote warned, Gladstone opposed the vote of want of confidence, but then joined the succeeding government such a course would 'not be intelligible to the world at large at first sight and it [was] always a disadvantage to be thrown upon explanations'. Moreover, a motion of want of confidence 'in that simple *negative* sense' could only be wisely given in a very extreme case, while opposition to such a motion was not to be taken as 'actual support' of the government 'in their specific acts'. Earle advised Disraeli that 'the tone of the Tories would almost seem to justify overtures to Lowe', and recommended Stanley to negotiate.[80] Horsman might also be expected to support the government, while Roebuck reported that Brooks's was in 'open revolt' and the government's prospects were 'good'.[81] Horsman was known to be in correspondence with Roebuck about the 'rumoured reconciliations between P. and J.R. and subsequent arrangements; disparaging them; and enquiring whether there was any spirit of resistance in the new House'.[82] The cabinet's task, as Earle saw it, was to keep their own ranks in order. 'The difficulty [was] to work on [their] own people without exciting alarm. Copious thanking for past support [was] perhaps the best and safest way to fix them.' In all events, Earle declared: '*The game is still alive.*'[83]

At a cabinet meeting on 27 May, discussing finance and ways and means, it was unanimously decided not to raise a loan.[84] This decision kept government policy in line with Gladstonian practice. At subsequent cabinet meetings on 30 and 31 May it was decided to avoid any detailed reference to reform in the Queen's Speech, but to express a non-committal readiness to consider a new scheme if it seemed desirable.[85] The Queen's Speech also provided the cabinet with an opportunity to refute 'a general impression, industriously circulated by the opposition, that the court and ministry [were] favourable to Austria'.[86] Disraeli was insistent that all 'distrust in the public mind' on this question should be 'averted' to prevent the opposition raising 'a colourable point on Austrian bias, or imminence of war from [their] policy'. Derby informed the Queen that the Austro–French war was 'one subject on which, more than any other, the mind of the country was unanimous' and desired 'an entire abstinence from participation in the struggle now going on in Italy'.[87] The reference to foreign affairs in the Queen's Speech was composed so as to pledge the cabinet to strict neutrality as long as the contest was confined to the present combatants.[88] 'With prudence', Disraeli confidently predicted, the government might 'have a majority on any amendment'.[89]

I

The party meeting held at Willis's Rooms on 6 June 1859 was attended by about 280 former Peelite, Whig, Liberal and Radical MPs. Many still had doubts about the expediency of moving a vote of no confidence, but most responded enthusiastically to the public affirmation of collaboration amongst prominent opposition figures. The news that Bright and Ellice, as well as Palmerston, Russell, Herbert and Milner Gibson, would speak heightened expectation. At the beginning of the gathering Palmerston ascended the platform to begin proceedings, noticed that the step was too high for Lord John, and helped him up amidst the cheers and laughter of the whole room.[90] Poignant symbolism had come to exist therein.

Palmerston began the meeting by alluding to the government's legislative failure, the danger of them taking the country into a war, and concluded with a declaration of his readiness to cooperate with Russell in a motion against the government and the formation of a cabinet. Greville saw in the speech ominous signs of Palmerston's 'pro-Gallican sympathies' which might result in a policy 'hateful to many who will be colleagues'.[91] But the demonstration of a new unity of purpose was enthusiastically received. Russell followed and expressed his willingness to cooperate with Palmerston, if Palmerston was asked by the Queen to form a government on a 'broad basis etc. – and then Pam whispered to him, and he added as much for Pam'.[92] Bright followed, 'wanted some clearer assurance about war, but upon the whole, promised cooperation'. Herbert 'preached union' as did Ellice and Milner Gibson.

Roebuck spoke *'against'* forwarding a motion, and Horsman counselled delay. Lindsay also objected to the proposed attack on the government. The general impression, however, was that the meeting 'went off as well as [Palmerston or Russell] could expect or desire'.[93] The majority of Whig and Liberal backbenchers willingly endorsed the public affirmation of private arrangements. The twenty-six year old Lord Hartington, who had just entered parliament in the preceding election, was chosen as an inoffensive yet reputable newcomer to propose the no confidence motion when the Commons reassembled on 7 June. Even so, the result of any division remained uncertain. Conservatives comforted themselves 'with the certainty that the division must be so close, that the successful Whigs will be able to form no government which will have a certain working majority'.[94] Equally importantly, Wood noted that the Willis's Rooms meeting further constricted Russell's freedom of action; it would be 'difficult for Lord John not to concur in any arrangement after what he said'.[95]

When parliament reassembled on 7 June, immediately after the Address from the Throne, Hartington moved a motion of 'want of confidence' in the government citing the Conservative precedent of 1841.[96] Speaking after Hartington, Disraeli, in 'a wonderfully able and adroit speech, full of live and good hits particularly against Graham, suggested the House divide immediately upon the motion'.[97] This was a well prepared tactical move. Anticipating the opposition motion, Disraeli had ensured all Conservative members were present on the first night of the debate:[98] seventeen new members of the opposition had not yet taken their seats.[99] An immediate division would guarantee a government majority. Caught unprepared by this 'dodge',[100] with Conservatives declining to rise and speak, the opposition, frantically scouring the Commons' tearooms, 'put up one man after another to keep the debate open, and eventually obtained an adjournement'.[101]

The continued debate revealed the significance that events during the recess had granted to the question of Italy. On 4 June, French and Sardinian forces had defeated the Austrians at Magenta, and taken possession of the plains of Lombardy. Foreign affairs emerged as a matter of domestic controversy alongside reform. Disraeli reaffirmed the declared objects of government policy as carefully framed in the Queen's Speech: to endeavour by all means in their power to preserve peace in Europe.[102] Palmerston insisted that the cabinet had exhibited an alarming ignorance of the real state of affairs, having believed that the danger of war was imminent on the part of Sardinia and France and not on that of Austria, whereas the reverse was the truth.[103] If they had not been acting under this misapprehension the government, Palmerston maintained, would have held a very different language towards Austria and might have prevented hostilities. Significantly, Bright also devoted the greater part of his statement to foreign affairs. Questioning whether the cabinet's pledge to neutrality was real or pretended, Bright observed that there was no reason to distrust the Emperor of the French, yet in Germany and France the government was suspected of a disposition towards Austria.[104] To the surprise of the Conservative frontbench, Horsman declared his support for the motion on the grounds of foreign policy. Without the information to judge whether the cabinet had, in grave complications, shown capacity, energy, foresight and impartiality, the Commons, Horsman pronounced, would be unable to protect the government from the motion.[105] These statements revealed the unity that might be achieved over foreign policy by sections alienated over reform.

Accusations of diplomatic bias were accompanied by charges of incompetency in domestic affairs. Bright suggested there was still sufficient time in the present session to bring forward a measure of reform: a line of argument not echoed by Palmerston. Graham expressed a strong condemnation of the late dissolution which had risked national interests, postponed measures of importance and forestalled decisions 'upon questions of the gravest kind'. The course of the government upon the subject of reform, Graham concluded, rendered it impossible for him to give them his support.[106] Milner Gibson, assuming Bright's role in the debate, avowed his distrust of the vague professions of the government on reform.[107] On the question of neutrality he did not charge the government with a direct desire to support by patent acts either side in the war, but he believed they harboured Austrian sympathies. Herbert delivered the barb that the government, in forgetfulness of its principles, 'were general merchants, who had samples of every kind'.[108] He expressed a preference to see the reform question in the hands of reformers, to waiting for the fulfilment of the promises the government had made. Referring to the state of parties, he saw no prospect of any ministry that would not be weak in point of supporters: the justification of his vote for the amendment would be that they might have one stronger in point of composition. It was a choice of difficulties.

During the course of the debate there were 'various rumours as to the decision – some giving the majority to one side some to the other – but all saying it would be small either way'.[109] The balance was seen to lie with the loyalty of some moderate Liberals and the Irish Brigade. Horsman's speech made it clear that one source of support for the government was gone. Lindsay, however, made it known that there were '15 or 16 of us who are determined to pull you through, but you must give us time – we cannot vote with you without making speeches for our constituents'.[110] In his speech to the Commons, Lindsay declared that as an advocate for reform he would best perform his duty to his Liberal constituents by voting against the motion. The government had pledged themselves to a substantial measure of reform, which he thought more likely to pass at the hands of the party now in power than by that of Lord John Russell.[111] The Liberal party, he insisted, had fallen victim to the conflict between different sections of Liberals upon various aspects of policy. The question remained, however, how many would follow Lindsay's deliberate neglect of Palmerston? Derby made some exertions 'to keep those Irish Members up to the mark'.[112] Together Derby and Jolliffe compiled a list of forty-four members of the opposition who might support the government in a division.[113] Of the Irish Brigade, Derby counted on Blake, Bowyer, Brady, Ennis, McEvoy and Maguire as certain votes. The result would therefore depend upon those Whig and Liberal votes swayed by Lindsay's portrayal of a stark choice between Derby and Russell.

Russell attempted to affirm a simple bi-partisan alignment of opinion with a forceful reiteration of Liberal wisdom on reform and a markedly moderate statement upon foreign affairs.[114] Russell characterised the government reform bill as a measure which diminished the popular strength in the constituency and which, after its implementation, would have gone far to repeal the first Reform Act. In their foreign policy Russell admitted that the government might have been sincerely attempting to prevent the outbreak of hostilities and, while the whole policy of Austria had been directed to the dominance of all Italy, Sardinia had not been justified in the course she had taken. All were for neutrality, but he had no confidence that the government would prove sufficiently competent to maintain a neutral position. The country had not that weight in the councils of Europe which it ought to have and, with the view of giving it its proper influence, he was ready to vote a want of confidence in the present ministers. Roebuck's counter was to highlight the divergence of opinion over reform amongst the opposition.[115] Palmerston was not a reformer and, even if Palmerston and Russell agreed over the question, the Lords would resist their bill. The Conservative cabinet, he continued, would introduce as good a bill as Palmerston or Russell which would also be certain of acceptance in the other House. He would therefore support the present government because it was better than any that might be formed by the opposition. This distinctive line of Radical argument encouraged ministerial hope.

Derby experienced alternating confidence and doubt. On 8 June he optimistically observed that 'the hopes of a majority on the part of the opposition [were] not as high as they were', while Gladstone's course was 'said to be unknown, even to himself!'[116] The following day, however, he noted that the 'junction' between the 'sections of the Liberal party [would] make it very difficult to effect what Lord Derby had very earnestly desired; a reconstruction of the government on such a basis as should include some of the leading *Whigs*, as contra-distinguished from the more advanced Liberals'.[117] Even men as 'moderate as Lord Euston [were] prepared to join in overthrowing the government'. In any event, although the 'majority either way [would] be very small . . . the result [would] be very decisive'.

As 'the tone of the government agents in the H. of Commons' became 'less sanguine', Disraeli gave new form to the hope for reconstruction.[118] Unable to 'tell how this thing [would] exactly end', and confident that sending 'for Palmerston or John Russell [was] no solution of the difficulty', there existed the opportunity 'for a third man'.[119] Disraeli bluntly suggested to Derby that there was 'only one man . . . who could combine the whole of the Conservative party and would immediately obtain a considerable section of the opposition. *It is Stanley*. He would *reconstruct the cabinet*: which you cannot.' His own and Derby's 'united withdrawal', Disraeli opined, 'would give authority and sanction to Stanley' and 'would entirely sell the Whigs'. Clarendon would replace Malmesbury and a considerable section of backbench Liberal votes would be secured. The advantage in such a course, Disraeli concluded, would be that despite their being out of office both Derby and he would be able to influence the new premier. '[I]t is better than Mr Addington, for Stanley is a clever fellow, and his Pitt and Dundas would be his father and his friend.'[120] Neither time, Stanley's temperament, nor opposition intention, lent any credi-bility to Disraeli's fancy. A different aspect of Conservative front-bench anxiety was revealed when Malmesbury advised Clarendon that 'a large number of Conservatives' might support a Palmerston government, if the 'opposition leaders [did] not in debate use language towards the party which would make it dishonourable for them to quit their ranks – in fact that a bridge should not be lost sight of'.[121] For good measure Malmesbury added that 'he was dead sick of office which he only retained out of deference to Derby'.

After three nights of debate, on 10 June, preparations were made for a division on Hartington's motion. Granville found it 'almost certain that there [would] be a majority against the government', yet 'Lord John [was] still supposed to decline serving under Palmerston' and there was 'a good deal of heart-burning already'.[122] In the division lobbies, 323 supported Hartington's want of confidence motion and 310 supported the government. Wood found the result 'quite as good as [they] expected' as 'Brand had made a minimum of 9 in the morning'.[123] The influence of Lindsay's appeal was revealed by the presence of fourteen members of the opposition in the government lobby.[124] A cabinet meeting was held on the morning of 11 June at which 'there was no doubt as to [their] course'.[125] At midday Derby went to the Queen and tendered the resignation of his government. He seemed 'much agitated', but stated that the Conservatives 'had never been more united . . . and would therefore be powerful'.[126]

The end of Derby's second ministry added a final footnote to the personal resentment between Disraeli and Malmesbury. Malmesbury had informed Disraeli at the beginning of the month that by 5 June a blue book would be published refuting allegations of pro-Austrian bias in British foreign policy. Malmesbury produced the blue book in the Lords, but Disraeli never presented it to the Commons. Subsequently Malmesbury claimed that twelve to fourteen opposition MPs admitted to him that, if they had read the blue book prior to the division, they would not have supported Hartington's motion. Returning to London from Windsor, after surrendering their seals of office, Malmesbury noted that all his colleagues praised the blue book on Italy except Disraeli 'who never said a word'.[127] Sullen silence was an appropriate conclusion to official relations between Disraeli and Malmesbury in 1859, as Disraeli kept to himself a loyalty that should have gone to his party.

The afternoon of 11 June, much to his own surprise, the Queen sent for Granville and charged him with the formation of a government. The Queen disliked Russell and feared that Palmerston as premier would produce a 'bad effect' in Europe, so 'thought it would be less invidious to choose neither'.[128] Yet it would be 'very mortifying to them to be invited to accept office under a man they [had] raised from the ranks, and who [was] young enough to be the son to either, and almost to be the grandson of the elder of the two'.[129] Granville expressed doubts about his being able to form a ministry, but the Queen insisted the attempt be made, stating a preference for Palmerston as Leader of the Commons and Clarendon at the Foreign Office. Granville anticipated that such an arrangement would be unacceptable to Russell, observed that a government formed without Russell 'would not be a strong one', but agreed to make the attempt.[130]

After leaving the Queen, Granville visited Cambridge House and offered Palmerston the lead of the House of Commons.[131] Palmerston cordially accepted, well aware that such an arrangement would be unpalatable to Russell. Palmerston also promptly wrote to the Queen expressing his readiness to join Granville provided he could 'form a strong government', i.e. a cabinet of which Russell was a member.[132] Granville then saw Russell who declined to serve under him unless he had the lead in the Commons 'which he considered necessary for carrying out his own views'. As Russell made clear to Granville 'with Palmerston I would only have to consider who is to have the first and who the second office in the State – with you I could only occupy the third'.[133] Returning to Cambridge House, Granville found Palmerston displaying 'dissatisfaction at not having been sent for' by the Queen and refusing to go to the Lords.[134] Cornewall Lewis, Gladstone and Herbert were 'anxious that Lord J. Russell should be comprised, but thought a government might be formed without him'.[135] Milner Gibson, however, 'said Lord John's being in the government was a *sine qua non* of support of Liberals below the gangway (extreme Liberals)'.[136] This impasse sealed the fate of Granville's attempt to form a ministry. After, on George Grey's advice, obtaining in writing the grounds for Russell's refusal, Granville saw the Queen in the early afternoon of 12 June and surrendered his commission.

Seemingly Palmerston had behaved 'very properly' while Russell had been forced to declare his 'personal feelings'.[137] Palmerston had agreed to serve under Granville, while Russell's obstinacy was the apparent cause for the breakdown in negotiation. To enhance this impression Palmerston wrote to the Queen that Granville's failure to secure Russell had prevented the formation of a government adding that he himself 'as chief and leading the C.' could form a 'stronger' government than 'only as leader'.[138] As a consequence the Queen became increasingly dismissive of 'selfish, peevish Johnny'.[139] To Cornewall Lewis, Palmerston insisted that nothing could induce him to go to the Lords as prime minister leaving Russell as Leader of the Commons. He 'could not trust Lord John who never knew his own mind, and only said what he had last heard from Bright'.[140] Such insinuations purposively emphasised Palmerston's standing as a moderate conciliatory figure. George Grey made it known that Palmerston 'might do what no one else perhaps could, namely form a government relying for much support from the opposite side and including probably some men from that side'.[141]

Since 10 June, Russell had remained 'hesitating about joining with Palmerston'.[142] Russell had informed Herbert 'he did not feel sure whether he could join Lord Palmerston!! on account of reform!!'[143] But Herbert answered that 'after what had passed at the [Willis's Rooms] meeting [Russell] could be in a great difficulty if he refused'.[144] Moreover, 'Palmerston was not a man to give up the government and that if he did not make the government with one man, he would with another'. This was precisely Russell's dilemma by 12 June: to secure an office and personal following within the cabinet, while not demanding too much so as to exclude himself from a new government and offering Palmerston the chance to form a centrist coalition isolating Russell and the Radicals. Russell's one remaining trump card was Radical insistence on his presence in a new cabinet as a necessary condition for Radical support. Moreover, 'Bright "explicitly" assured [Granville] that the Radicals would never consent to the Sir W. Molesworth dodge again; that one place in a cabinet was worse than none'.[145] Sustained by Radical commitment Russell informed Granville that 'he expected that if P. was sent for, to have the offer of any place (except P.M.) and the option of going to the Lords'.[146]

In the early evening of 12 June the Queen sent for Palmerston and charged him with the formation of a ministry. Palmerston, she believed, might form a government with or without Russell, might secure Clarendon at the Foreign Office and had behaved 'very properly' during recent negotiations.[147] Palmerston immediately pointed to the importance and difficulty of appeasing Russell. Russell would make conditions. But Palmerston again insisted that he could not go to the Lords leaving Russell as Leader in the Commons. He expressed a preference for Clarendon at the Foreign Office and Russell as Secretary for India in an office of prestigious political isolation. This, however, was an arrangement he expected Russell to reject. In any event, Palmerston reassured the Queen that 'even if Lord John did not join, he would undertake to form a government'.

That evening Palmerston drove down to Pembroke Lodge. Russell agreed to serve under Palmerston if he were given the Foreign Office.[148] Palmerston observed that 'there were many reasons why Clarendon who was perfectly conversant with all foreign affairs should resume them'.[149] In reply Russell admitted that 'he might not at another time have wished for it; but that taking such interest in foreign affairs at present he wished for that place'. Russell's insistence on the Foreign Office obliged Palmerston to consent. It was a feeling of Russell's 'own dignity which [Russell] wished to keep up', and Palmerston understood that Russell meant 'to settle Europe and then give up'.[150] Russell's insistence on the Foreign Office, in the circumstances of mid-June 1859, betrayed sound political sense. Italy had emerged as the prominent issue upon which Gladstone, Palmerston, Radicals and Russell himself could agree. From the Foreign Office, Russell could be seen to be healing political wounds, he could confirm his personal commitment to the great 'liberal' cause of Italian liberty, and also, as hoped in 1855, recover credibility by acting a leading diplomatic role on the grander political stage of Europe. Meanwhile, the divisive question of reform might be allowed to fragment a cabinet composed of Palmerston, Peelites, Whigs, Liberals and Radicals. Palmerston's letter to the Queen, informing her of Russell's successful request, betrayed a sense of irritation that attested to the astuteness of Russell's demand.[151]

On the morning of 13 June, Palmerston held a meeting at Cambridge House attended by Clarendon, Granville, G. Grey, Cornewall Lewis and Wood resulting in 'a long conference . . . on the arrangements to be made'.[152] Russell was not invited. Clarendon expressed 'great anxiety' at not being able to join the government as Foreign Secretary was the only appointment he could accept. Palmerston 'strongly press[ed] the Colonial Office on him, and Granville urged him 'to take the Presidency of the Council and the leadership of the House of Lords', but Clarendon refused both these offers.[153] In private, Clarendon admitted that he 'gladly recognised [Russell's] right and the superiority of his claims', and saw 'no necessity' to take another appointment.[154] Clarendon's 'extreme reluctance to take office' showed how far conversations with Malmesbury had led him away from the body of Liberal sentiment as he withstood earnest requests from the Queen to join the government.[155] Following Clarendon's refusal, Granville accepted the Presidency of the Council and resumed the leadership in the Lords. The arrangement of other government offices, however, promised continued difficulties. Wood complained loudly that 'there were more candidates for places than places'. Yet Broughton, noting that Wood himself was an aspirant, alighted on the irony and likened it 'to the fat man complaining of the crowd'.[156]

Vernon Smith, Labouchere and Lord Panmure were immediately dismissed as 'out of the question' as cabinet appointments.[157] Similarly Lord Stanley of Alderley and Benjamin Hall were discarded. After 'a long discussion' Palmerston tentatively selected Bethell as Lord Chancellor, 'rather from the inconvenience of having him discontented and against [them], than from any wish to have him as a colleague'. After further consideration, however, Palmerston appointed Lord Campbell as Chancellor and made Bethell Attorney-General. In the event Campbell proved 'first-rate in court, and useful in the cabinet'. But as he was eighty years of age, retirement was near and Granville feared that it would be 'impossible to prevent that clever but coxcombical Bethell from succeeding him'.[158] George Grey, after Wood expressed reluctance to join the cabinet if Grey were not a member, was offered and accepted the Duchy of Lancaster.[159]

Palmerston received word that Herbert and Gladstone were prepared to join his cabinet. Herbert's agreement, after his taking such a prominent part in arranging the Willis's Rooms meeting, was 'long expected'.[160] Gladstone's exact intentions, however, remained uncertain. The Conservative and former Peelite, Heathcote, impressed upon Gladstone the dangers of any precipitious decision by which he might find himself 'snared'.[161] If he joined a Palmerston cabinet, Heathcote warned, Gladstone would find himself 'alone' and this 'isolation would be fatal to [his] doing that good which nothing but the presence of one man on the Treasury bench [had] prevented of late'. Moreover, the time when Gladstone would find himself forced to resign from such a cabinet could not be 'very distant'. Gladstone's reply was full of the anguish of prolonged political ostracism. 'For thirteen years, the middle space of my life, I have been cast out of party connection: severed from my old party and loath irrevocably to join a new one.'[162] During those years Gladstone admitted that he had 'adhered to the vague hope of a reconstruction', but Derby's uncompromising attitude had denied any such hope. The offer of a cabinet position from Palmerston thus appeared his sole means of ending isolation and resuming executive responsibility. On the question of reform, which he had admitted to Herbert strongly influenced his course, Gladstone believed Derby had, by the decision to dissolve, lost the opportunity of proposing a settlement. 'I desire to see it settled [and] it seems a duty to assist those who may perhaps settle it'. On the question of Italy he found himself in 'close harmony of sentiment' with both Palmerston and Russell.

The one condition Gladstone made in his acceptance of a post in Palmerston's cabinet was that he be given the Chancellorship of the Exchequer. To this Palmerston agreed, in spite of the fact that he had originally chosen Cornewall Lewis for that office. Lady Clarendon could only note with incredulous surprise that he 'who voted in the last division with the Derby ministry should not only be asked to join, but allowed to *choose his office*'.[163] The reason for it lay in Gladstone's 'power of speaking'; Palmerston wanted his oratory to help the government and 'dread[ed] it in opposition'. Clarendon pointedly observed that the appointment would 'dissatisfy the City people who like[d] truth in matters of account and taxation'.[164] Cornewall Lewis agreed to go to the Home Office and, with Russell's concurrence, Palmerston appointed Herbert to the War Department and Wood accepted the India Office. Herbert, 'vain enough to believe anything', had hoped he might succeed Lytton as Colonial Secretary.[165] Elcho expressed a preference for Wood as Indian Secretary rather than at the Admiralty: 'it [was] better that he should raise India than loose England'.[166] But, as Broughton noted, 'the extreme unpopularity of the man and of his manners [would] account for anything said against him'. Cardwell accepted the Secretaryship of Ireland which was accompanied by a seat in cabinet. There was 'great discussion' as to whether Somerset or Newcastle should be appointed to the Admiralty. Both Herbert and Gladstone, however, urged that Newcastle would be 'much fitter for the Colonies from his slowness rendering him unfit for rapid decision and work'.[167] Granville also reminded his colleagues that after the criticisms of Newcastle's administration during the Crimean War 'it would be objectionable putting him at the Admiralty'.[168] In consequence, the Duke of Somerset went to the Admiralty and Newcastle became Secretary for the Colonies. On 15 June, Argyll accepted the Privy Seal and Elgin became Postmaster General.[169]

On 14 June, Herbert learnt from Milner Gibson that Bright 'had become very much dissatisfied with matters, that he repented of turning out the government [and] that places in the cabinet ought to have been offered to Cobden, Milner Gibson and himself'.[170] Milner Gibson, the more committed to Liberal reunion, 'softened' Bright by observing that 'his conduct had been prudent enough in the House, but that his speeches in the autumn had alarmed people very much, and that he could not accept office now'. Bright then talked of the 'incompatibility' of any warlike preparations to be sanctioned by him as a member of the government with 'the *sect*' to which he belonged.

In his conversations with Palmerston, Russell was insistent upon the inclusion of Cobden and Milner Gibson in the cabinet.[171] Yielding to Russell's demands, Palmerston agreed that Cobden should be offered the Board of Trade upon his return from the United States at the end of the month. Milner Gibson could be given the Poor Law Board with a seat in cabinet. Despite initial hesitation, on Russell's advice, Milner Gibson accepted the Poor Law Board. Once it was certain that Milner Gibson would be in the cabinet, Russell confirmed that he would accept the Foreign Office with 'the assurance that he would not be passed over again'.[172] Russell also made clear his strong dissatisfaction with the general political situation. He retained 'the liberty of withdrawing from the government if the [reform] bill or bills agreed to [by the cabinet] should in [his] opinion be unsatisfactory'.[173] He made clear his wish not to remain long at the Foreign Office, and expressed sharp criticism of the manner in which Palmerston had formed the government. 'I thought you would have acted as Ld. Melbourne and Ld. Aberdeen did, instead of assembling a caucus . . . As it is, much discontent will be felt in the H. of C. and some of it will, I fear, find expression. The ministry will be too much of a Restoration.'

While Russell was struggling to have Cobden and Milner Gibson included in the cabinet, Bright was reported to be in 'very bad humour' and finding it hard 'to reconcile himself to not being considered as capable of taking office'.[174] Ellice sensed in this desire for official recognition a conservative side to Bright's nature, later perceived by Bagehot.[175] While Cobden was seen as 'a safe man', Ellice judged 'Bright himself safe . . . He has only been made wild through exclusion. If only he had had six months experience in office in his earlier career, and learnt the difficulties in the way of his theories, of their application . . . and of the responsibilities of office, his great scorn would by this time have made him as tame as any of them.'[176] It was exactly this judgement which led Disraeli to speculate on a Conservative–Radical fusion throughout the 1850s. Palmerston, however, as Russell reported, declined to offer Bright a cabinet post because of his attacks on the aristocracy and his resort to the language of 'class' antagonism the previous November and December.[177] Russell's alternative suggestion, supported by Gladstone, of 'sending

[Bright] as Governor-General to Canada' also found little favour with Palmerston.[178] Ellice accurately judged the difficulty of Palmerston's situation. In attempting to form a government 'from all shades of opinion' he was 'in danger of opposition from the admission of Radicals into the cabinet, from uniting the party opposite and a hollow support from [the] upper benches', or by 'excluding them, from the opposition of the gentlemen below the gangway – and still taking Gibson and excluding the two others [was] an indifferent compromise'.[179]

When Cobden landed at Liverpool on 29 June he received a note from Russell that if he accepted office under Palmerston, Bright might enter the cabinet at a later date. But if he refused then Russell did 'not see the prospect of amalgamating the Liberal party during [his] life-time'.[180] Russell's letter was accompanied by a communication from Palmerston offering the Presidency of the Board of Trade.[181] On reaching London, Cobden had a private interview with Palmerston at which he explained his position. He felt, after twelve years of being the 'systematic and constant assailant of the principle on which [Palmerston's] foreign policy [had] been carried on', and feeling 'a general want of confidence in [Palmerston's] domestic politics', it was impossible to serve in his cabinet.[182] Despite Palmerston's forceful and candid argument that the only means of influencing foreign policy was to be in the cabinet, parliament never being consulted until after foreign questions were settled, Cobden repeated his refusal. Bright immediately made known his approval of Cobden's decision, while Cobden himself 'was looking well and seemed in spirits'.[183] Upon Cobden's refusal Palmerston appointed Milner Gibson to the Board of Trade and chose Charles Villiers, as a respectable representative of the 'extreme' Liberals, and Clarendon's brother, to be Chief Commissioner for the Poor Law Board with a seat in the cabinet. Villier's inclusion was an attempt at cabinet comprehensiveness avoiding a repeat of the Molesworth 'dodge'.

The junior appointments revealed the same earnest aspiration, injured pride, and zealous tact evidenced in the formation of the cabinet. During 14 June, Lowe was 'abusing the formation of the government, fuming about himself, had heard nothing, would not accept this or that, *certainly not the Education office*, which he took the next day'.[184] Carlisle 'would have cried himself to death if he had not been reappointed to Ireland and as nobody wished for the suicide of that beautiful boy' Palmerston chose him as his Lord Lieutenant of Ireland.[185] Headlam, as a legalistic and loyal backbencher, was appointed Judge-Advocate General. Henry Fitzroy, as a backbench Whig, was appointed Chief Commissioner of Works. The advanced Liberal, Charles Gilpin, was appointed Secretary to the Poor Law Board, despite Delane's dismissal of him as 'a jobber'.[186]

The list of new government appointments completed by the end of June 1859 was a judicious representation of non-Conservative opinion. Sufficiently broad bottomed so as to provide a passable assurance of Liberal reunion, it was carefully composed so as to avoid a powerful Russell lobby within the cabinet. If the cabinet did represent a Liberal reunion it embodied a Palmerstonian, not Russellite, alignment of non-Conservative sentiment. As Palmerston cheerfully remarked to Granville: 'A pretty mess I would have been in with Johnny alone, and objecting to all his proposals with no one to back me up'.[187]

Conclusion

I do not think we shall be very long lived, and after that I shall make my bow, under any circumstances, for I am heartily sick of it. (Wood to Panmure, 16 June 1859, Dalhousie Mss. GD/45/14/689)

In scrutinising parliamentary behaviour within its own terms this study has, in Pater's poetic words, teased political experience from 'the impressions of the individual in his isolation, each mind keeping as a solitary prisoner its own dream of a world' which 'are in perpetual flight'.[1] Consciousness is not quite a prison, and politics is a social activity with language as the pliable medium of the art. Yet it was the constant interaction of shifting perceptions that shaped parliamentary politics in the late 1850s. Lord Briggs has noted that 'the survival of parliamentary reform during these years . . . is best explained in terms of a delicately balanced political situation within parliament itself rather than in terms of sustained public pressure from outside'.[2] Within this context the Conservative pursuit of credible centrism and the jostling for effectiveness of prominent non-Conservative politicians assumed a profound importance.

The events of June 1859 did not guarantee Palmerston's retention of the premiership until his death in 1865. Nor did they ensure the continued union of those disparate sections of opinion associated with Palmerston's second government. Events between 1855 and 1859 only rendered such eventualities possible. In June 1859 the instability of party connection continued to threaten existing arrangements. 'Palmerston was the most popular man two years ago. He has become much the reverse . . . But as the Duke of Bedford said truly Lord John has not gained the other's losses.'[3] Panmure informed Palmerston:

The circumstances of the government which you are now forming are very different from that one over which you presided from 1855–1858. That government was composed of men well known to each other in the walks of private life, having the same political aspirations, and desiring from nothing of friendship as well as duty but to support you and each other. The very nature of the conditions under which the new government is being formed precludes the hope of any such spirit existing in it. The cabinet will contain

266

sections of all different parties – more than one 'open question' must exist in it, and where that is the case you start with the seeds of disunion sown, to vegetate at some future hour.[4]

Panmure himself, it was reported, was 'angry, and talks of sitting on the cross benches on account of the Puseyite principles of Gladstone and S. Herbert'.[5] Within the cabinet Russell, as before, was a focus for suspicion. Newcastle, for one, was 'keen against Lord John'.[6] 'Spider' Wood was increasingly unpopular, and Granville found Cornewall Lewis 'too much an old Company man'.[7] Elgin seemed 'discontented with the Post Office, very amiable in the House of Lords, but huffy at not being asked to take more part, and always afraid of taking anything which is not to be the means of a splash'.[8] Villiers appeared to have 'combed a little, grown fat, and a shade pompous on the strength of it'. Gladstone was an obvious source of disquiet.

Outside the cabinet disappointed hopes continued to rankle. Stanley of Alderley made 'the most praiseworthy attempts to be magnanimous, but *ça lui sort par tous les pores*'.[9] Benjamin Hall accepted the title Lord Llanover, 'but declines parting with his grievance'. Cranworth was 'much annoyed', and Grey 'furious'. Aberdeen reportedly disliked the new government's foreign policy and was 'grown more grumpy than formerly'. Before the cabinet appointments were completed Hall observed that 'the Liberal party are very angry at the arrangement . . . I sadly fear that we shall all be in confusion very soon again. . . . The two men most objected to by the Liberal party are Gladstone and C. Wood. . . . The tories are in high glee and bets were freely offered that the government would be upset or remodelled in 6 months.'[10] Granville gloomily noted 'the imminent unpopularity of the present government in the clubs and parliament' and expressed his personal 'annoyance at finding [himself] between Elgin and Newcastle, instead of between Lord Lansdowne, Ben [Stanley of Alderley] and Clarendon'.[11] When Granville informed the Lords 'that those friends whom Palmerston could not take into his government had behaved in the handsomest way possible, Clarendon and Stanley of Alderley, sitting below the gangway, did *not* laugh – but [Broughton] saw a smirk on Derby's lips'.[12]

Stanley of Alderley, as the 1859 session drew to a close, noted the significance of ministerial unease:

All this makes the Tory party stick together so much the closer, and if the session had lasted three months the government might have been in trouble, as the Peelites' overwhelming preponderance in the government gives them the accession of strength in the rank and file, and does not altogether increase the good will and confidence of their old friends and supporters.[13]

In late June, Derby was assuring his backbenchers that 'it would be easy to get a majority against the present government as large as that which turned him out'.[14] When he spoke at a party meeting early in July, attended by 'upward of 300 Conservatives', it became 'clear Derby intend[ed] to have another trial'.[15] As in 1855, Palmerston's premiership was seen as a temporary arrangement of party connection promising future realignment. 'There is a general impression that the government will not last – not a year many say. Indeed Palmerston's age forbids a long term of office for him.'[16] That such expectation was not fulfilled is the supreme achievement of Palmerston's last years. That achievement allows us, with the help of hindsight, to see the Willis's Rooms meeting of 6 June 1859 as 'the formal foundation of the Liberal Party'.[17]

The events surrounding the fall of the Aberdeen coalition in January and February 1855 had confirmed the basic difficulties of party politics in the 1850s. They revealed the disorder amongst Whig, Liberal and Radical ranks created by a surfeit of leadership. They affirmed the difficulties of a Conservative party that, although unified, was both in a minority and intentionally non-committal in its policy. Between 1855 and 1858 Palmerston appeared to overcome these problems with the tenets of Palmerstonian rhetoric: a preoccupation with foreign policy, the minimising of legislative domestic issues, and an executive notion of government that, while imputing inadequacy to other politicians, described a national community of interest enjoying material prosperity. This rhetoric, however, never secured Palmerston's position in parliament. 'Palmerstonianism' within Westminster remained, to a significant degree, a function of disgust with Russell, Radical impotence, Derby's passivity, the compliance of colleagues, and flattering social attentions carried off with zest and finesse. The appearance of political affairs differed because Palmerstonian policy was effective out-of-doors and because, for a variety of reasons, those posing the greatest threat in parliament were content for a while to acquiesce. The popular reading of the 1857 election confirmed the discrepancy between appearance and reality. Interpreted by *The Times* as a triumph for Palmerston, the election, in fact, brought into parliament a significant body of Liberal opinion of advanced views concerned with the issue of parliamentary reform. Such parliamentary opinion was more naturally inclined to Russell than Palmerston.[18] But a consensual strategy of watching and waiting, adopted by Palmerston, Russell and Derby deferred events, ensured inactivity and preserved the appearance of Palmerstonian dominance. During the winter of 1857–58, however, hostile compliance dissolved in the face of developing crises over India and reform. The true weakness of Palmerston's position became clear. Historians have remarked upon the sudden and surprising collapse of Palmerstonian support in February 1858. But one should appreciate Palmerston's achievement in surviving as long as he did. In less than a year he suffered parliamentary defeat on two issues; the latter chosen as decisive by Palmerston himself because it was preferable to more debilitating defeats on other questions. The deceptive apparent ease of Palmerston's ascendancy after 1855 is as worthy of note as his dramatic defeat over the Orsini crisis. Once again, in February 1858, a non-Conservative government was brought down by Whig, Liberal and Radical disarray, and Conservative unanimity.

The advent of a Conservative government in February 1858 brought matters to a head. Indeed, the climax of high political activity between the death of Peel in 1850 and the death of Palmerston in 1865 came during 1858 and 1859. The difficulties of Conservative policy and Whig–Liberal leadership were inevitably intensified once the Conservatives, in office, had to propose a policy, and non-Conservatives, in opposition, needed effective leaders. The Conservative response to this challenge only made opposition difficulties worse. By adopting moderate progressivism, Derby aggravated Whig, Liberal and Radical differences. This emphasised the rivalry between Palmerston and Russell, the danger of Whigs and moderate Liberals moving towards a centrist coalition, the divergence of Peelite intent, and frustrated the Radical need for a polarisation of opinion. It also marked out 1859 as a critical parliamentary session.

The year 1859 should have been, and nearly was, Russell's year. After computer analysis of party opinion and division voting between 1857 and 1859, R. G. Watt comments that in 'retrospect it is difficult to determine why Palmerston was the accepted Liberal leader and not Bright or Russell'.[19] The obstacles to Bright's leadership were obvious to nearly all. But during 1858 Russell's claim to the leadership was becoming increasingly convincing. By January 1859 Russell seemed poised to achieve that which had eluded him ten years before: the forging of a progressive alliance, embracing Peelites and Radicals, fired with Liberal rectitude, legislative zeal and Foxite ideals. In short, a progressive party of such elements as only Russell could lead. The political agenda for 1859 seemed ideal: reform the main business with Italy a supplementary issue. All this, Conservative concession, Radical reticence and Palmerston's patience denied in the critical weeks between January and June 1859.

Concession rehabilitated the Conservatives as moderates in office and a credible party of government. It also forced Russell, in March, to pre-empt a general reform debate with a motion focusing discussion upon the freehold voter. Conservative concession denied Russell and Liberals the cry of equalising the borough and county franchise. In 1858 no other political reform commanded a more unanimous Liberal, Whig and Radical support. But after 1859 Liberals could no longer assemble around that principle. Derby usurped Locke King and dispossessed non-Conservatives of a ready guide through the labyrinth of parliamentary reform. Reticence secured Radicals a high value in political negotiation. This had an important and beneficial effect upon Radical fortunes, but it also denied Russell the forthright endorsement of Radical support. Patience resurrected Palmerston's political career. This finally dashed Russell's hopes.

Russell's failure should not conceal how close he came to success. Nor should one underestimate the difficulty of the task that he set himself. During the 1850s Russell was often dismissed as impulsive and lacking in judgement. But he was attempting to pull together Peelites, Whigs, Liberals and Radicals. Actions seeming misguided to some were often pleasing to others. In offering differing opinions to different audiences Russell's correspondence reveals him attempting to placate Whig anxieties, Peelite earnestness and Radical enthusiasms. This was an onerous brokership. Two observations confirm the extent of Russell's success. First, between 1857 and 1859 a hard core of seventy MPs voted with Russell in nearly all divisions. Only thirty-six MPs were as faithful to Palmerston during the same period. Moreover, thirty of those MPs who voted with Palmerston also voted with Russell.[20] Secondly, two issues cohered Liberal opinion as much as any others in the late 1850s: abolition of the Church rates and the admission of Jews into parliament. Both issues were closely associated with Russell.[21] Prior to 1858 Palmerston's ministry fobbed off the Commons over the former and skirted the latter issue.[22] That Russell came so close to success was testimony to his political skill. It gives credence to Peel's incisive observation that Russell was 'the most ingenious tactician of his time'.[23] But Russell's behaviour also confirms that the parameters of his tactical ingenuity were rigidly confined by his cherished Foxite birthright to the half-closed world of Westminster, St James's and the country residence. Russell's liberal, if strategically complex, impulses were contained in a way that neglected those wider audiences that Palmerston, Stanley, Disraeli, Bright, and later Gladstone, were to address. Russell's ultimate failure in 1859 withheld the fruits of victory until 1865 when old age and ill-health soured their taste.

The major political event of 1859 was the coming together of non-Conservative opinion under Palmerstonian, not Russellite, leadership. Around the anti-climax of what Russell failed to do, the importance of what did occur arranged itself. The year 1859 has long been recognised as that important moment when the Peelite leadership, particularly Gladstone, merged with the Liberal party. Gladstone's absorption into the Liberal party did, indeed, have momentous results for British party politics, but three further points need to be made. First, to see the significance of 1859 in purely Gladstonian terms teases one thread out of the weave and disrupts the broad design. Much else happened of crucial importance for the future. Secondly, looking at Gladstone in isolation can suggest a pattern of consistent and increasing Liberal commitment in the 1850s. The Aberdeen coalition becomes a trial marriage with 1859 as the final consummation. Not only Gladstone in later life, but John Morley in his biography of the GOM, encouraged belief in such an underlying process. But this retrospective reading ignores a number of other, more influential, configurations; in particular a potential Derby–Palmerston–Whig alignment which underlay much manoeuvering and speculation. More importantly, contemporary evidence suggests Gladstone's uncertainty, the ambiguity of his actions, his lingering preference for Derby, and vehement dislike of Palmerston.

The third point to be made concerns the immediate circumstances of Gladstone's merger with the Liberals in May and June 1859. At the beginning of May, while Russell's hopes were still high, Gladstone saw reform as the crucial issue. In the event of Russell forming a progressive alliance with extreme Liberals and Radicals, reform promised a position in a centrist coalition including Conservatives, Whigs and moderate Liberals. By the end of May, circumstances had drastically changed. Derby had closed off immediate negotiations with the Conservatives. Russell's hopes were fading fast, and with them the prospect of a simple bi-partisan alignment over reform. Palmerston moved back to centre stage. For over a week after 19

May, Gladstone vacillated. Finally he brought forward the issue of Italy, because it offered a bridge to a reconstituted non-Conservative majority whether led by Russell or Palmerston. Gladstone entered Palmerston's cabinet in June emphasising the Italian question because he had no other choice. Certainly he had no choice if he wished to remain an active and influential politician. Circumstances forced Gladstone's hand. Similarly the events of 1859 shattered the Peelite pretence that they could determine the future of party politics. Graham and Aberdeen had consistently sought Russell's return to the Liberal leadership. Russell's failure confirmed that the Peelites did not control affairs, unless like Herbert they picked up on a resurgent Palmerstonian current.

Nor were Radicals leading the way so that others might follow. Rather, Radicals found themselves reacting to the initiatives of others. It was not they who transformed parliamentary reform into a major issue in 1857. What Radicals did do effectively was define the limits of progress and determine how little need be done to reassure moderate opinion. It became clear that Cobden was more advanced, if far less active, than Bright and that, contrary to Bright's memory, significant differences existed between them.[24] Yet even though in theory Cobden supported more extensive reform than Bright, he believed Bright to be pushing the wrong issue at the wrong time during the autumn of 1858. The camaraderie between the two men, built on shared bitterness and misfortune during the Crimean War, dissolved. Milner Gibson replaced Bright as Cobden's voice in parliament and took the active part in negotiations during the first half of 1859 on behalf of the Radicals and Pembroke Lodge.

Radical fortunes during 1859 did much to vindicate Bright's silence, owed much to Milner Gibson's mediation, and confirmed the extent of Russell's achievement. That a Liberal ministry should contain a significant Radical presence was one of the preconditions to Russell's resumption of leadership. That Palmerston was obliged to have Radicals in his cabinet in June 1859 was a testament to Russell's near success. Palmerston and the Whigs could no longer define a collective purpose out of disdain for Radicalism. The appointments of Milner Gibson and Villiers to the cabinet, and Headlam, Clive and Gilpin to junior office were followed by Layard becoming Under-Secretary to the Foreign Office in 1861. Between 1846 and 1859 Radicals (with the exception of one token member of Aberdeen's cabinet) were ostracised from the Whig–Liberal frontbench. After 1859, for clever and ambitious young men such as Charles Dilke and

G. O. Trevelyan, Radicalism was a means to office as well as an emotive cause. It no longer led to that political wilderness in which Cobden and Bright had suffered. Radicalism began to lose its urban coarseness and acquired a sleeker gloss to be personified by Dilke and Henry Labouchere. In short, Radicalism could be respectable. The Liberal assimilation of Radical aims became apparent at another level when by 1865, despite Palmerstonian quiescence, an increasing number of Liberal MPs declared that not just the domestic legislative questions of parliamentary reform and Church rates, but also the ballot were pressing issues.[25] Whatever his own wishes in 1859 Palmerston was forced to acknowledge that the reconstituted Liberal party embraced Radical opinion.

The pattern of Bright's career came to illustrate the point. His early political life was spent as a minor member of the Anti-Corn Law League. Isolated and abused for his denunciation of the Crimean War, he experienced a nervous breakdown and in 1857 was rejected by the middle classes of Manchester. Subsequently, he found himself drifting further away from his Manchester School colleagues to be replaced by Milner Gibson as Cobden's delegate in parliament. It was a career lacking in consequence. But during the winter of 1858–59 this began to change. His reform campaign established him as the foremost Radical presence in parliament and a man demanding consideration in any projected progressive alliance. It is surprising that Bright should have expected cabinet office in June 1859, but it was a striking indication of his renewed confidence and suggests why he was reluctant to commit himself prematurely during May. Although not offered a cabinet position Bright had through attack, provocative language and notoriety gained recognition. An unwavering commitment to the issue of reform over the next eight years consolidated his standing. In the 1860s he became associated with working-class aspirations and political Dissent. What was essential, however, was that Bright could claim sources of Radical sympathy amongst the Liberal leadership. The year 1859 marked a crucial stage in Bright's transition from political outcast to Liberal elder statesman. After 1859 fear of Radicalism was no longer a means of defining a broad Liberal movement.

The fate of prominent Peelites, the increase of Radical influence, as well as Russell's dramatic failure and Palmerston's subsequent success, point to significant aspects of 1859. Conservative experience identifies other consequences of equal importance. Derby's greatest achievement was to prevent the defining of a broad Liberal move-

ment out of easy contempt for the Conservative party shorn of
Peelites. Derby's public doctrine identified clear objectives for his
leadership.[26] First, to keep the Conservative party united and avoid
fragmenting backbench opinion. Peel was a recent and salutary
memory. Secondly, to establish the Conservatives as a credible party
of government. Finally, to assimilate additional parliamentary support when it offered the prospect of being a permanent alignment.
His strategies of masterly inactivity in opposition and moderate
progressivism in office prove that, despite historiographical conven-
tion, Derby was a serious politician with a doctrinal purpose of
substance when in office, a committed player of the parliamentary
game, and a significant Conservative leader for reasons other than
longevity.

Derby's handling of the reform issue during the recess of 1858–59
is an instructive example of his unobtrusive mastery over Conservative front and backbenches. He initiated ministerial discussion
immediately the recess began and formed a cabinet committee to
frame a measure. This allowed Derby to pre-empt Disraeli, Stanley,
Pakington, and more cautious cabinet figures, to postpone the disruptive discussion of general principles in cabinet, to determine the
character of the reform measure in his selection of committee members, to allow some to believe him to be either much more cautious
than he actually was, or else the victim of Disraelian intrigue, and to
assemble statistics and data relevant to his own preferences. In the
event, Derby successfully safeguarded the principles he committed
himself to in the autumn of 1858, seeing them form the basis of a
government measure in March 1859 at the cost of only two cabinet
resignations, while preventing others raising alternative issues that
might overshadow reform. Derby was master of his own cabinet.

Derby could claim a large degree of success between 1855 and
1859. The Conservative party possessed the single largest unified
body of votes in the Commons during the 1850s. It was a far more
cohesive group than Peelites, Liberals or Radicals. As Clarendon
confided in November 1859, the Conservatives were 'so compact and
well organised and above all so ready to admit the necessity of
discipline that they are sure to say they are pleased, and to act as if
they were so, by whatever is said or done by the individual whom they
acknowledge as their leader; and that is just what a party ought to be
– there is no union and consequently no strength in a set of men like
the Liberals who are jealous of each other, who recognize no chief,
who have different objects and no principle of cohesion. Derby

knows how to keep his forces together.'²⁷ Despite reform it was a unified party that Derby led into the session of 1860. Moreover, the immediate prospects of a moderate–radical split in Palmerstonian support encouraged a resumption of the tactic of killing with kindness. In opposition, Derby returned to a passive policy that brought Whig, Liberal and Radical differences to the fore in the void created by Conservative non-commitment. The three occasions that Derby came to power in 1852, 1858 and 1866 were opportunities presented by conflict within non-Conservative opinion, not Conservative offensives.²⁸ In 1852 Palmerston attacked Russell. In 1858 Russell and the Radicals attacked Palmerston. In 1866 the Adullamites attacked Gladstone and Russell. Once in power, however, Derby forsook astute inactivity for an official policy of moderate progressivism that was more than that demanded by the exigencies of minority government. In office Derby re-established the Conservatives as a credible party of government. Moreover, in pursuing legislation on those issues unifying non-Conservative opinion Derby blended moderate Conservative progressivism into the solvent of Whig–Liberal party connection. Derby's second ministry sought the legislative resolution of precisely those issues cohering non-Conservative sentiment such as Church rates and the admission of Jews into parliament. Such strategy betrayed Derby's keen political instinct.

The legislative achievement of sixteen months of minority Conservative government during 1858 and 1859 was significant.²⁹ The government of India was reformed. Disraeli's 1858 budget reinstated Gladstone's 1853 settlement. Legislation abolishing the property qualification for MPs (a Chartist demand) and allowing practising Jews to sit in the Commons was safeguarded. Reforms affecting Roman Catholics were passed. A conciliatory Church rates scheme was proposed. A more extensive reform bill was proposed than Palmerston's previous ministry had contemplated. Acts facilitating the drainage of the Thames, conferring self-governing status on British Columbia, and extending municipal government were also passed. At the same time Anglo–French relations were calmed in the wake of the Orsini crisis. Anglo–American relations were soothed over central America. Mediation was pursued in the affair of the *Charles et Georges*. The Caligari incident was resolved, and a policy of careful neutrality adopted in the face of a growing Italian crisis. This was effective substantiation of government rhetoric.

Contrary to Beaconsfield myth, Disraeli was not the frustrated genius of the mid-Victorian Conservative party hampered by the dead weight of Derby's social prominence. Rather Disraeli was a restless presence spurred to constant activity by his own insecurity. All Disraeli's initiatives were subject to Derby's authoritative endorsement. Disraeli's attempts to exploit the allegation of a secret treaty in February 1857, parliamentary reform in April 1857, the Indian Mutiny during the summer, as well as his attempt to push forward the questions of finance and foreign policy during the recess of 1858–59 all failed, because Derby stifled them. Yet Derby's restraint was not a symptom of apathy or inertia, but astute recognition of the persistent irritant that Disraeli's strategic ingenuity proved to Conservative sensibility. It was Derby who pushed forward the question of reform during 1858–59, against the wishes of Disraeli. Derby was to do the same in 1866.[30] In short, the Conservative party was led from Knowsley not Hughenden. Moreover, the Reform Act of 1867 was as much the product of Derby's vision of ministerial Conservatism as it was the result of Disraeli's brilliant short-term tactics. It was Derby, not Disraeli, who educated the mid-Victorian Conservative party. Disraeli offered oratorical talent and an obvious target upon which to deflect the resentment created by Derby's alternating strategies of inactivity and progressivism.

Derby rehabilitated the Conservatives as a party of government. Two factors prevented immediate recognition of his achievement in 1859. First, his resuming a patience policy in opposition that looked to reform and the paper duties in 1860, and later Dissent, the Italian question and the Schleswig Holstein crisis as the occasion of internal Palmerstonian fracture.[31] This was keeping 'the cripples on their legs'.[32] Secondly, Palmerston remained active for longer than anyone had good reason to expect. Palmerston's longevity obscured Derby's accomplishment.

The recovery of belief in the Conservative ability to govern also had much to do with Derby's son, Lord Stanley. Stanley was the coming man of the 1850s. In 1853 Malmesbury recognised him as the Conservative heir apparent and two years later he was offered a position in Palmerston's cabinet. In 1858 he firmly established himself as a politician of intelligence and integrity. Conservative credibility was associated with Stanley's bright prospects. Some saw in Stanley the leader of a centrist coalition once Palmerston was gone. With regard solely to the expectations of others, just as 1859 should have been Russell's year, so 1866 could have been Stanley's opportunity. Why it was not has as much to do with Stanley's interior life as his public actions. Stanley's distancing of himself from strategic considerations and his strong sense of filial duty prevented him from fulfilling his anticipated role. Nevertheless, Stanley's presence in his father's party was perceived as a guarantee of enlightened counsel that enhanced Conservative credibility and offered one more threat to Disraeli's position.

The Stanley family achievement, a Radical revival, a Peelite presence and Russell's near success, determined the difficulties of Palmerston's triumph in 1859. Palmerston headed a broad alliance of non-Conservatives denied those collective attitudes that had formerly cohered progressive opinion. Lord Shaftesbury observed his father-in-law's dilemma. Palmerston's ministry was formed 'on a very wide basis. To form a ministry in any other way would have been impossible, it was a choice of evils, a choice of dangers; and Palmerston wisely took the lesser of the two.' The government included Radicals, Peelites, and Whigs, 'elements of discord, rivalry, intrigue, ambition', and 'if Palmerston were removed the whole thing would be an agglomeration (and nothing more) of molecules floating in various, and ever opposite, directions'.[33] Derby prevented the cohering of progressive opinion out of contempt for atavistic Conservatism. Conservatism had shown itself to be the vehicle of moderate reform at home and diplomatic sobriety abroad. In terms of foreign policy, in contrast to the Conservative *via media*, non-Conservatives represented a range of opinion from 'aggressive chauvinism to pacifism'.[34] Nor was it possible to describe a collective Liberal purpose out of fear of Radicalism. This much Russell had achieved, and this was the price Palmerston had to pay for pre-eminence in June 1859. Liberalism had to incorporate Radicalism. Furthermore, Palmerston had to accommodate himself to the high morality and administrative concerns of Peelism as personified by Gladstone, Herbert and Cardwell. Prior to 1858 Palmerston had cohered Liberal opinion with an executive notion of government preoccupied with foreign affairs that dismissed domestic legislative concerns. This had been necessary in order to subjugate Russell. It had been possible because Liberal purpose was sustained in a collective contempt for Conservatism, fear of Radicalism, and a secure self-regard as the natural party of government. By 1859 none of these attitudes survived as easy assumptions with which to define a progressive parliamentary purpose. This was the extent of the challenge Palmerston faced.

After 1859, the inadequacy of previous dispositions of mind in defining a coherent Liberal intent required an idiomatic shift in political rhetoric. The full implications of this need to redefine and integrate progressive opinion were postponed by Palmerston's longevity. Palmerston 'is tolerated because he is cheerful and wounds no pride, and because he is old and excites no envy'.[35] As in 1855 Palmerston's success after 1859 did not entail solving pressing political problems, but deferring them. Between 1859 and 1865 he held the tensions between Whigs, Radicals and Peelites in check. Longevity elevated deferment and temporary accommodation into what appeared a permanent achievement. Yet the dramatic theme in the politics of the early 1860s is how Gladstone's transition from Peelite to 'People's William' became aligned with the Liberal party's search for new resolve in a world where earlier attitudes were no longer credible. Gladstone reaped the parliamentary harvest of Russell's near success in 1859 in the form of a Liberal party embracing Radicalism, Peelism and Whiggism. After 1868, through the intensity of his rhetoric, Gladstone identified that parliamentary configuration with audiences beyond Westminster and clubland, and defined a new collective Liberal purpose out of administrative and legislative moral zeal.

The intensity of parliamentary politics after 1865 was, in important ways, a delayed response to the challenges posed by the events of 1859. The melée of 1866 reaffirmed the antagonism within non-Conservative opinion. Robert Lowe ruthlessly exposed the absence of any progressive consensus over parliamentary reform. Unable to defer the problem, like Palmerston, neither Russell nor Gladstone responded effectively to the immediate critical need for a common Liberal sense of direction. As Derby anticipated, this crisis created a Conservative opportunity and 1867 crowned Derby's achievement of 1858–59. The second reform act asserted both the Conservative claim to credible centrism, and embarrassed a broad non-Conservative alliance incapacitated by internal dissension. Gladstone fashioned the disestablishment of the Church of Ireland into an effective, if belated, response. In 1868 Gladstonian vision and Liberal need met. Gladstone's 'Chapter of Autobiography' formed a new Liberal text, concession on the ballot secured Bright's support, and Gladstone's ministry of 1868 to 1874 became the energetic executive of a recharged progressive alliance. Although Disraeli adopted a more Palmerstonian livery after 1868, the events of 1871–74 proved a posthumous vindication of Derby's fundamental conviction that in pursuing a collective policy a broad non-Conservative coalition would discover its incompatible differences. Religion, education, Nonconformism, foreign affairs, and an Irish University scheme divided a

Liberal movement that prior to 1873 had seized upon the issues of the Irish Church, Irish land, the ballot and university and army reform. The alliance of opinion that came together in Willis's Rooms, however, was rescued by the resurgent power of Gladstone's oratory after 1876. Not until the Home Rule crisis of 1886 was the alignment of parliamentary party connection redrawn. This emphasised the importance of what occurred in 1859. Events between 1855 and 1859 shaped that alignment of parliamentary opinion that characterised the classic period of two-party politics after 1867. Moreover, they identified the deeper tensions within that configuration of political sentiment. Those events also offer up one final historical paradox. Appreciation of the true nature of Liberal union in 1859 lies in a recognition of the contingent circumstances of disunion and discord.

Notes

INTRODUCTION

1. W. Bagehot, *The English Constitution*, R. Crossman (ed.) (London, 1963) p. 158.
2. G. Kitson Clark, *The Making of Victorian England* (London, 1965) p. 208.
3. Gladstone memo, n.d. (? 12 April 1855) Gladstone Mss. 44745, fol. 203.
4. Kitson Clark, *Making of Victorian England*, pp. 210–11.
5. See G. H. L. LeMay, *The Victorian Constitution* (London, 1979) pp. 17–39; L. B. Namier, 'Monarchy and the Party System', in *Personalities and Power* (London, 1955); J. P. Mackintosh, *The British Cabinet* (London, 1962); A. S. Foord, 'The Waning of the Influence of the Crown', *EHR*, 62 (1947) pp. 484–526.
6. Bagehot, *The English Constitution*, p. 158.
7. See A. Mitchell, *The Whigs in Opposition 1815–30* (Oxford, 1967); A. Aspinall, *Lord Brougham and the Whig Party* (London, 1972); J. Cannon, *Parliamentary Reform* (Cambridge, 1972); J. Derry, *Charles James Fox* (London, 1972); E. Smith, *Whig Principles and Party Politics* (Manchester, 1976); N. Gash, *Reaction and Reconstruction in English Politics 1832–52* (Oxford, 1965); A. D. Kriegel (ed.) *The Holland House Diaries* (London, 1977); and L. Mitchell, *Holland House* (London, 1980).
8. See N. Gash, *Mr. Secretary Peel* (London, 1961) p. 9; and J. C. D. Clark, 'A General Theory of Party, Opposition and Government, 1688–1832', *HJ*, 23:2 (1980) pp. 307–11.
9. In I. D. C. Newbould, 'Whiggery and the Dilemma of Reform: Liberals, Radicals, and the Melbourne Administration, 1835–9', *BIHR*, 53 (1980) pp. 229–41, the Whigs' embarrassment of purpose is kindly interpreted as an attempt at compromise. The translation of an opposition tradition into government policy, however, was an obligation calculated to distress.
10. See N. Gash, *Sir Robert Peel* (London, 1972) and *Reaction and Reconstruction* by the same author. See also G. I. T. Machin, *Politics and the Churches in Great Britain 1832–1868* (Oxford, 1977); R. Blake, *The Conservative Party from Peel to Churchill* (London, 1970); Lord Butler (ed.) *The Conservatives: A History of their Origins to 1965* (London, 1977); D. Southgate (ed.) *The Conservative Leadership 1832–1932* (London, 1974; and R. Stewart, *The Foundation of the Conservative Party 1830–1867* (London, 1978).
11. See N. Gash, *Sir Robert Peel* (London, 1972) pp. 283–4; N. Gash,

'Peel and the Party System, 1830–50', *TRHS*, 5th series (1950) pp. 47–59; A. B. Hawkins, 'Lord Derby and Victorian Conservatism: A Reappraisal', forthcoming *Parliamentary History Yearbook*.

12. See Gash, 'Peel and the Party System', p. 56.

13. This was Namier's observation as developed by Richard Pares, *King George III and the Politicians* (Oxford, 1953).

14. N. Gash, *Aristocracy and People: Britain 1815–1865* (London, 1979) p. 163. See also D. E. D. Beales, 'Parliamentary Parties and the "Independent" Member, 1810–1860', in R. Robson (ed.) *Ideas and Institutions of Victorian Britain* (London, 1967) pp. 1–19; D. Close, 'The Formation of a Two-Party System in the House of Commons Between 1832 and 1841', *EHR* (1969) pp. 257–77; H. Berrington, 'Partisanship and Dissidence in the 19th century House of Commons', *Parliamentary Affairs* (1968) pp. 338–73; D. Large, 'The Decline of the "Party of the Crown" and the Rise of Parties in the House of Lords 1783–1837', *EHR* (1963) pp. 669–95; F. O'Gorman, 'The Problem of Party in Modern British History: 1725–1832', *Government and Opposition* (1981) pp. 447–70. See J. C. D. Clark, 'A General Theory of Party, Opposition and Government, 1688–1832', *HJ*, 23:2 (1980) pp. 295–325, for an important discussion of the development of successive party systems after 1688 and their attendant conventions of rhetoric and behaviour.

15. See T. L. Crosby, *Sir Robert Peel's Administration 1841–46* (Newton Abbot, 1970); and R. Stewart, *The Politics of Protection: Lord Derby and the Protectionist Party, 1841–1852* (Cambridge, 1971).

16. See Stewart, *Foundation of the Conservative Party*, pp. 128–46. In a consciously revisionist argument, R. H. Cameron, 'Parties and Politics in Early Victorian Britain', *Canadian Journal of History*, 13:3 (1979) pp. 375–93, alights on the discrepancy between rhetoric and sentiment and suggests that party leaders differed little and, ideologically, differed over means rather than ends. The discerning of consensus is astute. But the perception of political positions was framed within a deliberately adversarial rhetoric which was itself a reality shaping intent and behaviour.

17. See G. A. Cahill, 'Irish Catholicism and English Toryism', *Review of Politics*, 19 (1957) pp. 62–76.

18. As well as works cited above, the following articles contain much of value: W. O. Aydelotte, 'The Country Gentlemen and the Repeal of the Corn Laws', *EHR*, 82 (1967); G. Kitson Clark, 'The Electorate and the Repeal of the Corn Laws', *TRHS*, 5th series, 1 (1951); and M. Lawson-Tancred, 'The Anti-League and the Corn Law Crisis of 1846', *HJ*, 3 (1960).

19. H. E. Maxwell, *Life and Letters of G. W. Frederick, Fourth Earl of Clarendon*, 2 vols (London, 1913) I, pp. 265–7. See also, F. A. Dreyer, 'The Whigs and the Political Crisis of 1845', *EHR*, 80 (July 1965) pp. 514–37.

20. Gash, *Reaction and Reconstruction*, pp. 189–200; and J. Prest *Lord John Russell* (London, 1972) pp. 219–344. See T. F. Gallagher, 'The Second Reform Movement, 1848–1867', *Albion* 12:2 (1980) pp.

147–63, for a discussion of the vitality of the reform issue despite public indifference.

21. For a discussion of the changing political climate of the 1850s see M. Bentley, *Politics without Democracy* (London, 1984) pp. 143–63.

22. There exists only one substantial study of this neglected parliamentary group; J. H. Whyte, *The Independent Irish Party, 1850–1859* (Oxford, 1958).

23. Russell to Panmure, 26 August 1851, Dalhousie Mss. GD45/8/632, fol. 62. See also C. S. Parker, *Life and Letters of Sir James Graham*, (London, 1907) II, pp. 132–135.

24. Roebuck to Graham, 20 July 1852, Graham Mss. Bundle 119.

25. Graham to Aberdeen, 6 August 1852, Aberdeen Mss 43191, cited in Parker, *Graham*, II, p. 172.

26. Clarendon to Cornewall Lewis, 1 September 1852, cited in Maxwell, *Clarendon*, I, p. 346.

27. Stanley Diary, 1 March, 1853, Stanley Mss. 920 DER (15) 43/3; see also Stanley to Disraeli, 28 January 1853, Hughenden Mss. B/XX/S/588.

28. See C. H. Stuart, 'The Formation of the Coalition Cabinet of 1852', *TRHS*, 5th series (1954) pp. 45–68.

29. Ostrogorski originally coined the phrase 'the golden age of the back-bencher' in order to lament the contrasting restrictions of party discipline and an oppressive executive on individual conscience later in the century. M. Ostrogorski, *Democracy and the Organization of Political Parties* (London, 1902). Richard Crossman echoed this thought in his introduction to Bagehot's *English Constitution* by suggesting 'the existence of a solid centre, composed of the majority of solid, sensible, independent M.P.s, collectively able to unmake ministries, to defy when necessary their own Whips, and above all to frustrate the growth of constituency government outside', R. Crossman introduction to Bagehot, *The English Constitution*, p. 40. This interpretation dangerously distorts Bagehot's own emphasis on party connection. Attacks on party 'amend parliamentary government by striking out the very elements which make parliamentary government possible. At present the majority of parliament obey certain leaders; what those leaders propose they support, what those leaders reject they reject', Bagehot, *The English Constitution*, p. 157.

30. 'Opposition Government', *The Edinburgh Review*, January 1855, p. 3; R. Cecil, 'Independent Voting and Parliamentary Government', *The Saturday Review*, 28 February 1857.

31. Graham to Ellice, 7 January 1859, Ellice Mss. 15019, fol. 46, cited in Parker, *Graham*, II, p. 365.

32. Gladstone to Northcote, 9 October 1856, Iddesleigh Mss. 50014, fol. 340.

33. Gladstone to Aberdeen, 13 March 1856, Aberdeen Mss. 44089.

34. Disraeli, 5 March 1857, *Hansard*, 3rd series, CXLIV, 1897. R. E. McGowen and W. L. Arnstein in 'The Mid-Victorians and the Two Party System', *Albion*, 11:3 (1979) pp. 242–58, suggest a disillusion-

ment with party during the mid-Victorian period based upon the comment of some Whig–Liberal journals of the period. Therein lies a danger. Political journals took their cue from parliamentary circumstance. The quiescent survival of Conservative Party connection, and the disorder of non-Conservative (Peelite, Whig, Liberal and Radical) connection after 1850 forced some sort of coherent response from a partisan journalism looked to for intelligent comment. As a result the Conservative journals (the *Quarterly Review*, *Blackwood's* and *Fraser's Magazine*) upheld the virtues of party even when, through the acerbic pen of Lord Robert Cecil and the inclinations of the Rev. Elwin, the *Quarterly Review* became the vehicle of anti-Disraelian sentiment. At the same time Whig–Liberal journals, floundering in the confusion attending the Whig–Liberal disarray, sought a coherent position in eulogising the welcome end of party government. The *Edinburgh Review*, *Westminster Review*, *North British Review* and *Economist* described a partisanship in extolling non-partisanship. A consensus of intelligent opinion was defined based upon Whig axioms of contempt for the Conservatives and fear of Radicalism. The shift such a delineation of commonsense entailed, from legislative to executive preoccupations, was astutely exploited by Palmerston after 1855. By 1865, however, when circumstances created the opportunity to celebrate distinct party cleavages, those same journals eagerly seized the moment.

35. The Queen to the King of the Belgians, 17 March 1852, cited in A. C. Benson and Viscount Esher (eds) *The Letters of Queen Victoria*, 3 vols, 1st series, (London, 1907) II, p. 464. Beales has observed that despite the disorganisation of political connection after 1846 'the true "non-party" man is hard to find'. Beales, 'Parliamentary Parties and the "Independent" member, 1810–1860', in R. Robson (ed.) *Ideas and Institutions of Victorian Britain*, p. 13.

36. Beales, 'Parliamentary Parties', p. 13. Confirmation of general two-party voting in the Commons after 1859 is provided through multi-dimensional scaling by Valerie Cromwell, 'Mapping the Political World of 1861: A Multidimensional Analysis of House of Commons Division Lists', *Legislative Studies Quarterly*, 7:2 (1982) pp. 281–97.

37. R. Blake *Disraeli* (London, 1966) p. 406. See also D. E. D. Beales, *England and Italy, 1859–60* (London, 1961) pp. 79–84.

38. D. Southgate, '*The Most English Minister . . .*': *The Policies and Politics of Palmerston* (London, 1966) pp. 455–6. Gash comments: 'The liberal meeting in Willis's Rooms on 6 June 1859, which united whigs, moderate liberals, Peelites and radicals, was in its own way a refounding of the Victorian Liberal party.' He points to the Lichfield House Compact of 1835 as marking the genesis of the Liberal Party. Gash, *Aristocracy and People*, p. 268.

39. See J. Vincent, *The Formation of the Liberal Party, 1857–1868* (London, 1966); and R. T. Shannon, *Gladstone and the Bulgarian Agitation 1876* (London, 1963).

40. See P. Smith, *Disraelian Conservatism and Social Reform* (London, 1967); Blake, *Disraeli*; and H. J. Hanham, *Elections and Party Man-*

agement. Politics in the Time of Disraeli and Gladstone (London, 1959).

41. W. E. Gladstone, 'The History of 1852–60 and Greville's Latest Journals', *EHR*, 2 (1887) pp. 294–5.

42. J. McCarthy, *A History of Our Times*, 4 vols (London, 1881) III, p. 11.

43. G. M. Trevelyan, *British History in the Nineteenth Century and After* (London, 1922) chap. 21; and J. R. M. Butler, *A History of England: 1818–1914* (London, 1928) chap. IV, p. 90.

44. G. M. Young, *Portrait of an Age* (Oxford: 1936) chap. XII, p. 81.

45. J. B. Conacher, *From Waterloo to the Common Market* (London, 1977), although Conacher first used the phrase in 'Party Politics in the Age of Palmerston', in E. Appleman, W. A. Madden and M. Wolff (eds) *1859: Entering an Age of Crisis* (Bloomington, Indiana, 1959) p. 163.

46. Greville Diary, 23 May 1858, Greville Mss. 41122, cited in C. C. F. Greville, *The Greville Memoirs*, H. Reeve (ed.) 8 vols (London, 1888) VIII, p. 199.

47. Gladstone memo, n.d. (? September 1858) Gladstone Mss. 44689, fol. 52.

48. Disraeli to Mrs Brydges Willyams, 22 May 1858, cited in W. F. Monypenny and G. E. Buckle, *The Life of Benjamin Disraeli, Earl of Beaconsfield* 6 vols (London, 1910–20) IV, p. 149.

49. Lytton to Rose, 6 December 1858, Hughenden Mss. B/XX/Ly/106.

50. W. O. Aydelotte, 'The House of Commons in the 1840's', *History*, 39 (1954) p. 252. For a very persuasive statistical response to the aforementioned difficulties in defining ideological patterns see Valerie Cromwell's use of multidimensional scaling, V. Cromwell, 'Mapping the Political World of 1861: A Multidimensional Analysis of House of Commons' Division Lists', *Legislative Studies Quarterly*, 7:2 (1982) pp. 281–98.

51. Overstone to Granville, 23 March 1856, Granville Mss. PRO 30/39/18/1.

52. Elliot to Minto, 4 April 1853, Minto Mss. 1174, fol. 339.

53. Graham to Cardwell, 26 February 1856, Cardwell Mss PRO 30/29/18/1, fol. 117.

54. Senior Diary, 11 September 1856, cited in M. C. M. Simpson (née Senior) *Many Memories of Many People* (London, 1898) p. 241.

55. Bagehot, *The English Constitution*. pp. 159–60.

56. Palmer to Gordon, 9 November 1856, Selborne Mss. 1872, fol. 90.

57. Lord R. Cecil to Lord E. Cecil, 12 July 1853, Salisbury Mss.

58. Milner Gibson, 25 July 1856, *Hansard*, 3rd series, CXLIII, 1470.

59. W. O. Aydelotte, 'The House of Commons in the 1840's', *History*, 39 (1954) pp. 240–62. See also, W. O. Aydelotte, 'Voting Patterns in the British House of Commons in the 1840s', *Comparative Studies in History and Society*, 5 (1963) pp. 134–63.

60. W. O. Aydelotte, 'Parties and Issues in Early Victorian England', *JBS*, 5 (1966) pp. 95–114. The data presented in Table III, on p. 107, bears close examination. The three categories of division distribution yield,

surprisingly effectively, to chronological criteria. What we may be looking at here is less consistent ideological cleavages than shifting party connection wrought by changing circumstance. First, a period of Conservative cohesion and Whig–Liberal disarray, 1841–43; secondly, a period of strong cohesion amongst both Conservatives and Whig–Liberals, 1843–45; thirdly, a period of Whig–Liberal cohesion and Conservative disarray, 1845–47. The votes on the drainage of lands bill, 31 March 1843, and Russell's education proposals, 22 April 1847, remain as special cases.

61. W. O. Aydelotte, 'The Disintegration of the Conservative Party in the 1840s: A Study of Political Attitudes', in W. Aydelotte, A. G. Bogue and R. W. Fogel (eds) *The Dimensions of Quantitative Research in History* (London, 1972) p. 346. In this article Aydelotte is examining a temporal process of disintegration. The essential chronological dimension is therefore granted its appropriate importance.

62. Sotheron-Estcourt to Jolliffe, 1 January 1856, Hylton Mss. 24/11, fol. 13.

63. J. R. Bylsma, 'Party Structure in the 1852–1857 House of Commons: A Scalogram Analysis', *Journal of Interdisciplinary History*, 7:4 (1977) pp. 617–35; J. R. Bylsma, 'Political Issues and Party Unity in the House of Commons, 1852–1857: A Scalogram Analysis', unpublished PhD thesis, University of Iowa, 1968; R. G. Watt, 'Parties and Politics in Mid-Victorian Britain, 1857–1859; A Study in Quantification', unpublished PhD thesis, University of Minnesota, 1975. For discussion of the resilience of two-party voting see G. M. Gurowich, 'The Continuation of War by Other Means: Party and Politics, 1855–1865', *HJ*, 27:3 (1984) pp. 603–31.

64. See Bylsma, 'Party Structure', *passim*; and Watt, op. cit., pp. 261–5.

65. For Russell's overt support of Palmerston see Watt, op. cit., p. 138. Citing Watt's statistics, Gurowich, op. cit., p. 611 compounds this misreading stating that Russell enjoyed no defined backbench following distinct from the main parties. Watt's own figures, however, show that between 1857–59 Russell had a 'hard core' of support numbering 70 MPs. Palmerston had 36 consistent supporters, 30 of whom also supported Russell. Even while prime minister between March 1857 and February 1858, Palmerston received consistent support from only 110 MPs. This group included 3 Conservatives, 2 Liberal Conservatives, 4 Whigs, no avowed Radicals and included Russell, Watt, op. cit., p. 130–8. As what follows makes clear, Russell was looking to a redefinition of bi-polarity, and Gurowich seriously underestimates this possibility.

66. Graham to Aberdeen, 12 September 1852, Aberdeen Mss. 43190, fol. 331.

67. Gladstone to Aberdeen, n.d. (? March 1857) Gladstone Mss. 44747, fol. 53.

68. Gladstone memo, n.d. (? 12 April 1855) Gladstone Mss. 44745, fol. 198, cited in Conacher, 'Party Politics in the Age of Palmerston', p. 164.

69. Elliot to Minto, 17 December 1852, Minto Mss. 11754, fol. 330.

70. Cornewall Lewis to Head, 5 November 1856, cited in G. F. Lewis (ed.) *Letters of the Rt. Hon. Sir George Cornewall Lewis to Various Friends* (London, 1870) p. 318.

71. Granville to Canning, 30 January 1856, Granville Mss. PRO 30/39/31/1.

72. A. D. Kriegel, 'Liberty and Whiggery in Early Nineteenth Century England', *Journal of Modern History*, 52:2 (1980) pp. 253–78, examines the Whig notion of 'liberty' which was subordinated to 'the inviolability of property, aristocratic honour, and the preservation of a hierarchically ordered society'.

73. Cobden to Lindsay, 23 March 1858, Cobden Mss. 43669.

74. See J. Vincent, *Formation of the Liberal Party, 1857–1868*, pp. 8–9; and H. J. Hanham, *Elections and Party Management*.

75. Gladstone memo, 28 February 1855, Gladstone Mss. 44745, fol. 149.

76. Russell to Graham, 2 November 1852, Graham Mss. Bundle 122.

77. See Bylsma, 'Political Issues and Party', pp. 187–8, and Watt, op. cit., p. 263.

78. Dallas to Gilpin, 30 January 1857, cited in G. M. Dallas, *Letters from London, 1856–1860*, 2 vols (London, 1870) I, p. 38.

79. See Vincent, *Formation of the Liberal Party*, pp. 28–30.

80. Parkes to Ellice, 16 June 1856, Ellice Mss. 15042, fol. 14.

81. A. Briggs, *Victorian People: A Reassessment of People and Themes, 1851–67* (London, 1954) p. 73.

82. Cobden to Bright, 2 September 1851, Cobden Mss. 43649, cited in Norman McCord, 'Cobden and Bright in Politics, 1846–1857', in R. Robson (ed.) *Ideas and Institutions of Victorian Britain* (London, 1967) p. 103. In 1851 Bright believed Russell to be sinking into 'a state of hopeless imbecility . . . I believed him to be incurable, and the sooner he is banished from politics, the better for the country.' Bright to Wilson, 12 March 1851, Wilson Mss., cited in McCord, 'Cobden and Bright in Politics', p. 102.

83. Cobden to Bright, 9 September 1852, Cobden Mss. 43649, fol. 249.

84. Gladstone memo, n.d. (? 12 April 1855) Gladstone Mss. 44745, fol. 209.

85. Mrs E. Twisleton, *The Letters of Mrs Edward Twisleton to her Family: 1852–1862* (London, 1928) p. 128.

86. Parkes to Ellice, 30 December 1852, Ellice Mss. 15041, fol. 64. Clarendon saw the Peelites as 'a little bank of conceited colonels without general officers and no rank and file'. Clarendon to Cornewall Lewis, 10 November 1851, cited in Maxwell, *Clarendon*, I, p. 328.

87. C. R. Dod, *The Parliamentary Companion for 1855* (London, 1855) p. 278. See also, Baron Sanderson and E. S. Roscoe, *The Speeches and Addresses of Edward Henry, XVth Earl of Derby K. G.*, 2 vols (London, 1894); and J. Vincent (ed.) *Disraeli, Derby and the Conservative Party* (Hassocks, 1978).

88. Beresford to Derby, n.d. Derby Mss. 149/1, cited in Stewart, *The Politics of Protection*, p. 127.

89. The mood of 'ultra-Toryism' was poignantly expressed in the private confession that 'the great world is very much more corrupt than I ever

believed it to be'. M. Newdegate Diary, 11 January 1853. Newdegate Mss. The best study of the Victorian 'ultra-Tory' mind is W. L. Arnstein, *Protestant versus Catholic in Mid-Victorian England: Mr. Newdegate and the Nuns* (University of Missouri, Columbia, 1982).

90. Derby's purpose was clear: 'Wait – don't attack Ministers – that will only bind them together – if left alone they must fall to pieces by their own disunion.' This strategy was also referred to as killing the government 'with kindness'. Stanley Diary, 20 and 14 December 1852, Stanley Mss. 920 DER (15), 43/2, cited in Vincent (ed.) *Disraeli, Derby and the Conservative Party*, pp. 91–4. See also, Derby to Disraeli, 30 January 1853, Hughenden Mss. B/XX/S/111.

91. See D. Read, *Cobden and Bright: A Victorian Political Partnership* (London, 1967) pp. 109–49. See also, Vincent, *Formation of the Liberal Party*, pp. 33–4.

92. For a discussion of the patriotic Radical tradition see Hugh Cunningham, 'The Language of Patriotism? 1750–1914', *History Workshop Journal*, 12 (1981) pp. 8–33. See also, A. F. Cruickshank, 'J. A. Roebuck, MP: A Reappraisal of Liberalism in Sheffield, 1849–1879', *Northern History*, 16 (1980) pp. 196–214.

93. After his computer analysis of the 1852–57 parliament, Bylsma observes that 'it is very difficult to determine any common thread which runs through the foreign affairs issue other than the demand of the MPs and the country that the government conduct foreign affairs successfully'. Bylsma 'Political Issues and Party Unity', p. 188. See also Vincent, *Formation of the Liberal Party*, pp. 247–8.

94. For a discussion of the cross-party nature of mid-Victorian moral reform issues see Brian Harrison, *Peaceable Kingdom: Stability and Change in Modern Britain* (Oxford, 1982) pp. 152–4. For social legislation of the 1840s see W. O. Aydelotte, 'The Conservative and Radical Interpretations of Early Victorian Social Legislation', *Victorian Studies*, 11 (1967) pp. 225–36. See Gash's comment on Aydelotte's statistics in Gash, *Reactions and Reconstruction*, p. 217. See also W. O. Aydelotte, 'Voting Patterns in the British House of Commons in the 1840s', *Comparative Studies in Society and History*, 5:2 (1963); and Vincent, *Formation of the Liberal Party*, pp. 241–6.

95. See Bylsma, 'Political Issues and Party Unity', p. 146.

96. Clarendon to his wife, 10 January 1853, cited in Maxwell, *Clarendon*, I, p. 361.

97. Wood to Russell, 7 December 1854, Russell Mss. PRO 30/22/11/F.

98. Graham to Aberdeen, 31 October 1856, Aberdeen Mss. 43192, fol. 35.

99. Disraeli memo, n.d., Hughenden Mss. A/X/A/47.

100. Bentinck to Croker, 26 December 1847, cited in Stewart, *Politics of Protection*, p. 124.

101. See Bylsma, 'Political Issues and Party Unity', pp. 140–54.

102. Ibid. See also Watt, op. cit., pp. 141–76.

103. Sotheron-Estcourt to Jolliffe, 1 January 1856, Hylton Mss. DD/HY/24/11, fol. 13.

104. Gladstone memo, 27 December 1852, Gladstone Mss. 44778, fol. 48.

105. Prince Albert memo, 21 February 1855, *QVL*, 1st series, III, p. 137.
In a meeting with Gladstone that same day Prince Albert 'observed on
the great practical mischiefs that resulted from having one party
overcharged with Rt. Honorables i.e. candidates for ministerial
offices . . .' Gladstone memo, 21 February 1855, Gladstone Mss.
44745, fol. 140, cited in W. E. Gladstone, *The Gladstone Diaries*
H. C. G. Matthew (ed.) (Oxford, 1978) V, p. 28.

106. Gladstone memo, n.d. (? 12 April 1855) Gladstone Mss. 44745,
fol. 203.

107. Palmerston Diary, 19 March 1852, Broadlands Mss. D/13. See also
Palmerston Diary, 15 September 1852, Broadlands Mss. D/13.

108. Broughton Diary, 25 December 1852, Broughton Mss. 43757, fol. 83.
See also, Wood Diary, 23 December 1852, Hickleton Mss. A8/A; and
Greville Diary, 28 December 1852, Greville Mss. 41119, cited in
Greville, *Memoirs*, VII, p. 25–6.

109. Broughton Diary, 25 December 1852, Broughton Mss. 43757, fol. 83.

110. Gladstone to Aberdeen, 30 July 1852, Aberdeen Mss. 43070,
fol. 250.

111. Stanley Diary, 17 February 1853, Stanley Mss. 43/3, cited in Vincent
(ed.) *Disraeli, Derby and the Conservative Party*, p. 99.

112. See J. B. Conacher, *The Aberdeen Coalition 1852–1855: A Study in
Mid-Nineteenth Century Party Politics* (Cambridge, 1968) for a detailed
modern narrative of the coalition.

113. Ellice to Aberdeen, n.d. (? 24 February 1854) Aberdeen Mss. 43200,
fol. 122. See also Argyll to Russell, 9 February 1854, Russell Mss.
PRO 30/22/11/C, fol. 736.

114. Gordon Diary, 22 January 1855, cited in *Lord Aberdeen's Correspondence 1854–55*, p. 378: a privately printed selection from A. Gordon,
Baron Stanmore's diary not extant in the Stanmore Mss.

115. Stanley Diary, 17 December 1853, Stanley Mss. 920 DER (15) 43/3.

116. See Bylsma, 'Political Issues and Party Unity', pp. 77-80 and 185-6.

117. See J. Vincent, 'The Parliamentary Dimension of the Crimean War',
TRHS, 5th series, 31 (1981) pp. 37–49.

118. Clarendon commented in February 1855: 'The government may do
well for a short time, because Palmerston has prestige in the country,
and people believe the war will be conducted with more vigour; but
this won't last very long. P. is not a good man for general business: he
is apt to mistake popular applause for real opinion, and I doubt his
having the particular talent, or the vigourous health necessary for
leading the House of Commons.' (Clarendon to Cowley, 7 February
1855, Cowley Mss. FO 519/172.) Wood thought no 'man of sense'
could believe Palmerston's popularity would last. He 'thought it a
bubble, and told [Palmerston] so,' (Wood to Herbert, 24 February
1855, cited in A. H. Gordon, Baron Stanmore, *Sidney Herbert, Lord
Herbert of Lea: A Memoir*, 2 vols (London, 1906) I, p. 267.) Gladstone observed that the government had little strength in the Commons, and 'such would be the case with any government Lord Palmerston could form.' (Prince Albert memo, 21 February 1855, *QVL*, 1st
series, III, p. 136.) The *Edinburgh Review* found 'the new government

was formed mainly of the same elements [as the former); and did little more than continue the remedial measures which had already been begun.' R. Lowe (anon.) 'The Sebastopol Committee and Vienna Conferences', *Edinburgh Review*, 102 (1855) p. 274.

CHAPTER 1

1. Derby, 8 February 1855, *Hansard* 3rd series, CXXXVI, 1339. See also Palmerston to Temple, 15 February 1855, cited in E. Ashley, *Life of Viscount Palmerston, 1846–1865*, 2 vols (London, 1876) II, pp. 76–9. Palmerston told the Commons that his 'government [had] arisen in consequence of the failure of others'. Palmerston, 19 February 1855, *Hansard*, 3rd series, CXXXVI, 1538.

2. See Vernon Smith at Northampton, *The Times*, 6 March 1855, p. 8, and Robert Peel at Tamworth, *The Times*, 15 March 1855, p. 10. For Palmerston's use of the press see S. Koss, *The Rise and Fall of the Political Press in Britain: The Nineteenth Century* (London, 1981) pp. 112–13.

3. Robert Lowe was a regular editorial writer for *The Times*. Upon receiving news of his appointment Lowe wrote an editorial for the next morning's edition that began the paper's more favourable comment on the government. See Delane's Diary of leader writers for 1855, Delane Mss. Lord Goderich observed that Lowe had 'certainly played *his* cards well for his purposes'. Goderich to Layard, 25 August 1855, cited in *The History of 'The Times'* (London, 1939) II, p. 555. Both Goderich and Layard had good reason for rancour. Lowe's conversion to Palmerstonianism took the steam out of the administrative reform movement with which they had all been associated.

4. *The Times*, 6 October 1855, p. 6. Lowe in his editorials commented that 'Lord John has gone on in a headlong career of self destruction till he seems scarcely the shadow of that important personage on whom all eyes were fixed a few months ago'. *The Times*, 14 August 1855, p. 8.

5. Herbert to Clarendon, 7 October 1853, cited in A. H. Gordon, Baron Stanmore, *Sidney Herbert, Lord Herbert of Lea: A Memoir*, 2 vols (London, 1906) I, p. 204.

6. See Aberdeen to Palmerston, ? December 1853, cited in *Lord Aberdeen's Correspondence 1854–55*, B.P. 12 (10). See J. B. Conacher, *The Aberdeen Coalition 1852–1855: A Study in Mid-Nineteenth Century Party Politics* (Cambridge, 1968) pp. 137–268.

7. Palmerston Diary, 6 February 1855, Broadland Mss. D/16.

8. See J. R. Bylsma 'Political Issues and Party Unity in the House of Commons, 1852–1857: A Scalogram Analysis', unpublished PhD thesis, University of Iowa, 1968, p. 188; and J. R. Vincent, *The Formation of the Liberal Party 1857–1868* (London, 1966) p. 247.

9. Granville to Russell, 12 January 1852, Granville Mss. PRO 30/29/

18/1. See also H. C. F. Bell, *Lord Palmerston*, 2 Vols (London, 1936) II, p. 52.

10. Palmerston to Russell, 20 June 1852, Russell Mss. PRO 30/22/11/A, fol. 94–8. Part of a long memorandum on the Eastern Question, sections of which are printed in G. P. Gooch (ed.) *The Later Correspondence of Lord John Russell 1840–1878*, 2 vols (London, 1925) II, pp. 150–1.

11. Bright to Ellice, 4 February 1857, Ellice Mss. 15006, fol. 76.

12. Derby's remark that 'nine in ten of the House of Commons care nothing about [foreign policy]' was born of long parliamentary experience. Derby to Malmesbury, 15 December 1856, Derby Mss. 183/2, fol. 133.

13. Clarendon protested that Palmerston's resignation 'had nothing to do with the Eastern Question, though we may swear that till we are black in the face and nobody will believe us either at home or abroad'. Clarendon to Cowley, 16 December 1853, Cowley Mss. FO 715. For a detailed discussion of this episode see D. F. Krein, 'War and Reform: Russell, Palmerston and the Struggle for Power in the Aberdeen Cabinet, 1853–4', *Maryland Historian*, 7:2 (1976) pp. 67–84. Also Conacher, *Aberdeen Coalition*, pp. 215–32.

14. Duke of Argyll, *George Douglas, 8th Duke of Argyll: Autobiography and Memoirs*, 2 vols (London, 1906) 1, p. 527. While prime minister in the early 1860s, Palmerston was again to use the popular perception of cabinet differences to dissociate himself from difficult policies, in particular Gladstonian finance. See P. M. Gurowich, 'The Continuation of War by Other Means: Party and Politics, 1855–1865', *HJ*, 27:3 (1984) p. 618.

15. See J. Vincent, 'The Parliamentary Dimension of the Crimean War', *TRHS*, 5th series, 31 (1981) pp. 37–49.

16. Dallas to Marcy, 11 July 1856, cited in G. M. Dallas *Letters from London, 1856–1860* (London, 1870) I, p. 60.

17. A copy of Palmerston's speech at Manchester on the 6 November 1856 is part of the Broadlands Mss. SP/B, fol. 4. See also D. Steele, 'Gladstone and Palmerston, 1855–65', in P. J. Jagger (ed.) *Gladstone, Politics and Religion* (London, 1985) pp. 119–21.

18. Ibid.

19. Note Sidney Herbert's response: 'Palmerston seems to have flourished at Manchester and the papers are in a chorus of delight at a man making three commonplace speeches in one day.' Herbert to Gladstone, 10 November 1856, cited in Gordon, *Herbert*, II, p. 56.

20. See Cobden to Hargreaves, 7 April 1857, Cobden Mss. 43255, fol. 57. Lady Cowper noted that Palmerston was 'not popular, except out of doors among the people who say he is a fine Englishman'. Lady Cowper to Cowper, 28 February 1855, cited in J. Ridley, *Lord Palmerston* (London, 1972) p. 589. One foreign observer saw public opinion as 'a kite which rises or falls with every breath of air, and which none can fly but those who understand the game to be a game'. Palmerston proved himself a master. Count V. F. Vitzthum Eckstaedt, *St. Petersburg and London in the Years 1852 to 1864*, 2 vols (London,

1887) I, pp. 140–4. For other comments on the volatile nature of popular opinion see Gordon, *Herbert*, I, p. 448.

21. *The Times*, 21 October 1865, p. 9. For Palmerston's earlier career see K. Bourne's authoritative study, *Palmerston: The Early Years 1784–1841* (London, 1984).

22. Clarendon to Granville, 16 September 1855, Clarendon Mss. c. 138. Clarendon continued that Palmerston was no longer able to 'act upon his impulses at the F.O.', but was 'more immediately responsible to parliament than he ever was before'.

23. W. White, *The Inner Life of the House of Commons*, 2 vols (London, 1897) I, p. 2. Lady Palmerston reported that 'the House of Commons took up so much of [Palmerston's] time, that he went but very little into general society'. Lady Palmerston to Lady Holland, 16 August 1856, Holland House Mss. See also Granville to Canning, 31 January 1856, Granville Mss. PRO 30/29/21/1.

24. See Bernal Osborne Diary, 19 February 1858, cited in P. H. Bagenal, *The Life of Ralph Bernal Osborne M.P.* (London, 1884) p. 249. In a significant association of thought Lord Breadalbane at once 'thought well' of public affairs, 'and praised Palmerston for his attention to everyone small or great'. Broughton Diary, 21 May 1856, Broughton Mss. 43759, fol. 112. See also Clarendon to Brougham, 30 July 1856, Brougham Mss. 30157.

25. M. C. M. Simpson (née Senior) *Many Memories of Many People* (London, 1898) p. 134.

26. See Ashley, *Palmerston*, I, pp. 58–228.

27. See Bell, *Palmerston*, II, pp. 73–80.

28. See O. Anderson, 'The Wensleydale Peerage Case and the Position of the House of Lords in the Mid-Nineteenth Century', *EHR*, 82 (1967) pp. 486–502; Bell, *Palmerston*, II, p. 158; Bylsma 'Issues and Party Unity', pp. 203–13.

29. See Bylsma, 'Issues and Party Unity', p. 123.

30. Palmerston, 4 March 1856, *Hansard*, 3rd series, CXL, 1846.

31. Derby, 31 January 1856, *Hansard*, 3rd series, CXL, 18.

32. Bright to Cobden, 27 September 1856, Bright Mss. 43384, fol. 73.

33. Cobden to Bright, 3 April 1856, Cobden Mss. 43650, fol. 203.

34. Disraeli, 25 July 1856, *Hansard*, 3rd series, CXLIII, 1430–61.

35. Two divisions occurred during the Kars debate on 29 April and 1 May 1856: Bylsma, 'Issues and Party Unity', pp. 81–3. See also White, *Inner Life of the House of Commons*, I, p. 11.

36. Aberdeen to Gladstone, 3 August 1856, Gladstone Mss. 44089. For a discussion of how diplomatic material presented to parliament in blue books contained omissions, alterations and selected quotations intended to influence popular opinion and justify decisions see Valerie Cromwell, 'The Administrative Background to the Presentation of Parliamentary Papers on Foreign Affairs in the Mid-Nineteenth Century', in F. Ranger (ed.) *Prisca Munimenta: Studies in Archival and Administrative History* (London, 1973) pp. 184–201.

37. See Sir H. Maxwell, *The Life and Letters of the Fourth Earl of Clarendon* (London, 1913) II, pp. 123–5.

38. Palmerston, 31 January 1856, *Hansard*, 3rd series, CXC 77. See also Bell, *Palmerston*, II, pp. 143–5.

39. Disraeli, 25 July 1856, *Hansard*, 3rd series, CXLIII, 1430–61.

40. Parkes to Ellice, 10 January 1856, Ellice Mss. 15042, fol. 3.

41. Bedford to Brougham, 17 September 1856, Brougham Mss. 30405. The 'contest is not what should be done, but who should do it'. Elwin to Brougham, 27 May 1856, Brougham Mss. 1548.

42. See Bell, *Palmerston*, II, pp. 143–5.

43. Palmerston, 16 June 1856, *Hansard*, 3rd series, CXCII, 1508. See also Argyll, *Autobiography and Memoirs*, II, pp. 47–8. For an important discussion of the Anglo–American crisis see K. Bourne, 'Lord Palmerston's "Ginger Beer" Triumph, 1 July 1856', in K. Bourne and D. C. Watt (eds) *Studies in International History: Essays Presented to W. Norton Medlicott* (London, 1967) pp. 145–71.

44. See Owen Chadwick, *The Victorian Church*, 2 vols (London, 1966) I, pp. 468–76. Bell, *Palmerston*, II, p. 157 and Gurowich, 'The Continuation of War', p. 619.

45. Fortescue Diary, 31 October 1857, Carlingford Mss. 358. 'Many of the disputes in the cabinet spent themselves in private letters which were never brought before the cabinet at all.' Argyll, *Autobiography and Memoirs*, I, p. 455.

46. Lady Clarendon Diary, 13 April 1853, cited in Maxwell, *Clarendon*, II, p. 11; Gordon Diary, 22 January 1855, cited in *Lord Aberdeen's Correspondence, 1854–55*, B.P. 12 (11) p. 378; Granville to Canning, 3 December 1856, Granville Mss. PRO 30/29/21/1, fol. 117.

47. Clarendon, Disraeli noted, although associated with the party of reform resembled 'a high-stepping horse [that] made no progress'. Disraeli memo, n.d. Hughenden Mss. A/X/A/1, cited in H. M. Swartz and M. Swartz (eds) *Disraeli's Reminiscences* (London, 1975) p. 89.

48. *Vanity Fair* described Granville as master of that tact by which power is kept, while counteracting those means by which it was won or lost. Spy cartoon, *Vanity Fair*, 13 March 1869, p. 236. See also The Queen to Aberdeen, 5 September 1853, cited in *Aberdeen Correspondence*, B.P. 12 (10) p. 206.

49. Parkes to Ellice, 'Xmas Day' 1852, Ellice Mss. 15041, fol. 60; Wood Diary, 23 December 1852, Hickleton Mss. A8/A. See also Cornewall Lewis to Hayward, 8 February 1863, cited in Lewis Sir G. C., *Letters of the Rt. Hon. Sir George Cornewall Lewis to Various Friends* (London, 1870) p. 425.

50. Parkes to Ellice, 17 October 1855, Ellice Mss, 15041, fol. 168; Wood to Carlisle, 29 December 1852, Carlisle Mss. See also, Wood to his wife, 6 September 1855, Hickleton Mss. A2/32; and Senior Diary, 14 July 1855, cited in Simpson, *Many Memories*, p. 223.

51. Cornewall Lewis to Head, 29 November 1849, cited in Lewis, *Letters of Cornewall Lewis*, p. 218.

52. Greville Diary, 21 August 1855, Greville Mss. 41121, cited in C. C. F. Greville, *The Greville Memoirs*, H. Reeve (ed.) (London, 1888) VIII, p. 288. See also Palmerston to the Queen (? June 1855) cited in B. Connell (ed.) *Regina vs. Palmerston: The Correspondence Between*

Queen Victoria and Her Foreign and Prime Minister, 1837–1865 (London, 1962) pp. 204–6.

53. Bright to Cobden, 11 January 1856, Bright Mss. 43384, fol. 50. See David Smith, 'Sir George Grey at the Mid-Victorian Home Office', *Canadian Journal of History*, 19 (1984) pp. 361–86.

54. G. Grey to Russell, 25 December 1851, Russell Mss. PRO 30/22/9/J. See J. Prest, *Lord John Russell* (London, 1972) pp. 337–41.

55. Wood Diary, 22 December 1852, Hickleton Mss. A8/A. See also, Wood Diary, 20 December 1852, Hickleton Mss. A8/A.

56. M. Creighton, *Memoir of Sir George Grey Bart, G.C.B.* (London, 1901) p. 158.

57. Cornewall Lewis obituary, *The Times*, 14 April 1863.

58. Simpson, *Many Memories*, p. 132. See also, Stanley Diary, 13 February 1857, Stanley Mss. 920 DER (15) 46/1, cited in J. Vincent (ed.) *Disraeli, Derby and the Conservative Party* (Hassocks, 1978) p. 149.

59. Argyll, *Autobiography and Memoirs*, II, p. 72; W. Bagehot, 'Sir George Cornewall Lewis', cited in E. I. Barrington (ed.) *The Life and Works of Walter Bagehot*, 10 vols (London, 1915) IV, p. 189. A remark characteristic of Cornewall Lewis was that 'life would be tolerable but for its amusements'. E. I. Barrington, *The Servant of All: Pages from the Family, Social and Political Life of My Father James Wilson*, 2 vols (London, 1927) I, p. 169.

60. Granville to Canning, 10 March 1857, Granville Mss. PRO 30/29/21/ 2, fol. 7, cited in Lord E. Fitzmaurice, *Life of Granville George Leveson Gower, Second Earl Granville K.G.*, 2 vols (London, 1905) I, p. 226.

61. Argyll to Aberdeen, 27 February 1852. Aberdeen Mss. 43198.

62. Argyll, *Autobiography and Memoirs*, II, p. 65.

63. Argyll to Aberdeen, 9 October 1856, Aberdeen Mss. 43199, fol. 64.

64. Granville to Canning, 10 March 1857, Granville Mss. PRO 30/29/21/ 2, fol. 7, cited in Fitzmaurice, *Granville*, I, p. 226: Wood Diary, 7 February 1857, Hickleton Mss. A8/D.

65. Greville Diary, 25 February 1855, Greville Mss. 41121, cited in Greville, *Memoirs*, VII, p. 251.

66. Derby to Jolliffe, 20 November 1855, Hylton Mss. /HY, 18/1. See also Stanley memo, November 1855, Stanley Mss. 920 DER (15) 43/3, cited in Vincent (ed.) *Disraeli, Derby and the Conservative Party*, pp. 134–41.

67. Palmerston to the Queen, 10 November 1855, cited in *QVL*, 1st series, III, p. 190.

68. Broughton Diary, 29 April 1856, Broughton Mss. 43759, fol. 95.

69. Argyll to Aberdeen, 15 September 1858, Aberdeen Mss. 43199, fol. 136. See also, Argyll, *Autobiography and Memoirs*, II, p. 10.

70. Broughton Diary, 21 April 1858, Broughton Mss. 43761, fol. 67.

71. Broughton Diary, 19 April 1856, Broughton Mss. 43759, fol. 93.

72. Clarendon to Brougham, 30 July 1856, Broughan Mss. 30157.

73. Parkes to Ellice, 31 October 1855, Ellice Mss. 15041, fol. 177.

74. Vitzthum, *St. Petersburg and London*, I, p. 177.

75. Parkes to Ellice, 31 October 1855, Ellice Mss, 15041, fol. 177.

76. W. F. Monypenny and G. E. Buckle, *The Life of Benjamin Disraeli, Earl of Beaconsfield* (London, 1910–20) IV, p. 15.

77. Stanley memo, November 1855, Stanley Mss. 920 DER (15) 43/3, cited in Vincent (ed.) *Disraeli, Derby and the Conservative Party*, pp. 134–41.

78. Shaftesbury Diary, 19 February 1855, Broadlands Mss. SHA/PD6.

79. Clanricarde to Canning, 3 March 1856, Canning Mss. Box 4; Broughton Diary, 19 April 1856, Broughton Mss. 43759, fol. 93.

80. Cobden to Bright, 11 August 1856, Cobden Mss. 43650, fol. 211.

81. Clarendon to Brougham, 30 July 1856, Brougham Mss. 30157.

82. Prince Albert memo, 19 December 1852, cited in *QVL*, 1st series, II, p. 503. See also S. Walpole, *The Life of Lord John Russell*, 2 vols (London, 1889); and Prest, *Russell*. Whig–Liberal difficulties are discussed in N. Gash, *Reaction and Reconstruction in English Politics 1832–1852* (Oxford, 1965) pp. 189–200. Russell was executor of Charles Fox's papers, and in 1853 his edition of 'The Memorials and Correspondence of Charles James Fox' was published. In the years immediately after 1853 Russell was preparing *The Life and Times of Charles James Fox*, in three volumes, for publication.

83. See Walpole, *Russell*, II, pp. 90–142; and Prest, *Russell*, pp. 303–41.

84. Wood memo, 1846, Hickleton Mss. A8/A.

85. Parkes to Ellice, 6 January 1856, Ellice Mss. 15042, fol. 2.

86. Parkes to Ellice, 11 January 1856, Ellice Mss, 15042, fol. 12. See also Greville Diary, 25 June 1854, Greville Mss. 41120, cited in Greville, *Memoirs*, VII, p. 168.

87. G. Grey to Panmure, 13 July 1853, Dalhousie Mss. GD45/14/686.

88. Parkes to Ellice, 28 October 1856, Ellice Mss. 15042, fol. 35.

89. Parkes to Ellice, 29 December 1856, Ellice Mss. 15042, fol. 45.

90. Fortescue Diary, 4 February 1855, Carlingford Mss. DD/SH 358.

91. Broughton Diary, 7 March 1857, Broughton Mss. 43760, fol. 76. See also, Wood Diary, 10 December 1854, Hickleton Mss. A8/B; and Gladstone to Gordon, 12 October 1854, Gladstone Mss. 44319, fol. 77. A more affectionate portrait is provided in D. MacCarthy and A. Russell (eds) *Lady John Russell: A memoir with Selections from her Diary and Correspondence* (London, 1910).

92. Queen Victoria memo, 30 January 1855, cited in *QVL*, 1st series, III, p. 93.

93. Herbert to Gladstone, 4 February 1855, Gladstone Mss., cited in Gordon, *Herbert*, I, p. 398.

94. Broughton memo, n.d. (? September 1855) Broughton Mss. 47320, fol. 76.

95. Herbert to Gladstone, 4 February 1855, Gladstone Mss., cited in Gordon, *Herbert*, I, p. 398.

96. Broughton Diary, 17 November 1855, Broughton Mss. 43759, fol. 50. See also, Vitzthum, *St. Petersburg and London*, I, p. 150.

97. Palmerston to Russell, 13 July 1855, Russell Mss. PRO 30/22/12/D, cited in Walpole, *Russell*, II, p. 267.

98. Parkes to Ellice, 21 August 1856, Ellice Mss. 15042, fol. 18, cited in Prest, *Russell*, p. 376.

99. Russell to Minto, 22 July 1855, Minto Mss. 11775, fol. 102. See also Elliot to Minto, 13 July 1855, Minto Mss. 11754, fol. 380.
100. Clarendon to Newcastle, 11 August 1855, Newcastle Mss. NeC 12566.
101. Ibid. See J. Vincent, 'The Parliamentary Dimension of the Crimean War', *TRHS*, 5th series, 3 (1981) p. 46.
102. Parkes to Ellice, 6 January 1856, Ellice Mss. 15042, fol. 2.
103. Holland to Brougham, 14 July (? 1856) Brougham Mss. 16295. In September 1856 Russell told Palmerston: 'I must in fairness say that G. Grey's Church Rates scheme and Granville's peerage bill have convinced me that you are not to be trusted on reform.' Russell to Palmerston, 6 September 1856, cited in G. P. Gooch (ed.) *The Later Correspondence of Lord John Russell, 1840–1878* (London, 1925) II, p. 219.
104. Disraeli to Lady Londonderry, 2 February 1855, cited in Monypenny and Buckle, *Disraeli*, III, p. 567.
105. Parkes to Ellice, 21 August 1856, Ellice Mss. 15042, fol. 18, cited in Prest, *Russell*, p. 376.
106. Romilly to Minto, 31 January 1855, Minto Mss. 11776, fol. 51.
107. Romilly to Minto, 3 February 1855, Minto Mss. 11776, fol. 66.
108. Parkes to Ellice, 21 August 1856, Ellice Mss. 15042, fol. 16.
109. Russell to Dean of Bristol, 27 November 1856, Russell Mss. PRO 30/22/13/B, cited in Gooch (ed.) *The Later Correspondence of Lord John Russell* II, p. 220.
110. Parkes to Ellice, 29 December 1856, Ellice Mss. 15042, fol. 40.
111. Fourth Earl Grey memo, 23 April 1888, Grey Mss.
112. Wood Diary, 5 February 1855, Hickleton Mss. A8/D. See Prest, *Russell*, p. 152.
113. Grey Diary, 4 April 1853, Grey Mss. C3/17. See also, Stanley Diary, 10 January 1853, Stanley Mss. 920 DER (15) 43/3, cited in Vincent (ed.) *Disraeli, Derby and the Conservative Party*, p. 95; and Ponsonby to Grey, 3 April 1853, Grey Mss. 116/19.
114. Grey Diary, 17 February 1858, Grey Mss. C3/18A. See also, Grey Diary, 31 December 1855, Grey Mss. C3/18A.
115. Bright to his wife, 18 September 1856, Ogden Mss. 65.
116. Grey to Ellice, 27 June 1856, Ellice Mss. 15025, fol. 119.
117. Cobden to Bright, 2 September 1851, Cobden Mss. 43649.
118. Bright, 31 March 1854, *Hansard*, 3rd series, cxxxii, 257. See also D. Read, *Cobden and Bright: A Victorian Political Partnership* (London, 1967) pp. 109–48; N. McCord 'Cobden and Bright in Politics, 1846–1857', in R. Robson (ed.) *Ideas and Institutions of Victorian Britain* (London, 1967) pp. 87–114.
119. Herbert to Aberdeen, 17 May 1855, Aberdeen Mss., cited in Gordon, *Herbert*, I, p. 425. Palmerston remembered Cobden as 'the political fanatic . . . who proposed once in the House of Commons that England and France should lead their fleets into the middle of the Channel and there burn them'. Palmerston to Brand, 15 January 1861, Brand Mss.
120. Roebuck, 6 July 1855, *Hansard*, 3rd series, cxxxix, 593; and

Roebuck, 26 January 1855, *Hansard*, 3rd series, cxxxvi, 979. See also R. E. Leader, *Life and Letters of John Arthur Roebuck, P.C., Q.C., M.P.* (London, 1897).

121. Cobden to Baines, 11 December 1854, Baines Mss.
122. Bright Diary, 19 January 1853, cited in J. Bright, *The Diaries of John Bright* RA. J. Walling (ed.) (London, 1930).
123. Cobden to Bright, 20 December 1856, Cobden Mss. 43650, fol. 240. See, Cobden to Bright, 22 July 1856, Cobden Mss. 43650, fol. 211. See also McCord 'Cobden and Bright in Politics', p. 108.
124. Cobden to Bright, 8 January 1853, Cobden Mss. 43650.
125. Cobden to Wilson, 23 September 1856, Wilson Mss., cited in McCord, 'Cobden and Bright in Politics', p. 113.
126. Bright to Cobden, 31 March 1856, Bright Mss. 43384, fol. 51.
127. Bright to his wife, 9 February 1856, Ogden Mss. 65. Cobden to Parkes, 21 December 1856, Cobden Mss. 43664, fol. 65.
128. Malmesbury Diary, 23 December 1852, Malmesbury Mss. 9M73. See also, Bright Diary, 22 December 1852, cited in *Diaries of Bright*, p. 131.
129. Stanley Diary, 17 March 1854, Stanley Mss. 920 DER (15) 43/3.
130. Wood Diary, 20 December 1852, Hickleton Mss. A8/A.
131. Greville Diary, 22 May 1853, Greville Mss. 41120, cited in Greville, *Memoirs*, VII, p. 64.
132. Greville Diary, 4 October 1853, Greville Mss. 41120, cited in Greville, *Memoirs*, VII, p. 94.
133. Stanley Diary, 23 February 1854, Stanley Mss. 920 DER (15) 43/3, cited in Vincent (ed.) *Disraeli, Derby and the Conservative Party*, p. 121.
134. White, *Inner Life of the House of Commons*, I, p. 16.
135. Shaftesbury Diary, 3 September 1856, Broadlands Mss. SHA/PD6. Ten months earlier Shaftesbury had recorded that 'any day, humanly speaking, may carry off Palmerston, he is advanced in years, tho' thank God singularly strong'. Shaftesbury Diary, 13 November 1855, Broadlands Mss. SHA/PD6.
136. Parkes to Ellice, 21 August 1856, Ellice Mss. 15042, Fol. 16. See also Wood Diary, 20 December 1852, Hickleton Mss. A8/A.
137. Stanley Diary, 9 February 1854, Stanley Mss. 920 DER (15) 43/3. cited in Vincent (ed.) *Disraeli, Derby and the Conservative Party*, p. 120.
138. Stanley memo, November 1855, Stanley Mss. 920 DER (15) 43/3, cited in Vincent (ed.) *Disraeli, Derby and the Convservative Party*, p. 139.

CHAPTER 2

1. Newcastle to Gladstone, 8 March 1852, Newcastle Mss. Ne C 11713; Gladstone to Aberdeen, 12 August 1852, Aberdeen Mss. 43070, fol. 262. See also, J. B. Conacher, *The Peelites and the Party System*

1846–52, (Newton Abbot, 1972); and W. D. Jones and A. B. Erickson, *The Peelites, 1846–1857* (Ohio, 1972).

2. Gladstone to Aberdeen, 30 July 1852, Aberdeen Mss. 43070, fol. 250. See also, Conacher, *The Aberdeen Coalition 1852–1855: A Study in Mid-Nineteenth Century Party Politics* (Cambridge, 1968) p. 8.

3. Stanley Diary, 22 December 1853, Stanley Mss. 920 DER (15) 43/3, cited in J. Vincent (ed.) *Disraeli, Derby and the Conservative Party* (Hassocks, 1978) p. 114. See also, Elliot to Minto, 17 December 1852, Minto Mss. 11754, fol. 329; Parkes to Ellice, 30 December 1852, Ellice Mss. 15041, fol. 64; Broughton memo (? September 1855) Broughton Mss. 47230, fol. 58.

4. Taylor to Jolliffe, n.d. (? February 1855) Hylton Mss. DD/HY 18/13, fol. 52.

5. B. To Granville, 17 July 1856, Granville Mss. PRO 30/29/19/21, fol. 195. One Peelite described his colleagues as being 'like Mohammet's coffin, nowhere; neither in heaven, nor upon earth'. Palmer to Gordon, 9 November 1856, Selborne Mss. 1872, fol. 86.

6. Palmer to Gordon, 9 November 1856, Selborne Mss. 1872, fol. 86.

7. Lowe to Ellice, 13 September 1856, Ellice Mss. 15034, fol. 33. See also, Jones and Erickson, *The Peelites*.

8. Cardwell to Aberdeen, 18 November 1856, Aberdeen Mss. 43197, fol. 316. There are difficulties in precisely identifying Peelites during the 1850s. For a discussion of this problem see Conacher, *Peelites and the Party System*, pp. 119–22. Jones and Erickson, *The Peelites*, p. 182 list forty-six Peelites at the beginning of 1855. See also P. M. Gurowich, 'The Continuation of War by other Means: Party and Politics, 1855–1865', *HJ*, 27:3 (1984) pp. 603–31, p. 606 n. 24.

9. Aberdeen to Gladstone, 3 December 1856, Gladstone Mss. 44089. Gladstone felt that 'the pain and strain of acts of public duty are multiplied tenfold by the want of a clear and firm ground from which visibly to act'. Gladstone to Graham, 10 November 1856, cited in C. S. Parker, *Life and Letters of Sir James Graham, Second Baronet of Netherby* (London, 1907) II, p. 289.

10. Gladstone's budget of 1853 was innovatory both in content and scope. He re-imposed the income tax on a basis of annual reduction until 1860, while reducing tariffs and duties. For a brilliant commentary on the substantive content of the budget see H. C. G. Matthew, 'Disraeli, Gladstone and the Politics of Mid-Victorian Budgets', *Historical Journal*, 22 (1979) 615–43. See also, J. B. Conacher, *The Aberdeen Coalition, 1852–1855: A Study in Mid-Nineteenth Century Party Politics* (Cambridge, 1968) pp. 58–78, and P. Stansky, *Gladstone: a Progress in Politics* (London, 1979) pp. 69–89. J. Morley, *The Life of William Ewart Gladstone*, 3 vols (London, 1903) I, pp. 457–75 remains a necessary reference.

11. Cornewall Lewis financed the war effort through loans and indirect taxation. This was a fundamental departure from Gladstone's policy of 1853–54. See the commentary of S. H. Northcote, *Twenty Years of Financial Policy: A Summary of the Chief Financial Measures Passed Between 1842 and 1861* (London, 1862).

12. Aberdeen to Gladstone, 17 March 1856, Gladstone Mss. 44089. See also Morley, *Life of Gladstone*, 1, pp. 552–5, and Parker, *Graham*, II, pp. 299–302.

13. Graham to Aberdeen, 11 November 1856, Aberdeen Mss. 43192, fol. 43, cited in Parker, *Graham*, II, p. 288; Graham to Aberdeen, 22 November 1856, Aberdeen Mss. 43192, fol. 56.

14. Cornewall Lewis' 1856 budget had maintained the income tax at the wartime rate of 1s 4d in the pound. This was a basic departure from the seven-year schedule of income tax reduction proposed in 1853. Graham to Gladstone, 1 January 1857, Gladstone Mss. 44164, fol. 91.

15. Graham to Gladstone, 27 December 1856, Gladstone Mss. 44164, fol. 83.

16. Graham to Aberdeen, 20 December 1856, Aberdeen Mss. 43192, fol. 76. 'If we can but relieve the Income Tax, Palmerston's teeth will be drawn, and he will be as mild and gentle as a dove.' Graham to Aberdeen, 27 December 1856, Aberdeen Mss. 43192, fol. 86.

17. Aberdeen to Gladstone, 11 December 1856, Aberdeen Mss. 43071, fol. 342.

18. Gladstone memo. n.d. (? December 1856) Gladstone Mss. 44685, fol. 254 appeared as an anonymous article in the *Quarterly Review*, 101, January 1857, pp. 243–84.

19. L. A. Tollemache, *Talks with Mr. Gladstone* (London, 1898) p. 31.

20. Aberdeen to Gladstone, 5 December 1856, Gladstone Mss. 44089.

21. Broughton memo (? September 1855) Broughton Mss. 47230, fol. 100.

22. Parkes to Brougham, 9 August 1856, Brougham Mss. 20876.

23. Gordon Diary, 22 January 1855, cited in *Lord Aberdeen's Correspondence 1854–55*, Appendix, pp. 278–9, cited in Conacher, *Aberdeen Coalition*, p. 532.

24. Palmer to Gordon, 9 November 1856, Selborne Mss. 1872, fol. 93. Certain recent works are essential to an understanding of Gladstone's early political career: R. Shannon *Gladstone: 1809–1865* (London, 1982); W. E. Gladstone, *The Gladstone Diaries, 1825–1868* M. R. D. Foot and H. C. G. Matthew (eds) 6 vols (Oxford, 1968, 1974 and 1978); and Matthew 'Disraeli, Gladstone, and the Politics of Mid-Victorian Budgets', *HJ*, 22:3 (1979) pp. 615–43.

25. 'The desire for office is the desire of ardent minds for a larger space and scope within which to serve the country, and for access to the command of that powerful machinery for information and practice, which the public departments supply.' Gladstone memo, n.d., cited in Morley, *Gladstone*, I, p. 554. See also Angus Hawkins, 'A Forgotten Crisis: Gladstone and the Politics of Finance During the 1850s', *Victorian Studies*, 26:3 (1983) pp. 287–320.

26. Graham to Aberdeen, 11 November 1856, Aberdeen Mss. 43192, fol. 43 cited in Parker, *Graham*, II, p. 288.

27. A. R. Ashwell and R. G. Wilberforce, *Life of Samuel Wilberforce* 3 vols (London, 1881) II, p. 349. For a discussion of Gladstone's financial programme see Shannon, *Gladstone*, pp. 318–20; *Glad-*

stone's Diaries, V, p. XXVI and pp. 104–7. For a discussion of Gladstone's religious and intellectual development see P. Butler, *Gladstone: Church, State and Tractarianism* (Oxford, 1982); Agatha Ramm, 'Gladstone's Religion', *HJ*, 28:2 (1985) pp. 327–40; and Boyd Hilton, 'Gladstone's Theological Politics', in M. Bentley and J. Stevenson (eds) *High and Low Politics in Modern Britain* (Oxford, 1983) pp. 28–57.

28. Gladstone memo, 25 February 1852, Gladstone Mss. 44778, fol. 5, cited in Matthew *Gladstone Diaries*, IV, p. 398. See also, Gladstone memo, 27 February 1852, Gladstone Mss. 44778, fol. 13, cited in *Gladstone Diaries*, IV, p. 402.

29. Gladstone to Aberdeen, 13 October 1856, Aberdeen Mss. 43071, fol. 321; Gladstone memo, n.d., Gladstone Mss. 44685, fol. 235. See also Gladstone to Graham, 2 December 1856, cited in Parker, *Graham*, II, p. 295.

30. Gladstone to Aberdeen, 10 November 1856, Aberdeen Mss. 43071, fol. 324. See also, Gladstone memo, n.d. (? August 1856) Gladstone Mss. 44685, fol. 212, the manuscript draft of an anonymous article, 'The Declining Efficiency of Parliament', *Quarterly Review*, 99, September 1856, pp. 521–70.

31. Graham to Aberdeen, 1 December 1856, Aberdeen Mss. 43192, fol. 61.

32. Aberdeen to Graham, 16 December 1856, Aberdeen Mss. 43192, fol. 70. See Morley, *Gladstone*, I, pp. 554–6.

33. Malmesbury Diary, 28 November 1852, Malmesbury Mss. 9M73. In his published *Memoirs of An Ex-Minister*, Malmesbury found it prudent to alter this entry: 'I cannot make Gladstone out who seems to me a dark horse.' Lord Malmesbury, *Memoirs of an Ex-Minister* (London, 1885) p. 282.

34. Derby to Ellenborough, 3 February 1855, Ellenborough Mss. PRO 30/12/21/4. See also the important comment provided by J. R. Jones, 'The Conservatives and Gladstone in 1855', *EHR*, 77 (1962) pp. 95–8.

35. Taylor to Jolliffe, n.d. (? Feburary 1855) Hylton Mss. DD/HY 18/13, fol. 52.

36. Derby to Ellenborough, 3 February 1855, Ellenborough Mss. PRO 30/12/21/4.

37. Cardwell to Palmer, 6 November 1856, Selborne Mss. 1862, fol. 63.

38. Derby to Elwin, 26 November 1856, Derby Mss. 183/2, fol. 130.

39. Elwin to Gladstone, 28 October 1856, Gladstone Mss. 44152, fol. 23. See also, Elwin to Gladstone, 29 November 1856, Gladstone Mss. 44152, fol. 27.

40. Gladstone to Aberdeen, 2 December 1856, Gladstone Mss. 44089.

41. Derby to Gladstone, 25 January 1857, Gladstone Mss. 44140, fol. 205.

42. Derby to Jolliffe, 11 January 1857, Hylton Mss. DD/HY 18/2. See also, W. D. Jones, *Lord Derby and Victorian Conservatism* (Oxford, 1956) pp. 215–16.

43. Jolliffe to Disraeli, 29 January 1857, Hughenden Mss. B/XX/J/43. See also, W. F. Monypenny and G. E. Buckle, *The Life of Benjamin Disraeli, Earl of Beaconsfield* (London, 1910–20) IV, pp. 59–60.

44. Graham to Aberdeen, 18 December 1856, Aberdeen Mss. 43192, fol. 72.

45. See J. T. Ward, *Sir James Graham* (London, 1967) pp. 259–81.

46. Gordon Diary, 22 January 1855, *Aberdeen Correspondence*, Appendix, p. 378, cited in Conacher, *Aberdeen Coalition*, p. 532. See also, Croker to Herries, 15 August 1853, cited in E. Herries, *Memoir of the Public Life of the Rt. Honourable John Charles Herries*, 2 vols (London, 1880) II, p. 279.

47. Osborne Diary, ? March 1855, cited in P. H. D. Bagenal, *The Life of Ralph Berual Osborne M.P.* (London, 1884) p. 148.

48. Ibid.

49. Stanley Diary, 25 January 1854, Stanley Mss. 920 DER (15) 43/3, cited in Vincent (ed.) *Disraeli, Derby and the Conservative Party*, p. 117.

50. Wood Diary, 3 February 1855, Hickleton Mss. A8/B.

51. Greville Diary, 30 May 1853, Greville Mss. 41120, cited in Greville, *Memoirs*, VII, p. 66. See Ward, *Graham*, pp. xi–xviii.

52. Gladstone memo, 26 February 1852, Gladstone Mss. 44778, fol. 5, cited in *Gladstone Diaries*, IV, p. 398. See also Parker, *Graham*, II, p. 156–60; and Ward, *Graham*, pp. 245–64.

53. Gladstone memo, 26 February 1852, Gladstone Mss. 44778, fol. 5, cited in *Gladstone Diaries*, IV, p. 398.

54. Graham to Russell, 17, 22 and 26 July 1852 Russell Mss. PRO 30/22/10/C; see S. Walpole, *The Life of Lord John Russell* (London, 1889), II, pp. 153–6.

55. Wood Diary, 22 December 1852, Hickleton Mss. A8/A.

56. Bedford to Aberdeen, 21 December 1856, Aberdeen Mss. 43225, fol. 117.

57. Aberdeen to Bedford, 25 December 1856, Aberdeen Mss. 43225, fol. 181. See also Graham to Aberdeen, 28 December 1856, Aberdeen Mss. 43192, fol. 91.

58. Russell to Graham, 2 January 1857, Graham Mss. Bundle 131.

59. Graham to Aberdeen, 2 January 1857, Aberdeen Mss. 43192, fol. 94.

60. Graham to Aberdeen, 20 January 1857, Aberdeen Mss. 43192, fol. 104.

61. Graham to Herbert, 29 January 1857, Graham Mss. Bundle 131, cited in A. H. Gordon, Baron Stanmore, *Sidney Herbert, Lord Herbert of Lea: A Memoir*, 2 vols (London, 1906) II, p. 62.

62. Senior Diary, 29 January 1855, cited in M. C. M. Simpson (née Senior) *Many Memories of Many People* (London, 1898) p. 150. See also, Goulburn to Mrs Herbert, 29 June 1855, cited in Gordon, *Herbert*, I, p. 459.

63. Wood Diary, 5 December 1854, Hickleton Mss. A8/A.

64. Herbert to Gladstone, 18 November 1856, cited in Gordon, *Herbert*, II, p. 59.

65. Gladstone memo, 9 September 1897, Gladstone Mss. 44791, cited in

J. Brooke and M. Sorenson (eds) *The Prime Minister's Papers: W. E. Gladstone. 1: Autobiographica* (London, 1971) p. 72.

66. Senior Diary, 29 January 1855, cited in Simpson, *Many Memories*, p. 150.
67. Palmerston to Temple, 15 February 1855, cited in E. Ashley *The Life and Correspondence of Henry John Temple, Viscount Palmerston*, 2 vols (London, 1879) II, p. 76.
68. Aberdeen to Newcastle, 28 August 1856, Newcastle Mss. NeC 12447.
69. Newcastle to Aberdeen, 24 November 1856, Aberdeen Mss. 43197, fol. 76. For fuller discussion of Newcastle's career see J. Martineau, *The Life of Henry Pelham, Fifth Duke of Newcastle, 1811–1864* (London, 1908) and F. Darrell Munsell, *The Unfortunate Duke: Henry Pelham, Fifth Duke of Newcastle, 1811–1864* (Columbia, Missouri, 1985).
70. Gordon to Aberdeen, 25 October 1856, Aberdeen Mss. 43226, fol. 234. See also, Aberdeen to Graham, 9 November 1856, Graham Mss. Bundle 130.
71. Aberdeen to Gladstone, 18 November 1856, Gladstone Mss. 44089. See also, Graham to Gladstone, 15 November 1856, Gladstone Mss. 44164, fol. 51; Aberdeen to Graham, 24 November 1856, Graham Mss. Bundle 130.
72. Aberdeen to Gladstone, 20 December 1856, Gladstone Mss. 44089.
73. Graham to Gladstone, 18 December 1856, Gladstone Mss. 44164, fol. 72.
74. Graham to Gladstone, 27 December 1856, Aberdeen Mss. 43192, fol. 86.
75. Aberdeen to Graham, 17 January 1857, Aberdeen Mss. 43192, fol. 102.
76. Graham to Aberdeen, 1 February 1857, Aberdeen Mss. 43192, fol. 116.
77. Graham to Herbert, 29 January 1857, Graham Mss. Bundle 131, cited in Gordon, *Herbert*, II, p. 62.
78. Gathorne Hardy Diary, 3 May 1856, Cranbrook Mss. T501/290, p. 393.
79. Elwin to Brougham, 27 May 1856, Brougham Mss. 1548. See also R. Blake, *The Conservative Party from Peel to Churchill* (London, 1970) pp. 90–1; R. Stewart, *The Foundation of the Conservative Party 1830–1867* (London, 1978) pp. 310–12.
80. Sotheron-Estcourt to Jolliffe, 1 January 1856, Hylton Mss. DD/HY 11, fol. 13, cited in Stewart, *Foundation of the Conservative Party*, p. 311.
81. Taylor to Jolliffe, 20 August 1856, Hylton Mss. DD/HY 24; and Walpole to Pakington, 19 October 1856, Hampton Mss. 4372/2.
82. Charles Greville, who felt 'the greatest political and personal repugnance' towards Derby, and T. E. Kebbel, writing a Beaconsfield tradition, were formative influences on posterity. See Greville, *Memoirs*, VIII, p. 192; and T. E. Kebbel, *A History of Toryism* (London, 1886) pp. 302–32.
83. Conacher, 'Party Politics in the Age of Palmerston', in P. Appleman,

W. A. Madden and M. Wolf (eds) *1859: Entering An Age of Crisis* (Bloomington, Indiana, 1959) p. 166. W. D. Jones, *Lord Derby and Victorian Conservatism* (Oxford, 1956) was written without access to the Derby Mss. As a result Jones' portrait is often the view of Knowsley from Hughenden.

84. W. Pollard, *The Stanleys of Knowsley* (London, 1968) p. 177.

85. Lytton memo, n.d. (? 1869) Lytton Mss. C. 13, fol. 21.

86. Stanley Diary, June 1852, Stanley Mss. 920 DER (15) 43/2, cited in Vincent (ed.) *Disraeli, Derby and the Conservative Party*, p. 92.

87. See Stanley to Disraeli, 6 January 1849, Hughenden Mss. B/XX/S/3, cited in Monypenny and Buckle, *Disraeli*, III, p. 128; Stanley to Herries (copy), 6 January 1849, Derby Mss. 178/1. See also A. Hawkins, 'Lord Derby and Victorian Conservatism: A Reappraisal', forthcoming in *Parliamentary History Yearbook*.

88. Stanley Diary, 28 December 1852, Stanley Mss. DER (15) 37/2, cited in Vincent (ed.) *Derby, Disraeli and the Conservative Party*, p. 94.

89. Malmesbury, 27 April 1855, *Memoirs*, II, p. 21. One famous letter from Lord Henry Lennox to Disraeli complains that Derby is 'devoted to whist, billiards, racing, betting, and making a fool of himself with either Ladies Emily Peel or Mary Yorke'. (Lennox to Disraeli, 7 January 1857, Hughenden Mss. B/XX/Lx/86 cited in R. Blake, *Disraeli* (London, 1966) p. 369.) This letter is often quoted as proof of Derby's lack of political seriousness or commitment. All it shows, however, is Derby's disinclination to talk politics with Lennox. After complaining of Derby's evasiveness Lennox adds, in unconscious irony, that in talking to Bulwer Lytton 'of course I only told him as much as was good for him'.

90. Derby's strategy was alternatively described as 'killing with kindness', 'armed neutrality', or as 'a patience policy'.

91. Stanley Diary, 20 December 1852, Stanley Mss. 920 DER (15) 43/2, cited in Vincent (ed.) *Disraeli, Derby and the Conservative Party*, p. 92. An important statement of Derby's policy is contained in Derby to Disraeli, 30 January 1853, cited in Monypenny and Buckle, *Disraeli*, III, p. 483.

92. Grey Diary, 16 December 1854, Grey Mss. C3/18A.

93. Wood Diary, 19 December 1853, Hickleton Mss. A/8A. See also Greville Diary, 28 August 1853, Greville Mss. 41120, cited in Greville, *Memoirs*, VII, p. 83.

94. Taylor to Jolliffe, n.d. (? February 1855) Hylton Mss. DD/HY 13, fol. 52.

95. Stanley memo, 30 January 1855, Stanley Mss. 920 DER (15) 43/3, cited in Vincent (ed.) *Disraeli, Derby and the Conservative Party*, p. 130. See also, Disraeli memo, n.d., Hughenden Mss. A/X/A/43.

96. Stanley to Disraeli, 31 January 1855, Hughenden Mss. B/XX/S617, cited in Monypenny and Buckle, *Disraeli*, III, p. 563; see also, Walpole memo, n.d. (? February 1855) Walpole Mss; and J. Vincent, 'Parliamentary Dimension of the Crimean War', *TRHS*, 5th series, 31 (1981) p. 47.

97. Derby to Jolliffe, 2 November 1855, Hylton, Mss. DD/HY 18/1.

98. Derby to Disraeli, 14 November 1853, Hughenden Mss. B/XX/S/122.

99. Stanley memo, 22 November 1856, Stanley Mss. 920 DER (15) 43/3.

100. Taylor to Jolliffe, 25 November 1856, Hylton Mss. DD/HY 24, cited in Stewart, *Foundation of the Conservative Party*, p. 312.

101. Jolliffe to Derby, 3 January 1857, Derby Mss. 158/10.

102. See Blake, *Disraeli*, pp. 365 and 426; and D. Southgate (ed.) *The Conservative Leadership, 1832–1932* (London, 1974) p. 84.

103. Stanley Diary, 5 April 1853, Stanley Mss. 920 DER (15) 43/3, cited in Vincent (ed.) *Disraeli, Derby and the Conservative Party*, p. 104. See also, C. J. Lewis, 'Theory and Expediency in Disraeli's Policy', *Victorian Studies*, 4 (1961) pp. 237–58; Blake, *Disraeli*, pp. 278–84; and J. Vincent, 'Benjamin Disraeli', in H. Van Thal (ed.) *The Prime Ministers*, 2 vols (London, 1975) II, pp. 83–108.

104. Malmesbury Diary, 24 December 1852, Malmesbury Mss. 9M73. See also Blake, *Disraeli*, p. 343.

105. Stanley Diary, 4 April 1853, Stanley Mss. 920 DER (15) 43/3, cited in Vincent (ed.) *Disraeli, Derby and the Conservative Party*, p. 104.

106. Bright Diary 20 February 1855, cited in J. Bright, *The Diaries of John Bright*, R. A. J. Walling (ed.) (London, 1930) p. 186.

107. Bright Diary, 15 December 1852, cited in *Diaries of Bright*, p. 130.

108. Stanley Diary, 22 November 1856, Stanley Mss. 920 DER (15) 43/3.

109. Stanley Diary, June 1852, Stanley Mss. DER (15) 43/2, cited in Vincent (ed.) *Disraeli, Derby and the Conservative Party*, p. 72.

110. Greville Diary, 25 February 1853, Greville Mss. 41120, cited in Greville, *Memoirs*, VII, p. 44.

111. Holland to Brougham, 19 September 1856, Brougham Mss. 16298.

112. Jolliffe to Derby, 1 December 1856, Derby Mss. 158/10.

113. Holland to Brougham, 12 December 1856, Brougham Mss. 16301.

114. Stanley Diary, 22 November 1856, Stanley Mss. 920 DER (15) 43/3.

115. Carnavon to Heathcote, 26 October 1855, cited in A. H. Hardinge, *Life of Henry Edward Molyneux Herbert, Fourth Earl of Carnavon*, 3 vols (London, 1925) I, p. 112.

116. Lytton memo, n.d. (? 1867) Lytton Mss. C. 13, fol. 44.

117. Broughton Diary, 19 April 1856, Broughton Mss. 43759, fol. 93.

118. Stanley Diary, 30 June 1853, Stanley Mss. 920 DER (15) 43/3, cited in Vincent (ed.) *Disraeli, Derby and the Conservative Party*, p. 108.

119. Stanley Diary, 22 November 1853, Stanley Mss. 920 DER (15) 43/3, cited in Vincent (ed.) *Disraeli, Derby and the Conservative Party*, p. 112.

120. See Baron Sanderson and E. S. Roscoe, *The Speeches and Addresses of Edward Henry, XVth Earl of Derby K.G.* (London, 1894).

121. Shaftesbury Diary, 13 September 1855, Broadlands Mss. SHA/PD 6. See the commentary of Vincent (ed.) *Disraeli, Derby and the Conservative Party*.

122. Malmesbury Diary, 25 June 1853, Malmesbury Mss. 9M73, cited in Malmesbury, *Memoirs*, p. 310.

123. Greville Diary, 7 November 1855, Greville Mss. 41121, cited in Greville, *Memoirs*, VII, p. 299.

124. Hayward to Cornewall Lewis, 28 March 1855, Harpton Court Mss.

C/1479, cited in H. E. Carlisle (ed.) *Selection from the Correspondence of Abraham Hayward* 2 vols (London, 1886) I, p. 250.

125. Stanley Diary, 30 June 1853, Stanley Mss. 920 DER (15) 43/3, cited in Vincent (ed.) *Disraeli, Derby and the Conservative Party*, p. 109.

126. Derby to Jolliffe, 6 November 1855, Hylton Mss. DD/HY 18/1.

127. Stanley Diary, June 1852, Stanley Mss. 920 DER (15) 43/2, cited in Vincent (ed.) *Disraeli, Derby and the Conservative Party*, p. 71.

128. Stanley Diary, 28 November 1852, Stanley Mss. 920 DER (15) 43/2, cited in Vincent (ed.) *Disraeli, Derby and the Conservative Party*, p. 85.

129. Stanley Diary, 23 February 1854, Stanley Mss. 920 DER (15) 43/3, cited in Vincent (ed.) *Disraeli, Derby and the Conservative Party*, p. 121. Disraeli also suspected that Pakington had designs on the party leadership in the Commons.

130. Pakington to Disraeli, 16 December 1853, Hampton Mss. 3835/7.

131. Disraeli to Pakington, 5 January 1855, Hampton Mss. 3835/7. See also Monypenny and Buckle, *Disraeli*, IV, p. 63, and Vincent (ed.) *Disraeli, Derby and the Conservative Party*, pp. 143–5.

132. Pakington to Russell, 26 March 1856, Hampton Mss. 4732/1. See also, Russell to Pakington, 26 March 1856, Hampton Mss. 4732/1 and Pakington to Cobden, 23 November 1856, Cobden Mss. 43669, fol. 59. For Pakington's contribution to the education question see R. Aldrich, 'Sir John Pakington and the Newcastle Commission', *History of Education*, 8:1 (1979) pp. 21–31.

133. Heathcote to Northcote, 1 January 1857, Iddesleigh Mss. 50035.

134. Jolliffe to Disraeli, 29 January 1857, Hughenden Mss. B/XX/J/43.

135. Malmesbury, *Memoirs*, II, p. 57.

136. Sotheron-Estcourt to Jolliffe, 1 January 1856, Hylton Mss. DD/HY 24/11, fol. 13.

137. Jolliffe to Disraeli, 27 December 1856, Hughenden Mss. B/XX/J/40, cited in Monypenny and Buckle, *Disraeli*, IV, p. 59.

138. Derby to Malmesbury, 15 December 1856, Derby Mss. 183/2, fol. 133, cited in Malmesbury, *Memoirs*, II, p. 54.

139. Derby to Disraeli, 23 January 1857, Hughenden Mss. B/XX/S/140.

140. Pakington to Disraeli, 23 January 1857, Hughenden Mss. B/XX/P/23.

141. Pakington to Disraeli, 26 January 1857, Hughenden Mss. B/XX/P/24. See also Derby to Disraeli, 25 January 1857, Hughenden Mss. B/XX/S/141.

142. Stanley to Disraeli, 27 January 1857, Hughenden Mss. B/XX/S/626, cited in Monypenny and Buckle, *Disraeli*, IV, p. 62.

143. Stanley Diary, 2 February 1857, Stanley Mss. 920 DER (15) 4/6/1, cited in Vincent (ed.) *Disraeli, Derby and the Conservative Party*, p. 148.

144. Ibid.

145. Jolliffe to Disraeli, 29 January 1857, Hughenden Mss. B/XX/J/43.

146. See J. H. Whyte, *The Independent Irish Party 1850–1859* (Oxford, 1958).

147. G. Cornewall Lewis, *A Treatise on Observation and Method in Politics*, (London, 1852) p. 321.

148. Hamilton to Jolliffe, 17 December 1856, Hylton Mss. DD/HY 24/10, fol. 27.
149. Hayward to Gladstone, 17 December 1856, cited in Carlisle (ed.) *Hayward Correspondence*, I, p. 301; Lennox to Disraeli, 2 January 1857, Hughenden Mss. B/XX/LX/85.
150. Broughton Diary, 7 June 1857, Broughton Mss. 43760, fol. 119.
151. Aberdeen to Newcastle, 27 November 1856, Newcastle Mss. NeC. 12448. See also, Granville to Canning, 26 December 1856, Granville Mss. PRO 30/29/21/1, fol. 122, cited in Lord E. Fitzmaurice, *The Life of Granville George Leveson-Gower, Second Earl Granville, K.G.*, 2 vols (London, 1905) I, p. 224.
152. Clarendon to Normanby, 16 December 1856 Clarendon Mss. C. 137 fol. 539.
153. Russell to Dean of Bristol, 27 November 1856, Russell Mss. PRO 30/22/13/B, fol. 241, cited in Lord J. Russell, *The Later Correspondence of Lord Russell*, G. P. Gooch (ed.) (London, 1925) II, p. 220.
154. Clarendon to Normanby, 26 December 1856, Clarendon Mss. C. 137, fol. 539.
155. Clarendon to Cowley, 29 January 1857, Clarendon Mss. C. 138, fol. 127.
156. Clarendon to Palmerston, 1 February 1857, Broadlands Mss. GC/CL 1004.
157. Hamilton to Jolliffe, 17 December (? 1856) Hylton Mss. DD/HY 24/10, fol. 27.

CHAPTER 3

1. Cornewall Lewis to Clarendon, 4 January 1857, Clarendon Mss. C. 70, fol. 139.
2. Cornewall Lewis to Clarendon, 9 January 1857, Clarendon Mss. C. 70, fol. 152. See also Cornewall Lewis to Palmerston, 17 January 1857, Broadlands Mss. GC/LE, fol. 92.
3. Duke of Argyll, *George Douglas, 8th Duke of Argyll: Autobiography and Memoirs* (London, 1906) II, p. 72.
4. Cornewall Lewis to Clarendon, 4 January 1857, Clarendon Mss. C. 70, fol. 139.
5. Clarendon to his wife, 2 February 1857, cited in Sir H. Maxwell, *The Life and Letters of the Fourth Earl of Clarendon* (London, 1913) II, p. 138. See also, Aberdeen to Graham, 31 January 1857, Graham Mss. Bundle 131.
6. Aberdeen to Graham, 31 January 1857, Graham Mss. Bundle 131.
7. Ibid.
8. Clarendon to his wife, 2 February 1857, cited in Maxwell, *Clarendon*, II, p. 138.
9. Dallas to Cass, 3 February 1857, cited in G. M. Dallas, *Letters from London, 1856–1860*, (London, 1870) I, p. 140.
10. Queen's Speech, 3 February 1857, *Hansard*, 3rd series, CXLIV.

11. Lord Malmesbury, *Memoirs of an Ex-Minister* (London, 1885) II, p. 58.
12. Gathorne Hardy Diary, 3 February 1857, Cranbrook Mss. T501/290, fol. 458.
13. Derby, 3 February 1857, *Hansard*, 3rd series, CXLIV, 21.
14. Disraeli, 3 February 1857, *Hansard*, 3rd series, CXLIV, 106.
15. Grey Diary, 4 February 1857, Grey Mss. C3/19.
16. 3 February 1857, *Hansard*, 3rd series, CXLIV, 79.
17. Malmesbury, *Memoirs*, II, p. 59.
18. Disraeli, 3 February 1857, *Hansard*, 3rd series, CXLIV, 124–33.
19. Malmesbury, *Memoirs*, II, p. 58. For a discussion of this diplomatic initiative that proved politically disappointing for Disraeli, see W. F. Monypenny and G. E. Buckle, *The Life of Benjamin Disraeli, Earl of Beaconsfield* (London, 1910–20) IV, pp. 64–9; and R. Blake, *Disraeli* (London, 1966) pp. 370–3.
20. Gladstone, 3 February 1857, *Hansard*, 3rd series, CXLIV, 137–58.
21. Milner Gibson, 3 February 1851, *Hansard*, 3rd series, CXLIV, 197.
22. Russell, 3 February 1857, *Hansard*, 3rd series, CXLIV, 175–86.
23. Greville Diary, 11 February 1857, Greville Mss. 41122, cited in C. C. F. Greville *The Greville Memoirs*, H. Reeve (ed.) (London, 1888) VIII, p. 86.
24. Grey Diary, 4 February 1857, Grey Mss. C3/19.
25. Palmerston to Granville, 6 February 1857, Granville Mss. PRO 30/29/19/22, fol. 3.
26. Palmerston to Panmure, 7 February 1857, Dalhousie Mss. GD45/18/150, fol. 82.
27. Grey Diary, 9 February 1857, Grey Mss. C3/19.
28. Malmesbury to Derby, 4 February (? 1857) Derby Mss. 144/1.
29. Grey Diary, 4 February 1857, Grey Mss. C3/19.
30. Gladstone memo, n.d. (? 4 February 1857) Gladstone Mss. 44747, fol. 2, cited in W. E. Gladstone, *The Gladstone Diaries*, H. C. G. Matthew and M. R. D. Foot (eds) (Oxford, 1968–82) V, p. 193. See also J. Morley, *The Life of William Ewart Gladstone*, (London, 1903) I, pp. 558–9.
31. Malmesbury, *Memoirs*, II, p. 57.
32. Disraeli to Derby, 4 February 1857, Derby Mss. 145/3.
33. Derby to Disraeli, 4 February 1857, Hughenden Mss. B/XX/S/144.
34. Malmesbury, *Memoirs*, II, p. 59. See also, W. D. Jones, *Lord Derby and Victorian Conservatism*, (Oxford, 1956) p 216.
35. Ibid.
36. Gladstone Diary, 10 February 1857, cited in *Gladstone Diaries*, V, p. 196. See also, Derby to Gladstone, 11 February 1857, Gladstone Mss. 44140, fol. 214.
37. Derby to Gladstone, 11 February 1857, Gladstone Mss. 44140, fol. 214.
38. Graham memo, 6 February 1857, Graham Mss. Bundle 131. See also, Newcastle to Gladstone, 10 February 1857, Gladstone Mss. 44263, fol. 5.
39. Clarendon to Ellice, 11 February 1857, Ellice Mss. 15059, fol. 115.

40. Greville Diary, 11 February 1857, Greville Mss. 41122, cited in Greville, *Memoirs*, VIII, p. 86. See also, Greville Diary, 14 February 1857, Greville Mss. 41122, cited in Greville, *Memoirs*, VIII, p. 86-7.

41. Greville Diary, 8 February 1857, Greville Mss. 41122, cited in Greville, *Memoirs*, VIII, p. 86.

42. Clarendon to Howard de Walden, 14 February 1857, Clarendon Mss. C. 541.

43. Cornewall Lewis, 13 February 1857, *Hansard*, 3rd series, CXLIV, 629-64.

44. Grey Diary, 14 February 1857, Grey Mss. C3/19.

45. Stanley Diary, 13 February 1857, Stanley Mss. 920 DER (15) 46/1.

46. Gladstone memo, n.d. (? 14 February 1851) Gladstone Mss. 44747, cited in Morley, *Gladstone*, I, p. 561.

47. Trewen to Jolliffe, 15 February 1857, Hylton Mss. DD/HY 18/5, fol. 16.

48. Derby to Disraeli, 11 February 1857, Hughenden Mss. B/XX/S/146. See also, Grey Diary, 11 February 1857, Grey Mss. C3/19.

49. T. Carlyle, 'On History', *Frasers Magazine*, November 1830, cited in A. Shelton (ed.) *Thomas Carlyle: Selected Writings* (Harmondsworth, 1971) p. 55.

50. Romilly to Minto, 19 February 1857, Minto Mss. 11776, fol. 165.

51. Broughton Diary, 18 February 1857, Broughton Mss. 43760, fol. 62.

52. Romilly to Minto, 19 February 1857, Minto Mss. 11776, fol. 115.

53. Broughton Diary, 18 February 1857, Broughton Mss. 43760, fol. 62.

54. Locke King, 19 February 1857, *Hansard*, 3rd series, CXLIV, 841-3.

55. Russell, 19 February 1857, *Hansard*, 3rd series, CXLIV, 847-50.

56. Grey to Palmerston, 19 February 1857, Broadlands Mss. 9C/9R, fol. 2485.

57. Palmerston, 19 February 1857, *Hansard*, 3rd series, CXLIV, 843-5.

58. Palmerston, 19 February 1857, *Hansard*, 3rd series, CXLIV, 916-19.

59. Argyll, *Autobiograpby and Memoirs*, II, p. 73.

60. Fortescue Diary, 20 February 1857, Carlingford Mss. SH/358. See also, Gladstone, 20 February 1857, *Hansard*, 3rd series, CXLIV, 985-1018.

61. Overstone to Granville, 21 Februar 1857, Granville Mss. PRO 30/29/19/2, fol. 51.

62. Argyll, *Autobiography and Memoirs*, II, p. 73.

63. Bentinck, 23 February 1857, *Hansard*, 3rd series, CXLIV, 1077-8.

64. Bentinck to Derby, 20 February 1857, Derby Mss. 111/B. See also, Derby to Bentinck, 20 February 1857, Derby Mss. 183/2, fol. 174. At the beginning of February rumours had spread quickly when Derby, Gladstone and Graham were seen to meet in the Commons tea-room. Diary of 1st Baron Hatherton, 19 February 1857, Hatherton Mss. D260/M/F/5/26/71.

65. Malmesbury, *Memoirs*, II, p. 61.

66. Graham, 19 February 1857, *Hansard*, 3rd series, CXLIV, 852-7; and Herbert, 19 February 1857, *Hansard*, 3rd series, CXLIV, 857-9.

67. Gladstone Diary, 19 February 1857, cited in *Gladstone Diaries*, V, p. 200.

68. *Hansard*, 3rd series, CXLIV, 1148.
69. Argyll, *Autobiography and Memoirs*, II, p. 73.
70. Derby to Disraeli, 11 February 1857, Hughenden Mss. B/XX/S/146.
71. Argyll, *Autobiography and Memoirs*, II, p. 68.
72. Clarendon to Palmerston, 10 January 1857, Broadlands Mss. GC/CL, fol. 994.
73. Greville Diary, 27 February 1857, Greville Mss. 41122, cited in Greville, *Memoirs*, VIII, p. 93.
74. Grey Diary, 11 February 1857, Grey Mss. C3/19.
75. Greville Diary, 17 February 1857, Greville Mss. 41122, cited in Greville, *Memoirs*, VIII, p. 87.
76. Gladstone Diary, 24 February 1857, cited in *Gladstone Diaries*, V, p. 201.
77. Derby, 24 February 1857, *Hansard*, 3rd series, CXLIV, 1155–94.
78. Grey Diary, 28 February 1857, Grey Mss. C3/19.
79. Carnavon, 26 February 1857, *Hansard*, 3rd series, CXLIV, 1311–21.
80. Malmesbury, 26 February 1857, *Hansard*, 3rd series, CXLIV, 1341–52.
81. Clarendon, 24 February 1857, *Hansard*, 3rd series, CXLIV, 1195–212.
82. 26 February 1857, *Hansard*, 3rd series, CXLIV, 1385.
83. Cobden, 27 February 1857, *Hansard*, 3rd series, CXLIV, 1391–421.
84. Greville Diary, 27 February 1857, Greville Mss. 41122, cited in Greville, *Memoirs*, VIII, p. 93.
85. Palmerston to Clarendon, 27 February 1857, Clarendon Mss. C. 69, fol. 154.
86. Shaftesbury Diary, 17 February 1857, Broadlands Mss. SHA/PD.
87. Dunfermline to Panmure, 27 February 1857, Dalhousie Mss. GD45/14/631.
88. Ibid.
89. Elliot to Minto, 27 February 1857, Minto Mss. 11754, fol. 424.
90. Goderich, 27 February 1857, *Hansard*, 3rd series, CXLIV, 1543–8.
91. Bulwer Lytton, 26 February 1857, *Hansard*, 3rd series, CXLVI, 1434–46.
92. Cecil, 27 February 1857, *Hansard*, 3rd series, CXLIV, 1538–41.
93. Warren, 27 February 1857, *Hansard*, 3rd series, CXLVI, 1496–503.
94. Whiteside, 27 February 1857, *Hansard*, 3rd series, CXLIV, 1518–31.
95. Malmesbury, *Memoirs*, II, p. 62.
96. Ibid. See also, Jones, *Lord Derby and Victorian Conservatism*, p. 216.
97. Ibid. See also, Blake, *Disraeli*, p. 374.
98. Clarendon to Cowley, 28 February 1857, Clarendon Mss. C. 138, fol. 306.
99. Greville Diary, 27 February 1857, Greville Mss. 41122, cited in Greville, *Memoirs*, VIII, p. 94.
100. Graham, 27 February 1857, *Hansard*, 3rd series, CXLIV, 1552–69.
101. Herbert, 2 March 1857, *Hansard*, 3rd series, CXLIV, 1667–80.
102. Bruce to his wife, 3 March 1857, cited in H. A. Bruce, *Letters of the Rt. Hon. H. A. Bruce, Lord Aberdare of Duffryn*, 2 vols (London, 1902) I, p. 150.

103. Palmerston to Clarendon, 3 March 1857, Clarendon Mss. C. 69, fol. 160.
104. Grey Diary, 28 February 1857, Grey Mss. C3/19.
105. Broughton Diary, 3 March 1857, Broughton Mss. 43760, fol. 71.
106. Greville Diary, 3 March 1857, Greville Mss. 41122, cited in Greville, *Memoirs*, VIII, p. 97.
107. Palmerston, 3 March 1857, *Hansard*, 3rd series, CXLIV, 1809–34.
108. Greville Diary, 4 March 1857, Greville Mss. 41122, cited in Greville, *Memoirs*, VIII, p. 97.
109. Grey Diary, 28 February 1857, Grey Mss. C3/19.
110. Milner Gibson, 3 March 1857, *Hansard*, 3rd series, CXLIV, 1745–52.
111. Roebuck, 3 March 1857, *Hansard*, 3rd series, CXLIV, 1782–7; Disraeli, 3 March 1857, *Hansard*, 3rd series, CXLIV, 1834–40.
112. Greville Diary, 4 March 1857, Greville Mss. 41122, cited in Greville, *Memoirs*, VIII, p. 97.
113. Gladstone Diary, 3 March 1857, cited in *Gladstone Diaries*, V, p. 202.
114. Jolliffe to Derby, 4 March 1857, Derby Mss. 158/10, cited in R. Stewart, *The Foundation of the Conservative Party 1830–1867* (London, 1978) p. 313.
115. Derby to Jolliffe, 4 March 1857, Hylton Mss. DD/HY 18/2, fol. 2.
116. 'The Past Session and the New Parliament', *Edinburgh Review*, 204 (April 1857) p. 562. Bylsma compares the votes of the budget division on 23 February (in which the government gained a majority of eighty) with the division on Cobden's motion (in which the government were in a minority of sixteen). He reveals two important aspects of the ministerial defeat. First, government votes were lost from all non-Conservative sections of opinion. It was not the revolt of one group that brought about defeat. Secondly, many more Conservatives voted in the division on Cobden's motion than had done over the budget. This confirmed Derby's political strategy in choosing China as the issue with which to confront the government. See J. R. Bylsma, 'Political Issues and Party Unity', in the House of Commons, 1852–1857: A Scalogram Analysis', unpublished PhD thesis, University of Iowa, 1968, pp. 88–91.
117. Clarendon to Seymour, 4 March 1857, cited in Maxwell, *Clarendon*, II, p. 139.
118. Clarendon to Howard, 7 March 1857, Clarendon Mss. C. 137, fol. 339.
119. Clarendon to Delane, 4 March 1857, Delane Mss. 8/9.
120. Clarendon to Seymour, 4 March 1857, cited in Maxwell, *Clarendon*, II, p. 139.
121. Cobden to Bright, 6 March 1857, Cobden Mss. 43650, fol. 244.
122. Argyll, *Autobiography and Memoirs*, II, p. 70.
123. Palmerston, 5 March 1857, *Hansard*, 3rd series, CXLIV, 1894–7.
124. Disraeli, 5 March 1857, *Hansard*, 3rd series, CXLIV, 1897–8.
125. Russell, 5 March 1857, *Hansard*, 3rd series, CXLIV, 1907–11. Gladstone, 5 March 1857, *Hansard*, 3rd series, CXLIV, 1913–19.
126. Argyll, *Autobiography and Memoirs*, II, p. 70.

127. Clarendon to Howard de Walden, 7 March 1857, Clarendon Mss. C. 541. See also, Granville to Canning, 10 March 1857, Granville Mss. PRO 30/29/21/2, fol. 7.

128. Bruce to his wife, 8 March 1857, cited in Bruce, *Aberdare*, I, p. 150.

129. Clarendon to Clanricarde, 13 March 1857, Clanricarde Mss. 33. See also, Clanricarde, 13 March 1857, *Hansard*, 3rd series, CXLIV, 2278–80.

130. Clarendon, 13 March 1857, *Hansard*, 3rd series, CXLIV, 2280–2.

131. Cobden to Bright, 6 March 1857, Cobden Mss. 43650, fol. 243.

132. Gladstone Diary, 6 March 1857, cited in *Gladstone Diaries*, V, p. 203. See also, Gladstone memo, 6 March 1857, Gladstone Mss. 44747, fol. 14; and Stanley Diary, 6 March 1857, Stanley Mss. 920 DER (15) 46/1, cited in J. Vincent (ed.) *Disraeli, Derby and the Conservative Party* (Hassocks, 1978) p. 149–50.

133. Malmesbury, *Memoirs*, II, p. 64. See also, Malmesbury, *Memoirs*, II, p. 65.

134. Stanhope to Jolliffe, 9 March 1857, Hylton Mss. DD/HY 18/5, fol. 75.

135. Bulwer Lytton to Salisbury, 9 March 1857, Salisbury Mss.

136. Gathorne Hardy Diary, 6 March 1857, Cranbrook Mss. T501/290, fol. 468.

137. Broughton Diary, 11 March 1857, Broughton Mss. 437/60, fol. 79.

138. Derby, 16 March 1857, *Hansard*, 3rd series, CXLIV, 2311–43.

139. Malmesbury, *Memoirs*, II, p. 64.

140. Lady Palmerston to Goderich, 19 March 1857, cited in L. Wolf, *The Life of the First Marquess of Ripon*, 2 vols (London, 1921) I, p. 130.

141. Disraeli to Mrs Brydges Willyams, 23 March 1857, cited in Monypenny and Buckle, *Disraeli*, IV, p. 75.

142. *The Annual Register for 1857* (London, 1858) p. 84 provided an uncompromising statement of subsequent orthodoxy. Since then the perception of the 1857 election as a personal triumph for Palmerston has been almost universal.

143. See F. W. S. Craig, *British Parliamentary Election Results, 1832–1855* (London, 1978) pp. 621–4. Apart from the local press, two studies are indispensible for this election, J. K. Glynn, 'The Private Member of Parliament, 1833 to 1868', unpublished PhD thesis, University of London, 1949; and R. G. Watt 'Parties and Politics in Mid-Victorian Britain, 1857–1859: A Study in Quantification' unpublished PhD thesis, University of Minnesota, 1975, pp. 32–97. Both dispell the myth of a Palmerstonian triumph.

144. The *Sun*, 10 April 1857, noted that 153 MPs who had voted with Cobden were returned, and only 89 were defeated or else retired. This confirms Glynn's analysis that over two-thirds of the Liberals who voted against Palmerston were successfully returned. Four-fifths of the Palmerstonian vote were returned, Glynn, 'The Private Member'. Watt calculates that in fact a mere 38 MPs who voted against Palmerston on Cobden's motion were defeated in contested elections. The remaining 51 non-returning MPs who voted with Cobden retired and did not stand for election, Watt, 'Parties and Politics', p. 53. The

papers of Sir Henry Shiffner, Conservative electoral agent, give a well documented picture of the election in East Sussex, see Watt, 'Parties and Politics', pp. 58–62. For other comments on the absence of a clear Palmerstonian/anti-Palmerstonian cleavage in popular electoral opinion, see A. Miall, *The Life of Edward Miall* (London, 1884) p. 216; J. R. Vincent, *Formation of the Liberal Party, 1857–1868* (London, 1966) pp. 112–18; R. W. Davis, *Political Change and Continuity 1760–1885: A Buckinghamshire Study* (Newton Abbot, 1972) p. 195.

145. See Watt, 'Parties and Politics', p. 54. Roebuck, who had voted with Cobden, swept to an easy victory at Sheffield, as did Graham at Carlisle. Religion dominated the elections at Aylesbury, Windsor, Bodmin and Middlesex. Reform was prominent at Shrewsbury, Harwich and the City of London. The weaknesses and strengths of local organisations were crucial factors at Manchester and Bristol. Personalities dominated in Tewkesbury and Coventry, while there were also pocket boroughs such as Dartmouth, Newark and North Nottingham. See Watt, 'Parties and Politics', pp. 54–92. For the revival of aristocratic influence in north Lancashire after 1857, see D. Foster, 'The Politics of Uncontested Elections: North Lancashire 1832–1865', *Northern History*, 13 (1977) pp. 232–47.

146. See Watt, 'Parties and Politics', pp. 81–2.

147. Religion and reform were important at Glasgow and Dundee, lack of local organisation important in Leith, and Maynooth important generally. See Watt, 'Parties and Politics', pp. 82–9.

148. See K. T. Hoppen, *Elections, Politics and Society in Ireland 1832–1885* (Oxford, 1984); and K. T. Hoppen, 'National Politics and Local Realities in Mid-Nineteenth Century Ireland', in A. Cosgrove and D. McCartney, *Studies in Irish History: Presented to R. Dudley Edwards* (Dublin, 1979) pp. 190–227.

149. Bedford to Brougham, n.d. (? March 1857) Brougham Mss. 28122. At the Mansion House, on the 20 March, Palmerston declared that some party ties had been remembered on the occasion of Cobden's motion, 'but one party tie was wholly forgotten – the tie that ought to bind every Englishman to the interests, the honour and the glory of his country'. *The Times*, 21 March 1857, p. 9. See also Monck at Portsmouth, *The Times*, 12 March 1857, p. 12, and Wood at Halifax, *The Times*, 13 March 1857, p. 12.

150. Normanby to Brougham n.d. (? March 1857) Brougham Mss. 28122.

151. Watt comments that 'Palmerston's popularity was an issue in the election, but except for Norfolk it was not central in the local elections. . . . The election of 1857 had all the marks of being a national election, fought with the vigour of a national party, organised in each local constituency. But as we have seen, the obvious was not true.' Watt, 'Parties and Politics', pp. 96–7.

152. Bruce to Granville, 29 April 1857, Granville Mss. PRO 20/39/19/22, fol. 209.

153. Palmerston to Granville, 25 March 1857, Granville Mss. PRO 30/29/19/22, fol. 10, cited in Bell, *Palmerston*, II, p. 170.

154. Palmerston to Granville, 24 March 1857, Granville Mss. PRO 30/29/ 19/22, fol. 13, cited in H. C. F. Bell, *Lord Palmerston* (London, 1936) II, p. 170.
155. See *The Times*, 12 March 1857, p. 12.
156. Although the government and *The Times* portrayed the defeats of Cobden, Bright, Milner Gibson and Miall as a national revulsion to Radicalism, Watt shows that a significant body of advanced Liberals and Radicals were returned in the election. He identifies a hard core of 104 Radical or like-minded Liberal MPs and another 121 MPs who voted with this group in most divisions, Watt, 'Parties and Politics', p. 127.
157. *The Times*, 13 April, 1857, p. 13.
158. Jolliffe memo, n.d. (? April 1857) Hylton Mss. DD/HY 24/11.
159. Granville to Canning, 8 April 1857, Granville Mss. PRO 30/29/21/2, fol. 11, cited in Lord E. Fitzmaurice, *The Life of Granville George Leveson-Gower, Second Earl Granville, K.G.* (London, 1905) I, pp. 227–30.
160. Clarendon to Seymour, 1 April 1857, Clarendon Mss. C. 138, fol. 471.
161. Clarendon to Cornewall Lewis, 28 March 1857, Clarendon Mss. C. 533.
162. Paget at Nottingham, *The Times*, 14 March 1857, p. 9; and Windham in East Norfolk, *The Times*, 19 March 1857, p. 5.
163. Russell in the City of London, *The Times*, 20 March 1857, p. 7.
164. Granville to Canning, 8 April 1857, Granville Mss. PRO 30/39/21/2 fol. 11, cited in Fitzmaurice, *Granville*, I, pp. 227–30.
165. Argyll to Palmerston, 10 April 1857, Broadlands Mss. GC/AR, fol. 14.
166. Clarendon to Palmerston, 25 April 1857, Clarendon Mss. C. 138, fol. 585.
167. Granville to Canning, 8 April 1857, Granville Mss. PRO 30/29/21/2, fol. 11, cited in Fitzmaurice, *Granville*, I, pp. 227–30.
168. Clarendon to Palmerston, 25 April 1857, Clarendon Mss. C. 138, fol. 585.
169. Argyll, *Autobiography and Memoirs*, II, p. 76.
170. Broughton Diary, 29 March 1857, Broughton Mss. 43760, fol. 91.
171. Palmerston at Tiverton, *The Times*, 24 March 1857, p. 9.
172. Palmerston at Tiverton, *The Times*, 28 March 1857, p. 10.
173. Broughton Diary, 28 April 1857, Broughton Mss. 43760, fol. 99.
174. Dunfermline to Ellice, 26 May (? 1857) Ellice Mss. 15001, fol. 172. For Derby's attack on Palmerston's domestic policy see Jones, *Lord Derby and Victorian Conservatism*, p. 217.
175. Broughton Diary, 23 May 1857, Broughton Mss. 43760, fol. 116.
176. Newcastle to Hayward, 10 April 1857, Newcastle Mss. NeC12369, cited in H. E. Carlisle (ed.) *Selections from the Correspondence of Abraham Hayward* (London, 1886) I, pp. 312–13.
177. Dallas to Cass, 2 April 1857, cited in Dallas, *Letters from London*, I, p. 149.
178. Dallas to Cass, 10 April 1857, cited in Dallas, *Letters from London*, I, p. 156. See also, Bell, *Palmerston*, II, p. 170.

179. Newcastle to Hayward, 20 April 1857, Newcastle Mss. NeC 12369.
180. Clark to Dean of Bristol, n.d. (? April 1857) Russell Mss. PRO 30/22/13/C, fol. 19.
181. Ibid. See also, J. Prest, *Lord John Russell* (London, 1972) p. 380.
182. Russell to Panmure, 20 April 1857, Dalhousie Mss. GD45/8/632, fol. 94.
183. Clarendon to Palmerston, 20 May 1857, Broadlands Mss. GC/CL, fol. 1052.
184. Russell to Layard, 7 April 1857, Layard Mss. 38985, fol. 217.
185. Russell to Ellice, 25 March 1857, Ellice Mss. 15052, fol. 189.
186. Russell to Dean of Bristol, 8 April 1857, Russell Mss. PRO 30/22/13/C, fol. 201.
187. Russell to Dean of Bristol, n.d. (? April 1857) Russell Mss. PRO 30/22/13/C, fol. 223.
188. Russell to Ellice, 7 April 1857, Ellice Mss. 15052, fol. 191.
189. Dallas to Cass, 7 April 1857, cited in Dallas *Letters from London*, I, p. 149.
190. Clark to Dean of Bristol, 10 April 1857, Russell Mss. PRO 30/22/13/C, fol. 242.
191. Marwick to Russell, 1 April 1857, Russell Mss. PRO 30/22/13/C, fol. 180.
192. Holland to Brougham, 12 April 1857, Brougham Mss. 16306.
193. Clark to Dean of Bristol, n.d. (? April 1857) Russell Mss. PRO 30/22/13/C, fol. 19.
194. Ibid. See also, Prest, *Russell*, p. 380.
195. Holland to Brougham, 12 April 1857, Brougham Mss. 16306.
196. Clark to Dean of Bristol, n.d. (? April 1857) Russell Mss. Pro 30/22/13/C, fol. 27.
197. Clark to Dean of Bristol, 21 April 1857, Russell Mss. PRO 30/22/13/C, fol. 261.
198. Newcastle to Hayward, 10 April, 1857, Newcastle Mss. NeC 12369, cited in Carlisle (ed.) *Hayward Correspondence*, I, p. 312. See also, Clarendon to Howard, 9 May 1857 Clarendon Mss. C. 541.
199. Jolliffe memo. n.d. (? April 1857) Hylton Mss. DD/HY 24/11, cited in Stewart *Foundation of the Conservative Party*, p. 341.
200. Disraeli to Mrs Brydges Willyams, 13 April 1857, cited in Monypenny and Buckle, *Disraeli*, IV, p. 76.
201. Ibid. See also, Blake, *Disraeli*, p. 375.
202. Hamilton to Disraeli, 25 April 1857, Hughenden Mss. B/XX/H/62.
203. Jolliffe to Derby, 13 April 1857, Derby Mss. 158/10.
204. Derby to Disraeli, 24 April 1857, Hughenden Mss. B/XX/S/148, cited
205. Disraeli to Derby, 21 April 1857, Derby Mss. 145/3. See also Disraeli at Aylesbury, *The Times*, 1 April 1857, p. 10. For comment on a speech Disraeli made at Newport-Pagnell suggesting judicious changes in the representative system see 'Representative Reform', *Edinburgh Review*, 215 (July 1857) pp. 254–86.
206. Derby to Disraeli, 24 April 1857, Hughenden Mss. B/XX/S/148, cited in Monypenny and Buckle, *Disraeli*, IV, pp. 80–1.
207. Ibid.

208. Herbert to Aberdeen, 12 April 1857, Aberdeen Mss. 43197, fol. 153, cited in A. H. Gordon, Baron Stanmore, *Sidney Herbert, Lord Herbert of Lea: A Memoir* (London, 1906) II, p. 86–92. See also, W. D. Jones and A. B. Erickson, *The Peelites* (Iowa, 1973) pp. 201–5.

209. Graham at Carlisle, *The Times*, 19 March 1857, p. 5.

210. Granville to Canning, 8 April 1857, Granville Mss. PRO 30/29/21/2, fol. 11, cited in Fitzmaurice, *Granville*, I, pp. 227–30.

211. Gladstone to Herbert, 22 March 1857, Gladstone Mss. 44210, fol. 306. Gladstone's own sympathies remained firmly focused upon Derby. Gladstone wrote to Elwin that 'looking upon *dishonour* as the great characteristic of Lord Palmerston's government [he] would not willingly run the *risk* of wounding Lord Derby or any friend of his'. Gladstone to Elwin, 12 March 1857, cited in *Gladstone Diaries*, V, p. 207.

212. Herbert to Gladstone, 18 March 1857, Gladstone Mss. 44210, fol. 303, cited in Gordon, *Herbert*, II, p. 82.

213. Graham to Herbert, 15 April 1857, cited in Gordon, *Herbert*, II, pp. 95–6.

214. Aberdeen to Gladstone, 3 April 1857, Aberdeen Mss. 43071, fol. 364.

215. Gladstone to Herbert, 22 March 1857, Gladstone Mss. 44210, fol. 306, cited in Morley, *Gladstone*, I, pp. 565–6.

216. Graham to Herbert, 15 April 1857, cited in Gordon, *Herbert*, II, pp. 95–6.

217. Aberdeen to Gladstone, 3 April 1857, Aberdeen Mss. 43071, fol. 364.

218. Graham to Cobden, 26 April 1857, Cobden Mss. 43669.

219. Herbert to Aberdeen, 12 April 1857, Aberdeen Mss. 43197, fol. 153, cited in Gordon, *Herbert*, II, pp. 86–92.

220. Gladstone to Aberdeen, 31 March 1857, Aberdeen Mss. 43071, fol. 358.

221. Ibid.

222. Argyll, *Autobiography and Memoirs*, II, p. 73.

223. Gladstone memo, 7 May 1857, cited in *Gladstone Diaries*, V, p. 221.

224. Gladstone to Herbert, 22 March 1857, Gladstone Mss. 44210, fol. 306, cited in Gordon, *Herbert*, II, pp. 82–5.

225. Gladstone to Aberdeen, 4 April 1857, Aberdeen Mss. 43071, fol. 367.

226. Gladstone to Aberdeen, 31 March 1857, Aberdeen Mss. 43071, fol. 358.

227. Cobden to Graham, 16 March 1857, cited in C. S. Parker, *Life and Letters of Sir James Graham, Second Baronet of Netherby* (London, 1907) II, p. 303.

228. Cobden at Manchester, *The Times*, 20 March 1857, p. 5.

229. Cobden at Huddersfield, *The Times*, 23 March 1857, p. 9.

230. Bright Diary, 19 March 1857, cited in J. Bright, *The Diaries of John Bright* R. A. J. Walling (ed.) (London, 1930) p. 224.

231. Bright to Cobden, 16 April 1857, Bright Mss. 43384, fol. 92.

232. Ibid.

233. Cobden to Lindsay, 7 April 1857, cited in John Morley, *The Life of*

Richard Cobden (London, 1879) II, p. 662. See also, Cobden to Hargreaves, 7 April 1857, Cobden Mss. 43655, fol. 57.

234. Bright to Cobden, 16 April 1857, Bright Mss. 43384, fol. 93.
235. Ibid.
236. Cobden to Moffat, 7 April 1857, Cobden Mss. 43669, cited in Morley, *Cobden*, II.
237. Bright to Cobden, 16 April 1857, Bright Mss. 43384, fol. 93.
238. Ibid.
239. Roebuck at Sheffield, *The Times*, 23 March 1857, p. 9.
240. Morley to Cobden, 13 April 1857, Cobden Mss. 43669, fol. 107.
241. Ibid.
242. Lindsay to Cobden, 3 April 1857, Cobden Mss. 43669, fol. 101.
243. Cobden to Morley, 15 April 1857, Cobden Mss. 43669, fol. 109.

CHAPTER 4

1. Queen's speech, 1 May 1857, *Hansard*, 3rd series, CXLV, 16–18.
2. Dallas to Cass, 8 May 1957, cited in G. M. Dallas, *Letters from London, 1856–1860* (London, 1870) I, p. 163.
3. Stanley Diary, 7 May 1857, Stanley Mss. 920 DER (15) 46/1.
4. Queen's speech, 1 May 1857, *Hansard*, 3rd series, CXLV, 16–18.
5. Buchanan, 7 May 1857, *Hansard*, 3rd series, CXLV, 54–9.
6. Palmerston Diary, 7 May 1857, Broadlands Mss. D/17.
7. Palmerston, 7 May 1857, *Hansard*, 3rd series, CXLV, 65–8.
8. Ibid. See also, H. C. F. Bell, *Lord Palmerston* (London, 1936) II, p. 176–8.
9. Dallas to Cass, 10 April 1857, cited in Dallas, *Letters from London*, I, p. 156. See also, Bell, *Palmerston*, II, p. 170. As an indication of moderate Liberal opinion, in July the *Edinburgh Review* recommended the establishment of a uniform vote, with the adoption of Locke King's proposal of a £10 county and borough franchise. See 'Representative Reform', *Edinburgh Review*, 215 (July 1857) p. 278.
10. Clark to Dean of Bristol, 21 April 1857, Russell Mss. PRO 30/22/13/C.
11. Greville Diary, 10 May 1857, Greville Mss. 41122, cited in C. C. F. Greville, *The Greville Memoirs* H. Reeve (ed.) (London, 1888) VIII, p. 109.
12. Russell to Dean of Bristol, 8 April 1857, Russell Mss. PRO 30/22/13/C, fol. 201.
13. Greville Diary, 3 June 1857, Greville Mss. 41122, cited in Greville, *Memoirs*, VIII, p. 111.
14. Malmesbury to Derby, 8 May 1857, Derby Mss. 144/1.
15. Malmesbury to Derby, 4 May 1857, Derby Mss. 144/1.
16. Derby to Disraeli, 12 May 1857, Hughenden Mss. B/XX/S/149.
17. Dallas to Cass, 12 June 1857, cited in Dallas, *Letters from London*, I, p. 173. For comment on 1857 legislation see E. A. G. Clark, 'Sir Stafford Northcote's "Omnibus": The Genesis of the Industrial

Schools Act 1857', *Journal of Educational and Administrative History*, 14:1 (1982) pp. 27–45; and M. J. D. Roberts, 'Morals, Art and the Law: The Passing of the Obscene Publications Act, 1857', *Victorian Studies*, 28:4 (1985) pp. 609–30.

18. Spooner, 21 May 1857, *Hansard* 3rd series, CXLV, 644–63.

19. Roebuck, 21 May 1857, *Hansard*, 3rd series, CXLV, 671.

20. Dallas to Cass, 28 July 1857, cited in Dallas, *Letters from London*, I, p. 183.

21. Stanley Diary, 4 July 1857, Stanley Mss. 920 DER (15) 46/1, cited in J. Vincent (ed.) *Disraeli, Derby and the Conservative Party* (Hassocks, 1978) p. 151.

22. Gladstone to Cobden, 16 June 1857, Gladstone Mss. 44135, fol. 9. See also, Graham to Gladstone, 13 June 1857, Gladstone Mss. 44164, fol. 103; and Graham to Gladstone, 23 June 1857, Gladstone Mss. 44164, fol. 107.

23. Lindsay to Cobden, 18 June 1857, Cobden Mss. 43669, fol. 160.

24. Gladstone, 31 July 1857, *Hansard*, 3rd series, CXLVII, 851. See also Sir P. Magnus, *Gladstone: A Biography* (London, 1954) pp. 130–1; and M. L. Shanley, 'One Must Ride Behind: Married Women's Rights and the Divorce Act of 1857', *Victorian Studies*, 25:3 (1983) pp. 355–76.

25. Denison to Ellice, 19 August 1857, Ellice Mss. 15012, fol. 1.

26. Granville to Canning, 26 August 1857, Granville Mss. PRO 30/29/19/2, fol. 29, cited in Lord E. Fitzmaurice, *The Life of Granville George Leveson-Gower, Second Earl Granville, K.G.* (London, 1905) I, p. 258.

27. Dunfermline to Brougham, 25 October 1857, Brougham Mss. 13602.

28. Gladstone Diary, 29 December 1857, cited in W. E. Gladstone, *The Gladstone Diaries*, H. C. G. Matthew and M. R. D. Foot (eds) (Oxford, 1968–82) V, p. 270.

29. Stanley Diary, 4 June 1857, Stanley Mss. 920 DER (15) 46/1, cited in Vincent (ed.) *Disraeli, Derby and the Conservative Party*, p. 151.

30. Parkes to Brougham, 14 June 1857, Brougham Mss. 20886.

31. See P. Spear, *A History of India*, vol. 2 (London, 1970) pp. 129–44 for a consideration of the implications and importance of the mutiny within an Indian perspective. For detailed treatments see the standard work, G. B. Malleson, *History of the Indian Mutiny*, 3 vols (London, 1878–80); and the more recent studies of S. N. Sen, *1857*, and C. Hibbert, *The Great Mutiny: India 1857* (London, 1978). For a perceptive Indian viewpoint see S. Ahmad Khan, *The Indian Revolt* (London, 1873). Biographical perspectives are provided in W. Lee Warner, *Life of Lord Dalhousie*, 2 vols (London, 1904) and Marquess of Dalhousie, *The Private Letters of the Marquess of Dalhousie*, J. A. Baird (ed.) (London, 1910). See also, S. B. Smith, *Life of Lord Lawrence*, 2 vols (London, 1883): J. L. Morrison, *Life of Henry Lawrence* (London, 1934); M. Maclagan, *'Clemency' Canning: Charles John, 1st Earl Canning, Governor-General and Viceroy of India, 1856–1862* (London, 1962).

32. Palmerston to the Queen, 26 June 1857, *QVL*, 1st series, III, pp.

297-8. See also, Granville to Canning, 10 July 1851, Granville Mss. PRO 30/29/2, fol. 17, cited in Fitzmaurice, *Granville*, I, pp. 251-2; Wood to Grey, 22 September 1857, Grey Mss; Wood to Ellice, 6 October 1857, Ellice Mss. 15060, fol. 180; Palmerston to Granville, 19 September 1857, Granville Mss. PRO 30/29/21/2, fol. 2.

33.   Clarendon to Palmerston, 11 September 1857, Broadlands Mss. GC/ CL, 1087. See also, Clarendon to Cornewall Lewis, 20 September 1857, Clarendon Mss. C. 533. Clarendon to his wife, 1 October 1857, cited in Sir H. Maxwell, *The Life and Letters of the Fourth Earl of Clarendon* (London, 1913) II, p. 153. Argyll to Aberdeen, 25 August 1857, Aberdeen Mss. 43192, fol. 122. Granville to Canning, 9 September 1857, Granville Mss. PRO 30/29/21/2, fol. 32. Clarendon feared that 'if great disasters occur . . . the first thing that John Bull will as usual do is to look for a victim and that victim will be the government who is more to be charged with want of energy and for having lagged behind public opinion and for not having availed itself of the readiness which the country has manifested'. Clarendon to Palmerston, 1 September 1857, Broadlands Mss. GC/CL 1083. Argyll feared that sufficiently active and vigorous measures were not '*being carried into effect with the necessary expedition*'. Argyll to Palmerston, 29 September 1857, Broadlands Mss. GC/AR 16.

34.   Ellenborough, 29 June 1857, *Hansard*, 3rd series, CXLVI, 512-60. See also, Disraeli, 29 June 1857, *Hansard*, 3rd series, CXLVI, 536-60. Granville, 23 July 1857, *Hansard*, 3rd series, CXLVI, 1331-3. Palmerston, 13 July, 1857, *Hansard*, 3rd series, CXLVI, 2367-71. During the mutiny two preoccupations influenced Palmerston's understanding of the situation in India. First, 'the suspicion . . . that our Indian disturbances were not without some Russian origin'. In October the premier conveyed to Canning 'some information . . . received from a secret agent as to Russian intrigues in India as to the names of persons engaged in plots and as to certain hidden stores of arms and ammunition at Calcutta, held ready for insurrection'. Also Palmerston held information that an insurrection was imminent in Ireland, 'not wholly without foundation'. The Irish militia were stationed in England 'away from the influence of Priests and Traitors', and the Guards regiment, a 'sufficient Anglo-Saxon' force to quell any 'Celtic movement', were not sent to India so that 'the best troops could be kept in England to form the foundation of an Irish force in case of need'. Palmerston to Clarendon, 12 July 1857, Clarendon Mss. C. 69, fol. 346. Palmerston to Canning 11 October 1857, Canning Mss. 2/10. Palmerston to Panmure, 5 October 1857, Dalhousie Mss. GD45/8/50, fol. 93. Palmerston to Panmure, 11 October 1857, Dalhousie Mss. GD45/8/50, fol. 95.

35.   Edward Law, second Baron Ellenborough (1790-1871) had been Governor-General of India from 1841 to 1844, but because of his rather stringent and summary manner the East India Company requested his resignation and he returned to England and a place in Peel's cabinet in 1844. Thereafter, as a Peelite in outlook but a Conservative by habit, Ellenborough concerned himself with Indian

military affairs and education. On 9 June 1857 Ellenborough, speaking in the Lords, had drawn notice to the apprehension felt among the native troops in India that the government intended to interfere with their religion, warning that if this was attempted 'the most bloody revolution will occur'. Ellenborough, 9 June 1857, *Hansard*, 3rd series, CXLV 1393–6; see also, Ellenborough, 29 June 1857, *Hansard*, 3rd series, CXLVI, 512–20. Disraeli argued that the forcible destruction of native Princedoms, the disturbance of the traditional settlement of property and interference with the religion of the people had prompted a national revolt which the government insisted on regarding as merely a military mutiny. Disraeli, 27 July 1857, *Hansard*, 3rd series, CXLVII, 440–81. See also commentary in W. F. Monypenny and G. E. Buckle, *The Life of Benjamin Disraeli, Earl of Beaconsfield* (London, 1910–20) IV, pp. 83–94; and R. Blake, *Disraeli* (London, 1966) pp. 375–7.

36.	Baring, 27 July 1857, *Hansard*, 3rd series, CXLVII, 542–3. See also, Palmerston, 27 July 1857, *Hansard*, 3rd series, CXLVII, 543–5.

37.	Denison to Ellice, 6 August 1857, Ellice Mss. 15012, fol. 5; Dallas to Cass, 7 August 1857, cited in Dallas, *Letters from London*, I, p. 191.

38.	Denison to Ellice, 6 August 1857, Ellice Mss. 15012, fol. 5.

39.	Granville to Canning, 26 August 1857, Granville Mss. PRO 30/29/21/2, fol. 2, cited in Fitzmaurice, *Granville*, I, p. 258.

40.	Dallas to Cass, 14 September 1857, cited in Dallas, *Letters from London*, I, p. 201.

41.	Parkes to Ellice, 20 October 1857, Ellice Mss. 15042, fol. 80. The cabinet was beginning to be 'assailed for absenting themselves on grouse plains, stalking moors and watching places, at a moment when the Empire was being shaken to its foundations'. Dallas to Cass, 14 September 1857, cited in Dallas *Letters from London*, I, p. 201. Those outside the cabinet noted and repeated Clarendon's complaints 'of a want of energy and exertion'. Aberdeen to Newcastle, 15 September 1857, Newcastle Mss. NeC, 12,450. Russell observed that Palmerston 'thought little evidently of the danger'. Russell to Dean of Bristol, 1 October 1857, Russell Mss. PRO 30/29/21/2, fol. 29. Dallas perceived 'much effort and dexterity in preventing really bad news from striking too suddenly upon the public mind'. Dallas to Cass, 5 October 1857, cited in Dallas, *Letters from London*, I, p. 210. The cabinet's 'puzzled' rejoinder that 'the India business had not yet reached a stage at which anything could be attributed to the fault of the Home Government' was sounding distinctly lame. Argyll to Aberdeen, 3 September 1857, Aberdeen Mss. 43199, fol. 95. Wood's choice of vessels for conveying reinforcements to India also came to cause much concern. Prince Albert commented bitterly upon Palmerston's 'juvenile levity', cited in Bell, *Palmerston*, II, p. 173.

42.	Granville to Canning, 24 October 1857, Granville Mss. PRO 30/29/21/2, fol. 41, cited in Fitzmaurice, *Granville*, I, p. 262.

43.	Granville to Argyll, 8 October 1857, cited in Duke of Argyll, *George Douglas, 8th Duke of Argyll: Autobiography and Memoirs* (London, 1906) II, p. 94.

44. Clarendon to Palmerston, 23 September 1857, Broadlands Mss. GC/CL 1096. See also, Clarendon to Palmerston, 28 September 1857, Broadlands Mss. GC/CL 1099.
45. Osborne to Ellice, 14 October 1857, Ellice Mss. 15040, fol. 62.
46. Granville to Canning, 10 October 1857, Granville Mss. PRO 30/29/21/2, fol. 3. The system of 'double government' Palmerston wished to do away with shared the governing of India between the East India Company and the government in London. Prior to 1857, however, the East India Company 'had long been little more than an administrative corporation working under government direction, and had even lost its right of patronage when entry to the services was thrown open to competition in 1853'. Spear, *India: A Modern History*, p. 277.
47. Cornewall Lewis to Clarendon, 20 October 1857, Clarendon Mss. C. 70, fol. 214.
48. Palmerston to Clarendon, 14 November 1857, Clarendon Mss. C. 69, fol. 583.
49. Cornewall Lewis to Clarendon, 20 October 1857, Clarendon Mss. C. 70, fol. 214.
50. Parkes to Ellice, 28 November 1857, Ellice Mss. 15042, fol. 94.
51. Dunfermline to Panmure, 22 September 1857, Dalhousie Mss. GD45/14/631.
52. Granville to Canning, 26 August 1857, Granville Mss. PRO 30/29/21/2, fol. 29, cited in Fitzmaurice, *Granville*, I, p. 258.
53. Malmesbury to Derby, 1 May 1857, Derby Mss. 144/1.
54. Greville Diary, 20 June 1857, Greville Mss. 41122, cited in C. C. F. Greville, *The Greville Memoirs*, H. Reeve (ed.) (London, 1888) VIII, p. 113.
55. Palmerston Diary, n.d., Broadlands Mss. D/17.
56. Dunfermline to Panmure, 22 September 1857, Dalhousie Mss. GD/45/14/631.
57. Gressley to Ellice, 16 November 1857, Ellice Mss. 15034, fol. 23.
58. Aberdeen to Russell, 3 November 1857, Russell Mss. PRO 30/22/13/D, fol. 221.
59. Aberdeen to Newcastle, 15 September 1857, Newcastle Mss. NeC 12,450.
60. Granville to Canning, 24 October 1857, Granville Mss. PRO 30/29/21/2, fol. 41. In Fitzmaurice, *Granville*, I, p. 262 the passage is transcribed as 'nothing could be more fatal than to attempt to burke all reform'.
61. Wood to Grey, 27 November 1857, Grey Mss.
62. 'There is a general opinion that we must introduce some measure, which is rendered necessary by the decision of the House on Locke King's motion. Only ½ a dozen of the Liberal party voted with us against it, the large body including all our friends, Baring etc ... We cannot depend upon Tory support against our friends for long.' Wood to Grey, 28 November 1857, Grey Mss.
63. Grey Diary, 20 November 1857, Grey Mss. C3/20.
64. Granville to Canning, 24 October 1857, Granville Mss. PRO 30/29/21/2, fol. 41, cited in Fitzmaurice, *Granville*, I, p. 262.

65. Grey to Brougham, 1 August 1857, Brougham Mss. 7083; Aberdeen to Graham, 24 August 1857, Graham Mss. Bundle 135.

66. Grey to Brougham, 1 August 1857, Brougham Mss. 7083. See Henry George Grey, Third Earl, *Parliamentary Government Considered with Reference to a Reform of Parliament*, (London, 1858). Grey's essay was 'not a plan, but rather an attempt to show what ought *not* to be done'. Grey to Russell, 24 November 1857, Russell Mss. PRO 30/22/13/D, fol. 262. See also, Grey to Brougham, 30 September 1857, Brougham Mss. 7084; and Grey to Brougham, 22 October 1857, Brougham Mss. 14566.

67. Dunfermline to Brougham, 18 August 1857, Brougham Mss. 35145.

68. Graham to Aberdeen, n.d. (? August 1857) Aberdeen Mss. 43192, fol. 126. Clarendon noted that the Queen 'expects to have to *subir* Lord John one of these days'. Maxwell, *Clarendon*, II, p. 140.

69. Parkes to Ellice, n.d. (? September 1857) Ellice Mss. 15042, fol. 54.

70. Graham to Aberdeen, 11 September 1857, Aberdeen Mss. 43192, fol. 127.

71. Russell to Graham, 3 September 1857, Graham Mss. Bundle 132. See also, Graham to Russell, 11 September 1857, Russell Mss. PRO 30/22/13/D, fol. 130. Russell to Graham, 16 September 1857, Graham Mss. Bundle 132. Graham to Russell, 22 September 1857, Russell Mss. PRO 30/22/13/D, fol. 144. Important correspondence between Russell and Graham is transcribed in C. S. Parker, *Life and Letters of Sir James Graham, Second Baronet of Netherby* (London, 1907) II, pp. 313–20.

72. Graham to Russell, 11 September 1857, Russell Mss. PRO 30/22/13/D, fol. 130.

73. Graham to Aberdeen, 23 September 1857, Aberdeen Mss. 43192, fol. 129.

74. Russell to Graham, 29 September 1857, Graham Mss. Bundle 132; and Russell to Graham, 11 October 1857, Graham Mss. Bundle 132. See also, Graham to Russell, 8 October 1857, Russell Mss. PRO 30/22/13/D, fol. 175; and Parker, *Graham*, II, pp. 313–20.

75. Graham to Aberdeen, 12 October 1857, Aberdeen Mss. 43192, fol. 139.

76. Russell to Dean of Bristol, 24 October 1857, Russell Mss. PRO 30/22/13/D, fol. 194.

77. Fortescue Diary, 31 October 1857, Carlingford Mss. DD/SH 358.

78. Russell to Dean of Bristol, 10 November 1857, Russell Mss. PRO 30/22/13/D, fol. 254.

79. Russell to Dean of Bristol, 21 November 1857, Russell Mss. PRO 30/22/13/D, fol. 254.

80. Cobden to Bright, 24 August 1857, Cobden Mss. 43650, fol. 258. See Cobden to Hargreaves, 8 June 1857, Cobden Mss. 43655, fol. 61; Cobden to Bright, 6 July 1857, Cobden Mss. 43650, fol. 249.

81. Cobden to Bright, 11 August 1857, Cobden Mss. 43650, fol. 256.

82. Bright to Cobden, 24 November 1857, Bright Mss. 43384, fol. 113.

83. Morley to Cobden, 17 June 1857, Cobden Mss. 43669, fol. 158.

84. *The Times*, 18 November 1857, p. 7.

85. The 'Manifesto' recommended a borough franchise for all adult males who were owners or tenants of premises rated to the relief of the poor; a county franchise to all £10 occupiers; the assimilation of the franchise in Scotland and Ireland to those of England and Wales; vote by ballot; a redistribution of seats making such an approach to an equalisation of constituencies as would give a majority of members to a majority of electors; the abolition of property qualifications for MPs and triennial parliaments. *The Times*, 18 November 1857, p. 7.

86. Granville to Canning, 10 November 1857, Granville Mss. PRO 30/29/21/2, fol. 54, cited in Fitzmaurice, *Granville*, I, p. 265. See also, Bell, *Palmerston*, II, pp. 278–80.

87. Bell suggests this scheme represents Palmerston's own wishes, but no indication is given of who participated in drafting the proposal. Palmerston to the Queen, 18 October 1857, cited in H. C. Bell, 'Palmerston and Parliamentary Representation', *Journal of Modern History*, 4 (1932) pp. 186–213.

88. Walpole to Heathcote, 7 April 1857, Walpole Mss. See also Jolliffe to Derby, 13 April 1857, Derby Mss. 158/10; Jolliffe to Derby, 16 April 1857, Derby Mss. 158/10; and Jolliffe to Disraeli, n.d. (? April 1857) Hughenden Mss. B/XX/J/50.

89. Stanley to Disraeli, 10 October 1857, Hughenden Mss. B/XX/S/630.

90. Disraeli to Pakington, 6 October 1857, Hampton Mss. 3835/7.

91. Disraeli to Lennox, 7 November 1857, cited in Monypenny and Buckle, *Disraeli*, IV, p. 101.

92. Disraeli to Pakington, 6 October 1857, Hampton Mss. 3835/7.

93. Derby to Disraeli, 12 May 1857, Hughenden Mss. B/XX/S/149.

94. Malmesbury Diary, 16 May 1857, Malmesbury Mss. 9M73.

95. Malmesbury Diary, 9 September 1857, Malmesbury Mss. 9M73.

96. Dallas to Cass, 20 October 1857, cited in Dallas, *Letters from London*, I, p. 217.

97. Cornewall Lewis to Palmerston, 8 November 1857, Broadlands Mss. GC/LE 104. See also, Cornewall Lewis to Palmerston, 3 November 1857, Broadlands Mss. GC/LE 103.

98. Palmerston Diary, 12 November 1857, Broadlands Mss. D/17.

99. Grey to Ellice, 5 October 1857, Ellice Mss. 15025, fol. 122.

100. Delane to Ellice, 20 November 1857, Ellice Mss. 15011, fol. 7.

101. Lennox to Disraeli, 30 November 1857, Hughenden Mss. B/XX/LX/95.

102. Herbert to Newcastle, 29 November 1857, Newcastle Mss. NeC 12,553.

103. Newcastle to Hayward, 24 November 1857, Newcastle Mss. NeC 12,370, cited in H. E. Carlisle (ed.) *Selections from the Correspondence of Abraham Hayward* (London, 1886) I, p. 316.

104. Lennox to Disraeli, 19 November 1857, Hughenden Mss. B/XX/LX/94.

105. Derby to Disraeli, 15 November 1857, Hughenden Mss. B/XX/S/150. See also, Derby to Jolliffe, 25 November 1857, Hughenden Mss. B/XX/S/152; Derby to Disraeli, 29 November 1857, Hughenden Mss.

B/XX/S/153; and Derby to Disraeli, n.d. (? November 1857) Hughenden Mss. B/XX/S/156.

106. Russell to Dean of Bristol, 26 November 1857, Russell Mss. PRO 30/22/13/D, fol. 264.
107. Herbert to Newcastle, 29 November 1857, Newcastle Mss. NeC 12,553.
108. Graham to Gladstone, 23 November 1857, Gladstone Mss. 44164, fol. 124.
109. Parkes to Ellice Jr 22 November 1857, Ellice Mss. 15043, fol. 68.
110. Aberdeen to Gladstone, 13 December 1857, Graham Mss. Bundle 132. See also, Palmerston 3 December 1857, *Hansard*, 3rd series, CXLVIII, 127–31; and Palmerston, 7 December 1857, *Hansard*, 3rd series, CXLVIII, 273–4.
111. Bessborough to Granville, 8 December (? 1857) Granville Mss. PRO 30/29/23/10, fol. 729.
112. Granville to Canning, 23 December 1857, Granville Mss. PRO 30/29/21/2, fol. 72, cited in Fitzmaurice, *Granville*, I, p. 278.
113. Graham to Cardwell, 13 December 1857, Cardwell Mss. PRO 30/48/8/47, fol. 39.

CHAPTER 5

1. Palmerston to Sulivan, 7 October 1857, cited in K. Bourne (ed.) *The Letters of the Third Viscount Palmerston to Laurence and Elizabeth Sulivan, 1804–1863*, Camden Fourth Series, vol. 23 (London, Royal Historical Society, 1979) p. 315. Staying at Broadlands most of the autumn, Palmerston was suffering from a painful attack of shingles, as well as a nagging foot infection.
2. Bedford to Russell, 26 December 1857, Russell Mss. PRO 30/22/13/D, fol. 299. The minister referred to was probably Cornewall Lewis.
3. Greville Diary, 3 February 1858, Greville Mss. 41122, cited in C. C. F. Greville, *The Greville Memoirs*, H. Reeve (ed.) (London, 1888) VIII, p. 162.
4. Grey Diary, 29 December 1857, Grey Mss. C3/20.
5. Cornewall Lewis to Palmerston, 2 January 1858 Broadlands Mss. GC/LE, fol. 109.
6. Greville Diary, 21 December 1857, Greville Mss. 41122, cited in Greville, *Memoirs*, VIII, p. 147.
7. Ibid.
8. Argyll to Clarendon, 19 January 1858, Clarendon Mss. C. 82, fol. 204.
9. Ibid.
10. 'Before we broke up last evening I suggested to Palmerston that it might be well to have our other bill – namely, reform – put in the form of a draft as soon as possible. He replied: "Oh, there will be time enough for that; we cannot introduce it before Easter!" I said I thought it extremely probable that we should not be able to introduce

it at all if the India bill made heavy progress, but that it *was* important to be able to say that it was ready. I greatly fear that he may not have the importance of this sufficiently before him. I think that we shall feel rather uncomfortable under the accusation of insincerity about reform, unless we can say with truth that the measure is ready and prepared to be introduced, whenever the state of public business gives any hope of possible success. Pray, if you can, let this necessity be put fully before Palmerston.' Argyll to G. Grey, 15 January 1858, cited in Duke of Argyll, *George Douglas, 8th Duke of Argyll: Autobiography and Memoirs* (London, 1906) II, p. 97.

11. Argyll to G. Grey, 26 January 1858, cited in Argyll, *Autobiography and Memoirs*, II, p. 98. See also, Cornewall Lewis to Palmerston, 24 January 1858, Broadlands Mss. GC/LE, fol. 110.

12. Bethell to Clarendon, 29 January 1858, Clarendon Mss. C.82, fol. 244.

13. Ibid.

14. Herbert to Graham, 17 January 1858, Graham Mss. Bundle 133, cited in A. H. Gordon, *Sidney Herbert, Lord Herbert of Lea: A Memoir*, II, p. 105.

15. Grey Diary, 17 January 1858, Grey Mss. C3/20.

16. Grey Diary, 26 January 1858, Grey Mss. C3/20.

17. Greville Diary, 16 January 1858, Greville Mss. 41122, cited in Greville, *Memoirs*, VIII, p. 155.

18. Greville Diary, 28 January 1858, Greville Mss. 41122, cited in Greville, *Memoirs*, VIII, p. 159.

19. Greville Diary, 20 February 1858, Greville Mss. 41122, cited in Greville, *Memoirs*, VIII, p. 165.

20. Parkes to Ellice, 14 January 1858 Ellice Mss. 15042 fol. 102.

21. Parkes to Ellice, 30 January 1858, Ellice Mss. 15043, fol. 108. In such circumstances Palmerston's health was always of great concern. Granville noted that Palmerston was 'always asleep, both in the cabinet and in the House of Commons, where he endeavour[ed] to conceal it by wearing his hat over his eyes.' Greville Diary, 3 February 1858, Greville Mss. 41122, cited in Greville, *Memoirs*, VIII, p. 162.

22. Palmerston Diary, 9 December 1857, Broadlands Mss. D/17.

23. Clanricarde to Palmerston, 22 December 1857, Clanricarde Mss. 130/44.

24. Palmerston to Clanricarde, 24 December 1857, Clanricarde Mss. 130/44.

25. Clanricarde to Granville, 2 November 1857, Clanricarde Mss. 33. See also, Granville to Clanricarde, 4 November 1857, Clanricarde Mss. 33.

26. For all the letters and court transcripts of Hancock *vs.* Delacorn see Clanricarde Mss. 126 and 130.

27. Grey Diary, 4 February 1855, Grey Mss. C3/18A.

28. Herbert to Graham, 17 January 1858, Graham Mss. Bundle 133. Gordon, *Herbert*, II, p. 105 transcribes this passage as Lansdowne asking Palmerston if he was 'out of his mind'.

29. Granville to Canning, 9 January 1858, Granville Mss. PRO 30/29/

21/2, fol. 78. Fitzmaurice omitted all references to Clanricarde in his transcripts of Granville's correspondence of this period. See Lord Fitzmaurice, *The Life of Granville George Leveson-Gower, Second Earl Granville, K.G.* (London, 1905) I, pp. 286–7.

30. Granville to Canning, 24 January 1858, Granville Mss. PRO 30/29/ 21/2, fol. 80.

31. Granville to Canning, 1 February 1858, Granville Mss. PRO 30/29/ 21/2, fol. 83. The *Illustrated London News* observed that Clanricarde's appointment 'demonstrates the infinitesimal regard entertained by great persons for popular opinion'. It was also suggested that the appointment was an act of gratitude for Clanricarde's exertions in putting his eldest son, Lord Dunkellin, into the Commons as a supporter of the ministry. *Illustrated London News*, 2 January 1858, No. 896, Vol. XXXII p. 7.

32. Parkes to Ellice, 29 December 1857, Ellice Mss. 15042, fol. 97.

33. Grey Diary, 17 January 1858, Grey Mss. C3/20.

34. Greville Diary, 28 January 1858, Greville Mss. 41122, cited in Greville, *Memoirs*, VIII, p. 159.

35. Parkes to Ellice, 29 December 1857, Ellice Mss. 15042, fol. 97.

36. Disraeli to Lady Londonderry, 7 January 1858, cited in Marchioness of Londonderry (ed.) *Letters from Benjamin Disraeli to Francis Anne, Marchioness of Londonderry, 1837–61* (London, 1938).

37. Granville to Canning, 26 January 1858, Granville Mss. PRO 30/29/ 21/2, fol. 80, cited in Fitzmaurice, *Granville*, I, p. 287.

38. Parkes to Ellice, 16 January 1858, Ellice Mss. 15042, fol. 106.

39. Broughton Diary, 1 December 1857, Broughton Mss. 43761, fol. 27.

40. Broughton Diary, 22 December 1857, Broughton Mss. 43761, fol. 53.

41. Bedford to Russell, 20 October 1857, Russell Mss. PRO 30/22/13/D. It may have been in Bedford's mind that an annual allowance would enable Russell to accept a peerage from Palmerston. The immediate result, however, was to establish Russell's independence from Palmerston.

42. Comments on the Duke of Bedford's miserliness were legion. It was Clarendon's joke that the Duke was so mean that every time he came to see you he would ask for money to pay the cab. Sir H. Maxwell, *The Life and Letters of the Fourth Earl of Clarendon* (London, 1913) II, p. 194.

43. Russell to Graham, 13 December 1857, Graham Mss. Bundle 132, cited in C. S. Parker, *Life and Letters of Sir James Graham, Second Baronet of Netherby* (London, 1907) II, p. 324.

44. Ibid.

45. Graham to Russell 16 December 1857, Graham Mss. Bundle 132. Part of this letter is transcribed in Parker, *Graham*, II, pp. 324–5.

46. Ibid.

47. Ibid.

48. Graham to Aberdeen, 17 December 1857, Aberdeen Mss. 43192, fol. 156.

49. Ibid.

50. Aberdeen to Graham, 19 December 1857, Graham Mss. Bundle 132.

51. Russell to Graham, 21 December 1857, Graham Mss. Bundle 132, cited in Parker, *Graham*, II, p. 325.

52. Graham to Russell, 23 December 1857, Graham Mss. Bundle 132, cited in Parker, *Graham*, II, p. 326-7.

53. Graham to Aberdeen, 23 December 1857, Aberdeen Mss. 43192, fol. 156.

54. Russell to Graham, 25 December 1857, Graham Mss. Bundle 132, cited in Parker, *Graham*, II, p. 327.

55. Russell to Vernon Smith, 4 December 1857, cited in Lord J. Russell, *The Later Correspondence of Lord John Russell 1840–1878*, G. P. Gooch (ed.) (London, 1925) II, p. 223-4.

56. Graham to Aberdeen, 27 December 1857, Aberdeen Mss. 43192, fol. 160. See also, Aberdeen to Graham, 29 December 1857, Graham Mss. Bundle 132; and Aberdeen to Graham, 2 January 1858, Graham Mss. Bundle 133.

57. Greville Diary, 16 January 1858, Greville Mss. 41122, cited in Greville, *Memoirs*, VIII, p. 155-6.

58. Russell to Dean of Bristol, 8 January 1858, Russell Mss. PRO 30/22/13/E, fol. 148, cited in J. Prest, *Lord John Russell* (London, 1972) p. 380.

59. Ibid.

60. Graham to Aberdeen, 17 December 1857, Aberdeen Mss. 43192, fol. 156.

61. Graham to Cardwell, 12 January 1858, Cardwell Mss. PRO 30/48/8/47.

62. Graham to Aberdeen, 25 January, 1858, Aberdeen Mss. 43192, fol. 183. See also, Russell to Ellice 23 January 1858, Ellice Mss. 15052, fol. 201; and Graham to Ellice, 24 January 1858, Ellice Mss. 15019, fol. 11.

63. Aberdeen to Graham, 2 January 1858, Graham Mss. Bundle 133.

64. Aberdeen to Graham, 13 January 1858, Graham Mss. Bundle 133.

65. Graham to Aberdeen, 13 January 1858, Aberdeen Mss. 43192, fol. 170.

66. Graham to Russell, 13 January 1858, Graham Mss. Bundle 133. Russell himself wrote that 'Palmerston no doubt will be tenacious, but others will jump into a boat alongside to save themselves. They are not all seventy-three.' Russell to Graham, 12 January 1858, Graham Mss. Bundle 133, cited in Parker, *Graham*, II, p. 329.

67. Aberdeen to Graham, 15 January 1858, Graham Mss. Bundle 133.

68. Russell to Graham, 16 January 1858, Graham Mss. Bundle 133, cited in Parker, *Graham*, II, pp. 330-1.

69. Graham to Aberdeen, 4 February 1858, Aberdeen Mss. 43192, fol. 199. See also, Graham to Aberdeen, 17 January 1858, Aberdeen Mss. 43192, fol. 175; and Aberdeen to Graham, 27 January 1858, Graham Mss. Bundle 133.

70. Palmerston Diary, 17 January 1858, Broadlands Mss. D/18.

71. Aberdeen to Graham, 18 January 1858, Graham Mss. Bundle 133.

72. Ibid.
73. Graham to Aberdeen, 22 January 1858, Aberdeen Mss. 43192, fol. 178.
74. Parliamentary Papers, 1857–58, LX, p. 113. The best commentary on this affair is B. Porter, *The Refugee Question in Mid-Victorian Politics* (Cambridge, 1979) who discusses fully the legal and diplomatic aspects of the issue.
75. See Porter, *The Refugee Question*, pp. 170–8.
76. Bethell to Clarendon, 23 January 1858, Clarendon Mss. C-82, fol. 239–42.
77. Palmerston memo, 21 January 1858, Broadlands Mss. CAB/A/S. 89.
78. Palmerston memo, 'Political Refugees in Britain', n.d. (? 22 January 1858) Broadlands Mss. CAB/A, fol. 89–101.
79. The bill proposed to make conspiracy to murder a felony punishable with penal servitude, to apply to all persons involved in a conspiracy wherever the murder was to take place. In Ireland conspiracy to murder was already a felony, so the bill proposed the law be made uniform in this respect throughout the United Kingdom. Palmerston, 8 February 1858, *Hansard*, 3rd series, CXLVIII, 933–42.
80. Greville Diary, 3 February 1858, Greville Mss. 41122, cited in Greville, *Memoirs*, VIII, p. 162.
81. Bethell to Clarendon, 29 January 1858, Clarendon Mss. C. 82, fol. 244.
82. Palmerston to Clarendon, 21 January 1858, Clarendon Mss. C. 82, fol. 64. See also, Greville Diary, 3 February 1858, Greville Mss. 41122, cited in Greville, *Memoirs*, VIII, p. 162.
83. Jolliffe to Disraeli, 29 December 1857, Hughenden Mss. B/XX/J/49.
84. Derby to Disraeli, 2 January 1858, Hughenden Mss. B/XX/S/158.
85. Greville Diary, 23 January 1858, Greville Mss. 41122, cited in Greville, *Memoirs*, VIII, p. 158. See also, Taylor to Jolliffe, 25 January 1858, Hylton Mss. DD/HY 24.
86. Clarendon to Palmerston, 30 January 1858, Broadlands Mss. GC/CL 1146. See also, Porter, *Refugee Question*, p. 176.
87. Clarendon to Cowley, 19 January 1858, Clarendon Mss. C. 139, fol. 601.
88. Clarendon to Palmerston, 30 January 1858, Broadlands Mss. GC/CL 1146.
89. G. Grey to Clarendon, 31 January 1858, Clarendon Mss. C-82, fol. 194.
90. G. Grey to Clarendon, 1 February 1858, Clarendon Mss. C-82, fol. 154. 'The success of the bill on the continent depended upon its being thought more than it was; its success in England depended upon its being thought less than it was.' Porter, *Refugee Question*, p. 177.
91. Lennox to Disraeli, 1 February 1858, Hughenden Mss. B/XX/LX/104.
92. G. Grey to Russell, 2 February 1858, Russell Mss. PRO 30/22/13/E, fol. 212.
93. Russell to G. Grey, 2 February 1858, Russell Mss. PRO 30/22/13/E, fol. 216.
94. Graham to Russell, 4 February 1858, Graham Mss. Bundle 133, cited

in Parker, *Graham*, II, p. 336. See also, Russell to Graham, 2 February 1858, Graham Mss. Bundle 133.

95. Palmerston to Clarendon, 4 February 1858, Clarendon Mss. C-82, fol. 76.
96. Palmerston to Clarendon, 9 February 1858, Clarendon Mss. C-82, fol. 82.
97. *Morning Chronicle*, 22 February 1858, p. 4, cited in Porter, *Refugee Question*, p. 185.
98. Abercromby to Melgund, 8 February 1858, Minto Mss. 12252.
99. Greville Diary, 11 February 1858, Greville Mss. 41122, cited in Greville, *Memoirs* VIII, p. 162-3.
100. Roebuck, 5 February 1858, *Hansard*, 3rd series, CXLVIII, 762-6.
101. Broughton Diary, 7 February 1858, Broughton Mss. 43761, fol. 39.
102. Russell to Graham, 6 February 1858, Graham Mss. Bundle 133. See also, Graham to Aberdeen, 7 February 1858, Aberdeen Mss. 43192, fol. 201.
103. Palmerston memo, n.d. (? 22 January 1858) Broadlands Mss. CAB/A, fol. 89-101.
104. Palmerston, 8 February 1858, *Hansard*, 3rd series, CXLVIII, 933-42.
105. Kinglake, 8 February 1858, *Hansard*, 3rd series, CXLVIII, 933-42.
106. Horsman, 8 February 1858, *Hansard*, 3rd series, CXLVIII, 941.
107. Bruce, to his wife, 9 February 1858, cited in H. A. Bruce, *Letters of the Rt. Hon. H. A. Bruce, Lord Aberdare of Duffryn*, 2 vols (London, 1902) I, p. 150.
108. Elcho, 8 February 1858, *Hansard*, 3rd series, CXLVIII, 955-7.
109. Roebuck, 8 February 1858, *Hansard*, 3rd series, CXLVIII, 957-64.
110. Derby to Warren, 12 February 1858, Derby Mss. 183/1, fol. 31.
111. Russell, 9 February 1858, *Hansard*, 3rd series, CXLVIII, 1035-49. Lady Russell could not remember Russell being more moved, more mortified, more indignant, than he was at the prospect of the 'conspiracy to murder bill'. Russell was 'resolved to oppose to the utmost of his power what he consider[ed] as only the first step in a series of unworthy concessions'. Lady Russell to Lady Abercromby, 4 February 1858, cited in D. McCarthy and A. Russell (eds) *Lady John Russell: A Memoir with Selections from her Diaries and Correspondence* (London, 1910) p. 173.
112. Graham to Gladstone, 9 February 1858, Gladstone Mss. 44164, fol. 158, cited in Parker, *Graham*, II, pp. 337-8.
113. Graham to Aberdeen, 10 February 1858, Aberdeen Mss. 43192, fol. 203.
114. Gathorne Hardy Diary, 10 February 1858, Cranbrook Mss. T501/291, fol. 108. See also, Disraeli, 9 February 1858, *Hansard*, 3rd series, CXLVIII, 1053-63.
115. Based upon the division lists in *Hansard* and *The Times*, and using the designations in C. R. Dod, *Parliamentary Companion, 1857*, I calculate the pattern of party voting in the division as follows. For the bill: 177 Whigs, Liberals and Radicals; 115 Conservatives; 4 Peelites and 3 Irish Brigade. Against the bill: 81 Whigs, Liberals and Radicals; 18 Conservatives. Watt calculates a cohesion index for the division

showing the extent to which MPs of the same party voted together; the higher the percentage figure, the greater the degree of unity: Radicals 23%, Liberals 42%, Whigs 14%, Liberal Conservatives 73%, and Conservatives 68%. R. G. Watt, 'Parties and Politics in Mid-Victorian Britain, 1857–1859: A Study in Quantification', unpublished PhD thesis, University of Minnesota, 1975, pp. 289–308. In opposing the first reading of the conspiracy bill Aberdeen believed that Russell had been 'carried away by zealous friends'. Aberdeen to Graham, 10 February 1858, Graham Mss. Bundle 133.

116. Lyndhurst, 8 February 1858, *Hansard*, 3rd series, CXLVIII, 807–8.
117. Dallas to Cass, 9 February 1858 cited in G. M. Dallas, *Letters from London, 1856–1860*, (London, 1870) I, p. 258.
118. Vernon Smith, 5 February 1858, *Hansard*, 3rd series, CXLVIII, 780–4.
119. Cornewall Lewis, 5 February 1858, *Hansard*, 3rd series, CXLVIII, 787–91.
120. Panmure, 8 February 1858, *Hansard*, 3rd series, CXLVIII, 810–827; and Palmerston, 8 February 1858, *Hansard*, 3rd series, CXLVIII, 868–71.
121. Lord Malmesbury, *Memoirs of an Ex-Minister* (London, 1885) 12 February 1858, p. 416.
122. Grey, 11 February 1858, *Hansard*, 3rd series, CXLVIII, 1121–37.
123. Baring, 9 February 1858, *Hansard*, 3rd series, CXLVIII, 970–5.
124. Palmerston, 12 February 1858, *Hansard*, 3rd series, CXLVIII, 1276–93. The bill proposed to replace the Court of Directors and Court of Proprietors with a President and a council with a Secretary capable of sitting in parliament. The President would be a cabinet member. The council would be made up of eight members nominated for eight years. The decision of the President would be final in all matters brought before the council. Patronage and local appointments would remain unaltered, except that members of the council would be nominated by the Governor-General rather than the home government.
125. Baring, 12 February 1858, *Hansard*, 3rd series, CXLVIII, 1293–1304.
126. Monckton Milnes, 12 February 1858, *Hansard*, 3rd series, CXLVIII, 1308–16; and Vansittart, 12 February 1858, *Hansard*, 3rd series, CXLVIII, 1316–19.
127. Elphinstone, 12 February 1858, *Hansard*, 3rd series, CXLVIII, 1329–30; and Mangles, 12 February 1858, *Hansard*, 3rd series, CXLVIII, 1353–9.
128. Cornewall Lewis, 12 February 1858, *Hansard*, 3rd series, CXLVIII, 1330–53.
129. Roebuck, 15 February 1858, *Hansard*, 3rd series, CXLVIII, 1373–81.
130. Graham to Gladstone, 13 February 1858, Gladstone Mss. 44164, fol. 160.
131. Knatchbull-Hugessen Diary, 16 February 1858, Brabourne Mss. F.19. See also Bulwer Lytton, 18 February 1858, *Hansard*, 3rd series, CXLVIII, 1696–1709.
132. Russell, 18 February 1858, *Hansard*, 3rd series, CXLVIII, 1687–96.
133. Minto to Melgund, 17 February 1858, Minto Mss. 12241.

134. Based upon *Dod's Parliamentary Companion*, I calculate that 283 Whigs, Liberals and Radicals, 27 Conservatives, 2 Peelites and 7 Irish Brigade supported the bill; 132 Conservatives, 37 Whigs, Liberals and Radicals and 4 Peelites opposed it. Watt calculates the following indices of cohesion: Radicals 43%, Liberals 79%, Whigs 100%, Liberal Conservatives 5%, and Conservatives 58%.
135. Palmerston Diary, 18 February 1858, Broadlands Mss. D/18.
136. Palmerston, 19 February 1858, *Hansard*, 3rd series, CXLVIII, 1741–5.
137. Palmerston to the Queen, 19 February 1858, *QVL*, 1st series, III, p. 336.
138. Broughton Diary, 21 February 1858, Broughton Mss. 43761, fol. 41; and Milner Gibson, 19 February 1858, *Hansard*, 3rd series, CXLVIII, 1745–58.
139. Grey Diary, 20 February 1858, Grey Mss. C3/20.
140. Ibid.
141. Knatchbull-Hugessen Diary, 19 February 1858, Brabourne Mss. F. 29.
142. Derby to Clarendon (copy), 20 February 1858, Derby Mss. 184/1, fol. 37.
143. Ibid.
144. Granville to Canning, 24 February 1858, Granville Mss. 30/29/21/2, fol. 93. Palmerston reported the same sequence of events, see Palmerston Diary, 19 February 1858, Broadlands Mss. D/18.
145. Palmerston to the Queen, 19 February 1858, cited in *QVL*, 1st series, III, p. 337.
146. Knatchbull-Hugessen Diary, 19 February 1858, Brabourne Mss. F. 29. Lord Palmerston, Malmesbury noted, 'made a very intemperate speech and actually shook his fist at the Manchester clique'. Malmesbury, *Memoirs*, 20 February 1838, p. 417.
147. Broughton Diary, 21 February 1858, Broughton Mss. 43761, fol. 41. See also, Palmerston, 19 February 1858, *Hansard*, 3rd series, CXLVIII, 1837–44; and W. White, *The Inner Life of the House of Commons* (London, 1897) I, p. 46.
148. Greville Diary, 20 February 1858, Greville Mss. 41122, cited in Greville, *Memoirs*, VIII, p. 167.
149. Grey Diary, 20 February 1858, Grey Mss. C3/20.
150. Russell to Dean of Bristol, 19 February 1858, Russell Mss. PRO 30/22/13/E, fol. 232.
151. 'Lord Clanricarde's presence in the House of Commons during the debate, and in a conspicuous place, enraged many supporters of Lord Palmerston', Prince Albert memo, 21 February 1858, cited in *QVL*, 1st series, III, p. 331.
152. Knatchbull-Hugessen calculated the number as 93. Knatchbull-Hugessen Diary, 19 February 1858, Brabourne Mss. F. 29. Lord Broughton estimated the number at 'about 80'. Broughton Diary, 21 February 1858, Broughton Mss. 43761, fol. 41.
153. Based upon *Hansard*, *The Times* and C. R. Dod, *Parliamentary Companion*, I calculate the following voting pattern. Supporting Milner Gibson's motion: 140 Conservatives, 89 Whigs, Liberals and Radicals,

4 Peelites and 1 Irish Brigade. Opposing the motion: 195 Whigs, Liberals and Radicals, 18 Conservatives, 2 Irish Brigade. Watt calculates the following cohesion indices; Radicals 23%, Liberals 39%, Whigs 14%, Liberal Conservatives 18%, and Conservatives 66%, Watt, 'Parties and Politics', pp. 289–308.

154. Derby to Clarendon, 20 February 1858, Derby Mss. 184/1, fol. 37.
155. Grey Diary, 20 February 1858, Grey Mss. C3/20.
156. White, *The Inner Life of the House of Commons*, I, p. 43.
157. Malmesbury, *Memoirs*, 20 February 1858, p. 417.
158. Bright to Cobden, 20 February 1858, Cobden Mss. 43384, fol. 119.
159. Ibid.
160. Grey Diary, 20 February 1858, Grey Mss. C3/20.
161. Palmerston Diary, 20 February 1858, Broadlands Mss. D/18.
162. Lady Palmerston to Palmerston, 21 February 1858, cited in Countess of Airlie, *Lady Palmerston and Her Times*, 2 vols (London, 1922) II, p. 169–70. In brackets Lady Palmerston added: 'I am very glad that you have had no time to bring in a Reform Bill.'
163. Prince Albert memo, 21 February 1858, cited in *QVL*, 1st series, III, p. 337.
164. Palmerston Diary, 20 February 1858, Broadlands Mss. D/18.
165. Ibid.
166. Derby to Disraeli, 20 February 1858, Hughenden Mss. B/XX/S/158, cited in W. F. Monypenny and G. E. Buckle, *The Life of Benjamin Disraeli, Earl of Beaconsfield*, (London, 1910–20) IV, p. 114.
167. Prince Albert memo, 21 February 1858, cited in *QVL*, 1st series, III, p. 338.
168. Ibid.
169. Derby to Disraeli, 20 February 1858, Hughenden Mss. B/XX/S/158, cited in Monypenny and Buckle, *Disraeli*, IV, p. 114.
170. Prince Albert memo, 21 February 1858, cited in *QVL*, 1st series, III, p. 339. Southgate comments that Derby's statement was clearly an *argumentum ad feminam*. D. Southgate, *'The Most English Minister...': The Policies and Politics of Palmerston* (London, 1966) p. 602.
171. Derby to Disraeli, 20 February 1858, Hughenden Mss. B/XX/S/158, cited in Monypenny and Buckle, *Disraeli*, IV, p. 114.
172. Bright to his wife, 20 February 1858, Ogden Mss. 65.
173. Bright to Cobden, 20 February 1858, Bright Mss. 43384, fol. 119.
174. Ibid.
175. Goderich to Forster, 20 February 1858, Ripon Mss. 43536, fol. 121.
176. Newcastle to Aberdeen, 21 February 1858, cited in Bruce, *Aberdare*, I, p. 150.
177. Queen to Derby, 21 February 1858, *QVL*, 1st series, III, p. 340.
178. Derby to Disraeli, 21 February 1858, Hughenden Mss. B/XX/S/159, cited in Monypenny and Buckle, *Disraeli*, IV, p. 115.
179. Derby to the Queen, 21 February 1858, *QVL*, 1st series, III, p. 340.
180. Derby to Newcastle, 21 February 1858, Newcastle Mss. NeC12530.
181. Derby to Gladstone, 21 February 1858, Gladstone Mss. 44140, fol. 232 cited in J. Morley, *The Life of William Ewart Gladstone* (London, 1903) I, p. 577.

182. Graham to Aberdeen, 21 February 1858, Aberdeen Mss. 43192 fol. 205.

183. Gladstone to Derby, 21 February 1858, Gladstone Mss. 44140, fol. 236, cited in Morley, *Gladstone*, I, pp. 577–8.

184. Ibid.

185. Galway to Jolliffe, n.d. (? 24 February 1858) Hylton Mss. DD/HY 24/B, fol. 47.

186. See the draft copy of this letter, Gladstone to Derby, 21 February 1858, Gladstone Mss. 44140, fol. 236.

187. Gladstone to Derby, 21 February 1858, Gladstone Mss. 44140, fol. 236, cited in Morley, *Gladstone*, I, p. 578.

188. Bright to Gladstone, 21 February 1858, cited in Morley, *Gladstone*, I, pp. 578–80.

189. Stanley Diary, 27 March 1854, Stanley Mss. 920 DER (15) 43/3, cited in J. Vincent (ed.) *Disraeli, Derby and the Conservative Party* (Hassocks, 1978) p. 123.

190. Gladstone to Bright, 22 February 1858, cited in Morley, *Gladstone*, I, p. 580.

191. Malmesbury, *Memoirs*, 2 March 1858, p. 419. Three months later Grey 'was amazed by the bitterness with which Mrs. Gladstone spoke of Palmerston and her horror of his being again prime-minister. It is very obvious that if Derby had thrown over Dizzy ... Gladstone would have been too happy to join him and probably Sidney Herbert and Cardwell would have done the same.' Grey Diary, 15 May 1858, Grey Mss. C3/21.

192. Grey Diary, 22 February 1858, Grey Mss. C3/20.

193. This was a saying attributed to Lady Clanricarde. Graham to Aberdeen, 31 March 1858, cited in Parker, *Graham*, II, p. 340.

194. Newcastle to Derby, 21 February 1858, Newcastle Mss. NeC 12531. See also, Newcastle to Hayward, 21 February 1858, cited in H. E. Carlisle (ed.) *Selections from the Correspondence of Abraham Hayward* (London, 1886) II, p. 3.

195. Broughton Diary, 6 March 1858, Broughton Mss. 43761, fol. 46.

196. Grey Diary, 21 February 1858, Grey Mss. C3/20.

197. Ibid.

198. Grey to Derby, 21 February 1959, cited in *QVL*, 1st series, III, p. 342.

199. Grey Diary, 21 February 1858, Grey Mss. C3/20.

200. Derby to the Queen, 21 February 1858, cited in *QVL*, 1st series, III, p. 342.

201. Derby to Northumberland, 22 February 1858, Derby Mss. 184/1. See also, Prince Albert memo, 22 February 1858, *QVL*, 1st series, III, p. 339.

202. Stanley Diary, 21 February 1858, Stanley Mss. 920 DER (15) 46/1, cited in Vincent (ed.) *Disraeli, Derby and the Conservative Party*, p. 155–6. See also, Derby to Disraeli, 21 February 1858, Hughenden Mss. B/XX/S/160, cited in Monypenny and Buckle, *Disraeli*, IV, p. 117.

203. Disraeli to Derby, 22 February 1858, Derby Mss. 145/3, cited in Monypenny and Buckle, *Disraeli*, IV, p. 117–18.

204. Knatchbull-Hugessen Diary, 12 March 1858, Brabourne Mss. F. 29.

205. This was a popular appointment amongst members of the Bar. Thesiger entered the law after his father lost the family fortune following a volcanic eruption on the island of St Vincent. Thesiger defended O'Connell in his election for the City of Dublin before a committee of the House of Commons in 1835; became member for Woodstock in 1840; formerly Attorney General, 1845–6 and 1852. He had a reputation for dignity, acuteness, energy and accuracy.

206. Walpole to Derby, 23 February 1858, Derby Mss. 153/2.

207. Derby to Disraeli, 25 February 1858, Hughenden Mss. B/XX/S/161, cited in Monypenny and Buckle, *Disraeli*, IV, p. 118.

208. Disraeli to Derby, 25 February 1858, Derby Mss. 145/3, cited in Monypenny and Buckle, *Disraeli*, IV, p. 118.

209. Carnarvon Memo. n.d. (? February 1858), cited in Sir A. Hardinge, *Life of H. E. M. Herbert, Fourth Earl of Carnarvon, 1831–1890* (London, 1925) I, p. 119.

210. Disraeli to Derby, 25 February 1858, Derby Mss. 145/3, cited in Monpenny and Buckle, *Disraeli*, IV, p. 118.

211. Derby to the Queen, 25 February 1858, *QVL*, 1st series, III, p. 344.

212. Malmesbury, *Memoirs*, 26 February 1858, II, p. 98.

213. Newdegate to his mother, 24 February 1858, Newdegate Mss. B. 3276.

214. Disraeli to Jolliffe, n.d. (? 23 February 1858) Hylton Mss. DD/HY 24/13, fol. 30.

215. Dundas to Jolliffe, 2 March 1858, Hylton Mss. DD/HY 18/2.

216. Sotheron-Estcourt Diary, 24 February 1858, Sotheron-Estcourt Mss. F. 408. Born in 1801, he assumed the name of Sotheron on the death of his father-in-law in 1839, and in 1855, by Royal Licence, resumed the name Estcourt. Educated at Oriel College, Oxford, he received an honorary DCL in 1857; Magistrate and Deputy-Lieutenant of Wilts. He first entered the Commons in 1829. The family held considerable estates in Gloucestershire and Wiltshire.

217. Gathorne Hardy Diary, 25 February 1858, Cranbrook Mss. T501/291, fol. 114. He was born in 1814 and educated at Oriel College, Oxford; called to the Bar at Inner Temple in 1840, but ceased to practice; elected MP for Leominster in February 1856.

218. See *The Times*, 22 February 1858, and *The Times*, 23 February 1858.

219. Disraeli to Delane, 22 February 1858, Delane Mss. 9/34. See also, R. Blake, *Disraeli* (London, 1966) pp. 380–1.

220. See *The Times*, 23 and 24 February 1858.

221. Disraeli to Delane, 25 February 1858, Delane Mss. 9/34.

222. *The Times*, 26 February 1858.

223. Malmesbury, *Memoirs*, II, p. 107.

224. Newcastle to Canning, 26 February 1858, Canning Mss. 4.

225. Granville to Delane, 23 February 1858, Delane Mss. 9/32. See also, Lowe to Delane, 23 February 1858, Delane Mss. 9/32.

226. Granville to Canning, 24 February 1858, Canning Mss. 3, cited in Fitzmaurice, *Granville*, I, p. 293.

227. Grey Diary, 24 February 1858, Grey Mss. C3/20.

228. Grey Diary, 28 February 1858, Grey Mss. C3/20.

229. Clarendon to Howard, 26 February 1858, Clarendon Mss. C. 541.
230. Ellice Jnr. memo, 23 April 1858, Ellice Mss. 15052, fol. 205.
231. Russell to Dean of Bristol, 23 February 1858, Russell Mss. PRO 30/33/13/E, fol. 234.
232. Russell to Dean of Bristol, 26 February 1858, Russell Mss. PRO 30/22/13/E, fol. 238. See also Broughton Diary, 9 March 1858, Broughton Mss. 43761, fol. 47.
233. Minto to Melgund, 24 February 1858, Minto Mss. 12241.
234. Minto to Melgund, 25 February 1858, Minto Mss. 12241.
235. Russell to Graham, 28 February 1858, Graham Mss. Bundle 133.
236. Graham to Russell, 2 March 1858, Russell Mss. PRO 30/22/13/E, fol. 268.
237. Graham to Ellice, 25 February 1858, Ellice Mss. 15014, fol. 17.
238. Gladstone to Northcote, 17 March 1858, Iddesleigh Mss. 50014.
239. White, *Inner Life of the House of Commons*, I, p. 49.
240. Ibid., p. 47.
241. Granville to Canning, 10 March 1858, Granville Mss. PRO 30/29/21/2, fol. 101, cited in Fitzmaurice, *Granville*, I, p. 295.
242. White, *Inner Life of the House of Commons*, I, p. 47.
243. *Illustrated London News*, 6 March 1858, No. 906, Vol. XXXII, p. 243.
244. White, *Inner Life of the House of Commons*, I, p. 47.
245. Granville to Canning, 10 March 1858, Granville Mss. PRO 30/29/21/2, fol. 101, cited in Fitzmaurice, *Granville*, I, p. 295.

CHAPTER 6

1. Count Vitzhum, *St. Petersburg and London in the Years 1852 to 1865* (London, 1887) I, p. 235. The 'Palmerstonians' looked 'upon the office as their birthright, and upon those who deprive them of it as brigands who have robbed them of their property'. Lord Malmesbury, *Memoirs of an Ex-Minister* (London, 1885) II, p. 103.
2. Greville Diary, 10 March 1858, Greville Mss. 41122, cited in C. C. F. Greville, *The Greville Memoirs*, H. Reeve (ed.) (London, 1888) VII, p. 179.
3. Derby, 1 March 1858, *Hansard*, 3rd series, CXLIX, 41.
4. Dallas to Cass, 5 March 1858, cited in G. M. Dallas, *Letters from London, 1856–1860* (London, 1870) I, p. 262.
5. Grey Diary, 1 March 1858, Grey Mss. C3/20.
6. Derby, 1 March 1858, *Hansard*, 3rd series, CXLIV, 22–44.
7. Goderich to Bruce, 2 March 1858, Ripon Mss. 43534.
8. Palmerston Diary, 1 March 1858, Broadlands Mss. D/18.
9. Cairns at Belfast, *The Times*, 8 March 1858, p. 4.
10. Pakington at Droitwich, *The Times*, 4 March 1858.
11. Sotheron-Estcourt in North Wilts, *The Times*, 6 March 1858.
12. Stanley at Kings Lynn, *The Times*, 5 March 1858, p. 8.
13. Disraeli at Aylesbury, *The Times*, 9 March 1858, p. 7.
14. Bernal Osborne, 15 March 1858, *Hansard*, 3rd series, CXLIX, 181–92.

15. Broughton Diary, 18 March 1858, Broughton Mss. 43761, fol. 54. Although the attack was a personal initiative on Osborne's part Palmerston had indicated beforehand that he would not object to such an attack being made. Broughton Diary, 13 March 1858, Broughton Mss. 43761, fol. 50.

16. Disraeli, 15 March 1858, *Hansard*, 3rd series, CXLIX, 198.

17. Wemyss, *Memories* (privately printed in 1912). A copy forms part of the Wemyss Mss, 2 vols, I, p. 369.

18. Horsman, 15 March 1858, *Hansard*, 3rd series, CXLIX, 204–12.

19. Ibid.

20. Greville Diary, 10 March 1858, Greville Mss. 41122, cited in Greville, *Memoirs*, VIII, p. 178–9.

21. Greville noted: 'I gather from what I hear that Lord Palmerston is preparing to buckle on his armour, and to wage war against the new Government with the hope and expectation of forcing himself back into office speedily, and that the new Opposition mean to attack the new Government as quickly and as vehemently as they can. John Russell says they "ought not to be recklessly or prematurely opposed".' Greville Diary, 6 March 1858, Greville Mss. 41122, cited in Greville, *Memoirs*, VIII, p. 177.

22. Horsman, 15 March 1858, *Hansard*, 3rd series, CXLIX, 204–12.

23. Palmerston to Panmure, 16 March 1858, Dalhousie Mss. GD 45/14/660.

24. Russell, 15 March 1858, *Hansard*, 3rd series, CXLIX, 212–18.

25. Palmerston, 15 March 1858, *Hansard*, 3rd series, CXLIX, 218–22.

26. Greville Diary, 17 March 1858, Greville Mss. 41122, cited in Greville, *Memoirs*, VIII, p. 181.

27. Greville Diary, 11 March 1858, Greville Mss. 41122, cited in Greville, *Memoirs*, VIII, p. 179.

28. Bruce to his wife, 23 February 1858, cited in H. A. Bruce, *Letters of the Rt. Hon. H. A. Bruce, Lord Aberdare of Duffryn* (Oxford, 1902) I, p. 150.

29. Greville faithfully recorded the anxiety felt by some. 'The Whigs are in great perplexity. Some talk of Palmerston coming back again, others want to bring about a reunion between him and Lord John, and others still talk of setting them both aside and electing a new leader of the party.' Greville Diary, 2 March 1858, Greville Mss. 41122, cited in Greville, *Memoirs*, VIII, p. 176.

30. Bright to Cowen, 1 March 1858, cited in H. J. Leech (ed.) *The Public Letters of the Rt. Hon. John Bright* (London, 1885) p. 60.

31. Cobden to Parkes, 11 December 1856, Cobden Mss. 43664, fol. 63, cited in J. Morley, *The Life of Richard Cobden*, 1 vol. (London, 1903) p. 650.

32. Malmesbury, *Memoirs*, II, p. 104. On receiving news of the French answer Disraeli rushed in to see Derby 'in a state of great excitement'. Disraeli's 'delight was indescribably and amazingly demonstrative considering the usual phlegmatic manner in which he receives news of all kinds'.

33. Disraeli to the Queen, 22 March 1858, cited in *QVL*, 1st series, III,

p. 349. The previous week, anxiety about diplomatic relations with France and the *Caligari* affair had unsettled political feeling in the Commons. The *Caligari* had been 'a Sardinian ship freighted and manned by the Carbonari, and intended to land a party in Calabria to stir up that part of Italy'. The ship had been seized and some English engineers on board found themselves in Neopolitan prisons. See Malmesbury, *Memoirs*, II, p. 105, and Disraeli to the Queen, 12 March 1858, cited in *QVL*, 1st series, III, p. 348.

34. Broughton Diary, 18 March 1858, Broughton Mss. 43761, fol. 54.

35. Greville Diary, 3 March 1858, Greville Mss. 41122, cited in Greville, *Memoirs*, VIII, p. 177. The diplomatic resolution of the Caligari affair enhanced the government's standing. On 16 April they announced that £3000 compensation would be paid as well as Watt and Park released. Disraeli's announcement of the completion of this arrangement, on 11 June, was 'received with enthusiastic cheers. The ex-Ministers and their adherents were completely taken by surprise, and would not even pretend to be pleased that a quarrel which at one moment threatened a general war should have terminated in a manner so satisfactory.' Malmesbury, *Memoirs*, II, p. 123.

36. Dallas to Cass, 26 March 1858, cited in Dallas, *Letters from London*, II, p. 7.

37. Butt to Hamilton, 23 March 1858, Hughenden Mss. B/XX/H/70. From the same letter Disraeli also learnt that 'Roebuck is not anxious that Lord Palmerston should have an opportunity of doing mischief ... It is [Roebuck's] resolve to put his foot on any movement for patching up, for the purpose of mischief, the [India bill] of Lord P.'

38. 'I have no doubt you will act upon the principle of considering the politics of a man's family as of no account whatever in the making of appointments.' Ellenborough to Pakington, 25 March 1858, Ellenborough Mss. PRO 30/12/9, fol. 1607.

39. Carnarvon memo, n.d. (? March 1858) cited in Sir A. Hardinge *Life of H. E. M. Herbert, Fourth Earl of Carnarvon, 1831–1890* (London, 1925) I, p. 115. See also Ellenborough to Derby, 29 March 1858, Ellenborough Mss. PRO 30/12/9, fol. 1891.

40. Palmerston's India bill became referred to as India bill No. 1.

41. Disraeli, 26 March 1858, *Hansard*, 3rd series, CXLIX, 818–33.

42. Roebuck, 26 March 1858, *Hansard*, 3rd series, CXLIX, 842–3. See also, Derby to Ellenborough, 25 March 1858, Ellenborough Mss. PRO 30/12/9, fol. 1640.

43. Bright, 26 March 1858, *Hansard*, 3rd series, CXLIX, 843–5.

44. Bright to Cobden, 31 March 1858, Bright Mss. 43384, fol. 121.

45. Greville Diary, 30 March 1858, Greville Mss. 41123, cited in Greville, *Memoirs*, VIII, p. 185. See also, Argyll to Granville, 25 March 1858, cited in Duke of Argyll, *George Douglas, 8th Duke of Argyll: Autobiography and Memoirs* (London, 1906) II, p. 111.

46. Broughton Diary, 27 March 1858, Broughton Mss. 43761, fol. 57.

47. Forster to Goderich, 7 April 1858, Ripon 43536, fol. 128.

48. Gathorne Hardy Diary, 28 March 1858, Cranbrook Mss. T501/291, fol. 123.

49. Greville Diary, 21 March 1858, Greville Mss. 41123, cited in Greville, *Memoirs*, VIII, pp. 183–4.

50. Greville Diary, 25 March 1858, Greville Mss. 41123, cited in Greville, *Memoirs*, VIII, p. 184.

51. Russell to Aberdeen, 29 March 1858, Aberdeen Mss. 43068, fol. 289.

52. Broughton Diary, 9 March 1858, Broughton Mss. 43761, fol. 47.

53. Aberdeen to Russell, 30 March 1858, Aberdeen Mss. 43068, fol. 291.

54. Graham to Aberdeen, 31 March 1858, Aberdeen Mss. 43192, fol. 207, cited in C. S. Parker, *Life and Letters of Sir James Graham, Second Baronet of Netherby* (London, 1907) II, p. 340.

55. Newcastle to Hayward, 3 April 1858, Newcastle Mss. NeC 12,372.

56. Ibid. 'The "Great Minister", who but yesterday rode on the topmost crest of the waves of popularity, is sunk so low that there is hardly a man of his former friends to say, "God save him". Nor do men think of him in their speculations as to the future. That further changes are ahead everyone believes, but nobody seems to imagine that Lord Palmerston can be reinstated.' W. White, *Inner Life of the House of Commons* (London, 1897) I, p. 50. See also, H. C. F. Bell, *Lord Palmerston* (London, 1936) II, p. 184.

57. Russell to Aberdeen, 1 April 1858, Aberdeen Mss. 43068, fol. 293.

58. Fortescue Diary, 29 March 1858, Carlingford Mss. DD/SH 358.

59. Greville Diary, 30 March 1858, Greville Mss. 41123, cited in Greville, *Memoirs*, VIII, p. 186.

60. Palmerston Diary, 30 March 1858, Broadlands Mss. D/18. Palmerston's diary seems to misdate the meeting as all other sources show the meeting to have been held on 29 March.

61. Granville to Stanley of Alderley, 31 March 1858, Granville Mss. PRO 30/39/19/12, fol. 13.

62. Palmerston Diary, 30 March 1858, Broadlands Mss. D/18. Granville subsequently expressed his caution to Canning. 'I am sure our danger is being too impatient. Pam has no time to wait. The opinion which in this case is almost as serious as the fact, is rapidly growing that he is no longer the same man. Johnny is impatient by nature. The Peelites have been wittily described as perpetually offering themselves for sale, and always buying themselves in. The Radicals are disunited among themselves. Their only able man, Bright, is incapable of real work.' Granville to Canning, 1 April 1858, cited in Lord E. Fitzmaurice, *The Life of Granville George Leveson-Gower, Second Earl Granville, K.G.* (London, 1905) I, p. 300.

63. Granville to Byng, 29 March 1858, Granville Mss PRO 30/29/19/23, fol. 9.

64. Greville Diary, 2 April 1858, Greville Mss. 41123, cited by Greville, *Memoirs*, VIII, p. 187.

65. Granville to Stanley of Alderley, 31 March 1858, Granville Mss. PRO 30/29/19/23, fol. 13.

66. Granville to Byng, 29 March 1858, Granville Mss. PRO 30/29/19/23, fol. 9.

67. Clarendon to Palmerston, 31 March 1858, Broadlands Mss. GC/CL 1161.

68. Stanley of Alderley to Granville, 1 April 1858, Granville Mss. PRO 30/29/19/23.

69. Russell to Dean of Bristol, 2 April 1858, Russell Mss. PRO 30/22/13/F, fol. 5.

70. Cornewall Lewis to Granville, 31 March 1858, Granville Mss. PRO 30/29/19/23, fol. 33.

71. Palmerston Diary, 31 March 1858, Broadlands Mss. D/18.

72. Earle to Disraeli, 28 March 1858, Hughenden Mss. B/XX/E/34A. For a discussion of Earle, and some of his dubious activity, see R. Blake, *Disraeli* (London, 1966) pp. 370–4.

73. Ibid.

74. Ellenborough to Derby, 29 March 1858, Ellenborough Mss. PRO 30/12/19, fol. 1891.

75. During 1858 Bulwer Lytton earnt the gratitude of Ernest Jones by loaning him £5!

76. Bulwer Lytton to Derby, 30 March 1858, Hughenden Mss. B/XX/S/166A.

77. Bright to Cobden, 31 March 1858, Bright Mss. 43384, fol. 121.

78. Smith to Bright, 31 March 1858, Bright Mss. 43388, fol. 179.

79. Smith to Bright, 1 April 1858, Bright Mss. 43388, fol. 181.

80. Bulwer Lytton to Derby, 1 April 1858, Hughenden Mss. B/XX/S/169A.

81. Milner Gibson to Russell, 3 April 1858, Russell Mss. PRO 30/22/13/F, fol. 13.

82. Milner Gibson to Bright, 1 April 1858, Bright Mss. 43388, fol. 75.

83. Milner Gibson to Bright, 4 April 1858, Bright Mss. 43388, fol. 77.

84. Disraeli to Derby, n.d. (? 2 April 1858) Derby Mss. 145/5, cited by W. F. Monypenny and G. E. Buckle, *The Life of Benjamin Disraeli, Earl of Beaconsfield* (London, 1910–20) IV, pp. 129–30.

85. Derby at the Mansion House, 6 April, 1858, cited in *The Times*, 7 April 1858.

86. Ellenborough to Derby, 29 March 1858, Ellenborough Mss. PRO 30/12/9, fol. 1891.

87. Clarendon to Palmerston, 9 April 1858, Broadlands Mss. GC/CL 1162. 'Derby made a striking speech at the Mansion House . . . The inference deducible from his speech (and in which I have since been confirmed) is that, happen what may, he does not mean to resign, and that the Government will not go out, unless they are positively turned out.' Greville Diary, 8 April 1858, Greville Mss. 41123, cited in Greville, *Memoirs*, VIII, p. 188. See also, Grey Diary, 7 April 1858, Grey Mss. C3/21.

88. Russell to Cornewall Lewis, 5 April 1858, Broadlands Mss. GC/LE 111.

89. Ibid. See also, Grey Diary, 2 April 1858, Grey Mss. C3/21. For the confusion caused by Russell's change of intention see Cornewall Lewis to Palmerston, 5 April 1858, Broadlands Mss. GC/LE 111; Cornewall Lewis to Palmerston, 8 April 1858, Broadlands Mss. GC/LE 112; and Clarendon to Palmerston, 9 April 1858, Broadlands Mss. GC/CL 1162.

90. Russell to Aberdeen, 7 April 1858, Aberdeen Mss. 43068, fol. 297.
91. Graham to Aberdeen, 8 April 1858, Aberdeen Mss. 43192, fol. 214.
92. Graham to Ellice, 8 April 1858, Graham Mss. Bundle 133. Graham also observed that 'there is always a disposition to do too much, when you have a living fish on the hook – he will kill himself if you let him: and Ellenborough and his India bill are harpooned'.
93. Russell to Dean of Bristol, 9 April 1858, Russell Mss. PRO 30/22/13/F, fol. 24.
94. Stanley to Disraeli, n.d. (? April 1858) Hughenden Mss. B/XX/S/662.
95. Disraeli, 12 April 1858, *Hansard*, 3rd series, CXLIX, 857.
96. Russell, 12 April 1858, *Hansard*, 3rd series, CXLIX, 858–61.
97. Disraeli to the Queen, 12 April 1858, cited in *QVL*, 1st series, III, p. 354.
98. Ibid.
99. Disraeli, 12 April 1858, *Hansard*, 3rd series, CXLIX, 861–4.
100. For a transcript of a letter Russell wrote, but did not send, to Derby outlining a compromise see S. Walpole, *The Life of Lord John Russell* (London, 1889) II, pp. 295–6.
101. Wood, 12 April 1858, *Hansard*, 3rd series, CXLIX, 864–6.
102. Disraeli, 12 April 1858, *Hansard*, 3rd series, CXLIX, 873.
103. Disraeli to the Queen, 12 April 1858, cited in *QVL*, 1st series, III, p. 354.
104. Palmerston, 12 April 1858, *Hansard*, 3rd series, CXLIX, 871–3.
105. Palmerston, 26 April 1858, *Hansard*, 3rd series, CXLIX, 1674. As H. C. F. Bell has commented there was more than one corpse after the debate. The introduction of the resolutions prevented any attempt by the 'Palmerstonians' to revive India bill No. 1. The debate pushed aside India bill No. 2. Yet Wood's intervention also denied Russell the authoritative role he had been looking to play. The real victors of the debate were Disraeli and the government. See Bell, *Palmerston*, II, p. 187.
106. Palmerston to Clarendon, 13 April 1858, Clarendon Mss. C. 82, fol. 123. Russell went to a party held by Lady Derby on 14 April, 'and Lord Derby seeing him said "Here comes my confederate", a joke which J. R. did not seem to like.' Broughton Diary, 15 April 1858, Broughton Mss. 43761, fol. 64.
107. Russell to Dean of Bristol, 14 April 1858, Russell Mss. PRO 30/22/13/F, fol. 47.
108. Greville Diary, 16 April 1858, Greville Mss. 41123, cited in Greville, *Memoirs*, VIII, p. 189.
109. Ibid.
110. Russell to Dean of Bristol, 9 March 1858, Russell Mss. PRO 30/22/13/E.
111. Greville Diary, 16 April 1858, Greville Mss. 41123, cited in Greville, *Memoirs*, VIII, p. 189.
112. Russell to Dean of Bristol, 28 April 1858, Russell Mss. PRO 30/22/13/F, fol. 62.
113. Disraeli to Pakington, 3 April 1858, Hampton Mss. 3835/7. Stanley recognised 'the inconvenience of having nothing to propose, and also

that which arises from "open questions", but of the two, it is a lesser evil to admit that we could not act than to attempt what must fail.' Stanley to Disraeli, n.d. (? 31 March 1858) Hughenden Mss. B/XX/S/563.

114. Ibid. See also Walpole memo, 8 April 1858, Walpole Mss. 77B.
115. G. I. T. Machin, *Politics and the Churches in Great Britain 1832 to 1868*, (Oxford, 1977) p. 290.
116. Henley to Derby, 7 April 1858, Derby Mss. 156/14. For discussion of the Newcastle Commission, see F. D. Munsell, *The Unfortunate Duke: Henry Pelham, Fifth Duke of Newcastle, 1811–1864* (Missouri, 1985) pp. 234–5; and R. Aldrich, 'Sir John Pakington and the Newcastle Commission', *History of Education*, 8:1 (1979) pp. 23–31.
117. Sir S. Northcote, *Twenty Years of Financial Policy* (London, 1862) p. 339.
118. Disraeli, 19 April 1858, *Hansard*, 3rd series, CXLIX, 1286.
119. Earle observed to Disraeli that 'a Tory government can only exist by Liberal budgets'. Earle to Disraeli, 15 July 1858, Hughenden Mss. B/XX/E/39.
120. Greville Diary, 24 April 1868, Greville Mss. 41123, cited in Greville, *Memoirs*, VIII, p. 190.
121. Gladstone, 19 April 1858, *Hansard*, 3rd series, CXLIX, 1312–16.
122. Cornewall Lewis to Clarendon, 11 April (1858) Clarendon Mss. C. 531.
123. Disraeli to the Queen, 19 April 1858, cited in Monypenny and Buckle, *Disraeli*, IV, p. 135.
124. Derby to Disraeli, 20 April 1858, Hughenden Mss. B/XX/S/170.
125. Dallas to Cass, 23 April 1858, cited in Dallas, *Letters from London*, II, p. 14. See also, Grey Diary, 13 May 1858, Grey Mss. C3/21.
126. Ellice to Panmure, 19 (? April 1858) Dalhousie Mss. GD 45/14/644.
127. Derby to Disraeli, 30 April 1858, Hughenden Mss. B/XX/S/171, cited in Monypenny and Buckle, *Disraeli*, IV, pp. 137–9.
128. Disraeli, 26 April 1858, *Hansard*, 3rd series, CXLIX, 1654–73.
129. Palmerston, 26 April 1858, *Hansard*, 3rd series, CXLIX, 1762–80.
130. Gladstone, 26 April 1858, *Hansard*, 3rd series, CXLIX, 1680–7.
131. Gladstone to Graham, 23 April 1858, cited in Parker, *Graham*, II, p. 340.
132. Russell, 26 April 1858, *Hansard*, 3rd series, CXLIX, 1695–1701.
133. Walpole, 26 April 1858, *Hansard*, 3rd series, CXLIX, 1707–8; and Horsman, 26 April 1858, *Hansard*, 3rd series, CXLIX, 1710–13.
134. Graham to Russell, 25 April 1858, Russell Mss. PRO 30/22/13/F, fol. 58, cited in Parker, *Graham*, II, p. 341.

CHAPTER 7

1. Dallas to Cass, 30 April 1858, cited in G. M. Dallas, *Letters from London, 1856–1860* (London, 1870) II, p. 15.
2. *The Times*, 6 May 1858.

3. Granville to Ellenborough, 23 February 1858, Ellenborough Mss. PRO 30/12/9, fol. 276.
4. Ellenborough to Derby, 13 May 1858, cited in W. F. Monypenny and G. E. Buckle, *The Life of Benjamin Disraeli, Earl of Beaconsfield* (London 1910–20) IV, p. 141.
5. Broughton Diary, 7 May 1858, Broughton Mss. 43761, fol. 76.
6. Granville to Canning, 10 May 1858, Granville Mss. PRO 30/29/21/2, fol. 118, cited in Lord E. Fitzmaurice, *The Life of Granville George Leveson-Gower, Second Earl Granville, K.G.* (London, 1905) I, p. 306.
7. Granville to Canning, 17 May 1858, Granville Mss. PRO 30/29/21/2, fol. 124.
8. Greville Diary, 13 May 1858, Greville Mss. 41123, cited in C. C. F. Greville, *The Greville Memoirs*, H. Reeve (ed.) (London, 1888) VIII, p. 197.
9. Ibid.
10. Granville to Canning, 10 May 1858, Granville Mss. PRO 30/29/21/2, fol. 118, cited in Fitzmaurice, *Granville*, I, p. 306.
11. Lennox to Disraeli, 1 May 1858, Hughenden Mss. B/XX/LX/109.
12. Grey Diary, 24 May 1858, Grey Mss. C3/21. See also, Fortescue Diary, 11 May 1858, Carlingford Mss. DD/SH 358.
13. Ellenborough, 10 May 1858, *Hansard*, 3rd series, CL, 323–4.
14. Grey, 10 May 1858, *Hansard*, 3rd series, CL, 324.
15. Ellenborough, 10 May 1858, *Hansard*, 3rd series, CL, 324. See also, Malmesbury, 10 May 1858, *Hansard*, 3rd series, CL, 325.
16. Derby, 11 May 1858, *Hansard*, 3rd series, CL, 405–7.
17. Granville, 11 May 1858, *Hansard*, 3rd series, CL, 407–8; and Ellenborough, 11 May 1858, *Hansard*, 3rd series, CL, 409–12.
18. Derby to the Queen, 11 May 1858, Derby Mss. 183/1, fol. 151. Before the announcement the Duke of Bedford 'called on Lady Derby and said that there were three courses to pursue. Resign – Dissolve – Turn out Ellenborough. She said she should like to have been in office a little longer, and as to the three courses she preferred turning out Ellenborough.' Broughton Diary, 10 May 1858, Broughton Mss. 43/61, fol. 77.
19. Derby to the Queen, 11 May 1858, Derby Mss. 184/1, fol. 151.
20. Grey Diary, 13 May 1858, Grey Mss. C3/21.
21. Granville to Canning, 10 May 1858, Granville Mss. PRO 30/29/21/2, fol. 118, cited in Fitzmaurice, *Granville*, I, p. 306. See also, Rose to Disraeli, 12 May 1858, Hughenden Mss. B/XX/R/9.
22. Dallas to Cass, 11 May 1858, cited in Dallas, *Letters from London*, II, p. 18. Vernon Smith and Benjamin Hall were talking excitedly at Brooks's of a great majority over Cardwell's motion. Neither of them, however, had 'any notion as to what is to follow the downfall of Derby', although it was apparent that 'B.H. will take nothing short of the cabinet'. Broughton Diary, 11 May 1858, Broughton Mss. 43762, fol. 78.
23. Dallas to Cass, 14 May 1858, cited in Dallas, *Letters from London*, II, p. 20.

24. Dallas to Cass, 6 April 1848, cited in Dallas, *Letters from London*, II, p. 11. See also, Granville to Canning, 24 May 1858, cited in Fitzmaurice, *Granville*, I, pp. 308–9.

25. Prince Albert memo., 11 May 1858, cited in *QVL*, 1st series, III, p. 359. The constitutional propriety of Derby's request were uncertain. Both the Queen and Prince Albert had serious doubts. See Phipps memo (? 15 May 1858) cited in *QVL*, 1st series, III, pp. 363–4.

26. Phipps memo (? 15 May 1858) cited in *QVL*, 1st series, III, pp. 363–4. W. D. Jones has observed 'Aberdeen's attitude was of great consequence in this crisis. While his former intimacy with Derby had not been resumed after 1852, he still preferred the Conservative moderate foreign policy to the jingoism of Palmerston.' W. D. Jones, *Lord Derby and Victorian Conservatism* (Oxford, 1956) p. 236. In his audience with the Queen, Aberdeen 'seemed very low upon the state of public affairs. He said that the extreme Liberals were the only party that appeared to gain strength. Not only was the Whig party divided within itself, hated by the Radicals, and having a very doubtful support from the independent Liberals, but even the little band called the Peelites had entirely crumbled to pieces.' Phipps memo, (? 15 May 1858) cited in *QVL*, 1st series, III, p. 366.

27. Granville to Canning, 17 May 1858, Granville Mss. PRO 30/29/21/2, fol. 124, cited in Fitzmaurice, *Granville*, I, p. 307.

28. Lennox to Disraeli, 1 May 1858, Hughenden Mss. B/XX/LX/109.

29. Fortescue Diary, 12 May 1858, Carlingford Mss. DD/SH 358.

30. Greville Diary, 23 May 1858, Greville Mss. 41123, cited in Greville, *Memoirs*, VIII, p. 200.

31. Palmerston Diary, 13 May 1858, Broadlands Mss. D/18.

32. Fortescue Diary, 14 May 1858, Carlingford Mss. DD/SH 358.

33. Palmerston Diary, 14 May 1858, Broadlands Mss. D/18.

34. Cardwell, 14 May 1858, *Hansard*, 3rd series, CL, 674–86.

35. Greville Diary, 16 May 1858, Greville Mss. 41123, cited in Greville, *Memoirs*, VIII, p. 199. Disraeli described it as 'one of the greatest speeches since I have been in Parliament; perhaps, all things considered, the occasion, character of the man, etc., the greatest'. Disraeli to Derby (? 14 May 1858) Derby Mss. 145/5, cited in Monypenny and Buckle, *Disraeli*, IV, p. 143.

36. Cairns, 14 May 1858, *Hansard*, 3rd series, CL, 693–711.

37. Disraeli to Derby (? 14 May 1858) Derby Mss. 145/5, cited in Monypenny and Buckle, *Disraeli*, IV, p. 143.

38. Palmerston Diary, 14 May 1858, Broadlands Mss. D/18.

39. Greville Diary, 16 May 1858, Greville Mss. 41123, cited in Greville, *Memoirs*, VIII, p. 199.

40. Russell, 14 May 1858, *Hansard*, 3rd series, CL, 752–61.

41. Greville Diary, 23 May 1858, Greville Mss. 41123, cited in Greville, *Memoirs*, VIII, p. 200.

42. Disraeli to Derby, 16 May 1858, Derby Mss. 145/5, cited in Monypenny and Buckle, *Disraeli*, IV, p. 143.

43. Greville Diary, 23 May 1858, Greville Mss. 41123, cited in Greville, *Memoirs*, VIII, p. 200.

44. Disraeli to Derby, 16 May 1858, Derby Mss. 145/5, cited in Monypenny and Buckle, *Disraeli*, IV, p. 143.
45. Prince Albert memo, 16 May 1858, cited in *QVL*, 1st series, III, p. 367.
46. Ibid.
47. Disraeli to Derby, 16 May 1858, Derby Mss. 145/5, cited in Monypenny and Buckle, *Disraeli*, IV, p. 143.
48. Disraeli to Graham, 17 May 1858, cited in C. S. Parker, *Life and Letters of Sir James Graham, Second Baronet of Netherby* (London, 1907) II, p. 343.
49. Herbert to Gladstone, 17 May 1858, Gladstone Mss. 44211, fol. 10.
50. Grey Diary, 20 May 1858, Grey Mss. C3/21.
51. Broughton Diary, 18 May 1858, Broughton Mss. 43761, fol. 84. 'Roebuck ... very bitter against the Palmerstonians'. Grey Diary, 17 May 1858, Grey Mss. C3/21.
52. Bright, 20 May 1858, *Hansard*, 3rd series, CL, 944–62.
53. W. White, *The Inner Life of the House of Commons* (London, 1897) I, p. 70.
54. Elton, 20 May 1858, *Hansard*, 3rd series, CL, 974–6.
55. White, *Inner Life of the House of Commons*, I, p. 73.
56. Disraeli to the Queen, 21 May 1858, cited in *QVL*, 1st series, III, p. 369. See, Graham, 20 May 1858, *Hansard*, 3rd series, CL, 985–1003.
57. Fortescue Diary, 20 May 1858, Carlingford Mss. DD/SH 358.
58. Derby to Jolliffe, 20 May 1858, Derby Mss. 184/1, fol. 158.
59. Derby to the Queen, 21 May 1858, Derby Mss. 184/1, fol. 159.
60. Greville Diary, 23 May 1858, Greville Mss. 41123, cited in Greville, *Memoirs*, VIII, p. 201.
61. Palmerston Diary, 21 May 1858, Broadlands Mss. D/18.
62. Greville Diary, 23 May 1858, Greville Mss. 41123, cited in Greville, *Memoirs*, VIII, p. 201.
63. Clay, 21 May 1858, *Hansard*, 3rd series, CL, 1026–8.
64. White, *Inner Life of the House of Commons*, I, p. 75.
65. Bowyer, 21 May 1858, *Hansard*, 3rd series, CL, 1028–9.
66. Cardwell, 21 May 1858, *Hansard*, 3rd series, CL, 1029.
67. Duncombe, 21 May 1858, *Hansard*, 3rd series, CL, 1030–3.
68. Seymour, 21 May 1858, *Hansard*, 3rd series, CL, 1037–8.
69. Disraeli at Slough, *The Times*, 27 May 1858. 'I felt my tail between my legs when ... I came into the House of Commons just in time to hear Pam advise Cardwell to withdraw his motion. We cut rather a foolish figure. I believe that a hundred Radicals agreed at the last moment that they must do everything to prevent a dissolution ... I have had a correspondence with Aberdeen ... I believe that he and Gladstone ... were determined at all price to prevent Palmerston forming another Government.' Granville to Canning, 24 May 1858, cited in Fitzmaurice, *Granville*, I, pp. 308–9.
70. Palmerston, 21 May 1858, *Hansard*, 3rd series, CL, 1040–2.
71. Cardwell, 21 May 1858, *Hansard*, 3rd series, CL, 1042.
72. Disraeli, 21 May 1858, *Hansard*, 3rd series, CL, 1046–53.

73. Greville Diary, 23 May 1858, Greville Mss. 41123, cited in Greville, *Memoirs*, VIII, p. 201.
74. Gathorne Hardy Diary, 24 May 1858, Cranbrook Mss. T501/291, fol. 142. See also, Disraeli to Mrs Brydges Willyams, 22 May 1858, cited in Monypenny and Buckle, *Disraeli*, IV, p. 149.
75. Derby to the Queen, 23 May 1858, Derby Mss. 184/1, fol. 165.
76. Broughton Diary, 22 May 1858, Broughton Mss. 43761, fol. 86.
77. Knatchbull-Hugessen Diary, 30 July 1858, Brabourne Mss. U951, F.29.
78. Palmerston Diary, 21 May 1858, Broadlands Mss. D/18.
79. Grey Diary, 20 May 1858, Grey Mss. C3/21.
80. Graham to Aberdeen, 28 May 1858, Aberdeen Mss. 43192, fol. 218.
81. Greville Diary, 23 May 1858, Greville Mss. 41123, cited in Greville, *Memoirs*, VIII, p. 201–2.
82. Dallas to Cass, 25 May 1858, cited in Dallas, *Letters from London*, II, p. 25.
83. Carnarvon memo, 1858, cited in Sir A. Hardinge, *Life of H. E. M. Herbert, Fourth Earl of Carnarvon, 1831–1890*, I, p. 115.
84. Lyndhurst to Brougham, 23 July (1858), Brougham Mss. 13317.
85. Knatchbull-Hugessen Diary, 30 July 1858, Brabourne Mss. U951 F.29.
86. Grey Diary, 2 July 1858, Grey Mss. C3/21.
87. Knatchbull-Hugessen Diary, 30 July 1858, Brabourne Mss. U951, F.29.
88. Carnarvon memo, 1858, cited in Hardinge, *Carnarvon*, I, p. 115.
89. Disraeli to Mrs Brydges Willyams, 28 August 1858, cited in Monypenny and Buckle, *Disraeli*, IV, p. 175.
90. White, *Inner Life of the House of Commons*, I, p. 79.
91. Greville Diary, 4 November 1858, Greville Mss. 41123, cited in Greville, *Memoirs*, VIII, p. 216.
92. Graham to Gladstone, 25 May 1858, Gladstone Mss. 44164, fol. 165.
93. Ibid.
94. Ibid.
95. Graham to Aberdeen, 28 May 1858, Aberdeen Mss. 43192, fol. 218.
96. Disraeli to Gladstone, 25 May 1858, cited in John Morley, *The Life of William Ewart Gladstone* (London, 1903) I, p. 587.
97. Gladstone to Disraeli, 25 May 1858, cited in Morley, *Gladstone*, I, p. 589. Gladstone developed this point in his reply to Derby. If Derby could have raised 'fully the question whether those who were formerly my colleagues could again be brought into political relation' with the government, such a scheme would 'be considered deliberately and in a favourable spirit'. Gladstone to Derby, 28 May 1858, cited in Morley, *Gladstone*, I, p. 590.
98. Derby to Disraeli, 27 May 1858, Hughenden Mss. B/XX/S/175, cited in Monypenny and Buckle, *Disraeli*, IV, p. 160–1.
99. Disraeli to Stanley, 28 May 1858, cited in Monypenny and Buckle, *Disraeli*, IV, p. 161.
100. Graham to Aberdeen, 28 May 1858, Aberdeen Mss. 43192, fol. 218, cited in Parker, *Graham*, II, pp. 352–3. Graham also commented 'The

truth is that Gladstone wishes to join, and to carry with him Herbert and his most intimate friends. He forgets that he is master of his own decision, but cannot rule theirs.'

101. For an authoritative discussion of this aspect of Gladstone's behaviour during 1858 see Richard Shannon, *Gladstone, 1809–1865* (London, 1982) pp. 352–4 upon which this paragraph is based. For a fascinating analysis of the relation between Gladstone's Roumanian speech and the Midlothian campaign see R. Shannon, 'Midlothian: 100 Years After', in P. J. Jagger (ed.) *Gladstone, Politics and Religion* (London, 1985) pp. 88–103.

102. Carnarvon memo, 1858, cited in Hardinge, *Carnarvon*, I, p. 119, and Broughton Diary, 30 May 1858, Broughton Mss. 43761, fol. 91.

103. Locke King, 22 April 1858, *Hansard*, 3rd series, CXLIX, 1543–4.

104. Walpole, 6 May 1858, *Hansard*, 3rd series, CL, 226–7.

105. Derby, 22 April 1858, *Hansard*, 3rd series, CXLIX, 1479–80.

106. Disraeli to Derby, 8 May 1858, Derby Mss. 145/5. See also, Derby to Disraeli, 9 May 1858, Derby Mss. 184/1, fol. 145.

107. Ellesmere to Derby, 18 May 1858, Derby Mss. 111.

108. Lucan, 31 May 1858, *Hansard*, 3rd series, CL, 1139–42.

109. Derby, 31 May 1858, *Hansard*, 3rd series, CL, 1156–68.

110. Derby memo, 9 June 1858, Salisbury Mss.

111. Lyndhurst, 1 July 1858, *Hansard*, 3rd series, CLI, 697–702. See also, Derby to Lyndhurst, 13 June 1858, Derby Mss. 184/1, fol. 192.

112. Drummond, 16 July 1858, *Hansard*, 3rd series, CLI, 1628–31.

113. G. I. T. Machin, *Politics and the Churches in Great Britain 1832–1868* (Oxford, 1977) p. 272. See M. C. N. Sabelstein, *The Emancipation of the Jews in Britain: The Question of the Admission of the Jews to Parliament 1828–60* (London, 1982); and Abraham Gilam, *The Emancipation of the Jews in England* (New York, 1982).

114. The proposal to grant a charter to a Roman Catholic University in Dublin, suggested by Disraeli, was opposed by Stanley: 'we should lose more on our side than we could hope to gain on the other'. Stanley to Disraeli, 10 January 1859, Hughenden Mss. B/XX/S/671.

115. Spooner, 29 April, 1858, *Hansard*, 3rd series, CXLIX, 1990–6.

116. Watt's calculation of the cohesion index for each parliamentary group clearly illustrates the point. For the ballot vote of 8 June, Watt calculates Radicals 85%, Liberals 51%, Whigs 33%, Liberal Conservatives 100% and Conservatives 100%. For Locke King's motion of 10 June, Watt calculates Radicals 83%, Liberals 90%, Whigs 100%, Liberal Conservatives 73% and Conservatives 96%. See R. G. Watt, 'Parties and Politics in Mid-Victorian Britain, 1857 to 1859: A Study in Quantification' unpublished PhD thesis, University of Minnesota, 1975, pp. 289–308. See also, Bruce L. Kinzer, 'The Failure of "Pressure From Without": Richard Cobden, the Ballot Society, and the Coming of the Ballot Act in England', *Canadian Journal of History*, 13:3 (1978) pp. 399–422; and Bruce L. Kinzer, *The Ballot Question in Nineteenth Century English Politics* (New York, 1982).

117. Disraeli to Mrs Brydges Willyams, 26 July 1858, cited in Monypenny and Buckle, *Disraeli*, IV, p. 168.

118. Dallas to Cass, 13 August 1858, cited in Dallas, *Letters from London*, II, p. 44. Prince Albert described the Derby ministry as a 'Tory Ministry, with a Radical programme, carrying out Republican measures, with a Conservative majority against a Liberal opposition', cited in H. C. F. Bell, *Lord Palmerston* (London, 1936) II, p. 191.

CHAPTER 8

1. Broughton Diary, 6 July 1858, Broughton Mss. 43761, fol. 104. In March 1858, anticipating 'a gloomy future', Herbert had declined to make comparisons between 'the faults of possible prime-ministers. There is too much material of that kind to make it either difficult or pleasant.' Herbert to Argyll, 15 March 1858, cited in Duke of Argyll, *George Douglas, 8th Duke of Argyll: Autobiography and Memoirs* (London, 1906) II, p. 121. See also, Bedford to Ellice, 18 April 1858, Ellice Mss. 15050, fol. 181.
2. Argyll to G. Grey, 21 October 1858, cited in Argyll, *Autobiography and Memoirs*, II, p. 124.
3. Broughton Diary, 1 November 1858, Broughton Mss. 43761, fol. 131.
4. Graham to Ellice, 7 January 1859, Ellice Mss. 15019, fol. 46.
5. Herbert to Graham, 10 January 1859, cited in A. H. Gordon, Baron Stanmore, *Sidney Herbert, Lord Herbert of Lea: A Memoir* (London, 1906) II, pp. 165–6.
6. Villiers to Bright, 8 December 1858, Bright Mss. 43389, fol. 224.
7. Clanricarde to Canning, 9 May 1858, Canning Mss. 4.
8. Broughton Diary, 20 May 1858, Broughton Mss. 43761, fol. 85.
9. Forster to Goderich, 23 May 1858, Ripon Mss. 43536, fol. 142. Prince Albert found the 'remarkable feature' of the 1858 session was 'the extraordinary unpopularity of Lord Palmerston . . . The man who was without rhyme or reason stamped the only *English* statesman . . . is now considered the head of a clique, the man of intrigue, past his work, etc., etc., – in fact hated! and this throughout the country.' Prince Albert memo, 4 September 1858, cited in *QVL*, 1st series, III, p. 381.
10. Broughton Diary, 6 July 1858, Broughton Mss. 43761, fol. 104. In October 1858 Clarendon found Palmerston 'very moderate in his tone about men and things, and prepared to wait a long time for another innings, if he believes in the possibility of such an event which I doubt'. Clarendon to Aberdeen, 27 October 1858, cited in *Lord Aberdeen's Correspondence, 1854–55*, B.P. 12 (12) p. 395.
11. Broughton Diary, 11 June 1858, Broughton Mss. 43761, fol. 98.
12. Russell to Dean of Bristol, 29 October 1858, Russell Mss. PRO 30/22/13/F, fol. 136. See also, Russell to Dean of Bristol, 6 November 1858, Russell Mss. PRO 30/22/13/F, fol. 147.
13. Wood to Panmure, 9 January 1858, Dalhousie Mss. GD/45/14/689.
14. Delane to Ellice, 14 May 1858, Ellice Mss. 15011, fol. 9.
15. Broughton Diary, 22 April 1858, Broughton Mss. 43761, fol. 69.

16. Broughton Diary, 8 June 1858, Broughton Mss. 43761, fol. 97.
17. Grey Diary, 16 December 1858, Grey Mss. C3/21.
18. Knatchbull-Hugessen Diary, 30 July 1858, Brabourne Mss. F.29.
19. Broughton Diary, 17 July 1858, Broughton Mss. 43761, fol. 121.
20. Herbert to Granville, 31 August 1858, Granville Mss. PRO 30/29/18/6, fol. 65.
21. Palmerston to Granville, 30 August 1858, Granville Mss. PRO 30/29/18/6, fol. 64 cited in H. C. F. Bell, *Lord Palmerston* (London, 1936) II, p. 191.
22. Graham to Aberdeen, 24 October 1858, Aberdeen Mss. 43192, fol. 255.
23. Russell to Graham, 29 July 1858, Graham Mss. Bundle 134.
24. Graham to Aberdeen, 20 August 1858, Aberdeen Mss. 43192, fol. 228.
25. Russell to Aberdeen, 15 August 1858, Aberdeen Mss. 43068, fol. 306. See also, Russell to Aberdeen, 23 August 1858, Aberdeen Mss. 43068, fol. 307. Russell expected reform to force Derby to choose between 'the friendship of the Tories and the Crown, and that of the Radicals and the people'. Russell to Graham, 30 July 1858, Graham Mss. Bundle 134.
26. Russell to Graham, 29 July 1858, Graham Mss. Bundle 134.
27. Russell to Graham, 30 July 1858, Graham Mss. Bundle 134. See also, Russell to Graham, 30 August 1858, Graham Mss. Bundle 134.
28. Graham to Aberdeen, 1 September 1858, Aberdeen Mss. 43192, fol. 234.
29. Aberdeen to Graham, 5 November 1858, Graham Mss. Bundle 134.
30. Graham to Russell, 1 September 1858, Russell Mss. PRO 30/22/13/F, fol. 113, cited in C. S. Parker, *Life and Letters of Sir James Graham, Second Baronet of Netherby* (London, 1907) II, pp. 159–60.
31. Graham to Aberdeen, 1 September 1858, Aberdeen Mss. 43192, fol. 234.
32. Herbert to Granville, 31 August 1858, Granville Mss. PRO 30/29/18/6, fol. 65.
33. Clarendon to Cornewall Lewis, 5 November 1858, Clarendon Mss. C.533. See also, Clarendon to Cornewall Lewis, 5 December 1858, Clarendon Mss. C.533.
34. Greville Diary, 5 September 1858, Greville Mss. 41123, cited in C. C. F. Greville, *The Greville Memoirs*, H. Reeve (ed.) (London, 1888) VIII, p. 213. See also, Russell to Graham, 30 August 1858, Graham Mss. Bundle 134. Leveson Gower to Granville, 23 September 1858, Granville Mss. PRO 30/29/19/23.
35. Bedford to Brougham, 25 September 1858, Brougham Mss. 10387. See also, Stanley to Russell, 10 September 1858, Russell Mss. PRO 30/22/13/F, fol. 116; Russell to Cornewall Lewis, 15 September 1858, Russell Mss. PRO 30/22/13/F, fol. 118. Russell 'told Stanley a good deal about the political affairs in which he has been engaged, especially with respect to the great reform bill, its history and incidents, which details no doubt were very interesting and useful to him'.

Greville Diary, 5 September 1858, Greville Mss. 41123, cited in Greville, *Memoirs*, VIII, p. 213.

36. Greville Diary, 5 September 1858, Greville Mss. 41123, cited in Greville, *Memoirs*, VIII, p. 213.
37. Wood to Panmure, 16 October 1858, Dalhousie Mss. GD45/14/689.
38. Bedford to Brougham, 19 October 1858, Brougham Mss. 30407. In his biography of Russell, Walpole claims that Russell, while at Knowsley, stated that he was as ready to accept a good measure from Derby as to introduce it himself. S. Walpole, *The Life of Lord John Russell* (London, 1889) II, p. 301. Walpole cites no source for this statement, nor have I found any. What does survive is Russell's statement, in January 1859, that he was not going to allow Reform to be 'hacked at the request of a sham mother'. Russell to Dean of Bristol, 21 January 1859, Russell Mss. PRO 30/22/13/9, cited in J. Prest, *Lord John Russell* (London, 1972) p. 382.
39. Stanley of Alderley to Granville, 23 October 1858, Granville Mss. PRO 30/29/19/23, fol. 25.
40. Wood to Panmure, 16 October 1858, Dalhousie Mss. GD45/14/689.
41. Cornewall Lewis to Clarendon, 30 October 1858, Clarendon Mss. C.531.
42. Stanley of Alderley to Granville, 23 October 1858, Granville Mss. PRO 30/29/19/25, fol. 25. Clarendon also believed that Russell wanted 'to try his hand at a Cabinet with Bright and Stanley'. Clarendon to Aberdeen, 27 October 1858, cited in *Aberdeen Correspondence*, B.P. 12 (12) p. 395.
43. Holland to Brougham, 24 September 1858, Brougham Mss. 16328. For other anxious Whigs it seemed 'fully clear that Derby is making up to [Russell], and that they intend to propitiate him through the person of Stanley, with reference to the introduction of their reform bill'. Shelbourne to Granville, 3 October 1858, Granville Mss. PRO 30/20/19/23, fol. 209.
44. Ellice to Panmure, 31 October 1858, Dalhousie Mss. GD45/14/689. Parkes expected 'the Conservative Dramatis Personae' to experience 'an inevitable split on a scheme of parliamentary reform. Dizzy and Stanley will blow up the administration.' In the event of Disraeli vacating the Conservative leadership Gladstone would 'replace the circumcized Christianised Jew'. Without Russell's help the government would no more 'get over reform than climb up to the moon'. Parkes to Ellice Jnr, 24 August 1858, Ellice Mss. 15043, fol. 82. See also, Parkes to Ellice Jnr, 2 November 1858, Ellice Mss. 15043, fol. 91.
45. Parkes to Ellice Jnr, 2 November 1858, Ellice Mss. 15043, fol. 91.
46. Graham to Aberdeen, 24 October 1858, Aberdeen Mss. 43192, fol. 255.
47. Graham to Russell, 27 November 1858, Russell Mss. PRO 30/22/13/F, fol. 171. Part of this letter is cited in Parker, *Graham*, II, pp. 360–1.
48. Bright to Cobden, 9 April 1858, Bright Mss. 43384, fol. 124. See also, Bright to his wife, 5 June 1858, Ogden Mss. 65; and D. Read *Cobden*

and Bright: A Victorian Political Partnership (London, 1967) pp. 152–3.

49. Graham to Aberdeen, 7 November 1858, Aberdeen Mss. 43192, fol. 262.
50. Ellice to Panmure, 31 October 1858, Dalhousie Mss. GD43/14/689.
51. Bright to Cobden, 26 September 1858, Bright Mss. 43384, fol. 137.
52. Cobden to Bright, 20 September 1858, Cobden Mss. 43650, fol. 197.
53. Bright to Cobden, 26 September 1858, Bright Mss. 43384, fol. 137.
54. Bright to Cobden, 24 October 1858, Bright Mss. 43384, fol. 141.
55. Ibid. See also Bruce Kinzer, 'Failure of "Pressure from Without": Richard Cobden, the Ballot Society, and the Coming of the Ballot Act in England', *Canadian Journal of History*, 13:3 (1978) pp. 339–422; and Bruce Kinzer, *The Ballot Question in Nineteenth-Century English Politics* (New York, 1982).
56. Bright to his wife, 27 October 1858, Ogden Mss. 65.
57. Bright at Birmingham, *The Times*, 28 October 1858, p. 7. See also, Read, *Cobden and Bright*, pp. 162–4.
58. Bright's stress on this point probably owed much to Cobden's conviction that parliament might be reformed through the organised purchase of 40s county freeholds. After 1848 Cobden enthusiastically advocated this scheme. 'A county or two quietly rescued from the landlords in this process will, when announced, do more to strike dismay into the camp of feudalism and inspire the people with the assurance of victory, than anything else we could do.' Cobden to Bright, 7 November 1851, Cobden Mss. 43649, cited in Read, *Cobden and Bright*, p. 157.
59. Stanley of Alderley to Granville, 23 October 1858, Granville Mss. PRO 30/29/19/23, fol. 25.
60. Ibid.
61. Graham to Aberdeen, 16 November 1858, Aberdeen Mss. 43192, fol. 258.
62. Bedford to Brougham, 28 November 1858, Brougham Mss. 30408; and Aberdeen to Clarendon, 2 November 1858, Clarendon Mss. C.525.
63. Clarendon to Cornewall Lewis, 5 November 1858, Clarendon Mss. C.533. Clarendon believed that Bright had 'overshot the mark'.
64. Cowan at Edinburgh, *The Times*, 5 November 1858, p. 4. See also, Wilson at Devonport, *The Times*, 30 October 1858, p. 7.
65. Shaftesbury at the Fishmongers' Hall, London, *The Times*, 10 November 1858, p. 9.
66. Argyll at Dundee, *The Times*, 15 November 1858, p. 4.
67. Bouverie at Kilmarnock, *The Times*, 24 November 1858, p. 5.
68. Bruce to Goderich, 6 November 1858, Ripon Mss. 43354, fol. 95.
69. Goderich to Bruce, 3 November 1858, Ripon Mss. 43534, fol. 89.
70. Bright at Birmingham, *The Times*, 30 October 1858, p. 7.
71. The meeting was reported in *The Times*, 6 November 1858, p. 9.
72. Bright to Cobden, 14 November 1858, Bright Mss. 43384, fol. 143.
73. Ibid. See also, Kinzer, *The Ballot Question*.

74. Bright to Cobden, 29 December 1858, Bright Mss. 43384, fol. 148. See also, Cobden to Bright, 26 December 1858, Cobden Mss. 43650, fol. 305.

75. Cobden to Bright, 26 December 1858, Cobden Mss. 43650, fol. 305.

76. Villiers to Bright, 14 January 1859, Bright Mss. 43386, fol. 227.

77. Cornewall Lewis to Wilson, 27 December 1858, cited in E. I. Barrington, *The Servant of All: Pages from the Family, Social and Political Life of my Father James Wilson* (London, 1927) II, p. 117.

78. Count Vitzhum, *St. Petersburg and London in the Years 1852 to 1865* (London, 1887) I, p. 117.

79. Bright at Manchester, *The Times*, 11 December 1858. Before this speech Villiers was urging Bright to 'say as little about America as possible' and not to risk his position 'by any unnecessary violence of expression'. Villiers to Bright, 8 December 1858, Bright Mss. 53386, fol. 224.

80. Bright at Glasgow, *The Times*, 22 December 1858.

81. Cornewall Lewis to Wilson, 19 December 1858, cited in Barrington, *Servant of All*, II, p. 105.

82. Cornewall Lewis to Clarendon, 28 December 1858, Clarendon Mss. C.531.

83. Villiers to Bright, 8 December 1858, Bright Mss. 43386, fol. 224.

84. Graham to Russell, 27 November 1858, Russell Mss. PRO 30/22/13/F, fol. 171, cited in Parker, *Graham*, II, p. 361.

85. Graham to Aberdeen, 12 December 1858, Aberdeen Mss. 43192, fol. 280.

86. Clarendon to Duchess of Manchester, 25 December 1858, cited in A. L. Kennedy (ed.) *'My Dear Duchess': Social and Political Letters to the Duchess of Manchester, 1858–1869* (London, 1956) p. 36.

87. Clarendon to Palmerston, 29 November 1858, Broadlands Mss. GC/LC 1178.

88. Argyll to Graham, 7 October 1858, Graham Mss. Bundle 134. Argyll noted that 'action with Bright [was] impossible', while Russell was talking of 'some fusion of Parties as necessary'. Argyll to Aberdeen, 12 October 1858, Aberdeen Mss. 43199, fol. 143.

89. Argyll to Russell, 29 November 1858, Russell Mss. PRO 30/22/13/F, fol. 176. During this period Argyll was also corresponding extensively with Aberdeen.

90. See Lord Grey's essay *Parliamentary Government Considered with Reference to Reform of Parliament* (London, 1858). See also, Grey to Granville, 4 September 1858, Granville Mss. PRO 30/29/19/23, fol. 155. Grey feared the country was 'drifting helplessly down the stream which threatens very speedily to carry us to complete democracy'. Grey to Ellice, 3 January 1859, Ellice Mss. 15025, fol. 123.

91. Grey, *Parliamentary Government*, p. 100.

92. Mrs Grote to Ellice, 30 January 1859, Ellice Mss. 15026, fol. 119.

93. Grey to Ellice, 14 January 1859, Ellice Mss. 15025, fol. 146.

94. Grey to Ellice, 10 January, 1859, Ellice Mss. 15025, fol. 144.

95. Grey Diary, 31 December 1858, Grey Mss. C3/21.

96. Cornewall Lewis to Clarendon, 10 August 1858, Clarendon Mss. C.531. See also, Clarendon to Cornewall Lewis, 21 September 1858, Clarendon Mss. C.533.

97. Clarendon to Cornewall Lewis, 16 November 1858, Clarendon Mss. C.533.

98. Clarendon to Cornewall Lewis, 5 December 1858, Clarendon Mss. C.533.

99. Clarendon to Palmerston, 29 November 1858, Broadlands Mss. GC/CL 1178.

100. Clarendon to Cornewall Lewis, 5 December 1858, Clarendon Mss. C.533.

101. Ibid.

102. Cornewall Lewis to Clarendon, 15 December 1858, Clarendon Mss. C.531.

103. Howden to Clarendon, 8 December 1858, Clarendon Mss. C.540.

104. Clarendon to Cornewall Lewis, 14 December 1858, Clarendon Mss. C.533.

105. Cornewall Lewis to Clarendon, 15 December 1858, Clarendon Mss. C.531.

106. Clarendon to Cornewall Lewis, 20 December 1858, Clarendon Mss. C.533. See also, Clarendon to Cornewall Lewis, 19 December 1858, Clarendon Mss. C.533.

107. Cornewall Lewis to Clarendon, 22 December 1858, Clarendon Mss. C.531.

108. Clarendon to Cornewall Lewis, 20 December 1858, Clarendon Mss. C.533.

109. Clarendon to Reeve, 21 December 1858, Clarendon Mss. C.535.

110. Cornewall Lewis to Palmerston, 28 December 1858, Broadlands Mss. GC/LE 115.

111. Cornewall Lewis to Clarendon, 7 December 1858, Clarendon Mss. C.531.

112. Cornewall Lewis to Palmerston, 28 December 1858, Broadlands Mss. GC/LE 115. See also, Cornewall Lewis to Wilson, 27 December 1858, cited in Barrington, *Servant of All*, II, p. 115.

113. Cornewall Lewis to Clarendon, 7 December 1858, Clarendon Mss. C.531.

114. Clarendon to Reeve, 28 November 1858, Clarendon Mss. C.535.

115. Cornewall Lewis to Wilson, 27 December 1858, cited in Barrington, *Servant of All*, II, p. 116.

116. Clarendon to Cornewall Lewis, 5 December 1858, Clarendon Mss. C.533.

117. Cornewall Lewis to Clarendon, 7 December 1858, Clarendon Mss. C.531.

118. Clarendon to Cornewall Lewis, 19 December 1858, Clarendon Mss. C.533.

119. Palmerston to Clarendon, 4 January 1859, Clarendon Mss. C.524.

120. Roebuck to his wife (? October 1858) cited in R. E. Leader, *The Life and Letters of John Arthur Roebuck* (London, 1879) p. 273.

121. Parkes to Ellice Jnr, 3 January 1859, Ellice Mss. 15043, fol. 99.

122. Russell to Dean of Bristol, 31 December 1858, Russell Mss. PRO 30/22/13/F, fol. 286.

123. Russell to Dean of Bristol, 9 January 1859, Russell Mss. PRO 30/22/13/9, fol. 78.

124. Russell to Dean of Bristol, 10 January 1859, Russell Mss. PRO 30/22/13/G, fol. 90.

125. Clarendon to Cornewall Lewis, 6 January 1859, Clarendon Mss. C.533.

126. Cornewall Lewis to Clarendon, 12 January 1859, Clarendon Mss. C.531.

127. Clarendon to Lady Cornewall Lewis, 13 January 1859, cited in Sir H. Maxwell, *The Life and Letters of the Fourth Earl of Clarendon* (London, 1913) II, p. 175.

128. Grey Diary, 31 December 1858, Grey Mss. C3/21.

129. Russell to Clarendon, 24 January 1859, Clarendon Mss. C.104, fol. 23.

130. Russell to Graham, 3 January 1859, Graham Mss. Bundle 135, cited in Parker, *Graham*, II, pp. 363–4.

131. Russell to Graham, 19 January 1859, cited in Parker, *Graham*, II, p. 367.

132. Graham to Russell, 21 January 1859, Russell Mss. PRO 30/22/13/G, fol. 118, cited in Parker, *Graham*, II, pp. 367–9.

133. Argyll to Russell, 24 January 1859, Russell Mss. PRO 30/22/13/G, fol. 132.

134. Villiers to Bright, n.d. (? 26 January 1859) Bright Mss. 43386, fol. 250.

135. Richard Bethell (1800–73), matriculated at Wadham College, Oxford, at the age of fourteen. In 1823 he was called to the Bar; elected for Aylesbury in 1851; Solicitor General in the Aberdeen Coalition; in 1856 became Attorney-General until February 1858. In 1861 he received the title of Baron Westbury. The *Dictionary of National Biography* notes 'he will probably be known rather as the author of audacious sayings, and as the mythical source of innumerable stories'. See also, T. A. Nash, *The Life of Lord Westbury*, 2 vols (London, 1888).

136. Bedford to Granville, 31 January 1859, Granville Mss. PRO 30/29/19/24, fol. 58.

137. Greville Diary, 16 June 1858, Greville Mss. 41123, cited in Greville, *Memoirs*, VIII, p. 203.

138. Russell to Dean of Bristol, 4 October 1858, Russell Mss. PRO 30/22/13/F, fol. 128.

139. Delane to Osborne, 25 November 1858, cited in A. I. Dasent, *John Thadeus Delane, Editor of 'The Times': His Life and Correspondence*, 2 vols (London, 1908) I, p. 304.

140. Lowe at Kidderminster, *The Times*, 10 December 1858, p. 6. Gladstone, in an anonymous article in the *Quarterly Review*, observed that Palmerston 'can hardly fail to see that a number of those who formerly supported him . . . have written this sentence upon the tablets of their heart: "*Come what may, Lord Palmerston shall not again be Minis-*

ter".' Gladstone (anon.) 'The Past and Present Administrations', *Quarterly Review*, 208 (October 1858) p. 528.

141. Palmerston to Clarendon, 31 October 1858, Clarendon Mss. C.524. See also, Palmerston to Clarendon, 2 November 1858, Clarendon Mss. C.524; Palmerston to Clarendon, 3 November 1858, Clarendon Mss. C.524. Clarendon communicated his misgivings to Palmerston. See Clarendon to Palmerston, 4 November 1858, Broadlands Mss. GC/LE 1175; and Clarendon to Palmerston, 5 November 1858, Broadlands Mss. GC/LE 1176.

142. Lady Cornewall Lewis, Clarendon's sister, observed that, by visiting Napoleon, Palmerston 'placed another very large nail in the coffin of his premiership', cited in Bell, *Palmerston*, II, p. 198. See also, Graham to Aberdeen, 7 November 1858, Aberdeen Mss. 43192, fol. 258; Lowe to Osborne, 14 November 1858, cited in P. H. D. Bagenal *The Life of Ralph Bernal Osborne M.P.* (London, 1884) p. 151; Wood to Ellice, 30 November 1858, Ellice Mss. 15060, fol. 188; Broughton Diary, 16 December 1858, Broughton Mss. 43761, fol. 138.

   Russell observed that Palmerston and Clarendon 'must thereafter be considered rather as courtiers of the Tuileries than as subjects of St. James's', cited in D. Southgate, *'The Most English Minister ...': The Policies and Politics of Palmerston* (London, 1966) p. 447.

143. Palmerston to Clarendon, 19 December 1858, Clarendon Mss. C.524.

144. Palmerston to Clarendon, 3 November 1858, Clarendon Mss. C.524.

145. Palmerston to Clarendon, 19 December 1858, Clarendon Mss. C.524.

146. Palmerston to Clarendon, 4 January 1859, Clarendon Mss. C.524. See also, Cornewall Lewis to Clarendon, 28 December 1858, Clarendon Mss. C.531.

147. Palmerston to Clarendon, 3 November 1858, Clarendon Mss. C.524.

148. Two studies are essential guides to the diplomatic and political background of this question. C. T. McIntire, *England Against the Papacy, 1858–1861: Tories, Liberals, and the Overthrow of Papal Temporal Power During the Italian Risorgimento* (Cambridge, 1983); and D. E. D. Beales, *England and Italy, 1859–60* (London, 1961) especially pp. 1–35. See also C. T. McIntire, 'Mid-Victorian Anti-Catholicism, English Diplomacy and Odo Russell in Rome', *Fides et Historia*, 13:1 (1980) pp. 23–33.

149. Gladstone (anon.) 'War in Italy', *Quarterly Review*, 105 (April 1859) p. 537.

150. Graham to Aberdeen, 1 January 1859, Aberdeen Mss. 43192, fol. 287.

151. Cornewall Lewis to Clarendon, 7 January 1859, Clarendon Mss. C.531.

152. Aberdeen to Clarendon, 2 November 1858, Clarendon Mss. C.525.

153. Aberdeen to Graham, 24 December 1858, Graham Mss. Bundle 134.

154. Aberdeen to Graham, 5 January 1859, Graham Mss. Bundle 135.

155. Graham to Aberdeen, 4 December 1858, Aberdeen Mss. 43192, fol. 275.

156. Newcastle to Gladstone, 22 January 1859, Gladstone Mss. 44263, fol. 82.

157. Minto to Russell, 19 January 1859, Russell Mss. PRO 30/22/13/G, fol. 103.
158. Clarendon to Russell, 23 January 1859, Russell Mss. PRO 30/22/13/G, fol. 126.
159. Cornewall Lewis to Russell, 12 January 1859, Russell Mss. PRO 30/22/13/G, fol. 98.
160. Graham to Russell, 22 December 1859, Russell Mss. PRO 30/22/13/F, fol. 113.
161. Villiers to Bright, 14 January 1859, Bright Mss. 43386, fol. 227.
162. Villiers to Bright, 25 January 1859, Bright Mss. 43386, fol. 237.
163. *The Times*, 8 January 1859, p. 8.
164. *The Times*, 10 January 1859, p. 6.
165. *The Times*, 7 February 1859, p. 6. In April 1859 the *Edinburgh Review*, the organ of orthodox Whig opinion, affirmed the consensus. 'The misfortune of the Italians is, that not content with pursuing objects which are desirable and affirmable, the great bulk of the patriotic party, in all its different shades, aims at changes which are at present of impossible attainment, and which would not be less impossible even if the great obstacle of foreign dominion were removed.' 'Austria, France and Italy', *Edinburgh Review*, 222 (April 1859) p. 596.
166. Russell to Dean of Bristol, 31 December 1858, Russell Mss. PRO 30/22/13/F, fol. 236.
167. Russell to Dean of Bristol, 9 January 1859, Russell Mss. PRO 30/22/13/G, fol. 78.
168. Russell to Cornewall Lewis, 10 January 1859, Russell Mss. PRO 30/22/13/G, fol. 89.
169. Russell to Dean of Bristol, 10 January 1859, Russell Mss. PRO 30/22/13/G, fol. 90.
170. Russell to Dean of Bristol, 27 January 1859, Russell Mss. PRO 30/22/13/G, fol. 139.
171. Russell to Dean of Bristol, 2 February 1859, Russell Mss. PRO 30/22/13/G, fol. 145.
172. Russell to Clarendon, 26 December 1858, Clarendon Mss. C.104, cited in G. P. Gooch (ed.), *The Later Correspondence of Lord Russell* (London, 1925) II, pp. 228–9.
173. Russell to Clarendon, 28 December 1858, Clarendon Mss. C.104.
174. Russell to Clarendon, 21 January 1859, Clarendon Mss. C.104.
175. Clarendon to Russell, 6 January 1859, Russell Mss. PRO 30/22/13/G, fol. 82.
176. Graham to Aberdeen, 23 December 1858, Aberdeen Mss. 43192, fol. 283; and Aberdeen to Graham, 24 December 1858, Graham Mss. Bundle 134.
177. Clarendon to Palmerston, 6 January 1859, Broadlands Mss. GC/CL 1180.
178. Russell to Cornewall Lewis, 18 January 1859, Russell Mss. PRO 30/22/13/G, fol. 116.
179. Russell to Dean of Bristol, 21 January 1859, Russell Mss. PRO 30/22/13/G, fol. 116.
180. Russell to Melgund, 8 January 1859, Minto Mss. 12254.

181. Cornewall Lewis to Clarendon, 12 January 1859, Clarendon Mss. C.531.
182. Russell to Dean of Bristol, 27 January 1859, Russell Mss. PRO 30/22/13/G, fol. 139.
183. Palmerston to Clarendon, 10 January 1859, Clarendon Mss. C.524.
184. Palmerston to Granville, 30 January 1859, Granville Mss. PRO 30/29/18/6, fol. 69.
185. Palmerston to Clarendon, 10 January 1859, Clarendon Mss. C.524.
186. Villiers to Bright, 25 January 1859, Bright Mss. 43386, fol. 237.
187. Villiers to Bright, 14 January 1859, Bright Mss. 43386, fol. 227.
188. Graham to Aberdeen, 23 December 1858, Aberdeen Mss. 43192, fol. 283.
189. Graham to Aberdeen, 12 December 1858, Aberdeen Mss. 43192, fol. 276.

CHAPTER 9

1. Cornewall Lewis to Clarendon, 7 December 1858, Clarendon Mss. C.531.
2. Lyndhurst to Brougham, 16 November 1858, Brougham Mss. 13319.
3. Derby to Disraeli, 4 October 1858, Hughenden Mss. B/XX/S/181. Hayward, an assiduous collector of gossip, confessed to Cornewall Lewis that he had heard 'nothing of Derbyite intentions regarding reform'. Hayward to Cornewall Lewis, 11 November 1858, Harpton Court Mss. C/1490.
4. Clarendon to Palmerston, 25 November 1858, Broadlands Mss. GC/CL 1177.
5. Ibid.
6. Parkes to Ellice Jnr, 1 January 1859, Ellice Mss. 15043, fol. 96.
7. Palmerston to Clarendon, 27 November 1858, Clarendon Mss. C.523.
8. Clarendon to Cornewall Lewis, 21 September 1858, Clarendon Mss. C.533. See also, Wood to Panmure, 16 October 1858, Dalhousie Mss. GD45/14/689.
9. Clarendon to Cornewall Lewis, 16 November 1858, Clarendon Mss. C.533.
10. Clarendon to Reeve, 28 November 1858, Clarendon Mss. C.535.
11. Clarendon to Palmerston, 17 November 1858, Broadlands Mss. GC/CL 1179.
12. Cornwall Lewis to Palmerston, 11 December 1858, Broadlands Mss. GC/CE 114.
13. Hayward to Cornewall Lewis, 15 January 1859, Harpton Court Mss. C/1498.
14. Russell to Aberdeen, 15 August 1858, Aberdeen Mss. 43068, fol. 306. See also, Graham to Ellice, 26 December 1858, Ellice Mss. 15019, fol. 43.
15. Derby to Jolliffe, 3 August 1858, Hylton Mss. DD/HY 18/2, fol. 32. For discussion of the Conservative reform bill see G. L. Stone, 'Derby,

Disraeli and the Reform Bill of 1859', unpublished PhD thesis, University of Illinois at Urbana-Champaign, 1975. There are two important flaws in Stone's study, however. First, Conservative concern with reform is examined in isolation from Whig, Liberal Peelite and Radical manoeuvre. Secondly, Disraeli is portrayed as the dominant force in the cabinet, and the mastermind behind the 1859 scheme. Stone therefore perpetuates the 'Beaconsfield' myth penned by Kebbel.

16. Disraeli to Derby, 16 August 1858, Derby Mss. 145/5.
17. Rose to Disraeli, 12 August 1858, cited in W. F. Monypenny and G. E. Buckle, *The Life of Benjamin Disraeli, Earl of Beaconsfield* (London, 1910–20) IV, p. 182.
18. Derby to Jolliffe, 3 August 1858, Hylton Mss. DD/HY 18/2, fol. 32.
19. Rose to Disraeli, 17 November 1853, cited in R. Stewart, *The Foundation of the Conservative Party, 1830–1867* (London, 1978) p. 280.
20. Stanley Diary, 15 March 1851, Stanley Mss. DER (15) 43/1.
21. Rose memo, 3 June 1858, Hughenden Mss. B/XX/S/639A.
22. Stanley to Disraeli, 3 August 1858, Hughenden Mss. B/XX/S/639.
23. Stanley to Disraeli, 12 August 1858, Hughenden Mss. B/XX/S/640.
24. Ibid. Taylor informed Jolliffe that Stanley was looked to as the man 'to keep the Reform Bill Committee straight'. Taylor to Jolliffe, 16 August 1858, Hylton Mss. DD/HY 18/2.
25. Derby to Disraeli, 25 August 1858, Hughenden Mss. B/XX/S/180, cited in Monypenny and Buckle, *Disraeli*, IV, p. 184. See W. D. Jones, *Lord Derby and Victorian Conservatism* (Oxford, 1956) p. 245.
26. Ibid.
27. Disraeli to Derby, 26 August 1858, Derby Mss. 145/5. See also, Stone, 'Derby, Disraeli and the Reform Bill of 1859', p. 118.
28. Gathorne Hardy Diary, 6 September 1858, Cranbrook Mss. T501/290, fol. 175, cited in A. E. Gathorne-Hardy, *Gathorne Hardy, First Earl of Cranbrook: A Memoir with Extracts from his Diary and Correspondence* 2 vols (London, 1910) I, p. 125. Gathorne Hardy continued: Disraeli 'will alienate his party and break it up. Permissive Ballot! Rose sent me papers on this point, I must put down my numerous objections.'
29. Walpole to Derby, 20 September 1858, Derby Mss. 153/2.
30. Ibid.
31. Pakington to Derby, 6 October 1858, Derby Mss. 141/10.
32. Pakington to Disraeli, 8 October 1858, Hughenden Mss. B/XX/P/33.
33. Disraeli to Malmesbury, 29 September 1858, Malmesbury Mss. 9M73 1858–9/1.
34. Disraeli to Mrs Brydges Willyams, 11 October 1858, cited in Monypenny and Buckle, *Disraeli*, IV, p. 186.
35. Lord Malmesbury, *Memoirs of an Ex-Minister* (London, 1885) II, p. 140, cited in Jones, *Derby and Victorian Conservatism*, p. 246.
36. Sotheron-Estcourt Diary, 20 October 1858, Sotheron-Estcourt Mss. F.408.
37. Derby to Disraeli, 26 October 1858, Hughenden Mss. B/XX/S/183.

38. Derby to Pakington, 25 October 1858, Hampton Mss. 3835/11(iii).

39. Jolliffe to Disraeli, 27 October 1858, Hughenden Mss. B/XX/J/60.

40. Stanley to Derby, 25 October 1858, Derby Mss. 105/5. Stanley, who had 'no confidence in Jolliffe's informants', observed that 'if unsuccessful, it would damage the cabinet: and even success would only substitute an unsafe seat for a safe one'.

41. Stanley to Jolliffe, 27 October 1858, Hylton Mss. DD/HY 24/13, fol. 89.

42. Disraeli to Jolliffe, 28 October 1858, Hylton Mss. DD/HY 24/13, fol. 34.

43. Stanley to Jolliffe, 27 October 1858, Hylton Mss. DD/HY 24/13, fol. 88.

44. Talbot to Jolliffe, 29 October (1858), Hylton Mss. DD/HY 18/6, fol. 172.

45. Gordon to Palmer, 27 September 1858, Stanmore Mss. 49217, fol. 61.

46. Graham to Aberdeen, 14 August 1858, Aberdeen Mss. 43192, fol. 226.

47. Gordon to Palmer, 27 September 1858, Stanmore Mss. 49217.

48. Gladstone to Brougham, 2 October 1858, Brougham Mss. 12968.

49. Lytton to Disraeli, 23 September 1858, Hughenden Mss. B/XX/LY/94. See also, Lytton to Disraeli, 25 September 1858, Hughenden Mss. B/XX/LY/95; and Lytton to Disraeli, 13 October 1858, Hughenden Mss. B/XX/LY/99.

50. Graham to Gladstone, 19 October 1858, Gladstone Mss. 44164, fol. 90. See W. E. Gladstone, *The Gladstone Diaries*, H. C. G. Matthew and M. R. D. Foot (eds) (Oxford, 1968–82) V, pp. lxix–lxxi.

51. Aberdeen to Gladstone, 8 October 1858, Gladstone Mss. 44089 fol. 275, cited in John Morley, *The Life of William Ewart Gladstone* (London, 1903) I, p. 596.

52. Gladstone to Aberdeen, 30 October 1858, Aberdeen Mss. 43071, fol. 393. See also, *Gladstone Diaries*, V, p. xxvii; and Morley, *Gladstone*, I, pp. 595–7.

53. Graham to Aberdeen, 21 October 1858, Aberdeen Mss. 43192, fol. 253.

54. Graham to Aberdeen 3 November 1858, Aberdeen Mss. 43192, fol. 258.

55. Cardwell to Gordon, 4 November 1858, cited in *Lord Aberdeen's Correspondence, 1854–55*, B.P. 12 (12) p. 399.

56. Heathcote to Gladstone, 4 November 1858, Gladstone Mss. 44209, fol. 19.

57. Graham to Aberdeen, 7 November 1858, Aberdeen Mss. 43192, fol. 262.

58. Russell to Aberdeen, 5 November 1858, Aberdeen Mss. 43068, fol. 311.

59. Hayward to Cornewall Lewis, 11 November 1858, Harpton Court Mss. C/1490. For a discussion of the diplomatic significance of the Ionian settlement and the absence of widespread separatist ideas, see C. C. Eldridge, 'The Myth of Mid-Victorian "Separatism": The Cession of the Bay Islands and the Ionian Islands in the Early 1860's',

Victorian Studies, 12:3 (1969) pp. 331–46. But see also Keith A. P. Sandiford, 'Gladstone and Liberal Nationalist Movements', *Albion*, 13 (1981) pp. 27–42 and Bruce Knox, 'British Policy and the Ionian Islands, 1847–1864: Nationalism and Imperial Administration', *EHR*, 99 (1984) pp. 503–30 for the importance of the Ionian experience in the development of Gladstone's views on European nationalism and Ireland.

60. Graham to Ellice, 13 November 1858, Ellice Mss. 15019, fol. 134.
61. Graham to Aberdeen, 13 December 1858, Aberdeen Mss. 43192, fol. 276. See also, Cornewall Lewis to Wilson, 16 November 1858, cited in E. I. Barrington, *The Servant of All: Pages from the Family, Social and Political Life of my Father James Wilson* (London, 1927) II, p. 95.
62. Malmesbury, *Memoirs*, 3 November 1858, p. 454. See Jones, *Derby and Victorian Conservatism*, p. 246.
63. Manners to Granby (? November) 1858, cited in C. Whibley, *Lord John Manners and his Friends* 2 vols (Edinburgh, 1925) II, p. 109.
64. Walpole to Derby, 8 November 1858, Derby Mss. 153/2.
65. Derby memo, 21 November 1858, Derby Mss. 47. See also, Jones, *Derby and Victorian Conservatism*, p. 246, although Jones, as well as Stone in 'Derby, Disraeli and the Reform Bill of 1859', overlook both the existence and purpose of the cabinet committee.
66. Derby memo, n.d. (? 21 November 1858) Hughenden Mss. B/XX/S/191.
67. Derby memo, n.d. (? 21 November 1858) Hughenden Mss. B/XX/S/190.
68. Derby memo, n.d. (? 21 November 1858) Hughenden Mss. B/XX/S/191.
69. Derby memo, 21 November 1858, Derby Mss. 47.
70. Derby to Disraeli, n.d. (? 21 November 1858) Hughenden Mss. B/XX/S/190.
71. Pakington to Derby, 23 November 1858, Derby Mss. 141/10.
72. Pakington to Disraeli, 23 November 1858, Hughenden Mss. B/XX/P/42.
73. Pakington to Disraeli, 29 November 1858, Hughenden Mss. B/XX/P/35.
74. Jolliffe to Disraeli, 29 November 1858, Hughenden Mss. B/XX/J/63.
75. Manners to Granby, 6 December 1858, cited in Whibley, *Lord John Manners and his Friends*, II, p. 109.
76. Derby to the Queen, 1 December 1858, Derby Mss. 186/1; and Derby to the Queen, n.d. (? 7 December 1858) Derby Mss. 186/1.
77. Derby to Redesdale, 11 December 1858, Redesdale Mss. (D2002) c.40.
78. Walpole to Derby, 17 December 1858, Derby Mss. 153/2.
79. Gathorne Hardy Diary, 15 December 1858, Cranbrook Mss. T501/290, fol. 204, cited in Gathorne-Hardy, *Gathorne Hardy First Earl of Cranbrook*, I, p. 125.
80. Malmesbury, *Memoirs*, 3 December 1858, p. 456.
81. Lytton to Derby, 16 December 1858, Derby Mss. 162/1.
82. Derby to Disraeli, 19 December 1858, Hughenden Mss. B/XX/S/187.

83. Derby to Lytton (copy), 19 December 1858, Hughenden Mss. B/XX/S/187.
84. Disraeli to Derby, 20 December 1858, Derby Mss. 145/5.
85. Derby to Disraeli, 19 December 1858, Hughenden Mss. B/XX/S/187.
86. Disraeli to Derby, 20 December 1858, Derby Mss. 145/5.
87. Derby to Disraeli, 21 December 1858, Hughenden Mss. B/XX/S/188. See also, Disraeli to Derby, 22 December 1858, Derby Mss. 145/5.
88. Henley to Derby, 24 December 1858, Derby Mss. 156/14.
89. Derby to Disraeli, 25 December 1858, Hughenden Mss. B/XX/S/189.
90. Disraeli to Derby, 27 December 1858, Derby Mss. 145/5.
91. Henley to Derby, 27 December 1858, Derby Mss. 156/4.
92. Derby to Disraeli, 30 December 1858, Hughenden Mss. B/XX/S/193.
93. Disraeli to Derby, 27 December 1858, Derby Mss. 145/5.
94. Disraeli to Derby, 1 January 1859, Derby Mss. 145/6.
95. Ibid.
96. Disraeli to Derby, 27 December 1858, Derby Mss. 145/5.
97. Disraeli to Derby, 22 December 1858, Derby Mss. 145/5.
98. Derby to Disraeli, 30 December 1858, Hughenden Mss. B/XX/S/193.
99. Disraeli to Malmesbury, 29 September 1858, Malmesbury Mss. 9M73 1858–9/1.
100. Derby to Pakington, 25 October 1858, Hampton Mss. 3835/11(iii).
101. Disraeli to Mrs Brydges Willyams, 11 October 1858, cited in Monypenny and Buckle, *Disraeli*, IV, p. 186.
102. Disraeli to Derby, 1 January 1859, Derby Mss. 145/5.
103. Derby to Malmesbury, 28 December 1858, Malmesbury Mss. 9M73 1858–9/1.
104. Derby to Disraeli, 12 January 1859, Hughenden Mss. B/XX/S/209.
105. Derby to Disraeli, 21 December 1858, Hughenden Mss. B/XX/S/188.
106. Derby to Malmesbury, 28 December 1858, Malmesbury Mss. 9M73 1858–9/1.
107. Derby to Disraeli, 12 January 1859, Hughenden Mss. B/XX/S/209.
108. Derby to Disraeli, 2 January 1859, Hughenden Mss. B/XX/S/205.
109. Pakington to Derby, 30 December 1858, Derby Mss. 141/10.
110. Derby to Disraeli, 2 January 1859, Hughenden Mss. B/XX/S/205.
111. Derby to Malmesbury, 5 January 1859, Malmesbury Mss. 9M73 1858–9/1.
112. Derby to Disraeli, 2 January 1859, Hughenden Mss. B/XX/S/205.
113. Malmesbury to Hudson, 24 April 1858, Malmesbury Mss. 9M73 1/5, fol. 112. See also, D. E. D. Beales, *England and Italy 1859–60* (London, 1961) pp. 38–61; and H. Hearder, 'The Foreign Policy of Lord Malmesbury, 1858–9', unpublished PhD thesis, University of London, 1954.
114. Malmesbury to Cowley, 16 April 1858, Malmesbury Mss. 9M73 1/5, fol. 106. See also, *Correspondence relating to the Affairs of Italy, January to May 1859*, State Papers. Session 31 May–13 August 1859, Vol. xxxii, Command Paper No. 2524.
115. Derby to Malmesbury, 16 August 1858, Malmesbury Mss. 9M73 1858–9/3.

116. Derby to Malmesbury, 2 September 1858, Malmesbury Mss. 9M73 1858–9/3.
117. Palmerston to Malmesbury, 2 September 1858, Malmesbury Mss. 9M73 1858–9/3.
118. Malmesbury to Cowley, 7 December 1858, Malmesbury Mss. 9M73 1/5, fol. 498. See also, Malmesbury to Cowley, 15 January 1859, Malmesbury Mss. 9M73 1/5, fol. 639.
119. Malmesbury to Cowley, 13 January 1859, cited in F. A. Wellesley, *The Paris Embassy During the Second Empire* (London, 1928) p. 175. See also, Beales, *England and Italy*, pp. 42–3.
120. Malmesbury to Hudson, 12 January 1859, Malmesbury Mss. 9M73, fol. 8.
121. Derby to Malmesbury, 30 December 1858, Malmesbury Mss. 9M73 1858–9/3.
122. Derby to Malmesbury, 28 December 1858, Malmesbury Mss. 9M73 1858–9/3.
123. See Monypenny and Buckle, *Disraeli*, IV, pp. 216–28. See also, G. B. Henderson, 'Ralph Anstruther Earle', *EHR*, 58 (1943) pp. 172–89. 'In December 1858, Disraeli dispatched Ralph to Paris with two objects: first, to wean Napoleon from his friendship with Palmerston; and, second to persuade him to postpone his designs on Italy (presuming he meant war) until Disraeli had got his budget safely through Parliament', p. 181.
124. Malmesbury, *Memoirs*, 11 March 1852, p. 329. See also, Hearder, 'Foreign Policy of Lord Malmesbury'.
125. Stanley Diary, 15 March 1851, Stanley Mss. 920 DER (15) 43/1.
126. Disraeli to Derby, 4 January 1859, Derby Mss. 145/6, cited in Monypenny and Buckle, *Disraeli*, IV, p. 221.
127. Disraeli to Derby, 7 January 1859, Derby Mss. 145/6, cited in Monypenny and Buckle, *Disraeli*, IV, p. 222. See also, Beales, *England and Italy*, pp. 45–6.
128. Ibid.
129. Derby to Malmesbury, 4 January 1859, Malmesbury Mss. 9M73 1858–9/3.
130. Derby to Malmesbury, 5 January 1859, Malmesbury Mss. 9M73 1858–9/3.
131. Derby to Disraeli, 6 January 1859, Hughenden Mss. B/XX/S/206.
132. Derby to Malmesbury, 6 January 1859, Malmesbury Mss. 9M73 1858–9/3. See also, Derby to Disraeli, 8 January 1859, Hughenden Mss. B/XX/S/208.
133. Malmesbury, *Memoirs*, 12 and 16 January 1859, pp. 458–60.
134. Malmesbury, *Memoirs*, 12 January 1859, p. 459. There was widespread reaction to Napoleon's bellicose remarks. *The Times* thought it 'need not enlarge on the grossness of the artifice which seeks, after so many years, to palm upon us the Emperor Louis Napoleon as the enemy of any abuse however inveterate, or the champion of any reform however necessary'. *The Times*, 10 January 1859; see also, Beales, *England and Italy*, p. 49.

135. Derby to Walpole (copy), 6 January 1859, Hughenden Mss. B/XX/S/ 207A. See also, Jones, *Derby and Victorian Conservatism*, p. 247.
136. Derby to Disraeli, 14 January 1859, Hughenden Mss. B/XX/S/211.
137. Stanley to Derby, 13 January 1859, Derby Mss. 105/5.
138. Derby to Stanley, 14 January 1859, Derby Mss. 187/1, fol. 83. See also, Jones, *Derby and Victorian Conservatism*, p. 248.
139. Malmesbury, *Memoirs*, 28 January 1859, p. 462; Walpole to Derby, 27 January 1859, Derby Mss. 153/2; and Henley to Derby, 28 January 1859, Derby Mss. 156/14.
140. Walpole to Derby, 28 January 1859, Derby Mss. 153/2.
141. Rose memo, 24 January 1859, Derby Mss. 48/3.
142. Ibid. Stone, 'Derby, Disraeli and the Reform Bill of 1859', p. 120, sees the figures and statistics Rose produced as the authoritative guide to the cabinet's formulation of a reform scheme. But they were only authoritative once Derby presented them as such. By late January Rose's memo had an important political purpose, amid shifting circumstances, providing the premier with a means of reconstructing cabinet unanimity.

CHAPTER 10

1. Graham to Aberdeen, 1 February 1859, Aberdeen Mss. 43192, fol. 304.
2. Clarendon to Reeve, 26 January 1859, Clarendon Mss. C.535.
3. Clarendon to Aberdeen, 2 February 1859, Aberdeen Mss. 43324, fol. 116. See also, Graham to Aberdeen, 1 February 1859, Aberdeen Mss. 43192, fol. 304; and D. E. D. Beales, *England and Italy 1859–60* (London, 1961) p. 53.
4. The Queen's Speech, 3 February 1859, *Hansard*, 3rd series, CLII. Though 'unusually long' the statement 'was extremely cautious both in what it said and what it left unsaid'. Dallas to Cass, 4 February 1859, cited in G. M. Dallas, *Letters from London 1856–1860* (London, 1870) II, p. 88.
5. Derby, 3 February 1859, *Hansard*, 3rd series, CLII, 34–49.
6. Grey, 3 February 1859, *Hansard*, 3rd series, CLII, 49–51; Brougham 3 February 1859, *Hansard*, 3rd series, CLII, 52–5.
7. Disraeli, 3 February 1859, *Hansard*, 3rd series, CLII, 82–93.
8. Broughton Diary, 4 February 1859, Broughton Mss. 43761, fol. 146.
9. Aberdeen to Gordon, 8 February 1859, Aberdeen Mss. 43226, fol. 353; Argyll to Aberdeen, 7 February 1859, Aberdeen Mss. 43199, fol. 163.
10. Herbert to Gladstone, 7 February 1859, Gladstone Mss. 44211, fol. 32. See also, Russell, 3 February 1859, *Hansard*, 3rd series, CLII, 93–102; Palmerston, 3 February 1859, *Hansard*, 3rd series, CLII, 72–78; and Beales, *England and Italy*, p. 51. For the favourable diplomatic effect of the debate in Paris see Cowley to Malmesbury, 6 February 1859, cited in *QVL*, 1st series, I, p. 405.

11. Russell to Clarendon, 10 February 1859, Clarendon Mss. C.104, fol. 25. For further comment on Russell's growing belief that a congress was the best solution to diplomatic difficulties see S. Walpole, *The Life of Lord John Russell* (London, 1889) II, p. 301.

12. Russell to Palmerston, 13 February 1859, Broadlands Mss. GC/RU 496, cited in C. T. McIntire, *England Against the Papacy, 1858–1861: Tories, Liberals, and the Overthrow of Papal Temporal Power During the Italian Risgorgimento* (Cambridge, 1983) p. 83.

13. In the Papal States, Austrian and French forces imposed, Russell argued, 'the very worst form of government that any country ever had'. Russell, 3 February 1859, *Hansard*, 3rd series, CLII, 93–102. See also Walpole, *Russell*, II, p. 302.

14. Russell to Dean of Bristol, 4 February 1859, Russell Mss. PRO 30/22/13/G, fol. 147.

15. Palmerston to Russell, 14 February 1859, Russell Mss. PRO 30/22/13/G, fol. 149. Part of this letter is cited in D. F. Krein, *The Last Palmerston Government: Foreign Policy, Domestic Politics, and the Genesis of 'Splendid Isolation'* (Iowa, 1978) p. 11.

16. Palmerston to Clarendon, 16 February 1859, Clarendon Mss. C.524.

17. Broughton Diary, 2 February 1859, Broughton Mss. 43761, fol. 146.

18. Palmerston Diary, 2 February 1859, Broadlands Mss. D/19.

19. Hayward to Lady Holland, 18 February 1859, Holland House Mss.

20. ? to Disraeli, n.d. (? February 1859) Hughenden Mss. B/XVIII/C/35.

21. ? to Disraeli, n.d. (? 4 March 1859) Hughenden Mss. B/XVIII/C/43.

22. Lennox to Disraeli, n.d. (? February 1859) Hughenden Mss. B/XX/LX/47.

23. Hayward to Lady Holland, 18 February 1859, Holland House Mss.

24. Palmerston, 25 February 1859, *Hansard*, 3rd series, CLII, 869–78. See also McIntire, *England Against the Papacy*, pp. 84–5.

25. Disraeli, 25 February, 1859, *Hansard*, 3rd series, CLII, 878–81. For discussion of the diplomacy associated with this see McIntire, *England Against the Papacy*, pp. 83–101.

26. Dallas to Cass, 1 March 1859, cited in Dallas, *Letters from London*, II, p. 93. See also, Beales, *England and Italy*, p. 40.

27. Russell, 25 February 1859, *Hansard*, 3rd series, CLII, 881–2.

28. Granville to Canning, 9 March 1859, Granville Mss. PRO 30/29/21/3, fol. 25.

29. Hayward to Lady Holland, 12 March 1859, Holland House Mss.

30. Argyll to Gladstone, 22 March 1859, Gladstone Mss. 44098, fol. 191.

31. Clarendon memo, n.d. (? March 1859) Clarendon Mss. C.555.

32. Gladstone to Hudson, 14 March 1859, Gladstone Mss. 44391, fol. 206, cited in Beales, *England and Italy*, p. 53. See also, D. M. Schreuder, 'Gladstone and Italian Unification 1848–1870: The Making of a Liberal', *EHR*, 85 (1970) pp. 475–501.

33. Aberdeen to Gordon, 28 February 1859, cited in *Aberdeen Correspondence*, B.P. 12 (12) p. 453.

34. Gladstone to Hudson, 14 March 1859, Gladstone Mss. 44391, fol. 206, cited in Beales, *England and Italy*, p. 53.

35. W. E. Gladstone (anon.) 'War in Italy', *Quarterly Review*, 105 (April

1859) pp. 527–64. In summarising his views Gladstone wrote: 'If we are to consider the case as between Italy at large and Austria, it presents a long and dismal score of misdeeds which call loudly, if not for retribution, yet for remedy. If we take it as between Austria and France, then the first menace undoubtedly proceeded from the latter. If we regard it as between Austria and Sardinia it appears that, as far as overt acts of recent date are concerned, it is Austria not Sardinia which has first given ground for remonstrance and for alarm. As respects the past, to say nothing of the sequestrations, the chain of treaties between Austria and the States coterminous with Sardinia, and the illegal extension of the fortifications of Piacenza, seem to throw upon that Empire a responsibility not the less heavy because it has been unacknowledged. But finally, if we view the question as between Sardinia and France, it must be plain to every impartial mind that the consequence of a prayer for military protection is an immediate and heavy loss in point of independence; and that, though time has in some degree weakened the remembrance of French occupation in Northern Italy, it cannot be viewed otherwise than with feelings of aversion and alarm by any friend either to freedom or to the Italian peninsula.' Gladstone concluded the article: 'As far as it is possible to forecast the attitude of parties at the opening of a conflict now too probable, it seems plain that the neutrality of England will in all likelihood be a matter not of prudence only, but of the highest moral obligation. The relief of Italy is an honourable end, but it must not be sought by unholy means, such as would be the case if countenance be given to schemes, in whatever quarter, of selfish and reckless ambition.' See also, R. Shannon, *Gladstone, 1809–1865* (London, 1982) pp. 378–9; Beales, *England and Italy*, pp. 56–7; and J. B. Conacher, 'Party Politics in the Age of Palmerston', in E. Appleman, W. A. Madden and M. Wolff (eds) *1859: Entering an Age of Crisis* (Bloomington, Indiana, 1959) pp. 175–6.

36.   Greville Diary, 24 March 1859, Greville Mss. 41123, cited in C. C. F. Greville, *The Greville Memoirs*, H. Reeve (ed.) (London, 1888) VIII, p. 236.

37.   The correspondence between Malmesbury and the French government relating to this affair was laid before parliament on 8 March. Subsequently Granville, Sir George Grey and Russell strongly criticised Malmesbury for his part in the negotiations. Malmesbury, 8 March 1859, *Hansard*, 3rd series, CLII, 1428–40; and ibid., 1440–1553.

38.   Granville to Canning, 9 March 1859, Granville Mss. PRO 30/29/21/3, fol. 12.

39.   Palmerston to Clarendon, 28 March 1859, Clarendon Mss. C.524.

40.   Sotheron-Estcourt Diary, 19 March 1859, Sotheron-Estcourt Mss. C.409.

41.   Cairns, 11 February 1859, *Hansard*, 3rd series, CLII, 277–304.

42.   For the subsequent debate see, 11 February 1859, *Hansard*, 3rd series, CLII, 304–14.

43.   Walpole, 21 February 1859, *Hansard*, 3rd series, CLII, 610–29.

44. Trelawny, 21 February 1859, *Hansard*, 3rd series, CLII, 629–33; Russell, 21 February 1859, *Hansard*, 3rd series, CLII, 648–52.
45. C. R. Dod, *Parliamentary Companion, 1862* (London, 1862).
46. Ball, 21 February 1859, *Hansard*, 3rd series, CLII, 638–9.
47. G. Grey, 21 February 1859, *Hansard*, 3rd series, CLII, 633–8; Cornewall Lewis, 21 February 1859, *Hansard*, 3rd series, CLII, 643–4. After further debate Trelawny secured the rejection of Walpole's bill, which postponed the settlement of the question until 1868.
48. Pakington, 25 February 1859, *Hansard*, 3rd series, CLII, 882–913; Wood, 25 February 1859, *Hansard*, 3rd series CLII, 913–22.
49. Stanley, 14 February 1859, *Hansard*, 3rd series, CLII, 346–80; see ibid., 380–4 for the subsequent debate.
50. Jolliffe to Disraeli, 22 February 1859, Hughenden Mss. B/XX/J/70.
51. Herbert to Gladstone, 7 February 1859, Gladstone Mss. 44211, fol. 32. See also, Disraeli, 3 February 1859, *Hansard*, 3rd series, CLII, 82–93. This was the significance of the remark by Dallas that the Queen's Speech was 'extremely cautious both in what it said and what it left unsaid'. Dallas to Cass, 4 February 1859, cited in Dallas, *Letters from London*, II, p. 88.
52. Derby, 3 February 1859, *Hansard*, 3rd series, CLII, 34–49.
53. Argyll to Aberdeen, 7 February 1859, Aberdeen Mss. 43199, fol. 163.
54. Herbert to Gladstone, 7 February 1859, Gladstone Mss. 44211, fol. 32. Disraeli, Herbert went on to comment, ran 'the risk of getting up an agitation in the country by appearing inclined to jockey them out of a thing they are not impatient for so long as they believe they are getting it, but which they will learn to demand loudly if they think they are to be duped'.
55. Russell, 3 February 1859, *Hansard*, 3rd series, CLII, 93–102. The opposition press naturally seized upon Disraeli's reticence and the difficulties of the reform question to lampoon the government. *The Examiner* described Disraeli as 'mere stucco, not half so ornamented as he is unsolid. The majority are nothing but lath and plaster. The crack of doom is visible before the house is opened for business.' *The Examiner*, 27 February 1859, p. 130. See also, *The Examiner*, 12 February 1859, p. 97.
56. Derby memo, 7 February 1859, Derby Mss. 47/3.
57. Ibid. Derby went on to comment upon the effect of excluding redistribution from the bill. 'No doubt we shall to a certain extent disappoint public *expectation*: but I question whether we shall not conciliate public and still more private *support*.'
58. Derby to Disraeli, 8 February 1859, Derby Mss. 145/6.
59. For the letters written by Disraeli, Lytton, Walpole, Salisbury, Peel and Hardwicke to Derby, 7 February 1859, see Derby Mss. 47/3. See also, Derby to Disraeli, 8 February 1859, Derby Mss. 145/6.
60. Stanley to Derby, 7 February 1859, Derby Mss. 47/3.
61. Such an omission, Manners believed, would 'leave a popular and dangerous part of the Reform question open for agitation hereafter'. Manners to Derby, 7 February 1859, Derby Mss. 47/3.
62. Derby to Disraeli, 8 February 1859, Derby Mss. 47/3.

63. Derby to Walpole, 9 February 1859, Derby Mss. 187/1.
64. Stanley to Disraeli, 9 February 1859, Hughenden Mss. B/XX/S/676, cited in W. F. Monypenny and G. E. Buckle, *The Life of Benjamin Disraeli, Earl of Beaconsfield* (London, 1910–20) IV, p. 197.
65. Disraeli also pointed to Russell's evasive stance on redistribution in his own reform bills. In 1852 Russell had avoided disfranchisement by 'grouping', and in 1854 disfranchisement had been proposed 'with the object of enfranchising the *minorities*'. Disraeli to Stanley, 10 February 1859, cited in Monypenny and Buckle, *Disraeli*, IV, p. 198. See also, Disraeli to Derby, 11 February 1859, Derby Mss. 145/6.
66. Derby to the Queen, 13 February 1859, Derby Mss. 186/2.
67. Derby to the Queen, 15 February 1859, Derby Mss. 187/1.
68. Derby to the Queen, 13 February 1859, Derby Mss. 186/2.
69. Derby memo, 16 February 1859, Derby Mss. 47/3.
70. Malmesbury to Derby, n.d. (? 16 February 1859) Derby Mss. 47/3. For the letters written by Disraeli, Lytton, Henley, Hardwicke, Peel, Manners, and Stanley to Derby, 16 February 1859, see Derby Mss. 47/3.
71. Derby to Disraeli, 8 February 1859, Derby Mss. 145/6.
72. Walpole to Derby, 8 February 1859, Derby Mss. 47/3.
73. Derby to Disraeli, 8 February 1859, Derby Mss. 145/6.
74. Derby to Lennox, 28 February 1859, Derby Mss. 186/2.
75. In September 1858 Disraeli declined to appoint Lennox's brother, Lord March, to a vacant Commissionership of Excise. See R. Blake, *Disraeli* (London, 1966) p. 390–1.
76. Derby to Pakington, 14 February 1859, Hampton Mss. 3835/11(iii).
77. Pakington to Derby, 15 February 1859, Derby Mss. 141/10.
78. Derby to Pakington, 14 February 1859, Hampton Mss. 3835/11(iii).
79. Derby to Disraeli, 25 February 1859, Hughenden Mss. B/XX/S/214. Financial considerations were paramount for Lord Chandos in 1859 because of the bankruptcy of his father, the Duke of Buckingham. See Blake, *Disraeli*, p. 400.
80. Disraeli to Derby, 23 February 1859, Derby Mss. 145/6. Richard John Hely-Hutchinson, fourth Earl of Donoughmore (1823–66) was educated at Harrow; Sheriff of County Tipperary, 1847; and had been Vice-President of the Board of Trade since April 1858.
81. Earle to Disraeli, 20 February 1859, Hughenden Mss. B/XX/E/150.
82. Disraeli to Derby, 20 December 1858, Derby Mss. 145/5. Estcourt had influence amongst those 'country gentlemen who in default of one of their set in the Cabinet are constrained to look to Walpole'.
83. Lord March's appointment might also prevent any damage being caused amongst the backbenches by Lord Henry Lennox's umbrage.
84. Disraeli to Derby, 23 February 1859, Derby Mss. 145/6. To further placate 'ultra Tory' opinion Earle suggested appointing either Newdegate or Bentinck to the Poor Law Board. This suggestion, however, found favour with neither Disraeli or Derby.
85. Earle to Disraeli, 20 February 1859, Hughenden Mss. B/XX/E/150. While at Balliol College, Oxford, Northcote experienced a religious evolution similar to Gladstone in his undergraduate days, and during

the South Devon election of 1855 was accused by being a Puseyite. In 1842 Northcote admitted he would sooner addict himself to Gladstone's opinions than those of any other person with whom he was acquainted. See A. Lang, *Life, Letters, and Diaries of Sir Stafford Northcote, first Earl of Iddesleigh*, 2 vols (Edinburgh, 1890).

86. See Lang, *Northcote*, I, p. 153.
87. Derby to Disraeli, 25 February 1859, Hughenden Mss. B/XX/S/214.
88. Derby to Pakington, 27 February 1859, Hampton Mss. 3835/11(iii). C. B. Adderley, C. Baillie, J. R. Mowbray and Gathorne Hardy were also considered as candidates for reappointment. Adderley, however, although 'a gentleman' and a frequent speaker in Parliament, was considered 'careless and wild and would be little use as a counsellor'; Disraeli had 'already planned the political extinction of Baillie'; Mowbray was discarded as being 'without distinguishing ability', while Hardy possessed 'a reputation which [had] not yet been justified. As a speaker at least he [had] failed' and he had 'no advantages of breeding'. Earle to Disraeli, 20 February 1859, Hughenden Mss. B/XX/E/150.
89. Earle to Disraeli, n.d. (? 11 February 1859) Hughenden Mss. B/XX/E/147.
90. Jolliffe memo, 21 February 1859, Hylton Mss. DD/HY 18/8, fol. 2.
91. Earle to Disraeli, n.d. (? 27 February 1859) Hughenden Mss. B/XX/E/156.
92. Henley to Walpole, n.d. (? February 1859) Walpole Mss. 5991.
93. Delane's Diary of leader writers, 21 February 1859, *The Times*, Mss.
94. *The Times*, 28 February 1859, p. 8.
95. Disraeli to Derby, 1 March 1859, Derby Mss. 145/6, cited in Monypenny and Buckle, *Disraeli*, IV, p. 200.
96. Disraeli to Lennox, 1 March 1859, cited in Monypenny and Buckle, *Disraeli*, IV, p. 200.
97. Disraeli to Derby, 1 March 1859, Derby Mss. 145/6.
98. Ellice to Panmure, 27 (? February 1859) Dalhousie Mss. GD/45/14/644.
99. Gathorne Hardy Diary, 2 March 1859, Cranbrook Mss. T501/291, fol. 236 cited in A. E. Gathorne-Hardy, *Gathorne Hardy 1st Earl of Cranbrook: A Memoir* (London, 1910) I, p. 128. It is probable that we will never know who informed Ellice of details of the bill. But it must also remain a moot point whether this cabinet 'leak' was an inspired attempt to reassure potential support immediately prior to the debate.
100. Ellice to Panmure, 27 (? February 1859) Dalhousie Mss. GD/45/14/644.
101. Gathorne Hardy Diary, 2 March 1859, Cranbrook Mss. T501/291, fol. 236, cited in Gathorne-Hardy, *Gathorne Hardy*, I, p. 128.
102. Disraeli, 28 February 1859, *Hansard*, 3rd series, CLII, 966–1005. The bill Disraeli introduced was exactly that unanimously agreed to by the cabinet on 16 February. Disraeli opened his speech by arguing that the tranquility of the country made this an appropriate moment for reform. He then went on to pay a tribute to Russell, and attack 'Brightism'. Population could never be the only principle of represen-

tation. Thus Disraeli proposed an equalisation of the borough and county franchises at £10; a number of merit franchises in the boroughs; the transfer of 40s county freeholders residing in boroughs to borough constituencies; the introduction of voting papers; and a limited redistribution scheme disfranchising fifteen boroughs with less than 6000 in population. See also, G. L. Stone, 'Derby, Disraeli and the Reform Bill of 1859', unpublished PhD thesis, University of Illinois at Urbana-Champaign, 1975, pp. 135–45; and Monypenny and Buckle, *Disraeli*, IV, pp. 200-1.

103. Granville to Canning, 3 March 1859, Granville Mss. PRO 30/29/21/3, fol. 13.

104. Sotheron-Estcourt Diary, 28 February 1859, Sotheron-Estcourt Mss. C.409.

105. Gathorne Hardy Diary, 2 March 1859, Cranbrook Mss. T501/291, fol. 236, cited in Gathorne-Hardy, *Gathorne Hardy*, I, p. 128.

106. Russell, 28 February 1859, *Hansard*, 3rd series, CLII, 1016–19.

107. Fortescue Diary, 28 February 1859, Carlingford Mss. DD/SH 358.

108. Ellice to Panmure, 2 March 1859, Dalhousie Mss. GD45/14/644.

109. Dallas to Cass, 4 March 1859, cited in Dallas, *Letters from London*, II, p. 95. Roebuck strengthened the apparent cleavage between 'Palmerstonian' Whigs and 'Russellite' Radicals when, speaking after Russell, he attacked the government measure as failing to give 'one iota of power' to the working classes. Roebuck, 28 February 1859, *Hansard*, 3rd series, CLII, 1019–22. Bright, too, immediately denounced the bill as disturbing everything and settling nothing. Bright, 28 February 1859, *Hansard*, 3rd series, CLII, 1022–9.

110. Ellice to Panmure, 2 March 1859, Dalhousie Mss. GD45/14/644.

111. Hamilton to Disraeli, 13 March 1859, Hughenden Mss. B/XX/H/?.

112. Hayward to Lady Holland, 4 March 1859, Holland House Mss.

113. ? to Disraeli, 3 March 1859, Hughenden Mss. B/XVIII/C/28.

114. Granville to Canning, 3 March 1859, Granville Mss. PRO 30/29/21/3, fol. 13. Hayter, in a strongly partisan mood, predicted that the bill would be 'thrown out' on the second reading and suggested that Palmerston would succeed Derby. Cardwell to Newcastle, 2 March 1859, Newcastle Mss. NeC 12,426.

115. Ellice to Panmure, 4 March 1859, Dalhousie Mss. GD45/14/644. See also, Roebuck memo (? March 1859) cited in R. E. Leader *The Life and Letters of John Arthur Roebuck* (London, 1879) p. 278; and Parkes to Hatherton, 4 March 1859, Hatherton Mss. D260/M/F/5/27/33.

116. Baring to Russell, 4 March 1859, Russell Mss. PRO 30/22/13/G, fol. 153.

117. Herbert to Russell, 9 March 1859, Russell Mss. PRO 30/22/13/G, fol. 159, cited in A. H. Gordon, Baron Stanmore, *Sidney Herbert, Lord Herbert of Lea: A Memoir* (London, 1906) II, pp. 170–2.

118. Russell memo, n.d. (? March 1859) Russell Mss. PRO 30/22/13/G, fol. 169.

119. Argyll to Russell, 8 March 1859, Russell Mss. PRO 30/22/13/G, fol. 155.

120. Ellice to Panmure, 4 March 1859, Dalhousie Mss. GD45/14/644.
121. Granville caustically noted that Russell seemed to be in 'a fool's paradise, thinking himself prime minister already'. Granville to Canning, 14 March 1859, Granville Mss. PRO 30/29/21/3, fol. 30, cited in Lord E. Fitzmaurice, *The Life of Granville George Leveson-Gower, Second Earl Granville, K.G.* (London, 1905) I, p. 325.
122. Granville to Canning, 14 March 1859, Granville Mss. PRO 30/29/21/3, fol. 33.
123. *The Times*, 12 March 1859, p. 6.
124. Granville to Canning, 14 March 1859, Granville Mss. PRO 30/29/21/3, fol. 33.
125. Granville to Canning, 3 March 1859, Granville Mss. PRO 30/29/21/3, fol. 17, cited in Fitzmaurice, *Granville*, I, p. 325.
126. Hayward to Lady Holland, 12 March 1859, Holland House Mss.
127. Ibid.
128. Granville to Canning, 3 March 1859, Granville Mss. PRO 30/29/21/3, fol. 17. Granville had a personal belief that 'the best arrangement would be for Pam to come to the House of Lords. Although Johnny has declared in the most positive manner that he will not serve under anyone, I think he can hardly object to the leadership of the House of Commons under a man who is already seventy-four, who consented to serve under him and under whom he has served.' Ibid., cited in Fitzmaurice, *Granville*, I, pp. 324–5.
129. Palmerston Diary, 7 March 1859, Broadlands Mss. D/19.
130. Granville to Canning, 21 March 1859, Granville Mss. PRO 30/29/21/3, fol. 53.
131. Ellice to Panmure, n.d. (? 11 March 1859) Dalhousie Mss. GD45/14/644. Ellice saw Graham as the source of Russell's indiscretion: 'the best one to get a man into a scrape–but the worst . . . to get him out of one'.
132. Granville to Canning, 10 February 1859, Granville Mss. PRO 30/29/21/3, fol. 10.
133. Broughton Diary, 8 March 1859, Broughton Mss. 43761, fol. 153.
134. Grey to Elcho, 12 March 1859, published in *The Times*, 15 March 1859, p. 9.
135. *The Times*, 15 March 1859, p. 9.
136. Hayward to Lady Holland, 12 March 1859, Holland House Mss.
137. Roebuck memo, n.d. (? March 1859) cited in Leader, *Roebuck*, p. 276.
138. Roebuck, 18 March 1859, *Hansard*, 3rd series, CLIII, 331–3.
139. *The Times*, 19 March 1859, p. 9.
140. Russell, 18 March 1859, *Hansard*, 3rd series, CLIII, 342–55. Prince Albert caustically observed that in 'our home affairs the confusion is perhaps even greater. A Radical Reform Bill of a Conservative Ministry is denounced as not Radical enough by the Liberal Party (who want no reform, and are especially afraid of a Radical one), headed by Lord John, whom they will not have as a leader.' Prince Albert to Stockmar, 23 March 1859, cited in T. Martin, *The Life of his Royal Highness The Prince Consort*, 5 vols (London, 1879) IV, p. 410.

141. Gathorne Hardy Diary, 28 February 1859, Cranbrook Mss. T501/ 291, fol. 236, cited in Gathorne-Hardy, *Gathorne Hardy*, I, 127.
142. Sotheron-Estcourt Diary, 28 February 1859, Sotheron-Estcourt Mss. C.409.
143. Greville Diary, 3 March 1859, Greville Mss. 41123, cited in Greville, *Memoirs*, VIII, p. 227.
144. Sotheron-Estcourt Diary, 1 March 1859, Sotheron-Estcourt Mss. C.409.
145. Dallas to Cass, 4 March 1859, cited in Dallas, *Letters from London*, II, p. 95.
146. Gathorne Hardy Diary, 2 March 1859, Cranbrook Mss. T501/291, fol. 236, cited in Gathorne-Hardy, *Gathorne Hardy*, I, p. 128.
147. Dallas to Cass, 4 March 1859, cited in Dallas, *Letters from London*, II, p. 95.
148. Sotheron-Estcourt Diary, 1 March 1859, Sotheron-Estcourt Mss. C.409.
149. See Gathorne Hardy Diary, 2 March 1859, Cranbrook Mss. T501/ 291, fol. 236, cited in Gathorne-Hardy, *Gathorne Hardy*, I, p. 128. Newdegate concluded that 'as usual Disraeli has succeeded in sacrificing his party'. Newdegate to his mother, 1 March 1859, Newdegate Mss. B.3277.
150. Derby to Disraeli, 5 March 1859, Hughenden Mss. B/XX/S/216. The only exception to the collective approval of the Conservative peerage was Lord Hardinge who submitted his resignation from the cabinet. Derby persuaded Hardinge that it would not be necessary to act upon this decision until the bill reached the Lords. For practical purposes this postponed the threat indefinitely. Derby to Hardinge, 2 March 1859, Derby Mss. 186/2.
151. ? to Disraeli, 3 March 1859, Hughenden Mss. B/XI/B/16.
152. DeLaWarr to Derby, 9 March 1859, Derby Mss. III. On 7 March the 'Liberal–Conservative' Andrew Stewart warned Disraeli that some Liberals, 'not generally supporters of the government', who had declared themselves 'favourable to the general scope of the bill', were deterred from supporting the measure because of the freeholders clause. Stewart to Disraeli, 7 March 1859, Hughenden Mss. B/VI/B/ 10.
153. Carlton Petition, 9 March 1859, Hughenden Mss. B/XI/B/13. The petitioners also hoped that 'Derby should consider himself absolved from any obligation to withdraw the Reform Bill in case that clause were negatived by the H. of C.'
154. Derby to Newdegate, 10 March 1859, Newdegate Mss. B.6642.
155. Newdegate to Derby, 9 March 1859, Newdegate Mss. B.6641. Prior to the introduction of the reform bill Newdegate suspected that he was 'to catch it, if they can give it me in the Reform debates, so I must have my eyes about me'. By 'they' Newdegate meant principally Disraeli. Newdegate saw the bill as confirmation of Disraeli's dishonesty and the intention that he should 'catch it'. Newdegate to his mother, 23 February 1859, Newdegate Mss. B.3275.
156. Derby to Newdegate, 10 March 1859, Newdegate Mss. B.6642.

157. Disraeli received a plea from the 'Conservative Land Society' to withdraw the clause relating to the 40s freeholder; a 'host of opposition would be disarmed by such a modification'. 'Conservative Land Society' to Disraeli, 5 March 1859, Hughenden Mss. B/XI/B/9.

158. Manners to Granby, 10 March 1859, cited in C. Whibley, *Lord John Manners and His Friends* (Edinburgh, 1925) II, p. 111.

159. Sotheron-Estcourt Diary, 10 March 1859, Sotheron-Estcourt Mss. C.409.

160. Derby to the Queen, 10 March 1859, Derby Mss. 187/2.

161. Newdegate to his mother, 10 March 1859, Newdegate Mss. B.3278.

162. Newdegate to his mother, 13 March 1859, Newdegate Mss. B.3279.

163. Earle to Disraeli, n.d. (? March 1859) Hughenden Mss. B/XX/E/155.

164. Newdegate to his mother, 15 March 1859, Newdegate Mss. B.3280.

165. Malmesbury Diary, 16 March 1859, Malmesbury Mss. 9M73.

166. Malmesbury Diary, 17 March 1859, Malmesbury Mss. 9M73.

167. Sotheron-Estcourt Diary, 12 March 1859, Sotheron-Estcourt Mss. C.409.

168. Derby to Disraeli, 16 March 1859, Derby Mss. 186/2, cited in W. D. Jones, *Lord Derby and Victorian Conservatism* (Oxford, 1956) p. 251.

169. Malmesbury Diary, 19 March 1859, Malmesbury Mss. 9M73. By 19 March, Derby was convinced that an unyielding commitment to Russell's motion as fatal to the bill if successful was the best strategy to adopt. 'We certainly *may* refuse to accept John Russell's resolution as the final decision of the House, and may even alter it, proceed to the 2nd reading of our Bill and fix a day for Committee; but in that case we must consider whether we should go to the country with the same advantages on a defeat on a clause, as we should on a factious opposition to the whole Bill, in an unusual and unparliamentary form.' Derby to Disraeli, 20 March 1859, Derby Mss. 186/2.

170. Derby to the Queen, 20 March 1859, Derby Mss. 187/2.

171. Fortescue Diary, 21 March 1859, Carlingford Mss. DD/SG 358. During his speech Russell quoted a statement made by Derby in 1854 defending the distinction between the county and borough franchise; contrasting it with the equalisation of the franchise embodied in the government measure. Russell also argued that the borough franchise should be lowered although he did not propose a specific qualification. Russell, 21 March 1859, *Hansard*, 3rd series, CLIII, 393–403.

172. Granville to Canning, 23 March 1859, Granville Mss. PRO 30/29/21/3, fol. 54.

173. Ibid. See also, Fortescue Diary, 21 March 1859, Carlingford Mss. DD/SH 358.

174. Newdegate, 21 March 1859, *Hansard*, 3rd series, CLIII, 473–5.

175. Gathorne Hardy Diary, 22 March 1859, Cranbrook Mss. T501/291, fol. 245, cited in Gathorne-Hardy, *Gathorne Hardy*, I, p. 128.

176. Disraeli to Elcho, 21 March 1859, Wemyss Mss. 3/11. See also, Fortescue Diary, 21 March, 1859, Carlingford Mss. DD/SH 358.

177. Derby to Campden, 23 March 1859, Derby Mss. 187/2.

178. Derby to the Queen, 23 March 1859, Derby Mss. 187/2.

179. Derby to Disraeli, 20 March 1859, Derby Mss. 186/2. By 20 March,

Cowley had returned to Paris from his mission to Vienna. Another factor in the diplomatic situation was then introduced by Russia suggesting a conference between England, France, Austria, Prussia and Russia. After 20 March, Malmesbury was seeking the diplomatic initiative in organising the conference as part of his self-appointed role as the neutral arbiter of European differences. See also, the Queen to Malmesbury, 20 March 1859, cited in *QVL*, 1st series, III, p. 416; and the Queen to Malmesbury, 22 March 1859, cited in *QVL*, 1st series, III, p. 416–7.

180. Derby to the Queen, 23 March 1859, Derby Mss. 187/2.
181. Lytton, 22 March 1859, *Hansard*, 3rd series, CLIII, 542–59. When Lytton delivered this colourful metaphor Hayter quickly rose from the opposition benches and hastily left the chamber amid great laughter. Lytton put further pressure on the opposition by offering to submit all the provisions of the bill to review in Committee.
182. Cairns, 22 March 1859, *Hansard*, 3rd series, CLIII, 600–23. Cairns also presented a conciliatory position suggesting the possibility of amendment in Committee if the bill were allowed to pass its second reading.
183. Pakington, 28 March 1859, *Hansard*, 3rd series, CLIII, 985–1004.
184. Derby to the Queen, 23 March 1859, Derby Mss. 187/2.
185. Heathcote to Gladstone, 23 March 1859, Gladstone Mss. 44209, fol. 27. See also, Mrs Heathcote to Gladstone, 24 March 1859, Gladstone Mss. 44209, fol. 29.
186. Gladstone, 29 March 1859, *Hansard*, 3rd series, CLIII, 1046–67. Gladstone objected to the equalisation of the franchise and the freeholder clause. He favoured a reduction of the borough franchise, but approved of the limited redistribution in the bill. He then forcefully defended 'pocket borough' constituencies and urged support for the second reading of the bill. See W. White, *The Inner Life of the House of Commons* (London, 1897) I, p. 96.
187. Grey Diary, 4 April 1859, Grey Mss. C3/21. See also, Shannon, *Gladstone*, p. 376.
188. Palmerston, 25 March 1859, *Hansard*, 3rd series, CLIII, 873–85. At the beginning of the speech Palmerston confessed he had changed his mind and though he had formerly opposed it, he now supported the lowering of the borough franchise. He also opposed the freehold clause as leading towards electoral districts. He approved, however, of the limited redistribution in the government measure.
189. 'Palmerston made a clever but most insolent speech of which nobody seems to understand the precise object; it appeared to me to express opinions which ought to have led him to support the 2nd reading of the Bill.' Grey Diary, 4 April 1859, Grey Mss. C3/21. See also, H. C. F. Bell, *Lord Palmerston* (London, 1936) II, pp. 207–8.
190. Palmerston, 25 March 1859, *Hansard*, 3rd series, CLIII, 873–85. Palmerston's agreement to a lowering of the borough franchise was a significant change from his previous statements on reform. 'Almost as inevitably', Bell comments, 'one concludes that his alleged change of heart represented nothing so much as the conviction that an amalga-

mation of Whigs, "liberals", and radicals into a Liberal party had become a political necessity, and that it could be achieved only by his own acceptance of a liberal programme for parliamentary reform. No doubt he also had in mind his own political future; but the consolidation of the party had to come first whether he viewed the situation selfishly or unselfishly.' H. C. Bell, 'Palmerston and Parliamentary Reform', *Journal of Modern History*, 4(1932) p. 208.

191. Dallas to Cass, 25 March 1859, cited in Dallas, *Letters from London*, II, p. 104.

192. Lansdowne to Brougham, 29 March (? 1859) Brougham Mss. 4199.

193. Grey to Lady Elcho, 29 March 1859, Wemyss Mss. 3/14.

194. Elcho, 28 March 1859, *Hansard*, 3rd series, CLIII, 932–47. Beaumont, a self-styled 'Palmerstonian', declared against the motion denouncing its sincerity. Wortley, a former Peelite and a member of Palmerston's ministry, observed that if the second reading were carried the House could amend the bill in Committee. The success of Russell's motion, however, might postpone indefinitely any settlement of the reform question. Beaumont, 28 March 1859, *Hansard*, 3rd series, CLIII, 928–32; Wortley, 25 March 1859, *Hansard*, 3rd series, CLIII, 861–73.

195. Northcote, 25 March 1859, *Hansard*, 3rd series, CLIII, 826–39.

196. Ellice, 28 March 1859, *Hansard*, 3rd series, CLIII, 948–54.

197. Walpole, 24 March 1859, *Hansard*, 3rd series, CLIII, 753–73. Henley argued that the first part of Russell's resolution regarding the freeholders was open to concession by the government, while the second part of the motion was so vague 'that no human being could assign any definite meaning to it'. Henley, 31 March 1859, *Hansard*, 3rd series, CLIII, 1211–23.

198. Graham, 28 March 1859, *Hansard*, 3rd series, CLIII, 970–85. Argyll supported Graham's comments apart from Graham's suggestion that the wish for the ballot was growing. Argyll to Graham, 29 March 1859, cited in C. S. Parker, *Life and Letters of Sir James Graham, Second Baronet of Netherby* (London, 1907) II, p. 372. For an ecstatic description of Graham's speech see White, *Inner Life of the House of Commons*, I, p. 95.

199. Bright, 24 March 1859, *Hansard*, 3rd series, CLIII, 773–92. On 9 March, at a meeting of various reform organisations, a resolution was passed instructing Bright to reject the government measure for inadequate enfranchisement of the working classes, the disfranchisement of county freehold votes, the withholding of the ballot and the preservation of small corrupt boroughs. *The Times*, 10 March 1859, p. 9. See also, J. Bright, *The Diaries of John Bright* (London, 1930) pp. 235–7; and G. B. Smith, *The Life and Speeches of the Rt. Hon. John Bright M.P.*, 2 vols (London, 1881) I, pp. 499–505.

200. Palmerston remained sceptical about Bright's conservative tone and remarked to Granville that 'the dog does not bark until he has got the ducks into the decoy'. Granville to Canning, 29 March 1859, Granville Mss. PRO 30/29/21/3, fol. 59. See also, G. M. Trevelyan, *The Life of John Bright* (London, 1913) pp. 279–80.

201. Roebuck, 31 March 1859, *Hansard*, 3rd series, CLIII, 1223–30.

202. Bright to his wife, 1 April 1859, Ogden Mss. 65.
203. White, *Inner Life of the House of Commons*, I, p. 99. Grey thought Disraeli's speech 'very superior indeed to any of his I ever heard before and any other in the debate. I am informed that it made a very powerful impression on the House,' Grey Diary, 4 April 1859, Grey Mss. C3/21.
204. Disraeli, 31 March 1859, *Hansard*, 3rd series, CLIII, 1230–57. See also, Monypenny and Buckle, *Disraeli*, IV, pp. 208–10.
205. Broughton Diary, 21 March 1859, Broughton Mss. 43761, fol. 156.
206. Malmesbury Diary, 23 March 1859, Malmesbury Mss. GM73. By 27 March it was noted by the opposition that Jolliffe was making preparations for a possible election. Parkes to Hatherton, 28 March 1859, Hatherton Mss. D260/M/F/5/27/33. Since 19 March, Malmesbury had been enlisting Odo Russell's help in influencing British Catholic opinion via Rome in anticipation of an election, see McIntire, *England Against the Papacy*, p. 107–8.
207. Derby to Eglinton, 31 March 1859, Derby Mss. 187/2. See also, Derby to Disraeli, n.d. (? March 1859) Hughenden Mss. B/XX/S/217.
208. Broughton Diary, 29 March 1859, Broughton Mss. 43761, fol. 158.
209. Broughton Diary, 31 March 1859, Broughton Mss. 43761, fol. 159.
210. Granville to Canning, 29 March 1859, Granville Mss. PRO 30/29/21/3, fol. 59.
211. Grey Diary, 28 March 1859, Grey Mss. C3/21.
212. ? to Disraeli, 30 March 1859, Hughenden Mss. B/XVIII/C/36.
213. Earle to Elcho, 28 March 1859, Wemyss Mss. 3/12.
214. Disraeli to Derby, 30 March 1859, Derby Mss. 145/6.
215. Stanley to Disraeli, 27 March 1859, Hughenden Mss. B/XX/S/680.
216. Carnarvon to Lady Portsmouth, 28 March 1859, cited in Sir A. Hardinge, *Life of H. E. M. Herbert, Fourth Earl of Carnarvon, 1831–1890* (London, 1925) I, p. 141.
217. See division list, 31 March 1859, *Hansard*, 3rd series, CLIII, 1257–61. Watt calculates the following cohesion index; Radicals 87%, Liberals 79%, Whigs 100%, Liberal Conservatives 61%, Conservatives 98%. R. G. Watt, 'Parties and Politics in Mid-Victorian Britain, 1857 to 1859: A Study in Quantification', unpublished PhD thesis, University of Minnesota, 1975, pp. 289–308.
218. Fortescue Diary, 31 March 1859, Carlingford Mss. DD/SH 358. Wyld's motion was defeated by 328 to 98; see, 31 March 1859, *Hansard*, 3rd series, CLIII, 1261–4.
219. Malmesbury Diary, 1 April 1859, Malmesbury Mss. 9M73. Both Walpole and Henley supported the government, as did Beresford and Newdegate.
220. Manners to Granby, n.d. (? 1 April 1859) cited in Whibley, *Manners*, II, p. 111. Bernal Osborne calculated that thirty-one Liberals voted with the government, but agreed that only two Conservatives supported the resolution. Osborne to Briggs, 1 April 1859, cited in P. H. D. Bagenall, *The Life of Ralph Bernal Osborne M.P.* (London, 1884) p. 157. Horsman, Beaumont and Elcho, as well as Gladstone, supported the government.

221. Gathorne Hardy Diary, 1 April 1859, Cranbrook Mss. T501/291, fol. 252, cited in Gathorne-Hardy, *Gathorne Hardy*, I, p. 131.

222. Derby to the Queen, 1 April 1859, Derby Mss. 186/2.

223. Carnarvon memo, n.d. (? 1859) cited in Hardinge, *Carnarvon*, I, p. 141. Manners believed that it was 'extremely creditable' that only two Conservatives, Lord Hotham and Capt. Gray, voted for Russell's motion.

224. Clarendon to Duchess of Manchester, 23 March 1859, cited in A. L. Kennedy (ed.) *'My Dear Duchess': Social and Political letters to the Duchess of Manchester, 1858–1869* (London, 1956) p. 46. See also, Stanley to Disraeli, 27 March 1859, Hughendon Mss. B/XX/S/680.

225. Clarendon to Duchess of Manchester, 28 March 1859, cited in Kennedy (ed.) *'My Dear Duchess'*, p. 48.

226. Dallas to Cass, 1 April 1859, cited in Dallas, *Letters from London*, II, p. 110.

227. Ibid. Palmerston, Disraeli was secretly informed, was 'speaking to those with whom he is not intimate that he has no desire to become Minister again and that Lord John will succeed Lord Derby, but the secret arrangement is that he will be Premier, Lord John Indian Minister'. ? to Disraeli, 2 April 1859, Hughenden Mss. F/XI/B/37.

228. Bright to his wife, 1 April 1859, Ogden Mss. 65. See also *The Diaries of John Bright*, p. 237.

229. Malmesbury Diary, 1 April 1859, Malmesbury Mss. 9M73.

230. The Queen to the Prince of Wales, 1 April 1859, cited in J. Prest, *Lord John Russell* (London, 1972) p. 383. Clarendon came to regard the behaviour of the Whigs during the spring of 1859 as 'shameful factiousness'. Clarendon to Lady Salisbury, 17 March 1866, cited in Maxwell, *Clarendon*, II, p. 310.

CHAPTER 11

1. Disraeli to Derby, 3 April 1859, Derby Mss. 145/6, cited in W. F. Monypenny and G. E. Buckle, *The Life of Benjamin Disraeli, Earl of Beaconsfield* (London, 1910–20) IV, p. 212.

2. Derby to Disraeli, 5 April 1859, Hughenden Mss. B/XX/S/220, cited in Monypenny and Buckle, *Disraeli*, IV, p. 213. As noted by W. D. Jones, *Lord Derby and Victorian Conservatism* (Oxford, 1956) p. 252, Derby was by now very tired and fatigued.

3. Derby, 4 April 1859, *Hansard*, 3rd series, CLIII, 1267–91. In this statement Derby made a bitter attack upon the political career of Russell that restated similar comments made by Disraeli in the Commons on 31 March. Never, it was observed, had there been a statesman who had overthrown so many governments. In 1835 Russell had turned out Peel upon an 'impracticable pretext'. In 1852 he overthrew Derby with 'an objectionless coalition'. In 1855 he overthrew Aberdeen's coalition with 'a personal *coup d'état*'. In 1858 he turned out Palmerston, only to combine with Palmerston in 1859 upon a 'cunning

resolution' to reject a moderate reform bill. See also, Disraeli, 31 March 1859, *Hansard*, 3rd series, CLIII, 1255.

4. Disraeli, 4 April 1859, *Hansard*, 3rd series, CLIII, 1301–7. It was no accident that in such language lay echoes of Peelite rhetoric.

5. Russell, 4 April 1859, *Hansard*, 3rd series, CLIII, 1316–22.

6. Parkes to Ellice, 30 March 1859, Ellice Mss. 15042, fol. 119A.

7. Broughton Diary, 10 April 1859, Broughton Mss. 43761, fol. 164.

8. Broughton Diary, 14 April 1859, Broughton Mss. 43761, fol. 166.

9. Russell to the Dean of Bristol, 12 April 1859, Russell Mss. PRO 30/22/13/G, fol. 181.

10. Palmerston, 4 April 1859, *Hansard*, 3rd series, CLIII, 1307–12.

11. Broughton Diary, 13 April 1859, Broughton Mss. 43761, fol. 165.

12. Wood to Palmerston, 16 April 1859, Broadlands Mss. GC/WO 128.

13. Ibid.

14. Palmerston memo, 30 march 1859, Broadlands Mss. GMC 136.

15. Broughton Diary, 8 April 1859, Broughton Mss. 43761, fol. 163.

16. Fortescue Diary, 4 April 1859, Carlingford Mss. DD/SH 358.

17. Moncrieff to Elcho, 10 April 1859, Wemyss Mss. 3/18.

18. Granville to Canning, 16 April 1859, Granville Mss. PRO 30/29/21/3, fol. 63.

19. Grey Diary, 5 April 1859, Grey Mss. C3/21.

20. Wood to Elcho, 3 April 1859, Wemyss Mss. 3/15.

21. Grey Diary, 7 April 1859, Grey Mss. C3/21.

22. Grey Diary, 28 April 1859, Grey Mss. C3/21. See also, Broughton Diary, 6 May 1859, Broughton Mss. 43761, fol. 173.

23. Granville to Canning, 16 April 1859, Ganville Mss. PRO 30/29/21/3, fol. 63.

24. Broughton Diary, 8 April 1859, Broughton Mss. 43761, fol. 163.

25. Moncrieff to Elcho, 10 April 1859, Wemyss Mss. 3/18.

26. Baines to his brother, 6 April 1859, Baines Mss. 46.

27. Malmesbury Diary, 3 April 1859, Malmesbury Mss. 9M73.

28. Malmesbury Diary, 9 April 1859, Malmesbury Mss. 9M73. See also, Derby to the Queen, 9 April 1859, Derby Mss. 187/2, fol. 159. See also, the Queen to Derby, 12 April 1859, *QVL*, 1st series, III, pp. 417–18.

29. Malmesbury Diary, 11 April 1859, Malmesbury Mss. 9M73. See also, Malmesbury Diary, 12 April 1859, Malmesbury Mss. 9M73.

30. Malmesbury Diary, 13 April 1859, Malmesbury Mss. 9M73.

31. Sotheron-Estcourt Diary, 16 April 1859, Sotheron-Estcourt Mss. C.409.

32. Malmesbury Diary, 14 April 1859, Malmesbury Mss. 9M73. See also, A. J. P. Taylor, *The Struggle for Mastery in Europe 1848–1918* (London, 1954) pp. 110–11. Taylor writes that 'since all the rights of treaties and of international law were on the side of Austria, Cavour was on weak technical ground; and after a month of manoeuvring he seemed to be losing the game'.

33. Malmesbury, 18 April 1859, *Hansard*, 3rd series, CLIII, 1830–9.

34. Derby, 18 April 1859, *Hansard*, 3rd series, CLIII, 1849–57. As confirmation of the consensus over foreign policy, Derby noticed that

Clarendon, speaking at the beginning of the debate, succeeded in 'laying down, in point of fact, every principle to which we had adhered'. Derby to the Queen, 19 April 1859, Derby Mss. 186/2, fol. 94.

35. Clarendon to Reeve, 13 April 1859, Clarendon Mss. C.535. The arrival in London at the beginning of April of a number of Neopolitan liberals, formerly prisoners of 'Bomba', led to some public expression of support for Italian unification. See the *Daily News*, 11 April 1859 and the *Saturday Review*, 9 April 1859, and Delane's meeting with Marliani, a supporter of Cavour, Delane to Panizzi, 4 April 1859, Panizzi Mss. 36719, cited in *The History of 'The Times'*, 5 vols (London, 1935–52) II, p. 332. Suspicion of Napoleon and opposition to military involvement, however, still constrained Italian sympathies. See also D. E. D. Beales, *England and Italy 1859–60* (London, 1961) pp. 56–7.

36. Russell at the London Tavern, Bishopsgate Street, cited in *The Times*, 16 April 1859, p. 5.

37. Palmerston to Clarendon, 17 April 1859, Clarendon Mss. C.524. See also, Palmerston to Clarendon, 10 April 1859, Clarendon Mss. C.524; and Palmerston to Clarendon, 15 April 1859, Clarendon Mss. C.524.

38. Disraeli, 18 April 1859, *Hansard*, 3rd series, CLIII, 1863–73.

39. Palmerston, 18 April 1859, *Hansard*, 3rd series, CLIII, 1873–9. The popular expressions of pro-Italian feeling at the beginning of April confirmed that in the right circumstances foreign policy could become a political issue. Malmesbury noticed 'a very strong Sardinian feeling in the House of Commons and nothing is required to make it blaze forth but the smallest act of injustice by Austria'. Malmesbury to Cowley, 20 April 1859, cited in Beales, *England and Italy*, p. 58.

40. Duncombe, 18 April 1859, *Hansard*, 3rd series, CLIII, 1879–81. See also, T. H. Duncombe (ed.) *Life and Correspondence of T. S. Duncombe*, 2 vols (London, 1868) II, pp. 220–50.

41. Clarendon to Reeve, 13 April 1859, Clarendon Mss. C.535.

42. Gladstone, 18 April 1859, *Hansard*, 3rd series, CLIII, 1881–6. Gladstone denied Austrian consistency and agreed with Palmerston that it was unreasonable to insist upon Piedmont's disarmament prior to a Congress.

43. Russell to Clarendon, 21 April 1859, Clarendon Mss. C.104, fol. 38 cited in Beales, *England and Italy*, p. 58.

44. Malmesbury Diary, 19 April 1859, Malmesbury Mss. 9M73. Cavour's acquiescence came after diplomatic pressure from Paris who feared Prussian involvement. See Taylor, *Struggle for Mastery in Europe*, p. 111.

45. Malmesbury Diary, 24 April 1859, Malmesbury Mss. 9M73.

46. Broughton Diary, 22 April 1859, Broughton Mss. 43761, fol. 167. The Austrian ultimatum meant that Vienna 'solved the problem which had baffled Napoleon and Cavour: [the Austrians] opened the door for the destruction of the settlement of 1815 and for the national reconstruction of central Europe'. Taylor, *The Struggle for Mastery in Europe*, p. 111.

47. Aberdeen to Graham, 26 April 1859, cited in *Aberdeen Correspondence*, B.P. 12 (12A) p. 107.
48. Palmerston to Clarendon, 24 April 1859, Clarendon Mss. C.524.
49. Russell at the Shaftesbury Hall, *The Times*, 25 April 1859, p. 12; and Russell at the Albion Hall, *The Times*, 30 April 1859, p. 5.
50. Derby to the Queen, 21 April 1859, Derby Mss. 187/2, fol. 201. See also, Beales, *England and Italy*, pp. 62–4.
51. Sotheron-Estcourt Diary, 21 April 1859, Sotheron-Estcourt Mss. C.409.
52. Derby at the Mansion House, 25 April 1859, *The Times*, 26 April 1859. See also, Malmesbury to Loftus, 21 April 1859, cited in *Correspondence Relating to the Affairs of Italy* (State Papers vol. xxxii, Command Paper no. 2524) p. 276; and Malmesbury Diary, 25 April 1859, Malmesbury Mss. 9M73.
53. Derby to Malmesbury, 26 April 1859, Malmesbury Mss. 9M73.
54. Grey Diary, 26 April 1859, Grey Mss. C3/21.
55. Ellice to Panmure, 26 April 1859, Dalhousie Mss. GD45/13/644.
56. Graham to Aberdeen, 27 April 1859, Aberdeen Mss. 43192, fol. 306.
57. Russell to Palmerston, 29 April 1859, Clarendon Mss. C.104, fol. 42.
58. Aberdeen to Graham, 26 April 1859, Graham Mss. Bundle 135.
59. Newcastle to Hayward, 24 April 1859, Newcastle Mss. NeC, 12, 379.
60. Broughton Diary, 23 April 1859, Broughton Mss. 43761, fol. 169.
61. Wood at Halifax, *The Times*, 23 April 1859, p. 2; and Wood to Palmerston, 16 April 1859, Broadlands Mss. GC/WO 128.
62. Graham at Carlisle, *The Times*, 30 April 1859, p. 6. See also, C. S. Parker, *Life and Letters of Sir James Graham, Second Baronet of Netherby* (London, 1907) II, pp. 380–1.
63. Bright at Birmingham, *The Times*, 26 April 1859, p. 5.
64. Palmerston at Tiverton, *The Times*, 28 April 1859, p. 5. Palmerston had drafted a speech on 7 April and sent a corrected copy to Borthwick of the *Morning Post*. It contained 'no foam and fury' and 'little more than the constitutional question as to whether the government ought to have resigned rather than dissolve parliament'. After 19 April, however, Palmerston completely rewrote the speech haranguing the cabinet for diplomatic incompetence, and concentrating on the Italian question. R. J. Lucas, *Lord Glenesk and the 'Morning Post'*, (London, 1910) pp. 181–2.
65. Aberdeen to Graham, 26 May 1859, cited in *Aberdeen Correspondence*, B.P. 12 (12A) p. 109, and Parker, *Graham*, II, p. 380.
66. Stanley at Kings Lynn, *The Times*, 2 May 1859, p. 7.
67. Disraeli at Aylesbury, *The Times*, 3 May 1859, p. 6.
68. Derby to Jolliffe, 25 April 1859, Hylton Mss. DD/HY 18/3, fol. 1. See also, Talbot to Cairns, 26 April 1859, Cairns Mss. PRO 30/51/13, fol. 60.
69. Northcote to Disraeli, 16 April 1859, Iddesleigh Mss. 50063. On 30 April, Gladstone found the Carlton Club, which he was still visiting, 'excited and more pleased than the facts quite seem to justify'. W. E. Gladstone, *The Gladstone Diaries*, H. C. G. Matthew and M. R. D. Foot (eds) (Oxford, 1968–82) V, p. 398.
70. Derby to the Queen, 2 May 1859, Derby Mss. 188/1, fol. 39.

71. Derby to the Queen, n.d. (? 5 May 1859) Derby Mss. 188/1.
72. Jolliffe memo, n.d. (? May 1859) Hylton Mss 24/1, cited in R. Stewart, *The Foundation of the Conservative Party, 1830–1867* (London, 1978) p. 340.
73. Disraeli to Mrs Brydges Willyams, 20 May 1859, cited in Monypenny and Buckle, *Disraeli*, IV, p. 233.
74. Derby to Eglinton, 9 May 1859, Derby Mss. 188/1, fol. 60.
75. See Stewart, *Foundation of the Conservative Party*, p. 340–1. It should be noted that 1859 was the quietest general election between 1832 and 1885. Most county elections were uncontested. A total of 237 constituencies in the United Kingdom were uncontested; the highest figure between 1832 and 1885. A total of 860 candidates stood for election; the lowest figure from 1832–85. See F. W. S. Craig (ed.) *British Parliamentary Election Results, 1832–1885* (London, 1977) pp. 621–4. Conservative gains, therefore may have been as much the result of a lack of opposition as change in popular opinion. For further comment on the 1859 election see W. L. Guttsman, 'The general election of 1859 in the cities of Yorkshire', *International Review of Social History*, 3 (1957) pp. 231–58; T. Lloyd, 'Uncontested Seats in British General Elections, 1852–1910', *HJ*, 8:2 (1965) pp. 250–6; J. Vincent and M. Stenton (eds) *McCalmont's Parliamentary Poll Book: British Election Results 1832–1918* (Hassocks, 1971).
76. Jolliffe calculated seven Conservative gains in Ireland. But Dublin Castle and Derby calculated the gain at eight. The Catholic vote also helped the Conservative cause in South Lancashire.
77. Derby to Lambert, 27 May 1859, Derby Mss. 188/1, fol. 115. For the authoritative study of this aspect of the election see K. T. Hoppen, 'Tories, Catholics, and the General Election of 1859', *HJ*, 13:1 (1970) pp. 48–67. C. T. McIntire *England Against the Papacy, 1858–1861: Tories, Liberals, and the Overthrow of Papal Temporal Power during the Italian Risorgimento* (Cambridge, 1983) pp. 106–13 reveals Conservative attempts to win Catholic support through the influence of the Vatican.
78. Derby to Eglinton, 18 May 1859, Derby Mss. 188/1, fol. 90. See also, Naas to Disraeli, 17 May 1859, cited in Monypenny and Buckle, *Disraeli*, IV, p. 242.
79. Eglinton to Derby, 27 May 1859, Hughenden Mss. B/XX/S/225.
80. Beresford to Newdegate, 21 May 1859, Newdegate Mss. B.6279.
81. Disraeli to Palmerston, n.d. (? 3 May 1859) cited in Monypenny and Buckle, *Disraeli*, IV, p. 235.
82. Palmerston to Disraeli, 3 May 1859, cited in Monypenny and Buckle, *Disraeli*, IV, p. 257.
83. Ellice to Panmure, 8 May 1859, Dalhousie Mss. GD45/14/644.
84. Graham to Aberdeen, 3 May 1859, Aberdeen Mss. 43192, fol. 311, cited in D. Krein, *The Last Palmerston Government: Foreign Policy, Domestic Politics and the Genesis of 'Splendid Isolation'* (Iowa, 1978) p. 12.
85. Graham to Russell, 9 May 1859, Graham Mss. Bundle 135, cited in Parker, *Graham*, II, p. 382.
86. Malmesbury Diary, 12 May 1859, Malmesbury Mss. 9M73.

87. Fortescue Diary, 19 April 1859, Carlingford Mss. DD/SH 358.
88. Clarendon to Brougham, 15 May 1859, Brougham Mss. 36344. See also, Clarendon to Duchess of Manchester, 3 May 1859, cited in A. L. Kennedy (ed.) *'My Dear Duchess': Social and Political Letters to the Duchess of Manchester, 1858–1869* (London, 1956) p. 56.
89. Disraeli to Horsman, n.d., cited in Monypenny and Buckle, *Disraeli*, IV, p. 238.
90. Disraeli to Derby, 8 May 1859, Derby Mss. 145/6, cited in Monypenny and Buckle, *Disraeli*, IV, pp. 238–41.
91. Disraeli to Palmerston, n.d. (? 3 May 1859) cited in Monypenny and Buckle, *Disraeli*, IV, p. 236.
92. Disraeli to Derby, 8 May 1859, Derby Mss. 145/6, cited in Monypenny and Buckle, *Disraeli*, IV, pp. 238–41.
93. Ibid.
94. Derby to Disraeli, 8 May 1859, Derby Mss. 186/2, fol. 108.
95. Gladstone to Derby, 19 May 1859, Hughenden Mss. B/XX/S/224.
96. Derby to Disraeli, 20 May 1859, Hughenden Mss. B/XX/S/224.
97. Malmesbury Diary, 14 May 1859, Malmesbury Mss. 9M73. See also, Derby to Disraeli, 8 May 1859, Derby Mss. 186/2, fol. 108.
98. Sotheron-Estcourt Diary, 14 May 1859, Sotheron-Estcourt Mss. C.409.
99. Derby to the Queen, 14 May 1859, Derby Mss. 188/1, fol. 76.
100. Manners memo., n.d. (? May 1859) cited in C. Whibley, *Lord John Manners and His Friends* (Edinburgh, 1925) II, p. 112.
101. Malmesbury Diary, 17 May 1859, Malmesbury Mss. 9M73. See also, Sotheron-Estcourt Diary, 17 May 1859, Sotheron-Estcourt Mss. C.409.

CHAPTER 12

1. Ellice to Panmure, 26 April 1859, Dalhousie Mss. GD45/14/644.
2. Broughton Diary, 27 April 1859, Broughton Mss. 43761, fol. 171.
3. Fortescue Diary, 19 April 1859, Carlingford Mss. DD/SH 358.
4. Clarendon to Cornewall Lewis, 1 May 1859, Clarendon Mss. C.533.
5. Granville to Canning, 7 May 1859, Granville Mss. PRO 30/29/21/3, fol. 76.
6. Russell to Clarendon, 26 April 1859, Clarendon Mss. C.104, fol. 40. See also, Clarendon to Duchess of Manchester, 27 April 1859, cited in A. L. Kennedy, *'My Dear Duchess': Social and Political Letters to the Duchess of Manchester, 1858–1869* (London, 1956) p. 52.
7. Graham to Ellice, 1 May 1859, Ellice Mss. 15019, fol. 54.
8. Lady Hatherton to Ellice, 3 May 1859, Ellice Mss. 15036, fol. 21.
9. Graham to Ellice, 4 May 1859, Ellice Mss. 15019, fol. 60.
10. G. Grey to Granville, 12 May 1859, Granville Mss. PRO 30/29/18/15, fol. 1.
11. Palmerston to Clarendon, 5 May 1859, Clarendon Mss. C.524.
12. Russell to Clarendon, 12 May 1859, Clarendon Mss. C.104, fol. 44.

13. Russell to Parkes, 10 May 1859, Russell Mss. PRO 30/22/13/G, fol. 202.

14. Granville to Palmerston, 10 May 1859, Broadlands Mss. GC/GR 1861.

15. Russell to Graham, 7 May 1859, Graham Mss. Bundle 135.

16. Ibid. This part of the letter is cited in C. S. Parker, *Life and Letters of Sir James Graham, Second Baronet of Netherby*, (London, 1907) II, pp. 381–2.

17. Russell's comments during mid-May must be seen within the context of his commitment to these two safeguards of his position. Russell declared himself 'quite willing to see Palmerston prime-minister, and to stand aloof'. Yet at the same time he noted that this 'would not suit Graham, Bright etc.' and 'an interregnum must settle the matter'. Russell to Dean of Bristol, 13 May 1859, Russell Mss. PRO 30/22/13/G, fol. 204. Similarly Russell protrayed Liberal party divisions as the result of backbench antagonism, rather than frontbench ambition. It was left to Wood to affirm that before any step could be taken it was necessary that Russell and Palmerston should be agreed. Wood memo, n.d. (? June 1859) Hickleton Mss. A8/D. See also, Wood to Russell, 16 May 1859, Russell Mss. PRO 30/22/13/G, fol. 214, cited in D. Krein, *The Last Palmerston Government: Foreign Policy, Domestic Politics and the Genesis of 'Splendid Isolation'* (Iowa, 1978) p. 11.

18. Russell to Graham, 16 May 1859, Graham Mss. Bundle 135. See also D. Southgate, *'The Most English Minister . . .': The Policies and Politics of Palmerston* (London, 1966) p. 455.

19. Cornewall Lewis to Palmerston, 16 May 1859, Broadlands Mss. GC/LE 116.

20. Russell to Graham, 17 May 1859, Graham Mss. Bundle 135, cited in Parker, *Graham*, II, pp. 384–5; also cited in S. Walpole, *The Life of Lord John Russell* (London, 1889) II, p. 305.

21. Graham to Russell, 18 May 1859, Russell Mss. PRO 30/22/13/G, cited in Parker, *Graham*, II, p. 385.

22. Graham to Russell, 17 May 1859, Russell Mss. PRO 30/22/13/G, fol. 222, cited in Parker, *Graham*, II, pp. 383–4.

23. Herbert to Russell, 17 May 1859, Russell Mss. PRO 30/22/13/G, fol. 218, cited in A. H. Gordon, Baron Stanmore, *Sidney Herbert of Lea: A Memoir* (London, 1906) II, pp. 182–4.

24. Russell to Dean of Bristol, 19 May 1859, Russell Mss. PRO 30/22/13/G, fol. 233.

25. Russell to Clarendon, 18 May 1859, Clarendon Mss. C.104, fol. 46.

26. Russell to Palmerston, 18 May 1859, Broadlands Mss. GC/RU 497.

27. The inclusion of Bright was, of course, a crucial safeguard of Russell's prospects. Of similar importance was Russell's comment to Parkes that 'it would be better for the Whigs to be reduced to an insignificant minority than to give up their principles for the sake of places. There has been too much of this of late years . . .' Russell to Parkes, 19 May 1859, cited in Lord J. Russell, *The Later Correspondence of Lord Russell*, G. P. Gooch (ed.) (London, 1925) II, p. 230.

28. Russell to Palmerston, 18 May 1859, Broadlands Mss. GC/RU 497.
29. Palmerston to Russell, 19 May 1859, Russell Mss. PRO 30/22/13/G.
    See also, Krein, *The Last Palmerston Government*, p. 12.
30. Russell to Dean of Bristol, 21 May 1859, Russell Mss. PRO 30/22/
    13/G, fol. 208. Herbert noted that Russell and Palmerston were
    'wonderously agreed'. Herbert to Gladstone, 22 May 1859, Gladstone
    Mss. 44211, fol. 62 cited in Gordon, *Herbert*, II, p. 187. For the fullest
    account of the meeting see Palmerston to Herbert, 24 May 1859, cited
    in Gordon, *Herbert*, II, pp. 190–2.
31. Russell to Graham, 23 May 1859, Graham Mss. Bundle 135, cited in
    Parker, *Graham*, II, pp. 386–7. Herbert warned Gladstone that 'Lord
    John reserves his entire freedom as to acceptance. So far for counting
    the chickens. Rest à voir about hatching them.' Herbert to Gladstone,
    22 May 1859, cited in Gordon, *Herbert*, II, p. 187.
32. In his correspondence Graham was talking of being 'very unwell' and
    in 'drooping spirits'. See Graham to Russell, 9 May 1859, and Graham
    to Russell, 17 May 1859, cited in Parker, *Graham*, II, pp. 382–4.
33. Wood Diary, 21 May 1859, Hickleton Mss. A8/D.
34. Wood to Palmerston, 24 May 1859, Broadlands Mss. GC/WO 131.
35. Wood Diary, 23 May 1859, Hickleton Mss. A8/D.
36. Greville Diary, 29 May 1859, Greville Mss. 41123, cited in C. C. F.
    Greville, *The Greville Memoirs*, H. Reeve (ed.) (London, 1888) VIII,
    p. 249.
37. Wood Diary, 25 May 1859, Hickleton Mss. A8/D.
38. Wood Diary, 26 May 1859, Hickleton Mss. A8/D.
39. Ibid.
40. Gladstone to Acton, 6 January 1864, Gladstone Mss. 44093, fol. 32.
    See also, John Morley, *The Life of William Ewart Gladstone* (London,
    1903) I, p. 628.
41. Gladstone to Herbert, 18 May 1859, Gladstone Mss. 44211, fol. 56,
    cited in Gordon, *Herbert*, II, p. 185. In his draft of the letter Glad-
    stone wrote, but later crossed out: 'As respects the former I was much
    dissatisfied with some declarations of the Government, but I think
    they have had a lesson and are doing better if not well.' For a different
    view of Gladstone's priorities see Morley, *Gladstone*, I, pp. 623–4.
42. Wood Diary, 20 May 1859, Hickleton Mss. A8/D.
43. Wood Diary, 22 May 1859, Hickleton Mss. A8/D, cited in Morley,
    Gladstone, I, p. 623. A significant indication of the intense anxiety
    Gladstone was feeling came on 25 May when, for the first time in two
    years, he scourged himself. *The Gladstone Diaries*, H. C. G. Matthew
    and M. R. D. Foot (eds) (Oxford, 1968–82) V, p. 396. The last
    occasion was in May 1857 when he passed through a period of
    profound political and personal crisis. On 6 June 1859 Gladstone
    found the Duchesse d'Aumale 'too Italian in feeling'. *Gladstone
    Diaries*, V, p. 399.
44. Gladstone to Herbert, 29 May 1859, Gladstone Mss. 44211, fol. 60,
    cited in Gordon, *Herbert*, II, p. 187.
45. Gladstone to Heathcote, 16 June 1859, Gladstone Mss. 44209, fol.
    38, cited in Morley, *Gladstone*, I, pp. 627–8. See also R. Shannon,

Gladstone, 1809–1865 (London, 1982) pp. 380–2; and *Gladstone Diaries*, V, p. xxvii.

46. Russell to Graham, 23 May 1859, Graham Mss. Bundle 135, cited in Parker, *Graham*, II, pp. 386–7.
47. Wood Diary, 26 May 1859, Hickleton Mss. A8/D.
48. Bright Diary, 5 June 1859, cited in J. Bright, *The Diaries of John Bright* (London, 1930) pp. 239–40.
49. Wood Diary, 19 May 1859, Hickleton Mss. A8/D.
50. See R. E. Leader, *The Life and Letters of John Arthur Roebuck* (London, 1879) p. 279.
51. Ibid.
52. Roebuck to Lindsay, 22 May 1859, cited in Monypenny and Buckle, *Disraeli*, IV, p. 243.
53. Graham to Russell, 24 May 1859, Russell Mss. PRO 30/22/13/G, fol. 243.
54. This section of the letter is cited in Parker, *Graham*, II, p. 387.
55. Russell to Graham, 26 May 1859, Graham Mss. Bundle 135, cited in Parker, *Graham*, II, p. 388.
56. Wood Diary, 27 May 1859, Hickleton Mss. A8/D.
57. Hayward to Lady Holland, 24 May 1859, Holland House Mss. The change in mood is clearly reflected in Greville's diary. On 26 May Greville records the optimism produced by the meeting on 20 May. His entry for 29 May, however, records the disillusion that rapidly overtook hope. See Greville Diary, 26 and 29 May 1859, Greville Mss. 41123, cit. Greville, *Memoirs*, VIII, pp. 247–9.
58. Ellice to Panmure, 25 May 1859, Dalhousie Mss. GD/45/14/644.
59. Aberdeen to Graham, 26 May 1859, Graham Mss. Bundle 135.
60. Broughton Diary, 28 May 1859, Broughton Mss. 43761, fol. 183.
61. Granville to Canning, 24 May 1859, Granville Mss. PRO 30/29/23/I, fol. 84.
62. Wood Diary, 31 May 1859, Hickleton Mss. A8/D.
63. Ibid. See also, Russell to Granville, n.d. (? 30 May 1859) Russell Mss. PRO 30/22/13/G, fol. 252.
64. Ibid.
65. Wood Diary, 1 June 1859, Hickleton Mss. A8/D.
66. Granville to Palmerston, 1 June 1859, Broadlands Mss. GC/GR 1862.
67. Clark to Dean of Bristol, n.d. Russell Mss. PRO 30/22/13/G, fol. 258.
68. Bright Diary, 2 June 1859, cited in *The Diaries of John Bright*, pp. 237–8.
69. Bright Diary, 5 June 1859, cited in *The Diaries of John Bright*, p. 239.
70. Wood Diary, 2 June 1859, Hickleton Mss. A8/D.
71. Ibid.
72. Wood Diary, 3 June 1859, Hickleton Mss. A8/D.
73. Herbert to his wife, 3 June 1859, cited in Gordon, *Herbert*, II, p. 197.
74. Broughton Diary, 4 June 1859, Broughton Mss. 43761, fol. 185.
75. Wood Diary, 31 May 1859, Hickleton Mss. A8/D.
76. Broughton Diary, 4 June 1859, Broughton Mss. 43761, fol. 185.
77. Wood Diary, 31 May 1859, Hickleton Mss. A8/D.

78. Granville to Canning, 4 June 1859, Granville Mss. PRO 30/29/23/I, fol. 91.
79. Heathcote to Gladstone, 5 June 1859, Gladstone Mss. 44209, fol. 32.
80. Earle to Disraeli, 27 May 1859, Hughenden Mss. B/XX/E/165.
81. Earle to Disraeli, n.d. (? June 1859) Hughenden Mss. B/XX/E/172.
82. Disraeli to Derby, 26 May 1859, Derby Mss. 145/6.
83. Earle to Disraeli, n.d. (? June 1859) Hughenden Mss. B/XX/E/172.
84. Sotheron-Estcourt Diary, 27 May 1859, Sotheron-Estcourt Mss. C.409. See also, Malmesbury Diary, 27 May 1859, Malmesbury Mss. 9M73.
85. Malmesbury Diary, 30 May 1859, Malmesbury Mss. 9M73. See also, Sotheron-Estcourt Diary, 30 May 1859, Sotheron-Estcourt Mss. C.409 and Sotheron Estcourt Diary, 31 May 1859, Sotheron Estcourt Mss. C.409.
86. Disraeli to Derby, 2 June 1859, Derby Mss. 145/6.
87. Derby to the Queen, n.d. (? 2 June 1859) Derby Mss. 188/1, fol. 127, cited in *QVL*, 1st series, III, p. 430.
88. Derby to the Queen, n.d (? 4 June 1859) Derby Mss. 188/1, fol. 137. See also, the Queen to Derby, 3 June 1859, cited in *QVL*, 1st series, III, pp. 433–4.
89. Disraeli to Derby, 2 June 1859, Derby Mss. 145/6, cited in Monypenny and Buckle, *Disraeli*, IV, p. 246.
90. Herbert to his wife, 6 June 1859, cited in Gordon, *Herbert*, II, p. 198.
91. Greville Diary, 7 June 1859, Greville Mss. 41123, cited in Greville, *Memoirs*, VIII, p. 251.
92. Herbert to his wife, 6 June 1859, cited in Gordon, *Herbert*, II, pp. 198–9. See also, H. C. F. Bell, *Lord Palmerston* (London, 1936) II, p. 214.
93. Greville Diary, 7 June 1859, Greville Mss. 41123, cited in Greville, *Memoirs*, VIII, p. 250. See also, Wood Diary, 6 June 1859, Hickleton Mss. A8/D.
94. Ibid.
95. Wood Diary, 6 June 1859, Hickleton Mss. A8/D. See also, Broughton Diary, 6 June 1859, Broughton Mss. 43761, fol. 186.
96. Hartington, 7 June 1859, *Hansard*, 3rd series, CLIV, 110–8.
97. Fortescue Diary, 7 June 1859, Carlingford Mss. DD/SH 358. See also, Disraeli, 7 June 1859, *Hansard*, 3rd series, CLIV, 122–46.
98. Disraeli to Derby, 26 May 1859, Derby Mss. 145/6.
99. Greville Diary, 9 June 1859, Greville Mss. 41123, cited in Greville, *Memoirs*, VIII, p. 251.
100. Fortescue Diary, 7 June 1859, Carlingford Mss. DD/SH 358.
101. Greville Diary, 9 June 1859, Greville Mss. 41123, cited in Greville, *Memoirs*, VIII, p. 251. See also, Knatchbull-Hugessen Diary, 28 January 1860, Brabourne Mss. U951, fol. 29.
102. Disraeli, 7 June 1859, *Hansard*, 3rd series, CLIV, 122–46.
103. Palmerston, 7 June 1859, *Hansard*, 3rd series, CLIV, 171–83.
104. Bright, 9 June 1859, *Hansard*, 3rd series, CLIV, 217–34.
105. Horsman, 9 June 1859, *Hansard*, 3rd series, CLIV, 246–51.
106. Graham, 9 June 1859, *Hansard*, 3rd series, CLIV, 262–77.
107. Milner Gibson, 10 June 1859, *Hansard*, 3rd series, CLIV, 298–311.

108. Herbert, 10 June 1859, *Hansard*, 3rd series, CLIV, 318–35.
109. Broughton Diary, 8 June 1859, Broughton Mss. 43762, fol. 3. See also, Broughton Diary, 10 June 1859, Broughton Mss. 43762, fol. 4.
110. Pakington to Disraeli, 6 June 1859, Hughenden Mss. B/XX/P/54.
111. Linsday, 10 June 1859, *Hansard*, 3rd series, CLIV, 311–18.
112. Derby to Jolliffe, n.d. (? 10 June 1859) Hylton Mss. DD/HY 18/4, fol. 7.
113. Derby to Jolliffe, n.d. (? 11 June 1859) Hylton Mss. DD/HY 18/4, fol. 14.
114. Russell, 10 June 1859, *Hansard*, 3rd series, CLIV, 374–90.
115. Roebuck, 10 June 1859, *Hansard*, 3rd series, CLIV, 390–5.
116. Derby to the Queen, 8 June 1859, Derby Mss. 186/2, fol. 125.
117. Derby to the Queen, 9 June 1859, Derby Mss. 188/1, fol. 148.
118. Derby to the Queen, 10 June 1859, Derby Mss. 186/2, fol. 126.
119. Disraeli to Derby, 10 June 1859, Derby Mss. 145/6, cited in Monypenny and Buckle, *Disraeli*, IV, pp. 259–60.
120. Ibid.
121. Clarendon to Palmerston, 5 June 1859, Broadlands Mss. GC/CL 1195.
122. Granville to Canning, 10 June 1859, Granville Mss. PRO 30/29/23/I, fol. 95.
123. Wood Diary, 11 June 1859, Hickleton Mss. A8/D.
124. Broughton Diary, 12 June 1859, Broughton Mss. 43762, fol. 6. See also, Bruce to his wife, 11 June 1859, cited in H. A. Bruce, *Letters of Rt. Hon. H. A. Bruce, Lord Aberdare of Duffryn* (Oxford, 1902) I.
125. Sotheron-Estcourt Diary, 11 June 1859, Sotheron-Estcourt Mss. C.409.
126. Queen Victoria Diary, 11 June 1859, cited in B. Connell (ed.) *Regina v. Palmerston: The Correspondence between Queen Victoria and her Foreign and Prime Minister, 1837–1865* (London, 1962) p. 255.
127. Lord Malmesbury, 18 June 1859, *Memoirs of an Ex-Minister* (London, 1885) II, pp. 189–91. See also Malmesbury to Disraeli, 2 June 1859, Hughenden Mss. B/xx/Hs/90. Disraeli's biographers suggest that he did not read the blue book because of his low opinion of Malmesbury. Kebbel noted that 'Disraeli turned on me rather sharply', when he enquired about the incident. Disraeli replied: 'Why, how could I produce them when they were not printed?' T. E. Kebbel, *Lord Beaconsfield and Other Tory Memories* (London, 1907) p. 18.
128. Queen Victoria Diary, 11 June 1859, cited in Connell, *Regina v. Palmerston*, pp. 255–6; and Greville Diary, 12 June, Greville Mss. 41123, cited in Greville, *Memoirs*, VIII, p. 252.
129. Greville Diary, 12 June 1859, Greville Mss. 41123, cited in Greville, *Memoirs*, VIII, p. 252. See also, Granville memo, n.d. (? 11 June 1859) cited in *QVL*, 1st series, III, pp. 438–9.
130. Queen Victoria Diary, 11 June 1859, cited in Connell, *Regina v. Palmerston*, p. 256.
131. Wood Diary, 12 June 1859, Hickleton Mss. A8/D.
132. Queen Victoria Diary, 12 June 1859, cited in Connell, *Regina v. Palmerston*, p. 256.
133. Russell to Granville, 12 June 1859, Russell Mss. PRO 30/22/13/G, fol. 266 cited in Lord E. Fitzmaurice, *The Life of Granville George*

Leveson-Gower, Second Earl Granville, K.G. (London, 1905) I, p. 337, also cited in Walpole, *Russell*, II, p. 308. See also, Fitzmaurice, *Granville*, I, pp. 340–1.

134. Granville to the Queen, 12 June 1859, cited in *QVL*, 1st series, III, p. 441.
135. Queen Victoria Diary, 12 June 1859, cited in Connell, *Regina v. Palmerston*, pp. 256–7.
136. Ibid. See also, Granville to Russell, 11 June 1859, Russell Mss. PRO 30/22/13/G, fol. 264, cited in Fitzmaurice, *Granville*, I, pp. 333–4, and Walpole, *Russell*, II, p. 307. See also, Wood Diary, 12 June 1859, Hickleton Mss. A8/D.
137. Queen Victoria Diary, 12 June 1859, cited in Connell, *Regina v. Palmerston*, p. 257.
138. Wood Diary, 12 June 1859, Hickleton Mss. A8/D.
139. The Queen to the King of the Belgians, 14 June 1859, cited in J. Prest, *Lord John Russell* (London, 1972) p. 384.
140. Wood Diary, 12 June 1859, Hickleton Mss. A8/D.
141. G. Grey to Granville, 12 June 1859, Granville Mss. PRO 30/29/18/5, fol. 21.
142. Wood Diary, 12 June 1859, Hickleton Mss. A8/D.
143. Queen Victoria Diary, 13 June 1859, cited in Connell, *Regina v. Palmerston*, p. 259.
144. Wood Diary, 12 June 1859, Hickleton Mss. A8/D.
145. Disraeli to Derby, n.d. (? 12 June 1859) Derby Mss. 145/6. Russell later made a similar comment to Bright: 'I fear there is not much chance for Reform in the new Cabinet. I see nobody in it but yourself and Milner Gibson who would not gladly smother the whole question if it were possible. I fear that you will find this the case before we are six months older. I hope I may be mistaken.' Russell to Bright, 16 June 1859, cited in *The Later Correspondence of Russell*, II, p. 233.
146. Wood Diary, 12 June 1859, Hickleton Mss. A8/D.
147. Queen Victoria Diary, 12 June 1859, cited in Connell, *Regina v. Palmerston*, pp. 257–8.
148. Palmerston to the Queen, 12 June 1859, cited in *QVL*, 1st series, III, p. 442. See also, Palmerston to Russell, 12 June 1859, cited in Walpole, *Russell*, II, p. 308.
149. Wood Diary, 12 June 1859, Hickleton Mss. A8/D.
150. Queen Victoria Diary, 13 June 1859, cited in Connell, *Regina v. Palmerston*, p. 258.
151. Palmerston to the Queen, 12 June 1859, cited in *QVL*, 1st series, III, p. 442.
152. Wood Diary, 13 June 1859, Hickleton Mss. A8/D.
153. Lady Clarendon Diary, 13 June 1859, cited in Sir H. Maxwell, *The Life and Letters of the Fourth Earl of Clarendon* (London, 1913) II, p. 185.
154. Clarendon to Reeve, 13 June 1859, Clarendon Mss. C.535.
155. Lady Clarendon Diary, 13 June 1859, cited in Maxwell, *Clarendon*, II, p. 185. See also, Queen Victoria Diary, 13 June 1859, cited in Connell, *Regina v. Palmerston*, p. 259.

156. Broughton Diary, 15 June 1859, Broughton Mss. 43762, fol. 9.
157. Wood Diary, 13 June 1859, Hickleton Mss. A8/D.
158. Granville to Canning, 23 August 1859, Granville Mss. PRO 30/29/ 23/I, cited in Fitzmaurice, *Granville*, I, p. 346.
159. Wood Diary, 13 June 1859, Hickleton Mss. A8/D.
160. Carnarvon to Heathcote, 12 June 1859, cited in Sir A. Hardinge, *Life of H. E. M. Herbert, Fourth Earl Carnarvon, 1831–1890* (London, 1925) I, p. 143.
161. Heathcote to Gladstone, 15 June 1859, Gladstone Mss. 44209, fol. 36.
162. Gladstone to Heathcote, 16 June 1859, Gladstone Mss. 44209, fol. 38.
163. Lady Clarendon Diary, 14 June 1859, cited in Maxwell, *Clarendon*, II, p. 185.
164. Clarendon to Duchess of Manchester (? 16 June 1859) cited in Kennedy, '*Dear Duchess*', p. 58.
165. Wood Diary, 16 June 1859, Hickleton Mss. A8/D.
166. Broughton Diary, 17 June 1859, Broughton Mss. 43762, fol. 10. For some caustic comments on the manner of 'Spider' Wood, see Granville to Canning, 27 June 1859, Granville Mss. PRO 30/29/23/I, cited in Fitzmaurice, *Granville*, I, p. 345.
167. Wood Diary, 14 June 1859, Hickleton Mss. A8/D.
168. Wood Diary, 15 June 1859, Hickleton Mss. A8/D.
169. Ibid.
170. Wood Diary, 14 June 1859, Hickleton Mss. A8/D.
171. Ibid.
172. Wood Diary, 15 June 1859, Hickleton Mss. A8/D.
173. Russell to Palmerston, 16 June 1859, Broadlands Mss. GC/RU. 498, cited in Krein, *The Last Palmerston Government*, pp. 16–17.
174. Wood Diary, 15 June 1859, Hickleton Mss. A8/D, cited in Morley, *Gladstone*, I, pp. 626–7.
175. W. Bagehot, 'The Conservative Vein in Mr. Bright', *The Economist*, 29 April 1876, xxxiv, pp. 506–7.
176. Ellice to Parkes, 17 June 1859, Ellice Mss. 15045, fol. 105.
177. Russell to Bright, 15 June 1859, G. M. Trevelyan, *The Life of John Bright* (London, 1913) p. 282.
178. Wood Diary, 15 June 1859, Hickleton Mss. A8/D.
179. Ellice to Parkes, 17 June 1859, Ellice Mss. 15045, fol. 105.
180. Russell to Cobden, 25 June 1859, Cobden Mss. 43669, fol. 206.
181. Palmerston to Cobden, 27 June 1859, Cobden Mss. 43669, fol. 208.
182. Cobden to Sale, 4 July 1859, Cobden Mss. 43669, fol. 217.
183. Bright to Cobden, 30 June 1859, Bright Mss. 43384, fol. 152; and Broughton Diary, 2 July 1859, Broughton Mss. 43762, fol. 23.
184. Fortescue Diary, 15 June 1859, Carlingford Mss. DD/SH 358.
185. Clarendon to Duchess of Manchester, n.d. (? 16 June 1859) cited in Kennedy, '*Dear Duchess*', p. 58.
186. Broughton Diary, 18 June 1859, Broughton Mss. 43762, fol. 14.
187. Granville to Gladstone, 11 November 1868, cited in Prest, *Russell*, p. 385.

CONCLUSION

1. W. H. Pater, *The Renaissance: Studies in Art and Poetry* (London, 1901) p. 235.
2. A. Briggs, *The Age of Improvement, 1783–1867* (London, 1959) p. 416.
3. Wood to Ellice, 17 June 1859, Ellice Mss. 15062, fol. 5.
4. Panmure to Palmerston, 15 June 1859, Broadlands Mss. GC.PA 170.
5. Granville to Canning, 10 August 1859, Granville Mss. PRO 30/29/31/I, cited in Lord E. Fitzmaurice, *The Life of Granville George Leveson-Gower, Second Earl Granville, K.G.* (London, 1905) I, p. 345.
6. Ibid.
7. Granville to Canning, 27 June 1859, Granville Mss. PRO 30/29/31/I, fol. 99, cited in Fitzmaurice, *Granville*, I, p. 345.
8. Granville to Canning, 10 August 1859, Granville Mss. PRO 30/29/31/I, cited in Fitzmaurice, *Granville*, I, p. 345.
9. Ibid.
10. Hall to Phipps, 15 June 1859, cited in H. C. F. Bell, *Lord Palmerston* (London, 1936) II, pp. 217–18.
11. Granville to Canning, 27 June 1859, Granville Mss. PRO 30/29/31/I, fol. 99, cited in Fitzmaurice, *Granville*, I, p. 345.
12. Broughton Diary, 30 June 1859, Broughton Mss. 43762, fol. 22.
13. Stanley of Alderley to Panmure, 30 July 1859, Dalhousie Mss. GD/45/14/655.
14. Broughton Diary, 21 June 1859, Broughton Mss. 43762, fol. 14.
15. Broughton Diary, 18 July 1859, Broughton Mss. 43762, fol. 19.
16. Broughton Diary, 25 June 1859, Broughton Mss. 43762 fol. 19.
17. D. Southgate, *'The Most English Minister . . .': The Policies and Politics of Palmerston* (London, 1966) p. 456. See also N. Gash, *Aristocracy and People: Britain 1815–1865* (London, 1979) p. 268.
18. R. G. Watt, 'Parties and Politics in Mid-Victorian Britain, 1857 to 1859: A Study in Quantification', unpublished PhD thesis, University of Minnesota, 1975, p. 127, identifies a hard core of 104 Radical or like-minded Liberal MPs in the Commons after the 1857 election. A total of 225 Radical and Liberal MPs voted with known Radicals in 85% or more of the major divisions during the parliament. This counters the Palmerstonian myth that the 1857 election purged Radicalism from the parliament.
19. Watt 'Parties and Politics', p. 139.
20. Ibid. pp. 130–7.
21. Ibid., p. 110.
22. In June 1857 Palmerston assured the Liberal backbencher Sir John Trelawny that the government intended to legislate upon the Church rates question. This prevented Trelawny introducing a private motion, but no government measure appeared. The Radical T. S. Duncombe asked Palmerston if the government was going to deal with the issue in December 1857. Palmerston's reply was evasive. Despairing of Palmerston's vague assurances, Trelawny subsequently introduced a pri-

vate motion on the Church rates question which was debated during February 1858. Russell raised the issue of the admission of Jews into parliament by introducing his own bill in 1857, and proposing a committee of enquiry for the 1857–58 recess. The committee, however, did not recommend the adoption of Russell's proposal.

23. Parkes to Brougham, 3 May 1859, Brougham Mss. 20080.
24. D. Read, *Cobden and Bright: A Victorian Political Partnership* (London, 1967) discusses this point fully, especially pp. 152–3.
25. W. L. Arnstein, 'The Religions Issue in Mid-Victorian Politics: A Note on a Neglected Source', *Albion*, 6:2 (1974) pp. 134–43.
26. For a fuller discussion of this point see A. Hawkins, 'Lord Derby and Victorian Conservatism: A Reappraisal', forthcoming in *Parliamentary History Yearbook*.
27. Clarendon to Duchess of Manchester, 6 November 1859, cited in A. L. Kennedy (ed.) *'My Dear Duchess': Social and Political Letters to the Duchess of Manchester, 1858–1869* (London, 1956) pp. 78–9. See Watt, 'Parties and Politics', p. 109. Over 80% of the Conservative party usually voted together. Both Radicals and Whigs had greater unity than avowed Liberals. Only Liberal Conservatives had a more disunited voting record than the Liberals. See also J. R. Bylsma, 'Political Issues and Party Unity in the House of Commons, 1852–1857: A Scalogram Analysis', unpublished PhD thesis, University of Iowa, 1968, pp. 78 and 88.
28. D. E. MacCracken, 'The Conservatives in "Power": The Minority Governments of 1852, 1858–9 and 1866–8', unpublished PhD thesis, University of Virginia, 1979; as well as R. Stewart, *The Foundation of the Conservative Party, 1830–1867* (London, 1978).
29. Stewart discusses Derby's second ministry in *Foundation of the Conservative Party*, pp. 318–24.
30. Derby to Disraeli, 16 September 1866, cited in W. F. Monypenny and G. E. Buckle, *The Life of Benjamin Disraeli, Earl of Beaconsfield* (London, 1910–20) IV, p. 453. See W. D. Jones, *Lord Derby and Victorian Conservatism* (Oxford, 1956) p. 298; and M. Cowling, *1867, Disraeli, Gladstone and Revolution* (Cambridge, 1967) pp. 306–9.
31. Derby to Malmesbury (copy), 25 December 1869, Derby Mss. 188/2; Derby to Disraeli, 27 January 1861, Hughenden Mss. B/xx/S/280; Derby to Disraeli, 6 August 1863, Hughenden Mss. B/xx/S/314, cited in P. M. Gurowich, 'The Continuation of War by Other Means: Party and Politics, 1855–1865', *HJ*, 27:3 (1984) p. 622: Disraeli to Derby, 13 May 1864, Derby Mss. 146/1 cited in Monypenny and Buckle, *Disraeli*, IV, pp. 344–5; Derby to Disraeli, 24 July 1865, Hughenden Mss. B/xx/S/334.
32. Malmesbury to Derby, 6 February 1860, cited in Lord Malmesbury, *Memoirs of an Ex-Minister* (London, 1885) II, p. 215.
33. Shaftesbury Diary, 21 June 1859, cited in E. Hodder, *The Life and Work of the Seventh Earl of Shaftesbury* (London, 1886) III, p. 88.
34. J. R. Vincent, *Formation of the Liberal Party, 1857–1868* (London, 1966) p. 248.
35. This is Lord Acton's observation in April 1862. He continues: 'The

opposition like him, and consider him a conservative. He suits the bad conservative instincts, just as he adopts the sins of the Liberals, and is strong because he is wrong. Gladstone could not hold the government together a week if Palmerston were to die because of his genius, of his principles, and of his pugnacity. The only man who could disarm opposition, in a different way from Palmerston, would be Lewis, who has gained ground wonderfully of late.' Acton to Simpson, 30 April 1862, cited in J. L. Althoz, D. McElrath and J. C. Holland (eds) *The Correspondence of Lord Acton and Richard Simpson*, 3 vols (Cambridge, 1973) II, p. 292.

Bibliography

The place of publication throughout is London, unless otherwise stated.

I MANUSCRIPT SOURCES

Those manuscript collections of letters, diaries, memoranda and private papers consulted in the preparation of this study.

Abercromby Mss: The correspondence of the 2nd Lord and Lady Dunfermline, the National Library of Scotland, Edinburgh.

Aberdare Mss: The correspondence of H. A. Bruce, 1st Lord Aberdare, the Glamorgan Record Office.

Aberdare Mss: The correspondence of H. A. Bruce, 1st Lord Aberdare, the Huntington Library, San Marino, California.

Aberdeen Mss: The correspondence of G. H. Gordon, the 4th Earl Aberdeen, the British Library.

Baines Mss: The correspondence of Edward Baines, the Leeds District Archives.

Brabourne Mss: The diaries, papers and correspondence of Sir E. Knatchbull-Hugessen, 1st Lord Brabourne, the Kent County Archives, Maidstone.

Brand Mss: The papers and correspondence of H. B. Brand, the House of Lords Record Office.

Bright Mss: The correspondence of John Bright, the British Library.

Broadlands Mss: The diary, papers and correspondence of Henry Temple, Viscount Palmerston, in Southampton University Library.

Broadlands Mss: The official correspondence of Henry Temple, Viscount Palmerston, the British Library.

Brougham Mss: The correspondence of Lord Brougham, University College, the University of London.

Broughton Mss: The diaries and correspondence of J. C. Hobhouse, Lord Broughton, in the British Library.

Buckingham Mss: The correspondence and papers of the 2nd Duke of Buckingham and Chandos, the Huntington Library, San Marino, California.

Cairns Mss: The papers and correspondence of Sir Hugh McCalmont Cairns, the Public Record Office.

Canning Mss: The papers and correspondence of Charles, Earl Canning, the Leeds District Archives.

Cardwell Mss: The correspondence of Edward Cardwell, the Public Record Office.

Carlingford Mss: The diary and correspondence of S. Chichester-Fortescue, 1st Lord Carlingford, form part of the Strachie collection, the Somerset County Record Office, Taunton.

Carnarvon Mss: The papers and correspondence of the 4th Earl of Carnarvon, the Public Record Office.

Clarendon Mss: The papers and correspondence of the 4th Earl Clarendon, the Bodleian Library, Oxford.

Clanricarde Mss: The papers and correspondence of the Marquess of Clanricarde and the correspondence of Lord Dunkellin, the Leeds District Archives.

Cobden Mss: The correspondence of Richard Cobden, the British Library.

Codrington Mss: The papers and correspondence of Sir C. W. Codrington, the Gloucestershire Record Office, Gloucester.

Cowley Mss: The correspondence of H. R. C. Wellesley, 1st Earl Cowley, the Public Record Office.

Cranbrook Mss: The diaries and correspondence of A. E. Gathorne Hardy, Lord Cranbrook, the East Suffolk Record Office, Ipswich.

Croker Mss: The correspondence of J. W. Croker, the British Library.

Cross Mss: The correspondence of R. A. Cross, the British Library.

Dalhousie Mss: The papers and correspondence of Lord Pamure later 11th Earl of Dalhousie, the Scottish Record Office, Edinburgh.

Delane Mss: The diaries and correspondence of J. T. Delane, *The Times* Archive, New Printing House Square, London.

Denison Mss: The diaries and correspondence of J. E. Denison, the University of Nottingham Library.

Derby Mss: The papers and correspondence of the 14th Earl of Derby, in the custody of Lord Blake, Queen's College, Oxford.

Elgin Mss: The papers and correspondence of James Bruce, 8th Earl of Elgin, the India Office Library and Records.

Ellenborough Mss: The papers and correspondence of Lord Ellenborough, the Public Record Office.

Ellice Mss: The correspondence of Edward Ellice Senior and the papers and correspondence of Edward Ellice Junior, the National Library of Scotland, Edinburgh.

Gladstone Mss: The papers and correspondence of W. E. Gladstone, the British Library.

Graham Mss: The correspondence of Sir J. Graham, seen on microfilm in the Bodleian Library, Oxford.

Granville Mss: The papers and correspondence of the 2nd Earl Granville, the Public Record Office.

Grey Mss: The diaries, papers and correspondence of the 3rd Earl Grey, the Department of Palaeography and Diplomatic, The University of Durham.

Greville Mss: The diaries of C. C. F. Greville, the British Library.

Hadfield Mss: The correspondence of G. Hadfield, the Manchester Central Library.

Hamilton Mss: The correspondence of G. A. Hamilton, the Public Record Office.

Hampton Mss: The papers and correspondence of Sir J. Pakington, the Worcestershire County Record Office, Worcester.

Hardwicke Mss: The correspondence of Charles Yorke, 4th Earl of Hardwicke, the British Library.

Harpton Court Mss: The papers and correspondence of Sir G. Cornewall Lewis, the National Library of Wales, Aberystwyth.

Hatherton Mss: The papers and correspondence of the 1st and 2nd Lord Hatherton, the Staffordshire County Record Office, Stafford.

Hickleton Mss: The diaries and correspondence of Sir Charles Wood, 1st Lord Halifax, consulted at the Borthwick Institute, York.

Holland House Mss: The correspondence of the 4th Lord and Lady Holland, the British Library.

Hughenden Mss: The papers and correspondence of Benjamin Disraeli, the Bodleian Library, Oxford.

Hylton Mss: The papers and correspondence of Sir William Jolliffe, 1st Lord Hylton, the Somerset County Record Office, Taunton.

Iddesleigh Mss: The papers and correspondence of Sir Stafford Northcote, the British Library.

Kinglake Mss: The correspondence of A. W. Kinglake, the University of Cambridge Library.

Knightley Mss: The diaries of Lady L. Knightley, the Northamptonshire County Record Office, Northampton.

Layard Mss: The correspondence of A. H. Layard, the British Library.

Londonderry Mss: The correspondence of Frances Anne, Marchioness of Londonderry, the Durham Record Office.

Lyndhurst Mss: The papers and correspondence of J. S. Copley, 1st Lord Lyndhurst, the Glamorgan Record Office.

Lytton Mss: The papers and correspondence of Sir Edward Bulwer Lytton, 1st Lord Lytton, the Hertfordshire County Record Office, Hertford.

Malmesbury Mss: The diaries, papers and correspondence of James Fitz-Harris, 3rd Earl of Malmesbury, the Hampshire County Record Office, Winchester.

Melville Mss: The correspondence of the 3rd Viscount Melville, the National Library of Scotland, Edinburgh.

Minto Mss: The correspondence of the 2nd Earl of Minto and the correspondence of Lord Melgund, the National Library of Scotland, Edinburgh.

Monk Bretton Mss: The correspondence of J. G. Dodson, 1st Lord Monk Bretton, the Bodleian Library, Oxford.

Newcastle Mss: The papers and correspondence of Henry Pelham Clinton, 5th Duke of Newcastle, the University of Nottingham Library.

Newdegate Mss: The correspondence of C. N. Newdegate and the diaries of his mother, M. Newdegate, the Warwickshire County Record Office, Warwick.

Ogden Mss: The correspondence of Mrs. J. Bright née Margaret Elizabeth Leatham, University College, the University of London.

Palfrey Mss: Foley scrapbooks containing political press cuttings, the Worcestershire County Record Office, Worcester.

Parkes Mss: The correspondence of J. Parkes, University College, the University of London.

Ramsay Mss: The papers and correspondence of Sir G. Dalhousie Ramsay, the British Library.

Redesdale Mss: The correspondence of J. T. Freeman-Mitford, 2nd Lord Redesdale, the Gloucestershire County Record Office, Gloucester.

Ripon Mss: The correspondence of the 1st Marquess of Ripon, the British Library.

Russell Mss: The papers and correspondence of Lord John Russell, the Public Record Office.

Salisbury Mss: The correspondence of Lord Robert Cecil and the papers and correspondence of the 2nd Marquis of Salisbury, Hatfield House, Hertfordshire.

Selborne Mss: The papers and correspondence of Roundell Palmer, 1st Lord Selborne, the Lambeth Palace Library.

Shaftesbury Mss: The diaries and correspondence of the 7th Earl Shaftesbury, form part of the Broadlands collection in Southampton University Library.

Sotheron-Estcourt Mss: The diary, papers and correspondence of T. H. S. Sotheron-Estcourt, the Gloucestershire County Record Office.

Stanley Mss: The diaries and correspondence of Edward Henry Stanley, later the 15th Earl of Derby, the Liverpool City Record Office.

Stanley of Alderley Mss: The correspondence of the 2nd Lord Stanley of Alderley, the Cheshire County Record Office.

Stanmore Mss: The papers and correspondence of Arthur Gordon, Lord Stanmore, the British Museum. A privately printed selection from Gordon's diary, not extant in the Stanmore Mss., in the British Library, Reference Division, catalogue number, B.P. 12 (10–12A).

Strachie Mss: The correspondence of Frances, Countess Waldegrave the Somerset County Record Office, Taunton.

The Times Mss: Diaries and papers of *The Times*, the Archives, New Printing House Square, London.

Walpole Mss: The papers and correspondence of S. H. Walpole, in the possession of Mr. D. C. L. Holland C.B.

Ward Hunt Mss: The papers and correspondence of G. Ward Hunt, the Northamptonshire County Record Office, Northampton.

Wemyss Mss: The correspondence of Lord Elcho, seen on microfilm at the National Register of Archives (Scotland), Edinburgh.

Westbury Mss: The correspondence and fragments of a journal of Sir Richard Bethell, 1st Lord Westbury, the Bodleian Library, Oxford.

II CONTEMPORARY PAMPHLETS AND PUBLICATIONS

Anon., *Lord Palmerston's Foreign Policy in and out of Europe. By a Late Resident in China* (1857).

Anon., *Palmerston for Premier. The Claims of Lord Palmerston to fill the Post of Prime Minister of England Considered* (1854).

Anon., *The Two Great Statesmen: A Plutarchian Parallel between Earl Russell and Viscount Palmerston* (1862).

Anon., *How Shall we Vote?* . . . (1859).

A Liberal MP, *The Contrast: or John Bright's support of the present Government justified* . . . (1859).

Abram, W. J., *Mr. Bright and his Schemes* (1859).

An English Liberal, *Italy: Its Condition. Gt. Britain: Its Policy* (1859).

Baring, F. T., Baron Northbrook, *Baron Northbrook, To the Electors of Portsmouth (An Election Address)* (1859).

Bright, J., *Mr. Bright's Speeches, revised by himself, at Birmingham, Manchester, London, Edinburgh, Glasgow, Bradford, and Rochdale. With the Schedules of Disfranchisement and Redistribution of Seats* (1859).

Bright, J., *The Letter of John Bright Esq., M.P. [to Absalom Watkin] on the War . . .* (1854).

Bright, J., *Speech on Legislation for India, delivered in the House of Commons on the Second Reading of the India Bill, June 24th, 1858* (1858).

Bright, J., *The National Protest against Manchester's Rejection of John Bright: being a selection from the comments of the press* (1857).

Cecil, Lord R., 'The Theories of Parliamentary Reform', in *Oxford Essays* (1858).

Cobden, R., *What Next and Next?* (1856).

Cocker, E. (pseud.), *What Share of Cocker and the Chancellor of the Exchequer. A Dialogue on the Income Tax* (?1856).

Fletcher, G., *Parliamentary Portraits of the Present Period* (1862).

F. M. E. [i.e. Frederick Milnes Edge], *Richard Cobden at Home . . .* (n.d.).

Francis, G. H., *The Right Honourable Benjamin Disraeli M.P. A Critical Biography* (1852).

Grey, Henry, Third Earl, *Parliamentary Government Considered with Reference to a Reform of Parliament* (1858).

Kebbel, T. E., *Essays upon History and Politics* (1864).

Lammer Moor (pseud.), *Bowring, Cobden and China etc . . .* (1857).

Lewis, G. Cornewall, *An Essay on the Influence of Authority in Matters of Opinion* (1849).

Lewis, G. Cornewall, *A Treatise on the Method of Observation and Reasoning in Politics* 2 vols (1852).

MacKnight, *The Right Honourable Benjamin Disraeli M. P. A Political and Literary Biography. Addressed to a New Generation* (1854).

Mill, J., *Disraeli the Author, Orator and Statesman* (1863).

Mill, J. S., *Who is the 'Reformer', John Stuart Mill or John Bright?* (1859).

Miller, J. C., *What? or Neither? An Examination of the Education Bills of Lord John Russell and Sir John S. Pakington* (1855).

Rickards, F. P., *Manchester and John Bright* (1859).

Russell, Lord J., *Russell and Burke Upon Party* (1850).

Russell, Lord J., *The Foreign Policy of England 1570 to 1870: A Historical Essay* (1871).

S. P. O., *The Life . . . of Viscount Palmerston* (1857).

Taylor, H., *The Statesman: An Ironical Treatise on the Art of Succeeding* (1827).

III CONTEMPORARY JOURNALS AND NEWSPAPERS

Blackwood's Magazine
Daily News

Economist
Edinburgh Review
Examiner
Illustrated London News
Morning Post
Punch
Quarterly Review
Saturday Review
Sun
The Times

IV AUTOBIOGRAPHIES, DIARIES, MEMOIRS AND BIOGRAPHIES CONTAINING CORRESPONDENCE

Edited documents are listed under the name of principal author.

Acland, Sir T. D., *The Memoirs and Letters of the Rt. Hon. Sir Thomas Acland* (1902) A. H. D. Acland (ed.).

Acton, John Edward Dalberg, *The Correspondence of Lord Acton and Richard Simpson*, 3 vols (Cambridge, 1971–3) J. Althoz, D. McElrath and J. C. Holland (eds).

Airlie, Countess of, Mabel, *Lady Palmerston and Her Times*, 2 vols (1922).

Argyll, Duke of, *George Douglas, 8th Duke of Argyll: Autobiography and Memoirs*, 2 vols (1906) Dowager Duchess of Argyll (ed.).

Ashley, E., *The Life and Correspondence of Henry John Temple, Viscount Palmerston*, 2 vols (1879).

Ashworth, H., *Recollections of Richard Cobden M.P. and the Anti-Corn Law League* (1877).

Awdry, F., *A Country Gentleman of the Nineteenth Century. Being a Short Memoir of the Rt. Hon. Sir William Heathcote, Bart. of Hursley. 1801–1881* (1906).

Bagenal, P. H. D., *The Life of Ralph Bernal Osborne M.P.* (1884).

Balfour, Lady Frances, *The Life of George, Fourth Earl of Aberdeen, K.G., K.T.* 2 vols (1923).

Baring, F. T. Lord Northbrook, *Journals and Correspondence of Francis Thornhill Baring, Lord Northbrook*, 2 vols (Winchester, 1905) Thomas George, Earl of Northbrook (ed.).

Barrington, E. I., *The Servant of All: Pages from the Family, Social and Political Life of my Father James Wilson*, 2 vols (1927).

Barrington, E. I., *The Life and Works of Walter Bagehot*, 10 vols (1915).

Bassett, A. T. (ed.), *Gladstone to his Wife*, (1936).

Bright, J., *The Diaries of John Bright* (1930) R. A. J. Walling (ed.).

Bright, J., *Speeches on the Public Affairs of the Last Twenty Years*, 2 vols (1869) J. E. Thorold Rogers (ed.).

Bright, J., *The Public Letters of the Rt. Hon. John Bright . . .* (1885) H. J. Leech (ed.).

Broughton, Lord, *Recollections of a Long Life by Lord Broughton*, 6 vols (1909) Lady Dorchester (ed.).

Bruce, H. A., *Letters of Rt. Hon. H. A. Bruce, Lord Aberdare of Duffryn*, 2 vols (Oxford, 1902).

Bulwer, Baron Dalling, *The Life of Henry John Temple, Viscount Palmerston with Selections from his Diaries and Correspondence*, 5 vols (1870–4).

Bunsen, Baroness Frances, *The Memoirs of Baron Bunsen*, 2 vols (1869).

Campbell, J. D. S., Duke of Argyll, *Viscount Palmerston K.G.* (1906).

Campbell, Lord, *The Lives of Lord Lyndhurst and Lord Brougham* (1869).

Cartwright, J. (ed.) *The Journals of Lady Knightley of Fawsley, 1856–1884* (1915).

Cavendish, E. C., *Anecdotes and Biographical Sketches* (1863).

Cavendish, Lady Frederick, *The Diary of Lady Frederick Cavendish*, 2 vols (1927) J. Bailey (ed.).

Cecil, Lady G., *The Life of Robert, Marquis of Salisbury*, 4 vols (1921–32).

Childe-Pemberton, W. S., *The Life of Lord Norton, 1814–1905: Statesman and Philanthropist* (1909).

Cobden, R., *The Political Writings of Richard Cobden*, 2 vols (1867).

Cobden, R., *The Speeches of Richard Cobden on Questions of Public Policy*, 2 vols (1870) J. Bright and J. E. Thorold Rogers (eds).

Colchester, Lord, Admiral Charles, *Memoranda of My Life from 1798 to 1859 inclusive* (1869).

Cox, Homersham, *Whig and Tory Administration During the Last Thirteen Years* (1868).

Creighton, M., *A Memoir of Sir George Grey* (1884).

Cunningham, Sir H. S., *Earl Canning* (Oxford, 1891).

Dalhousie, Marquess of, *The Private Letters of the Marquess of Dalhousie* (1910) J. G. A. Baird (ed.).

Dallas, G. M., *Letters from London, 1856–1860*, 2 vols (1870) J. Dallas (ed.).

Dallas, G. M., *The Diary of G. M. Dallas* (Philadelphia, 1892) S. Dallas (ed.).

Dasent, A. I., *John Thadeus Delane, Editor of 'The Times'*, 2 vols (1908).

Denison, J. E., Viscount Ossington, *Notes from my Journal when Speaker of the House of Commons* (1899).

Derby, E. H., *Speeches and Addresses of Edward Henry, XVth Earl of Derby*, 2 vols (1894) Sir T. H. Sanderson and E. S. Roscoe (eds).

Disraeli, B., *Parliamentary Reform. A Series of Speeches on that Subject delivered in the House of Commons by the Rt. Hon. B. Disraeli, 1848–1866* (1867) M. Corry (ed.).

Disraeli, B., *Letters from Benjamin Disraeli to Francis Anne, Marchioness of Londonderry 1837–61* (1938) Marchioness of Londonderry (ed.).

Drummond, H., *Speeches in Parliament and some Miscellaneous Pamphlets of the late Henry Drummond*, 2 vols (1860) Lord Lovaine (ed.).

Duncombe, T. H., *The Life and Correspondence of T. S. Duncombe*, 2 vols (1868).

Elcho, Lord, *Memories 1818–1912 by the Earl of March and Wemyss* (privately printed, 1912).

Elgin, Lord, *The Letters and Journals of Lord Elgin* (1872) T. Walrond (ed.).

Escott, T. H. S., *Edward Bulwer, First Baron Lytton of Knebworth: A Social, Personal and Political Monograph* (1910).

Fitzmaurice, Lord E., *The Life of Granville George Leveson-Gower, Second Earl Granville, K. G.*, 2 vols (1905).

Fortescue, F. C., '. . . and Mr. Fortescue': A Selection from the Diaries from 1851 to 1862 of Chichester Fortescue, Lord Carlingford, K. P.* (1958) O. W. Hewett (ed.).

Fraser, Sir William, *Disraeli and His Day* (1891).

Gathorne-Hardy, A. E., *Gathorne Hardy, 1st Earl of Cranbrook: A Memoir*, 2 vols (1910).

Gladstone, W. E., *The Gladstone Diaries*, 8 vols (Oxford, 1968–1982) H. C. G. Matthew and M. R. D. Foot (eds).

Gladstone, W. E., *The Prime-Minister's Papers: W. E. Gladstone 1. Autobiographica 2. Autobiographical Memoranda* (1971) J. Brooke and M. Sorenson (eds).

Gladstone, W. E., 'Gladstone-Gordon Correspondence, 1851–1896', *American Philosophical Society Transactions*, New Series 51, pt. 4 (1961).

Gordon, A. H., Baron Stanmore, *Gordon Diary, extracts from* . . ., Privately printed by Lord Stanmore, British Library ref. no. B.P. 12 (10–12A).

Gordon, A. H., Baron Stanmore, *The Earl of Aberdeen* (1893).

Gordon, A. H., Baron Stanmore, *Sidney Herbert, Lord Herbert of Lea: A Memoir*, 2 vols (1906).

Grant Duff, Sir Mountstuart Elphinstone, *Notes from a Diary, 1851–1872* (1897).

Greville, C. C. F., *A Journal of the Reigns of King George IV, King William IV and Queen Victoria*, 8 vols (1888) H. Reeve (ed.).

Greville, C. C. F., *The Letters of Charles Greville and Henry Reeve* (1924) Rev. A. H. Johnson (ed.).

Hardinge, Sir A., *Life of H. E. M. Herbert, Fourth Earl of Carnarvon, 1831–1890*, 3 vols (1925).

Hayward, A., *A Selection from the Correspondence of Abraham Hayward Q.C.* (1886) H. C. Carlisle (ed.).

Hayward, A., *Lord Landsdowne: A Biographical Sketch* (1872).

Hayward, A., *Lady Palmerston: A Biographical Sketch* (1872).

Hodder, E., *The Life and Work of the Seventh Earl of Shaftesbury*, 3 vols (1886).

Holyoake, G. J., *Sixty Years of an Agitator's Life*, 2 vols (1892).

Hunter, W., *The Life of the Earl of Mayo*, 2 vols (Oxford, 1875).

Kebbel, T. E., *English Statesmen Since 1815* (1868).

Kebbel, T. E., *A History of Toryism* (1886).

Kebell, T. E., *The Earl of Derby* (1890).

Kebbel, T. E., *Lord Beaconsfield and Other Tory Memories* (1907).

Kennedy, A. L. (ed.) *'My Dear Duchess': Social and Political Letters to the Duchess of Manchester, 1858–1869* (1956).

Lang, A., *Sir Stafford Northcote, First Earl of Iddesleigh*, 2 vols (1890).

Layard, Sir. A. H., *Autobiography and Letters of Sir A. Henry Layard* (1903) Hon. W. N. Bruce (ed.).

Leader, R. E., *The Life and Letters of John Arthur Roebuck* (1879).

Lewis, Sir G. C., *Letters of the Rt. Hon. Sir George Cornewall Lewis to Various Friends* (1870) G. F. Lewis (ed.).

Lorne, Marquis of, *Viscount Palmerston* (1892).

Lucas, E., *The Life of Frederick Lucas, M. P.* (1886).

MacCarthy, D. and Russell, A. (eds) *Lady John Russell: A Memoir with Selections from her Diaries and Correspondence* (1910).

Malmesbury, Lord, *Memoirs of an Ex-Minister*, 2 vols (1885).

Martin, A. P., *The Life and Letters of the Rt. Hon. Robert Lowe, Viscount Sherbrooke*, 2 vols (1893).

Martin, T., *A Life of Lord Lyndhurst* (1883).

Martineau, J., *The Life of Henry Pelham, Fifth Duke of Newcastle* (1908).

Maxwell, Sir H., *The Life and Letters of the Fourth Earl of Clarendon*, 2 vols (1913).

Meath, Earl of, *Memories of the 19th Century* (1923).

Miall, A., *Life of Edward Miall* (1884).

Miall, C. S., *Henry Richard, M. P.: A Biography* (1889).

Monypenny, W. F. and Buckle, G. E., *The Life of Benjamin Disraeli, Earl of Beaconsfield*, 6 vols (1910–20).

Moore, M. G., *An Irish Gentleman, George Henry Moore* (1913).

Morier, Sir R., *The Memoirs and Letters of the Rt. Hon. Sir R. Morier* (1911) Mrs R. Wemyss (ed.).

Morley, John, *The Life of Richard Cobden*, 2 vols (1879).

Morley, John, *The Life of William Ewart Gladstone*, 3 vols (1903).

Motley, J. L., *The Correspondence of J. L. Motley*, 3 vols (1889) G. W. Curtis (ed.).

Nash, T. A., *The Life of Lord Westbury* (1888).

Northcote, S. H., *Twenty Years of Financial Policy: A Summary of the Chief Financial Measures passed between 1842 and 1861, with a table of Budgets* (1862).

Palmerston, Viscount, *The Letters of the Third Viscount Palmerston to Laurence and Elizabeth Sullivan, 1804–1863* (1979) K. Bourne (ed.).

Palmerston, Lady, *The Letters of Lady Palmerston* (1957) T. Lever (ed.).

Panmure, Lord, *Panmure Papers*, 2 vols (1908) Sir G. Douglas and Sir G. D. Ramsay (eds).

Parker, C. S., *Life and Letters of Sir James Graham, Second Baronet of Netherby*, 2 vols (1907).

Reeve, H., *The Memoirs of Henry Reeve*, 2 vols (1898) J. K. Laughton (ed.).

Reid, Sir T. W., *The Life of Richard Monckton Milnes, First Lord Houghton*, 2 vols (1891).

Rogers, J. E. Thorold, *Cobden and Modern Political Opinion . . .* (1873).

Russell, Lord J., *The Later Correspondence of Lord Russell*, 2 vols (1925) G. P. Gooch (ed.).

Russell, Lord J., *Recollections and Suggestions, 1813–1873* (1875).

St Helier, Lady, *Memories of Fifty Years* (1909).

Saintsbury, G. E. B., *The Earl of Derby*, (1892).

Schwabe, Mrs. S., *Reminiscences of Richard Cobden* (1895).

Simpson, M. C. M. (née Senior), *Many Memories of Many People* (1898).

Somerset, Duke of, *The Letters, Remains and Memoirs of the 12th Duke of Somerset* (1893) W. H. Mallock and Lady G. Ramsden (eds).

Stanley, Lady Augusta, *Reminiscences* (1892) Mrs E. Charles (ed.).

Stanley, Lady Augusta, *Letters of Lady Augusta Stanley 1849–1863* (1927) Dean of Winsdor and Hector Bolitho (eds).

Times, The, *The History of 'The Times', The Tradition Established 1841–1884* (1939).

Tollemache, L. A., *Talks with Mr. Gladstone* (1898).

Trevelyan, G. O., *The Life and Letters of Lord Macaulay*, 2 vols (1883).

Victoria, Queen, *The Letters of Queen Victoria*, 1st Series, 3 vols (1907) A. C. Benson and Viscount Esher (eds).

Vitzhum, Count, *St. Petersburg and London in the Years 1852 to 1865: Reminiscences of Count Charles Frederick Vitzhum von Eckstaedt*, 2 vols (1887) E. F. Taylor (trans.) H. Reeve (ed.).

Walpole, S., *The Life of Lord John Russell*, 2 vols (1889).

Wellesley, H. R., *The Paris Embassy during the Second Empire* (1928) F. A. Wellesley (ed.).

Whibley, C., *Lord John Manners and His Friends*, 2 vols (Edinburgh, 1925).

White, W., *The Inner Life of the House of Commons*, 2 vols (1897) J. McCarthy (ed.).

Wolf, Lucien, *Life of the First Marquess of Ripon*, 2 vols (1921).

V SECONDARY SOURCES

Anderson, O., *A Liberal State at War: English Politics and Economics During the Crimean War* (1974).

Appleman, P., Madden, W. A. and Wolff, M. (eds), *1859: Entering an Age of Crisis* (Bloomington, Indiana, 1959).

Arnstein, W. L., *Protestant Versus Catholic in Mid-Victorian England: Mr. Newdegate and the Nuns* (Missouri, 1982).

Bagehot, W., *The English Constitution* (1963) R. Crossman (ed.).

Bagehot, W., *Historical Essays* (1971) N. St. John Stevas (ed.).

Battiscombe, Georgina, *Shaftesbury: A Biography of the Seventh Earl, 1801–1885* (1974).

Beales, D. E. D., *England and Italy, 1859–60* (1961).

Beattie, A., *English Party Politics*, 2 vols (1971).

Bell, H. C. F., *Lord Palmerston*, 2 vols (1936).

Bentley, Michael, *Politics Without Democracy: 1815–1914* (1984).

Best, G. F. A., *Shaftesbury* (1964).

Blake, R., *The Conservative Party from Peel to Churchill* (1970).

Blake, R., *Disraeli* (1966).

Bourne, K., *The Foreign Policy of Victorian England: 1830–1902* (1970).

Bourne, K., *Palmerston: The Early Years, 1784–1841* (1982).

Bradley, Ian, *The Optimists: Themes and Personalities in Victorian Liberalism* (1980).

Briggs, A., *Victorian People: Some Reassessments of People, Institutions, Ideas and Events 1851–1857* (1954).

Briggs, A., *The Age of Improvement* (1959).

Bulwer-Thomas, I., *The Growth of the British Party System*, I (1965).

Burn, W. L., *The Age of Equipoise* (1964).

Butler, D. (ed.) *Coalitions in British Politics* (1978).

Butler, G. G., *The Tory Tradition* . . . (1914).

Butler, Lord (ed.) *The Conservatives: A History from their Origins to 1965* (1977).

Butler, P., *Gladstone: Church, State and Tractarianism* (Oxford, 1982).

Chadwick, O., *The Victorian Church. Part 1, 1829–1860* (1967).

Chamberlain, M. E., *Lord Aberdeen: A Political Biography* (1983).

Clark, G. Kitson, *An Expanding Society* (1967).

Clark, G. Kitson, *The Making of Victorian England* (1963).

Conacher, J. B., *The Aberdeen Coalition 1852–1855: A Study in Mid-Nineteenth Century Party Politics* (Cambridge, 1968).

Conacher, J. B., *The Peelites and the Party System, 1846–52* (Newton Abbot, 1972).

Connell, B. (ed.) *Regina vs. Palmerston: The Correspondence between Queen Victoria and Her Foreign and Prime Minister, 1837–1865* (1962).

Cook, E., *Delane of 'The Times'* (1916).

Cowling, M., *1867: Disraeli, Gladstone and Revolution* (Cambridge, 1967).

Davis, R. W., *Political Change and Continuity, 1760–1885: A Buckinghamshire Study* (Newton Abbot, 1972).

Davis, R. W., *Disraeli* (1976).

Davis, W. W., *Gladstone and the Unification of Italy* (1918).

Denholm, A., *Lord Ripon 1827–1909: A Political Biography* (1982).

Erickson, A. B., *The Public Career of Sir James Graham* (1952).

Feuchtwanger, E. J., *Gladstone* (1975).

Finlayson, G., *The Seventh Earl of Shaftesbury* (1981).

Gash, N., *Reaction and Reconstruction in English Politics 1832–1852* (Oxford, 1965).

Gash, N., *Aristocracy and People: Britain, 1815–1865* (1979).

Gilam, A., *The Emancipation of the Jews in England* (New York, 1982).

Guedalla, P., *Palmerston* (1962).

Guedalla, P., *Gladstone and Palmerston* (1928).

Guttsman, W. L., *The British Political Elite* (1965).

Hammond, J. L. and Foot, M. R. D., *Gladstone and Liberalism* (1952).

Harrison, Brian, *Peaceable Kingdom: Stability and Change in Modern Britain* (Oxford, 1982).

Hirst, F. W., *Gladstone as Financier and Economist* (1931).

Holcombe, Lee, *Wives and Property: Reform of the Married Women's Property Law in Nineteenth-Century England* (1983).

Hollis, P., *Pressure from Without in Early Victorian England* (1974).

Hoppen, K. T., *Elections, Politics and Society in Ireland 1832–1885* (Oxford, 1984).

Howard, C., *Britain and the 'Casus Belli', 1822–1902: A Study of Britain's International Position from Canning to Salisbury* (1974).

Hugessen, H. Knatchbull, *A Kentish Family* (1960).

Imlah, Albert, H., *Lord Ellenborough: A Biography of Edward Law, Earl of Ellenborough, Governor-General of India* (Cambridge, Mass., 1939).

Iremonger, Lucille, *Lord Aberdeen: A Biography of the Fourth Earl of Aberdeen, K.G., K.T., Prime Minister, 1852–1855* (1978).

Jagger, Peter J. (ed.) *Gladstone, Politics and Religion* (1985).

Jones, W. D., *Lord Derby and Victorian Conservatism* (Oxford, 1956).

Jones, W. D., *'Prosperity' Robinson, The Life of Viscount Goderich, 1782–1859* (1967).

Jones, W. D., *The American Problem in British Diplomacy 1841–1861* (1974).

Jones, W. D. and Erickson, A. B., *The Peelites* (Iowa, 1973).

Kennedy, A. L., *Salisbury 1830–1903: Portrait of a Statesman* (1953).

Kinzer, Bruce, L., *The Ballot Question in Nineteenth-Century English Politics* (New York, 1982).

Kinzer, Bruce, L. (ed.) *The Gladstonian Turn of Mind* (Toronto, 1985).

Kirk, R., *The Conservative Mind* (1954).

Krein, David F., *The Last Palmerston Government: Foreign Policy, Domestic Politics, and the Genesis of 'Splendid Isolation'* (Iowa, 1978).

LeMay, G. H. L., *The Victorian Constitution: Conventions, Usages and Contingencies* (1979).

Lucas, R., *Lord Glenesk and 'The Morning Post'* (1910).

McCarthy, J., *A History of Our Times*, 4 vols (1905).

McCarthy, J., *Reminiscences*, 2 vols (1899).

McCarthy, J., *Modern England* (n.d.).

Maccoby, Simon, *English Radicalism, 1853–1886* (1938).

McDowell, R. B., *British Conservatism, 1832–1914* (1959).

McIntire, C. T., *England Against the Papacy, 1858–1861: Tories, Liberals, and the Overthrow of Papal Temporal Power during the Italian Risorgimento* (Cambridge, 1983).

Maclagan, Michael, *'Clemency' Canning: Charles John, 1st Earl Canning, Governor-General and Viceroy of India, 1856–1862* (1962).

Magnus, Sir P., *Gladstone: A Biography* (1954).

Marlow, J., *Mr. and Mrs. Gladstone: An Intimate Biography* (1977).

Marsh, Peter (ed.) *The Conscience of the Victorian State* (Hassocks, 1978).

Martin, B. K., *The Triumph of Lord Palmerston* (1924).

Mitchell, Leslie, *Holland House* (1980).

Molesworth, W. N., *A History of England, 1830–1874*, vol. III (1874).

Moore, D. C., *The Politics of Deference: A Study of the Mid-Nineteenth Century English Political System* (Hassocks, 1976).

Moore, R. J., *Sir Charles Wood's Indian Policy* (Manchester, 1966).

Mumford, W. A., *William Ewart M. P.: Portrait of A Radical* (1960).

Munsell, F. Darrell, *The Unfortunate Duke: Henry Pelham, Fifth Duke of Newcastle, 1811–1864* (Missouri, 1985).

Olien, D. D., *Morpeth: A Victorian Public Career* (Washington, 1983).

Olney, R. J., *Lincolnshire Politics, 1832–1885*, (Oxford, 1973).

Paul, H., *A History of Modern England*, 5 vols (1904–6).

Pemberton, N. W. B., *Lord Palmerston* (1954).

Petrie, Sir C., *The Carlton Club* (1955).

Pinto-Duschinsky, M., *The Political Thought of Lord Salisbury, 1854–1868* (1967).

Platt, D. C. M., *Finance, Trade and Politics: British Foreign Policy* (1971).

Pollard, W., *The Stanleys of Knowsley* (1868).

Porter, Bernard, *The Refugee Question in Mid-Victorian Politics* (Cambridge, 1979).

Prest, J., *Lord John Russell* (1972).
Read, D., *Cobden and Bright: A Victorian Political Partnership* (1967).
Reid, S. J., *Lord John Russell* (1906).
Rostow, W. W., *British Economy of the Nineteenth Century* (1948).
Robson, R. (ed.) *Ideas and Institutions of Victorian Britain* (1967).
Rothstein, A., *British Foreign Policy and its Critics* (1972).
Salbstein, M. C. N., *The Emancipation of the Jews in Britain: The Question of the Admission of the Jews to Parliament 1828–1860* (1982).
Seymour, C., *Electoral Reform in England and Wales* (Newton Abbot, 1970).
Shannon, Richard, *Gladstone, 1809–1865* (1982).
Smith, E. F. M., *Palmerston* (1935).
Southgate, D., *The Passing of the Whigs* (1962).
Southgate, D., *'The Most English Minister . . .': The Policies and Politics of Palmerston* (1966).
Southgate, D. (ed.) *The Conservative Leadership 1832–1932* (1974).
Stewart, R., *The Politics of Protection. Lord Derby and the Protectionist Party, 1841–1852* (Cambridge, 1971).
Stewart, R., *The Foundation of the Conservative Party, 1830–1867* (1978).
Swartz, H. M. and Swartz, M. (eds) *Disraeli's Reminiscences* (1975).
Taylor, A. J. P., *Essays in English History* (1976).
Taylor, A. J. P., *The Trouble-Makers: Dissent over Foreign Policy, 1792–1939* (1957).
Taylor, A. J. P., *The Struggle for Mastery in Europe: 1848–1918* (Oxford, 1954).
Thomas, J. A., *The House of Commons, 1832–1901* (1939).
Tilby, A. W., *Lord John Russell: A Study in Civil and Religious Liberty* (1930).
Vincent, J. R., *The Formation of the Liberal Party, 1857–1868* (1966).
Walker, Brian M. (ed.) *Parliamentary Election Results in Ireland, 1801–1922* (Dublin, 1978).
Walpole, S., *The History of Twenty-Five Years*, vol. I (1904).
Ward, J. T., *Sir James Graham* (1967).
Watson, G., *The English Ideology* (1973).
White, R. J., *The Conservative Tradition* (1950).
Whyte, J. H., *The Independent Irish Party, 1850–1859* (Oxford, 1958).
Williams, W. E., *The Rise of Gladstone to the Leadership of the Liberal Party, 1859–1868* (1934).
Winter, J., *Robert Lowe* (Toronto, 1976).
Woods, M., *A History of the Tory Party* (1924).
Young, G. M., *Victorian England, Portrait of an Age*, 2nd ed. (Oxford, 1953).

VI ARTICLES

Aldrich, R., 'Sir John Pakington and the Newcastle Commission', *History of Education*, 8:1 (1979) pp. 21–31.
Altholz, J. L., 'The Political Behaviour of the English Catholics, 1850–1867', *JBS*, 13 (1964) pp. 89–103.

Anderson, Olive, 'Cabinet Government and the Crimean War', *EHR*, 79 (1964) pp. 548–51.

Anderson, Olive, 'The Reactions of the Church and Dissent Towards the Crimean War', *Journal of Ecclesiastical History* 16 (1965) pp. 209–20.

Anderson, Olive, 'The Janus Face of Mid-Nineteenth Century English Radicalism: The Administrative Reform Association of 1855', *Victorian Studies*, 8:3 (1965) pp. 231–42.

Anderson, Olive, 'The Political Uses of History in Mid-Nineteenth Century England', *Past and Present*, 36 (1967) pp. 87–105.

Anderson, Olive, 'The Wensleydale Peerage Case and the Position of the House of Lords in the Mid-Nineteenth Century', *EHR*, 82 (1967) pp. 486–502.

Andrews, James R., 'The Rationale of Nineteenth Century Pacifism: Religious and Political Arguments in the Early British Peace Movement', *Quaker History*, 57:1 (1968) pp. 17–27.

Aydelotte, W. O., 'The House of Commons in the 1840s', *History*, 39 (1954) pp. 249–62.

Aydelotte, W. O., 'Parties and Issues in Early Victorian England', *JBS*, 5 (1966) pp. 95–114.

Aydelotte, W. O., 'The Conservative and Radical Interpretations of Early Victorian Social Legislation', *Victorian Studies*, 11 (1967) pp. 225–36.

Aydelotte, W. O., 'The Disintegration of the Conservative Party in the 1840s: A Study of Political Attitudes', in W. O. Aydelotte, A. G. Bogue and R. W. Fogel (eds) *The Dimensions of Quantitative Research in History* (1972) pp. 319–46.

Beales, D. E. D., 'Parliamentary Politics and the "Independent" Member 1810–1860', in R. Robson (ed.) *Ideas and Institutions of Victorian Britain* (1967) pp. 1–19.

Bell, H. C. F., 'Palmerston and Parliamentary Representation', *Journal of Modern History*, 4 (1932) pp. 186–213.

Berrington, Hugh, 'Partisanship and Dissidence in the Nineteenth Century House of Commons', *Parliamentary Affairs*, 21:4 (1968) pp. 338–74.

Bourne, K., 'Lord Palmerston's "Ginger Beer" Triumph, 1 July 1856', in K. Bourne and D. C. Watt (eds) *Studies in International History: Essays Presented to W. Norton Medlicott* (1967) pp. 145–71.

Bylsma, J. R., 'Party Structure in the 1852–1857 House of Commons: A Scalogram Analysis', *Journal of Interdisciplinary History*, 7:4 (1977) pp. 375–93.

Chadwick, Owen, 'Young Gladstone and Italy', *Journal of Ecclesiastical History*, 30:2 (1979) pp. 243–59.

Clark, E. A. G., 'Sir Stafford Northcote's "Omnibus": The Genesis of the Industrial Schools Act, 1857', *Journal of Educational and Administrative History*, 14:1 (1982) pp. 27–45.

Cromwell, Valerie, 'The Administrative Background to the Presentation to Parliament of Parliamentary Papers on Foreign Affairs in the Mid-Nineteenth Century', *Journal of the Society of Archivists*, 2 (1963) pp. 302–15.

Cromwell, Valerie, 'Mapping the Political World of 1861: A Multidimensional Analysis of House of Commons Division Lists', *Legislative Studies Quarterly*, 7:2 (1982) pp. 281–298.

Cruickchank, A. F., 'J. A. Roebuck, M. P.: A Reappraisal of Liberalism in Sheffield, 1849–1879', *Northern History*, 16 (1980) pp. 196–214.

Edsall, N. C., 'A Failed National Movement: The Parliamentary and Financial Reform Association, 1848–54', *BIHR*, 49 (1976) pp. 108–31.

Eldridge, C. C., 'The Myth of Mid-Victorian "Separatism", The Cession of the Bay Islands and the Ionian Islands in the Early 1860s', *Victorian Studies*, 12:3 (1969) pp. 331–46.

Erickson, Arvel B., 'Edward T. Cardwell: Peelite', *Transactions of the American Philosophical Society*, 49:2 (1959).

Finlayson, G. B. A. M., 'Joseph Parkes of Birmingham, 1796–1865: A Study in Philosophic Radicalism', *BIHR*, 46 (1973) pp. 186–201.

Flournoy, F. R., 'British Liberal Theories of International Relations, 1848–1898', *Journal of History Ideas*, 7 (1946) pp. 195–217.

Foster, D., 'The Politics of Uncontested Elections: North Lancashire 1832–1865', *Northern History*, 13 (1977) pp. 232–47.

Gallagher, Thomas, F., 'The Second Reform Movement. 1848–1867', *Albion*, 12 (1980) pp. 147–63.

Gilam, A., 'Anglo-Jewish Attitudes towards Benjamin Disraeli During the Era of Emancipation', *Jewish Social Studies*, 42:3–4 (1980) pp. 313–22.

Gosh, P. R., 'Disraelian Conservatism: A Financial Approach', *EHR*, 99 (1984) pp. 268–96.

Gurowich, P. M., 'The Continuation of War by Other Means: Party and Politics, 1855–1865', *HJ*, 27:3 (1984) pp. 603–31.

Guttsman, W. L., 'The General Election of 1859 in the Cities of Yorkshire', *International Review of Social History*, 2 (1957) pp. 231–58.

Harrison, Brian, 'The Sunday Trading Riots of 1855', *HJ*, 8:2 (1965) pp. 219–45.

Hawkins, Angus, 'A Forgotten Crisis: Gladstone and the Politics of Finance During the 1850s', *Victorian Studies*, 26:3 (1983) pp. 287–310.

Hawkins, Angus, 'British Parliamentary Party Alignment and the Indian Issue, 1857–1858', *JBS*, 23:2 (1984) pp. 79–105.

Hearder, H., 'Napoleon III's Threat to Break Off Diplomatic Relations with England During the Crisis Over the Orsini Attempt in 1858', *EHR*, 72 (1957) pp. 474–81.

Hearder, H., 'Queen Victoria and Foreign Policy: Royal Intervention in the Italian Question, 1859–1860', in K. Bourne and D. C. Watt (eds) *Studies in International History: Essays presented to W. Norton Medlicott* (1967) pp. 172–88.

Henderson, G. B., 'Ralph Anstruther Earle', *EHR*, 58 (1943) pp. 172–89.

Herrick, F. H., 'The Second Reform Movement in Britain, 1850–1865', *Journal of the History of Ideas*, 9:2 (1948) pp. 174–92.

Hoppen, K. T., 'Tories, Catholics, and the General Election of 1859', *HJ*, 13:1 (1970) pp. 48–67.

Hoppen, K. T., 'National Politics and Local Realities in Mid-Nineteenth Century Ireland', in A. Cosgrove and D. McCartney (eds) *Studies in Irish History*, pp. 190–227.

Jones, J. R., 'The Conservatives and Gladstone in 1855', *EHR*, 77 (1962) pp. 95–8.

Kinzer, Bruce L., 'The Failure of "Pressure From Without": Richard Cobden, the Ballot Society, and the Coming of the Ballot Act in England', *Canadian Journal of History*, 13:3 (1978) pp. 339–422.

Knox, Bruce, 'British Policy and the Ionian Islands 1847–1864: Nationalism and Imperial Administration', *EHR*, 99 (1984) pp. 503–29.

Krein, David F., 'War and Reform: Russell, Palmerston and the Struggle for Power in the Aberdeen Cabinet, 1853–4', *Maryland Historian*, 7:2 (1976) pp. 67–84.

Lloyd, Trevor, 'Uncontested Seats in British General Elections, 1852–1910', *HJ*, 8:2 (1965) pp. 260–5.

McCord, N., 'Cobden and Bright in Politics, 1846–1857', in R. Robson (ed.) *Ideas and Institutions of Victorian Britain*, pp. 87–114.

McDonald, T. A., 'Religion and Voting in an English Borough: Poole in 1859', *Southern History*, 5 (1983) pp. 221–37.

McGowen, R. E. and Arnstein, W. L., 'The Mid-Victorians and the Two Party System', *Albion*, 11:3 (1979) pp. 242–58.

McIntire, C. T., 'Mid-Victorian Anti-Catholicism, English Diplomacy and Odo Russell in Rome', *Fides et Historia*, 13:1 (1980) pp. 13–23.

Matthew, H. C. G., 'Disraeli, Gladstone and the Politics of Mid-Victorian Budgets', *HJ*, 22:3 (1979) pp. 615–43.

Moore, D. C., 'The Matter of the Missing Contests: Towards a Theory of the Mid-Nineteenth Century British Political System', *Albion*, 6:2 (1974) pp. 93–119.

Palmer, Stanley H., 'Sir George Cornewall Lewis, A Different Kind of Englishman', *Eire*, 16:3 (1981) pp. 118–33.

Prest, J. M., 'Gladstone and Russell', *TRHS*, 5th series, 16 (1966) pp. 43–64.

Ramm, Agatha, 'Gladstone's Religion', *HJ*, 28:2 (1985) pp. 327–40.

Roberts, M. J. D., 'Morals, Art and the Law: The Passing of the Obscene Publications Act, 1857', *Victorian Studies*, 28:4 (1985) pp. 609–30.

Roper, Jon, 'Party and Democracy in Nineteenth Century Britain', *Parliaments, Estates and Representation*, 3:1 (1983) pp. 22–33.

Sanderson, G. N., 'The "Swing of the Pendulum" in British General Elections, 1832–1966', *Political Studies*, 14:3 (1966) pp. 349–60.

Sandiford, Keith A. P., 'Gladstone and Liberal Nationalist Movements', *Albion*, 13 (1981) pp. 27–42.

Schreuder, D. M., 'Gladstone and Italian Unification, 1848–1870: The Making of a Liberal?', *EHR*, (1970) pp. 475–501.

Shanley, Mary Lyndon, 'One Must Ride Behind: Married Women's Right and the Divorce Act of 1857', *Victorian Studies*, 25 (1982) pp. 355–76.

Simpson, F. A., 'England and the Italian War of 1859', *HJ*, (1962) pp. 111–21.

Smith, David, 'Sir George Grey at the Mid-Victorian Home Office', *Canadian Journal of History*, 19 (1984) pp. 361–86.

Stephen, M. D., 'Gladstone and the Composition of the Final Court in Ecclesiastical Causes', *HJ*, 9:2 (1966) pp. 191–200.

Stuart, C. H., 'The Formation of the Coalition Cabinet of 1852' *TRHS*, 5th series, 4 (1954) pp. 45–68.

Stuart, C. H., 'The Prince Consort and Ministerial Politics, 1856–9', in H. R. Trevor Roper (ed.) *Essays in British History Presented to Sir Keith Feiling*, pp. 247–70.

Thomas, J. A., 'The System of Registration and the Development of Party Organisation, 1832–70', *History*, 35 (1950) pp. 81–98.

Varlaam, Carol, 'The 1858 Medical Act; The Origins and the Aftermath', *Bulletin of the Society for the Social History of Medicine*, 21 (1977) pp. 31–3.

Vincent, J. R., 'The Parliamentary Dimension of the Crimean War', *TRHS*, 31 (1981) pp. 31–49.

Wasson, E. A., 'The Spirit of Reform, 1832 and 1867', *Albion*, 12 (1980) pp. 164–74.

Whyte, J. H., 'The Influence of the Catholic Clergy on Elections in Mid-Nineteenth Century Ireland', *EHR*, 75 (1960) pp. 239–59.

Woodall, Robert, 'Orsini and the Fall of Palmerston', *History Today*, 26 (1976) pp. 636–43.

VII   UNPUBLISHED DISSERTATIONS CONSULTED

Bylsma, J. R., 'Political Issues and Party Unity in the House of Commons, 1852–1857: A Scalogram Analysis', PhD thesis, University of Iowa, 1968.

Chapman, J. K., 'The Career of Arthur Hamilton Gordon 1st Lord Stanmore', PhD thesis, University of London, 1954.

Denholm, A. F., 'Some Aspects of the Radical and Democratic Career of the 1st Marquess of Ripon', MA thesis, University of Wales, 1966.

Glynn, J. K., 'The Private Member of Parliament 1833–1868', PhD thesis, University of London, 1949.

Hearder, H., 'The Foreign Policy of Lord Malmesbury, 1858–9', PhD thesis, University of London, 1954.

Major, W. E., 'The Public Life of the Third Earl of Malmesbury', PhD thesis, University of Georgia, 1980.

McCracken, D. E., 'The Conservatives in "Power": the Minority Governments of 1852, 1858–9 and 1866–8', PhD thesis University of Virgina, 1981.

Synder, C. W., 'Liberty and Morality: A Political Biography of Edward Bulwer Lytton', PhD thesis, University of Virginia, 1979.

Watt, R. G., 'Parties and Politics in Mid-Victorian Britain, 1857 to 1859: A Study in Quantification', PhD thesis, University of Minnesota, 1975.

VIII   REFERENCE WORKS

The Annual Register, 1855–1859 (1856–60).
Bateman's Great Landowners of Great Britain and Ireland (1883).
Boase, F., *Modern English Biography*, 2nd edn, 6 vols (1965).
Burke's Peerage, Baronetage and Knightage (1963).

Cokayne, G. E., *Complete Peerage*, 14 vols (1910–59).

Craig, F. W. S. (ed.) *British Parliamentary Election Results 1832–1885* (1977).

Dictionary of National Biography, 22 vols (1908–9) Sir Leslie Stephen and Sir Sidney Lee (eds).

Dod, C. R., *Parliamentary Companion, 1852–9* (1852–9).

Stenton, M. (ed.) *Who was Who of British M.P.s, 1832–1885* (Hassocks, 1976).

Vincent, J. R. and Stenton, M. (eds) *McCalmont's Parliamentary Poll Book* (Hassocks, 1971).

Index

Since the terms Liberal, Whig, Radical, Peelite and Conservative appear constantly throughout the text this index contains references only to individuals associated with each of these groups.